SAT is a registered trademark of the College Entrance Examination Board, which neither sponsors nor endorses this book.

This book is designed to provide hundreds of question types of categorized SAT math for the students who aspire to achieve a high score on the SAT math sections. The books provide a lot of the fastest methods of solving the questions by Logical Step Form created by the author.

The book is published by Mad Math Publishing, a division of John's Learning Services, Inc.

October 8, 2018

10 9 8 7 6 5 4 3 2 1

ISBN-13: 978-1723493096

ISBN-10: 1723493090

Printed in the United States of America

Redesigned
For New SAT of 2016 March & Beyond

15

SAT Math

TESTS

(Practice Tests 1 to 15)

New Edition

Introduction

The College Board makes the SAT. So every person who wants to prepare the SAT should buy one book called "The official SAT Study Guide". "The official SAT Study Guide" covers many the questions of the SAT types. After using the book, you may buy some reference books like this book to obtain more chances to practice more the SAT type questions.

The SAT score is one of five main factors that universities or colleges look at when they consider an application. They look at applicant's GPA, special activity, application essay, and letters of recommendations.

In the mathematics sections 44 questions belong to multiple-choice form and 10 questions belong to Student-produced response (grid-ins) form. There are 54 mathematics questions in total. The time length of the total mathematics sections is 70 minutes (two sections each are 25 minutes and one section is 20 minutes).

The SAT tests are scheduled 7 times in October, November, December, January, March, May, and June each academic year. Each SAT test is always on Saturday. There is no any SAT test in July, August, and September. The SAT online registration is available at www.collegeboard.org.

This book provides a lot of the SAT math questions that include abundant the SAT math types. During the real test period, if the types of the most test questions examinee has met and practiced before, then the test result goes without saying.

The explorations of this book primarily use the logical steps to let users easily memorize the methods of solving questions. The essence of mathematics is logic. Human thinking naturally accepts the formula of "because" and "therefore". Hence, using mathematically logical steps to solve questions directly is in harmony with the natural function of human brain. Furthermore, it is helpful for memorizing because what you need to remember are the mathematically logical steps, which is refined and easily to be memorized, instead of the mixed explanations of English and math that are difficult to memorize.

Success mainly comes from diligence. In most of the schools nowadays, students study multiple subjects in the same period of time. Under such condition, it is impossible to succeed without diligence. If you are not diligent, you then will not have the chance to prove whether or not you are gifted and genius.

To save readers' time, this set of books uses the method, at the solution part, of completely replicating the original questions. The purpose of this design is to save time for readers from flipping back and forth through the pages to see the accurate descriptions of the original question. Even though the cost for the books will increase with such design, namely, it will cost you more, yet, it saves you enormous and precious amount of time.

This book belongs to the series of Mad Math books. This series includes SAT / PSAT Math Database, SAT Math, PSAT Math, SAT Subject Math Level 1 Database, SAT Subject Math Level 1, SAT Subject Math Level 2 Database, and SAT Subject Math Level 2.

SAT Math

Practice

Test 01

Redesigned for Tests in March 2016 and Beyond

Mad Math

Math Test – No Calculator

Time: 25 Minutes
20 Questions

Notes:

- The use of a calculator is not allowed.
- All numbers used in this section are the real number.
- Figures are provided for some problems in this test. Unless otherwise indicated under the figure "Note: Figure above not drawn to scale", all figures are drawn as accurately as possible.
- All figures lie in a plane EXCEPT otherwise specified.
- Unless otherwise indicated, the domain of any function f, g or j is assumed to be the set of all real numbers x for which $f(x)$, $g(x)$, or $j(x)$ is a real number.

Reference Information

$$A = \frac{1}{2}bh$$

$$A = lw$$

$$A = \pi r^2$$

$$V = \pi r^2 h$$

$$V = lwh$$

$$c^2 = a^2 + b^2$$

$$V = \frac{1}{3}\pi r^2 h$$

$$V = \frac{4}{3}\pi r^3$$

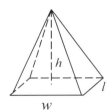

$$V = \frac{1}{3}lwh$$

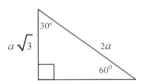

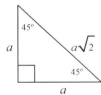

Copying or reuse of any portion of this page is illegal.

1. Monica has X dollars to spend and go on a shopping mall. First she spends three-fifths of her money on books. Then she spends three fourths of what's left on shoes. Finally she buys a bag that costs one-third of her remaining dollars. What fraction of X is left?

(A) $\dfrac{1}{15}$

(B) $\dfrac{3}{25}$

(C) $\dfrac{1}{5}$

(D) $\dfrac{1}{20}$

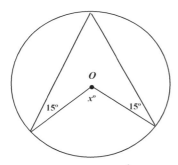

2. Point O is the center of the circle above. What is the value of x?

(A) 40

(B) 60

(C) 70

(D) 90

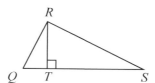 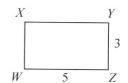

Note: Figure above not drawn to scale.

3. Triangle QRS and rectangle $WXYZ$ have eqaul areas. The length $\overline{RT}$ is 6. What is the length of $\overline{QS}$?

(A) $\dfrac{5}{2}$

(B) 5

(C) 9

(D) 10

4. When it is noon (12:00pm) Pacific Time (PT) in Los Angeles, it is 3:00pm Eastern Time (ET) in New Jersey. A jetliner left New Jersey at 1:00pm ET and arrived in Los Angeles at 5:00pm PT on the same day. If a second jetliner left New Jersey at noon ET and took exactly the same amount of time for the trip, what was the jetliner's arrival time (PT) in Los Angeles?

(A) 4:00pm PT
(B) 3:00pm PT
(C) 9:00pm PT
(D) 8:00pm PT

NEXT PAGE

5. If you take 2 less than a number x and then raise this result to the 4th power, it equals 81. What is one possible value of x ?

(A) -1

(B) -7

(C) 1

(D) -5

6. A cylindrical bucket has a height of 1 foot and a radius of 0.3 foot. How many such buckets can be completely filled from a full rectangular container whose length is 4 feet, width is 3 feet, and height is 6 feet?

(A) 255

(B) 253

(C) 252

(D) 254

7. The part of a walkway of a park consists of a continuous chain in the shape of hexagons, the beginning of which is shown in the diagram above. The chain consists of 100 the same size hexagons. Each hexagon, except the first and last ones, shares two of its sides with adjacent hexagons. The length of each side of each hexagon is four yards. What is the perimeter of the walkway?

(A) 400

(B) 402

(C) 486

(D) 1,608

8. What is the greatest 4-digit integer meeting the following three conditions?

I. The greatest digit is the sum of the remaining 3 digits.

II. All of the digits are distinct.

III. The product of the 4 digits is not equivalent to zero but is divisible by six.

(A) 3,216

(B) 6,321

(C) 6,311

(D) 1,236

NEXT PAGE

9. A and B both are constant and $3x^2 + Ax - 6$ equals $(3x - 2)(x + B)$. What is the value of A?

(A) 1

(B) 5

(C) 7

(D) -5

11. If $-1 < x < 0$, then which of the following must be true?

(A) $x^2 < x^6$

(B) $x^3 > x^5$

(C) $x^3 > x^6$

(D) $x^5 > x^3$

10. At Water High School, a history class has 25 students in it. Of those students, 12 are enrolled in biology and 14 are enrolled in chemistry. What is the minimum percent of the students in the history class who are also enrolled in biology and chemistry?

(A) 4
(B) 3
(C) 2
(D) 1

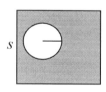

Note: Figure above not drawn to scale.

12. In the figure above, a circle inside a square. If the radius of the circle is r and $s = 4$, what is the area, in terms of r, of the shaded region?

(A) $16 - 2r\pi$

(B) $8 - r^2\pi$

(C) $16 - r^2\pi$

(D) $12 - 2r\pi$

NEXT PAGE

13. If the interior angles of triangle *ABC* are in the ratio of 4: 5: 6, then *ABC* is

(A) Obtuse Triangle
(B) Acute Triangle
(C) Right Triangle
(D) Isosceles Triangle

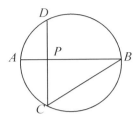

Note: Figure above not drawn to scale.

15. If $\overline{DC}$ is perpendicular to $\overline{AB}$, $AP = 5$, $DP = 12$, and $CP = 15$, what is CB ?

(A) 18
(B) 20
(C) 16
(D) 39

14. If $i = \sqrt{-1}$, which of the following equals $\sqrt{-5 + 12i}$?

(A) $-\dfrac{5}{2} - 6i$

(B) $2 + 3i$

(C) $-\dfrac{2}{3} - 3i$

(D) $2 - 3i$

NEXT PAGE

16. What is the probability of choosing a prime number at random from the set = [1, 2, 4, and 9].

17. If 3 distinct numbers are chosen, one from each of following sets, what is the greatest sum these numbers could have?

$S_1 = \{2, 3, 7\}$

$S_2 = \{4, 6, 8\}$

$S_3 = \{2, 5, 9\}$

18. How many square yards are in a floor that is 9 feet by 21 feet if there is no waste?

19. If x is an integer and $3 < x < 8$, how many distinct triangles are there with sides of lengths 3, 8, and x?

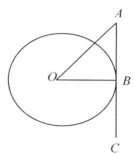

Note: Figure above not drawn to scale.

20. In the figure above, $\overline{AC}$ is tangent to the circle O at point B. BO is the radius of this circle $BO = AB = \sqrt{2}$. What is the AO?

STOP

Math Test – Calculator

Time: 55 Minutes
38 Questions

Notes:

- The use of a calculator is not allowed.
- All numbers used in this section are the real number.
- Figures are provided for some problems in this test. Unless otherwise indicated under the figure "Note: Figure above not drawn to scale", all figures are drawn as accurately as possible.
- All figures lie in a plane EXCEPT otherwise specified.
- Unless otherwise indicated, the domain of any function f, g or j is assumed to be the set of all real numbers x for which $f(x)$, $g(x)$, or $j(x)$ is a real number.

Reference Information

$A = \dfrac{1}{2}bh$

$A = lw$

$A = \pi r^2$

$V = \pi r^2 h$

$V = lwh$

$c^2 = a^2 + b^2$

$V = \dfrac{1}{3}\pi r^2 h$

$V = \dfrac{4}{3}\pi r^3$

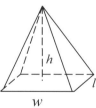

$V = \dfrac{1}{3}lwh$

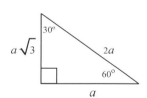

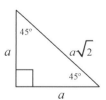

1. Jeff was 20 years old x years ago. Which of the following represents his age y years from now?

(A) $20 + x - y$

(B) $20 - x - y$

(C) $20 + x + y$

(D) $20 + y - x$

2. For which of the following values of x is $\dfrac{x^2 - 9}{x^2 + 2x - 3}$ undefined?

(A) 3 and -1
(B) -2
(C) -1
(D) -3 and 1

Questions 3 and 4 refer to all information of the following figure:

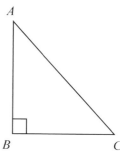

3.   What is $\cos A$?

(A) $\dfrac{BC}{AC}$ (B) $\dfrac{AB}{AC}$ (C) $\dfrac{AC}{BC}$ (D) $\dfrac{BC}{AB}$

4.   If $AC = 4$, what is the area of the triangle?

(A) $8 \sin C \cos C$ (B) $4 \sin C \cos C$

(C) $8 \sin A \cos A$ (D) $4 \sin A \cos A$

NEXT PAGE

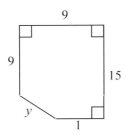

Note: Figure above not drawn to scale.

5. What is the perimeter of the figure shown above?

(A) 44
(B) 36
(C) 40
(D) 38

6. Which of the following is divisible by 3 and 5 but is not divisible by 9?

(A) 135
(B) 120
(C) 45
(D) 90

7. Mr. Wolf chooses watermelons for his supermarket. He will not choose the watermelons that weigh less than 10 pounds or more than 20 pounds. If n represents the weight of a watermelon, in pounds, he will not choose, which inequalities below represents all possible values of n?

(A) $|n-15| < 10$
(B) $|n-15| > 20$
(C) $|n-10| < 15$
(D) $|n-15| > 5$

$g(t)$	t
3	-3
-2	-2
4	-1
-3	0
0	1
2	2

8. The function g is defined by the chart above. For what value of t does $g(t) + t = 0$?

(A) 2
(B) 0
(C) -1
(D) -3

9. Line *m* is perpendicular to a segment *PQ* at point *W* and *PW = WQ*. How many points on line *m* have the same distance from point *P* as from point *Q*?

(A) 1
(B) 4
(C) 3
(D) > 4

10. If segment *PQ* in the coordinate plane has endpoint *P* (-8, 6) and midpoint (-4, 10), then endpoint *Q* of $\overline{PQ}$ has coordinates

(A) (0, 26)
(B) (0, 14)
(C) (12, 8)
(D) (16, 14)

11. A rectangle was changed by increasing its length by *P*% and decreasing its width by 10%. If these changes increased the area of the rectangle to 108% of its original area, what is the value of *P* ?

(A) 20
(B) 15
(C) 30
(D) 22

12. If $\dfrac{a}{b}$ of *x*, *b* > *a* > 0, is 15, then $\dfrac{2}{15}$ of *x* =

(A) $\dfrac{2a}{b}$

(B) $\dfrac{2b}{a}$

(C) $\dfrac{4a}{b}$

(D) $\dfrac{a}{4b}$

NEXT PAGE

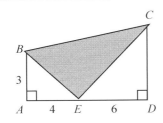

Note: Diagram above not drawn to scale.

13. The diagram above shows a trapezoid divided into 3 right triangles. What is the the area of the shaded region?

(A) 20

(B) 25

(C) 30

(D) 35

14. Set P_1 consists of the positive factors of 15 and P_2 consists of the positive factors of 18. What is the intersection of P_1 and P_2 ?

(A) (1, 2, 3, 5, 6, 9, 15, 18)
(B) (2, 5, 6, 9, 15, 18)
(C) (1, 3, 5, 9, 15)
(D) (1, 3)

15. If the line $y = 3$ intersects the graph of the equation $y = x^2 - 14x + 52$ at one point only, which of the following is the coordinates of the point?

(A) $(-7, \ 3)$

(B) $(7, \ 7)$

(C) $(-7, -7)$

(D) $(7, \ 3)$

NEXT PAGE

16. If the six cards shown above are placed in a row so that

, and are never at either end, how many possible distinct combinations exist?

(A) 24
(B) 30
(C) 132
(D) 144

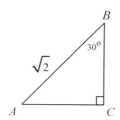

Note: Figure above not drawn to scale.

18. In the figure above, what is BC?

(A) $\dfrac{3}{\sqrt{2}}$

(B) $\dfrac{\sqrt{6}}{2}$

(C) $2\sqrt{2}$

(D) $4\sqrt{2}$

17. Car X's speed is 2 times Car Y's speed, and Car Z's speed is 3 times Car X's speed. If car Z's speed is 12 miles per hour, what is 2 times Car Y's speed, in miles per hour?

(A) 2
(B) 4
(C) 6
(D) 8

19. If 1.862 is rounded to the nearest tenth, the result is how much less than if 1.862 is rounded to nearest whole number?

(A) 0.01

(B) 0.02

(C) 0.1

(D) 0.2

NEXT PAGE

20. If p_1 represents the greatest prime number less than 96 and p_2 represents the least prime number greater than 8, which of the following is the value of $p_1 - p_2$?

(A) 81

(B) 80

(C) 78

(D) 82

Centimeters 2 3 2 3 2 3 ... 2 3

Note: Figure above not drawn to scale.

22. A 200-centimeter-long strip is shown in the figure above. By eliminating an equilateral triangle from the front of each 5-centimeter length on one side of the strip, the nicked side shown in bold is formed. Which of the following is the total length, in centimeters, of the bold nicked side on the 200-centimeter strip?

(A) 240

(B) 185

(C) 280

(D) 125

21. A banquet has 21 tables, which can seat a total of 140 people. Some of the tables seat 6 people and the rest seat 8 people. How many tables seat 8 people?

(A) 5
(B) 6
(C) 7
(D) 8

23. Two sides of a triangle have lengths 13 and 12, respectively. If the remaining side of the triangle has a value that is an integer, what is the smallest possible perimeter of this triangle?

(A) 25
(B) 21
(C) 45
(D) 27

NEXT PAGE

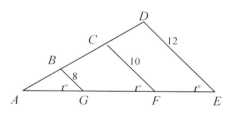

24. In the figure above, what are the values of $\dfrac{CF}{DE}$ and $\dfrac{AG}{AE}$?

(A) $\dfrac{5}{6}$ and $\dfrac{2}{3}$

(B) $\dfrac{5}{6}$ and $\dfrac{4}{5}$

(C) $\dfrac{5}{12}$ and $\dfrac{5}{6}$

(D) $\dfrac{6}{12}$ and $\dfrac{2}{3}$

The questions 25 and 26 refer to the following information.

Questions 25 and 26 refer to following information.

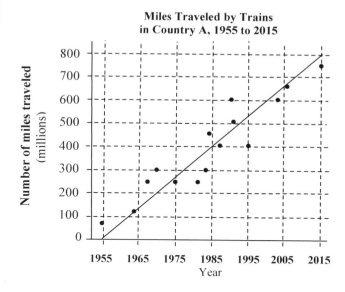

25. By the line of best fit above, which of the following best approximates the year in which the number of miles traveled by trains in Country A was estimated to be 600 millions?

(A) 1990

(B) 1996

(C) 2003

(D) 2000

26. By the line of best fit, which of the following best approximates the percent increasing in the millions of miles traveled in Country A from year 1985 to year 2015?

(A) 96.5%

(B) 89.3%

(C) 95%

(D) 100%

NEXT PAGE

27. How many positive factors, excluding 1 and m, does m have if a, b, and c are three distinct prime numbers greater than 2, and m is the product of a, b, and c ?

(A) 3

(B) 8

(C) 6

(D) 5

28. In the figure above, if the right circular cylinder has height $h = \pi$ and diameter d, which of the following represents the volume of the smallest rectangular prism that contains the entire cylinder?

(A) $d^2 \pi$

(B) $d\pi$

(C) $\dfrac{d\pi}{2}$

(D) $\dfrac{d^2 \pi}{2}$

NEXT PAGE

29. Mary has two jobs. She works as a waitress, which pays $15 per hour, and she works as a nurse, which pays $16 per hour. Mary can work less than 120 hours per month, and she plans to make greater than $1,200 per month. Which of the following system of inequalities describes this situation in terms of w and n, where w represents the number of hours she works as a waitress and n represents the number of hours she works as a nurse?

(A) $w + n < 120$
$15w + 16n > 1,200$

(B) $w + n > 120$
$16w + 15n \geq 1,200$

(C) $w + n \leq 120$
$15w + 16n \leq 1,200$

(D) $w + n > 120$
$15w + 16n \geq 1,200$

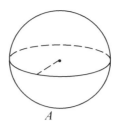 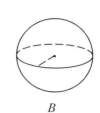

A B C

Figure 3

30. In Figure 3, sphere A and sphere C have a radius of 4 and 2, respectively. If the volume of sphere B is the mean of the volumes of sphere A and sphere C, which of the following is the diameter of sphere B?

(A) 6.0

(B) 12

(C) 6.6

(D) 6.4

NEXT PAGE

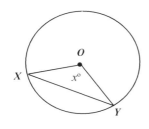

Note that figure not drawn to scale.

31. Point O is the center of the circle above and the area of sector OXY is $\dfrac{5}{12}$ of the area of the circle. What is the value of x?

$$1 + \frac{y}{2} = 2x - 1$$

32. What is the slope of the function above?

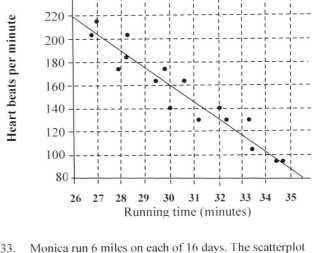

Relationship of Running Time and Heart Beats

33. Monica run 6 miles on each of 16 days. The scatterplot with the line of best fit above shows the relationship of her running time, in minutes, and heart beats per minute after each running. For this running that Monica run 30 minutes, her actual heart beats per minute or beat rate was around how many less than the heart beat rate predicted by the line of best fit?

34. Around what is the length of the radius of the sphere $x^2 + y^2 + z^2 + 4x - 4z = 12$?

NEXT PAGE

35.   Each of 6 boys played a computer game with each of five girls, and then each boy played a computer game with each of the other boys. How many computer games were played?

	Seniors	Juniors	Period-1	Period-2
Math	20	25	16	n
English	20	35	k	19

37. The chart above shows the number of seniors and juniors taking math and English classes at a high school and gives the enrollment for these classes in period-1 and period-2, which are the only periods math and English are taught. Only seniors and juniors take these classes. What is the total number of students who take math and English in period-1?

38.   In how many arrangements can people P_A, P_B, P_C, P_S and P_M stand in a straight line if P_M must be at the middle position and P_S must be at the second position?

36.   If $p = 10q = 2m = 5n,$ then $\dfrac{pq}{mn} =$

STOP

Answer Key
For
SAT Math Practice Test 01

Section 3

1	A
2	B
3	B
4	A
5	A
6	D
7	D
8	B
9	C
10	A
11	D
12	C
13	B
14	B
15	D

16	1/4 or .25
17	24
18	21
19	2
20	2

Section 4

1	C	16	D
2	D	17	B
3	B	18	B
4	A	19	C
5	A	20	C
6	B	21	C
7	D	22	C
8	D	23	D
9	D	24	A
10	B	25	D
11	A	26	D
12	B	27	C
13	B	28	A
14	D	29	A
15	D	30	C

31	150
32	4
33	20
34	4.47
35	45
36	1
37	52
38	6

SAT Math

Practice

Test 01

Explanations

Redesigned for Tests in March 2016 and Beyond

Mad Math

Math Test – No Calculator

Time: 25 Minutes
20 Questions

Notes:

- The use of a calculator is not allowed.
- All numbers used in this section are the real number.
- Figures are provided for some problems in this test. Unless otherwise indicated under the figure "Note: Figure above not drawn to scale", all figures are drawn as accurately as possible.
- All figures lie in a plane EXCEPT otherwise specified.
- Unless otherwise indicated, the domain of any function f, g or j is assumed to be the set of all real numbers x for which $f(x)$, $g(x)$, or $j(x)$ is a real number.

Reference Information

$$A = \frac{1}{2}bh$$

$$A = lw$$

$$A = \pi r^2$$

$$V = \pi r^2 h$$

$$V = lwh$$

$$c^2 = a^2 + b^2$$

$$V = \frac{1}{3}\pi r^2 h$$

$$V = \frac{4}{3}\pi r^3$$

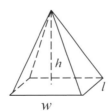

$$V = \frac{1}{3}lwh$$

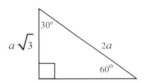

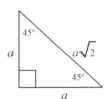

1. Monica has X dollars to spend and go on a shopping mall. First she spends three-fifths of her money on books. Then she spends three fourths of what's left on shoes. Finally she buys a bag that costs one-third of her remaining dollars. What fraction of X is left?

(A) $\dfrac{1}{15}$

(B) $\dfrac{3}{25}$

(C) $\dfrac{1}{5}$

(D) $\dfrac{1}{20}$

> Solution: Answer: (A)
>
> Let 1 = total dolars X.
>
> $\Downarrow$
>
> $\left(\dfrac{2}{5} \cdot 1\right) \cdot \dfrac{1}{4} \cdot \dfrac{2}{3} = \dfrac{1}{15}$

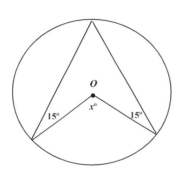

2. Point O is the center of the circle above. What is the value of x?

(A) 40

(B) 60

(C) 70

(D) 90

> Solution: Answer: (B)
>
> Draw one radius shown below.
>
>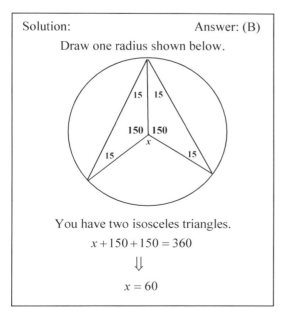
>
> You have two isosceles triangles.
>
> $x + 150 + 150 = 360$
>
> $\Downarrow$
>
> $x = 60$

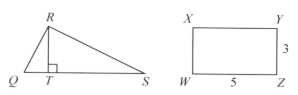

Note: Figure above not drawn to scale.

3. Triangle QRS and rectangle $WXYZ$ have eqaul areas. The length $\overline{RT}$ is 6. What is the length of $\overline{QS}$?

(A) $\dfrac{5}{2}$

(B) 5

(C) 9

(D) 10

> Solution: Answer: (B)
>
> $A_{\text{Tri}} = A_{\text{Rec}}$
>
> $\downarrow$
>
> $\dfrac{6 \times QS}{2} = 3 \times 5$
>
> $\Downarrow$
>
> $QS = 5$

4. When it is noon (12:00pm) Pacific Time (PT) in Los Angeles, it is 3:00pm Eastern Time (ET) in New Jersey. A jetliner left New Jersey at 1:00pm ET and arrived in Los Angeles at 5:00pm PT on the same day. If a second jetliner left New Jersey at noon ET and took exactly the same amount of time for the trip, what was the jetliner's arrival time (PT) in Los Angeles?

(A) 4:00pm PT
(B) 3:00pm PT
(C) 9:00pm PT
(D) 8:00pm PT

> Solution: Answer: (A)
>
> $PT = ET - 3$
>
> (1) Get the hours for one trip.
>
> 1pm ET – 3 = 10am PT
>
> 5:00pm PT– 10am ST= 7 hours
>
> (2) Get the second arrival time.
>
> 12pm ET – 3 = 9am PT
>
> $\Downarrow$
>
> 9am PT+ 7 = 4:00pm PT

NEXT PAGE

5. If you take 2 less than a number x and then raise this result to the 4th power, it equals 81. What is one possible value of x ?

(A) -1

(B) -7

(C) 1

(D) -5

> Solution: Answer: (A)
> $$x - 2, \quad (x-2)^4 = 81$$
> $$\downarrow$$
> $$\left((x-2)^4\right)^{\frac{1}{4}} = \pm\sqrt[4]{81}$$
> $$\downarrow$$
> $$x - 2 = \pm\sqrt[4]{3^4} = \pm 3$$
> $$\Downarrow$$
> $$x_1 = \boxed{5}, \text{ or } x_2 = \boxed{-1}$$

6. A cylindrical bucket has a height of 1 foot and a radius of 0.3 foot. How many such buckets can be completely filled from a full rectangular container whose length is 4 feet, width is 3 feet, and height is 6 feet?

(A) 255

(B) 253

(C) 252

(D) 254

> Solution: Answer: (D)
> $$\begin{cases} V_{\text{Cyl}} = r^2\pi \cdot h = 0.3^2\pi \cdot 1 = 0.09\pi \\ V_{\text{Rec}} = 4 \cdot 3 \cdot 6 = 72 \end{cases}$$
> $$\downarrow$$
> $$N_{\text{Buckets}} = \frac{V_{\text{Rec}}}{V_{\text{Cyl}}} = \frac{72}{0.09\pi}$$
> $$\downarrow$$
> $$\frac{72}{\frac{9}{100}\pi} = \frac{\cancel{72}^{8}00}{\cancel{9}\pi}$$
> $$\downarrow$$
> $$\frac{800}{\pi} \approx 254.65$$
> "be completely filled from"
> $$\Downarrow$$
> $$N_{\text{Buckets}} = 254$$

7. The part of a walkway of a park consists of a continuous chain in the shape of hexagons, the beginning of which is shown in the diagram above. The chain consists of 100 the same size hexagons. Each hexagon, except the first and last ones, shares two of its sides with adjacent hexagons. The length of each side of each hexagon is four yards. What is the perimeter of the walkway?

(A) 400

(B) 402

(C) 486

(D) 1,608

> Solution: Answer: (D)
> $$\# \text{ of sides} = (100 - 2) \times 4 + 2 \times 5 = 402$$
> $$\Downarrow$$
> $$\text{Perimeter} = 402 \times 4 = 1608$$

8. What is the greatest 4-digit integer meeting the following three conditions?

  I. The greatest digit is the sum of the remaining 3 digits.

  II. All of the digits are distinct.

  III. The product of the 4 digits is not equivalent to zero but is divisible by six.

(A) 3,216

(B) 6,321

(C) 6,311

(D) 1,236

> Solution: Answer: (B)
> According to the 3 conditions, 1236 and 6321 are the least and greatest integers, respectively.
> $$\Downarrow$$
> Answer is 6321.

NEXT PAGE

9. A and B both are constant and $3x^2 + Ax - 6$ equals $(3x-2)(x+B)$. What is the value of A?

(A) 1
(B) 5
(C) 7
(D) -5

> **Solution:**   **Answer: (C)**
>
> $$(3x-2)(x+B)$$
> $$\downarrow$$
> $$3x^2 - 2x + 3bx - 2B$$
> $$\begin{cases} 3x^2 + (3b-2)x - 2B \\ 3x^2 + \quad\quad Ax - 6 \end{cases}$$
>
> Corresponding coefficients are equal.
> $$\downarrow$$
> $$\begin{cases} 3B - 2 = A \\ -2B = -6 \end{cases}$$
> $$\Downarrow$$
> $$B = 3, \quad \boxed{A = 7}$$

10. At Water High School, a history class has 25 students in it. Of those students, 12 are enrolled in biology and 14 are enrolled in chemistry. What is the minimum percent of the students in the history class who are also enrolled in biology and chemistry?

(A) 4
(B) 3
(C) 2
(D) 1

> **Solution:**   **Answer: (A)**
>
> $$T = S1 + S2 - B + N$$
>
> T = total number of elements that overlap parts are eliminated
>
> $S1$ and $S2$ = number of elements in sets 1 and 2
>
> N = number of elements neither in set 1 nor set 2
>
> B = number of elements in both sets counted twice
> $$\downarrow$$
> $$25 = 12 + 14 - B + N$$
> $$B = 1 + N, \text{ when } N = 0, B = 1$$
> $$\Downarrow$$
> $$\frac{1}{25} \times 100\% = 4\%$$

11. If $-1 < x < 0$, then which of the following must be true?

(A) $x^2 < x^6$
(B) $x^3 > x^5$
(C) $x^3 > x^6$
(D) $x^5 > x^3$

> **Solution:**   **Answer: (D)**
>
> $$\underbrace{(C)\ x^3 > x^6}$$
> Negative values have no chance > positive values.
> $$\downarrow$$
> (C) is eliminated.
>
> Let $x = -\dfrac{1}{2}$ to test.
>
> $$\left(-\frac{1}{2}\right)^3 = -\frac{1}{8}, \quad \left(-\frac{1}{2}\right)^5 = -\frac{1}{32}$$
>
> $-\dfrac{1}{32}$ is More close to 0 than $-\dfrac{1}{8}$.
> $$\downarrow$$
> $$-\frac{1}{32} > -\frac{1}{8}$$
> $$\Downarrow$$
> Answer is (D).

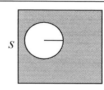

Note: Figure above not drawn to scale.

12. In the figure above, a circle inside a square. If the radius of the circle is r and $s = 4$, what is the area, in terms of r, of the shaded region?

(A) $16 - 2r\pi$
(B) $8 - r^2\pi$
(C) $16 - r^2\pi$
(D) $12 - 2r\pi$

> **Solution:**   **Answer: (C)**
> $$s = 4$$
> $$\begin{vmatrix} A_{\text{Cir}} = r^2\pi \\ A_{\text{Squ}} = s^2 = 16 \end{vmatrix}$$
> $$\Downarrow$$
> $$A_{\text{Sh}} = A_{\text{Squ}} - A_{\text{Cir}} = 16 - r^2\pi$$

NEXT PAGE ⟹

13. If the interior angles of triangle ABC are in the ratio of 4: 5: 6, then ABC is

(A) Obtuse Triangle
(B) Acute Triangle
(C) Right Triangle
(D) Isosceles Triangle

Solution: Answer: (B)

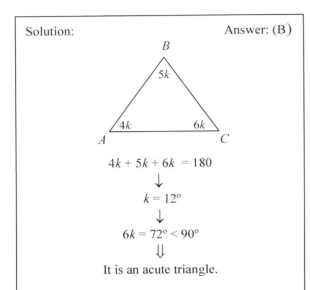

$$4k + 5k + 6k = 180$$
$$\downarrow$$
$$k = 12°$$
$$\downarrow$$
$$6k = 72° < 90°$$
$$\Downarrow$$

It is an acute triangle.

14. If $i = \sqrt{-1}$, which of the following equals $\sqrt{-5+12i}$?

(A) $-\dfrac{5}{2} - 6i$

(B) $2 + 3i$

(C) $-\dfrac{2}{3} - 3i$

(D) $2 - 3i$

Solution: Answer: (B)

$$\begin{cases} \sqrt{-5+12i} \text{ is the form } \sqrt{a}. \\ \text{One of the 5 choices is } \sqrt{a}. \end{cases}$$
$$\left(\sqrt{a}\right)^2 = a$$
$$\downarrow$$
Use plug-in method.
$$(2+3i)^2 = 2^2 + 12i + (3i)^2$$
$$\downarrow$$
$$4 + 12i - 9 = -5 + 12i$$
$$\Downarrow$$
$$\sqrt{-5+12i} = 2 + 3i$$

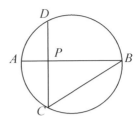

Note: Figure above not drawn to scale.

15. If $\overline{DC}$ is perpendicular to $\overline{AB}$, $AP = 5$, $DP = 12$, and $CP = 15$, what is CB ?

(A) 18
(B) 20
(C) 16
(D) 39

Solution: Answer: (D)

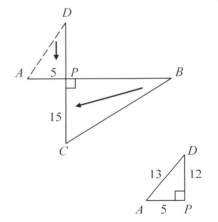

$\angle ADC$ and $\angle ABC$ face the same arc AC.
$$\downarrow$$
They have the same angle measure.
$$\downarrow$$
The 2 triangles have 3 pairs
of the same interior angles.
$$\downarrow$$
They are similar triangles.
$$\downarrow$$
The ratios of the corresponding sides are equal.
$$\Downarrow$$
$$\frac{CB}{AD} = \frac{15}{5}, \quad \frac{CB}{13} = \frac{15}{5}, \quad CB = 39$$

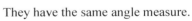

NEXT PAGE ⟹

16. What is the probability of choosing a prime number at random from the set = [1, 2, 4, and 9].

Solution: Answer: 1/4 or .25

Only number 2 is a prime number.

⇓

$$P = \frac{1}{4} = .25$$

17. If 3 distinct numbers are chosen, one from each of following sets, what is the greatest sum these numbers could have?

$S_1 = \{2, 3, 7\}$

$S_2 = \{4, 6, 8\}$

$S_3 = \{2, 5, 9\}$

Solution: Answer: 24

$$7 + 8 + 9 = 24$$

18. How many square yards are in a floor that is 9 feet by 21 feet if there is no waste?

Solution: Answer: 21
Change units first.

$$\frac{9}{3} = 3$$

$$\frac{21}{3} = 7$$

⇓

$$A = 3 \times 7 = 21$$

19. If x is an integer and $3 < x < 8$, how many distinct triangles are there with sides of lengths 3, 8, and x?

Solution: Answer: 2

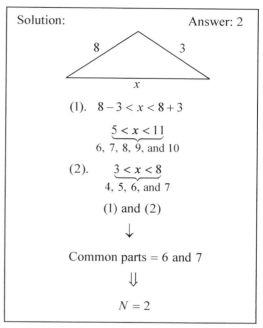

(1). $8 - 3 < x < 8 + 3$

$$\underbrace{5 < x < 11}$$
6, 7, 8, 9, and 10

(2). $\underbrace{3 < x < 8}$
4, 5, 6, and 7

(1) and (2)

↓

Common parts = 6 and 7

⇓

$$N = 2$$

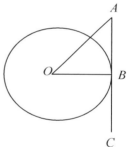

Note: Figure above not drawn to scale.

20. In the figure above, $\overline{AC}$ is tangent to the circle O at point B. BO is the radius of this circle $BO = AB = \sqrt{2}$. What is the AO?

Solution: Answer: 2

$\triangle AOB$ is a right triangle with 45°.

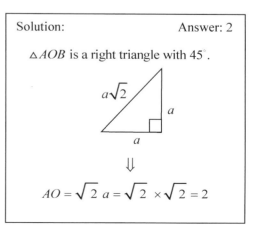

⇓

$$AO = \sqrt{2}\, a = \sqrt{2} \times \sqrt{2} = 2$$

STOP

Math Test – Calculator

Time: 55 Minutes
38 Questions

Notes:
- The use of a calculator is not allowed.
- All numbers used in this section are the real number.
- Figures are provided for some problems in this test. Unless otherwise indicated under the figure "Note: Figure above not drawn to scale", all figures are drawn as accurately as possible.
- All figures lie in a plane EXCEPT otherwise specified.
- Unless otherwise indicated, the domain of any function f, g or j is assumed to be the set of all real numbers x for which $f(x)$, $g(x)$, or $j(x)$ is a real number.

Reference Information

$$A = \frac{1}{2}bh$$

$$A = lw$$

$$A = \pi r^2$$

$$V = \pi r^2 h$$

$$V = lwh$$

$$c^2 = a^2 + b^2$$

$$V = \frac{1}{3}\pi r^2 h$$

$$V = \frac{4}{3}\pi r^3$$

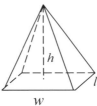

$$V = \frac{1}{3}lwh$$

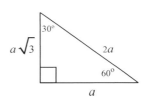

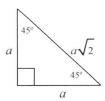

1. Jeff was 20 years old x years ago. Which of the following represents his age y years from now?

(A) $20 + x - y$

(B) $20 - x - y$

(C) $20 + x + y$

(D) $20 + y - x$

Solution: Answer: (C)

Current age $= 20 + x$

$\Downarrow$

y years from now $= 20 + x + y$

---

2. For which of the following values of x is $\dfrac{x^2 - 9}{x^2 + 2x - 3}$ undefined?

(A) 3 and -1
(B) -2
(C) -1
(D) -3 and 1

Solution: Answer: (D)

The defined or undefined values of x comes from the fraction before simplifying, not the fraction after simplifying.

$x^2 + 2x - 3 = 0$

$\downarrow$

$(x + 3)(x - 1) = 0$

$\Downarrow$

$x = -3$ and $x = 1$

Questions 3 and 4 refer to all information of the following figure:

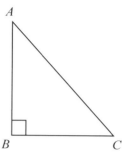

3. What is $\cos A$?

(A) $\dfrac{BC}{AC}$ (B) $\dfrac{AB}{AC}$ (C) $\dfrac{AC}{BC}$ (D) $\dfrac{BC}{AB}$

Solution   Answer: (B)
The definition of cosine

$\Downarrow$

$\cos A = \dfrac{AB}{AC}$ (for A, not for C)

---

4. If $AC = 4$, what is the area of the triangle?

(A) $8 \sin C \cos C$ (B) $4 \sin C \cos C$

(C) $8 \sin A \cos A$ (D) $4 \sin A \cos A$

Solution: Answer: (A)

$\sin C = \dfrac{AB}{AC}, \quad AB = AC \sin C$

$\cos C = \dfrac{BC}{AC}, \quad BC = AC \cos C$

$\downarrow$

$\begin{cases} A = \dfrac{AB \cdot BC}{2} = \dfrac{AC \sin C \cdot AC \cos C}{2} \\ AC = 4 \end{cases}$

$\Downarrow$

$A = \dfrac{\overset{8}{\cancel{16}} \sin C \cos C}{\cancel{2}} = 8 \sin C \cos C$

NEXT PAGE

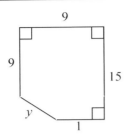

Note: Figure above not drawn to scale.

5. What is the perimeter of the figure shown above?

(A) 44
(B) 36
(C) 40
(D) 38

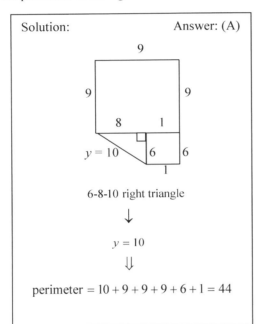

Solution: Answer: (A)

6-8-10 right triangle

$$\downarrow$$

$$y = 10$$

$$\Downarrow$$

perimeter $= 10 + 9 + 9 + 9 + 6 + 1 = 44$

6. Which of the following is divisible by 3 and 5 but is not divisible by 9?

(A) 135
(B) 120
(C) 45
(D) 90

Solution: Answer: (B)

Use plug-in method.

$$\downarrow$$

$$\frac{120}{3} = 40 = \text{integer}, \frac{120}{5} = 24 = \text{integer}$$

$$\frac{120}{9} \neq \text{integer}$$

$$\Downarrow$$

Answer is (B).

7. Mr. Wolf chooses watermelons for his supermarket. He will not choose the watermelons that weigh less than 10 pounds or more than 20 pounds. If n represents the weight of a watermelon, in pounds, he will not choose, which inequalities below represents all possible values of n?

(A) $|n - 15| < 10$
(B) $|n - 15| > 20$
(C) $|n - 10| < 15$
(D) $|n - 15| > 5$

Solution: Answer: (D)

Interpret English to math first.

$$n < 10, n > 20$$

Use plug-in method.

$$\downarrow$$

$$|n - 15| > 5$$

$$\downarrow$$

$$\left.\begin{array}{l} n - 15 > 5 \\ n - 15 < -5 \end{array}\right\}$$

$$\downarrow$$

$$\left.\begin{array}{l} n > 20 \\ n < 10 \end{array}\right\}$$

$$\Downarrow$$

Answer is (D).

$g(t)$	t
3	-3
-2	-2
4	-1
-3	0
0	1
2	2

8. The function g is defined by the chart above. For what value of t does $g(t) + t = 0$?

(A) 2
(B) 0
(C) -1
(D) -3

Solution: Answer: (D)

Refer to the chart above.

$$\downarrow$$

When $t = -3$, $g(-3) = 3$.

$$\downarrow$$

$$g(t) + t = 3 + (-3) = 0$$

$$\Downarrow$$

Answer is (D).

9. Line m is perpendicular to a segment PQ at point W and $PW = WQ$. How many points on line m have the same distance from point P as from point Q?

(A) 1
(B) 4
(C) 3
(D) > 4

Solution: Answer: (D)

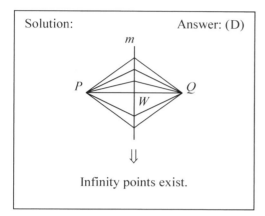

Infinity points exist.

10. If segment PQ in the coordinate plane has endpoint P (-8, 6) and midpoint (-4, 10), then endpoint Q of $\overline{PQ}$ has coordinates

(A) (0, 26)
(B) (0, 14)
(C) (12, 8)
(D) (16, 14)

Solution: Answer: (B)

$$\text{Midpoint} = \left(\frac{x_1 + x_2}{2} = x_m, \; \frac{y_1 + y_2}{2} = y_m \right)$$

$$M = \left(\frac{-8 + x_2}{2} = -4, \; \frac{6 + y_2}{2} = 10 \right)$$

$$\downarrow \qquad\qquad \downarrow$$

$$x_2 = -8 + 8, \qquad y_2 = 20 - 6$$
$$x_2 = 0, \qquad y_2 = 14$$

$$\Downarrow$$

Answer is (B).

11. A rectangle was changed by increasing its length by $P\%$ and decreasing its width by 10%. If these changes increased the area of the rectangle to 108% of its original area, what is the value of P?

(A) 20
(B) 15
(C) 30
(D) 22

Solution: Answer: (A)

$$\frac{\left(1 + \frac{P}{100}\right)\cancel{x} \cdot \frac{90}{100}\cancel{y}}{\cancel{xy}} = \frac{108}{100}$$

$$\downarrow$$

$$\left(\frac{100 + P}{\cancel{100}}\right) \cdot \frac{\cancel{9}}{10} = \frac{\cancel{108}^{12}}{\cancel{100}}$$

$$\Downarrow$$

$$100 + P = 120, \qquad P = 20$$

12. If $\dfrac{a}{b}$ of x, $b > a > 0$, is 15, then $\dfrac{2}{15}$ of $x =$

(A) $\dfrac{2a}{b}$

(B) $\dfrac{2b}{a}$

(C) $\dfrac{4a}{b}$

(D) $\dfrac{a}{4b}$

Solution: Answer: (B)

$$\frac{a}{b}x = 15 \rightarrow x = 15 \cdot \frac{b}{a}$$

$$\downarrow$$

$$\left(\frac{2}{15}\right) \cdot x = 15 \cdot \frac{b}{a} \cdot \left(\frac{2}{15}\right)$$

$$\Downarrow$$

$$\frac{2}{15}x = \frac{2b}{a}$$

NEXT PAGE

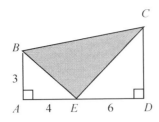

Note: Diagram above not drawn to scale.

13. The diagram above shows a trapezoid divided into 3 right triangles. What is the the area of the shaded region?

(A) 20

(B) 25

(C) 30

(D) 35

Solution: Answer: (B)

By the law: Measure of one exterior angle is equal to sum of measures of two non-adjacent interior angles.

↓

$\angle AEB + \angle BEC = \angle EDC + \angle DCE$

$\angle BEC = \angle EDC = 90°$

↓

$\angle AEB = \angle DCE$

$\angle ABE = \angle CED$

↓

ABE and DCE are similar triangles.

↓

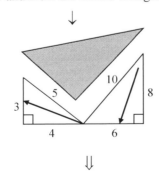

⇓

$A_{shaded} = \dfrac{5 \times 10}{2} = 25$

14. Set P_1 consists of the positive factors of 15 and P_2 consists of the positive factors of 18. What is the intersection of P_1 and P_2 ?

(A) (1, 2, 3, 5, 6, 9, 15, 18)
(B) (2, 5, 6, 9, 15, 18)
(C) (1, 3, 5, 9, 15)
(D) (1, 3)

Solution: Answer: (D)

$$P_1 = \{1, 3, 5, 15\}$$

$$P_2 = \{1, 2, 3, 6, 9, 18\}$$

⇓

$$P_1 \cap P_2 = (1, 3)$$

15. If the line $y = 3$ intersects the graph of the equation $y = x^2 - 14x + 52$ at one point only, which of the following is the coordinates of the point?

(A) (−7, 3)

(B) (7, 7)

(C) (-7, -7)

(D) (7, 3)

Solution: Answer: (D)

At an intersection point, $y = y$ and $x = x$.

↓

$$3 = x^2 - 14x + 52$$

↓

$$x^2 - 14x + 49 = 0$$

x -7

x -7

$$(x - 7)(x - 7)$$

⇓

$$x = 7$$

NEXT PAGE

16. If the six cards shown above are placed in a row so that

 , , and are never at either end, how

many possible distinct combinations exist?

(A) 24
(B) 30
(C) 132
(D) 144

Solution: Answer: (D)

The order does matter.
↓
(1) 4 cards between 2 end cards
4 positions, 4 elements
$\boxed{4} \times \boxed{3} \times \boxed{2} \times \boxed{1} = 24$
(2) 2 cards at either end
2 positions, 3 elements
$\boxed{3} \times \boxed{2} = 6$
(3)   2 element sets
They can be combined.
↓
Use fundamental counting principle.
⇓
Total = 24 · 6 = 144

17. Car X's speed is 2 times Car Y's speed, and Car Z's speed is 3 times Car X's speed. If car Z's speed is 12 miles per hour, what is 2 times Car Y's speed, in miles per hour?

(A) 2
(B) 4
(C) 6
(D) 8

Solution: Answer: (B)

Let x = Y's speed.
↓
$2x$ = X's speed
↓
$6x$ = Z's speed
↓
$6x = 12$, $x = 2$
⇓
$2x = \boxed{4}$

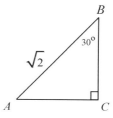

Note: Figure above not drawn to scale.

18. In the figure above, what is BC?

(A) $\dfrac{3}{\sqrt{2}}$

(B) $\dfrac{\sqrt{6}}{2}$

(C) $2\sqrt{2}$

(D) $4\sqrt{2}$

Solution: Answer: (B)

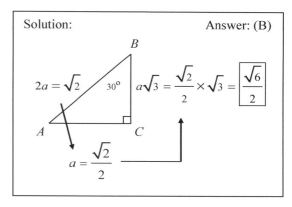

19. If 1.862 is rounded to the nearest tenth, the result is how much less than if 1.862 is rounded to nearest whole number?

(A) 0.01

(B) 0.02

(C) 0.1

(D) 0.2

Solution: Answer: (C)

Nearest tenth: $1.862 \to 1.9$

Nearest whole number: $1.862 \to 2.0$
⇓
$2.0 - 1.9 = 0.1$

NEXT PAGE

20. If p_1 represents the greatest prime number less than 96 and p_2 represents the least prime number greater than 8, which of the following is the value of $p_1 - p_2$?

(A) 81

(B) 80

(C) 78

(D) 82

Solution: Answer: (C)

$$91 = 13 \times 7$$
$$\downarrow$$
$$91 \text{ is not prime.}$$
$$p_1 = 89, \quad p_2 = 11$$
$$\Downarrow$$
$$p_1 - p_2 = 89 - 11 = 78$$

21.   A banquet has 21 tables, which can seat a total of 140 people. Some of the tables seat 6 people and the rest seat 8 people. How many tables seat 8 people?

(A) 5
(B) 6
(C) 7
(D) 8

Solution: Answer: (C)

$$8x + 6(21 - x) = 140$$
$$\downarrow$$
$$8x + 126 - 6x = 140$$
$$\downarrow$$
$$2x = 14$$
$$\Downarrow$$
$$x = 7$$

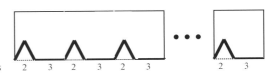

Centimeters   2   3   2   3   2   3   2   3

Note: Figure above not drawn to scale.

22. A 200-centimeter-long strip is shown in the figure above. By eliminating an equilateral triangle from the front of each 5-centimeter length on one side of the strip, the nicked side shown in bold is formed. Which of the following is the total length, in centimeters, of the bold nicked side on the 200-centimeter strip?

(A) 240

(B) 185

(C) 280

(D) 125

Solution: Answer: (C)

An equilateral triangle
$$\downarrow$$
2 centimeters increased
per 5 centimeters
$$\Downarrow$$
$$\text{Total length} = 200 + 2 \cdot \frac{200}{5} = 280$$

23.   Two sides of a triangle have lengths 13 and 12, respectively. If the remaining side of the triangle has a value that is an integer, what is the smallest possible perimeter of this triangle?

(A) 25
(B) 21
(C) 45
(D) 27

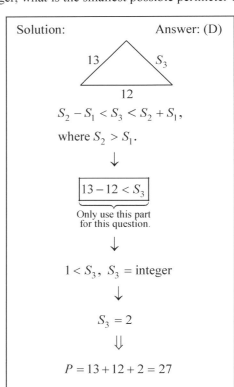

Solution: Answer: (D)

$$S_2 - S_1 < S_3 < S_2 + S_1,$$
where $S_2 > S_1$.
$$\downarrow$$
$$\boxed{13 - 12 < S_3}$$
Only use this part
for this question.
$$\downarrow$$
$$1 < S_3, \ S_3 = \text{integer}$$
$$\downarrow$$
$$S_3 = 2$$
$$\Downarrow$$
$$P = 13 + 12 + 2 = 27$$

NEXT PAGE ⟶

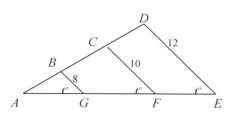

24. In the figure above, what are the values of $\dfrac{CF}{DE}$ and $\dfrac{AG}{AE}$?

(A) $\dfrac{5}{6}$ and $\dfrac{2}{3}$

(B) $\dfrac{5}{6}$ and $\dfrac{4}{5}$

(C) $\dfrac{5}{12}$ and $\dfrac{5}{6}$

(D) $\dfrac{6}{12}$ and $\dfrac{2}{3}$

Solution:　　　　　　　　　Answer: (A)

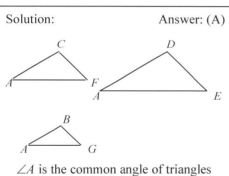

$\angle A$ is the common angle of triangles ABG, ACF, and ADE. The three triangles each have another angle t°.

↓

They are the similar triangles.

⇓

$$\dfrac{CF}{DE} = \dfrac{10}{12} = \boxed{\dfrac{5}{6}}$$

$$\dfrac{AG}{AE} = \dfrac{BG}{DE} = \dfrac{8}{12} = \boxed{\dfrac{2}{3}}$$

The questions 25 and 26 refer to the following information.

Questions 25 and 26 refer to following information.

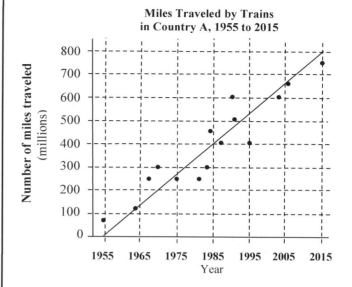

Miles Traveled by Trains in Country A, 1955 to 2015

25. By the line of best fit above, which of the following best approximates the year in which the number of miles traveled by trains in Country A was estimated to be 600 millions?

(A) 1990
(B) 1996
(C) 2003
(D) 2000

Solution:　　　　　　　　Answer: (D)

"By the line...", not "by the scatterplot"

⇓

It is not year 1990, it is year 2000.

26.　　By the line of best fit, which of the following best approximates the percent increasing in the millions of miles traveled in Country A from year 1985 to year 2015?

(A) 96.5%
(B) 89.3%
(C) 95%
(D) 100%

Solution:　　　　　　　　Answer: (D)

"percent increase" → format $\dfrac{b-a}{a} \cdot 100\%$

⇓

$$\dfrac{800-400}{400} \cdot 100\% = 100\%$$

NEXT PAGE

27. How many positive factors, excluding 1 and m, does m have if a, b, and c are three distinct prime numbers greater than 2, and m is the product of $a, b,$ and c ?

(A) 3

(B) 8

(C) 6

(D) 5

Solution: Answer: (C)

3, 5, 7   → 3

$3 \times 5 \times 7 = $ A certain #

Because 3, 5, and 7 is the factors of the certain #, the product of each pair of them still is the factors of the certain #.

3×5, 5×7, 3×7 → 3

3 is the maximun number of possible combinations.

↓

$3 + 3 = 6$

5, 7, 11   → 3

$5 \times 7 \times 11 = $ A certain #

Because 5, 7, and 11 is the factors of the certain #, the product of each pair of them still is the factors of the certain #.

5×7, 7×11, 5×11 → 3

3 is the maximun number of possible combinations.

↓

$3 + 3 = 6$

⋮

⇓

Conclusion: 6 factors

28. In the figure above, if the right circular cylinder has height $h = \pi$ and diameter d, which of the following represents the volume of the smallest rectangular prism that contains the entire cylinder?

(A) $d^2 \pi$

(B) $d \pi$

(C) $\dfrac{d \pi}{2}$

(D) $\dfrac{d^2 \pi}{2}$

Solution: Answer: (A)

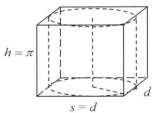

$h = \pi$

$s = d$

The bases of the prism are squares.

↓

$V = A \times h$

⇓

$d \times d \times \pi = d^2 \pi$

NEXT PAGE

29. Mary has two jobs. She works as a waitress, which pays $15 per hour, and she works as a nurse, which pays $16 per hour. Mary can work less than 120 hours per month, and she plans to make greater than $1,200 per month. Which of the following system of inequalities describes this situation in terms of w and n, where w represents the number of hours she works as a waitress and n represents the number of hours she works as a nurse?

(A) $w + n < 120$
$15w + 16n > 1,200$

(B) $w + n > 120$
$16w + 15n \geq 1,200$

(C) $w + n \leq 120$
$15w + 16n \leq 1,200$

(D) $w + n > 120$
$15w + 16n \geq 1,200$

Solution: Answer: (A)

$$\begin{cases} \text{"less than"} \rightarrow \text{Use sign } <. \\ \text{"greater than"} \rightarrow \text{Use sign } >. \end{cases}$$
$$\Downarrow$$
$$\begin{cases} w + y < 120 \\ 15w + 16n > 1200 \end{cases}$$

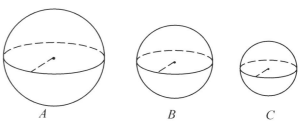

Figure 3

30. In Figure 3, sphere A and sphere C have a radius of 4 and 2, respectively. If the volume of sphere B is the mean of the volumes of sphere A and sphere C, which of the following is the diameter of sphere B?

(A) 6.0

(B) 12

(C) 6.6

(D) 6.4

Solution: Answer: (C)

$$V_B = \frac{V_A + V_C}{2}$$
$$\downarrow$$
$$\frac{4}{3} \pi r_B^3 = \frac{\frac{4}{3} \pi r_A^3 + \frac{4}{3} \pi r_C^3}{2}$$
$$\downarrow$$
$$r_B^3 = \frac{r_A^3 + r_C^3}{2}$$
$$\downarrow$$
$$r_B = \sqrt[3]{\frac{2^3 + 4^3}{2}} = \sqrt[3]{\frac{8 + 64}{2}} = \sqrt[3]{36}$$
$$r_B \approx 3.3$$
$$\Downarrow$$
$$2r = 2 \times 3.3 = \boxed{6.6}$$

NEXT PAGE

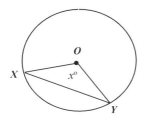

Note that figure not drawn to scale.

31. Point O is the center of the circle above and the area of sector OXY is $\dfrac{5}{12}$ of the area of the circle. What is the value of x?

> **Solution:**   **Answer: 150**
>
> In the same circle, arc, area, and measure of angle have the same ratio.
>
> $\begin{cases} \text{if getting ratio from area, you can use} \\ \text{it to obtain arc or angle measure.} \end{cases}$
>
> $\begin{cases} \text{if getting ratio from arc, you can use} \\ \text{it to obtain area or angle measure.} \end{cases}$
>
> $\begin{cases} \text{if getting ratio from angle measure,} \\ \text{you can use it to obtain area or arc.} \end{cases}$
>
> $\Downarrow$
>
> $\dfrac{5}{12} \times 360 = 150$

$$1 + \frac{y}{2} = 2x - 1$$

32. What is the slope of the function above?

> **Solution:**   **Answer: 4**
>
> $\dfrac{y}{2} = 2x - 2, \quad y = 4x - 4$
>
> $\underbrace{y = sx + b}_{\text{slope-intercept form}}$
>
> $\Downarrow$
>
> $s = 4$

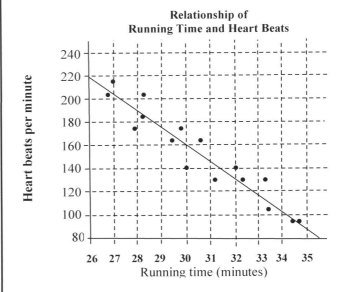

Relationship of Running Time and Heart Beats

33. Monica run 6 miles on each of 16 days. The scatterplot with the line of best fit above shows the relationship of her running time, in minutes, and heart beats per minute after each running. For this running that Monica run 30 minutes, her actual heart beats per minute or beat rate was around how many less than the heart beat rate predicted by the line of best fit?

> **Solution**   **Answer: 20**
>
> Actual heart beat rate is represented by the scatterplot.
>
> $\Downarrow$
>
> $160 - 140 = 20$

34. Around what is the length of the radius of the sphere $x^2 + y^2 + z^2 + 4x - 4z = 12$?

> **Solution:**   **Answer: 4.47**
>
> $\left(x^2 + 4x + 2^2\right) + y^2 + \left(z^2 - 4z + 2^2\right) = 12 + 2^2 + 2^2 = \left(\sqrt{20}\right)^2$
>
> $\downarrow$
>
> $\underbrace{(x+2)^2 + y^2 + (z-2)^2 = \left(\sqrt{20}\right)^2}_{\substack{\text{Radius is the target in this case. You} \\ \text{may not need to write down this step.}}}$
>
> $\Downarrow$
>
> $r = \sqrt{20} \approx 4.47$

NEXT PAGE

35. Each of 6 boys played a computer game with each of five girls, and then each boy played a computer game with each of the other boys. How many computer games were played?

Solution: Answer: 45

$\underbrace{\text{2 element sets}}_{\text{boys with girls}}$

↓

Use Fundamental Counting Principle.

↓

$\boxed{6} \times \boxed{5} = 30$

$\underbrace{\text{1 element set}}_{\text{boys with boys}}$

Order is not important.

2 positions, 6 elements

↓

Use the counting method of combinations.

↓

$\dfrac{\boxed{6} \cdot \boxed{5}}{2} = 15$

2 element sets

The elements of the 2 sets cannot be combined.

↓

Cannot use Fundamental Counting Principle.

⇓

Total number of games $= 30 + 15 = 45$

36. If $p = 10q = 2m = 5n$, then $\dfrac{pq}{mn} =$

Solution: Answer: 1

$\dfrac{mn}{pq} = \dfrac{m}{p} \times \dfrac{n}{q} \rightarrow \begin{cases} (1)\ p = 2m,\ \boxed{\dfrac{m}{p} = 2} \\[2ex] (2)\ 10q = 5n,\ \boxed{\dfrac{n}{q} = \dfrac{1}{2}} \end{cases}$

⇓

$\dfrac{mn}{pq} = 2 \times \dfrac{1}{2} = \boxed{1}$

	Seniors	Juniors	Period-1	Period-2
Math	20	25	16	n
English	20	35	k	19

37. The chart above shows the number of seniors and juniors taking math and English classes at a high school and gives the enrollment for these classes in period-1 and period-2, which are the only periods math and English are taught. Only seniors and juniors take these classes. What is the total number of students who take math and English in period-1?

Solution: Answer: 52

$\text{Total}_{\text{English}} = 20 + 35 = 55$

↓

$k = 55 - 19 = 36$

⇓

$\text{Total}_{\text{Period-1}} = 16 + k = 16 + 36 = 52$

38. In how many arrangements can people P_A, P_B, P_C, P_S and P_M stand in a straight line if P_M must be at the middle position and P_S must be at the second position?

Solution: Answer: 6

Two postions for p_M and p_S are fixed. They are always there. Their presence doesn't affect the # of the arrangements.

$5 - 2 = 3$ the remaining elements determine the number of the arrangements.

⇓

$\underbrace{\boxed{3} \cdot \boxed{2} \cdot \boxed{1}}_{\substack{\text{3 positions} \\ \text{3 elements} \\ \text{Order does matter.}}} = 6$

STOP

SAT Math

Practice

Test 02

Redesigned for Tests in March 2016 and Beyond

Mad Math

Math Test – No Calculator

Time: 25 Minutes
20 Questions

Notes:
- The use of a calculator is not allowed.
- All numbers used in this section are the real number.
- Figures are provided for some problems in this test. Unless otherwise indicated under the figure "Note: Figure above not drawn to scale", all figures are drawn as accurately as possible.
- All figures lie in a plane EXCEPT otherwise specified.
- Unless otherwise indicated, the domain of any function f, g or j is assumed to be the set of all real numbers x for which $f(x)$, $g(x)$, or $j(x)$ is a real number.

Reference Information

$$A = \frac{1}{2}bh$$

$$A = lw$$

$$A = \pi r^2$$

$$V = \pi r^2 h$$

$$V = lwh$$

$$c^2 = a^2 + b^2$$

$$V = \frac{1}{3}\pi r^2 h$$

$$V = \frac{4}{3}\pi r^3$$

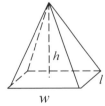

$$V = \frac{1}{3}lwh$$

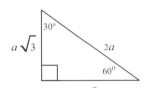

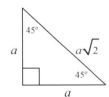

1. $\dfrac{1}{m+n}\left(\dfrac{1}{m+n}\right)^{-2} = ?$

(A) $\dfrac{1}{\left(m+n\right)^{3}}$

(B) $\dfrac{1}{\left(m+n\right)^{2}}$

(C) $\dfrac{\left(m+n\right)^{2}}{1}$

(D) $m+n$

2. In a parallelogram whose area is 72, the base is represented by $x + 3$ and the altitude is $x - 3$. What is the altitude of the parallelogram?

(A) 6
(B) 17
(C) 9
(D) 8

3. Which of the following does $E = 25^{\frac{3}{4}}$ equal?

(A) $\sqrt[5]{5}$
(B) $\sqrt[4]{5}$
(C) $5\sqrt{5}$
(D) $\sqrt[6]{5}$

4. If $i^{2} = -1$, which of the following expressions could $x^{2} + 2$ equal?

(A) $x^{2} - \left(\sqrt{2}\right)^{2}$

(B) $\left(x - \sqrt{2} \cdot i\right)\left(x + \sqrt{2} \cdot i\right)$

(C) $x^{2} + \left(\sqrt{2} \cdot i\right)^{2}$

(D) $(x - \sqrt{2} \cdot i)^{2}$

NEXT PAGE

5.   If $x^{-2} < \dfrac{1}{x^4}$ and $x > 0,$ which of the following is one possible value for x?

(A) $\dfrac{5}{2}$

(B) $\dfrac{1}{4}$

(C) $1\dfrac{1}{6}$

(D) $-\dfrac{1}{2}$

NUMBER OF FOOD COMPANY LOCATIONS

Company	USA Locations	Non-USA Locations
$X1$	6,200	1,909
$X2$	6,100	2,108
X3	4,998	2,199
$X4$	4,280	1,090

6.   In the chart above, it shows the number of the locations for 4 food companies. For which of following companies has the greatest ratio of the number of USA locations to the number of Non-USA locations?

(A) $X4$

(B) $X1$

(C) $X3$

(D) $X2$

7.   If $f(x) = \dfrac{1}{\csc x}$, which of the following must be true?

(A) $f(-x) = f(x)$

(B) $f(x) = f(-x)$

(C) $f(-x) = -f(x)$

(D) $f(x) = 2f(-x)$

NEXT PAGE

8. Which of the following equations must be true if $x + y = 90°$?

(A) $\dfrac{\sin x}{\cos x} = \dfrac{\sin y}{\cos y}$

(B) $\sin x = \sin y$

(C) $\sin x = -\sin y$

(D) $\dfrac{\sin x}{\cos x} = \dfrac{\cos y}{\sin y}$

9. Which of the following does $2 \le |x + 4| \le 3$ equal?

(A) $-2 \le x \le -1$, $-7 \le x \le -6$
(B) $-7 \le x \le -6$
(C) $-7 \le x \le -6$
(D) $1 \le x \le 2$, $6 \le x \le 7$

Questions 10 and 11 refer to the following graph.

HOUSES SOLD PER YEAR

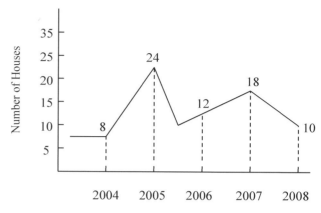

The line graph above shows the number of houses Mark sold in each of the 5 years.

10. Mark sold how many less houses in year 2007 than in years 2004 and 2008 combined?

(A) 0

(B) 1

(C) 2

(D) 3

11. If the information of the house sales from the 5 years were illustrated by a circle graph, what would be the degree measure of the central angle of the sector that represents the 2006?

(A) 20

(B) 60

(C) 40

(D) 50

NEXT PAGE

Number of Pets per Family in A Street

Number of Pets	Number of Families
0	5
1	5
2	2
3	1

12.   The chart above shows how many families in a street of 13 families had 0, 1, 2 or 3 pets. Recently, a new family moved into the street, and the average (arithmetic mean) number of pets per family became equal to the median number of pets per family. How many pets must the new family have?

(A) 0

(B) 4

(C) 3

(D) 2

13.   If $\dfrac{4x + 20y}{27} = \dfrac{16a - 32b}{81}$, then $a - 2b =$

(A) $\dfrac{3(x + 5y)}{4}$

(B) $\dfrac{4(x + 5y)}{3}$

(C) $\dfrac{3(x - 5y)}{4}$

(D) $\dfrac{4(x - 5y)}{3}$

NEXT PAGE

Mean	78
Median	83
Lower quartile	72
Upper quartile	92
Standard Deviation	9

14.   The statistical information above provides a summary of chemistry scores of 200 students at North Ridge High School. Round about 100 of the students in the statistical information have chemistry scores

(A) from 68 to 91.

(B) less than 72.

(C) less than 99.

(D) from 72 to 92..

15.   How must a and b be related so that the graph of $g(x+1)$ will be symmetrical about the y-axis if $g(x) = ax^2 + bx + c$?

(A) $2a = b$

(B) $4a = -b$

(C) $2a = -b$

(D) $5a = -b$

NEXT PAGE

16. How many multiples of 7 between 100 and 600 ?

17. When $2x^{(6m+1)} + 3x^{(4m+2)} - 4x^{(2m+3)} - 5$ is divided by $x + 1$, if m is an integer, what is the remainder?

18. If $f(x) = x - 5$, $g(x) = 10x$, and $j(x) = \dfrac{x}{5}$, what does $f(j(g(5)))$ equal?

19. At a college, in a class of 90 juniors, there are 4 girls for every 6 boys. In a senior class, there are 5 girls for every 2 boys. If the two classes are combined, and in the combined class, the number of girls is twice the number of boys, how many boys are in the senior class?

20. In how many ways can an SAT club of six be selected from eight students if the club always includes a certain student?

STOP

No Test Contents

On This Page

Go to Next Page

Math Test – Calculator

Time: 55 Minutes
38 Questions

Notes:

- The use of a calculator is not allowed.
- All numbers used in this section are the real number.
- Figures are provided for some problems in this test. Unless otherwise indicated under the figure "Note: Figure above not drawn to scale", all figures are drawn as accurately as possible.
- All figures lie in a plane EXCEPT otherwise specified.
- Unless otherwise indicated, the domain of any function f, g or j is assumed to be the set of all real numbers x for which $f(x)$, $g(x)$, or $j(x)$ is a real number.

Reference Information

$$A = \frac{1}{2}bh$$

$$A = lw$$

$$A = \pi r^2$$

$$V = \pi r^2 h$$

$$V = lwh$$

$$c^2 = a^2 + b^2$$

$$V = \frac{1}{3}\pi r^2 h$$

$$V = \frac{4}{3}\pi r^3$$

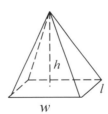

$$V = \frac{1}{3}lwh$$

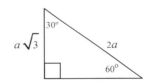

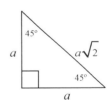

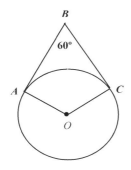

1. In the figure above, the center of the circle is point O, line segments AB and BC are tangent to the circle at points A and C, respectively, and the segments intersect at point B as shown. If the circomference of the circle is 10π, which of the following is the area of minor sector OAC?

(A) $\dfrac{22\pi}{5}$

(B) $\dfrac{20\pi}{3}$

(C) $\dfrac{25\pi}{4}$

(D) $\dfrac{25\pi}{3}$

2. If the point $(5, -7)$ is on the graph of a function f and if $f(-x) = f(x)$ for all x, which of the following points must also be on the graph of the function f ?

(A) $(-7, 5)$

(B) $(-5, -7)$

(C) $(-5, 7)$

(D) $(5, -7)$

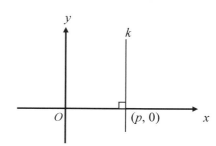

Figure 1

3. In Figure 1, the equation of line k is

(A) $y = p$

(B) $x = k$

(C) $x = p$

(D) $y = -p$

4. A truck is used to move boxes. The boxes each weigh either 50 pounds or 75 pounds. Let x represent the number of 50-pound boxes and y represent the 75-pound boxes. The truck can carry up to either 65 boxes or less than a weight of 4,600 pounds. Which system of inequalities below represents the conditions described?

(A) $\begin{cases} x + y \le 65 \\ 75x + 50y < 4,600 \end{cases}$

(B) $\begin{cases} x + y < 65 \\ 50x + 75y < 4,600 \end{cases}$

(C) $\begin{cases} x + y \le 65 \\ 50x + 75y < 4,600 \end{cases}$

(D) $\begin{cases} x + y < 4,600 \\ 75y - 50x \le 65 \end{cases}$

NEXT PAGE

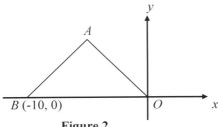

Figure 2

5. In the equilateral triangle in Figure 2, what is the slope of segment AO?

(A) $-\sqrt{3}$

(B) $\sqrt{3}$

(C) $-\dfrac{\sqrt{3}}{3}$

(D) $\dfrac{\sqrt{2}}{3}$

6. If $x^{\frac{2}{3}} = 27$, then $x^{\frac{4}{9}}$ is equal to

(A) 121

(B) $\dfrac{1}{9}$

(C) 9

(D) 81

7. If $\dfrac{n^{n+1}}{(n-1)!} = \dfrac{2nx}{n!}$, x is equal to

(A) $2n^{n}$

(B) $\dfrac{n^{n+1}}{2}$

(C) $n^{\frac{n}{2}}$

(D) n^{n-1}

8. At East North High School, 55 percent of the students are boys and 45 percent of the boys at the high school play basketball. If a student at the high school is selected randomly, which of the following is the probability that the student is a boy who plays basketball, to the nearest hundredth?

(A) 0.24

(B) 0.25

(C) 0.42

(D) 0.51

NEXT PAGE

9. If 5 girls A, B, C, D, and E line up in a row, what is the probability that girl E is at either end of the row?

(A) 15%

(B) 25%

(C) 35%

(D) 40%

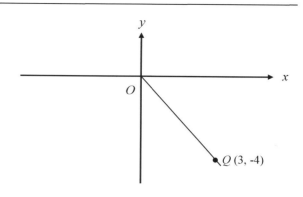

Note: Figure above not drawn to scale.

11. In the figure above, a ring with circumference π is placed on an incline. Point Q with coordinates (3, -4) is on the ring. The ring is rolled up the incline, and once point Q of the ring touches the origin, it is then rolled horizontally along the x-axis to the right. What is the x-coordinate of point Q, where point Q on the ring touches the x-axis or the incline for the 8th time?

(A) -16.99

(B) 26.99

(C) 19.96

(D) 16.99

10. Route 8 to Catharine's home is 8 miles longer than the direct route. When Catharine goes by Route 8 and returns by the direct route, the round trip is 88 miles. How many miles is the direct route?

(A) 30
(B) 56
(C) 40
(D) 54

NEXT PAGE

12. Line m is tangent to the circle whose center is at (-4, -1). If the tangent point is (-2, -4), what is the x-intercept of m?

(A) $\dfrac{1}{4}$

(B) 4

(C) 1

(D) -4

13. What is the sum of the volume of a cone and the volume of a sphere if the cone whose base radius is 6 is inscribed in the sphere of radius 10?

(A) 19,512

(B) 12,620

(C) 4,867

(D) 4,602

14. If $f(x) = -x^3 + 2k^2x^2 + 12x$ is divisible by $x - 6$, what is k equal to?

(A) ± 6.00

(B) ± 1.41

(C) ± 4.94

(D) ± 5.74

NEXT PAGE

15. For $x > 0$, what is $\dfrac{\dfrac{7x}{3}}{\dfrac{1}{9x}} \div 9x$?

(A) $149x^2$

(B) $\dfrac{7x^2}{3}$

(C) $63x$

(D) $\dfrac{7x}{3}$

16. For which of the following sets of numbers is the average (arithmetic mean) less than the median?

(A) [1, 2, 3, 4, 4]
(B) [1, 2, 3, 4, 5]
(C) [2, 3, 4, 5, 6]
(D) [3, 4, 5, 6, 8]

17. A cylindrical container has a height of two yards and a radius of 1 yard. How many such containers can completely fill up water into a rectangular container whose length is 4 yards, width is 4 yards, and height is 6 yards?

(A) 16

(B) 15

(C) 14

(D) 13

18. Burger Queen sold 10 percent in 2011 less hamburger sandwiches than in 2010, and the price of each hamburger sandwich they sold in 2011 was 10 percent more than in 2010. The total earnings from the sale of hamburger sandwiches were what percent change in 2011 than in 2010?

(A) 0%

(B) 1%

(C) 11%

(D) $\dfrac{1}{100}$ %

NEXT PAGE

19. Under which of the following conditions is $\dfrac{k_2(k_2 - k_1)}{k_1}$ greater than zero ?

(A) $1 < k_2 < k_1$

(B) $k_1 < 0 < k_2$

(C) $k_1 < 0 = k_2$

(D) $k_2 > k_1 > 0$

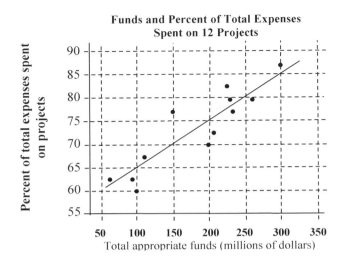

Funds and Percent of Total Expenses Spent on 12 Projects

20. The appropriate funds are alloted to 12 research projects. The scatterplot with the line of best fit above shows data for the 12 projects. For the project with the greatest percent of total expenses spent on projects, which of the following is closest to the difference of the percent predicted by the line of best fit and the actual percent?

(A) 2 percent

(B) 85 percent

(C) 4.5 percent

(D) 87.5 percent

NEXT PAGE

21. If n is $\dfrac{2}{3}$ of s and p is $\dfrac{4}{5}$ of s, what is the value of $\dfrac{n}{p}$?

(A) $\dfrac{5}{2}$

(B) $\dfrac{10}{3}$

(C) $\dfrac{5}{6}$

(D) $\dfrac{15}{8}$

x	$g(x)$	$f(x)$
2	-1	2
1	0	-1
0	1	-2
-1	2	3
-2	3	4

22. According to the chart above, what is the value of $g(-2) - f(1)$?

(A) 2

(B) 3

(C) 4

(D) -3

23. Line L passes through the points $(0, 0)$ and $(9, 9)$. Which of the following points is located in the region between the graph of the line L and positive part of the x-axis?

(A) $x > y$ and $y > 0$
(B) $x = y$ and $y < 0$
(C) $x \geq y$ and $y < 0$
(D) $x < y$ and $y > 0$

24. Mr. David Smith built a house at a cost of $800,000. He offers a discount of 10% to encourage sales after pricing the home for sale by adding 20% of his expenses. What does he make on his house?

(A) $0
(B) $64,000
(C) $46,000
(D) $4,600

NEXT PAGE

25.　If $x^2 + y^2 = 256$ and $xy = 25$, what is the value of $(x + y)^2$?

(A) 306
(B) 206
(C) 302
(D) 216

26.　If m is a positive number, which of the following is equal to $9m$?

(A) $3\sqrt{3m^2}$

(B) $3\sqrt{6m^2}$

(C) $3\sqrt{27m^2}$

(D) $3\sqrt{9m^2}$

27. How many 3-person committees formed from a group of five?

(A) 60
(B) 10
(C) 30
(D) 20

28.　If $\dfrac{1}{4}x = x^2$, then which of the following can be the value of x ?

　　I.　0

　　II. $-\dfrac{1}{4}$

　　III. $\dfrac{1}{4}$

(A) I only

(B) II only

(C) III only

(D) I and III only

NEXT PAGE

29. If the circle $x^2 + y^2 + 2x - 8y = r^2 - 17$ is tangent to the line $12y = 60$, what is the value of r ?

(A) 1

(B) 4

(C) 3

(D) 8

30. Circle O_1 is centered at (-2, k) and has a radius of 6. Circle O_2 is centered at (5, -5) and has a radius of 4. If circle O_1 is externally tangent to circle O_2, which of the following is the value of k ? Round to the nearest hundredth.

(A) 2.1

(B) 2.141

(C) 2.14

(D) 4.12

NEXT PAGE

31. May bought a ticket for a concert, and then she changed her mind because she needed more time to prepare the SAT test. May sold the ticket to Jackson for $12, thus she lost 25%. What is the original price?

33. A rectangle was changed by decreasing its length by 20% and increasing its width by 10%. If these changes decreased the area of the rectangle to X% of its original area, what is the value of X ?

x	$f(x)$
1	-2
2	3
3	0
4	-4
5	7
6	-3

32. Emily drove to work at an average speed of 30 miles per hour and returned along the same route at 50 miles per hour. If her total traveling time was 2 hours, what was the total number of miles in the round trip?

34. In the chart above, some values of the function f are shown. If the function is defined by $g(x) = f(2x + 3)$, what is the value of $g(1)$?

NEXT PAGE

35. How many different integers greater than 199 and less than 1000 have exactly one digit that is a zero?

37. In the similar triangles ABC and XYZ, $\overline{AC}$ and $\overline{XZ}$ are corresponding sides. If $AC = 6$, $XZ = 12$, and the area of ABC is 15, what is the area of XYZ?

36. The population of a city is tripled per 5 years. The population of the city in the year 2,020 will be how many times the population in the year 2,000?

38. If the total surface area of a cube is 96 square inches, what is the volume, in cubic inches, of the cube?

STOP

Answer Key
For
SAT Math Practice Test 02

Section 3

1	D
2	B
3	C
4	C
5	B
6	A
7	C
8	D
9	A
10	A
11	B
12	D
13	A
14	D
15	C

16	71
17	0
18	5
19	144
20	21

Section 4

1	D	16	A
2	C	17	A
3	C	18	B
4	B	19	D
5	A	20	A
6	C	21	C
7	B	22	C
8	B	23	A
9	D	24	B
10	C	25	A
11	D	26	D
12	B	27	B
13	C	28	D
14	B	29	A
15	D	30	C

31	16
32	75
33	88
34	7
35	144
36	81
37	60
38	64

SAT Math

Practice

Test 02

Explanations

Redesigned for Tests in March 2016 and Beyond

Mad Math

Math Test – No Calculator

Time: 25 Minutes
20 Questions

Notes:
- The use of a calculator is not allowed.
- All numbers used in this section are the real number.
- Figures are provided for some problems in this test. Unless otherwise indicated under the figure "Note: Figure above not drawn to scale", all figures are drawn as accurately as possible.
- All figures lie in a plane EXCEPT otherwise specified.
- Unless otherwise indicated, the domain of any function f, g or j is assumed to be the set of all real numbers x for which $f(x)$, $g(x)$, or $j(x)$ is a real number.

Reference Information

$$A = \frac{1}{2}bh$$

$$A = lw$$

$$A = \pi r^2$$

$$V = \pi r^2 h$$

$$V = lwh$$

$$c^2 = a^2 + b^2$$

$$V = \frac{1}{3}\pi r^2 h$$

$$V = \frac{4}{3}\pi r^3$$

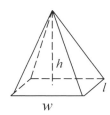

$$V = \frac{1}{3}lwh$$

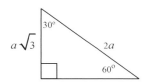

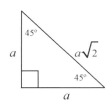

Copying or reuse of any portion of this page is illegal.

1. $\dfrac{1}{m+n}\left(\dfrac{1}{m+n}\right)^{-2} = ?$

(A) $\dfrac{1}{(m+n)^3}$

(B) $\dfrac{1}{(m+n)^2}$

(C) $\dfrac{(m+n)^2}{1}$

(D) $m+n$

Solution: Answer: (D)

$$\dfrac{1}{m+n}(m+n)^2$$

$$\Downarrow$$

$$\dfrac{(m+n)\,\cancel{(m+n)}}{\cancel{m+n}} = m+n$$

---

2. In a parallelogram whose area is 72, the base is represented by $x+3$ and the altitude is $x-3$. What is the altitude of the parallelogram?

(A) 6
(B) 17
(C) 9
(D) 8

Solution: Answer: (A)

$$\text{Area}_{\text{Parallelogram}} = \text{Base} \times \text{Altitude}$$

$$\downarrow$$

$$72 = (x+3)(x-3), \quad 72 = x^2 - 3^2$$

$$\downarrow$$

$$81 = x^2, \quad x = 9$$

$$\Downarrow$$

$$\text{Altitude} = x - 3 = 9 - 3 = 6$$

---

3. Which of the following does $E = 25^{\frac{3}{4}}$ equal?

(A) $\sqrt[5]{5}$

(B) $\sqrt[4]{5}$

(C) $5\sqrt{5}$

(D) $\sqrt[6]{5}$

Solution: Answer: (C)

$$25^{\frac{3}{4}} = \sqrt[4]{25^3} = \sqrt[4]{\left((5)^2\right)^3}$$

$$\downarrow$$

$$\sqrt[4]{5^6} = 5^{\frac{6}{4}} = 5^{\frac{3}{2}} = \sqrt{5}\sqrt{5}\sqrt{5}$$

$$\Downarrow$$

$$E = 5\sqrt{5}$$

---

4. If $i^2 = -1$, which of the following expressions could $x^2 + 2$ equal?

(A) $x^2 - \left(\sqrt{2}\right)^2$

(B) $\left(x - \sqrt{2}\cdot i\right)\left(x + \sqrt{2}\cdot i\right)$

(C) $x^2 + \left(\sqrt{2}\cdot i\right)^2$

(D) $(x - \sqrt{2}\cdot i)^2$

Solution: Answer: (B)

$$x^2 - 2 = \left(x - \sqrt{2}\right)\left(x + \sqrt{2}\right)$$

$$\Downarrow$$

$$\left(x - \sqrt{2}\cdot i\right)\left(x + \sqrt{2}\cdot i\right)$$

Proof:

$$x^2 + 2 = x^2 - (-2)$$

$$\downarrow$$

$$x^2 - \left(\sqrt{-2}\right)^2 = x^2 - \left(\sqrt{-1}\sqrt{2}\right)^2$$

$$\downarrow$$

$$x^2 - \left(i\sqrt{2}\right)^2$$

$$\Downarrow$$

$$(x - \sqrt{2}\cdot i)(x + \sqrt{2}\cdot i)$$

NEXT PAGE ⟩

5. If $x^{-2} < \dfrac{1}{x^4}$ and $x > 0$, which of the following is one possible value for x?

(A) $\dfrac{5}{2}$

(B) $\dfrac{1}{4}$

(C) $1\dfrac{1}{6}$

(D) $-\dfrac{1}{2}$

NUMBER OF FOOD COMPANY LOCATIONS

Company	USA Locations	Non-USA Locations
$X1$	6,200	1,909
$X2$	6,100	2,108
X3	4,998	2,199
$X4$	4,280	1,090

6. In the chart above, it shows the number of the locations for 4 food companies. For which of following companies has the greatest ratio of the number of USA locations to the number of Non-USA locations?

(A) $X4$

(B) $X1$

(C) $X3$

(D) $X2$

Solution: Answer: (A)

Estimate type

$$X4 \simeq \dfrac{4000}{1000} = 4, \ \text{Rest} \simeq 3$$

$\Downarrow$

Answer = (A)

Solution: Answer: (B)

$$x^{-2} < \dfrac{1}{x^4} \text{ and } x > 0$$

$\downarrow$

$$x^4 < \dfrac{1}{x^{-2}}$$

$\downarrow$

$$x^4 < x^2$$

$\begin{cases} \text{If } x > 1, \quad x^4 > x^2. \\ \text{For example, } 2^4 > 2^2 \end{cases}$

$\begin{cases} \text{If } 0 < x < 1, \ x^2 > x^4. \\ \text{For example, } \left(\dfrac{1}{2}\right)^2 > \left(\dfrac{1}{2}\right)^4 \end{cases}$

$\downarrow$

$$0 < x < 1$$

$\Downarrow$

Answer is (B)

7. If $f(x) = \dfrac{1}{\csc x}$, which of the following must be true?

(A) $f(-x) = f(x)$

(B) $f(x) = f(-x)$

(C) $f(-x) = -f(x)$

(D) $f(x) = 2f(-x)$

Solution: Answer: (C)

$$f(x) = \dfrac{1}{\csc x} = \sin x$$

$\sin x$ is an odd function.

(C) is the definition of odd function.

$\Downarrow$

Answer is (C).

8. Which of the following equations must be true if $x + y = 90°$?

(A) $\dfrac{\sin x}{\cos x} = \dfrac{\sin y}{\cos y}$

(B) $\sin x = \sin y$

(C) $\sin x = -\sin y$

(D) $\dfrac{\sin x}{\cos x} = \dfrac{\cos y}{\sin y}$

Solution: Answer: (D)

$$\tan x = \frac{\sin x}{\cos x}, \quad \cot y = \frac{\cos y}{\sin y}$$

They are complementary.

$$\tan x = \cot y$$

---

9. Which of the following does $2 \le |x + 4| \le 3$ equal?

(A) $-2 \le x \le -1, \; -7 \le x \le -6$
(B) $-7 \le x \le -6$
(C) $-7 \le x \le -6$
(D) $1 \le x \le 2, \; 6 \le x \le 7$

Solution: Answer: (A)

$$2 \le |x + 4| \le 3$$
It is equal to two inequalities.

↓

(1) $2 \le +(x + 4) \le 3$

↓

$-2 \le x \le -1$

(2) $2 \le -(x + 4) \le 3$
$-2 \ge x + 4 \ge -3$
$-3 \le x + 4 \le -2$

↓

$-7 \le x \le -6$

⇓

Answer is (A).

Questions 10 and 11 refer to the following graph.

HOUSES SOLD PER YEAR

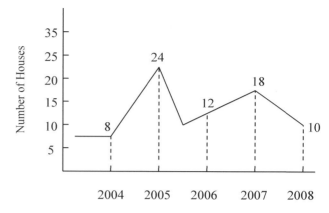

The line graph above shows the number of houses Mark sold in each of the 5 years.

10. Mark sold how many less houses in year 2007 than in years 2004 and 2008 combined?

(A) 0
(B) 1
(C) 2
(D) 3

Solution: Answer: (A)

2007: 18
2004 and 2008: $8 + 10 = 18$

$18 - 18 = 0$

---

11. If the information of the house sales from the 5 years were illustrated by a circle graph, what would be the degree measure of the central angle of the sector that represents the 2006?

(A) 20
(B) 60
(C) 40
(D) 50

Solution: Answer: (B)

Total $= 8 + 24 + 12 + 18 + 10 = 72$

$$\text{Ratio} = \frac{12}{72} = \frac{1}{6}$$

⇓

$$360° \times \frac{1}{6} = 60°$$

NEXT PAGE ⇨

Number of Pets per Family in A Street

Number of Pets	Number of Families
0	5
1	5
2	2
3	1

12. The chart above shows how many families in a street of 13 families had 0, 1, 2 or 3 pets. Recently, a new family moved into the street, and the average (arithmetic mean) number of pets per family became equal to the median number of pets per family. How many pets must the new family have?

(A) 0

(B) 4

(C) 3

(D) 2

Solution: **Answer: (D)**

(1). Determine the median.

$$\underbrace{0\ 0\ 0\ 0\ 0\ 1\ 1\ 1\ 1\ 1\ 2\ 2\ 3}_{\text{13 families}}$$

↓

After adding either 0, 1, 2, or 3 pets,

Median = 1

(2). $\underbrace{\text{Determine the average.}}_{\text{After a new family added}}$

$$\underbrace{5 \times 1 + 2 \times 2 + 1 \times 3 = 12}$$

The number of pets before
the new family moved into.

After the new family moved into,

# of pets = $12 + x$, # of families = $13 + 1$

$$\frac{12 + x}{13 + 1} = 1, \qquad 12 + x = 14$$

⇓

$$x = 14 - 12 = \boxed{2}$$

---

13.   If $\dfrac{4x + 20y}{27} = \dfrac{16a - 32b}{81}$, then $a - 2b =$

(A) $\dfrac{3(x + 5y)}{4}$

(B) $\dfrac{4(x + 5y)}{3}$

(C) $\dfrac{3(x - 5y)}{4}$

(D) $\dfrac{4(x - 5y)}{3}$

Solution: **Answer: (A)**

$$\frac{\cancel{4}\,(x + 5y)}{\cancel{27}} = \frac{\cancel{16}^{\,4}\,(a - 2b)}{\cancel{27}\cdot 3}$$

⇓

$$\frac{3(x + 5y)}{4} = a - 2b$$

NEXT PAGE

Mean	78
Median	83
Lower quartile	72
Upper quartile	92
Standard Deviation	9

14.   The statistical information above provides a summary of chemistry scores of 200 students at North Ridge High School. Round about 100 of the students in the statistical information have chemistry scores

(A) from 68 to 91.

(B) less than 72.

(C) less than 99.

(D) from 72 to 92..

Solution: Answer: (D)

Quartiles/Median: 72   83   92
# of Students: 1,..., 50,51 ...100,101...150,151...200

About 100 students
have scores from 72 to 92

Note: 72 represents lower quartile;
          92 represents upper quartile.

15.   How must a and b be related so that the graph of $g(x+1)$ will be symmetrical about the y-axis if $g(x) = ax^2 + bx + c$?

(A) $2a = b$

(B) $4a = -b$

(C) $2a = -b$

(D) $5a = -b$

Solution: Answer: (C)

$$g(x) = ax^2 + bx + c$$

When $x = -\dfrac{b}{2a}$, $g(x)$ has maximum

or minimum value. And $x = -\dfrac{b}{2a}$ is the

symmetrical line. The graph of $g(x+1)$ is the translation of $g(x)$ 1 units to the left. If $g(x)$ is symmetric about $x = +1$, $g(x+1)$ will be symmetric about the y-axis.

$$\Downarrow$$

$$-\dfrac{b}{2a} = 1 \text{ or } 2a = -b$$

NEXT PAGE

16. How many multiples of 7 between 100 and 600 ?

> Solution: Answer: 71
>
> "multiples of 7"
>
> $\downarrow$
>
> Arithmetic seq. with $d = 7$
>
> $$a_n = a_1 + (n-1)d$$
>
> $a_1 = 105, \qquad \underbrace{a_n = 595}$
> $\qquad\qquad\qquad$ Result from $\frac{\text{Top numbers}}{7}$
>
> $$595 = 105 + (n-1)7$$
>
> $\Downarrow$
>
> $$\frac{490}{7} + 1 = 71$$

17. When $2x^{(6m+1)} + 3x^{(4m+2)} - 4x^{(2m+3)} - 5$ is divided by $x+1$, if m is an integer, what is the remainder?

> Solution: Answer: 0
>
> By remainder theorem, the remainder is $P(\text{-}1)$.
>
> $$P(\text{-}1) = 2(\text{-}1)^{(6m+1)} + 3(\text{-}1)^{(4m+2)} - 4(\text{-}1)^{(2m+3)} - 5$$
>
> $\downarrow$
>
> $$2(\text{-}1)^1 + 3(\text{-}1)^2 - 4(\text{-}1)^3 - 5$$
>
> $\Downarrow$
>
> $$\text{-}2 + 3 + 4 - 5 = 0$$

18. If $f(x) = x - 5$, $g(x) = 10x$, and $j(x) = \dfrac{x}{5}$, what does $f(j(g(5)))$ equal?

> Solution: Answer: 5
>
> $$g(5) = 10 \cdot 5 = 50$$
>
> $\downarrow$
>
> $$j(50) = \frac{50}{5} = 10$$
>
> $\Downarrow$
>
> $$f(10) = 10 - 5 = 5$$

19. At a college, in a class of 90 juniors, there are 4 girls for every 6 boys. In a senior class, there are 5 girls for every 2 boys. If the two classes are combined, and in the combined class, the number of girls is twice the number of boys, how many boys are in the senior class?

> Solution: Answer: 144
>
> $\begin{cases} \text{4 girls for every 6 boys} \\ \text{Number of } A \text{ for every number of } B \end{cases}$
>
> $\downarrow$
>
> This is a ratio question.
>
> (1) $\quad 90 \cdot \dfrac{4}{10} = 36, \ 90 \cdot \dfrac{6}{10} = 54$
>
> (2). $\qquad$ Girls is twice boys.
>
> $\downarrow$
>
> $$36 + 5k = 2(54 + 2k)$$
>
> $$36 + 5k = 108 + 4k$$
>
> $$k = 72$$
>
> $\Downarrow$
>
> $$2k = 2 \cdot 72 = 144$$

20. In how many ways can an SAT club of six be selected from eight students if the club always includes a certain student?

> Solution: Answer: 21
>
> A certain student must be on the club.
>
> $\downarrow$
>
> A club of 5 is chosen 7.
>
> $\downarrow$
>
> 5 positions, 7 elements
>
> Order doesn't matter.
>
> $\downarrow$
>
> $\boxed{7} \cdot \boxed{6} \cdot \boxed{5} \cdot \boxed{4} \cdot \boxed{3}$
>
> 5!
>
> $\Downarrow$
>
> $$\frac{\boxed{7} \cdot \cancel{\boxed{6}} \cdot \cancel{\boxed{5}} \cdot \cancel{\boxed{4}} \cdot \boxed{3}}{\cancel{5} \cdot \cancel{4} \cdot \cancel{3} \cdot 2} = 21$$

STOP

No Test Contents

On This Page

Go to Next Page

Math Test – Calculator

Time: 55 Minutes
38 Questions

Notes:

- The use of a calculator is not allowed.
- All numbers used in this section are the real number.
- Figures are provided for some problems in this test. Unless otherwise indicated under the figure "Note: Figure above not drawn to scale", all figures are drawn as accurately as possible.
- All figures lie in a plane EXCEPT otherwise specified.
- Unless otherwise indicated, the domain of any function f, g or j is assumed to be the set of all real numbers x for which $f(x)$, $g(x)$, or $j(x)$ is a real number.

Reference Information

$$A = \frac{1}{2}bh$$

$$A = lw$$

$$A = \pi r^2$$

$$V = \pi r^2 h$$

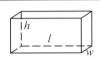

$$V = lwh$$

$$c^2 = a^2 + b^2$$

$$V = \frac{1}{3}\pi r^2 h$$

$$V = \frac{4}{3}\pi r^3$$

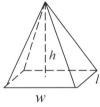

$$V = \frac{1}{3}lwh$$

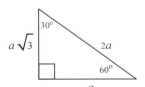

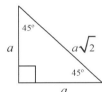

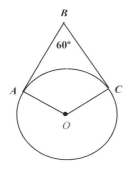

1. In the figure above, the center of the circle is point O, line segments AB and BC are tangent to the circle at points A and C, respectively, and the segments intersect at point B as shown. If the circomference of the circle is 10π, which of the following is the area of minor sector OAC?

(A) $\dfrac{22\pi}{5}$

(B) $\dfrac{20\pi}{3}$

(C) $\dfrac{25\pi}{4}$

(D) $\dfrac{25\pi}{3}$

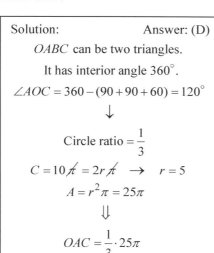

Solution: Answer: (D)

$OABC$ can be two triangles.

It has interior angle $360°$.

$\angle AOC = 360 - (90 + 90 + 60) = 120°$

↓

Circle ratio $= \dfrac{1}{3}$

$C = 10\pi = 2r\pi \rightarrow r = 5$

$A = r^2\pi = 25\pi$

⇓

$OAC = \dfrac{1}{3} \cdot 25\pi$

2. If the point (5, -7) is on the graph of a function f and if $f(-x) = f(x)$ for all x, which of the following points must also be on the graph of the function f ?

(A) (-7, 5)

(B) (-5, -7)

(C) (-5, 7)

(D) (5, -7)

Solution: Answer: (B)

(1) $(5, -7) \rightarrow f(5) = -7$

(2) $f(-x) = f(x)$

(The definition of even function)

$f(-5) = f(5) = -7$

$(-5, -7)$ must be a point on the

graph of the even function f.

⇓

Correct answer $= $ (B)

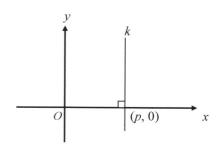

Figure 1

3. In Figure 1, the equation of line k is

(A) $y = p$

(B) $x = k$

(C) $x = p$

(D) $y = -p$

Solution: Answer: (C)

The value of x of any point on line $k = p$

⇓

$x = p$

4. A truck is used to move boxes. The boxes each weigh either 50 pounds or 75 pounds. Let x represent the number of 50-pound boxes and y represent the 75-pound boxes. The truck can carry up to either 65 boxes or less than a weight of 4,600 pounds. Which system of inequalities below represents the conditions described?

(A) $\begin{cases} x + y \leq 65 \\ 75x + 50y < 4,600 \end{cases}$

(B) $\begin{cases} x + y < 65 \\ 50x + 75y < 4,600 \end{cases}$

(C) $\begin{cases} x + y \leq 65 \\ 50x + 75y < 4,600 \end{cases}$

(D) $\begin{cases} x + y < 4,600 \\ 75y - 50x \leq 65 \end{cases}$

Solution: Answer: (C)

"carry up to" and "less than"

↓

Use the signs $\leq$ and $<$.

⇓

Answer is (C).

NEXT PAGE

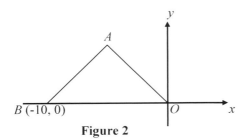

Figure 2

5. In the equilateral triangle in Figure 2, what is the slope of segment AO?

(A) $-\sqrt{3}$

(B) $\sqrt{3}$

(C) $-\dfrac{\sqrt{3}}{3}$

(D) $\dfrac{\sqrt{2}}{3}$

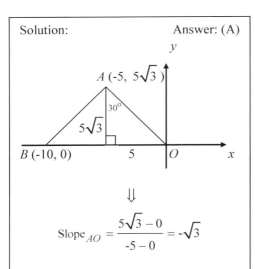

6. If $x^{\frac{2}{3}} = 27$, then $x^{\frac{4}{9}}$ is equal to

(A) 121

(B) $\dfrac{1}{9}$

(C) 9

(D) 81

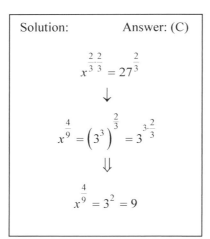

7. If $\dfrac{n^{n+1}}{(n-1)!} = \dfrac{2nx}{n!}$, x is equal to

(A) $2n^{n}$

(B) $\dfrac{n^{n+1}}{2}$

(C) $n^{\frac{n}{2}}$

(D) n^{n-1}

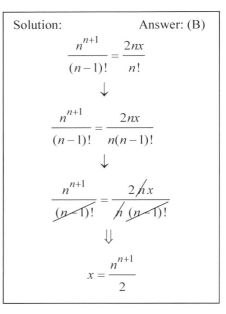

8. At East North High School, 55 percent of the students are boys and 45 percent of the boys at the high school play basketball. If a student at the high school is selected randomly, which of the following is the probability that the student is a boy who plays basketball, to the nearest hundredth?

(A) 0.24

(B) 0.25

(C) 0.42

(D) 0.51

Solution: Answer: (B)
Let x = number of entire students

$$\Downarrow$$

$$P = \frac{\dfrac{55}{100}x \cdot \dfrac{45}{100}}{x} = \frac{55 \cdot 45}{10000} \approx 0.2475$$

$$\Downarrow$$

$$P \approx 0.25$$

NEXT PAGE

9. If 5 girls A, B, C, D, and E line up in a row, what is the probability that girl E is at either end of the row?

(A) 15%

(B) 25%

(C) 35%

(D) 40%

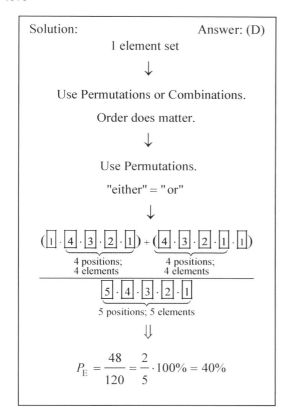

Solution: Answer: (D)

1 element set

↓

Use Permutations or Combinations.

Order does matter.

↓

Use Permutations.

"either" = "or"

↓

$\left(\boxed{1}\cdot\boxed{4}\cdot\boxed{3}\cdot\boxed{2}\cdot\boxed{1}\right) + \left(\boxed{4}\cdot\boxed{3}\cdot\boxed{2}\cdot\boxed{1}\cdot\boxed{1}\right)$

4 positions; 4 elements   4 positions; 4 elements

$\boxed{5}\cdot\boxed{4}\cdot\boxed{3}\cdot\boxed{2}\cdot\boxed{1}$

5 positions; 5 elements

⇓

$P_E = \dfrac{48}{120} = \dfrac{2}{5}\cdot 100\% = 40\%$

10. Route 8 to Catharine's home is 8 miles longer than the direct route. When Catharine goes by Route 8 and returns by the direct route, the round trip is 88 miles. How many miles is the direct route?

(A) 30
(B) 56
(C) 40
(D) 54

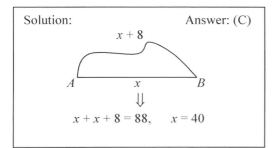

Solution: Answer: (C)

$x + 8$

A x B

⇓

$x + x + 8 = 88,$ $x = 40$

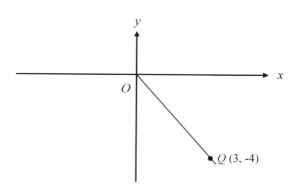

Q (3, -4)

Note: Figure above not drawn to scale.

11. In the figure above, a ring with circumference π is placed on an incline. Point Q with coordinates (3, -4) is on the ring. The ring is rolled up the incline, and once point Q of the ring touches the origin, it is then rolled horizontally along the x-axis to the right. What is the x-coordinate of point Q, where point Q on the ring touches the x-axis or the incline for the 8th time?

(A) -16.99

(B) 26.99

(C) 19.96

(D) 16.99

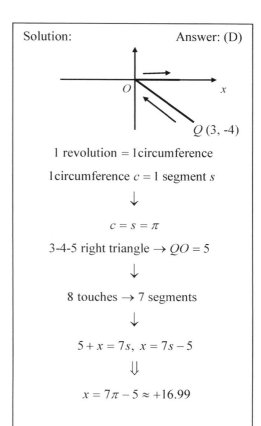

Solution: Answer: (D)

O x

Q (3, -4)

1 revolution = 1 circumference

1 circumference c = 1 segment s

↓

$c = s = \pi$

3-4-5 right triangle → $QO = 5$

↓

8 touches → 7 segments

↓

$5 + x = 7s,\ x = 7s - 5$

⇓

$x = 7\pi - 5 \approx +16.99$

NEXT PAGE ⟹

12. Line m is tangent to the circle whose center is at (-4, -1). If the tangent point is (-2, -4), what is the x-intercept of m?

(A) $\dfrac{1}{4}$

(B) 4

(C) 1

(D) -4

Solution: Answer: (B)

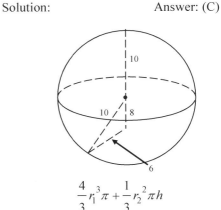

(1). Get slope from "triangle" and direction.

$$S_{\text{radius}} = \dfrac{-3}{2}$$

The line is perpendicular to the radius.

$$S_{\text{line}} = -\dfrac{1}{S_{\text{radius}}} = \dfrac{2}{3}$$

(2). Get slope from "triangle" and direction again.

$$\dfrac{4}{2+x} = \dfrac{2}{3}, \quad \cancel{4}^2 \times 3 = \cancel{2}(2+x)$$

$$\Downarrow$$

$$x = 4$$

The result can be obtained by using slope formula.

13. What is the sum of the volume of a cone and the volume of a sphere if the cone whose base radius is 6 is inscribed in the sphere of radius 10?

(A) 19,512

(B) 12,620

(C) 4,867

(D) 4,602

Solution: Answer: (C)

$$\dfrac{4}{3} r_1^3 \pi + \dfrac{1}{3} r_2^2 \pi h$$

$$\dfrac{4}{3} \cdot 10^3 \pi + \dfrac{1}{3} \cdot 6^2 \pi (8+10)$$

$$\text{Sum} = \dfrac{4000\pi + 648\pi}{3} \approx 4867$$

14. If $f(x) = -x^3 + 2k^2 x^2 + 12x$ is divisible by $x - 6$, what is k equal to?

(A) ± 6.00

(B) ± 1.41

(C) ± 4.94

(D) ± 5.74

Solution: Answer: (B)

Factor Theorem

$$\downarrow$$

$x - 6$ is a factor of $f(x)$, then $f(6) = 0$.

$$\downarrow$$

$$-6^3 + 2k^2 6^2 + 12 \cdot 6 = 0$$

$$\Downarrow$$

$$72k^2 = 144, \quad k = \pm\sqrt{2} \approx \pm 1.41$$

NEXT PAGE

15. For $x > 0$, what is $\dfrac{\frac{7x}{3}}{\frac{1}{9x}} \div 9x$?

(A) $149x^2$

(B) $\dfrac{7x^2}{3}$

(C) $63x$

(D) $\dfrac{7x}{3}$

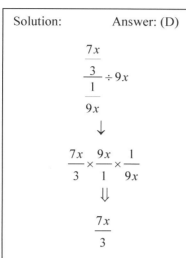

Solution:　　　　Answer: (D)

$$\dfrac{\frac{7x}{3}}{\frac{1}{9x}} \div 9x$$

$$\downarrow$$

$$\dfrac{7x}{3} \times \dfrac{9x}{1} \times \dfrac{1}{9x}$$

$$\Downarrow$$

$$\dfrac{7x}{3}$$

16. For which of the following sets of numbers is the average (arithmetic mean) less than the median?

(A)[1, 2, 3, 4, 4]
(B)[1, 2, 3, 4, 5]
(C)[2, 3, 4, 5, 6]
(D)[3, 4, 5, 6, 8]

Solution:　　　　Answer: (A)

If the number of total terms of consecutive integers is odd, its median equals to its average.

Median of $[1,\ 2,\ 3,\ 4,\ 5] = 3$

$$\Downarrow$$

Average of $[1,\ 2,\ 3,\ 4,\ 4] < 3$

17. A cylindrical container has a height of two yards and a radius of 1 yard. How many such containers can completely fill up water into a rectangular container whose length is 4 yards, width is 4 yards, and height is 6 yards?

(A) 16
(B) 15
(C) 14
(D) 13

Solution:　　　　Answer: (A)

$$\begin{cases} V_{\text{Cyl}} = r^2\pi \cdot h = 1^2\pi \cdot 2 = 2\pi \\ V_{\text{Rec}} = 4 \cdot 4 \cdot 6 = 96 \end{cases}$$

$$\downarrow$$

$$N_{\text{Cyl-containers}} = \dfrac{V_{\text{Rec}}}{V_{\text{Cyl}}} = \dfrac{\overset{48}{\cancel{96}}}{\cancel{2}\pi}$$

$$\downarrow$$

$$\dfrac{48}{\pi} \approx 15.28$$

"completely fill up"

$$\Downarrow$$

$$N_{\text{Cyl-containers}} = 16$$

18. Burger Queen sold 10 percent in 2011 less hamburger sandwiches than in 2010, and the price of each hamburger sandwich they sold in 2011 was 10 percent more than in 2010. The total earnings from the sale of hamburger sandwiches were what percent change in 2011 than in 2010?

(A) 0%
(B) 1%
(C) 11%
(D) $\dfrac{1}{100}$%

Solution:　　　　Answer: (B)

$$\dfrac{\left| xy - \left(0.9x\right) \cdot \left(1.1y\right) \right|}{xy}$$

$$\downarrow$$

$$\dfrac{xy - 0.99xy}{xy} = \dfrac{\cancel{xy}\,(1 - 0.99)}{\cancel{xy}} = 0.01$$

$$\Downarrow$$

$$0.01 \times 100\% = 1\%$$

19. Under which of the following conditions is $\dfrac{k_2(k_2 - k_1)}{k_1}$ greater than zero ?

(A) $1 < k_2 < k_1$

(B) $k_1 < 0 < k_2$

(C) $k_1 < 0 = k_2$

(D) $k_2 > k_1 > 0$

Solution: Answer: (D)

Do not forget to consider all 4 states of k.

$$\begin{cases} \text{If } k > 0, \text{ then} \quad 0 < k < 1 \ \text{ or } \ k > 0. \\ \text{If } k < 0, \text{ then} \ -1 < k < 0 \text{ or } k < -1. \end{cases}$$

Use plug-in method. Order: (D) → (A).

(E) $k_2 < k_1 < 0$

(1) $-1 < n < 0$

Let $k_1 = -\dfrac{1}{3}, \ k_2 = -\dfrac{1}{2}$

$$\dfrac{-\dfrac{1}{2}\left(-\dfrac{1}{2} - \left(-\dfrac{1}{3}\right)\right)}{-\dfrac{1}{3}}, \quad \dfrac{3}{2}\left(-\dfrac{1}{2} + \dfrac{1}{3}\right) = \dfrac{3}{2} \cdot \dfrac{-1}{6} < 0$$

↓

(E) is not the correct answer.

(D) $k_2 > k_1 > 0$

Let $k_1 = \dfrac{1}{3}, \ k_2 = \dfrac{1}{2}$

$$\dfrac{\dfrac{1}{2}\left(\dfrac{1}{2} - \left(\dfrac{1}{3}\right)\right)}{\dfrac{1}{3}} > 0$$

Let $k_1 = 2, \ k_2 = 3$

$$\dfrac{3(3-2)}{2} > 0$$

⇓

(D) is the correct answer.

Funds and Percent of Total Expenses Spent on 12 Projects

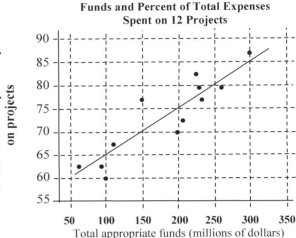

20. The appropriate funds are alloted to 12 research projects. The scatterplot with the line of best fit above shows data for the 12 projects. For the project with the greatest percent of total expenses spent on projects, which of the following is closest to the difference of the percent predicted by the line of best fit and the actual percent?

(A) 2 percent

(B) 85 percent

(C) 4.5 percent

(D) 87.5 percent

Solution: Answer: (A)

When the total funds are 300 million dollars, the funds have the greatest %

⇓

$$|87\% - 85\%| = 2\%$$

---

21. If n is $\dfrac{2}{3}$ of s and p is $\dfrac{4}{5}$ of s, what is the value of $\dfrac{n}{p}$?

(A) $\dfrac{5}{2}$

(B) $\dfrac{10}{3}$

(C) $\dfrac{5}{6}$

(D) $\dfrac{15}{8}$

Solution: Answer: (C)

Target: s will be eliminated.

Let $s = 15$.

$\downarrow$

$$\begin{cases} n = \dfrac{2}{3}s = \dfrac{2}{3} \cdot 15 = 10 \\[2mm] p = \dfrac{4}{5}s = \dfrac{4}{5} \cdot 15 = 12 \end{cases}$$

$\Downarrow$

$$\dfrac{n}{p} = \dfrac{10}{12} = \dfrac{5}{6}$$

x	$g(x)$	$f(x)$
2	-1	2
1	0	-1
0	1	-2
-1	2	3
-2	3	4

22. According to the chart above, what is the value of $g(-2) - f(1)$?

(A) 2

(B) 3

(C) 4

(D) -3

Solution: Answer: (C)

$$\begin{cases} g(-2) = 3 \\ f(1) = -1 \end{cases}$$

$\Downarrow$

$$g(-2) - f(1) = 3 - (-1) = 4$$

23. Line L passes through the points $(0, 0)$ and $(9, 9)$. Which of the following points is located in the region between the graph of the line L and positive part of the x-axis?

(A) $x > y$ and $y > 0$
(B) $x = y$ and $y < 0$
(C) $x \geq y$ and $y < 0$
(D) $x < y$ and $y > 0$

Solution: Answer: (A)

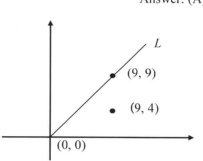

Choose one point with the same x-value between the graph of the line L and positive part of the x-axis.

$$x = 9, y = 4$$
$\Downarrow$
$$x > y \text{ and } y > 0$$

24. Mr. David Smith built a house at a cost of \$800,000. He offers a discount of 10% to encourage sales after pricing the home for sale by adding 20% of his expenses. What does he make on his house?

(A) \$0
(B) \$64,000
(C) \$46,000
(D) \$4,600

Solution: Answer: (B)

$$800000 \times 1.2 \times 0.9$$

$\Downarrow$

$$864,000 - 800000 = 64,000$$

NEXT PAGE

25.　If $x^2 + y^2 = 256$ and $xy = 25,$ what is the value of $(x + y)^2$?

(A) 306
(B) 206
(C) 302
(D) 216

Solution:　　　　　　　Answer: (A)

$$x^2 + 2xy + y^2 = 256 + 2xy$$

$$\Downarrow$$

$$(x + y)^2 = 256 + 2 \times 25 = 306$$

26. If m is a positive number, which of the following is equal to $9m$?

(A) $3\sqrt{3m^2}$

(B) $3\sqrt{6m^2}$

(C) $3\sqrt{27m^2}$

(D) $3\sqrt{9m^2}$

Solution:　　　Answer: (D)
Use plug-in method.

$$\downarrow$$

$$3\sqrt{9m^2} = \sqrt{9 \cdot 9m^2}$$

$$\downarrow$$

$$\sqrt{81m^2} = 9m$$

$$\Downarrow$$

Answer is (D).

27. How many 3-person committees formed from a group of five?

(A) 60
(B) 10
(C) 30
(D) 20

Solution:　　　　　　Answer: (B)

1 element set.

$$\downarrow$$

Use the counting method of Permutations or Combinations.

Order doesn't matter.

$$\downarrow$$

Use the counting method of Combinations.

$$\Downarrow$$

$$\frac{\boxed{5} \times \boxed{4} \times \boxed{3}}{3!} = 10$$

28.　If $\frac{1}{4}x = x^2,$ then which of the following can be the value of x ?

　I.　0

　II. $-\frac{1}{4}$

　III. $\frac{1}{4}$

(A) I only

(B) II only

(C) III only

(D) I and III only

Solution:　　　Answer: (D)
Method 1.

$$x^2 - \frac{1}{4}x = 0$$

$$x\left(x - \frac{1}{4}\right) = 0$$

$$\downarrow$$

$$x = 0, \ x = \frac{1}{4}$$

$$\Downarrow$$

Answer is (D).

Method 2.

I. $(0)^2 = \frac{1}{4} \cdot (0)$

$$\Downarrow$$

$$0 = 0$$

So III is true.

II. $\left(-\frac{1}{4}\right)^2 = \frac{1}{4} \cdot \left(-\frac{1}{4}\right)$

$$\Downarrow$$

$$\frac{1}{16} = -\frac{1}{16}$$

So II is false.

III. $\left(\frac{1}{4}\right)^2 = \frac{1}{4} \cdot \frac{1}{4}$

$$\Downarrow$$

$$\frac{1}{16} = \frac{1}{16}$$

So III is true.

NEXT PAGE

29. If the circle $x^2 + y^2 + 2x - 8y = r^2 - 17$ is tangent to the line $12y = 60$, what is the value of r?

(A) 1

(B) 4

(C) 3

(D) 8

30. Circle O_1 is centered at $(-2, k)$ and has a radius of 6. Circle O_2 is centered at $(5, -5)$ and has a radius of 4. If circle O_1 is externally tangent to circle O_2, which of the following is the value of k? Round to the nearest hundredth.

(A) 2.1

(B) 2.141

(C) 2.14

(D) 4.12

Solution: Answer: (A)

$$\left(x^2 + 2x + 1\right) + \left(y^2 - 8y + 4^2\right) = r^2 - 17 + 1 + 4^2$$

$$(x+1)^2 + (y-4)^2 = r^2$$

$$12y = 60 \rightarrow y = 5$$

The center is at (-1, 4).

Line y is tangent to the radius.

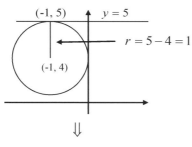

$$r = 5 - 4 = 1$$

⇓

Answer is (A).

Solution: Answer: (C)

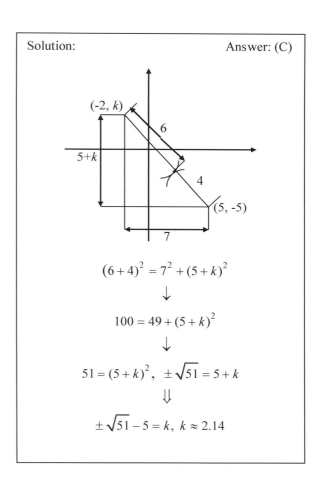

$$(6+4)^2 = 7^2 + (5+k)^2$$

↓

$$100 = 49 + (5+k)^2$$

↓

$$51 = (5+k)^2, \ \pm\sqrt{51} = 5 + k$$

⇓

$$\pm\sqrt{51} - 5 = k, \ k \approx 2.14$$

NEXT PAGE

31. May bought a ticket for a concert, and then she changed her mind because she needed more time to prepare the SAT test. May sold the ticket to Jackson for $12, thus she lost 25%. What is the original price?

Solution: Answer: 16

$$12 = 0.75x \qquad x = 16$$

32. Emily drove to work at an average speed of 30 miles per hour and returned along the same route at 50 miles per hour. If her total traveling time was 2 hours, what was the total number of miles in the round trip?

Solution: Answer: 75

$$\begin{cases} \text{distance}_1 = \text{distance}_2 & Y \\ \text{distance}_1 + \text{distance}_2 = \text{distance}_3 & N \end{cases}$$

$$\downarrow$$

$$30x = 50(2 - x), \quad x = \frac{5}{4}$$

$$\Downarrow$$

$$2 \times 30x = 2 \times 30 \times \frac{5}{4} = 75$$
round trip

33. A rectangle was changed by decreasing its length by 20% and increasing its width by 10%. If these changes decreased the area of the rectangle to $X\%$ of its original area, what is the value of X?

Solution: Answer: 88

$$\frac{80}{100} \not{x} \cdot \frac{110}{100} \not{y} = \frac{X}{100}$$
$$\frac{}{\not{xy}}$$

$$\downarrow$$

$$\frac{8\not{0}}{\not{100}} \cdot \frac{11\not{0}}{\not{100}} = \frac{X}{\not{100}}$$

$$\Downarrow$$

$$X = 88$$

x	$f(x)$
1	-2
2	3
3	0
4	-4
5	7
6	-3

34.   In the chart above, some values of the function f are shown. If the function is defined by $g(x) = f(2x + 3)$, what is the value of $g(1)$?

Solution: Answer: 7

$$g(x) = f(2x + 3)$$

$$\downarrow$$

When $x = 1$,

$$g(1) = f(2 \times 1 + 3) = f(5)$$

$$\Downarrow$$

$$f(5) = 7, \quad g(1) = 7$$

NEXT PAGE

35. How many different integers greater than 199 and less than 1000 have exactly one digit that is a zero?

> Solution: Answer: 144
>
> 3 digits
>
> ↓
>
> 3 element sets
>
> ↓
>
> Use Fundamental Counting Principle.
>
> ↓
>
> $\boxed{8} \cdot \boxed{1} \cdot \boxed{9} = 72$
> $\quad$ 2~9 $\quad$ 0 $\quad$ 1~9
>
> $\boxed{8} \cdot \boxed{9} \cdot \boxed{1} = 72$
>
> ⇓
>
> $72 + 72 = 144$

36. The population of a city is tripled per 5 years. The population of the city in the year 2,020 will be how many times the population in the year 2,000?

> Solution: Answer: 81
>
> "in the year 2,020"
>
> ↓
>
> Use the formula of exponential function:
>
> $$f(t) = a_1 b^t .$$
>
> $$t = \frac{2020 - 2000}{5} = \frac{20}{5} = 4$$
>
> ⇓
>
> $$\frac{f(4)}{f(0)} = \frac{\cancel{a_1} r^4}{\cancel{a_1} r^0} = \frac{r^4}{1} = 3^4 = 81$$

37. In the similar triangles ABC and XYZ, $\overline{AC}$ and $\overline{XZ}$ are corresponding sides. If $AC = 6$, $XZ = 12$, and the area of ABC is 15, what is the area of XYZ?

> Solution: Answer: 60
>
>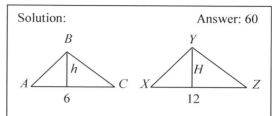
>
> $$A_{ABC} = \frac{AC \cdot h}{2}, \ 15 = \frac{6h}{2}, \ h = 5$$
>
> The ratio of corresponding heights of similar triangles is the same ratio as their sides.
>
> ↓
>
> $$\frac{H}{h} = \frac{12}{6}, \ H = \frac{12 \cdot h}{6} = \frac{12 \cdot 5}{6} = 10$$
>
> ⇓
>
> $$A_{XYZ} = \frac{XZ \cdot H}{2} = \frac{12 \cdot 10}{2} = 60$$

38. If the total surface area of a cube is 96 square inches, what is the volume, in cubic inches, of the cube?

> Solution: Answer: 64
>
> A cube has 6 faces.
>
> ↓
>
> $$A_{\frac{1}{6}} = \frac{96}{6} = 16$$
>
> ↓
>
> $$S = \sqrt{A_{\frac{1}{6}}} = \sqrt{16} = 4$$
>
> ⇓
>
> $$V = S^3 = 4^3 = 64$$

STOP

SAT Math

Practice

Test 03

Redesigned for Tests in March 2016 and Beyond

Mad Math

Math Test – No Calculator

Time: 25 Minutes
20 Questions

Notes:
- The use of a calculator is not allowed.
- All numbers used in this section are the real number.
- Figures are provided for some problems in this test. Unless otherwise indicated under the figure "Note: Figure above not drawn to scale", all figures are drawn as accurately as possible.
- All figures lie in a plane EXCEPT otherwise specified.
- Unless otherwise indicated, the domain of any function f, g or j is assumed to be the set of all real numbers x for which $f(x)$, $g(x)$, or $j(x)$ is a real number.

Reference Information

$A = \dfrac{1}{2}bh$

$A = lw$

$A = \pi r^2$

$V = \pi r^2 h$

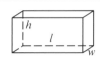

$V = lwh$

$c^2 = a^2 + b^2$

$V = \dfrac{1}{3}\pi r^2 h$

$V = \dfrac{4}{3}\pi r^3$

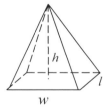

$V = \dfrac{1}{3}lwh$

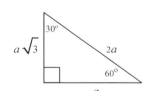

1. If three distinct numbers are chosen, one from each of following sets, what is the smallest sum of the 3 numbers?

$S_1 = \{1, 4, 6\}$

$S_2 = \{5, 6, 8\}$

$S_3 = \{1, 5, 9\}$

(A) 7
(B) 11
(C) 10
(D) 9

2. If $i = \sqrt{-1}$, then $|-6 + 3i| =$

(A) $\sqrt{95}$

(B) 35

(C) $3\sqrt{5}$

(D) 19

3. A list of numbers has been arranged such that each number in the list is 15 more than the number that precedes it. If number 298 is the tenth number in the list, what is the third number in the list?

(A) 202
(B) 193
(C) 311
(D) 180

4.
$$\begin{cases} y > x^2 + 2 \\ y < x + 5 \end{cases}$$

If $(2, k)$ is a solution to the system of inequalities above, which of the following could be the value of k ?

(A) 7.0

(B) 6.1

(C) 8.1

(D) 6.0

NEXT PAGE

5. A rectangular container has a length of 8, a width of 6, a height of 7, and a volume of V_1. Which of the following represents the volume of a rectangular container with dimensions length 16, width 2, and height 7 in terms of V_1?

(A) $\dfrac{2}{3}V_1$

(B) $\dfrac{1}{2}V_1$

(C) $3V_1$

(D) $2V_1$

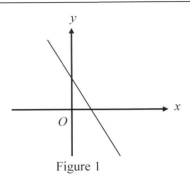

Figure 1

7. In Figure 1, the graph of equation $y = mx + b$ is the line. Which of the following must be true?

(A) $b + m > 0$

(B) $b - m < 0$

(C) $b - m \neq 0$

(D) $b - m > 0$

6. If $9x^2 - 24x + k = 0$ has $\dfrac{4}{3}$ as a double root, $k =$

(A) 5

(B) 16

(C) 8

(D) $\dfrac{1}{8}$

NEXT PAGE

8. If $a > 0$, what is the domain of function $f(x) = \dfrac{a}{x^2 + a}$?

(A) $x \neq -a$

(B) $x \neq -\dfrac{1}{a}$

(C) $-a \leq x \leq a$

(D) All real numbers including $-a$

9. If a = the number of primes from 16 to 41,

    b = the number of primes divisible by 5,

    c = the number of even primes,

    d = the number of primes divisible by 7,

what is the sum of a, b, c, and d ?

(A) 7

(B) 6

(C) 5

(D) 10

10. Line m is tangent to the circle whose center is at (5, -1). If the tangent point is (-2, 4), what is the y-intercept of m ?

(A) -6.8

(B) 6.8

(C) 3.4

(D) 8.6

11. Which of the following is not the equation of a function?

(A) $y = 0$

(B) $y = |x|$

(C) $y = -|x|$

(D) $x = 0$

NEXT PAGE

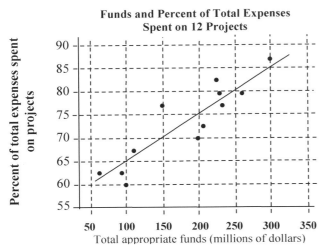

**Funds and Percent of Total Expenses
Spent on 12 Projects**

12. The appropriate funds are alloted to 12 research projects. The scatterplot with the line of best fit on the left shows data for the 12 projects. If the vertical axis represents y-axis and the horizontal axis represents the x-axis, what is the equation of the line of best fit?

(A) $f(x) = 10x + 55$

(B) $f(x) = (1/10)x + 59$

(C) $f(x) = (1/10)x + 55$

(D) $f(x) = (2/3)x + 59$

13. Fastest Bikes sold 10 percent in 2011 more bikes than in 2010, and the price of each bike they sold in 2011 was 10 percent more than in 2010. The total profit from the sale of bikes was what percent increase in 2011 than in 2010 ?

(A) 20%

(B) 0.21%

(C) 21%

(D) 79%

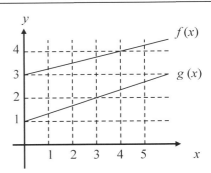

14. The graph of the functions f and g are lines, as shown above. What is the value of $f(4) - g(3)$?

(A) 2.6

(B) 4.3

(C) 3

(D) 2

15. A rectangular living room is 90 feet length and 50 feet width. How many square yards of carpeting are needed to cover the floor?

(A) 4,500

(B) 1,500

(C) 800

(D) 500

NEXT PAGE

16.   If $3^2 = 81^x$, then $2x =$

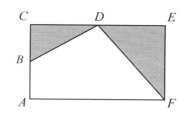

19.   In the rectangle $ACEF$ above, B and D are midpoints of sides $\overline{AC}$ and $\overline{CE}$, respectively. What is the ratio of the area of the shaded portion to the area of the rectangle?

17.   If 3 less than 4 times a certain number is 9 more than the number, what is the number?

18.   If x is an integer and $2 < x < 10$, how many distinct triangles are there with sides of lengths 5, 8, and x?

20. The average (arithmetic mean) of a list of 15 scores is 79. If one of the scores is removed, the average of the remaining scores is 81. What is the score that was removed?

STOP

Math Test – Calculator

Time: 55 Minutes
38 Questions

Notes:
- The use of a calculator is not allowed.
- All numbers used in this section are the real number.
- Figures are provided for some problems in this test. Unless otherwise indicated under the figure "Note: Figure above not drawn to scale", all figures are drawn as accurately as possible.
- All figures lie in a plane EXCEPT otherwise specified.
- Unless otherwise indicated, the domain of any function f, g or j is assumed to be the set of all real numbers x for which $f(x)$, $g(x)$, or $j(x)$ is a real number.

Reference Information

$$A = \frac{1}{2}bh$$

$$A = lw$$

$$A = \pi r^2$$

$$V = \pi r^2 h$$

$$V = lwh$$

$$c^2 = a^2 + b^2$$

$$V = \frac{1}{3}\pi r^2 h$$

$$V = \frac{4}{3}\pi r^3$$

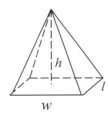

$$V = \frac{1}{3}lwh$$

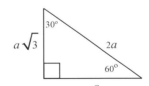

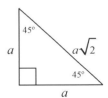

1. The expression $\dfrac{4x-1}{3} - \dfrac{x-5}{3}$ is how much greater than x?

(A) -2

(B) $\dfrac{4}{3}$

(C) 2

(D) $-\dfrac{4}{3}$

2. What is a single discount, which is equal to 2 successive discounts of 10% and 20%?

(A) 28%
(B) 19%
(C) 18%
(D) 20%

3. If the line $y = -3$ intersects the graph of the equation $f(x) = x^2 - 11x + 25$, which of the following is a possible pair of the coordinates of the intersection points?

(A) (-3, 7)

(B) (-4, -3)

(C) (7, 4)

(D) (7, -3)

4. The acceleration of a motorcycle is a function involving time elapsed. If $A(T) = 15T^2 + 120T + 86$ represents the acceleration of the motorcycle and T represents the time lapsed, what is the acceleration of the motorcycle 10 seconds after the motorcycle started to accelerate?

(A) 1786
(B) 2786
(C) 3786
(D) 4786

NEXT PAGE

f(x)	x
82	−2
25	−1
12	0
13	1

5. The chart above provides selected values of the function $f(x)$ and x. Which of the following functions could be the $f(x)$?

(A) $11x^2 - 11x$

(B) $12x - 15$

(C) $f(x) = 12x^2 - 11x - 12$

(D) $f(x) = 12x^2 - 11x + 12$

6. Which of the following does $e = 4^{\frac{3}{4}}$ equal?

(A) $\sqrt[5]{2}$

(B) $2\sqrt{2}$

(C) $\sqrt[4]{2}$

(D) $\sqrt[6]{2}$

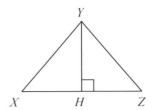

7. Triangle XYZ above is an equilateral triangle. If the length of side, S, is 10, what is the area of triangle XYZ?

(A) $\dfrac{5\sqrt{3}}{2}$

(B) 30

(C) 40

(D) $25\sqrt{3}$

8. The first term of set A is −3, and each term thereafter is 3 greater than the previous term. The Nth term of set B is given by the formula $-N + 22$. Which one is the term of set A that first exceeds the value of its corresponding term in set B?

(A) 6

(B) 8

(C) 7

(D) 10

NEXT PAGE

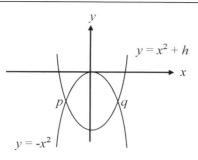

9. The figure above shows the graphs $y = -x^2$ and $y = x^2 + h$. h is a certain constant. p and q separately represent the intersecting points of the two graphs in the xy-plane. If the length of the distance between p and q is 10, what is the value of h?

(A) -50
(B) 98
(C) 82
(D) -98

10. The quantity y is proportional to the cube root of the quantity x, and y is 5 units if x is 216 units. What is the formula for y in terms of x?

(A) $A = \dfrac{5}{6} \cdot \sqrt[3]{B}$

(B) $A = \dfrac{6}{5} \cdot \sqrt[3]{B}$

(C) $A = \dfrac{5}{6 \cdot \sqrt[3]{B}}$

(D) $A \geq \dfrac{5}{6} \cdot \sqrt[3]{B}$

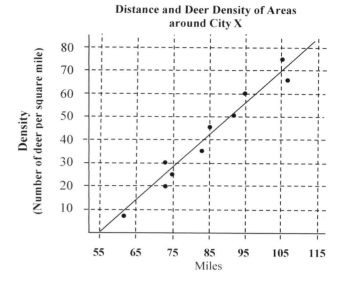

The scatterplot with line of best fit above shows the deer density of 10 areas, in number of deers per square mile, with respect to their distances from City X.

11. By the scatterplot, which of the following statements is true about the relationship between a distance of an area from City X and its deer density?

(A) The areas that are lesser distance from City X tend to have more deer densities.

(B) The areas that are more distance from City X tend to have more or lesser deer densities.

(C) The areas that are more distance from City X tend to have more deer densities.

(D) None above

NEXT PAGE

12.   Three fair cubes each are one that is labeled with the numbers 1, 2, 3, 4, 5, and 6, such that there is an equal chance of rolling each of these numbers. If you roll these three cubes at the same time, what is the probability that the sum of the three numbers you roll will be greater than seventeen?

(A) $\dfrac{1}{108}$

(B) $\dfrac{1}{216}$

(C) $\dfrac{1}{36}$

(D) $\dfrac{1}{72}$

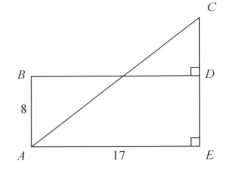

14. In the figure above, the area of triangle ACE equals the area of rectangle $ABDE$. What is the length of segment $\overline{CD}$?

(A) 6

(B) 7

(C) 8

(D) 9

13.   Monica has two jobs. She works as a waitress, which pays $15 per hour, and she works as a nurse, which pays $16 per hour. Monica can work no more than 120 hours per month, and she plans to make at least $1,200 per month. Which of the following system of inequalities describes this situation in terms of w and n, where w represents the number of hours she works as a waitress and n represents the number of hours she works as a nurse?

(A) $w + n < 120$
    $15w + 16n \geq 1,200$

(B) $w + n \leq 120$
    $15w + 16n \geq 1,200$

(C) $w + n \leq 120$
    $15w + 16n \leq 1,200$

(D) $w + n \leq 120$
    $15w + 16n > 1,200$

NEXT PAGE

15. If $x \neq \pm 1$, which of the following is the reduced form for

$$\frac{x^2 - 1}{(x+1)^2 (x-1)}?$$

(A) $\dfrac{1}{x-1}$

(B) $\dfrac{1}{x+1}$

(C) $\dfrac{x+1}{(x^2 + 2x + 1)}$

(D) $x + 1$

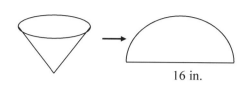

16 in.

Note: Figure above not drawn to scale.

17. In the figure above, if the semicircle with diameter 16 inches is made from a cone, what is the radius of the cone?

(A) 2

(B) 9

(C) 8

(D) 4

16. A computer program at random chooses a positive 3-digit integer. If the integer chosen is even, twice the value of the integer is printed. If the integer printed is 204, which of the following could have been the integer chosen?

    I.   306
    II. 102
    III. 204

(A) II and III only
(B) II only
(C) III only
(D) I only

NEXT PAGE

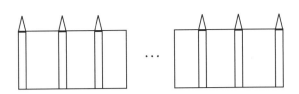

18. The figure above represents a stretch of wall, which is 1,120 yards long. The wall posts are placed at two ends and also placed every 5.6 yards along the wall. How many the posts totally are there in the wall stretch?

(A) 200

(B) 100

(C) 101

(D) 201

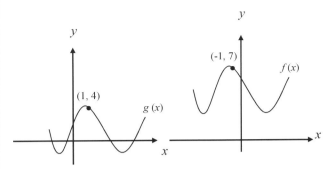

20. The figures above show the graphs of the functions $g(x)$ and $f(x)$. The function $f(x)$ is defined by $f(x) = g(x + k) + h$, where k and h are constants. What is the value of $\dfrac{h}{k}$?

(A) 3/2
(B) -1
(C) -2
(D) 2

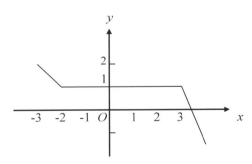

19. The graph of $f(x)$ is shown above. If $f(a) = 1$, which of the following is possible value of a?

(A)-3
(B)-2.5
(C) 2.5
(D)-3.5

NEXT PAGE

21. If $f(x) = \sqrt{7 - x^2}$, what is the domain of f ?

(A) $-\sqrt{7} \geq x, \ x \geq \sqrt{7}$

(B) $-\sqrt{7} < x < \sqrt{7}$

(C) $-\sqrt{7} < x, \ x > \sqrt{7}$

(D) $-\sqrt{7} \leq x \leq \sqrt{7}$

Questions 22 and 23 refer to the information below.

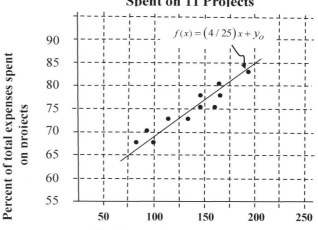

Funds and Percent of Total Expenses Spent on 11 Projects

The appropriate funds are alloted to 11 research projects. The scatterplot with the line of best fit above shows data for the 11 projects.

22. What is the value of y_o of the equation of the line of best fit?

(A) $y_o = 54$

(B) $y_o = 53$

(C) $y_o = 55$

(D) $y_o = 56$

23. If one of the total funds is changed to 275 million dollars, what is the predicted percent?

(A) 95

(B) 98

(C) 96

(D) 97

NEXT PAGE

24.　If 0.003 percent of *m* is 3, what is 3 percent of *m*?

(A) 1,000

(B) 2,000

(C) 3,000

(D) 4,000

25.　The cost of some computer of a computer retail store is $700. After discount 30%, the retail store still wants to make a profit of 10% from the computer. What is the selling price in dollars?

(A) 1,070
(B) 770
(C) 1,100
(D) 1,200

26.   Five actresses try out for the 3 roles in an opera. If each actress can perform any one role, but she cannot perform more than one role in the same play, how many distinct arrangements of the actresses are possible?

(A) 20
(B) 14
(C) 9
(D) 60

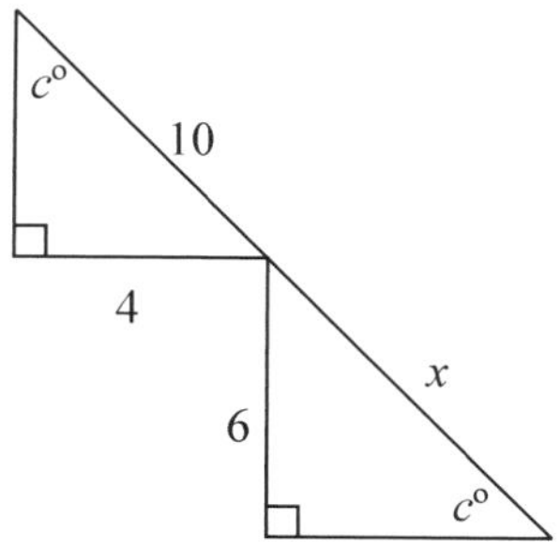

Note: Figure above not drawn to scale.

27.   In the figure above, what is the value of x?

(A) $6\dfrac{2}{3}$

(B) 15

(C) 12

(D) $\dfrac{40}{5}$

NEXT PAGE

28. A group of five people is to be selected from five boys and seven girls. If the selection is made at random, what is the probability that the group consists of 2 boys and 3 girls?

(A) 0.22

(B) 0.41

(C) 0.44

(D) 0.93

29. Which of the following is the sum of the positive 3-digit integers ending in 6?

(A) 45,590

(B) 49,950

(C) 49,590

(D) 49,509

30. Tom owns the shares of his company including $15,000 in cash and $35,000 in other holdings. If Tom redistributes his holdings in order to make 90 percent of the entire shares be in other holdings, how many dollars of cash must Tom change to other holdings?

(A) 10,000

(B) 11,000

(C) 20,000

(D) 100

NEXT PAGE

31. If $4 = \dfrac{16}{\sqrt{x}}$, where $x > 0$, what is the value of x?

32. If $m = \dfrac{1}{p}$, $n = \dfrac{1}{q}$, $p = 3$, $q = 1$, what is the value of $\dfrac{1}{m} + \dfrac{2}{n}$?

33. A spherical container has a radius of 3 cm. How many such spherical containers can be completely filled from a full rectangular container whose length is 6 cm, width is 4 cm, and height is 10 cm?

34. Shirley, Kathie and Cynthia are on a trip. Shirley drives during the first three hours at an average rate of 48 miles per hour. Kathie drives during the next one hour at an average rate of 52 miles per hour. Cynthia drives for the next four hours at an average rate of 51 miles per hour. They reach their destination after exactly eight hours. The average rate of their entire trip, in miles per hour, was

35. If $\dfrac{1}{2}$ of a cup pineapple juice is filled to $1\dfrac{1}{2}$-cup mark of a measuring container with a mixture containing equal amounts of apple and pineapple juices, what is the ratio of pineapple juice to final mixture?

NEXT PAGE

36.   If $3^{x+3} = 3$, then $3^x =$

37. The pizza-topping list:

Potato	Tomato	Mushrooms	Sausage
Garlic	Onion	Green Peppers	Meatballs

If a pizza must have 4 toppings chosen from the list above,
and no topping can be used more than once, how many
different kinds of pizza may be made?

38.   Sarah herself can clean a room in 14 minutes, and Jay
himself can clean the same room in 21 minutes. After Sarah

begins the job and does $\dfrac{3}{7}$ of the job, Jay takes over and

finishes the job. What is the entire time, in minutes, that takes
Sarah and Jay to clean the room?

STOP

Answer Key
For
SAT Math Practice Test 03

Section 3

1	C
2	C
3	B
4	B
5	A
6	B
7	D
8	D
9	D
10	B
11	D
12	C
13	C
14	D
15	D

16	1
17	4
18	6
19	3/8 or .375
20	51

Section 4

1	B	16	B
2	A	17	D
3	D	18	D
4	B	19	C
5	D	20	A
6	B	21	D
7	D	22	B
8	B	23	D
9	A	24	C
10	A	25	C
11	C	26	D
12	B	27	B
13	B	28	C
14	C	29	C
15	B	30	A

31	16
32	5
33	2
34	50
35	2/3 or .666 or .667
36	1/9 or .111
37	70
38	18

SAT Math

Practice

Test 03

Explanations

Redesigned for Tests in March 2016 and Beyond

Mad Math

Math Test – No Calculator

Time: 25 Minutes
20 Questions

Notes:
- The use of a calculator is not allowed.
- All numbers used in this section are the real number.
- Figures are provided for some problems in this test. Unless otherwise indicated under the figure "Note: Figure above not drawn to scale", all figures are drawn as accurately as possible.
- All figures lie in a plane EXCEPT otherwise specified.
- Unless otherwise indicated, the domain of any function f, g or j is assumed to be the set of all real numbers x for which $f(x)$, $g(x)$, or $j(x)$ is a real number.

$$A = \frac{1}{2}bh$$

$$A = lw$$

$$A = \pi r^2$$

$$V = \pi r^2 h$$

$$V = lwh$$

$$c^2 = a^2 + b^2$$

$$V = \frac{1}{3}\pi r^2 h$$

$$V = \frac{4}{3}\pi r^3$$

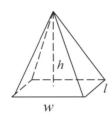

$$V = \frac{1}{3}lwh$$

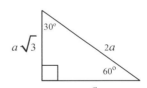

Reference Information

1. If three distinct numbers are chosen, one from each of following sets, what is the smallest sum of the 3 numbers?

$S_1 = \{1, 4, 6\}$

$S_2 = \{5, 6, 8\}$

$S_3 = \{1, 5, 9\}$

(A) 7
(B) 11
(C) 10
(D) 9

Solution: Answer: (C)

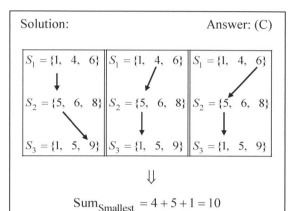

$$\text{Sum}_{\text{Smallest}} = 4 + 5 + 1 = 10$$

2. If $i = \sqrt{-1}$, then $|{-6 + 3i}| =$

(A) $\sqrt{95}$
(B) 35
(C) $3\sqrt{5}$
(D) 19

Solution: Answer: (C)

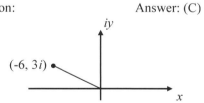

The absolute value $|a + bi|$ of a complex number $a + bi$ is the distance between origin $(0, 0)$ and point (a, bi).

$$\downarrow$$

$$|a + bi| = \sqrt{(a-0)^2 + (b-0)^2} = \sqrt{a^2 + b^2}$$

$$\Downarrow$$

$$|6 + 3i| = \sqrt{(-6)^2 + 3^2} = \sqrt{45} = 3\sqrt{5}$$

3. A list of numbers has been arranged such that each number in the list is 15 more than the number that precedes it. If number 298 is the tenth number in the list, what is the third number in the list?

(A) 202
(B) 193
(C) 311
(D) 180

Solution: Answer: (B)

It is an arithmetic sequence.

Use the formula: $a_n = a_1 + (n-1)d$.

$$298 = a_1 + 9 \cdot 15$$

$$\downarrow$$

$$a_1 = 163$$

$$\Downarrow$$

$$a_3 = 163 + 2 \cdot 15 = 193$$

4.
$$\begin{cases} y > x^2 + 2 \\ y < x + 5 \end{cases}$$

If $(2, k)$ is a solution to the system of inequalities above, which of the following could be the value of k ?

(A) 7.0
(B) 6.1
(C) 8.1
(D) 6.0

Solution: Answer: (B)

Substitute 2 for x and k for y.

$$\downarrow$$

$$k > 6 \text{ and } k < 7$$

or

$$6 < k < 7$$

$$\Downarrow$$

Answer is (B) 6.1

NEXT PAGE

5. A rectangular container has a length of 8, a width of 6, a height of 7, and a volume of V_1. Which of the following represents the volume of a rectangular container with dimensions length 16, width 2, and height 7 in terms of V_1?

(A) $\dfrac{2}{3}V_1$

(B) $\dfrac{1}{2}V_1$

(C) $3V_1$

(D) $2V_1$

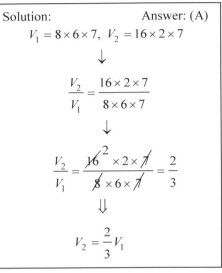

Solution: Answer: (A)

$$V_1 = 8 \times 6 \times 7, \; V_2 = 16 \times 2 \times 7$$
$$\downarrow$$
$$\frac{V_2}{V_1} = \frac{16 \times 2 \times 7}{8 \times 6 \times 7}$$
$$\downarrow$$
$$\frac{V_2}{V_1} = \frac{16^2 \times 2 \times 7}{8 \times 6 \times 7} = \frac{2}{3}$$
$$\Downarrow$$
$$V_2 = \frac{2}{3}V_1$$

6. If $9x^2 - 24x + k = 0$ has $\dfrac{4}{3}$ as a double root, $k =$

(A) 5

(B) 16

(C) 8

(D) $\dfrac{1}{8}$

Solution: Answer: (B)

Method 1

$$b^2 - 4ac = 0$$
$$24^2 - 4 \cdot 9k = 0, \; 576 = 36k$$
$$\Downarrow$$
$$k = 16$$

Method 2

$$9x^2 - 24x + k = 0$$

"$\dfrac{4}{3}$ as a double root"

$$\downarrow$$
$$\left(x - \frac{4}{3}\right)\left(x - \frac{4}{3}\right) = 0, \; x - \frac{4}{3} = 0$$
$$\downarrow$$
$$(3x - 4)(3x - 4) = (3x - 4)^2$$
$$9x^2 - 24x + 16 = 0$$
$$\Downarrow$$
$$k = 16$$

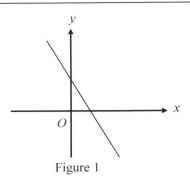

Figure 1

7. In Figure 1, the graph of equation $y = mx + b$ is the line. Which of the following must be true?

(A) $b + m > 0$

(B) $b - m < 0$

(C) $b - m \neq 0$

(D) $b - m > 0$

Solution: Answer: (D)

The direction of the line in Figure 1
$$\downarrow$$
slope $m < 0$

The position of the y-intercept of the line in Figure 1
$$\downarrow$$
y-intercept $b > 0$
$$\Downarrow$$
$$b > m \to \boxed{b - m > 0}$$

NEXT PAGE

8. If $a > 0$, what is the domain of function $f(x) = \dfrac{a}{x^2 + a}$?

(A) $x \neq -a$

(B) $x \neq -\dfrac{1}{a}$

(C) $-a \leq x \leq a$

(D) All real numbers including $-a$

Solution: Answer: (D)

The denominator has no any chance to be 0.

⇓

All real numbers

---

9. If a = the number of primes from 16 to 41,

b = the number of primes divisible by 5,

c = the number of even primes,

d = the number of primes divisible by 7,

what is the sum of a, b, c, and d ?

(A) 7

(B) 6

(C) 5

(D) 10

Solution   Answer: (D)

$a = 7$ $(17, 19, 23, 29, 31, 37, 41)$

$b = 1$ (5)

$c = 1$ (2)

$d = 1$ (7)

⇓

$a + b + c + d = 7 + 1 + 1 + 1 = 10$

---

10. Line m is tangent to the circle whose center is at (5, -1). If the tangent point is (-2, 4), what is the y-intercept of m ?

(A) -6.8

(B) 6.8

(C) 3.4

(D) 8.6

Solution: Answer: (B)

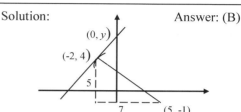

$$\begin{cases} S_{\text{Radius}} = -\dfrac{5}{7} \\ \text{The line is perpendicular to the radius.} \\ S_{\text{Line}} = -\dfrac{1}{S_{\text{Radius}}} = \dfrac{7}{5} \end{cases}$$

$$\begin{cases} \dfrac{y-4}{0-(-2)} = \dfrac{7}{5}, & \dfrac{y-4}{0-(-2)} = \dfrac{7 \times 2}{5} + 4 \end{cases}$$

⇓

$y = 6.8$

---

11. Which of the following is not the equation of a function?

(A) $y = 0$

(B) $y = |x|$

(C) $y = -|x|$

(D) $x = 0$

Solution: Answer: (D)

If an equation is not a function, then a x-value has more than one value of y corresponding the x-value.

$x = 0$ → It is the y-axis.

On y-axis, each distinct point has the same x-value, but has different y-value corresponding the x-value 0.

⇓

Anser is (D).

 NEXT PAGE

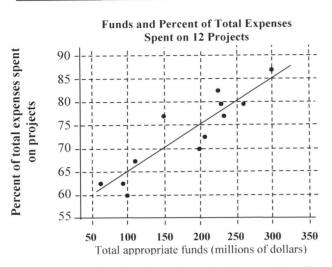

Funds and Percent of Total Expenses Spent on 12 Projects

Percent of total expenses spent on projects (vertical axis)
Total appropriate funds (millions of dollars) (horizontal axis)

12. The appropriate funds are alloted to 12 research projects. The scatterplot with the line of best fit on the left shows data for the 12 projects. If the vertical axis represents y-axis and the horizontal axis represents the x-axis, what is the equation of the line of best fit?

(A) $f(x) = 10x + 55$

(B) $f(x) = (1/10)x + 59$

(C) $f(x) = (1/10)x + 55$

(D) $f(x) = (2/3)x + 59$

Solution: Answer: (C)

Slope and y-intercept form of linear function:

$$f(x) = sx + y_0. \quad s = \frac{85-65}{300-100} = \frac{1}{10}$$

$$y_0 = f(x) - \frac{1}{10}x, \quad y_0 = f(100) - \frac{1}{10}\cdot 100$$

$$\Downarrow$$

$$y_0 = 65 - 10 = 55, \quad f(x) = \frac{1}{10}x + 55$$

13. Fastest Bikes sold 10 percent in 2011 more bikes than in 2010, and the price of each bike they sold in 2011 was 10 percent more than in 2010. The total profit from the sale of bikes was what percent increase in 2011 than in 2010 ?

(A) 20%

(B) 0.21%

(C) 21%

(D) 79%

Solution: Answer: (C)

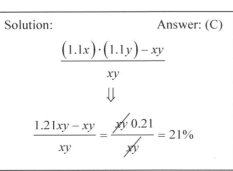

$$\frac{(1.1x)\cdot(1.1y) - xy}{xy}$$

$$\Downarrow$$

$$\frac{1.21xy - xy}{xy} = \frac{xy\,0.21}{xy} = 21\%$$

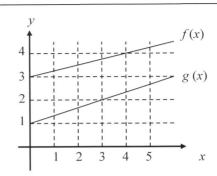

14. The graph of the functions f and g are lines, as shown above. What is the value of $f(4) - g(3)$?

(A) 2.6

(B) 4.3

(C) 3

(D) 2

Solution: Answer: (D)

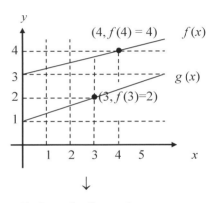

Refer to the figure above.

$$\Downarrow$$

$$f(4) - g(3) = 4 - 2 = 2$$

15. A rectangular living room is 90 feet length and 50 feet width. How many square yards of carpeting are needed to cover the floor?

(A) 4,500

(B) 1,500

(C) 800

(D) 500

Solution: Answer: (D)

feet → yards

$$\Downarrow$$

$$\frac{90}{3}, \frac{50}{3}$$

$$\Downarrow$$

$$\text{Area}_{\text{yards}} = \frac{90}{3} \times \frac{50}{3} = 500$$

NEXT PAGE →

16.   If $3^2 = 81^x$, then $2x =$

> Solution: Answer: 1
>
> $$3^2 = \left(3^4\right)^x \rightarrow 3^2 = 3^{4x}$$
>
> $$\Downarrow$$
>
> $$2 = 4x, \quad 2x = 1$$

17.   If 3 less than 4 times a certain number is 9 more than the number, what is the number?

> Solution: Answer: 4
>
> $$4x - 3 = x + 9$$
>
> $$\Downarrow$$
>
> $$3x = 12, \quad x = 4$$

18.   If x is an integer and $2 < x < 10$, how many distinct triangles are there with sides of lengths 5, 8, and x?

> Solution: Answer: 6
>
>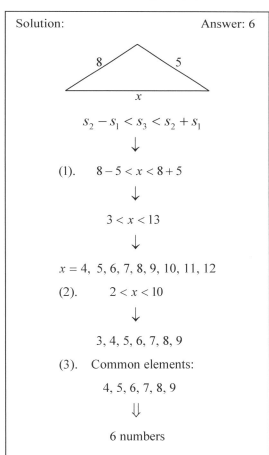
>
> $$s_2 - s_1 < s_3 < s_2 + s_1$$
>
> $$\downarrow$$
>
> (1). $8 - 5 < x < 8 + 5$
>
> $$\downarrow$$
>
> $$3 < x < 13$$
>
> $$\downarrow$$
>
> $$x = 4, 5, 6, 7, 8, 9, 10, 11, 12$$
>
> (2). $2 < x < 10$
>
> $$\downarrow$$
>
> $$3, 4, 5, 6, 7, 8, 9$$
>
> (3).   Common elements:
>
> $$4, 5, 6, 7, 8, 9$$
>
> $$\Downarrow$$
>
> 6 numbers

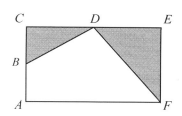

19.   In the rectangle $ACEF$ above, B and D are midpoints of sides $\overline{AC}$ and $\overline{CE}$, respectively. What is the ratio of the area of the shaded portion to the area of the rectangle?

> Solution: Answer: 3/8 or .375
>
> $$\text{Ratio} = \frac{A_{\text{Tri-1}} + A_{\text{Tri-2}}}{A_{\text{rectangle}}} = \frac{\dfrac{BC \cdot CD}{2} + \dfrac{DE \cdot EF}{2}}{AC \cdot AF}$$
>
> $$\downarrow$$
>
> $$\frac{\dfrac{BC \cdot CD}{2} + \dfrac{CD \cdot 2BC}{2}}{2BC \cdot 2CD} = \frac{\cancel{BC \cdot CD} \cdot \left(\dfrac{1}{2} + 1\right)}{\cancel{BC \cdot CD} \cdot 4}$$
>
> $$\Downarrow$$
>
> $$\text{Ratio} = \frac{\dfrac{3}{2}}{4} = \frac{3}{8}$$

20. The average (arithmetic mean) of a list of 15 scores is 79. If one of the scores is removed, the average of the remaining scores is 81. What is the score that was removed?

> Solution: Answer: 51
>
> $$\frac{15 \times 79 - x}{14} = 81$$
>
> $$\downarrow$$
>
> $$1185 = x + 1134$$
>
> $$\Downarrow$$
>
> $$x = 51$$

STOP

Math Test – Calculator

Time: 55 Minutes
38 Questions

Notes:
- The use of a calculator is not allowed.
- All numbers used in this section are the real number.
- Figures are provided for some problems in this test. Unless otherwise indicated under the figure "Note: Figure above not drawn to scale", all figures are drawn as accurately as possible.
- All figures lie in a plane EXCEPT otherwise specified.
- Unless otherwise indicated, the domain of any function f, g or j is assumed to be the set of all real numbers x for which $f(x)$, $g(x)$, or $j(x)$ is a real number.

Reference Information

$$A = \frac{1}{2}bh$$

$$A = lw$$

$$A = \pi r^2$$

$$V = \pi r^2 h$$

$$V = lwh$$

$$c^2 = a^2 + b^2$$

$$V = \frac{1}{3}\pi r^2 h$$

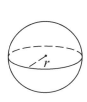
$$V = \frac{4}{3}\pi r^3$$

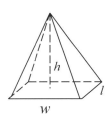
$$V = \frac{1}{3}lwh$$

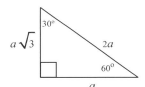

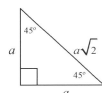

1. The expression $\dfrac{4x-1}{3} - \dfrac{x-5}{3}$ is how much greater than x?

(A) -2

(B) $\dfrac{4}{3}$

(C) 2

(D) $-\dfrac{4}{3}$

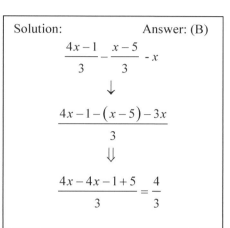

Solution: Answer: (B)

$$\dfrac{4x-1}{3} - \dfrac{x-5}{3} - x$$

$$\downarrow$$

$$\dfrac{4x-1-(x-5)-3x}{3}$$

$$\Downarrow$$

$$\dfrac{4x-4x-1+5}{3} = \dfrac{4}{3}$$

2. What is a single discount, which is equal to 2 successive discounts of 10% and 20%?

(A) 28%
(B) 19%
(C) 18%
(D) 20%

Solution: Answer: (A)

Method 1

Work with an easy number such as $100.

$$100 \cdot 0.9 \cdot 0.8 = 72$$

$$100 - 72 = 28, \ 28/100 = 28\%$$

Method 2

$$0.9 \times 0.8x = 0.72x = \dfrac{72}{100}x$$

$$\Downarrow$$

$$100 - \dfrac{72}{100} = \dfrac{28}{100} = 28\%$$

3. If the line $y = -3$ intersects the graph of the equation $f(x) = x^2 - 11x + 25$, which of the following is a possible pair of the coordinates of the intersection points?

(A) (-3, 7)

(B) (-4, -3)

(C) (7, 4)

(D) (7, -3)

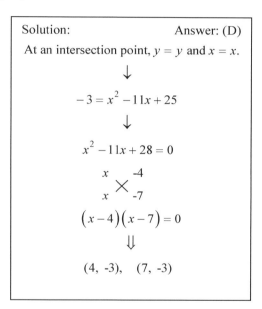

Solution: Answer: (D)

At an intersection point, $y = y$ and $x = x$.

$$\downarrow$$

$$-3 = x^2 - 11x + 25$$

$$\downarrow$$

$$x^2 - 11x + 28 = 0$$

$$x \overset{-4}{\underset{-7}{\times}} x$$

$$(x-4)(x-7) = 0$$

$$\Downarrow$$

$$(4, -3), \quad (7, -3)$$

4. The acceleration of a motorcycle is a function involving time elapsed. If $A(T) = 15T^2 + 120T + 86$ represents the acceleration of the motorcycle and T represents the time lapsed, what is the acceleration of the motorcycle 10 seconds after the motorcycle started to accelerate?

(A) 1786
(B) 2786
(C) 3786
(D) 4786

Solution: Answer: (B)

$$A(10) = 15 \cdot 10^2 + 120 \cdot 10 + 86$$

$$\Downarrow$$

$$2786$$

NEXT PAGE

$f(x)$	x
82	−2
25	−1
12	0
13	1

5. The chart above provides selected values of the function $f(x)$ and x. Which of the following functions could be the $f(x)$?

(A) $11x^2 - 11x$

(B) $12x - 15$

(C) $f(x) = 12x^2 - 11x - 12$

(D) $f(x) = 12x^2 - 11x + 12$

Solution: Answer: (D)

Use plug-in method.

↓

$(D) f(0) = 12 \cdot 9^2 - 11 \cdot 0 + 12 = 12$

You may not continue to do following because when $x = 0$, only (D) has $f(0) = 12$ among the five choices.

$f(-2) = 12 \cdot (-2)^2 - 11 \cdot (-2) + 12 = 82$

$f(-1) = 12 \cdot (-1)^2 - 11 \cdot (-1) + 12 = 25$

$f(1) = 12 \cdot 1^2 - 11 \cdot 1 + 12 = 13$

⇓

Answer is (D).

6. Which of the following does $E = 4^{\frac{3}{4}}$ equal?

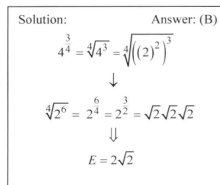

(A) $\sqrt[5]{2}$

(B) $2\sqrt{2}$

(C) $\sqrt[4]{2}$

(D) $\sqrt[6]{2}$

Solution: Answer: (B)

$$4^{\frac{3}{4}} = \sqrt[4]{4^3} = \sqrt[4]{\left((2)^2\right)^3}$$

↓

$$\sqrt[4]{2^6} = 2^{\frac{6}{4}} = 2^{\frac{3}{2}} = \sqrt{2}\sqrt{2}\sqrt{2}$$

⇓

$$E = 2\sqrt{2}$$

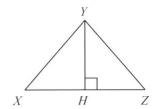

7. Triangle XYZ above is an equilateral triangle. If the length of side, S, is 10, what is the area of triangle XYZ?

(A) $\dfrac{5\sqrt{3}}{2}$

(B) 30

(C) 40

(D) $25\sqrt{3}$

Solution: Answer: (D)

$$Area = \frac{S^2\sqrt{3}}{4}$$

⇓

$$Area = \frac{10^2\sqrt{3}}{4} = 25\sqrt{3}$$

8. The first term of set A is −3, and each term thereafter is 3 greater than the previous term. The Nth term of set B is given by the formula $-N + 22$. Which one is the term of set A that first exceeds the value of its corresponding term in set B?

(A) 6

(B) 8

(C) 7

(D) 10

Solution: Answer: (B)

$A = (-3, 0, 3, 6, 9, 12, 15, 18 \ldots)$

$B = (-N + 22)$

Because N represents the term number, N must represent underline positive integers.

$N = 1, 2, 3 \ldots$

$B = (21, 20, 19, 18, 17, 16, 15, 14 \ldots)$

8th term of A = 18

8th term of B = 14

⇓

The underline term = 8

NEXT PAGE ⟩

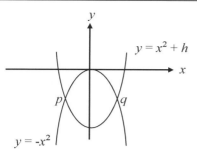

9. The figure above shows the graphs $y = -x^2$ and $y = x^2 + h$. h is a certain constant. p and q separately represent the intersecting points of the two graphs in the xy-plane. If the length of the distance between p and q is 10, what is the value of h?

(A) -50
(B) 98
(C) 82
(D) -98

Solution: Answer: (A)

(1) At the intersection points

$$y = y$$
$$-x^2 = x^2 + h$$

(2) $pq = 10 \rightarrow x = \pm 5$

↓

$$-(\pm 5)^2 = (\pm 5)^2 + h$$

⇓

$$h = -50$$

10. The quantity y is proportional to the cube root of the quantity x, and y is 5 units if x is 216 units. What is the formula for y in terms of x?

(A) $A = \dfrac{5}{6} \cdot \sqrt[3]{B}$

(B) $A = \dfrac{6}{5} \cdot \sqrt[3]{B}$

(C) $A = \dfrac{5}{6 \cdot \sqrt[3]{B}}$

(D) $A \geq \dfrac{5}{6} \cdot \sqrt[3]{B}$

Solution: Answer: (A)

$$A = k\sqrt[3]{B}$$

↓

$$k = \frac{A}{\sqrt[3]{B}} = \frac{5}{\sqrt[3]{216}} = \frac{5}{6}$$

⇓

$$A = \frac{5}{6} \cdot \sqrt[3]{B}$$

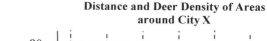

Distance and Deer Density of Areas around City X

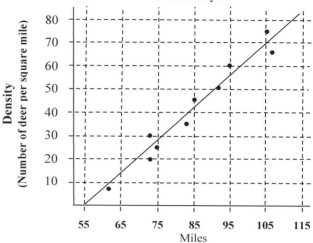

The scatterplot with line of best fit above shows the deer density of 10 areas, in number of deers per square mile, with respect to their distances from City X.

11.   By the scatterplot, which of the following statements is true about the relationship between a distance of an area from City X and its deer density?

(A) The areas that are lesser distance from City X tend to have more deer densities.

(B) The areas that are more distance from City X tend to have more or lesser deer densities.

(C) The areas that are more distance from City X tend to have more deer densities.

(D) None above

Solution: Answer: (C)
    According to the scatterplot,
        the distances increase, the densities increase.

⇓

Answer is (C).

NEXT PAGE

12. Three fair cubes each are one that is labeled with the numbers 1, 2, 3, 4, 5, and 6, such that there is an equal chance of rolling each of these numbers. If you roll these three cubes at the same time, what is the probability that the sum of the three numbers you roll will be greater than seventeen?

(A) $\dfrac{1}{108}$

(B) $\dfrac{1}{216}$

(C) $\dfrac{1}{36}$

(D) $\dfrac{1}{72}$

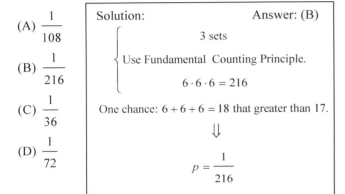

Solution: Answer: (B)

$\begin{cases} \text{3 sets} \\ \text{Use Fundamental Counting Principle.} \\ \quad 6 \cdot 6 \cdot 6 = 216 \end{cases}$

One chance: $6 + 6 + 6 = 18$ that greater than 17.

$\Downarrow$

$p = \dfrac{1}{216}$

13. Monica has two jobs. She works as a waitress, which pays \$15 per hour, and she works as a nurse, which pays \$16 per hour. Monica can work no more than 120 hours per month, and she plans to make at least \$1,200 per month. Which of the following system of inequalities describes this situation in terms of w and n, where w represents the number of hours she works as a waitress and n represents the number of hours she works as a nurse?

(A) $w + n < 120$
  $15w + 16n \geq 1,200$

(B) $w + n \leq 120$
  $15w + 16n \geq 1,200$

(C) $w + n \leq 120$
  $15w + 16n \leq 1,200$

(D) $w + n \leq 120$
  $15w + 16n > 1,200$

Solution: Answer: (B)

$\begin{cases} \text{"no more than"} \rightarrow \text{Use sign } \leq. \\ \quad \text{"at least"} \rightarrow \text{Use sign } \geq. \end{cases}$

$\Downarrow$

$\begin{cases} w + y \leq 120 \\ 15w + 16n \geq 1200 \end{cases}$

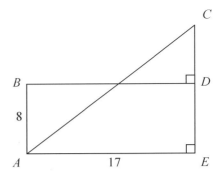

14. In the figure above, the area of triangle ACE equals the area of rectangle $ABDE$. What is the length of segment $\overline{CD}$?

(A) 6

(B) 7

(C) 8

(D) 9

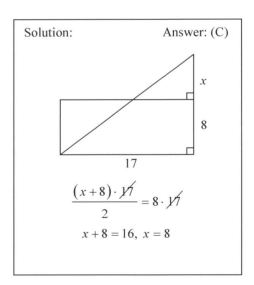

Solution: Answer: (C)

$\dfrac{(x+8) \cdot \cancel{17}}{2} = 8 \cdot \cancel{17}$

$x + 8 = 16, \; x = 8$

NEXT PAGE ⟫

15. If $x \neq \pm 1$, which of the following is the reduced form for

$$\frac{x^2 - 1}{(x+1)^2 (x-1)}?$$

(A) $\dfrac{1}{x-1}$

(B) $\dfrac{1}{x+1}$

(C) $\dfrac{x+1}{(x^2 + 2x + 1)}$

(D) $x + 1$

Solution: Answer: (B)

$$\frac{x^2 - 1}{(x+1)^2 (x-1)}$$

↓

$$\frac{(x-1)(x+1)}{(x+1)^2 (x-1)}$$

↓

$$\frac{(x+1)}{(x+1)^2}$$

⇓

$$\frac{1}{x+1}$$

16. A computer program at random chooses a positive 3-digit integer. If the integer chosen is even, twice the value of the integer is printed. If the integer printed is 204, which of the following could have been the integer chosen?

   I.   306
   II.   102
   III.   204

(A) II and III only
(B) II only
(C) III only
(D) I only

Solution: Answer: (B)

I. The integer printed is 204. The number chosen should be 102, which is even. Twice 102 = 204 should be printed and triple 102 = 306 should not be printed.

⇓

I is false.

II. The integer printed is 204. The number chosen should be 102, which is even.

⇓

II is true.

III. The integer printed is 204. The number chosen should be 102, which is even. 204 is the number printed, not the number chosen.

⇓

III is false.

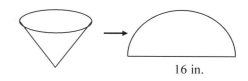

16 in.

Note: Figure above not drawn to scale.

17. In the figure above, if the semicircle with diameter 16 inches is made from a cone, what is the radius of the cone?

(A) 2

(B) 9

(C) 8

(D) 4

Solution: Answer: (D)

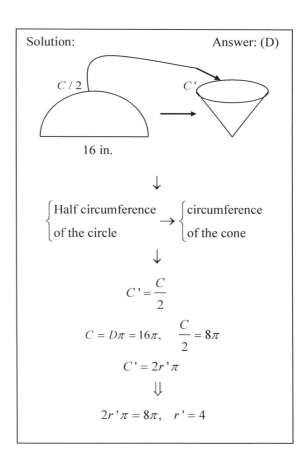

16 in.

↓

$\begin{cases} \text{Half circumference} \\ \text{of the circle} \end{cases} \rightarrow \begin{cases} \text{circumference} \\ \text{of the cone} \end{cases}$

↓

$$C' = \frac{C}{2}$$

$$C = D\pi = 16\pi, \qquad \frac{C}{2} = 8\pi$$

$$C' = 2r'\pi$$

⇓

$$2r'\pi = 8\pi, \quad r' = 4$$

NEXT PAGE

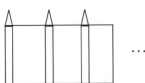 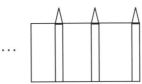

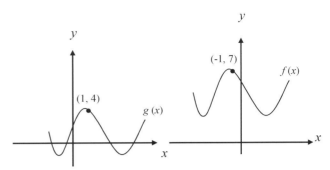

18. The figure above represents a stretch of wall, which is 1,120 yards long. The wall posts are placed at two ends and also placed every 5.6 yards along the wall. How many the posts totally are there in the wall stretch?

(A) 200

(B) 100

(C) 101

(D) 201

Solution: Answer: (D)

$$\frac{1120}{5.6}+1$$

↓

$$\frac{11200}{56}+1$$

⇓

$$200+1=201$$

20. The figures above show the graphs of the functions $g(x)$ and $f(x)$. The function $f(x)$ is defined by $f(x) = g(x+k) + h$, where k and h are constants. What is the value of $\dfrac{h}{k}$?

(A) 3/2

(B) -1

(C) -2

(D) 2

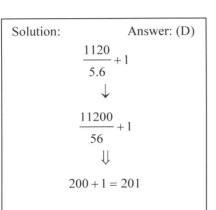

19. The graph of $f(x)$ is shown above. If $f(a) = 1$, which of the following is possible value of a?

(A) -3
(B) -2.5
(C) 2.5
(D) -3.5

Solution: Answer: (C)

$$y = f(a)$$

When $f(a) = 3$, $-2 \le a \le 3$.
Whereas, among the 5 choices, only

⇓

$$-2 \le 2.5 \le 3$$

Solution: Answer: (A)

$$k = 2 \text{ and } h = 3$$

⇓

$$\frac{h}{k} = \frac{3}{2}$$

NEXT PAGE

21. If $f(x) = \sqrt{7 - x^2}$, what is the domain of f ?

(A) $-\sqrt{7} \geq x, \ x \geq \sqrt{7}$

(B) $-\sqrt{7} < x < \sqrt{7}$

(C) $-\sqrt{7} < x, \ x > \sqrt{7}$

(D) $-\sqrt{7} \leq x \leq \sqrt{7}$

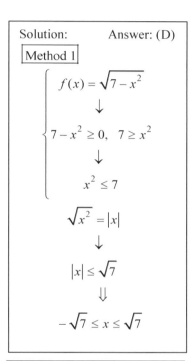

Solution: Answer: (D)

Method 1

$$f(x) = \sqrt{7 - x^2}$$
$$\downarrow$$
$$7 - x^2 \geq 0, \quad 7 \geq x^2$$
$$\downarrow$$
$$x^2 \leq 7$$
$$\sqrt{x^2} = |x|$$
$$\downarrow$$
$$|x| \leq \sqrt{7}$$
$$\Downarrow$$
$$-\sqrt{7} \leq x \leq \sqrt{7}$$

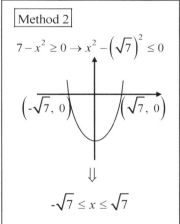

Method 2

$$7 - x^2 \geq 0 \rightarrow x^2 - \left(\sqrt{7}\right)^2 \leq 0$$

$\left(-\sqrt{7}, \ 0\right)$ $\left(\sqrt{7}, \ 0\right)$

$$\Downarrow$$
$$-\sqrt{7} \leq x \leq \sqrt{7}$$

Questions 22 and 23 refer to the information below.

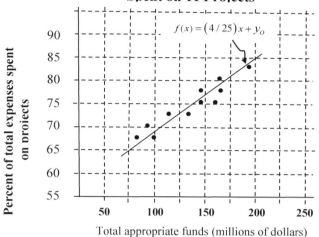

Funds and Percent of Total Expenses Spent on 11 Projects

$f(x) = (4/25)x + y_o$

The appropriate funds are alloted to 11 research projects. The scatterplot with the line of best fit above shows data for the 11 projects.

22. What is the value of y_o of the equation of the line of best fit?

(A) $y_o = 54$

(B) $y_o = 53$

(C) $y_o = 55$

(D) $y_o = 56$

Solution: Answer: (B)

$$f(x) = \left(4/25\right)x + y_o$$
$$\downarrow$$
According to the line of best fit,
$$f(200) = 85.$$
$$\Downarrow$$
$$85 = \frac{4}{25} \cdot 200 + y_o, \quad y_o = 85 - 32 = 53$$

23. If one of the total funds is changed to 275 million dollars, what is the predicted percent?

(A) 95

(B) 98

(C) 96

(D) 97

Solution: Answer: (D)

$$f(x) = \left(4/25\right)x + 53$$
$$\Downarrow$$
$$f(275) = \frac{4}{25} \cdot 275 + 53 = 97$$

NEXT PAGE

24. If 0.003 percent of m is 3, what is 3 percent of m?

(A) 1,000

(B) 2,000

(C) 3,000

(D) 4,000

Solution: Answer: (C)

$$\frac{0.003}{100}m = 3, \quad 0.003m = 300$$

$$\downarrow$$

$$m = \frac{300}{0.003} = \frac{300}{\frac{3}{1000}} = 10^5$$

$$\Downarrow$$

$$\frac{3}{100}m = \frac{3}{100} \times 10^5 = 3000$$

25. The cost of some computer of a computer retail store is $700. After discount 30%, the retail store still wants to make a profit of 10% from the computer. What is the selling price in dollars?

(A) 1,070

(B) 770

(C) 1,100

(D) 1,200

Solution: Answer: (C)

$$700 \times 1.1 = 770$$

$$\downarrow$$

The value 770 includes a 10% profit.

$$\downarrow$$

$$770 = 0.7x$$

$$\Downarrow$$

$$x = 1100$$

NEXT PAGE

26. Five actresses try out for the 3 roles in an opera. If each actress can perform any one role, but she cannot perform more than one role in the same play, how many distinct arrangements of the actresses are possible?

(A) 20
(B) 14
(C) 9
(D) 60

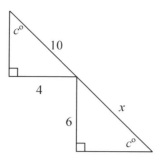

Note: Figure above not drawn to scale.

27. In the figure above, what is the value of x?

(A) $6\dfrac{2}{3}$

(B) 15

(C) 12

(D) $\dfrac{40}{5}$

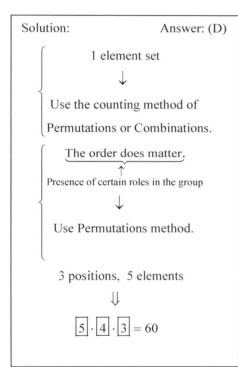

Solution: Answer: (D)

⎧ 1 element set

↓

Use the counting method of

Permutations or Combinations. ⎭

⎧ The order does matter.

↑

Presence of certain roles in the group

↓

Use Permutations method. ⎭

3 positions, 5 elements

⇓

$\boxed{5} \cdot \boxed{4} \cdot \boxed{3} = 60$

Solution: Answer: (B)

The 2 triangles have the same

3 pairs of interior angles.

↓

They are similar triangles.

↓

Ratios of corresponding sides are equal.

⇓

$\dfrac{x}{10} = \dfrac{6}{4},\ x = \boxed{15}$

NEXT PAGE

28. A group of five people is to be selected from five boys and seven girls. If the selection is made at random, what is the probability that the group consists of 2 boys and 3 girls?

(A) 0.22

(B) 0.41

(C) 0.44

(D) 0.93

Solution: Answer: (C)

$\left\{\begin{array}{l}\text{2 element sets}\\ \text{The elements can be combined in this case.}\end{array}\right.$

↓

Use Fundamental Counting Principle.

$\left\{\begin{array}{l}\text{1 set}\\ \text{2 postions}\\ \text{5 elements}\\ \text{Order doesn't matter.}\end{array}\right.$ $\left\{\begin{array}{l}\text{1 set}\\ \text{3 postions}\\ \text{7 elements}\\ \text{Order doesn't matter.}\end{array}\right.$

$$P = \dfrac{\dfrac{\boxed{5}\cdot\boxed{4}}{2!} \times \dfrac{\boxed{7}\cdot\boxed{6}\cdot\boxed{5}}{3!}}{\dfrac{\boxed{12}\cdot\boxed{11}\cdot\boxed{10}\cdot\boxed{9}\cdot\boxed{8}}{5!}}$$

$\left\{\begin{array}{l}\text{1 set}\\ \text{5 postions}\\ \text{12 elements}\\ \text{Order doesn't matter.}\end{array}\right.$

⇓

$$\dfrac{\dfrac{\boxed{5}\cdot\cancel{\boxed{4}}^{2}}{\cancel{2!}} \times \dfrac{\boxed{7}\cdot\cancel{\boxed{6}}\cdot\boxed{5}}{\cancel{3!}}}{\dfrac{\cancel{\boxed{12}}\cdot\boxed{11}\cdot\cancel{\boxed{10}}\cdot\boxed{9}\cdot\boxed{8}}{\cancel{5\cdot2}\cdot\cancel{4\cdot3}}} = \dfrac{350}{99\cdot8} \approx 0.44$$

29. Which of the following is the sum of the positive 3-digit integers ending in 6?

(A) 45,590

(B) 49,950

(C) 49,590

(D) 49,509

Solution: Answer: (C)

$$106,\ 116,\ 126,\ \cdots,\ 996 \rightarrow d = 10$$

↓

Arithmetic seq.

$$a_n = a_1 + (n-1)d$$

$$996 = 106 + (n-1)10, \quad n = \dfrac{890}{10} + 1 = 90$$

$$S_n = \dfrac{n(a_1 + a_n)}{2}$$

⇓

$$S_{90} = \dfrac{90(106 + 996)}{2} = 49590$$

30. Tom owns the shares of his company including $15,000 in cash and $35,000 in other holdings. If Tom redistributes his holdings in order to make 90 percent of the entire shares be in other holdings, how many dollars of cash must Tom change to other holdings?

(A) 10,000

(B) 11,000

(C) 20,000

(D) 100

Solution: Answer: (A)

$$\dfrac{35+x}{15+35} = \dfrac{9\cancel{0}}{10\cancel{0}}$$

↓

$$\dfrac{35+x}{5\cancel{0}} = \dfrac{9}{1\cancel{0}}, \quad 35+x = 45$$

$$x = 10$$

⇓

$$x = 10 \times 10^{3} = 10000$$

NEXT PAGE ⟩

31. If $4 = \dfrac{16}{\sqrt{x}}$, where $x > 0$, what is the value of x?

Solution: Answer: 16

$$4 = \frac{16}{\sqrt{x}} \;\rightarrow\; \cancel{4}\sqrt{x} = \cancel{16}^{4}$$

$$\Downarrow$$

$$\sqrt{x} = 4, \quad \left(\sqrt{x}\right)^2 = 4^2, \quad x = \boxed{16}$$

32. If $m = \dfrac{1}{p}$, $n = \dfrac{1}{q}$, $p = 3$, $q = 1$, what is the value of $\dfrac{1}{m} + \dfrac{2}{n}$?

Solution: Answer: 5

$$\frac{1}{m} + \frac{2}{n} = \frac{1}{m} + \frac{1}{n} \times 2$$

$$\Downarrow$$

$$3 + 1 \times 2 = 5$$

33. A spherical container has a radius of 3 cm. How many such spherical containers can be completely filled from a full rectangular container whose length is 6 cm, width is 4 cm, and height is 10 cm? $\left(\text{The volume of a sphere is } V = \dfrac{4}{3} r^3 \pi.\right)$

Solution: Answer: 2

$$\begin{cases} V_{\text{Sph}} = \dfrac{4}{3} r^3 \pi = \dfrac{4}{3} 3^3 \pi = \dfrac{4}{\cancel{3}} \cdot \cancel{3} \cdot 3^2 \pi = 36\pi \\[2mm] V_{\text{Rec}} = 6 \cdot 4 \cdot 10 = 240 \end{cases}$$

$$\downarrow$$

$$N_{\text{Sph-containers}} = \frac{V_{\text{Rec}}}{V_{\text{Sph}}} = \frac{240}{36\pi}$$

$$\downarrow$$

$$\frac{240}{36} = \frac{20}{3\pi} \approx 2.11$$

"$\cdots$ filled from a $\cdots$ rectangular container"

$$\Downarrow$$

$$N_{\text{Sph-containers}} = 2$$

34. Shirley, Kathie and Cynthia are on a trip. Shirley drives during the first three hours at an average rate of 48 miles per hour. Kathie drives during the next one hour at an average rate of 52 miles per hour. Cynthia drives for the next four hours at an average rate of 51 miles per hour. They reach their destination after exactly eight hours. The average rate of their entire trip, in miles per hour, was

Solution: Answer: 50

$$\underbrace{\text{Average rate}}_{\text{For entire trip}} = \frac{\text{Total distance}}{\text{Total time}}$$

$$\Downarrow$$

$$x = \frac{3 \times 48 + 1 \times 52 + 4 \times 51}{8} = 50$$

35. If $\dfrac{1}{2}$ of a cup pineapple juice is filled to $1\dfrac{1}{2}$-cup mark of a measuring container with a mixture containing equal amounts of apple and pineapple juices, what is the ratio of pineapple juice to final mixture?

Solution: Answer: 2/3 or .666 or .667

Before $\dfrac{1}{2}$ of a cup apple juice was filled to

$1\dfrac{1}{2}$-cup mark of the container, the container

had contained $\left(\dfrac{3}{2} - \dfrac{1}{2}\right)$ cup mixed juice.

$$\downarrow$$

$$\text{Ratio} = \frac{\dfrac{1}{2} + \left(\dfrac{\dfrac{3}{2} - \dfrac{1}{2}}{2}\right)}{\dfrac{3}{2}}$$

$$\Downarrow$$

$$\frac{\dfrac{1}{2} + \dfrac{1}{2}}{\dfrac{3}{2}} = \boxed{\dfrac{2}{3}}$$

NEXT PAGE ➡

36. If $3^{x+3} = 3$, then $3^x =$

Solution: Answer: 1/9 or .111

Method 1:

$$3^{x+3} = 3 \rightarrow 3^x \cdot 3^3 = 3$$

$$\Downarrow$$

$$3^x = \frac{3}{3^3} = \frac{3}{27} = \frac{1}{9}$$

Method 2:

$$3^{x+3} = 3^1$$

$$\downarrow$$

$$3^{x+3-3} = 3^{1-3}$$

$$\Downarrow$$

$$3^x = 3^{-2} = \frac{1}{3^2} = \frac{1}{9}$$

37. The pizza-topping list:

Potato	Tomato	Mushrooms	Sausage
Garlic	Onion	Green Peppers	Meatballs

If a pizza must have 4 toppings chosen from the list above, and no topping can be used more than once, how many different kinds of pizza may be made?

Solution: Answer: 70

1 element set

$$\downarrow$$

Use the method of Permutations or Combinations.
The order doesn't matter or is not important.

$$\downarrow$$

Use the counting method of Combination.
4 positions, 8 elements

$$\Downarrow$$

$$\frac{\boxed{8} \cdot \boxed{7} \cdot \boxed{6} \cdot \boxed{5}}{4!} = 70$$

Note: The order doesn't matter so that the result should be divided by the factorial, whose number equals the number of positions, to eliminate the arrangements counted repeatedly.

38. Sarah herself can clean a room in 14 minutes, and Jay himself can clean the same room in 21 minutes. After Sarah begins the job and does $\frac{3}{7}$ of the job, Jay takes over and finishes the job. What is the entire time, in minutes, that takes Sarah and Jay to clean the room?

Solution: Answer: 18

$$"\frac{3}{7} \text{ of the job}" = "\frac{3}{7} \text{ of the time}"$$

$$\downarrow$$

1 as fraction is the entire job.

1 as fraction is the entire time.

$$1 - \frac{3}{7} = \frac{4}{7}$$

$$\downarrow$$

$$\begin{cases} \cancel{14}^{\,2} \times \frac{3}{\cancel{7}} = 6 \\ \cancel{21}^{\,3} \times \frac{4}{\cancel{7}} = 12 \end{cases}$$

$$\Downarrow$$

$$T_{\text{Entire}} = 6 + 12 = 18$$

STOP

SAT Math

Practice

Test 04

Redesigned for Tests in March 2016 and Beyond

Mad Math

Math Test – No Calculator

Time: 25 Minutes
20 Questions

Notes:
- The use of a calculator is not allowed.
- All numbers used in this section are the real number.
- Figures are provided for some problems in this test. Unless otherwise indicated under the figure "Note: Figure above not drawn to scale", all figures are drawn as accurately as possible.
- All figures lie in a plane EXCEPT otherwise specified.
- Unless otherwise indicated, the domain of any function f, g or j is assumed to be the set of all real numbers x for which $f(x)$, $g(x)$, or $j(x)$ is a real number.

Reference Information

$$A = \frac{1}{2}bh$$

$$A = lw$$

$$A = \pi r^2$$

$$V = \pi r^2 h$$

$$V = lwh$$

$$c^2 = a^2 + b^2$$

$$V = \frac{1}{3}\pi r^2 h$$

$$V = \frac{4}{3}\pi r^3$$

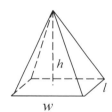

$$V = \frac{1}{3}lwh$$

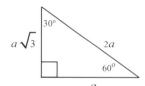

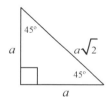

1.   Which of the following is NOT equal to the others?

(A) $(0.2)(0.008)$

(B) 0.016

(C) 1.6×10^{-2}

(D) $(0.2)(0.08)$

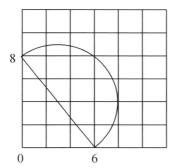

2.   In the figure above, what is the arc of the semicircle?

(A) $\dfrac{25\pi}{4}$

(B) $\dfrac{25\pi}{2}$

(C) 5π

(D) $\dfrac{5\pi}{2}$

3. In a right triangle ABC, if angle C is $90°$ and $\cos A = 0.3$, which of the following is $\sin(90° - A)$ equal to ?

(A) 0.7

(B) 0.5

(C) 0.3

(D) 0.4

4. 2 sides of a triangle have lengths 8.1 and 12, respectively. If the remaining side of the triangle has a value that is an integer, what is the smallest possible perimeter of this triangle?

(A) 41.1
(B) 25.1
(C) 24.1
(D) 40.1

5. $g(f(x)) = \dfrac{\sqrt{e^x - 1} + 3}{4\sqrt{e^x - 1} - 3}$ and $g(x) = \dfrac{x + 3}{4x - 3}$, $f(x) =$

(A) $\sqrt{e^x}$

(B) $\sqrt{x}$

(C) $e^x - 1$

(D) $\sqrt{e^x - 1}$

6. If $f(x) = ax^2 + bx + c$ for all real numbers x and if $f(1) = -1$ and $f(0) = 2$, what is the sum of a and b?

(A) -1

(B) 2

(C) -3

(D) 0

7. If the average (arithmetic mean) of 21 consecutive even integers is $n - 7$, what is the median of the twenty-one integers?

(A) 21
(B) $n - 3$
(C) $n - 7$
(D) $n - 2$

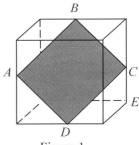

Figure 1

8. Figure 1 shows a cube with edge of length 2 units. If points A, B, C and D are midpoints of the edges of the cube, what is the sum of DC and BC?

(A) $\sqrt{2} + \sqrt{6}$

(B) $\sqrt{5} + \sqrt{3}$

(C) $\sqrt{13}$

(D) $\sqrt{2} + \sqrt{5}$

NEXT PAGE

9. The menu of a certain restaurant lists 8 items in the first page and 7 items in the second page. A family plans to share 4 items from the first page and 4 items from the second page. If none of the items is found in both pages, how many distinct possibilities of items could the family choose?

(A) 2,450

(B) 1,178

(C) 4,116

(D) 6,820

10. If $\dfrac{-4x + 20y}{125p} = \dfrac{-16c - 48d}{625p}$, then $c + 3d =$

(A) $\dfrac{4(x - 5y)}{5}$

(B) $\dfrac{5(x - 5y)}{4}$

(C) $\dfrac{5(x + 5y)}{4}$

(D) $\dfrac{4(x + 5y)}{5}$

NEXT PAGE

11. The relationship between A and B is $A = \dfrac{2}{3}(B - 23)$, and the relationship between A and C is $C = A - 32$. Which of the following is the relationship between B and C ?

(A) $C = \dfrac{2}{3}(B - 23) - 32$

(B) $C = \dfrac{2}{3}(B + 23) - 32$

(C) $C = \dfrac{2}{3}(B - 23) + 32$

(D) $C = \dfrac{3}{2}(B + 23) - 32$

12. If a sequence $p - 2, p + 2, 2p - 3$ forms an arithmetic sequence, what is the value of p?

(A) 6
(B) -3
(C) 8
(D) 9

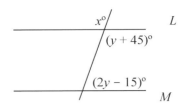

Note: Figure bellow not drawn to scale.

13. In the figure above, lines L and M are parallel. What is the value of x?

(A) 45

(B) 95

(C) 65

(D) 80

14. If $x^2 - 31 = 3^2 \times 10$, then x could be equal to

(A) -15

(B) 16

(C) 14

(D) 11

15. Which of the following is the complete solution set for the inequality $|x - 5| \geq 3$?

(A) $2 \leq x \leq 8$
(B) $x \geq 8, x \leq 3$
(C) $x \geq 8, x \leq 2$
(D) $x \leq 1$

NEXT PAGE

16. Eight cards in a pot are numbered 1 through 8. One card is drawn at random. The ones digit of the sum of the numbers on the remaining cards is 8. What is the number on the drawn card?

17. Stephanie is now five times as old as her brother Steve. After 2 years, Stephanie will be 3 times as old as Steve will be. How old was Stephanie five year ago?

18. In class A, each of the 35 students contributed either a nickel or dime to the Child Foundation. If the total amount collected was $2.05, how many students contributed a nickel?

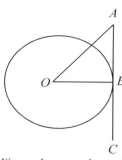

Note: Figure above not drawn to scale.

19. In the figure above, $\overline{AC}$ is tangent to circle O at point B. $\overline{BO}$ is radius of the circle. If $BO = AB = \sqrt{2}$, what is the area of the triangle AOB?

20. If x and y are different nonnegative integers and $3x + y = 22$, what is the number of all possible values of x?

STOP

Math Test – Calculator

Time: 55 Minutes
38 Questions

Notes:
- The use of a calculator is not allowed.
- All numbers used in this section are the real number.
- Figures are provided for some problems in this test. Unless otherwise indicated under the figure "Note: Figure above not drawn to scale", all figures are drawn as accurately as possible.
- All figures lie in a plane EXCEPT otherwise specified.
- Unless otherwise indicated, the domain of any function f, g or j is assumed to be the set of all real numbers x for which $f(x)$, $g(x)$, or $j(x)$ is a real number.

Reference Information

$$A = \frac{1}{2}bh$$

$$A = lw$$

$$A = \pi r^2$$

$$V = \pi r^2 h$$

$$V = lwh$$

$$c^2 = a^2 + b^2$$

$$V = \frac{1}{3}\pi r^2 h$$

$$V = \frac{4}{3}\pi r^3$$

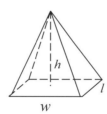
$$V = \frac{1}{3}lwh$$

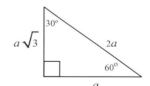

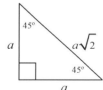

1. If $f(-x) = -f(x)$ for all real numbersE x and if $(5, 7)$ is a point on the graph of function f, which of the following points must also be on the graph of the function ?

(A) (-7, 5)

(B) (-5, -7)

(C) (7, -5)

(D) (7, 5)

2. A function is defined by $f(t) = 3^t + 2$. Which of the following is the sketch of $g(t) = f(-t)$?

(A)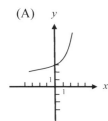

(B)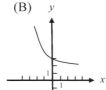

(C)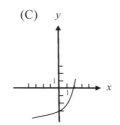

(D)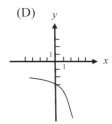

3. What is $f(3)$ equal to if $f(x) = |6 - 5x|$?

(A) $f(-3)$

(B) $f\left(\dfrac{3}{5}\right)$

(C) $f\left(\dfrac{5}{7}\right)$

(D) $f\left(-\dfrac{3}{5}\right)$

4. A student group at a middle school is planing a trip to a park that has a ticket cost of \$10 each person. The student group members must share the \$260 cost of a bus plus the ticket cost for one administrator who will accompany the group. Which of the following functions expresses the cost, in dollars, for each group member as a function of s, the number of the group members ?

(A) $C(s) = \dfrac{260 + 10s}{s - 1}$

(B) $C(s) = \dfrac{260 + 10s}{s + 1}$

(C) $C(s) = \dfrac{270 + 10s}{s - 1}$

(D) $C(s) = \dfrac{270 + 10s}{s}$

NEXT PAGE

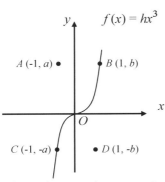

$f(x) = hx^3$

Note: Figure above not drawn to scale

5. In the figure above, A, B, C, and D are the points of the vertices of a rectangle (not shown). Points B and C lie on the curve of $f(x) = hx^3$, where h is a constant. If area of $ABCD$ is 10, what is the value of h?

(A) 2.5

(B) 4.5

(C) 3.5

(D) 5.5

6. In triangle ABC, if $\angle C$ is a right angle and $\tan A = \dfrac{\sqrt{3}}{3}$, what is the value of $\dfrac{\sin B}{\sin A}$?

(A) -0.37

(B) -1.23

(C) 1.37

(D) 1.73

7. Which of the following is $e = 4^{\frac{3}{5}}$ equal to?

(A) $2\sqrt[3]{2}$

(B) $\sqrt[5]{2}$

(C) $3\sqrt[5]{2}$

(D) $2\sqrt[5]{2}$

NEXT PAGE

8. Which of the following could be the equation of the circle with x-intercept $(-2, 0)$ and y-intercept $(0, 2)$, which center is in the second quadrant?

(A) $(x-2)^2 + (y+2)^2 = 4$

(B) $(x+2)^2 + (y-2)^2 = 4$

(C) $(x+2)^2 + (y+2)^2 = 2$

(D) $(x-2)^2 + (y-2)^2 = 4$

\

9. If the height, length, and width of a rectangular solid are 9, 5, and 8, respectively, what is the length of the longest line segment whose two end points are vertices of the rectangular solid?

(A) $\sqrt{170}$

(B) $\sqrt{145}$

(C) $\sqrt{89}$

(D) $\sqrt{106}$

10. What is the number that satisfies the following 3 conditions?

1. It is an integer greater than 2000 and less than 3,200.
2. The sum of its digits is 29.
3. It tens and units digits are the same.

(A) 2099

(B) 3019

(C) 2999

(D) 2019

11. Burger Queen sold 15 percent in 2011 more hamburger sandwiches than in 2010, and the price of each hamburger sandwich they sold in 2011 was 10 percent less than in 2010. The total earnings from the sale of hamburger sandwiches were what percent change in 2011 than in 2010?

(A) 0.0035

(B) 0.35

(C) 35%

(D) 3.5%

NEXT PAGE

12. If the roots of the equation $x^2 + bx + c = 0$ are p and q,

the value of $\dfrac{pq}{(p+q)^2}$ in terms of b and c is

(A) $\dfrac{c}{b^2}$

(B) $\dfrac{c^2}{b}$

(C) $-\dfrac{b}{c^2}$

(D) $\dfrac{b^2}{c}$

13. Mike cuts a cake into m equal pieces, where $m>4$, and eats four pieces. In terms of m, what percentage of the cake is left?

(A) $\dfrac{m-4}{100m}\%$

(B) $100(m-4)\%$

(C) $\dfrac{100(m-4)}{m}\%$

(D) $\dfrac{m-4}{m}\%$

NEXT PAGE

14.   In the *xy*-plane, the distance between points R (1, 12) and point Q (4, *h*) is $\sqrt{178}$. What is one possible value of *h*?

(A) 1
(B) -20
(C) 2
(D) 25

16. In a department store, Maria bought 8 items from aisles 1 through 6 and 10 items from aisles 4 through 11. Which of the following could be the total number of items that Maria bought?

(A) 8
(B) 20
(C) 9
(D) 17

15.   In triangle ABC, $m\angle C$ is $90°$. Which of the following must be true?

I. $\sin A < \sin B$

II. $\cos A = \sin B$

III. $\cos^2 A + \sin^2 B = 1$

IV. $\dfrac{\cos A}{\sin A} = \dfrac{\sin B}{\cos B}$

(A) I only   (B) II only   (C) III only   (D) II and IV only

NEXT PAGE

Questions 17 and 19 refer to the information below.

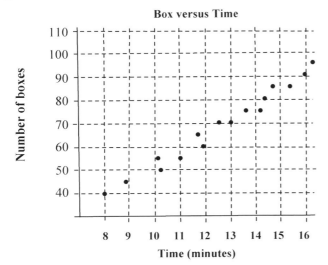

Box versus Time

Group	Rate of Packing (boxes per minute)
group 1	3.50
group 2	2.50
group 3	4.25
group 4	6.00
group 5	5.00
group 6	7.00
group 7	4.00

Calculating the approximate number, N, of the boxes packed by people is easy: N = Time × Rate of packing. The scatterlpot and table above provide the relationship of time and box, and the names of seven packing groups and their rates of packing.

17.   According to the information of the scatterplot and table, if group 2 and group 7 both have finished 1/6 hour for packing boxes, then each of them now has 10 boxes to pack, which of the following will be closest to the absolute difference, in minutes, of their time?

(A) 2.5   (B) 3.0   (C) 1.5   (D) 2.5

18.   The scatterplot provides the time ploted against box for 16 people of a single group. The packing rate of this group is closest to that of which the following groups?

(A) group 2

(B) group 5

(C) group 4

(D) group 3

19.   By the information in the table, which of the following is the approximate number of boxes of group 3 with time of 11 minutes?

(A) 47

(B) 45

(C) 48

(D) 46

NEXT PAGE ⟹

20.   Fastest Bikes sold 15 percent in 2011 less bikes than in 2010, and the price of each bike they sold in 2011 was 15 percent less than in 2010. The total profit from the sale of bikes was what percent decrease in 2011 than in 2010 ?

(A) $\left(\dfrac{85}{100}\right)^2 - 1$

(B) $\dfrac{70}{100}$

(C) $1 - \left(\dfrac{85}{100}\right)^2$

(D) $100\left(1 - \left(\dfrac{85}{100}\right)^2\right)$

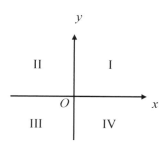

Figure 4

21. In Figure 4, if $\cos\theta < 0$ and $\sin\theta\,\cos\theta < 0$, then θ must be in which quadrant(s) ?

(A) I only

(B) III only

(C) IV only

(D) II only

NEXT PAGE

22. If segment PQ in the coordinate plane has endpoint P (-8, 6) and midpoint (8, 10), then endpoint Q of $\overline{PQ}$ has coordinates

(A) (0, 26)
(B) (0, 14)
(C) (12, 8)
(D) (24, 14)

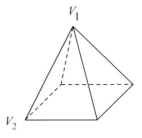

24. In the figure above, the pyramid has a square base and four congruent triangular surfaces. If the height of the pyramid is $\sqrt{5.5}$ feet and each side of the base is 5 feet, what is the length of segment $\overline{V_1 V_2}$?

(A) $3\sqrt{2}$

(B) $2\sqrt{3}$

(C) $2\sqrt{2}$

(D) $5.5\sqrt{3}$

23. If the total surface area of a cube is 24 square inches, what is the volume, in cubic inches, of the cube?

(A) 16
(B) 8
(C) 56
(D) 32

NEXT PAGE

25. A ship travels 34 miles, and then travels back in 4 hours 48 minutes. If the speed of this ship in still water is 15 miles per hour, which of the following is the speed of the current?

(A) $\pm 5\dfrac{\sqrt{2}}{2}$

(B) $\dfrac{5\sqrt{2}}{2}$

(C) $\dfrac{5}{2\sqrt{2}}$

(D) $5\sqrt{2}$

$g(x)$	x
0	-1
1	0
0	3

26. Three of whose values are shown in the chart above. If g is a polynomial of degree 3, what could $g(x)$ be equal to ?

(A) $(x-3)\left(x-\dfrac{3}{2}\right)(x+3)$

(B) $(x+1)(x-3)(x+3)$

(C) $(x-1)\left(x-\dfrac{3}{2}\right)(x+3)$

(D) $(x+1)(x-3)\left(x-\dfrac{1}{3}\right)$

NEXT PAGE

27. A car rental company offers their customers two rental schemes. Scheme-1 costs $30 as the basic charge and then $3 per hour to use the car. Scheme-2 costs $12 as the basic charge and then $6 per hour to use the car. After how many hours of use would the cost Scheme-1 be the same as the cost of Scheme-2?

(A) 2

(B) 4

(C) 6

(D) 8

28. The cost of some computer of a computer retail store is $900. After discount 10%, the retail store still wants to make a profit of 10% from the computer. What is the selling price in dollars?

(A) 1,090
(B) 990
(C) 1,100
(D) 1,200

29. If $x^2 + y^2 = (x + y)^2$, then x must be equal to

(A) It cannot be determined from the information given.
(B) -1
(C) $-y$
(D) y

30. If $(\pi, -2)$ is a point on the graph of function f and if $f(x) = 2 \cos x$ for all real numbers x, which of the following must also be a point of the graph of f ?

(A) $(-\pi, -2)$

(B) $(\pi, \pm 2)$

(C) $(\pm \pi, 2)$

(D) $(\pi, 2)$

NEXT PAGE

31. What number should be added to any one of the three numbers 2, 6, and 15 so that the resulting three numbers form a geometric sequence ?

32. If 21st term of an arithmetic sequence is 160 and the 61st term of the sequence is 200, what is the second term of this sequence?

Note: Figure above not drawn to scale.

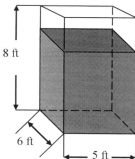

8 ft

6 ft

5 ft

33. The figure above shows the dimensions of a rectangular container closed. There is 96 cubic feet of non-sand in the container. The container will be repositioned on level ground so that the container rests on one, which has the greatest area, of the six surfaces. If it has been repositioned, what will be the entire surface area of the sand?

34. John wants to buy a mixture of two kinds of teas, red tea and green tea. Its price is $20/lb. He has 3 pounds of red tea at $18 per pound. How many pounds of green tea at $26 per pound does John have to purchase?

35. The number 202 is separated into two parts. The larger part exceeds five times the smaller by 22. The smaller part is

36. The average (arithmetic mean) of the exam scores of a class of r students is 75, and the average of the exam score of the class of s students is 91. When the scores of both classes are combined, the average score is 89. What is the value of $\dfrac{r}{s}$?

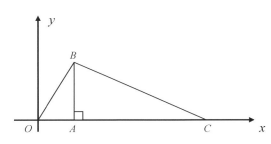

Note: Figure above not drawn to scale.

37. In the coordinate plane, the area of triangle OBC is 30, the length of segment $\overline{AO}$ is 5, and the coordinates of C are $(20, 0)$, what is the slope of segment $\overline{BO}$?

38. What is the least positive integer x for which $13x$ is the cube of an integer?

STOP

Answer Key
For
SAT Math Practice Test 04

Section 3

1	A
2	C
3	C
4	C
5	D
6	C
7	C
8	A
9	A
10	B
11	A
12	D
13	B
14	D
15	C

16	8
17	5
18	29
19	1
20	8

Section 4

1	B	16	D
2	B	17	C
3	D	18	C
4	D	19	D
5	A	20	D
6	D	21	D
7	D	22	D
8	B	23	B
9	A	24	A
10	C	25	B
11	D	26	D
12	A	27	C
13	C	28	C
14	D	29	A
15	D	30	A

31	6/5 or 1.2
32	141
33	180
34	1
35	30
36	1/7 or .142 or .143
37	3/5 or .6
38	169

SAT Math

Practice

Test 04

Explanations

Redesigned for Tests in March 2016 and Beyond

Mad Math

Math Test – No Calculator

Time: 25 Minutes
20 Questions

Notes:
- The use of a calculator is not allowed.
- All numbers used in this section are the real number.
- Figures are provided for some problems in this test. Unless otherwise indicated under the figure "Note: Figure above not drawn to scale", all figures are drawn as accurately as possible.
- All figures lie in a plane EXCEPT otherwise specified.
- Unless otherwise indicated, the domain of any function f, g or j is assumed to be the set of all real numbers x for which $f(x)$, $g(x)$, or $j(x)$ is a real number.

Reference Information

$A = \dfrac{1}{2}bh$

$A = lw$

$A = \pi r^2$

$V = \pi r^2 h$

$V = lwh$

$c^2 = a^2 + b^2$

$V = \dfrac{1}{3}\pi r^2 h$

$V = \dfrac{4}{3}\pi r^3$

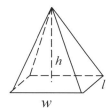
$V = \dfrac{1}{3}lwh$

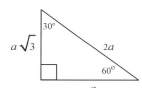

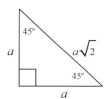

1. Which of the following is NOT equal to the others?

(A) $(0.2)(0.008)$

(B) 0.016

(C) 1.6×10^{-2}

(D) $(0.2)(0.08)$

> **Solution:**　　　　　　　　　Answer: (A)
>
> Each choice = 0.016 except (A).
>
> ⇓
>
> Answer is (A).

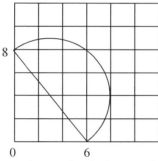

0　　　　　6

2. In the figure above, what is the arc of the semicircle?

(A) $\dfrac{25\pi}{4}$

(B) $\dfrac{25\pi}{2}$

(C) 5π

(D) $\dfrac{5\pi}{2}$

> **Solution:**　　　　　　　　　Answer: (C)
>
> There is a 6-8-10 right triangle.
> Diameter = 10
> ↓
>
> $C_{\text{semicircle}} = \dfrac{C_{\text{circle}}}{2} = \dfrac{D_{\text{circle}}\pi}{2} = \dfrac{10\pi}{2}$
>
> ⇓
>
> $C_{\text{semicircle}} = 5\pi$

3. In a right triangle ABC, if angle C is $90°$ and $\cos A = 0.3$, which of the following is $\sin(90° - A)$ equal to?

(A) 0.7

(B) 0.5

(C) 0.3

(D) 0.4

> **Solution:**　　　　　　　　　Answer: (C)
>
> $\cos A = \sin(90° - A)$
>
> ⇓
>
> $\sin(90° - A) = 0.3$

4. 2 sides of a triangle have lengths 8.1 and 12, respectively. If the remaining side of the triangle has a value that is an integer, what is the smallest possible perimeter of this triangle?

(A) 41.1

(B) 25.1

(C) 24.1

(D) 40.1

> **Solution:**　　　　　　　　　Answer: (C)
>
> 8.1　　　$x = 4$ ←
>
> 12
>
> $s_2 - s_1 < s_3 < s_2 + s_1$
>
> where $s_2 > s_1$.
>
> ↓
>
> $12 - 8.1 < x = s_3$
>
> ↓
>
> $3.9 < x$
>
> ↓
>
> x is an integer. $x = 4$ ——
>
> ⇓
>
> Perimeter = $12 + 8.1 + 4 = 24.1$

NEXT PAGE ⇨

5. $g(f(x)) = \dfrac{\sqrt{e^x - 1} + 3}{4\sqrt{e^x - 1} - 3}$ and $g(x) = \dfrac{x + 3}{4x - 3}$, $f(x) =$

(A) $\sqrt{e^x}$

(B) $\sqrt{x}$

(C) $e^x - 1$

(D) $\sqrt{e^x - 1}$

Solution: Answer: (D)

$$g(x) = \frac{x + 3}{4x - 3}$$

$$\downarrow$$

$$g\left(\sqrt{e^x - 1}\right) = \frac{\sqrt{e^x - 1} + 3}{4\sqrt{e^x - 1} - 3}$$

$$\Downarrow$$

$$f(x) = \sqrt{e^x - 1}$$

6. If $f(x) = ax^2 + bx + c$ for all real numbers x and if $f(1) = -1$ and $f(0) = 2$, what is the sum of a and b?

(A) -1

(B) 2

(C) -3

(D) 0

Solution: Answer: (C)

$$f(x) = ax^2 + bx + c$$

$$f(1) = -1 \text{ and } f(0) = 2$$

$$\downarrow$$

$$f(0) = a \cdot 0^2 + b \cdot 0 + c = 2$$

$$f(1) = a \cdot 1^2 + b \cdot 1 + 2 = -1$$

$$\Downarrow$$

$$a + b = -3$$

7. If the average (arithmetic mean) of 21 consecutive even integers is $n - 7$, what is the median of the twenty-one integers?

(A) 21

(B) $n - 3$

(C) $n - 7$

(D) $n - 2$

Solution: Answer: (C)

Directly use the conclusion:

If the number of terms of consecutive integers, consecutive odd integers, or consecutive even integers is odd, then median = mean.

$$\Downarrow$$

Mean = average = median = $n - 7$

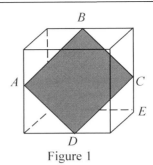

Figure 1

8. Figure 1 shows a cube with edge of length 2 units. If points A, B, C and D are midpoints of the edges of the cube, what is the sum of DC and BC?

(A) $\sqrt{2} + \sqrt{6}$

(B) $\sqrt{5} + \sqrt{3}$

(C) $\sqrt{13}$

(D) $\sqrt{2} + \sqrt{5}$

Solution: Answer: (A)

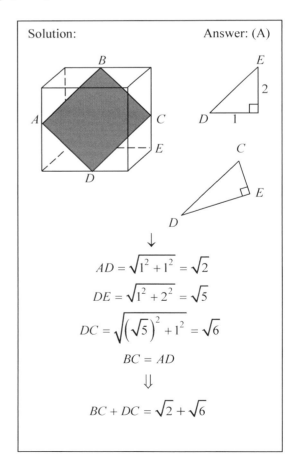

$$AD = \sqrt{1^2 + 1^2} = \sqrt{2}$$

$$DE = \sqrt{1^2 + 2^2} = \sqrt{5}$$

$$DC = \sqrt{\left(\sqrt{5}\right)^2 + 1^2} = \sqrt{6}$$

$$BC = AD$$

$$\Downarrow$$

$$BC + DC = \sqrt{2} + \sqrt{6}$$

NEXT PAGE

9. The menu of a certain restaurant lists 8 items in the first page and 7 items in the second page. A family plans to share 4 items from the first page and 4 items from the second page. If none of the items is found in both pages, how many distinct possibilities of items could the family choose?

(A) 2,450

(B) 1,178

(C) 4,116

(D) 6,820

---

10. If $\dfrac{-4x + 20y}{125p} = \dfrac{-16c - 48d}{625p}$, then $c + 3d =$

(A) $\dfrac{4(x - 5y)}{5}$

(B) $\dfrac{5(x - 5y)}{4}$

(C) $\dfrac{5(x + 5y)}{4}$

(D) $\dfrac{4(x + 5y)}{5}$

Solution: Answer: (A)

(1).

$\begin{cases} \text{1 element set} \\ \text{4 positions, 8 elements} \\ \text{Order does not matter.} \end{cases}$

↓

Use the counting method of Combinations.

↓

$\dfrac{\cancel{8}^{2} \cdot \boxed{7} \cdot \cancel{6} \cdot \boxed{5}}{\cancel{4} \cdot \cancel{3} \cancel{2} \cdot 1} = 70 \text{ elements}$

$\begin{cases} \text{1 element set} \\ \text{4 positions, 7 elements} \\ \text{Order does not matter.} \end{cases}$

↓

Use the counting method of Combinations.

↓

$\dfrac{\boxed{7} \cdot \cancel{6} \cdot \boxed{5} \cdot \cancel{4}}{\cancel{4} \cdot \cancel{3} \cancel{2} \cdot 1} = 35 \text{ elements}$

(2).   2 element sets

The elements can be combined in this case.

Use Fundamental Counting Principle.

⇓

$n \times m = 70 \times 35 = 2450$

Solution: Answer: (B)

$\dfrac{\cancel{4}\,(x - 5y)}{\cancel{5}\,\cancel{p}} = \dfrac{\cancel{16}^{4}\,(c + 3d)}{\cancel{5} \cdot 5\,\cancel{p}}$

⇓

$\dfrac{5(x - 5y)}{4} = c + 3d$

NEXT PAGE ▷

11. The relationship between A and B is $A = \dfrac{2}{3}(B-23)$, and the relationship between A and C is $C = A - 32$. Which of the following is the relationship between B and C ?

(A) $C = \dfrac{2}{3}(B-23)-32$

(B) $C = \dfrac{2}{3}(B+23)-32$

(C) $C = \dfrac{2}{3}(B-23)+32$

(D) $C = \dfrac{3}{2}(B+23)-32$

Solution: Answer: (A)

Target: Let A be cancelled.

$$\begin{cases} A = \dfrac{2}{3}(B-23) \\ C = A - 32 \end{cases} \rightarrow \begin{cases} A = \dfrac{2}{3}(B-23) \\ A = C + 32 \end{cases}$$

$$A = A$$

$$\downarrow$$

$$C + 32 = \dfrac{2}{3}(B-23)$$

$$\Downarrow$$

$$C = \dfrac{2}{3}(B-23)-32$$

12. If a sequence $p-2$, $p+2$, $2p-3$ forms an arithmetic sequence, what is the value of p?

(A) 6
(B) -3
(C) 8
(D) 9

Solution: Answer: (D)

Let a, b, and c is an arithmetic sequence.

$$\downarrow$$

$$b - a = c - b.$$

$$\downarrow$$

$$(p+2)-(p-2)=(2p-3)-(p+2)$$

$$\Downarrow$$

$$4 = p-5, \ p = 9$$

Note: Figure bellow not drawn to scale.

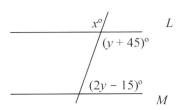

13. In the figure above, lines L and M are parallel. What is the value of x?

(A) 45
(B) 95
(C) 65
(D) 80

Solution: Answer: (B)

$$(2y-15)+(y+45)=180$$

$$3y = 180 - 30$$

$$y = 50$$

$$\Downarrow$$

$$x = y + 45 = 50 + 45 = 95$$

14. If $x^2 - 31 = 3^2 \times 10$, then x could be equal to

(A) -15
(B) 16
(C) 14
(D) 11

Solution: Answer: (D)

$$x^2 - 31 = 3^2 \times 10$$

$$\downarrow$$

$$x^2 = 90 + 31 = 121$$

$$\Downarrow$$

$$x = \pm\sqrt{121} = \pm 11$$

15. Which of the following is the complete solution set for the inequality $|x-5| \geq 3$?

(A) $2 \leq x \leq 8$
(B) $x \geq 8$, $x \leq 3$
(C) $x \geq 8$, $x \leq 2$
(D) $x \leq 1$

Solution: Answer: (C)

Type : $|x - a| \geq b$

$$\downarrow$$

$$\begin{cases} x - a \geq b \\ x - a \leq -b \end{cases}$$

$$(a > 0, \ b > 0)$$

$$\Downarrow$$

(1) $x - 5 \geq 3$, $x \geq 8$
(2) $x - 5 \leq -3$, $x \leq 2$

NEXT PAGE

16. Eight cards in a pot are numbered 1 through 8. One card is drawn at random. The ones digit of the sum of the numbers on the remaining cards is 8. What is the number on the drawn card?

> Solution: Answer: 8
>
> Note: "through" = "from… to…".
> (Including two ends)
>
> (1). Sum $= 1 + 2 + 3 + 4 + 5 + 67 + 7 + 8 = 36$
>
> (2). $\text{Sum}_{\text{Remaining}} = 36 - x = \begin{cases} 28 \\ 18 \\ 8 \end{cases}$
>
> $\Downarrow$
>
> $x = 8$
>
> (Only 8 is one of the numbers 1 through 8.)

17. Stephanie is now five times as old as her brother Steve. After 2 years, Stephanie will be 3 times as old as Steve will be. How old was Stephanie five year ago?

> Solution: Answer: 5
>
> $x + 2 = 3\left(\dfrac{1}{5}x + 2\right) \rightarrow 5x + 10 = 3(x + 10)$
>
> $\Downarrow$
>
> $5x + 10 = 3x + 30,\ 2x = 20,\ x = 10,\ x - 5 = 5$

18. In class A, each of the 35 students contributed either a nickel or dime to the Child Foundation. If the total amount collected was $2.05, how many students contributed a nickel?

> Solution: Answer: 29
>
> Let x = number of nickel-students;
> $35 - x$ = number of dime-students.
> $5x + 10(35 - x) = 205$
> $\Downarrow$
> $x = 29$

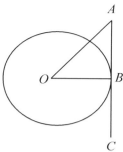

Note: Figure above not drawn to scale.

19. In the figure above, $\overline{AC}$ is tangent to circle O at point B. $\overline{BO}$ is radius of the circle. If $BO = AB = \sqrt{2}$, what is the area of the triangle AOB?

> Solution: Answer: 1
>
> $\triangle AOB$ is a right triangle with $45°$.
>
>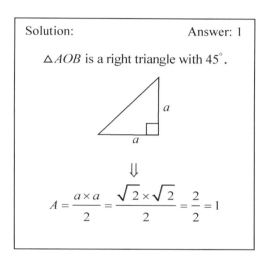
>
> $\Downarrow$
>
> $A = \dfrac{a \times a}{2} = \dfrac{\sqrt{2} \times \sqrt{2}}{2} = \dfrac{2}{2} = 1$

20. If x and y are different nonnegative integers and $3x + y = 22$, what is the number of all possible values of x?

> Solution: Answer: 8
>
> $3x + y = 22$
>
> $3 \cdot 7 + 1 = 22$
>
> $3 \cdot 6 + 4 = 22$
>
> $\vdots$
>
> $3 \cdot 1 + 19 = 22$
>
> $3 \cdot 0 + 22 = 22$
>
> $\Downarrow$
>
> $N = 8$

STOP

Math Test – Calculator

Time: 55 Minutes
38 Questions

Notes:
- The use of a calculator is not allowed.
- All numbers used in this section are the real number.
- Figures are provided for some problems in this test. Unless otherwise indicated under the figure "Note: Figure above not drawn to scale", all figures are drawn as accurately as possible.
- All figures lie in a plane EXCEPT otherwise specified.
- Unless otherwise indicated, the domain of any function f, g or j is assumed to be the set of all real numbers x for which $f(x)$, $g(x)$, or $j(x)$ is a real number.

Reference Information

$$A = \frac{1}{2}bh$$

$$A = lw$$

$$A = \pi r^2$$

$$V = \pi r^2 h$$

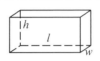

$$V = lwh$$

$$c^2 = a^2 + b^2$$

$$V = \frac{1}{3}\pi r^2 h$$

$$V = \frac{4}{3}\pi r^3$$

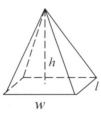

$$V = \frac{1}{3}lwh$$

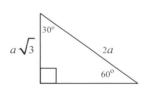

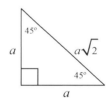

1. If $f(-x) = -f(x)$ for all real numbersE x and if $(5, 7)$ is a point on the graph of function f, which of the following points must also be on the graph of the function ?

(A) (-7, 5)

(B) (-5, -7)

(C) (7, -5)

(D) (7, 5)

Solution: Answer: (B)
$$f(-x) = -f(x)$$
↓

$f(x)$ is an odd function.

The set of points is $(x, f(x))$.

↓

$$(-x, -f(x))$$
⇓

$$(5, 7) \rightarrow (-5, -7)$$

2. A function is defined by $f(t) = 3^t + 2$. Which of the following is the sketch of $g(t) = f(-t)$?

(A) y

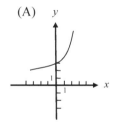

(B) y

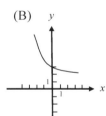

(C) y

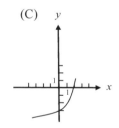

(D) y

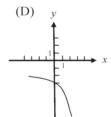

Solution: Answer: (B)

The sketch of f is (A).

$$g(x) = f(-x)$$
↓

The sketch of f flips about y-axis

⇓

The sketch of g is (B).

3.   What is $f(3)$ equal to if $f(x) = |6 - 5x|$?

(A) $f(-3)$

(B) $f\left(\dfrac{3}{5}\right)$

(C) $f\left(\dfrac{5}{7}\right)$

(D) $f\left(-\dfrac{3}{5}\right)$

Solution: Answer: (D)
$$f(x) = |6 - 5x|$$
↓

$$f(3) = |6 - 5 \cdot 3| = |6 - 15| = |-9| = 9$$

Use plug-in method.

↓

$$f\left(-\frac{3}{5}\right) = \left|6 - \cancel{5} \cdot \left(-\frac{3}{\cancel{5}}\right)\right| = |6 + 3| = 9$$

⇓

$$(D) f\left(-\frac{3}{5}\right) = f(3)$$

4.   A student group at a middle school is planing a trip to a park that has a ticket cost of \$10 each person. The student group members must share the \$260 cost of a bus plus the ticket cost for one administrator who will accompany the group. Which of the following functions expresses the cost, in dollars, for each group member as a function of s, the number of the group members ?

(A) $C(s) = \dfrac{260 + 10s}{s - 1}$

(B) $C(s) = \dfrac{260 + 10s}{s + 1}$

(C) $C(s) = \dfrac{270 + 10s}{s - 1}$

(D) $C(s) = \dfrac{270 + 10s}{s}$

Solution: Answer: (D)
$$\frac{260 + 10s + 10}{s}$$
⇓
$$\frac{270 + 10x}{s}$$

NEXT PAGE

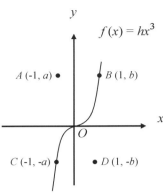

Note: Figure above not drawn to scale

5. In the figure above, *A, B, C,* and *D* are the points of the vertices of a rectangle (not shown). Points *B* and *C* lie on the curve of $f(x) = hx^3$, where *h* is a constant. If area of *ABCD* is 10, what is the value of *h*?

(A) 2.5

(B) 4.5

(C) 3.5

(D) 5.5

Solution: Answer: (A)

$$Area = 10 = L \cdot W = (1+1) \cdot 2b$$

$$\downarrow$$

$$10 = 2 \cdot 2b, \ b = 2.5$$

$$\downarrow$$

$$point \ B = (1, \ 2.5)$$

Point *B* is on the graph of $y = hx^3$

$$\downarrow$$

$$y = 2.5, \ x = 1$$

$$\Downarrow$$

$$2.5 = h(1)^3, \ h = 2.5$$

6. In triangle *ABC*, if $\angle C$ is a right angle and $\tan A = \dfrac{\sqrt{3}}{3}$, what is the value of $\dfrac{\sin B}{\sin A}$?

(A) -0.37

(B) -1.23

(C) 1.37

(D) 1.73

Solution: Answer: (D)

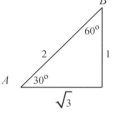

$$\Downarrow$$

$$\frac{\sin B}{\sin A} = \frac{\dfrac{\sqrt{3}}{2}}{\dfrac{1}{2}} = \sqrt{3} \approx 1.73$$

7. Which of the following is $e = 4^{\frac{3}{5}}$ equal to?

(A) $2\sqrt[3]{2}$

(B) $\sqrt[5]{2}$

(C) $3\sqrt[5]{2}$

(D) $2\sqrt[5]{2}$

Solution: Answer: (D)

Refer to the choices, a target

is $\sqrt[3]{2}$ or $\sqrt[5]{2}$ something.

$$4^{\frac{3}{5}} = \sqrt[5]{4^3} = \sqrt[5]{\left((2)^2 \right)^3}$$

$$\downarrow$$

$$\sqrt[5]{2^6} = \sqrt[5]{2^5 2^1} = \sqrt[5]{2^5} \cdot \sqrt[5]{2}$$

$$\Downarrow$$

$$e = 2 \cdot \sqrt[5]{2}$$

NEXT PAGE

8. Which of the following could be the equation of the circle with x-intercept $(-2, 0)$ and y-intercept $(0, 2)$, which center is in the second quadrant?

(A) $(x-2)^2 + (y+2)^2 = 4$

(B) $(x+2)^2 + (y-2)^2 = 4$

(C) $(x+2)^2 + (y+2)^2 = 2$

(D) $(x-2)^2 + (y-2)^2 = 4$

Solution: Answer: (B)

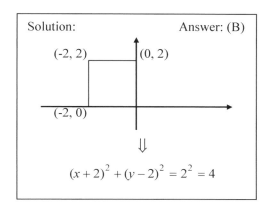

$$(x+2)^2 + (y-2)^2 = 2^2 = 4$$

9. If the height, length, and width of a rectangular solid are 9, 5, and 8, respectively, what is the length of the longest line segment whose two end points are vertices of the rectangular solid?

(A) $\sqrt{170}$

(B) $\sqrt{145}$

(C) $\sqrt{89}$

(D) $\sqrt{106}$

Solution: Answer: (A)

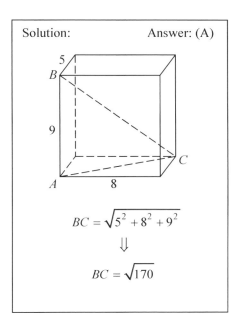

$$BC = \sqrt{5^2 + 8^2 + 9^2}$$

$$\Downarrow$$

$$BC = \sqrt{170}$$

10. What is the number that satisfies the following 3 conditions?

1. It is an integer greater than 2000 and less than 3,200.
2. The sum of its digits is 29.
3. It tens and units digits are the same.

(A) 2099

(B) 3019

(C) 2999

(D) 2019

Solution: Answer: (C)

$$\begin{cases} 2 + \underbrace{9+9+9}_{3 \times 9 = 27} = 29 \\ 2000 < 2999 < 3200 \end{cases}$$

$$\Downarrow$$

$$x = 2999$$

11. Burger Queen sold 15 percent in 2011 more hamburger sandwiches than in 2010, and the price of each hamburger sandwich they sold in 2011 was 10 percent less than in 2010. The total earnings from the sale of hamburger sandwiches were what percent change in 2011 than in 2010?

(A) 0.0035

(B) 0.35

(C) 35%

(D) 3.5%

Solution: Answer: (D)

$$\frac{\left| xy - (1.15x) \cdot (0.9y) \right|}{xy}$$

$$\downarrow$$

$$\frac{\left| xy - 1.035xy \right|}{xy} = \frac{\cancel{xy}\, 0.035}{\cancel{xy}}$$

$$\downarrow$$

$$0.035 \times 100\% = (0.035 \times 100)\%$$

$$\Downarrow$$

$$x = 3.5\%$$

NEXT PAGE ⇨

12. If the roots of the equation $x^2 + bx + c = 0$ are p and q, the value of $\dfrac{pq}{(p+q)^2}$ in terms of b and c is

(A) $\dfrac{c}{b^2}$

(B) $\dfrac{c^2}{b}$

(C) $-\dfrac{b}{c^2}$

(D) $\dfrac{b^2}{c}$

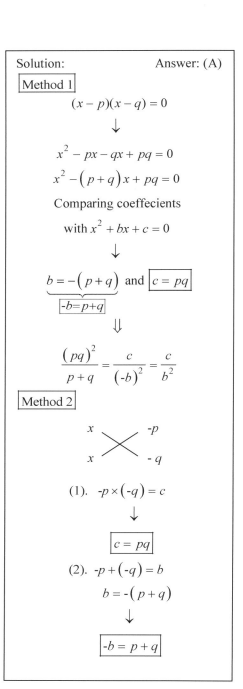

Solution: Answer: (A)

Method 1

$$(x - p)(x - q) = 0$$
$$\downarrow$$
$$x^2 - px - qx + pq = 0$$
$$x^2 - (p + q)x + pq = 0$$

Comparing coeffecients

with $x^2 + bx + c = 0$
$$\downarrow$$

$\underbrace{b = -(p + q)}_{-b = p+q}$ and $\boxed{c = pq}$

$$\Downarrow$$

$$\frac{(pq)^2}{p + q} = \frac{c}{(-b)^2} = \frac{c}{b^2}$$

Method 2

$$\begin{array}{c} x \quad\quad -p \\ \times \\ x \quad\quad -q \end{array}$$

(1). $-p \times (-q) = c$
$$\downarrow$$
$$\boxed{c = pq}$$

(2). $-p + (-q) = b$
$$b = -(p + q)$$
$$\downarrow$$
$$\boxed{-b = p + q}$$

13. Mike cuts a cake into m equal pieces, where $m > 3$, and eats four pieces. In terms of m, what percentage of the cake is left?

(A) $\dfrac{m - 4}{100m}\%$

(B) $100(m - 4)\%$

(C) $\dfrac{100(m - 4)}{m}\%$

(D) $\dfrac{m - 4}{m}\%$

Solution: Answer: (C)

$$\frac{m - 4}{m} = \frac{m - 4}{m} \times 100\%$$
$$\Downarrow$$
$$\frac{100 \times (m - 4)}{m}\%$$

NEXT PAGE ⇨

---

14. In the xy-plane, the distance between points $R\,(1,\,12)$ and point $Q\,(4,\,h)$ is $\sqrt{178}$. What is one possible value of h?

(A) 1
(B) -20
(C) 2
(D) 25

Solution: Answer: (D)

$$d^2 = (x_2 - x_1)^2 + (y_2 - y_1)^2$$

$$\downarrow$$

$$178 = 3^2 + h^2 - 2 \cdot 12 \cdot h + 12^2$$

$$\downarrow$$

$$178 = h^2 - 24h + 153$$

$$\downarrow$$

$$h^2 - 24h - 25 = 0$$

$$\begin{matrix} k & & -25 \\ & \times & \\ k & & 1 \end{matrix}$$

$$(h - 25)(k + 1) = 0$$

$$\Downarrow$$

$$h = -1, \quad h = 25$$

15. In triangle ABC, $m\angle C$ is $90°$. Which of the following must be true?

  I. $\sin A < \sin B$

  II. $\cos A = \sin B$

  III. $\cos^2 A + \sin^2 B = 1$

  IV. $\dfrac{\cos A}{\sin A} = \dfrac{\sin B}{\cos B}$

(A) I only   (B) II only   (C) III only   (D) II and IV only

Solution: Answer: (D)

$$m\angle C = 90°$$

$$\downarrow$$

$\angle A$ and $\angle B$ are complementary angles

$$\downarrow$$

$$\begin{cases} \cos A = \sin B \\ \cot A = \tan B \end{cases}$$

$$\Downarrow$$

II and IV must be true only.

16. In a department store, Maria bought 8 items from aisles 1 through 6 and 10 items from aisles 4 through 11. Which of the following could be the total number of items that Maria bought?

(A) 8
(B) 20
(C) 9
(D) 17

Solution: Answer: (D)

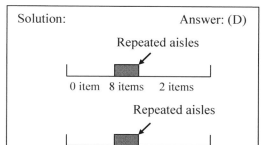

Consider 2 situations (1) and (2) below.
(1). The 8 items of 10 items came from repeated aisles.

$$\downarrow$$

The least number of items $= 10$
(2). All the 10 items from aisles 4 through 13 were bought from not repeated aisles.

$$\downarrow$$

The greatest number of items $= 8 + 10 = 18$.

$$\downarrow$$

$$10 \le x \le 18$$

$$\Downarrow$$

Answer is (D).

NEXT PAGE ⇨

Questions 17 and 19 refer to the information below.

Box versus Time

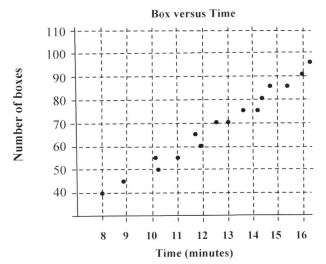

Group	Rate of Packing (boxes per minute)
group 1	3.50
group 2	2.50
group 3	4.25
group 4	6.00
group 5	5.00
group 6	7.00
group 7	4.00

Calculating the approximate number, N, of the boxes packed by people is easy: N = Time × Rate of packing. The scatterlpot and table above provide the relationship of time and box, and the names of seven packing groups and their rates of packing.

17. According to the information of the scatterplot and table, if group 2 and group 7 both have finished 1/6 hour for packing boxes, then each of them now has 10 boxes to pack, which of the following will be closest to the absolute difference, in minutes, of their time?

(A) 2.5   (B) 3.0   (C) 1.5   (D) 2.5

Solution: Answer: (C)

$$(1/6) \text{ hour} = 10 \text{ minutes}$$

$$\begin{cases} \text{Rate of group 2 is } \dfrac{5}{2}. \text{ That means } \dfrac{2}{5} \text{ minute per box.} \\ \text{Rate of group 7 is 4. That means } \dfrac{1}{4} \text{ minute per box.} \end{cases}$$

$$\Downarrow$$

$$\left(10 + \frac{2}{5} \times 10\right) - \left(10 + \frac{1}{4} \times 10\right) = 4 - 2.5 = 1.5$$

18. The scatterplot provides the time ploted against box for 16 people of a single group. The packing rate of this group is closest to that of which the following groups?

(A) group 2
(B) group 5
(C) group 4
(D) group 3

Solution: Answer: (C)

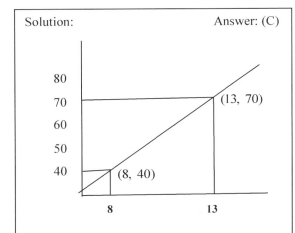

$$\text{Rate of packing } = \text{slope} = \frac{70 - 40}{13 - 8} = \frac{30}{5} = 6$$

$$\Downarrow$$

By the table, it is group 4.

19. By the information in the table, which of the following is the approximate number of boxes of group 3 with time of 11 minutes?

(A) 47
(B) 45
(C) 48
(D) 46

Solution: Answer: (D)

$$N = \text{Time} \times \text{Rate of packing}$$
$$N = 11 \times 4.25 = 46.75$$
A box cannot be 0.75 one.

$$\Downarrow$$

$$N \neq 47, \quad N = 46$$

NEXT PAGE

20. Fastest Bikes sold 15 percent in 2011 less bikes than in 2010, and the price of each bike they sold in 2011 was 15 percent less than in 2010. The total profit from the sale of bikes was what percent decrease in 2011 than in 2010 ?

(A) $\left(\dfrac{85}{100}\right)^2 - 1$

(B) $\dfrac{70}{100}$

(C) $1 - \left(\dfrac{85}{100}\right)^2$

(D) $100\left(1 - \left(\dfrac{85}{100}\right)^2\right)$

Solution: Answer: (D)

$$\dfrac{xy - \left(\dfrac{85}{100}x\right)\cdot\dfrac{85}{100}y}{xy}$$

↓

$$\dfrac{xy - \left(\dfrac{85}{100}\right)^2 xy}{xy}$$

↓

$$\dfrac{\cancel{xy}\left(1 - \left(\dfrac{85}{100}\right)^2\right)}{\cancel{xy}}$$

↓

$$\left(1 - \left(\dfrac{85}{100}\right)^2\right)\times 100\%$$

⇓

$$100\left(1 - \left(\dfrac{85}{100}\right)^2\right)\%$$

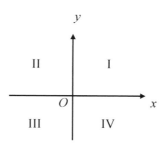

Figure 4

21. In Figure 4, if $\cos\theta < 0$ and $\sin\theta\cos\theta < 0$, then θ must be in which quadrant(s) ?

(A) I only

(B) III only

(C) IV only

(D) II only

Solution: Answer: (D)

Method 1
  Condition 1: $\sin\theta\cos\theta < 0$

  ↓

  Q II and Q IV

  Condition 2: $\cos\theta < 0$

  ⇓

  Q II only

Method 2

	I	II	III	IV
sin	+	+	−	−
cos	+	−	−	+

↑

$\begin{cases} \sin\theta\cos\theta < 0 \\ \cos\theta < 0 \end{cases}$

⇓

Answer is (D).

NEXT PAGE ⟩

22. If segment PQ in the coordinate plane has endpoint P (-8, 6) and midpoint (8, 10), then endpoint Q of $\overline{PQ}$ has coordinates

(A) (0, 26)
(B) (0, 14)
(C) (12, 8)
(D) (24, 14)

Solution: **Answer: (D)**

$$\text{Midpoint} = (\frac{x_1 + x_2}{2} = x_m, \frac{y_1 + y_2}{2} = y_m)$$

$$M = (\frac{-8 + x_2}{2} = 8, \frac{6 + y_2}{2} = 10)$$

$$\downarrow \qquad\qquad \downarrow$$

$$x_2 = 8 + 16 \qquad y_2 = 20 - 6$$

$$\Downarrow$$

$$x_2 = 24, \qquad y_2 = 14$$

---

23. If the total surface area of a cube is 24 square inches, what is the volume, in cubic inches, of the cube?

(A) 16
(B) 8
(C) 56
(D) 32

Solution: **Answer: (B)**

A cube has 6 faces.

$$A_{\frac{1}{6}} = \frac{24}{6} = 4$$

$$\downarrow$$

$$S = \sqrt{A_{\frac{1}{6}}} = \sqrt{4} = 2$$

$$\Downarrow$$

$$V = S^3 = 2^3 = 8$$

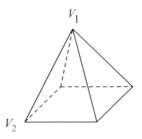

24. In the figure above, the pyramid has a square base and four congruent triangular surfaces. If the height of the pyramid is $\sqrt{5.5}$ feet and each side of the base is 5 feet, what is the length of segment $\overline{V_1V_2}$?

(A) $3\sqrt{2}$

(B) $2\sqrt{3}$

(C) $2\sqrt{2}$

(D) $5.5\sqrt{3}$

Solution: **Answer: (A)**

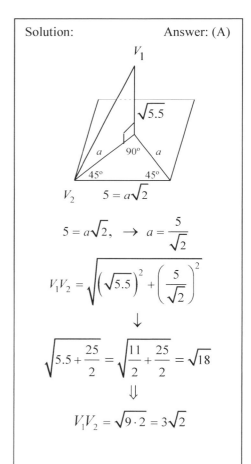

$$5 = a\sqrt{2}, \ \rightarrow \ a = \frac{5}{\sqrt{2}}$$

$$V_1V_2 = \sqrt{\left(\sqrt{5.5}\right)^2 + \left(\frac{5}{\sqrt{2}}\right)^2}$$

$$\downarrow$$

$$\sqrt{5.5 + \frac{25}{2}} = \sqrt{\frac{11}{2} + \frac{25}{2}} = \sqrt{18}$$

$$\Downarrow$$

$$V_1V_2 = \sqrt{9 \cdot 2} = 3\sqrt{2}$$

NEXT PAGE

25. A ship travels 34 miles, and then travels back in 4 hours 48 minutes. If the speed of this ship in still water is 15 miles per hour, which of the following is the speed of the current?

(A) $\pm 5\dfrac{\sqrt{2}}{2}$

(B) $\dfrac{5\sqrt{2}}{2}$

(C) $\dfrac{5}{2\sqrt{2}}$

(D) $5\sqrt{2}$

$g(x)$	x
0	-1
1	0
0	3

26. Three of whose values are shown in the chart above. If g is a polynomial of degree 3, what could $g(x)$ be equal to ?

(A) $(x-3)\left(x-\dfrac{3}{2}\right)(x+3)$

(B) $(x+1)(x-3)(x+3)$

(C) $(x-1)\left(x-\dfrac{3}{2}\right)(x+3)$

(D) $(x+1)(x-3)\left(x-\dfrac{1}{3}\right)$

Solution: Answer: (B)

$$\frac{d}{r}=t, \quad t_1+t_2=t_3$$

$$4\text{ h }48\text{m} = 4+\frac{48}{60}=\frac{24}{5}$$

↓

$$\frac{34}{15-c}+\frac{34}{15+c}=\frac{24}{5}$$

↓

$$34\left(\frac{1}{15-c}+\frac{1}{15+c}\right)=\frac{24}{5}$$

↓

$$34\left(\frac{15+c+15-c}{15^2-c^2}\right)=\frac{24}{5}$$

↓

$$5\times 34\left(15+\cancel{c}+15-\cancel{c}\right)=24\left(15^2-c^2\right)$$

$$\frac{5\times 34\times \cancel{30}^{\,5}}{\cancel{24}_{\,4}}-225=-c^2$$

$$\frac{25\times \cancel{34}^{\,17}}{\cancel{4}_{\,2}}-225=\frac{25\times 17-450}{2}=-c^2$$

$$c^2=\frac{25}{2}\quad c=\pm\sqrt{\frac{25}{2}}=\pm 5\cdot\frac{1}{\sqrt{2}}$$

⇓

$$c=5\frac{\sqrt{2}}{2}$$

Solution: Answer: (D)

$$g(-1)=0 \text{ and } g(3)=0$$

↓

$(x+1)$ and $(x-3)$ are factors of $g(x)$. This means that $g(x)$ can be written as $g(x)=(x+1)(x-3)(x-k)$ for a certain real number k.

↓

(A) and (C) are cancelled.
When $x=0$, $g(0)=1$.

↓

$$(0+1)(0-3)(0-k)=1, \rightarrow k=\frac{1}{3}$$

⇓

$$(x+1)(x-3)\left(x-\frac{1}{3}\right)$$

NEXT PAGE ⟶

27. A car rental company offers their customers two rental schemes. Scheme-1 costs $30 as the basic charge and then $3 per hour to use the car. Scheme-2 costs $12 as the basic charge and then $6 per hour to use the car. After how many hours of use would the cost Scheme-1 be the same as the cost of Scheme-2?

(A) 2

(B) 4

(C) 6

(D) 8

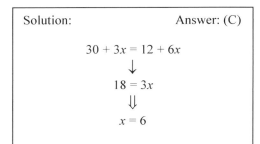

Solution: Answer: (C)

$$30 + 3x = 12 + 6x$$
$$\downarrow$$
$$18 = 3x$$
$$\Downarrow$$
$$x = 6$$

28. The cost of some computer of a computer retail store is $900. After discount 10%, the retail store still wants to make a profit of 10% from the computer. What is the selling price in dollars?

(A) 1,090
(B) 990
(C) 1,100
(D) 1,200

Solution: Answer: (C)

$$900 \times 1.1 = 990$$
$$\downarrow$$

The value 990 includes a 10% profit.
$$\downarrow$$
$$990 = 0.9x$$
$$\Downarrow$$
$$x = 1100$$

29. If $x^2 + y^2 = (x+y)^2$, then x must be equal to

(A) It cannot be determined from the information given.
(B) -1
(C) -y
(D) y

Solution: Answer: (A)

$$x^2 + y^2 = (x+y)^2$$
$$\downarrow$$
$$x^2 + y^2 = x^2 + \underline{2xy} + y^2$$
$$\downarrow$$
$$2xy = 0$$
$$\downarrow$$
$$x = 0 \text{ and/or } y = 0$$
$$\Downarrow$$

(A) It cannot be determined
from the information given.

30. If $(\pi, -2)$ is a point on the graph of function f and if $f(x) = 2\cos x$ for all real numbers x, which of the following must also be a point of the graph of f ?

(A) $(-\pi, -2)$
(B) $(\pi, \pm 2)$
(C) $(\pm\pi, 2)$
(D) $(\pi, 2)$

Solution: Answer: (A)

1. $f(x) = 2\cos x$
$$\downarrow$$
$$\begin{cases} f(x) \text{ is an even function.} \\ f(-x) = f(x) \end{cases}$$

2. $\begin{cases} (\pi, -2) \text{ is a point on} \\ \text{the graph of the even } f. \\ f(\pi) = -2 \end{cases}$
$$\downarrow$$
$$f(-\pi) = -2 \text{ or point } (-\pi, -2)$$
$$\Downarrow$$
Answer is (A).

NEXT PAGE

31. What number should be added to any one of the three numbers 2, 6, and 15 so that the resulting three numbers form a geometric sequence ?

Solution: Answer: 16/5 or .2

$$\begin{cases} a,\ b,\ c \\ \dfrac{b}{a} = \dfrac{c}{b} \end{cases} \rightarrow \begin{cases} 2+x,\ 6+x,\ 15+x \\ \dfrac{6+x}{2+x} = \dfrac{15+x}{6+x} \end{cases}$$

$$\downarrow$$

$$(6+x)^2 = (2+x)(15+x)$$

$$\downarrow$$

$$36 + 12x + \cancel{x^2} = 30 + 15x + 2x + \cancel{x^2}$$

$$\Downarrow$$

$$5x = 6,\ x = \frac{6}{5} = 1.2$$

32. If 21st term of an arithmetic sequence is 160 and the 61st term of the sequence is 200, what is the second term of this sequence?

Solution: Answer: 141

$$a_n = a_1 + (n-1)d$$

$$\downarrow$$

$$\begin{cases} 160 = a_1 + 20d \quad (1) \\ 200 = a_1 + 60d \quad (2) \end{cases}$$

$$(2) - (1)$$

$$\downarrow$$

$$d = 1 \rightarrow (1), \rightarrow a_1 = 140$$

$$\Downarrow$$

$$a_2 = 140 + 1 = 141$$

Note: Figure above not drawn to scale.

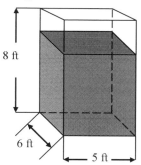

8 ft

6 ft   5 ft

33. The figure above shows the dimensions of a rectangular container closed. There is 96 cubic feet of non-sand in the container. The container will be repositioned on level ground so that the container rests on one, which has the greatest area, of the six surfaces. If it has been repositioned, what will be the entire surface area of the sand?

Solution: Answer: 180

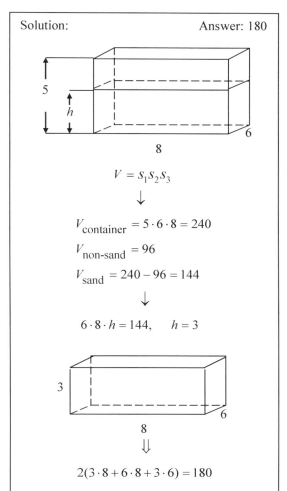

5

h

8   6

$$V = s_1 s_2 s_3$$

$$\downarrow$$

$$V_{container} = 5 \cdot 6 \cdot 8 = 240$$

$$V_{non\text{-}sand} = 96$$

$$V_{sand} = 240 - 96 = 144$$

$$\downarrow$$

$$6 \cdot 8 \cdot h = 144, \quad h = 3$$

3

8   6

$$\Downarrow$$

$$2(3 \cdot 8 + 6 \cdot 8 + 3 \cdot 6) = 180$$

NEXT PAGE

34. John wants to buy a mixture of two kinds of teas, red tea and green tea. Its price is $20/lb. He has 3 pounds of red tea at $18 per pound. How many pounds of green tea at $26 per pound does John have to purchase?

Solution: Answer: 1

$$A + B = M$$

$$\downarrow$$

$$3 \times 18 + 26x = 20(3 + x)$$

$$\Downarrow$$

$$x = 1$$

35. The number 202 is separated into two parts. The larger part exceeds five times the smaller by 22. The smaller part is

Solution: Answer: 30

$$202 = (5S + 22) + S$$

$$\Downarrow$$

$$S = 30$$

36. The average (arithmetic mean) of the exam scores of a class of r students is 75, and the average of the exam score of the class of s students is 91. When the scores of both classes are combined, the average score is 89. What is the value of $\dfrac{r}{s}$?

Solution: Answer: 1/7, .143 or .142

$$\frac{75r + 91s}{r + s} = 89$$

$$\downarrow$$

$$75r + 91s = 89(r + s)$$

$$\downarrow$$

$$89r - 75r = 91s - 89s$$

$$\Downarrow$$

$$\frac{r}{s} = \frac{2}{14} = \frac{1}{7}$$

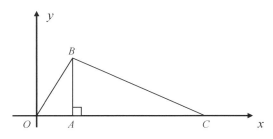

Note: Figure above not drawn to scale.

37. In the coordinate plane, the area of triangle OBC is 30, the length of segment $\overline{AO}$ is 5, and the coordinates of C are (20, 0), what is the slope of segment $\overline{BO}$?

Solution: Answer: 3/5 or .6

$$30 = \frac{OC \cdot AB}{2}$$

$$\downarrow$$

$$30 = \frac{20 \cdot AB}{2}, \quad AB = 3$$

Point $B = (5, 3)$, and

$\overline{BO}$ rises from left to right.

$$\Downarrow$$

$$\text{Slope}_{\overline{BO}} = + \frac{\text{Change of } y\text{-value}}{\text{Change of } x\text{-value}} = \frac{3}{5}$$

38. What is the least positive integer x for which $13x$ is the cube of an integer?

Solution: Answer: 169

$$13x = I^3, \quad x = \frac{I^3}{13}$$

13 is a prime number

$$\downarrow$$

It is divisible by 1 and itself.

$$\Downarrow$$

$$x = \frac{I^3}{13} = \frac{13^3}{13} = 13^2 = 169 = \text{integer}$$

STOP

SAT Math

Practice

Test 05

Redesigned for Tests in March 2016 and Beyond

Mad Math

Math Test – No Calculator

Time: 25 Minutes
20 Questions

Notes:
- The use of a calculator is not allowed.
- All numbers used in this section are the real number.
- Figures are provided for some problems in this test. Unless otherwise indicated under the figure "Note: Figure above not drawn to scale", all figures are drawn as accurately as possible.
- All figures lie in a plane EXCEPT otherwise specified.
- Unless otherwise indicated, the domain of any function f, g or j is assumed to be the set of all real numbers x for which $f(x)$, $g(x)$, or $j(x)$ is a real number.

Reference Information

$A = \dfrac{1}{2}bh$

$A = lw$

$A = \pi r^2$

$V = \pi r^2 h$

$V = lwh$

$c^2 = a^2 + b^2$

$V = \dfrac{1}{3}\pi r^2 h$

$V = \dfrac{4}{3}\pi r^3$

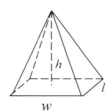

$V = \dfrac{1}{3}lwh$

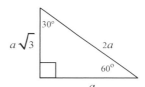

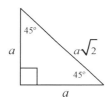

1. If $x^2 - 31 = 3^2 \times 10$, then x could be equal to

(A) -15

(B) 11

(C) 14

(D) 12

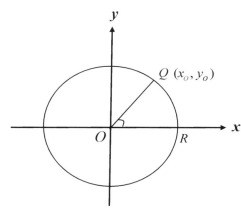

3. In the xy-plane above, O is the center of the circle, $(1, \sqrt{3})$ is the point Q. If $\dfrac{\pi}{k}$ radians is the measure of the angle QOR, what is the value of k?

(A) 6

(B) 4

(C) π

(D) 3

2. Which of the following is the complete solution set for the inequality $|x - 5| \geq 3$?

(A) $2 \leq x \leq 8$
(B) $x \geq 8, x \leq 3$
(C) $x \geq 8, x \leq 2$
(D) $x \leq 1$

4. Which of the following does $E = 25^{\frac{3}{5}}$ equal?

(A) $3\sqrt[5]{5}$

(B) $\sqrt[5]{5}$

(C) $5\sqrt[5]{5}$

(D) $5\sqrt[3]{5}$

NEXT PAGE

5. A function is defined by $f(t) = -3^t + 2$. Which of the following is the sketch of $g(t) = f(-t)$?

(A)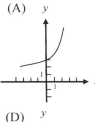

(B)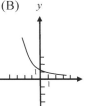

(C)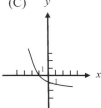

(D)

6. Mike cuts a cake into m equal pieces, where $m > 2$, and eats two pieces. In terms of m, what percentage of the cake is left?

(A) $\dfrac{m-2}{100m}\%$

(B) $\dfrac{100(2-m)}{m}\%$

(C) $\dfrac{100(m-2)}{m}\%$

(D) $\dfrac{m-2}{m}\%$

7. If a sequence $p-2, p+2, 2p-3$ forms an arithmetic sequence, what is the value of p?

(A) 6
(B) -3
(C) 8
(D) 9

8. In the figure above, O is the center of the circle and 6 is the radius of the circle. If the length of minor arc XY is between 4 and 5, what is one possible integer x-value?

(A) 40
(B) 38
(C) 37
(D) 36

NEXT PAGE

9. If the parabola with equation $y = (x - 12)^2$ intersects the line with equation $y = 16$ at two points, Q and R, in the xy-plane, what is the length of $\overline{QR}$?

(A) 20

(B) 4

(C) 8

(D) 12

10. Machine A itself can finish a job in k_1 hours, and Machine B itself can finish a job in k_2 hours, where $k_1 > 0$ and $k_2 > 0$. After Machine A begins the job and does $5/6$ of the job, Machine B takes over and finishes the remaining job. Which of the following is the entire time, in hours, that takes Machine A and Machine B to finish the job?

(A) $\dfrac{5k_1 + k_2}{6}$

(B) $\dfrac{3k_1 - k_2}{6}$

(C) $\dfrac{5k_1 + 2k_2}{6}$

(D) $\dfrac{3k_1 + k_2}{6}$

11. Let $f(t)$ give the entire amount earned, in dollars, in a week by James as a function of the number of hours worked. James earns \$10.5 per hour and must work 3 to 5 days each week from 6 to 8 hours each day. What is the domain of function f ?

(A) $18 < t < 40$

(B) $18 < t \le 40$

(C) $18 \le t, t \ge 40$

(D) $18 \le t \le 40$

12. The angle formed by the hour hand and minute hand of a clock at 5:15 is

(A) 78°
(B) 67.5°
(C) 72.5°
(D) 125°

13. If $x^2 = 7$, what is the value of $\left(x - \sqrt{7}\right)\left(x + \sqrt{7}\right)$?

(A) 0
(B) 9
(C) 7
(D) 5

14. If p is inversely proportional to q and if $p = 20$ when $q = 5$, what is the value of p when $q = 10$?

(A) 36
(B) 2.5
(C) 5
(D) 10

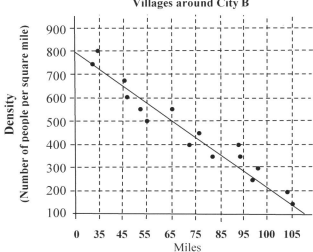

Distance and Population Density of Villages around City B

The scatterplot with line of best fit above shows the population density of 16 villages, in number of people per square mile, with respect to their distances from City B.

15. By the scatterplot, which of the following statements is true about the relationship between a distance of a village from City B and its population density?

(A) The villages that are more distance from City B tend to have more population densities.

(B) The villages that are lesser distance from City B tend to have more population densities.

(C) The villages that are more distance from City B tend to have lesser or more population densities.

(D) The villages that are lesser distance from City B tend to have lesser population densities.

NEXT PAGE

16. If $p = 3q$, $q = 4r$, $3r = s$, and $s \neq 0$, then $\dfrac{p}{s} =$

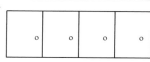

19. The figure above represents four offices, which will be arranged at random to 4 teachers, one tercher per office. If Dr. Smith and Ms. Bush are 2 of the 4 teachers, what is the probability that each of the two teachers will be arranged an office at either end?

17. John wants to buy a mixture of two kinds of teas, red tea and green tea. Its price is $20/lb. He has 3 pounds of red tea at $18 per pound. How many pounds of green tea at $26 per pound does John have to purchase?

20. If x and y are positive integers, $x + y < 19$, what is the greatest possible value of $x - y$?

18. The number 202 is separated into two parts. The larger part exceeds five times the smaller by 22. The smaller part is

STOP

Math Test – Calculator

Time: 55 Minutes
38 Questions

Notes:
- The use of a calculator is not allowed.
- All numbers used in this section are the real number.
- Figures are provided for some problems in this test. Unless otherwise indicated under the figure "Note: Figure above not drawn to scale", all figures are drawn as accurately as possible.
- All figures lie in a plane EXCEPT otherwise specified.
- Unless otherwise indicated, the domain of any function f, g or j is assumed to be the set of all real numbers x for which $f(x)$, $g(x)$, or $j(x)$ is a real number.

Reference Information

$$A = \frac{1}{2}bh$$

$$A = lw$$

$$A = \pi r^2$$

$$V = \pi r^2 h$$

$$V = lwh$$

$$c^2 = a^2 + b^2$$

$$V = \frac{1}{3}\pi r^2 h$$

$$V = \frac{4}{3}\pi r^3$$

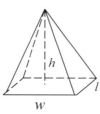
$$V = \frac{1}{3}lwh$$

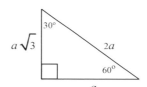

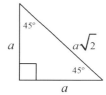

1. Jack makes $7 for each odd job he does during the month, plus a monthly pin money of $30. If he obtains no other money, which of the following expression represents the total amount, in dollars, Jack obtains for a month in which he has done j odd job?

(A) $30 + 7j$

(B) $30j + 7$

(C) $j(30 + 7)$

(D) $7(25 + j)$

2. If $n > 0$, what is $\dfrac{3}{7n} \div \dfrac{1}{7n}$?

(A) $\dfrac{3}{49n^2}$

(B) 3

(C) $49n$

(D) $\dfrac{49n}{2}$

3. If $b^4 + 4 = \dfrac{b^{12}}{b^8} + a$, then $a =$

(A) Can not be determined.

(B) 2^2

(C) 16

(D) 2^3

4. If $p = 1 + \dfrac{1}{3} + \dfrac{1}{9} + \dfrac{1}{27}$ and $q = 1 + \dfrac{1}{3}p$, then q exceeds p by

(A) $-\dfrac{1}{81}$

(B) $\dfrac{40}{27}$

(C) $\dfrac{121}{81}$

(D) $\dfrac{1}{81}$

NEXT PAGE ⇨

5. If $i = \sqrt{-1}$, what are the solutions to $6x^2 + 24x + 66 = 0$?

A) $\dfrac{-4 + \sqrt{7} \cdot i}{2}$

(B) $-2 \pm \sqrt{2}$

(C) $-2 \pm \sqrt{7} \cdot i$

(D) $\pm 2 + \sqrt{2} \cdot i$

6. Mike owns the shares of his company including $30,000 in cash and $45,000 in other holdings. If Mike redistributes his holdings in order to make 60 percent of the entire shares be in other holdings, how many dollars of cash must Mike change to other holdings?

(A) 1,500

(B) 30,000

(C) 0.000

(D) 15.000

7. Which scatterplot below shows a relationship that is approximately modeled with the equation $f(x) = ax^k$, where a is positive and k is even and positive?

(A)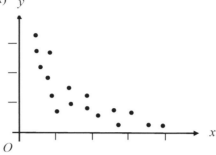

(B)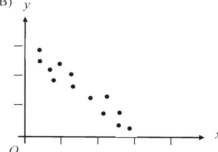

(C)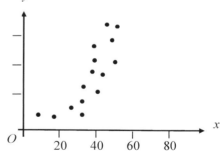

(D)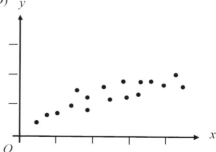

NEXT PAGE

8. What is an equation in point-slope form for the perpendicular bisector of the segment with endpoints $A(4, 2)$ and $B(1, -3)$?

(A) $y - \dfrac{1}{2} = \dfrac{3}{5}\left(x - \dfrac{5}{2}\right)$

(B) $y - \dfrac{1}{2} = -\dfrac{3}{5}\left(x - \dfrac{5}{2}\right)$

(C) $y + \dfrac{1}{2} = -\dfrac{3}{5}\left(x - \dfrac{5}{2}\right)$

(D) $y + \dfrac{1}{2} = -\dfrac{3}{5}\left(x + \dfrac{5}{2}\right)$

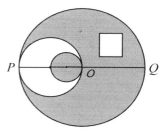

Note: Figure above not drawn to scale.

9. In the figure above, the centers of 3 circles are all lie on diameter PQ of the greatest circle with center O, the radius of the smallest circle is 1, and the area the square is 1. The smallest circle touches centers of greatest and white circles. What is the area of the entire shaded portion?

(A) $13\pi - 1$

(B) $13\pi - 4$

(C) $11\pi - 1$

(D) $11\pi + 4$

NEXT PAGE

10. A rectangular garden is twice as its length as its width. If its length is decreased by 3 meters and its width is increased by 1 meter. The new garden formed has an area of 33 square meters. Which of the following is the area, in square meters, of the original garden?

(A) 27

(B) $\dfrac{81}{2}$

(C) $\dfrac{85}{2}$

(D) 42

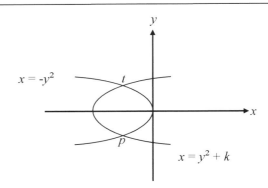

12. The figure above shows the graph $x = -y^2$ and $x = y^2 + k$. k is a certain constant. p and t separately represent the intersecting points of the 2 graphs in the xy-plane. If the length of the distance between t and p is 8, what is the value of k?

(A) -32
(B) 72
(C) 32
(D) 37

11.   If $x^2 + y^2 = (x + y)^2$, then x must be equal to

(A) It cannot be determined from the information given.
(B) -1
(C) $-y$
(D) y

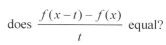
13. If $f(x) = -x^2 - 3x + 5$, then which of the following does $\dfrac{f(x-t) - f(x)}{t}$ equal?

(A) $2x - t + 3$

(B) $2x + t - 3$

(C) $2x - t - 3$

(D) $t - 2x + 3$

14. For which of the following sets of numbers is the median greater than the average (arithmetic mean)?

(A) [1, 2, 3, 4, 4]
(B) [1, 2, 3, 4, 5]
(C) [2, 3, 4, 5, 6]
(D) [3, 4, 5, 6, 8]

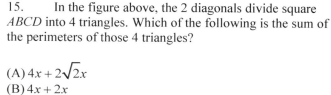

15. In the figure above, the 2 diagonals divide square $ABCD$ into 4 triangles. Which of the following is the sum of the perimeters of those 4 triangles?

(A) $4x + 2\sqrt{2}x$
(B) $4x + 2x$
(C) $4x + 4x$
(D) $4(x + \sqrt{2}x)$

NEXT PAGE

16. How many integers greater than 399 and less than 1,000 have exactly one digit 0 ?

(A) 162

(B) 108

(C) 144

(D) 128

17. If $j(x) = \sqrt{11 - x^2}$, what is the domain of j ?

(A) $-\sqrt{11} \geq x, \ x \geq \sqrt{11}$

(B) $-\sqrt{11} < x, \ x > \sqrt{11}$

(C) $-\sqrt{11} \leq x \leq \sqrt{11}$

(D) $x \geq -\sqrt{11}, \ \sqrt{11} \leq x$

18. If a rectangular solid has length 10 centimeters, width 2 centimeters, and height 50 centimeters, then how many of the rectangular solids have a volume of four cubic meters when they are combined?

(A) 200

(B) 4,000

(C) 2,000

(D) 400

NEXT PAGE

19. Two balls that have distinct weights are droped from a height of 81 inches. If one of the two balls rebounds $\frac{2}{3}$ the height that has fallen, and another ball rebounds $\frac{1}{3}$ the height that has fallen, after they hit the same floor for the fourth time, which of the following is the sum S, in inches, of measures of altitudes, between the floor and highest point that the balls can reach, respectively, of the two balls ?

(A) 15

(B) 16

(C) 17

(D) 18

Note: Figure below not drawn to scale.

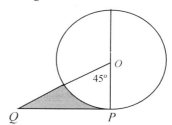

20. In the figure above, the center of the circle with a radius of 1 is at O and segment $\overline{PQ}$ is tangent to the circle at point P. What is the area of the shaded portion?

20. In the figure above, the center of the circle with a radius of 1 is at O and segment $\overline{PQ}$ is tangent to the circle at point P. What is the area of the shaded portion?

(A) $\frac{\sqrt{3}}{6} - \frac{\pi}{12}$

(B) $\frac{1}{2} - \frac{\pi}{4}$

(C) $\frac{\pi}{8} - \frac{1}{2}$

(D) $\frac{1}{2} - \frac{\pi}{8}$

NEXT PAGE

21. Which of the following is not the equation of a function?

(A) $y = 0$

(B) $y = |x|$

(C) $y = x^2$

(D) $|y| = x$

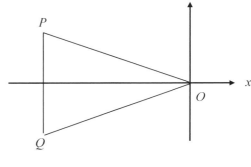

23. In the xy-coordinate plane above, points P, O, and Q are the 3 vertices of a certain triangle. The coordinates of P are $(-7, w)$ and the coordinates of Q are $(-7, -w)$, where w is a number greater than zero. Which of the following is one possible value of w if the area of triangle POQ is less than 6 and greater than 5 ?

(A) $\dfrac{6}{7}$

(B) $\dfrac{9}{14}$

(C) $\dfrac{11}{14}$

(D) $\dfrac{13}{14}$

22. If $x^2 > x^3$ and $x > 0$, what is one possible value for x?

(A) $\dfrac{3}{2}$

(B) $\dfrac{1}{2}$

(C) $1\dfrac{1}{5}$

(D) $-\dfrac{1}{2}$

NEXT PAGE

24. If a_1, a_2, and a_3 are numbers such that $\dfrac{a_1}{a_2} = 2$ and $\dfrac{a_2}{a_3} = 3$, then $\dfrac{a_1 - a_2}{a_2 + a_3}$ equals

(A) $\dfrac{4}{3}$

(B) $\dfrac{2}{5}$

(C) $\dfrac{5}{2}$

(D) $\dfrac{3}{4}$

Questions 25 and 26 refer to following figure.

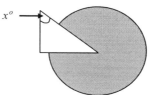

Note: Figure above not drawn to scale.

25. The circle and right triangle are shown above. The circle has a diameter of length 12. If the area of the shaded portion is 30π, what is the value of x?

(A) 20
(B) 30
(C) 36
(D) 60

26. The circle and right triangle are shown above. The circle has a radius of length 8. If the arc of the shaded portion is 14π, what is the value of x?

(A) 20
(B) 30
(C) 45
(D) 60

NEXT PAGE

27. The distance D, in yards, of a certain vehicle from a stop sign is given by the function $D(T) = 18T^{\frac{4}{3}}$, where T is the time in seconds. Which of the following is the average speed, in yards per second, of the vehicle from $T_1 = 8$ to $T_2 = 27$ seconds, to the closest whole number?

(A) 62

(B) 64

(C) 32

(D) 124

28. What is the greatest integer g for which the equation $x^2 + 7x + g = 0$ has real solutions?

(A) ± 13

(B) 12

(C) ± 11

(D) 13

29. If $f(x) = (2x + 3)(x + 7)$, which of the following is the possible sketch for the function f ?

(A) 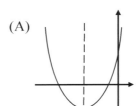   (B)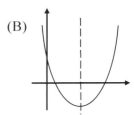

(C) 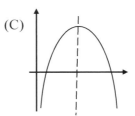   (D)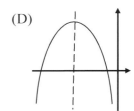

30. If Q, R, and S are positive integers greater than 1, where $Q \le R \le S$ and $Q + R + S < 107$, what is the greatest possible value for the median of these three integers?

(A) 51

(B) 53

(C) 52

(D) 50

NEXT PAGE

31. Point O is the center of the circle above. What is the value of x?

Note: Figure below not drawn to scale.

33. In the figure above, $x < 30$ and $y = z + 3$. z is an integer. What is the least possible value of y?

32. The average (arithmetic mean) of the exam scores of a class of r students is 75, and the average of the exam score of the class of s students is 91. When the scores of both classes are combined, the average score is 89. What is the value of $\dfrac{r}{s}$?

34. A process begins that if three fourths of the students in a class room leave at the end of every 15-minutes interval and at the end of 45 minutes the next to the last two students leave, how many students were in the room to start with?

NEXT PAGE

35. Al horizontally cuts a wooden cube with volume 216 in half. The two halves are glued together to form a rectangular solid, which is not a cube. What is the surface area of this new solid?

37. If the six cards shown above are placed in a row so that

♥ , ♦ and ♠ are never at either end, how

many possible distinct combinations exist?

36. If $64 = 2^{x+2}$, then $x^2 =$

38. At a supermarket, $\dfrac{2}{7}$ of the items are discounted by 70 percent,

$\dfrac{1}{7}$ of the items are discounted by 40 percent, $\dfrac{3}{7}$ of the items are

discounted by 50 percent, and rest items are not discounted. If one

item is to be selected randomly, wha is the probability that the item is

discounted by 40 percent and 50 percent?

STOP

Answer Key
For
SAT Math Practice Test 05

Section 3

1	B
2	C
3	D
4	C
5	D
6	C
7	D
8	A
9	C
10	A
11	D
12	B
13	A
14	D
15	B

16	4
17	1
18	30
19	1/6 or .166 or .167
20	16

Section 4

1	A	16	B
2	B	17	C
3	B	18	B
4	D	19	C
5	C	20	D
6	C	21	D
7	C	22	B
8	C	23	C
9	A	24	D
10	B	25	B
11	A	26	C
12	A	27	A
13	A	28	B
14	A	29	A
15	D	30	C

31	160
32	1/7 or .142 or .143
33	77
34	128
35	252
36	16
37	144
38	3/49 or .061

SAT Math

Practice

Test 05

Explanations

Redesigned for Tests in March 2016 and Beyond

Mad Math

Math Test – No Calculator

Time: 25 Minutes
20 Questions

Notes:
- The use of a calculator is not allowed.
- All numbers used in this section are the real number.
- Figures are provided for some problems in this test. Unless otherwise indicated under the figure "Note: Figure above not drawn to scale", all figures are drawn as accurately as possible.
- All figures lie in a plane EXCEPT otherwise specified.
- Unless otherwise indicated, the domain of any function f, g or j is assumed to be the set of all real numbers x for which $f(x)$, $g(x)$, or $j(x)$ is a real number.

Reference Information

$$A = \frac{1}{2}bh$$

$$A = lw$$

$$A = \pi r^2$$

$$V = \pi r^2 h$$

$$V = lwh$$

$$c^2 = a^2 + b^2$$

$$V = \frac{1}{3}\pi r^2 h$$

$$V = \frac{4}{3}\pi r^3$$

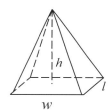

$$V = \frac{1}{3}lwh$$

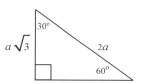

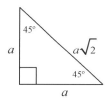

1. If $x^2 - 31 = 3^2 \times 10$, then x could be equal to

(A) -15

(B) 11

(C) 14

(D) 12

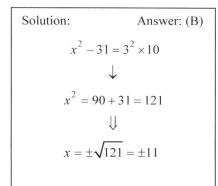

Solution: Answer: (B)

$$x^2 - 31 = 3^2 \times 10$$

$$\downarrow$$

$$x^2 = 90 + 31 = 121$$

$$\Downarrow$$

$$x = \pm\sqrt{121} = \pm 11$$

2. Which of the following is the complete solution set for the inequality $|x - 5| \geq 3$?

(A) $2 \leq x \leq 8$
(B) $x \geq 8, x \leq 3$
(C) $x \geq 8, x \leq 2$
(D) $x \leq 1$

Solution: Answer: (C)

$$\text{Type}: |x - a| \geq b$$

$$\downarrow$$

$$\begin{cases} x - a \geq b \\ x - a \leq -b \end{cases}$$

$$(a > 0, \quad b > 0)$$

$$\Downarrow$$

(1) $x - 5 \geq 3, \ x \geq 8$
(2) $x - 5 \leq -3, \ x \leq 2$

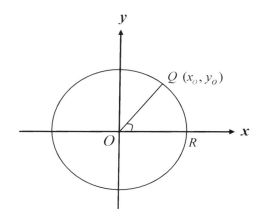

3. In the xy-plane above, O is the center of the circle, $(1, \sqrt{3})$ is the point Q. If $\dfrac{\pi}{k}$ radians is the measure of the angle QOR, what is the value of k?

(A) 6
(B) 4
(C) π
(D) 3

Solution: Answer: (D)

$(1, \sqrt{3})$ $(\sqrt{3}, 1)$

$$\tan\theta = \frac{\sqrt{3}}{1} \rightarrow \theta = 60°$$

$$60° = \frac{\pi}{3} \quad \text{and} \quad 30° = \frac{\pi}{6}$$

$$\Downarrow$$

$$k \neq 6, \quad k = 3$$

4. Which of the following does $E = 25^{\frac{3}{5}}$ equal?

(A) $3\sqrt[5]{5}$
(B) $\sqrt[5]{5}$
(C) $5\sqrt[5]{5}$
(D) $5\sqrt[3]{5}$

Solution: Answer: (C)

Refer to the choices, a target
is $\sqrt[3]{2}$ or $\sqrt[5]{2}$ something.

$$25^{\frac{3}{5}} = \sqrt[5]{25^3} = \sqrt[5]{\left((5)^2\right)^3}$$

$$\downarrow$$

$$\sqrt[5]{5^6} = \sqrt[5]{5^5 5^1} = \sqrt[5]{5^5} \cdot \sqrt[5]{5}$$

$$\Downarrow$$

$$E = 5 \cdot \sqrt[5]{5}$$

NEXT PAGE ⟹

5. A function is defined by $f(t) = -3^t + 2$. Which of the following is the sketch of $g(t) = f(-t)$?

(A)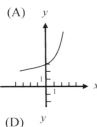

(B)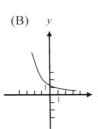

(C)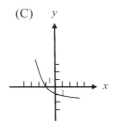

(D)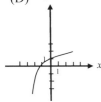

Solution: Answer: (D)

$$\begin{cases} f(t) = -3^t + 2 = -\left(3^t - 2\right) \\ g(t) = f(-t) = -\left(3^{-t} - 2\right) = -\left(\left(\frac{1}{3}\right)^t - 2\right) \end{cases}$$

$$h(t) = \left(\frac{1}{3}\right)^t \rightarrow \text{The sketch of } h \text{ is (B).}$$

$$j(t) = \left(\frac{1}{3}\right)^t - 2 \rightarrow \text{The sketch of } j \text{ is (C).}$$

$$g(t) = f(-t) = -j(t)$$
↓
The sketch of j flips about x-axis.
⇓
The sketch of g is (D).

6. Mike cuts a cake into m equal pieces, where $m > 2$, and eats two pieces. In terms of m, what percentage of the cake is left?

(A) $\dfrac{m-2}{100m}\%$

(B) $\dfrac{100(2-m)}{m}\%$

(C) $\dfrac{100(m-2)}{m}\%$

(D) $\dfrac{m-2}{m}\%$

Solution: Answer: (C)

$$\frac{m-2}{m} = \frac{m-2}{m} \times 100\%$$
⇓
$$\frac{100 \times (m-2)}{m}\%$$

7. If a sequence $p - 2, p + 2, 2p - 3$ forms an arithmetic sequence, what is the value of p?

(A) 6
(B) -3
(C) 8
(D) 9

Solution: Answer: (D)

Let a, b, and c is an arithmetic sequence.
↓
$$b - a = c - b.$$
↓
$$(p+2) - (p-2) = (2p-3) - (p+2)$$
⇓
$$4 = p - 5, \; p = 9$$

8. In the figure above, O is the center of the circle and 6 is the radius of the circle. If the length of minor arc XY is between 4 and 5, what is one possible integer x-value?

(A) 40
(B) 38
(C) 37
(D) 36

Solution: Answer: (A)

$$S = r\theta, \qquad 4 < r\theta < 5$$
$$\frac{4}{r} < \theta < \frac{5}{r}, \qquad \frac{4}{6} < x \cdot \frac{\pi}{180} < \frac{5}{6}$$
↓
$$\frac{180}{\pi} \cdot \frac{4}{6} < x < \frac{5}{6} \cdot \frac{180}{\pi}$$
↓
$$\frac{120}{\pi} < x < \frac{150}{\pi}, \quad 38.19 < x < 47.7$$
⇓
All integers: $39 \le x \le 47$

NEXT PAGE ⟹

9. If the parabola with equation $y = (x - 12)^2$ intersects the line with equation $y = 16$ at two points, Q and R, in the xy-plane, what is the length of $\overline{QR}$?

(A) 20

(B) 4

(C) 8

(D) 12

Solution: Answer: (C)

$16 = (x - 12)^2, \quad \pm 4 = x - 12$

$x = 4 + 12 \quad$ or $\quad x = -4 + 12$

↓

$x = 16 \quad$ or $\quad x = 8$

$x = 12$ is the symmetric

line of the parabola.

⇓

$QR = 16 - 8 = 8$

10. Machine A itself can finish a job in k_1 hours, and Machine B itself can finish a job in k_2 hours, where $k_1 > 0$ and $k_2 > 0$. After Machine A begins the job and does $5 / 6$ of the job, Machine B takes over and finishes the remaining job. Which of the following is the entire time, in hours, that takes Machine A and Machine B to finish the job?

(A) $\dfrac{5k_1 + k_2}{6}$

(B) $\dfrac{3k_1 - k_2}{6}$

(C) $\dfrac{5k_1 + 2k_2}{6}$

(D) $\dfrac{3k_1 + k_2}{6}$

Solution: Answer: (A)

Workload ratio = Time ratio

↓

1 is the entire job as fraction.

↓

$\begin{cases} T_{M-A} = \dfrac{5}{6}k_1 \\[2mm] 1 - \dfrac{5}{6} = \dfrac{1}{6} \\[2mm] T_{M-B} = \dfrac{1}{6}k_2 \end{cases}$

⇓

$T_{\text{Entire}} = \dfrac{5}{6}k_1 + \dfrac{1}{6}k_2 = \dfrac{5k_1 + k_2}{6}$

11. Let $f(t)$ give the entire amount earned, in dollars, in a week by James as a function of the number of hours worked. James earns $10.5 per hour and must work 3 to 5 days each week from 6 to 8 hours each day. What is the domain of function f ?

(A) $18 < t < 40$

(B) $18 < t \le 40$

(C) $18 \le t, t \ge 40$

(D) $18 \le t \le 40$

Solution: Answer: (D)

$\begin{cases} \text{Input = hours} \\ \text{Output = total dollars} \end{cases}$

↓

$\begin{cases} \text{Domain is about hours.} \\ \text{Range is about total dollars.} \end{cases}$

↓

$\begin{cases} \text{Domain:} \\ \text{The least} = 3 \times 6 = 18 \\ \text{The greatest} = 5 \times 8 = 40 \end{cases}$

⇓

$\boxed{18 \le t \le 40}$

12. The angle formed by the hour hand and minute hand of a clock at 5:15 is

(A) 78°

(B) 67.5°

(C) 72.5°

(D) 125°

Solution: Answer: (B)

Hour hand:

5 hours: $5 \cdot 30° = 150°$

15 minutes: $15 \cdot 0.5° = 7.5°$

$150 + 7.5 = 157.5°$

Minute hand:

15 minutes: $15 \cdot 6° = 90°$

The angle degrees between 2 hands:

⇓

$157.5° - 90° = 67.5°$

NEXT PAGE ⟩

13. If $x^2 = 7$, what is the value of $\left(x - \sqrt{7}\right)\left(x + \sqrt{7}\right)$?

(A) 0
(B) 9
(C) 7
(D) 5

> Solution: Answer: (A)
>
> $$\left(x-\sqrt{7}\right)\left(x+\sqrt{7}\right) = x^2 - \left(\sqrt{7}\right)^2$$
> $$\downarrow$$
> $$x^2 - 7$$
> $$\Downarrow$$
> $$x^2 = 7, \quad 7 - 7 = 0$$

14. If p is inversely proportional to q and if $p = 20$ when $q = 5$, what is the value of p when $q = 10$?

(A) 36
(B) 2.5
(C) 5
(D) 10

> Solution: Answer: (D)
>
> **Method 1**
>
> $\begin{cases} \text{"Inversely"} \\ \text{Question doesn't ask constant } k. \end{cases}$
>
> $$\downarrow$$
>
> Use the formula: $\boxed{} \cdot x = \boxed{} \cdot \boxed{}$
>
> A pair   A pair
> of values   of values
>
> $$\Downarrow$$
>
> $\cancel{10}\, p = \cancel{20}^{2} \times 5, \quad p = 10$
>
> **Method 2**
>
> $$A = \frac{k}{B}, \quad k = \text{constant}$$
>
> $$\downarrow$$
>
> (1) Use the first set of information to get k.
>
> $$p = \frac{k}{q}, \quad 20 = \frac{k}{5}, \quad k = 100$$
>
> (2) Use the second set of information to get p.
>
> $$\Downarrow$$
>
> $$p = \frac{100}{q} = \frac{100}{10} = 10$$

Distance and Population Density of Villages around City B

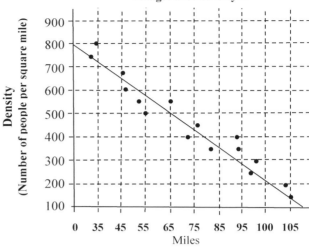

The scatterplot with line of best fit above shows the population density of 16 villages, in number of people per square mile, with respect to their distances from City B.

15. By the scatterplot, which of the following statements is true about the relationship between a distance of a village from City B and its population density?

(A) The villages that are more distance from City B tend to have more population densities.

(B) The villages that are lesser distance from City B tend to have more population densities.

(C) The villages that are more distance from City B tend to have lesser or more population densities.

(D) The villages that are lesser distance from City B tend to have lesser population densities.

> Solution: Answer: (B)
> According to the scatterplot,
> the distances increase, the densities decrease.
> $$\Downarrow$$
> Answer is (B).

NEXT PAGE ⟩

16. If $p = 3q$, $q = 4r$, $3r = s$, and $s \neq 0$, then $\dfrac{p}{s} =$

> Solution: Answer: 4
>
> $$"\frac{p}{s} = "$$
> $$\downarrow$$
> q and r should be eliminated.
> $$\downarrow$$
> Let $q = 4$.
> $$p = 3 \cdot 4, \quad \boxed{p = 12}$$
> $$4 = 4r, \quad r = 1$$
> $$3 \cdot 1 = s, \quad \boxed{s = 3}$$
> $$\Downarrow$$
> $$\frac{p}{s} = \frac{12}{3} = \boxed{4}$$

17. John wants to buy a mixture of two kinds of teas, red tea and green tea. Its price is $20/lb. He has 3 pounds of red tea at $18 per pound. How many pounds of green tea at $26 per pound does John have to purchase?

> Solution: Answer: 1
> $$A + B = M$$
> $$\downarrow$$
> $$3 \times 18 + 26x = 20(3 + x)$$
> $$\Downarrow$$
> $$x = 1$$

18. The number 202 is separated into two parts. The larger part exceeds five times the smaller by 22. The smaller part is

> Solution: Answer: 30
> $$202 = (5S + 22) + S$$
> $$\Downarrow$$
> $$S = 30$$

19. The figure above represents four offices, which will be arranged at random to 4 teachers, one tercher per office. If Dr. Smith and Ms. Bush are 2 of the 4 teachers, what is the probability that each of the two teachers will be arranged an office at either end?

> Solution: Answer: 1/6 or .166 or .167
>
> (1). Total possibilities
> 4 positions, 4 elements, and order does matter.
> $$\downarrow$$
> $$4 \cdot 3 \cdot 2 \cdot 1 = 24$$
> (2). Possibilities for the 2 teachers
>
>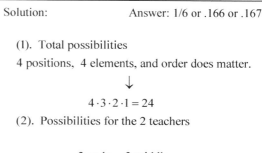
>
> (1) and (2)
> $$\Downarrow$$
> $$p = \frac{4}{24} = \frac{1}{6}$$

20. If x and y are positive integers, $x + y < 19$, what is the greatest possible value of $x - y$?

> Solution: Answer: 16
> $$x = 17, \quad y = 1$$
> $$\downarrow$$
> $$x + y = 17 + 1 = 18 < 19$$
> $$\Downarrow$$
> $$x - y = 17 - 1 = 16$$

STOP

Math Test – Calculator

Time: 55 Minutes
38 Questions

Notes:

- The use of a calculator is not allowed.
- All numbers used in this section are the real number.
- Figures are provided for some problems in this test. Unless otherwise indicated under the figure "Note: Figure above not drawn to scale", all figures are drawn as accurately as possible.
- All figures lie in a plane EXCEPT otherwise specified.
- Unless otherwise indicated, the domain of any function f, g or j is assumed to be the set of all real numbers x for which $f(x)$, $g(x)$, or $j(x)$ is a real number.

Reference Information

$A = \dfrac{1}{2}bh$

$A = lw$

$A = \pi r^2$

$V = \pi r^2 h$

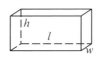

$V = lwh$

$c^2 = a^2 + b^2$

$V = \dfrac{1}{3}\pi r^2 h$

$V = \dfrac{4}{3}\pi r^3$

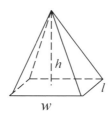

$V = \dfrac{1}{3}lwh$

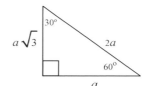

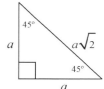

1. Jack makes \$7 for each odd job he does during the month, plus a monthly pin money of \$30. If he obtains no other money, which of the following expression represents the total amount, in dollars, Jack obtains for a month in which he has done j odd job?

(A) $30 + 7j$

(B) $30j + 7$

(C) $j(30 + 7)$

(D) $7(25 + j)$

> Solution: Answer: (A)
>
> j odd jobs $= \$7j$
> $$\Downarrow$$
> Total $= \$(7j + 30)$

2. If $n > 0$, what is $\dfrac{3}{7n} \div \dfrac{1}{7n}$?

(A) $\dfrac{3}{49n^2}$

(B) 3

(C) $49n$

(D) $\dfrac{49n}{2}$

> Solution: Answer: (B)
>
> $$\dfrac{3}{7n} \div \dfrac{1}{7n}$$
> $$\Downarrow$$
> $$\dfrac{3}{7n} \times \dfrac{7n}{1} = 3$$

3. If $b^4 + 4 = \dfrac{b^{12}}{b^8} + a$, then $a =$

(A) Can not be determined.

(B) 2^2

(C) 16

(D) 2^3

> Solution: Answer: (B)
>
> $$\cancel{b^4} + 4 = \cancel{b^4} + a$$
> $$\Downarrow$$
> $$a = 4 = 2^2$$

4. If $p = 1 + \dfrac{1}{3} + \dfrac{1}{9} + \dfrac{1}{27}$ and $q = 1 + \dfrac{1}{3}p$, then q exceeds p by

(A) $-\dfrac{1}{81}$

(B) $\dfrac{40}{27}$

(C) $\dfrac{121}{81}$

(D) $\dfrac{1}{81}$

> Solution: Answer: (D)
>
> $$\begin{cases} p = \dfrac{27 + 9 + 3 + 1}{27} = \dfrac{40}{27} \\ q = 1 + \dfrac{1}{3}\left(\dfrac{40}{27}\right) = \dfrac{81 + 40}{81} = \dfrac{121}{81} \end{cases}$$
> $$\Downarrow$$
> $$q - p = \dfrac{121}{81} - \dfrac{40}{27} = \dfrac{121 - 120}{81} = \dfrac{1}{81}$$

NEXT PAGE

5. If $i = \sqrt{-1}$, what are the solutions to $6x^2 + 24x + 66 = 0$?

A) $\dfrac{-4 + \sqrt{7} \cdot i}{2}$

(B) $-2 \pm \sqrt{2}$

(C) $-2 \pm \sqrt{7} \cdot i$

(D) $\pm 2 + \sqrt{2} \cdot i$

Solution: Answer: (C)

$$6\left(x^2 + 4x + 11\right) = 0$$

$$\downarrow$$

$$\text{Use } x_{1,2} = \frac{-b \pm \sqrt{b^2 - 4ac}}{2a}$$

$$\downarrow$$

$$x_{1,2} = \frac{-4 \pm \sqrt{16 - 44}}{2} = \frac{-4 \pm \sqrt{-28}}{2}$$

$$\downarrow$$

$$\frac{-4 \pm \sqrt{4}\sqrt{7} \cdot \sqrt{-1}}{2} = \frac{-4 \pm 2\sqrt{7} \cdot i}{2}$$

$$\Downarrow$$

$$x_{1,2} = -2 \pm \sqrt{7} \cdot i$$

6. Mike owns the shares of his company including $30,000 in cash and $45,000 in other holdings. If Mike redistributes his holdings in order to make 60 percent of the entire shares be in other holdings, how many dollars of cash must Mike change to other holdings?

(A) 1, 500

(B) 30, 000

(C) 0.000

(D) 15.000

Solution: Answer: (C)

$$\frac{45 + x}{30 + 45} = \frac{6\cancel{0}}{10\cancel{0}}$$

$$\downarrow$$

$$\frac{45 + x}{\cancel{75}^{15}} = \frac{3}{\cancel{5}}, \quad 45 + x = 45$$

$$\Downarrow$$

$$x = 0$$

7. Which scatterplot below shows a relationship that is approximately modeled with the equation $f(x) = ax^k$, where a is positive and k is even and positive?

(A) y

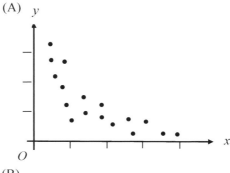

(B) y

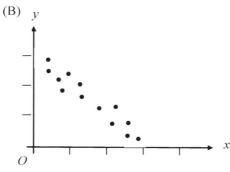

(C) y

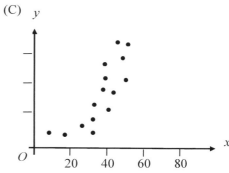

(D) y

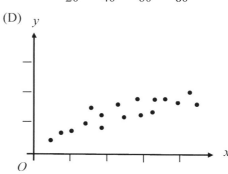

Solution: Answer: (C)

$f(x) = ax^k$ is a power function. It can be $y = x^2$. Its graph is a parent curve.

$$\Downarrow$$

Answer is (C).

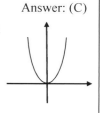

8. What is an equation in point-slope form for the perpendicular bisector of the segment with endpoints $A(4, 2)$ and $B(1, -3)$?

(A) $y - \dfrac{1}{2} = \dfrac{3}{5}\left(x - \dfrac{5}{2}\right)$

(B) $y - \dfrac{1}{2} = -\dfrac{3}{5}\left(x - \dfrac{5}{2}\right)$

(C) $y + \dfrac{1}{2} = -\dfrac{3}{5}\left(x - \dfrac{5}{2}\right)$

(D) $y + \dfrac{1}{2} = -\dfrac{3}{5}\left(x + \dfrac{5}{2}\right)$

Solution: Answer: (C)

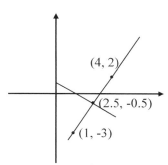

$$\left\{ \text{Midpoint of } \overline{AB} = \left(\frac{x_1 + x_2}{2}, \frac{y_1 + y_2}{2}\right) \right.$$

$$\left(\frac{4+1}{2}, \frac{2-3}{2}\right) = (2.5, -0.5)$$

$$\left\{\begin{array}{l} \text{Slope} = s = \dfrac{y_2 - y_1}{x_2 - x_1}, \quad s_2 = -\dfrac{1}{s_1} \\ s_1 = \dfrac{2-(-3)}{4-1} = \dfrac{5}{3}, \quad s_2 = \boxed{-\dfrac{3}{5}} \end{array}\right.$$

$$\left\{ \begin{array}{l} y - y_0 = s(x - x_0) \\ \text{The midpoint is on the perpendicular bisector.} \end{array} \right.$$

$$y + \frac{1}{2} = -\frac{3}{5}\left(x - \frac{5}{2}\right)$$

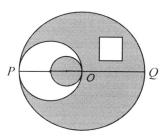

P · · · O · · · Q

Note: Figure above not drawn to scale.

9. In the figure above, the centers of 3 circles are all lie on diameter PQ of the greatest circle with center O, the radius of the smallest circle is 1, and the area the square is 1. The smallest circle touches centers of greatest and white circles. What is the area of the entire shaded portion?

(A) $13\pi - 1$

(B) $13\pi - 4$

(C) $11\pi - 1$

(D) $11\pi + 4$

Solution: Answer: (A)

$$\left\{\begin{array}{l} r_{\text{Small}} = r_s \\ r_{\text{Middle}} = 2r_s \\ r_{\text{Large}} = 4r_s \end{array}\right.$$

$$\downarrow$$

$$(4r_s)^2 \pi + r_s^2 \pi - (2r_s)^2 \pi - 1$$

$$\downarrow$$

$$16r_s^2 \pi + r_s^2 \pi - 4r_s^2 \pi - 1$$

$$\downarrow$$

$$\left\{\begin{array}{l} 13r_s^2 \pi - 1 \\ r_s = 1 \end{array}\right.$$

$$\Downarrow$$

$$13\pi - 1$$

NEXT PAGE ⟹

10. A rectangular garden is twice as its length as its width. If its length is decreased by 3 meters and its width is increased by 1 meter. The new garden formed has an area of 33 square meters. Which of the following is the area, in square meters, of the original garden?

(A) 27

(B) $\dfrac{81}{2}$

(C) $\dfrac{85}{2}$

(D) 42

Solution: Answer: (B)

$$(2w-3)(w+1)=33$$

$$2w^2 + 2w - 3w - 3 = 33$$

$$2w^2 - w - 36 = 0, \quad (2w-9)(w+4)=0$$

$$2w - 9 = 0, \rightarrow w = \boxed{\dfrac{9}{2}}$$

$$w + 4 = 0, \quad \rightarrow \quad w = -4$$

It doesn't exist in the real life.

$$\Downarrow$$

$$2w = \not{2} \cdot \dfrac{9}{\not{2}} = \boxed{9}, \quad A = 9 \times \dfrac{9}{2} = \boxed{\dfrac{81}{2}}$$

11. If $x^2 + y^2 = (x+y)^2$, then x must be equal to

(A) It cannot be determined from the information given.
(B) -1
(C) -y
(D) y

Solution: Answer: (A)

$$x^2 + y^2 = (x+y)^2$$
$$\downarrow$$
$$x^2 + y^2 = x^2 + \underline{2xy} + y^2$$
$$\downarrow$$
$$2xy = 0$$
$$\downarrow$$
$$x = 0 \text{ and/or } y = 0$$
$$\Downarrow$$

(A) It cannot be determined from the information given.

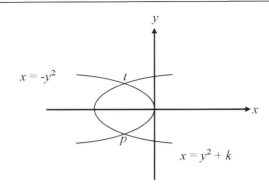

$x = -y^2$

$x = y^2 + k$

12. The figure above shows the graph $x = -y^2$ and $x = y^2 + k$. k is a certain constant. p and t separately represent the intersecting points of the 2 graphs in the xy-plane. If the length of the distance between t and p is 8, what is the value of k?

(A) -32
(B) 72
(C) 32
(D) 37

Solution: Answer: (A)

(1) At the intersection points

$$x = x$$

$$-y^2 = y^2 + k$$

(2) $tp = 8 \rightarrow x = \pm 4$

$$\downarrow$$

$$-(\pm 4)^2 = (\pm 4)^2 + k$$

$$\Downarrow$$

$$k = -32$$

NEXT PAGE

13. If $f(x) = -x^2 - 3x + 5$, then which of the following does $\dfrac{f(x-t) - f(x)}{t}$ equal?

(A) $2x - t + 3$

(B) $2x + t - 3$

(C) $2x - t - 3$

(D) $t - 2x + 3$

Solution: Answer: (A)

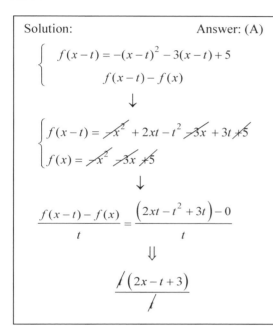

$$\begin{cases} f(x-t) = -(x-t)^2 - 3(x-t) + 5 \\ f(x-t) - f(x) \end{cases}$$

$$\downarrow$$

$$\begin{cases} f(x-t) = -x^2 + 2xt - t^2 - 3x + 3t + 5 \\ f(x) = -x^2 - 3x + 5 \end{cases}$$

$$\downarrow$$

$$\frac{f(x-t) - f(x)}{t} = \frac{\left(2xt - t^2 + 3t\right) - 0}{t}$$

$$\Downarrow$$

$$\frac{t\left(2x - t + 3\right)}{t}$$

---

14. For which of the following sets of numbers is the median greater than the average (arithmetic mean)?

(A) [1, 2, 3, 4, 4]
(B) [1, 2, 3, 4, 5]
(C) [2, 3, 4, 5, 6]
(D) [3, 4, 5, 6, 8]

Solution: Answer: (A)

If the number of total terms of consecutive integers is odd, its median equals its average.

$$\text{Median of } [1,\ 2,\ 3,\ 4,\ 5] = 3$$

$$\Downarrow$$

$$\text{Average of } [1,\ 2,\ 3,\ 4,\ 4] < 3$$

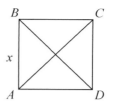

15. In the figure above, the 2 diagonals divide square *ABCD* into 4 triangles. Which of the following is the sum of the perimeters of those 4 triangles?

(A) $4x + 2\sqrt{2}x$
(B) $4x + 2x$
(C) $4x + 4x$
(D) $4(x + \sqrt{2}x)$

Solution: Answer: (D)

The diagonals of rhombus are perpendicular each other. Square is a special rhombus.

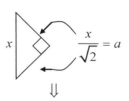

$$\frac{x}{\sqrt{2}} = a$$

$$\Downarrow$$

$$4(x + \frac{x}{\sqrt{2}} + \frac{x}{\sqrt{2}}) = 4(x + \sqrt{2}x)$$

NEXT PAGE

16. How many integers greater than 399 and less than 1,000 have exactly one digit 0 ?

(A) 162

(B) 108

(C) 144

(D) 128

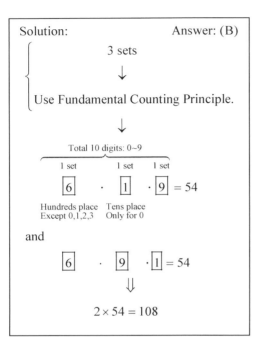

Solution: Answer: (B)

$\begin{cases} \quad\quad 3\ sets \\ \quad\quad\quad \downarrow \\ Use\ Fundamental\ Counting\ Principle. \end{cases}$

↓

Total 10 digits: 0~9

| 1 set | 1 set | 1 set |

$\boxed{6} \cdot \boxed{1} \cdot \boxed{9} = 54$

Hundreds place   Tens place
Except 0,1,2,3   Only for 0

and

$\boxed{6} \cdot \boxed{9} \cdot \boxed{1} = 54$

⇓

$2 \times 54 = 108$

17. If $j(x) = \sqrt{11 - x^2}$, what is the domain of j ?

(A) $-\sqrt{11} \geq x, \ x \geq \sqrt{11}$

(B) $-\sqrt{11} < x, \ x > \sqrt{11}$

(C) $-\sqrt{11} \leq x \leq \sqrt{11}$

(D) $x \geq -\sqrt{11}, \ \sqrt{11} \leq x$

Solution: Answer: (C)

$\begin{cases} \quad j(x) = \sqrt{11 - x^2} \\ \quad\quad\quad \downarrow \\ 11 - x^2 \geq 0, \quad 11 \geq x^2 \\ \quad\quad\quad \downarrow \\ \quad\quad x^2 \leq 11 \end{cases}$

$\sqrt{x^2} = |x|, \ |x| \leq \sqrt{11}$

⇓

$-\sqrt{11} \leq x \leq \sqrt{11}$

18. If a rectangular solid has length 10 centimeters, width 2 centimeters, and height 50 centimeters, then how many of the rectangular solids have a volume of four cubic meters when they are combined?

(A) 200

(B) 4,000

(C) 2,000

(D) 400

Solution: Answer: (B)

$\begin{cases} \quad\quad V = S_1 \cdot S_2 \cdot S_3 \\ 1\ meter = 100\ centimeters \end{cases}$

↓

$V = \dfrac{1\cancel{0}}{10\cancel{0}} \cdot \dfrac{2}{100} \cdot \dfrac{5\cancel{0}}{10\cancel{0}}$

↓

$\dfrac{1}{1000}$ cubic meter

⇓

$V = \dfrac{4}{\frac{1}{1000}} = \dfrac{4 \cdot 1000}{1} = 4000$

NEXT PAGE

19. Two balls that have distinct weights are droped from a height of 81 inches. If one of the two balls rebounds $\frac{2}{3}$ the height that has fallen, and another ball rebounds $\frac{1}{3}$ the height that has fallen, after they hit the same floor for the fourth time, which of the following is the sum S, in inches, of measures of altitudes, between the floor and highest point that the balls can reach, respectively, of the two balls ?

(A) 15

(B) 16

(C) 17

(D) 18

Solution: Answer: (C)

1st hit 2nd hit 3rd hit 4th hit

"$\frac{2}{3}$ or $\frac{1}{3}$ the height that has fallen"

↓

Use exponential function. $f(x) = a_o r^x$

↓

(1). $f(4) = 81 \cdot \left(\frac{2}{3}\right)^4 = \cancel{81} \cdot \frac{2^4}{\cancel{3^4}} = 16$

(2). $f(4) = 81 \cdot \left(\frac{1}{3}\right)^4 = \cancel{81} \cdot \frac{1^4}{\cancel{3^4}} = 1$

⇓

$S = 16 + 1 = 17$

Note: Figure below not drawn to scale.

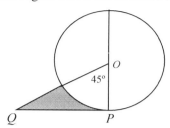

20. In the figure above, the center of the circle with a radius of 1 is at O and segment $\overline{PQ}$ is tangent to the circle at point P. What is the area of the shaded portion?

(A) $\frac{\sqrt{3}}{6} - \frac{\pi}{12}$

(B) $\frac{1}{2} - \frac{\pi}{4}$

(C) $\frac{\pi}{8} - \frac{1}{2}$

(D) $\frac{1}{2} - \frac{\pi}{8}$

Solution: Answer: (D)

$\begin{cases} 45°\text{-Right Triangle} \\ \quad\quad\downarrow \\ \quad PQ = 1 \end{cases} \rightarrow A_{triangle} = \frac{1 \cdot 1}{2} = \frac{1}{2}$

$A_{sector} = \frac{1}{2} r^2 \theta^r = \frac{1}{2} \cdot 1^2 \cdot 45 \cdot \frac{\pi}{180} = \frac{\pi}{8}$

⇓

$A_{shaded} = A_{triangle} - A_{sector} = \frac{1}{2} - \frac{\pi}{8}$

NEXT PAGE

21. Which of the following is not the equation of a function?

(A) $y = 0$

(B) $y = |x|$

(C) $y = x^2$

(D) $|y| = x$

Solution: Answer: (D)

If an equation is not a function, then one value of x has more than one value of y.

$$|y| = x$$

$\downarrow$

(1). $y = x$

(2). $y = -x$

$\downarrow$

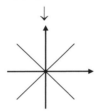

On the curve above, when $x = a$,

a has two values of y cooresponding a.

$\downarrow$

$|y| = x$ is not a function.

$\Downarrow$

Answer is (D).

22. If $x^2 > x^3$ and $x > 0$, what is one possible value for x?

(A) $\dfrac{3}{2}$

(B) $\dfrac{1}{2}$

(C) $1\dfrac{1}{5}$

(D) $-\dfrac{1}{2}$

Solution: Answer: (B)

$$x^2 > x^3 \text{ and } x > 0$$

$\downarrow$

$$0 < x < 1$$

$\Downarrow$

$$x = \frac{1}{2}$$

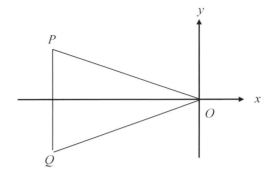

23. In the xy-coordinate plane above, points P, O, and Q are the 3 vertices of a certain triangle. The coordinates of P are $(-7, w)$ and the coordinates of Q are $(-7, -w)$, where w is a number greater than zero. Which of the following is one possible value of w if the area of triangle POQ is less than 6 and greater than 5 ?

(A) $\dfrac{6}{7}$

(B) $\dfrac{9}{14}$

(C) $\dfrac{11}{14}$

(D) $\dfrac{13}{14}$

Solution: Answer: (C)

It is an isosceles triangle of base $2w$ and height 7.

$\downarrow$

$$A = \frac{base \cdot height}{2}, \quad 5 < \frac{2w \cdot 7}{2} < 6$$

$\Downarrow$

$$\frac{5}{7} < w < \frac{6}{7}, \quad \frac{10}{14} < w < \frac{12}{14}$$

NEXT PAGE

24. If a_1, a_2, and a_3 are numbers such that $\dfrac{a_1}{a_2} = 2$ and $\dfrac{a_2}{a_3} = 3$, then $\dfrac{a_1 - a_2}{a_2 + a_3}$ equals

(A) $\dfrac{4}{3}$

(B) $\dfrac{2}{5}$

(C) $\dfrac{5}{2}$

(D) $\dfrac{3}{4}$

Solution: Answer: (D)

Let the top and bottom of the expression only keep one and the same unknown.

$$\begin{cases} \dfrac{a_1}{a_2} = 2 \;\rightarrow\; a_1 = 2a_2 \\[2mm] \dfrac{a_2}{a_3} = 3 \;\rightarrow\; a_3 = \dfrac{a_2}{3} \end{cases}$$

$$\Downarrow$$

$$\dfrac{a_1 - a_2}{a_2 + a_3} = \dfrac{2a_2 - a_2}{a_2 + \dfrac{a_2}{3}}, \quad \dfrac{\cancel{a_2}}{4\,\dfrac{\cancel{a_2}}{3}} = \boxed{\dfrac{3}{4}}$$

Questions 25 and 26 refer to following figure.

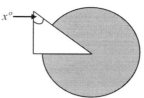

Note: Figure above not drawn to scale.

25. The circle and right triangle are shown above. The circle has a diameter of length 12. If the area of the shaded portion is 30π, what is the value of x?

(A) 20
(B) 30
(C) 36
(D) 60

Solution: Answer: (B)

$D = 12$, $r = 6$, $\quad A_{\text{entire}} = r^2 \pi = 36\pi$

$$\begin{cases} \text{Arc} \\ \text{Degree} \\ \text{Area} \end{cases} \boxed{\begin{array}{l} \text{Obtain the circle ratio from} \\ \text{area to be used for degree.} \end{array}}$$

$$\text{Ratio} = 1 - \dfrac{30\pi}{36\pi} = 1 - \dfrac{5}{6} = \dfrac{1}{6}$$

$$\dfrac{1}{6} \times 360^\circ = 60$$

$$\Downarrow$$

$$x = 90 - 60 = 30$$

26. The circle and right triangle are shown above. The circle has a radius of length 8. If the arc of the shaded portion is 14π, what is the value of x?

(A) 20
(B) 30
(C) 45
(D) 60

Solution: Answer: (C)

$$C = 2r\pi = 2 \cdot 8\pi = 16\pi$$

$$\begin{cases} \text{Arc} \\ \text{Degree} \\ \text{Area} \end{cases} \boxed{\begin{array}{l} \text{Obtain a ratio from arc} \\ \text{to be used for degree.} \end{array}}$$

$$\text{Ratio} = \dfrac{14\pi}{16\pi} = \dfrac{7}{8}, \quad 1 - \dfrac{7}{8} = \dfrac{1}{8}$$

$$\dfrac{1}{8} \times 360^\circ = 45$$

$$\Downarrow$$

$$x = 90 - 45 = 45$$

NEXT PAGE ⟹

27. The distance D, in yards, of a certain vehicle from a stop sign is given by the function $D(T) = 18T^{\frac{4}{3}}$, where T is the time in seconds. Which of the following is the average speed, in yards per second, of the vehicle from $T_1 = 8$ to $T_2 = 27$ seconds, to the closest whole number?

(A) 62

(B) 64

(C) 32

(D) 124

Solution: Answer: (A)

$$\frac{\text{Change of distance}}{\text{Change of time}}$$

$$\frac{D(T_2) - D(T_1)}{T_2 - T_1} = \frac{18 \cdot 27^{\frac{4}{3}} - 18 \cdot 8^{\frac{4}{3}}}{27 - 8}$$

$$\downarrow$$

$$\frac{18 \cdot \left(\sqrt[3]{27}\right)^4 - 18\left(\sqrt[3]{8}\right)^4}{19} = \frac{18\left(3^4 - 2^4\right)}{19}$$

$$\Downarrow$$

$$\frac{18(81 - 16)}{19} = \frac{18 \times 65}{19} = 62$$

28. What is the greatest integer g for which the equation $x^2 + 7x + g = 0$ has real solutions?

(A) ± 13

(B) 12

(C) ± 11

(D) 13

Solution: Answer: (B)

$x^2 + 7x + g = 0$, $a = 1$, $b = 7$

When $b^2 - 4ac > 0$, the equation has 2 real solutions.

$$\downarrow$$

$$7^2 - 4 \cdot 1g > 0$$

$$49 - 4g > 0, \ 49 > 4g$$

$$\downarrow$$

$$\frac{49}{4} > g, \ 12\frac{1}{4} > g \text{ or } g < 12\frac{1}{4}$$

$$\Downarrow$$

$$g = 12$$

29. If $f(x) = (2x + 3)(x + 7)$, which of the following is the possible sketch for the function f ?

(A)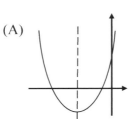

(B)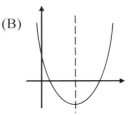

(C)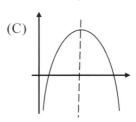

(D)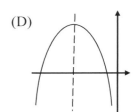

Solution: Answer: (A)

Use factored form (intercept form),

$$f(x) = a\left(x - x_1\right)\left(x - x_2\right)$$

$$f(x) = 2\left(x + \frac{3}{2}\right)\left(x + 7\right)$$

$$\begin{cases} a = 2 > 0 \ \rightarrow \ \text{Open up} \\ \\ x\text{-intercepts: } x_1 = -\frac{3}{2} \text{ and } x_2 = -7 \\ \\ \underbrace{x = \frac{x_1 + x_2}{2} = \frac{-1.5 - 7}{2} = -4.25}_{\text{equation of symmetric axis}} \end{cases}$$

$$\Downarrow$$

Answer is (A).

30. If Q, R, and S are positive integers greater than 1, where $Q \le R \le S$ and $Q + R + S < 107$, what is the greatest possible value for the median of these three integers?

(A) 51

(B) 53

(C) 52

(D) 50

Solution: Answer: (C)

$$\begin{cases} (1). \text{ "greater than 1"} \ \rightarrow \ \text{Can be 2.} \\ (2). \text{ If a median and all its following} \\ \text{integers have the same valu e, the} \\ \text{median is the greatest possible value.} \end{cases}$$

$$\Downarrow$$

$2 + 52 + 52 = 106$, The median $= 52$

NEXT PAGE

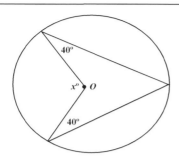

31. Point O is the center of the circle above. What is the value of x?

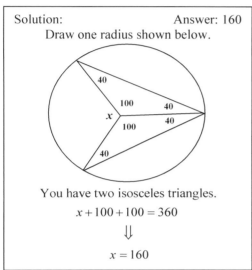

Solution: Answer: 160

Draw one radius shown below.

You have two isosceles triangles.

$$x + 100 + 100 = 360$$
$$\Downarrow$$
$$x = 160$$

32. The average (arithmetic mean) of the exam scores of a class of r students is 75, and the average of the exam score of the class of s students is 91. When the scores of both classes are combined, the average score is 89. What is the value of $\dfrac{r}{s}$?

Solution: Answer: 1/7, .143 or .142

$$\frac{75r + 91s}{r + s} = 89$$
$$\downarrow$$
$$75r + 91s = 89(r + s)$$
$$\downarrow$$
$$89r - 75r = 91s - 89s$$
$$\Downarrow$$
$$\frac{r}{s} = \frac{2}{14} = \frac{1}{7}$$

Note: Figure below not drawn to scale.

33. In the figure above, $x < 30$ and $y = z + 3$. z is an integer. What is the least possible value of y?

Solution: Answer: 77

(1). $x + y + z = 180$

$$x + y + (y - 3) = 180$$
$$\downarrow$$
$$2y = 183 - x, \quad y = \frac{183 - x}{2}$$

(2). $x \uparrow, \quad y \downarrow$
$$\downarrow$$
$$x = 29$$
$$\uparrow$$
$$x < 30 \text{ given}$$
$$\Downarrow$$
$$y = \frac{183 - 29}{2}, \quad y = \boxed{77}$$

34. A process begins that if three fourths of the students in a class room leave at the end of every 15-minutes interval and at the end of 45 minutes the next to the last two students leave, how many students were in the room to start with?

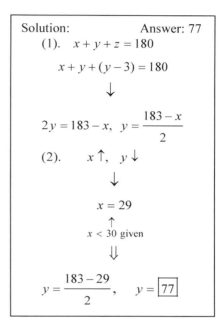

Solution: Answer: 128

Remaining: $x, \quad \dfrac{1}{4}x, \quad \dfrac{1}{4}\cdot\left(\dfrac{1}{4}x\right), \quad \dfrac{1}{4}\cdot\left(\dfrac{1}{4}\cdot\dfrac{1}{4}x\right)$

Minutes   0   15   30   45
$$\Downarrow$$
$$\frac{1}{4}\cdot\left(\frac{1}{4}\cdot\frac{1}{4}x\right) = 2, \quad x = 128$$

NEXT PAGE

35. Al horizontally cuts a wooden cube with volume 216 in half. The two halves are glued together to form a rectangular solid, which is not a cube. What is the surface area of this new solid?

37. If the six cards shown above are placed in a row so that

♥, ♦ and ♠ are never at either end, how many possible distinct combinations exist?

Solution: Answer: 252

$216 = s^3, \ s = 6$

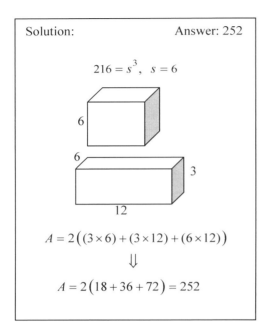

$A = 2\big((3 \times 6) + (3 \times 12) + (6 \times 12)\big)$

$\Downarrow$

$A = 2(18 + 36 + 72) = 252$

Solution: Answer: 144

One element set

$\downarrow$

Permutations or Combinations

The order does matter.

$\downarrow$

Permutations

(1) 4 cards between 2 end cards

4 positions, 4 elements

$\boxed{4} \times \boxed{3} \times \boxed{2} \times \boxed{1} = 24$

(2) 2 cards at either end

2 positions, 3 elements

$\boxed{3} \times \boxed{2} = 6$

(3) Use the fundamental counting principle.

$\Downarrow$

Total $= 24 \cdot 6 = 144$

36.   If $64 = 2^{x+2}$, then $x^2 =$

38. At a supermarket, $\dfrac{2}{7}$ of the items are discounted by 70 percent, $\dfrac{1}{7}$ of the items are discounted by 40 percent, $\dfrac{3}{7}$ of the items are discounted by 50 percent, and rest items are not discounted. If one item is to be selected randomly, wha is the probability that the item is discounted by 40 percent and 50 percent?

Solution: Answer: 16

$2^6 = 2^{x+2}$

$\downarrow$

$x + 2 = 6, \ x = 4$

$\Downarrow$

$x^2 = 16$

Solution: Answer: 3/49 or .061

"and" = "×"

$\Downarrow$

$\dfrac{1}{7} \times \dfrac{3}{7} = \dfrac{3}{49}$

STOP

SAT Math

Practice

Test 06

Redesigned for Tests in March 2016 and Beyond

Mad Math

Math Test – No Calculator

Time: 25 Minutes
20 Questions

Notes:
- The use of a calculator is not allowed.
- All numbers used in this section are the real number.
- Figures are provided for some problems in this test. Unless otherwise indicated under the figure "Note: Figure above not drawn to scale", all figures are drawn as accurately as possible.
- All figures lie in a plane EXCEPT otherwise specified.
- Unless otherwise indicated, the domain of any function f, g or j is assumed to be the set of all real numbers x for which $f(x)$, $g(x)$, or $j(x)$ is a real number.

Reference Information

$A = \dfrac{1}{2}bh$

$A = lw$

$A = \pi r^2$

$V = \pi r^2 h$

$V = lwh$

$c^2 = a^2 + b^2$

$V = \dfrac{1}{3}\pi r^2 h$

$V = \dfrac{4}{3}\pi r^3$

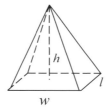

$V = \dfrac{1}{3}lwh$

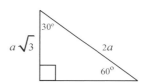

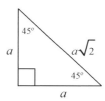

Copying or reuse of any portion of this page is illegal.

1. Cindy pays $R\%$ tax on merchandise at P dollars. How much does she pay for the taxes?

(A) $P \times \dfrac{R}{100}$

(B) $P + \dfrac{R}{100}$

(C) $\dfrac{R}{100}$

(D) $P + P \times R$

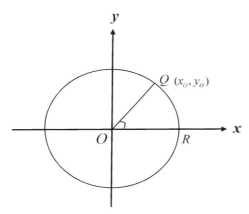

2. In the xy-plane above, O is the center of the circle, $(\sqrt{3}, \sqrt{3})$ is the point Q. If $\dfrac{\pi}{c}$ radians is the measure of the angle QOR, what is the value of c?

(A) 6
(B) 3
(C) $\sqrt{5}$
(D) 4

3. If a and b are positive even integers and $\sqrt{a} + \sqrt[3]{b} = 8$, what is one possible value of $a + b$?

(A) 222
(B) 80
(C) 136
(D) 46

4. Ray owns the shares of his company including $45,000 in cash and $30,000 in other holdings. If Ray redistributes his holdings in order to make 60 percent of the entire shares be in other holdings, how many dollars of cash must Ray change to other holdings?

(A) 1, 500
(B) 15, 000
(C) 30, 000
(D) 0.000

NEXT PAGE

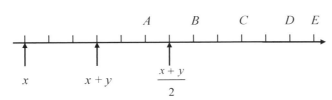

5. If on the number line above, the tick marks are equally spaced, which of the following lettered points represents y?

(A) C

(B) D

(C) B

(D) E

7. If $f(x) = (2x - 3)(x - 7)$, which of the following is the possible sketch for the function f?

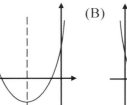

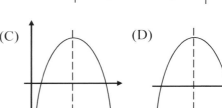

6. In the xy-plane, the distance between points $Q(k, 12)$ and point $P(3, 5)$ is $\sqrt{50}$. What is one possible value of k?

(A) -2
(B) -4
(C) 2
(D) 3

NEXT PAGE

8. If you take 4 less than a number x and then raise this result to the 5th power, the result equals 243. What is the value of x?

(A) -1

(B) 7

(C) 1

(D) 5

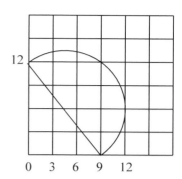

11. In the figure above, what is the area of the semicircle?

(A) $\dfrac{225\pi}{8}$

(B) $\dfrac{225\pi}{2}$

(C) 225π

(D) $\dfrac{5\pi}{2}$

9. If $f(x) = 2x^2 + 3$ and $g(x) = 2x^2 - 1$, what is the value of $\dfrac{f(-2) - g(2)}{f(2) - g(-2)}$?

(A) 2
(B) 1
(C) 3
(D) 5

10. If $x + y = 8$, $y + z = 16$, and $z + x = 18$, what is the average (arithmetic mean) of $x, y,$ and z ?

(A) 4
(B) 5
(C) 6
(D) 7

NEXT PAGE

12. If $f(x) = \sqrt{x^2 - 9}$, which of the following indicates the set of all values of x at which the function is not defined?

(A) $-3 < x < 3$

(B) $x < -3$

(C) $x > 3$

(D) $x > -3$

13. What is the 95th digit after the decimal point of the repeating decimal if the fraction $\dfrac{2}{26}$ is equal to the repeating decimal 0.0769230769230?

(A) 4
(B) 9
(C) 2
(D) 0

PRICES OF ITEMS

	Sofa	Tea Table
2005	$ 670	$105
2006	$ 850	$125
2007	$ 980	$135
2008	$ 990	$145

CAPACITY OF INVENTORY

	Warehouse		
	A	B	C
Sofas	42	93	40
Tea Tables	308	255	200

14. A furniture store sells one type of sofas and tea tables. The chart on the left above shows the prices of the sofas and tea tables in four years. The chart on the right above shows the maximum number of sofas and tea tables that can be stocked in each of three warehouses, A, B, and C. According to the prices shown in the chart above, what was the maximum possible value of the inventory of the sofas and tea tables in warehouse B in 2005 ?

(A) 66,200

(B) 58,870

(C) 39,400

(D) 89,085

15. If $3^y = x$, which of the following equals $3x$ in terms of y?

(A) 3^{2+y}

(B) 3^{1+2y}

(C) 3^{1+y}

(D) 3^{2+2y}

16. Robot-1 and Robot-2 stand shoulder-to-shoulder on one line. Then each of them takes 15 steps in opposite direction away and stops. And then Robot-1 goes back, walks toward Robot-2 and reaches Robot-2 in 24 steps. The size of one of Robot-1's steps is how many times the size of one of Robot-2's steps?

Note: By the designers of the robots, all of Robot-1's steps are the same size and all of Robot-2's steps are the same size also.

17. The first and sixth terms of a geometric sequence are 2 and 2048. What is the value of the fourth term?

18. For all positive integers g and h, let g ℜ h be defined as the integer remainder when g is divided by h. What is the value of x if 37 ℜ $x = 12$?

19. The vertices of a triangle are (-3, -2), (3, 2), and (3, -2). The area of the triangle is

20. What is the least positive integer x for which $13x$ is the cube of an integer?

STOP

Math Test – Calculator

Time: 55 Minutes
38 Questions

Notes:
- The use of a calculator is not allowed.
- All numbers used in this section are the real number.
- Figures are provided for some problems in this test. Unless otherwise indicated under the figure "Note: Figure above not drawn to scale", all figures are drawn as accurately as possible.
- All figures lie in a plane EXCEPT otherwise specified.
- Unless otherwise indicated, the domain of any function f, g or j is assumed to be the set of all real numbers x for which $f(x)$, $g(x)$, or $j(x)$ is a real number.

Reference Information

$$A = \frac{1}{2}bh$$

$$A = lw$$

$$A = \pi r^2$$

$$V = \pi r^2 h$$

$$V = lwh$$

$$c^2 = a^2 + b^2$$

$$V = \frac{1}{3}\pi r^2 h$$

$$V = \frac{4}{3}\pi r^3$$

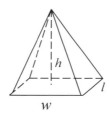

$$V = \frac{1}{3}lwh$$

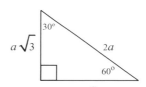

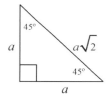

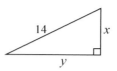

1. If $x^{-4} = 64$, then what is (are) the value(s) of x?

(A) $\dfrac{\sqrt{2}}{4}$

(B) $\pm\sqrt{2}$

(C) $\pm\dfrac{\sqrt{2}}{4}$

(D) $-\sqrt{2}$

Note: Figure below not drawn to scale.

3. Which of the following is true about the lengths x and y of the sides of the triangle above?

(A) $0 < (x + y)^2 \leq 196$

(B) $14 \leq (x + y)^2 < 40$

(C) $0 < (x + y)^2 < 196$

(D) $196 < (x + y)^2$

2. If $g(x) = \sqrt{x^2 - 11}$, what is the domain of g?

(A) $x \geq -\sqrt{11}, \ \sqrt{11} \geq x$

(B) $x \leq -\sqrt{11}, \ x \geq \sqrt{11}$

(C) $-\sqrt{11} < x, \ x > \sqrt{11}$

(D) $-\sqrt{11} \leq x \leq \sqrt{11}$

4. Jennifer's password consists of three two-digit numbers. The combination satisfies the 3 conditions below:

- One number is odd.
- One number is a multiple of 7.
- One number is day of month of Jennifer's brother's birthday.

Which of the following could be the combination to the password if every number satisfies exactly one of the conditions?

(A) 10-16-13
(B) 12-15-17
(C) 19-20-14
(D) 33-10-42

5. Pump-1 can fill up an oil tank in M hours. Pump-2 can fill up the same tank in N hours, how long would it take the two pumps working together to fill up the oil tank?

(A) $\dfrac{M - N}{N + M}$

(B) $\dfrac{MN}{N - M}$

(C) $\dfrac{MN}{M + N}$

(D) $\dfrac{MN}{M - N}$

6. In the xy-plan, if the lines with the equations $y = s_1 x - 5$ and $y = s_2 x + 3$ intersect to the quatrant IV, which of the following must be the relationship between s_1 and s_2 ?

(A) $s_1 \le s_2$

(B) $s_1 \ge s_2$

(C) $s_1 < s_2$

(D) $s_1 > s_2$

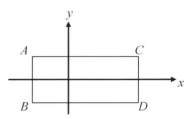

Note: Figure above not drawn to scale.

7. In the figure above, A, B, C, and D are the points of the vertices of a rectangle, where $A = (A1, A2)$, $B = (B1, B2)$, $C = (C1, C2)$, and $D = (D1, D2)$. What is the area of the rectangle?

(A) $(A1 + B1)(A2 + C2)$

(B) $(B1 + |D1|)(C2 + D2)$

(C) $(|A1| + C1)(A2 + |D2|)$

(D) $(C2 + D2)(B1 + D1)$

8. Tom bought a ticket for a concert, and then he changed his mind because he needed more time to prepare the SAT math subject test. Tom sold the ticket to Michael for $18, thus he lost 25%. What is the original price?

(A) 16

(B) 24

(C) 12

(D) 14

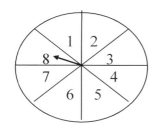

Note: Figure above not drawn to scale.

9. In the figure above, Stephanie spins the arrow twice. The fraction *m/n* is formed, where *m* is the number of the sector where the arrow stops after the first spin and *n* is the number of the sector where the arrow stops after the second spin. On every spin, if each of the numbered sectors has an equal chance that the arrow stops on the sector, what is the probability that the distinct fraction *m/n* is less than 1/2?

(A) $\dfrac{17}{64}$

(B) $\dfrac{5}{32}$

(C) $\dfrac{19}{64}$

(D) $\dfrac{5}{64}$

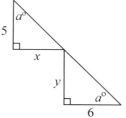

Note: Figure above not drawn to scale.

10. In the figure above, what is the value of $\dfrac{y}{x}$?

(A) $\dfrac{5}{6}$

(B) 30

(C) $\dfrac{6}{5}$

(D) 1

11. If Jackson bought *u* notebooks for *v* dollars each, and Jennifer bought *v* notebooks for *u* dollars each, what is the average price, in dollars, per notebook for all the notebooks that the two people bought?

(A) $\dfrac{2uv}{u + v}$

(B) $\dfrac{2(u + v)}{u + v}$

(C) $\dfrac{2u + v}{u + v}$

(D) $\dfrac{u + 2v}{u + v}$

NEXT PAGE ⇨

12.   For $y = 5x^2 + 3$, $h(x) = 0$, $g(x) = x + 3$, and j {(4, 2), (3, 2), (5, 1), (4, 1)},

(A) h is the only function
(B) g is the only function
(C) y, g, and h are all the functions.
(D) j and g are the only functions.

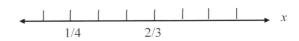

14. On the number line above, if the tick marks are equally spaced, what is the coordinate of midpoint point between 1/4 and 2/3 ?

(A) $\dfrac{5}{24}$

(B) $\dfrac{11}{24}$

(C) $\dfrac{6}{24}$

(D) $\dfrac{13}{24}$

13.   If a_1, a_2, and a_3 are numbers such that $\dfrac{a_1}{a_2} = 3$ and $\dfrac{a_2}{a_3} = 7$, then $\dfrac{a_1 + a_2}{a_2 - a_3}$ is equivalent to

(A) $\dfrac{14}{5}$

(B) $\dfrac{14}{3}$

(C) $\dfrac{3}{14}$

(D) 7

NEXT PAGE

15. In Container-1, there are 48 small balls that have only 2 colors, white and yellow. Among the 48 balls, there are 3 white balls for every 5 yellow balls. In Container-2, there are 3 white balls for every 2 yellow balls. If all the balls of the 2 containers are put into Container-3 that was empty, and then Container-3 has equal number of the white and yellow balls, how many balls were in Container-2 ?

(A) 50

(B) 60

(C) 70

(D) 80

16. An insect population is growing in such a way: number in each generation is approximately 3 times of the previous generation. If there are 300 insects in the first generation, approximately how many insects will there be in the third generation?

(A) 25,000

(B) 81,000

(C) 26,000

(D) 2,700

NEXT PAGE

17.   A 25-gallon mixture of ammonia and water contains two gallons of ammonia. If five more gallons of ammonia are added, what percent of the new mixture is ammonia?

(A) 33

(B) $33\dfrac{1}{3}$

(C) $23\dfrac{1}{3}$

(D) $66\dfrac{2}{3}$

18.   After $\dfrac{x^2-1}{x^2+2x-3}$ is simplified, what is the resulting form and for which of the following values of x is

$\dfrac{x^2-1}{x^2+2x-3}$ undefined?

(A) $\dfrac{x+3}{x+1}$, 3 and -1

(B) $\dfrac{x+1}{x+3}$, -3 and 1

(C) $\dfrac{x+1}{x+3}$, 3 and -1

(D) $\dfrac{x+1}{x+3}$, -1

19.   How many integers greater than or equal to 200 and less than 1,000 have exactly one digit 1 ?

(A) 162

(B) 128

(C) 144

(D) 142

20.   Which of the following is a simplified form of $\dfrac{a^2-8a+12}{a^2-36}$?

(A) $\dfrac{a-2}{a-6}$

(B) $\dfrac{a-2}{a+6}$

(C) $\dfrac{a+2}{a+6}$

(D) $\dfrac{a+2}{a-6}$

NEXT PAGE

21. At Milton School, there are as many twice math club members as biology club members and three times as many biology members as chemistry members. No member can be enrolled in more than one of the three clubs. There are sixty members in the 3 clubs, how many members are in the chemistry club?

(A) 12
(B) 24
(C) 6
(D) 36

22. Each of the following is equal to $\sqrt{x^{2008}}$ except

(A) $x\sqrt{x^{2006}}$
(B) $x^{101}\sqrt{x^{1806}}$
(C) $x^{333}\sqrt{x^{1342}}$
(D) $x^{18}\sqrt{x^{1990}}$

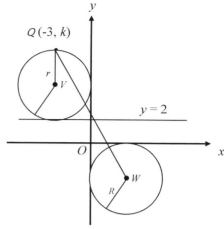

Note: Figure above not drawn to scale.

23. In the xy-plane above, points W and V are the centers of the identical circles, which are both tangent to the y-axis, one of them tangent to x-axis, and one tangent to line $y = 2$. What is the slope of $\overline{WQ}$?

(A) $-\dfrac{11}{6}$
(B) $\dfrac{11}{6}$
(C) 3
(D) -2

24. $f(x)$ is a linear function such that $f(6) = -7$, $f(10) = 2$, and $f(x) = 12.4$. What is the value of x?

(A) 41.6

(B) 55.1

(C) 33.2

(D) 14.6

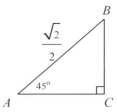

Note: Figure above not drawn to scale.

25.   In the figure above, what does the perimeter equal?

(A) $1 + \dfrac{\sqrt{2}}{2}$

(B) $2 + 2\sqrt{3}$

(C) 1

(D) $4\sqrt{3}$

26.   If the lines with the equations $y = s_1 x + 5$ and $y = s_2 x + 3$ intersect at quadrant II or III, which of the following must be the relationship between s_1 and s_2?

(A) $s_1 \leq s_2$

(B) $s_1 < s_2$

(C) $s_1 > s_2$

(D) $s_1 \geq s_2$

NEXT PAGE

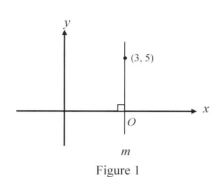

Figure 1

27. In Figure 1, the equation of line m is

(A) $y = 5$

(B) $x = 3$

(C) $y = 0$

(D) $y = 3$

28. $E = \sqrt[4]{\dfrac{1}{81}} = ?$

(A) $\dfrac{1}{3}$

(B) 9

(C) $\dfrac{1}{9}$

(D) 3

29. If x is a prime number greater than 8 and not more than 23, then $2x + 3$ may equal any of the following except

(A) 29
(B) 25
(C) 37
(D) 24

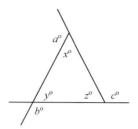

30. What is the value of $2(a + b + c)$ in the figure above?

(A) 180

(B) 360

(C) 720

(D) 380

31. A right triangle has one side of length $6\sqrt{2}$. If the lengths of the other two sides are equal, what is the area of the triangle?

Type	Number of Bells	Rings n Times on the nth hour	Rings once on the Hour	Rings Once on the Half Hour
X	9		√	√
Y	10	√		√

32. In the table of the bell information above, what is the total number of rings of bells in the 150-minute period from $6:25_{pm}$ to $8:55_{pm}$?

33. A list of numbers has been arranged such that each number in the list is 16 more than the number that precedes it. If number 398 is ninth number in the list, what is the third number in the list?

34. Stephanie is now five times as old as her brother Steve. After 2 years, Stephanie will be 3 times as old as Steve will be. How old was Stephanie five year ago?

NEXT PAGE

35. If the line $y = 3$ intersects the graph of the equation $y = x^2 - 3x - 25$, what is one possible x-coordinate of the intersection point of the two graphs?

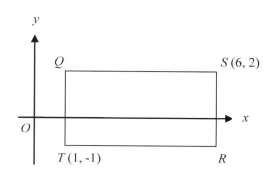

38. In the figure above, point $(a, 1)$ (not shown) is on the diagonal ST of rectangle $TQSR$. What is the value of a?

36. Eight cards in a pot are numbered 1 through 8. One card is drawn at random. The ones digit of the sum of the numbers on the remaining cards is 8. What is the number on the drawn card?

37. In class A, each of the 35 students contributed either a nickel or dime to the Child Foundation. If the total amount collected was $2.05, how many students contributed a nickel?

STOP

Answer Key
For
SAT Math Practice Test 06

Section 3

1	A
2	D
3	B
4	B
5	D
6	C
7	B
8	B
9	B
10	D
11	A
12	A
13	C
14	D
15	C

16	5/3 or 1.66 or 1.67
17	128
18	25
19	12
20	169

Section 4

1	C	16	D
2	B	17	C
3	D	18	B
4	D	19	C
5	C	20	B
6	D	21	C
7	C	22	D
8	B	23	A
9	B	24	D
10	C	25	A
11	A	26	C
12	C	27	B
13	B	28	A
14	B	29	D
15	B	30	C

31	18
32	225
33	302
34	5
35	7
36	8
37	29
38	13/3 or 4.33

SAT Math

Practice

Test 06

Explanations

Redesigned for Tests in March 2016 and Beyond

Mad Math

Math Test – No Calculator

Time: 25 Minutes
20 Questions

Notes:
- The use of a calculator is not allowed.
- All numbers used in this section are the real number.
- Figures are provided for some problems in this test. Unless otherwise indicated under the figure "Note: Figure above not drawn to scale", all figures are drawn as accurately as possible.
- All figures lie in a plane EXCEPT otherwise specified.
- Unless otherwise indicated, the domain of any function f, g or j is assumed to be the set of all real numbers x for which $f(x)$, $g(x)$, or $j(x)$ is a real number.

Reference Information

$$A = \frac{1}{2}bh$$

$$A = lw$$

$$A = \pi r^2$$

$$V = \pi r^2 h$$

$$V = lwh$$

$$c^2 = a^2 + b^2$$

$$V = \frac{1}{3}\pi r^2 h$$

$$V = \frac{4}{3}\pi r^3$$

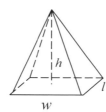

$$V = \frac{1}{3}lwh$$

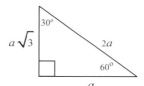

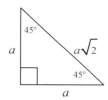

Copying or reuse of any portion of this page is illegal.

1. Cindy pays $R\%$ tax on merchandise at P dollars. How much does she pay for the taxes?

(A) $P \times \dfrac{R}{100}$

(B) $P + \dfrac{R}{100}$

(C) $\dfrac{R}{100}$

(D) $P + P \times R$

> Solution: Answer: (A)
>
> $$\% = \frac{1}{100}$$
>
> $$\Downarrow$$
>
> $$P \times \frac{R}{100}$$

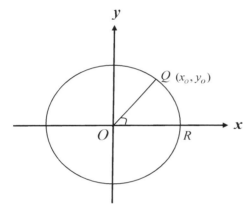

2. In the xy-plane above, O is the center of the circle, $(\sqrt{3}, \sqrt{3})$ is the point Q. If $\dfrac{\pi}{c}$ radians is the measure of the angle QOR, what is the value of c?

(A) 6

(B) 3

(C) $\sqrt{5}$

(D) 4

> Solution: Answer: (D)
>
>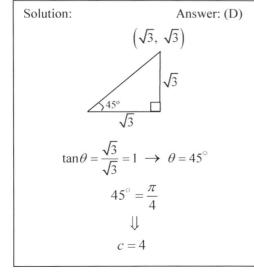
>
> $$\tan\theta = \frac{\sqrt{3}}{\sqrt{3}} = 1 \;\rightarrow\; \theta = 45^\circ$$
>
> $$45^\circ = \frac{\pi}{4}$$
>
> $$\Downarrow$$
>
> $$c = 4$$

3. If a and b are positive even integers and $\sqrt{a} + \sqrt[3]{b} = 8$, what is one possible value of $a + b$?

(A) 222

(B) 80

(C) 136

(D) 46

> Solution: Answer: (B)
>
> $$\begin{cases} \sqrt{a} + \sqrt[3]{b} = 8 \\ a \text{ and } b \text{ are positive even integers.} \end{cases}$$
>
> $$\downarrow$$
>
> $$\begin{cases} 2 + 6 = \sqrt{4} + \sqrt[3]{216} \\ 4 + 216 = 220 \\ 6 + 2 = \sqrt{36} + \sqrt[3]{8} \\ 36 + 8 = 44 \end{cases}$$
>
> or
>
> $$\begin{cases} 4 + 4 = \sqrt{16} + \sqrt[3]{64} \\ 16 + 64 = 80 \end{cases}$$
>
> $$\Downarrow$$
>
> $$a + b = 80$$

4. Ray owns the shares of his company including \$45,000 in cash and \$30,000 in other holdings. If Ray redistributes his holdings in order to make 60 percent of the entire shares be in other holdings, how many dollars of cash must Ray change to other holdings?

(A) 1,500

(B) 15,000

(C) 30,000

(D) 0.000

> Solution: Answer: (B)
>
> $$\frac{30 \cdot 10^3 + x \cdot 10^3}{45 \cdot 10^3 + 30 \cdot 10^3} = \frac{60}{100}$$
>
> $$\downarrow$$
>
> $$\frac{30 + x}{75} = \frac{3}{5}, \quad 30 + x = 45$$
>
> $$\Downarrow$$
>
> $$x = 15, \quad x = 15 \times \$1000$$

NEXT PAGE

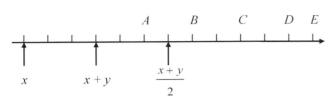

5. If on the number line above, the tick marks are equally spaced, which of the following lettered points represents y?

(A) C

(B) D

(C) B

(D) E

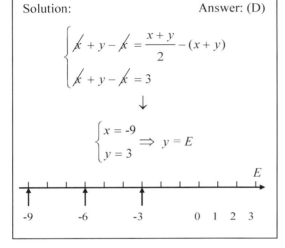

Solution: Answer: (D)

$$\begin{cases} \cancel{x} + y - \cancel{x} = \dfrac{x+y}{2} - (x+y) \\ \cancel{x} + y - \cancel{x} = 3 \end{cases}$$

$$\downarrow$$

$$\begin{cases} x = \text{-}9 \\ y = 3 \end{cases} \Rightarrow y = E$$

6. In the xy-plane, the distance between points $Q\,(k, 12)$ and point $P\,(3, 5)$ is $\sqrt{50}$. What is one possible value of k?

(A) -2
(B) -4
(C) 2
(D) 3

Solution: Answer: (C)

$$d^2 = (x_2 - x_1)^2 + (y_2 - y_1)^2$$

$$50 = (k - 3)^2 + (12 - 5)^2$$

$$0 = (k - 3)^2 - 1$$

$$\downarrow$$

$$(k - 3 - 1)(k - 3 + 1) = 0$$

$$\downarrow$$

$$(k - 4)(k - 2) = 0$$

$$\Downarrow$$

$$k = 2 \text{ or } k = 4$$

7. If $f(x) = (2x - 3)(x - 7)$, which of the following is the possible sketch for the function f ?

(A) 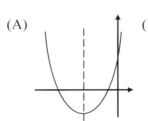   (B)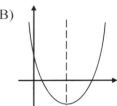

(C) 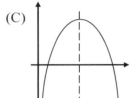   (D)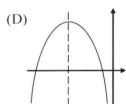

Solution: Answer: (B)

$$\begin{cases} \text{Target} \rightarrow \text{ factored form} \\ f(x) = a(x - x_1)(x - x_2) \end{cases}$$

$$f(x) = 2\left(x - \frac{3}{2}\right)(x - 7)$$

$$\downarrow$$

$$\begin{cases} a = 2 > 0 \rightarrow \text{ Open up} \\ x\text{-intercepts: } x_1 = \dfrac{3}{2} \text{ and } x_2 = 7 \end{cases}$$

$$\underbrace{x = \frac{x_1 + x_2}{2} = \frac{(1.5) + 7}{2} = 4.25}_{\text{equation of symmetric axis}}$$

$$\Downarrow$$

Answer is (B).

NEXT PAGE

8. If you take 4 less than a number x and then raise this result to the 5th power, the result equals 243. What is the value of x?

(A) -1

(B) 7

(C) 1

(D) 5

Solution:	Answer: (B)

$$x - 4, \qquad (x-4)^5 = 243$$

$$\downarrow$$

$$\left((x-4)^5\right)^{\frac{1}{5}} = \sqrt[5]{243}$$

$$\Downarrow$$

$$x - 4 = \sqrt[5]{3^5} = 3, \quad x = \boxed{7}$$

9. If $f(x) = 2x^2 + 3$ and $g(x) = 2x^2 - 1$, what is the value of $\dfrac{f(-2) - g(2)}{f(2) - g(-2)}$?

(A) 2

(B) 1

(C) 3

(D) 5

Solution:	Answer: (B)

$$\begin{cases} f(2) = 2 \times 2^2 + 3 = 11 \\ f(-2) = 2 \times (-2)^2 + 3 = 11 \end{cases}$$

$$\begin{cases} g(2) = 2 \times 2^2 - 1 = 7 \\ g(-2) = 2 \times (-2)^2 - 1 = 7 \end{cases}$$

$$\Downarrow$$

$$\frac{f(-2) - g(2)}{f(2) - g(-2)} = \frac{11 - 7}{11 - 7} = 1$$

10. If $x + y = 8$, $y + z = 16$, and $z + x = 18$, what is the average (arithmetic mean) of $x, y,$ and z?

(A) 4
(B) 5
(C) 6
(D) 7

Solution:	Answer: (D)

$$(x + y) + (y + z) + (z + x) = 8 + 16 + 18$$

$$\downarrow$$

$$2x + 2y + 2z = 42, \quad x + y + z = 21$$

$$\Downarrow$$

$$\text{Average} = \frac{21}{3} = 7$$

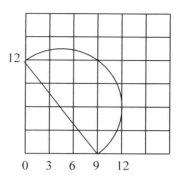

11. In the figure above, what is the area of the semicircle?

(A) $\dfrac{225\pi}{8}$

(B) $\dfrac{225\pi}{2}$

(C) 225π

(D) $\dfrac{5\pi}{2}$

Solution:	Answer: (A)

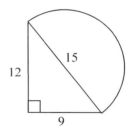

"Multiple" of 3-4-5 right triangle.

$$\text{Diameter} = 15, \quad \text{Radius} = \frac{15}{2}$$

$$A_{\text{semicircle}} = \frac{A_{\text{circle}}}{2}$$

$$\downarrow$$

$$A_{\text{semicircle}} = \frac{r^2 \pi}{2}$$

$$\Downarrow$$

$$\frac{\left(\frac{15}{2}\right)^2 \pi}{2} = \frac{225\pi}{8}$$

NEXT PAGE ⟩

12. If $f(x) = \sqrt{x^2 - 9}$, which of the following indicates the set of all values of x at which the function is not defined?

(A) $-3 < x < 3$

(B) $x < -3$

(C) $x > 3$

(D) $x > -3$

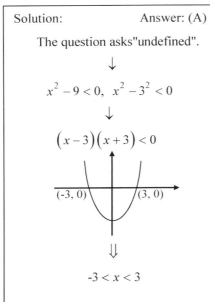

Solution: Answer: (A)

The question asks "undefined".

↓

$x^2 - 9 < 0, \quad x^2 - 3^2 < 0$

↓

$(x - 3)(x + 3) < 0$

(-3, 0)   (3, 0)

⇓

$-3 < x < 3$

13. What is the 95th digit after the decimal point of the repeating decimal if the fraction $\dfrac{2}{26}$ is equal to the repeating decimal 0.0769230769230?

(A) 4
(B) 9
(C) 2
(D) 0

Solution: Answer: (C)

Pattern = 076923
Number of pattern elements = 6

$$\frac{95}{6} = 15 + \frac{5}{6}$$

Remainder = 5 → at the fifth pattern position

⇓

95th digit = 2

PRICES OF ITEMS

	Sofa	Tea Table
2005	$ 670	$105
2006	$ 850	$125
2007	$ 980	$135
2008	$ 990	$145

CAPACITY OF INVENTORY

	Warehouse		
	A	B	C
Sofas	42	93	40
Tea Tables	308	255	200

14. A furniture store sells one type of sofas and tea tables. The chart on the left above shows the prices of the sofas and tea tables in four years. The chart on the right above shows the maximum number of sofas and tea tables that can be stocked in each of three warehouses, $A, B,$ and C. According to the prices shown in the chart above, what was the maximum possible value of the inventory of the sofas and tea tables in warehouse B in 2005 ?

(A) 66,200

(B) 58,870

(C) 39,400

(D) 89,085

Solution: Answer: (D)
$670 \times 93 + 105 \times 255$

⇓

$62310 + 26775 = 89085$

15. If $3^y = x$, which of the following equals $3x$ in terms of y?

(A) 3^{2+y}

(B) 3^{1+2y}

(C) 3^{1+y}

(D) 3^{2+2y}

Solution: Answer: (C)

$(3)^1 \cdot 3^y = x \cdot (3)$

⇓

$3x = 3^{1+y}$

NEXT PAGE ⇨

16. Robot-1 and Robot-2 stand shoulder-to-shoulder on one line. Then each of them takes 15 steps in opposite direction away and stops. And then Robot-1 goes back, walks toward Robot-2 and reaches Robot-2 in 24 steps. The size of one of Robot-1's steps is how many times the size of one of Robot-2's steps?

Note: By the designers of the robots, all of Robot-1's steps are the same size and all of Robot-2's steps are the same size also.

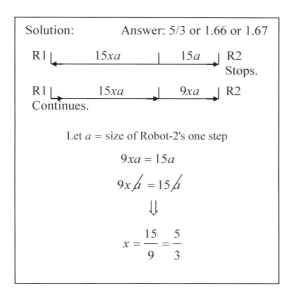

Solution: Answer: 5/3 or 1.66 or 1.67

R1 |⟵——— 15xa ———|—— 15a ——| R2
                                    Stops.

R1 |⟵——— 15xa ———|—— 9xa ——| R2
Continues.

Let a = size of Robot-2's one step

$$9xa = 15a$$

$$9x\cancel{a} = 15\cancel{a}$$

⟱

$$x = \frac{15}{9} = \frac{5}{3}$$

17. The first and sixth terms of a geometric sequence are 2 and 2048. What is the value of the fourth term?

Solution: Answer: 128

$$a_n = a_1 r^{n-1}$$

↓

$$2048 = 2 \cdot r^{6-1}$$

$$r^5 = 1024$$

$$r = \sqrt[5]{1024} = 4$$

$$a_4 = 2 \cdot 4^{4-1}$$

⟱

$$a_4 = 2 \cdot 4^3 = 2 \cdot 64 = 128$$

18. For all positive integers g and h, let $g \,\boxed{\Re}\, h$ be defined as the integer remainder when g is divided by h. What is the value of x if $37 \,\boxed{\Re}\, x = 12$?

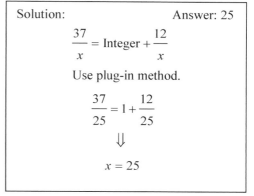

Solution: Answer: 25

$$\frac{37}{x} = \text{Integer} + \frac{12}{x}$$

Use plug-in method.

$$\frac{37}{25} = 1 + \frac{12}{25}$$

⟱

$$x = 25$$

19. The vertices of a triangle are (-3, -2), (3, 2), and (3, -2). The area of the triangle is

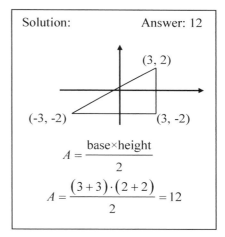

Solution: Answer: 12

$$A = \frac{\text{base} \times \text{height}}{2}$$

$$A = \frac{(3+3) \cdot (2+2)}{2} = 12$$

20. What is the least positive integer x for which $13x$ is the cube of an integer?

Solution: Answer: 169

$$13x = I^3, \quad x = \frac{I^3}{13}$$

13 is a prime number

↓

It is divisible by 1 and itself.

⟱

$$x = \frac{I^3}{13} = \frac{13^3}{13} = 13^2 = 169 = \text{integer}$$

STOP

4 ♪ ♪ ♪ ♪   ♪ ♪ ♪ ♪ **4**

Math Test – Calculator

Time: 55 Minutes
38 Questions

Notes:

- The use of a calculator is not allowed.
- All numbers used in this section are the real number.
- Figures are provided for some problems in this test. Unless otherwise indicated under the figure "Note: Figure above not drawn to scale", all figures are drawn as accurately as possible.
- All figures lie in a plane EXCEPT otherwise specified.
- Unless otherwise indicated, the domain of any function f, g or j is assumed to be the set of all real numbers x for which $f(x)$, $g(x)$, or $j(x)$ is a real number.

Reference Information

$$A = \frac{1}{2}bh$$

$$A = lw$$

$$A = \pi r^2$$

$$V = \pi r^2 h$$

$$V = lwh$$

$$c^2 = a^2 + b^2$$

$$V = \frac{1}{3}\pi r^2 h$$

$$V = \frac{4}{3}\pi r^3$$

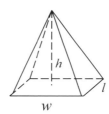

$$V = \frac{1}{3}lwh$$

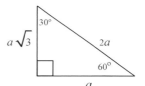

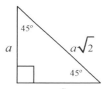

1. If $x^{-4} = 64$, then what is (are) the value(s) of x?

(A) $\dfrac{\sqrt{2}}{4}$

(B) $\pm\sqrt{2}$

(C) $\pm\dfrac{\sqrt{2}}{4}$

(D) $-\sqrt{2}$

Solution: Answer: (C)

$$\frac{1}{x^4} = 64 \ \rightarrow \ x^4 = \frac{1}{64}$$

$$x = \pm\left(\frac{1}{64}\right)^{\frac{1}{4}} = \pm\left(\left(\frac{1}{64}\right)^{\frac{1}{2}}\right)^{\frac{1}{2}}$$

$$\pm\left(\frac{1}{8}\right)^{\frac{1}{2}} = \pm\frac{1}{\sqrt{8}} = \pm\frac{1}{\sqrt{4\cdot 2}}$$

$$\pm\frac{1}{2\sqrt{2}} = \pm\frac{1}{2}\cdot\frac{1}{\sqrt{2}} = \pm\frac{1}{2}\cdot\frac{\sqrt{2}}{2} \Rightarrow x = \pm\frac{\sqrt{2}}{4}$$

2. If $g(x) = \sqrt{x^2 - 11}$, what is the domain of g?

(A) $x \geq -\sqrt{11}, \ \sqrt{11} \geq x$

(B) $x \leq -\sqrt{11}, \ x \geq \sqrt{11}$

(C) $-\sqrt{11} < x, \ x > \sqrt{11}$

(D) $-\sqrt{11} \leq x \leq \sqrt{11}$

Solution: Answer: (B)

$$\begin{cases} x^2 - 11 \geq 0, \ x^2 - \left(\sqrt{11}\right)^2 \geq 0 \\ \left(x - \sqrt{11}\right)\left(x + \sqrt{11}\right) \geq 0 \end{cases}$$

Consider $\left(x - \sqrt{11}\right)\left(x + \sqrt{11}\right) = 0$ first.

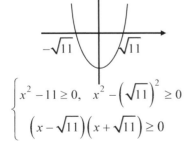

$$\begin{cases} x^2 - 11 \geq 0, \ x^2 - \left(\sqrt{11}\right)^2 \geq 0 \\ \left(x - \sqrt{11}\right)\left(x + \sqrt{11}\right) \geq 0 \end{cases}$$

Then consider $\left(x - \sqrt{11}\right)\left(x + \sqrt{11}\right) \geq 0$.

$$\Downarrow$$

$$x \leq -\sqrt{11}, \qquad x \geq \sqrt{11}$$

Note: Figure below not drawn to scale.

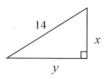

3. Which of the following is true about the lengths x and y of the sides of the triangle above?

(A) $0 < (x+y)^2 \leq 196$

(B) $14 \leq (x+y)^2 < 40$

(C) $0 < (x+y)^2 < 196$

(D) $196 < (x+y)^2$

Solution: Answer: (D)

$$s_1 + s_2 > s_3$$
$$\downarrow$$
$$x + y > 14$$
$$(x+y)^2 > 14^2$$
$$\Downarrow$$
$$196 < (x+y)^2$$

4. Jennifer's password consists of three two-digit numbers. The combination satisfies the 3 conditions below:

- One number is odd.
- One number is a multiple of 7.
- One number is day of month of Jennifer's brother's birthday.

Which of the following could be the combination to the password if every number satisfies exactly one of the conditions?

(A) 10-16-13
(B) 12-15-17
(C) 19-20-14
(D) 33-10-42

Solution: Answer: (D)
(A) No any number can be a multiple of 7.
(B) Two numbers are odd.
(C) 14, 19 or 20 may be a day in a month.
(D) Only number 33 is odd. Only number 10 can be a day of a month. Only number 42 is a multiple of 7.

NEXT PAGE

5. Pump-1 can fill up an oil tank in M hours. Pump-2 can fill up the same tank in N hours, how long would it take the two pumps working together to fill up the oil tank?

(A) $\dfrac{M-N}{N+M}$

(B) $\dfrac{MN}{N-M}$

(C) $\dfrac{MN}{M+N}$

(D) $\dfrac{MN}{M-N}$

Solution:　　　　Answer: (C)

$$T = \frac{W}{R_{a1} + R_{a1}}$$

↓

$$T = \frac{W}{\dfrac{W}{t_{a1}} + \dfrac{W}{t_{a2}}}$$

↓

$$T = \frac{W}{\dfrac{W}{M} + \dfrac{W}{N}} = \frac{\cancel{W}}{\cancel{W}\left(\dfrac{1}{M} + \dfrac{1}{N}\right)}$$

⇓

$$T = \frac{1}{\dfrac{N+M}{MN}} = \frac{MN}{N+M}$$

6. In the xy-plan, if the lines with the equations $y = s_1 x - 5$ and $y = s_2 x + 3$ intersect to the quatrant IV, which of the following must be the relationship between s_1 and s_2 ?

(A) $s_1 \le s_2$

(B) $s_1 \ge s_2$

(C) $s_1 < s_2$

(D) $s_1 > s_2$

Solution:　　　　Answer: (D)

$$y = s_1 x - 5 \text{ and } y = s_2 x + 3$$

intersect

↓

$$s_1 x - 5 = s_2 x + 3$$

$$s_1 x - s_2 x = 8$$

$$x\left(s_1 - s_2\right) = 8, \ s_1 - s_2 = \frac{8}{x}$$

Intersection point at the quatrant IV

↓

$$x > 0$$

⇓

$$\frac{8}{x} > 0, \ s_1 - s_2 > 0, \ \boxed{s_1 > s_2}$$

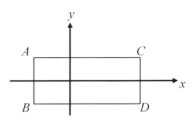

Note: Figure above not drawn to scale.

7. In the figure above, A, B, C, and D are the points of the vertices of a rectangle, where $A = (A1, A2)$, $B = (B1, B2)$, $C = (C1, C2)$, and $D = (D1, D2)$. What is the area of the rectangle?

(A) $(A1 + B1)(A2 + C2)$

(B) $(B1 + |D1|)(C2 + D2)$

(C) $(|A1| + C1)(A2 + |D2|)$

(D) $(C2 + D2)(B1 + D1)$

Solution:　　　　Answer: (C)

$$\text{Area} = A = \text{Length} \cdot \text{Width}$$

$$|A1| + C2 = \text{Width}$$

$$A2 + |D2| = \text{Length}$$

⇓

$$A = (|A1| + C2)(A2 + |D2|)$$

8. Tom bought a ticket for a concert, and then he changed his mind because he needed more time to prepare the SAT math subject test. Tom sold the ticket to Michael for $18, thus he lost 25%. What is the original price?

(A) 16

(B) 24

(C) 12

(D) 14

Solution:　　　　Answer: (B)

$$18 = 0.75x$$

↓

$$\frac{18}{\dfrac{75}{100}} = x$$

⇓

$$x = \frac{1800}{75} = 24$$

NEXT PAGE

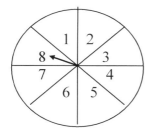

Note: Figure above not drawn to scale.

9. In the figure above, Stephanie spins the arrow twice. The fraction m/n is formed, where m is the number of the sector where the arrow stops after the first spin and n is the number of the sector where the arrow stops after the second spin. On every spin, if each of the numbered sectors has an equal chance that the arrow stops on the sector, what is the probability that the distinct fraction m/n is less than 1/2?

(A) $\dfrac{17}{64}$

(B) $\dfrac{5}{32}$

(C) $\dfrac{19}{64}$

(D) $\dfrac{5}{64}$

Solution: Answer: (B)

(1)   2 element sets

Use Fundamental Counting Principle.

$$8 \times 8 = 64$$

(2) $\dfrac{m}{n} < \dfrac{1}{2}$

$$\begin{vmatrix} \dfrac{1}{3}, \dfrac{1}{4}, \dfrac{1}{5}, \dfrac{1}{6}, \dfrac{1}{7}, \dfrac{1}{8} \\ \dfrac{2}{5}, \left(\dfrac{2}{6} = \dfrac{1}{3}\right), \dfrac{2}{7}, \left(\dfrac{2}{8} = \dfrac{1}{4}\right) \\ \dfrac{3}{7}, \dfrac{3}{8} \end{vmatrix}$$

↓

The total posssibilities = 10

⇓

(3) $P_{\text{fraction } \frac{m}{n} < \frac{1}{2}} = \dfrac{10}{64} = \dfrac{5}{32}$

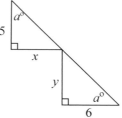

Note: Figure above not drawn to scale.

10.   In the figure above, what is the value of $\dfrac{y}{x}$?

(A) $\dfrac{5}{6}$

(B) 30

(C) $\dfrac{6}{5}$

(D) 1

Solution: Answer: (C)

The 2 triangles are similar triangles.

↓

The ratios of the corresponding sides are equal.

⇓

$$\dfrac{y}{x} = \dfrac{6}{5}$$

11. If Jackson bought u notebooks for v dollars each, and Jennifer bought v notebooks for u dollars each, what is the average price, in dollars, per notebook for all the notebooks that the two people bought?

(A) $\dfrac{2uv}{u+v}$

(B) $\dfrac{2(u+v)}{u+v}$

(C) $\dfrac{2u+v}{u+v}$

(D) $\dfrac{u+2v}{u+v}$

Solution: Answer: (A)

$$\dfrac{uv + vu}{u+v} = \dfrac{uv + uv}{u+v}$$

⇓

$$\dfrac{2uv}{u+v}$$

NEXT PAGE

12. For $y = 5x^2 + 3$, $h(x) = 0$, $g(x) = x + 3$, and $j\ \{(4, 2), (3, 2), (5, 1), (4, 1)\}$,

(A) h is the only function
(B) g is the only function
(C) y, g, and h are all the functions.
(D) j and g are the only functions.

> Solution: Answer: (C)
>
> j has points (4, 2) and (4, 1).
>
> ↓
>
> One value of x in j has 2 values of y corresponding x.
>
> ↓
>
> j is not a function.
>
> ⇓
>
> Answer is (C).

13. If a_1, a_2, and a_3 are numbers such that $\dfrac{a_1}{a_2} = 3$ and $\dfrac{a_2}{a_3} = 7$, then $\dfrac{a_1 + a_2}{a_2 - a_3}$ is equivalent to

(A) $\dfrac{14}{5}$

(B) $\dfrac{14}{3}$

(C) $\dfrac{3}{14}$

(D) 7

> Solution: Answer: (B)
> Let the top and bottom of the expression only keep one and the same unknown.
>
> $\begin{cases} \dfrac{a_1}{a_2} = 3 \ \rightarrow \ a_1 = 3a_2 \\[2mm] \dfrac{a_2}{a_3} = 7 \ \rightarrow \ a_3 = \dfrac{a_2}{7} \end{cases}$
>
> ↓
>
> $\dfrac{a_1 + a_2}{a_2 - a_3} = \dfrac{3a_2 + a_2}{a_2 - \dfrac{a_2}{7}}$
>
> ⇓
>
> $\dfrac{4\,\cancel{a_2}}{6\,\cancel{a_2}} = \dfrac{\cancel{4}^{\,2} \times 7}{\cancel{6}^{\,3}} = \dfrac{14}{3}$

14. On the number line above, if the tick marks are equally spaced, what is the coordinate of midpoint point between 1/4 and 2/3 ?

(A) $\dfrac{5}{24}$

(B) $\dfrac{11}{24}$

(C) $\dfrac{6}{24}$

(D) $\dfrac{13}{24}$

> Solution: Answer: (B)
>
> $\dfrac{\text{Distance}}{2} = \dfrac{\dfrac{2}{3} - \dfrac{1}{4}}{2} = \dfrac{\dfrac{8 - 3}{12}}{2} = \dfrac{5}{12 \times 2} = \dfrac{5}{24}$
>
> $\dfrac{5}{24}$ is not a coordinate.
>
> ⇓
>
> The coordinate $= \dfrac{1}{4} + \dfrac{5}{24} = \dfrac{6 + 5}{24} = \dfrac{11}{24}$

NEXT PAGE

15. In Container-1, there are 48 small balls that have only 2 colors, white and yellow. Among the 48 balls, there are 3 white balls for every 5 yellow balls. In Container-2, there are 3 white balls for every 2 yellow balls. If all the balls of the 2 containers are put into Container-3 that was empty, and then Container-3 has equal number of the white and yellow balls, how many balls were in Container-2 ?

(A) 50

(B) 60

(C) 70

(D) 80

Solution: Answer: (B)

$\begin{cases} \text{3 white balls for every 5 yellow balls} \\ \text{Number of } A \text{ for every number of } B \end{cases}$

$\downarrow$

This is a ratio question.

(1) $\dfrac{3}{8} \times 48 = 18, \quad \dfrac{5}{8} \times 48 = 30$

(2) Equal number of white and yellow balls

$\downarrow$

$18 + 3k = 30 + 2k, \quad k = 12$

$\Downarrow$

$3k + 2k = 5k, \ 5k = 5 \cdot 12 = 60$

---

16. An insect population is growing in such a way: number in each generation is approximately 3 times of the previous generation. If there are 300 insects in the first generation, approximately how many insects will there be in the third generation?

(A) $25,000$

(B) $81,000$

(C) $26,000$

(D) $2,700$

Solution   Answer: (D)

$\begin{cases} \begin{cases} \text{Exponential function } f(n) = a_0 r^n, \\ \text{where } n \text{ is an integer} \geq 0. \end{cases} \\ \begin{cases} \text{Geometric sequence } a_n = a_1 r^{n-1}, \\ \text{where } n \text{ is an integer} \geq 1 \text{ because 0} \\ \text{term should not exist.} \end{cases} \end{cases}$

Which formula above should we choose? Generally speaking, use the formula of exponential function for some problems involving population and investment; use the geometric sequence if a question includes the word "geometric sequence".

$\downarrow$

Use formula $f(n) = a_0 r^n$.

$n = 3 - 1 = 2$

$\Downarrow$

$f(2) = 300(3)^2 = 2700$

NEXT PAGE

17. A 25-gallon mixture of ammonia and water contains two gallons of ammonia. If five more gallons of ammonia are added, what percent of the new mixture is ammonia?

(A) 33

(B) $33\dfrac{1}{3}$

(C) $23\dfrac{1}{3}$

(D) $66\dfrac{2}{3}$

Solution: Answer: (C)

Create the direct proportion to get the percent of the 25-gallon mixture first.

$$\frac{P}{100} = \frac{2}{25}, \; P = \frac{2 \times 100}{25} = 2 \times 4 = 8$$

$$A + B = M$$

⇓

$$25 \times 8 + 5 \times \underset{\substack{\text{pure} \\ \text{ammonia}}}{100} = 30x$$

⇓

$$70\cancel{0} = 3\cancel{0}x, \; x = \frac{70}{3} = 23\frac{1}{3}$$

18. After $\dfrac{x^2 - 1}{x^2 + 2x - 3}$ is simplified, what is the resulting form and for which of the following values of x is $\dfrac{x^2 - 1}{x^2 + 2x - 3}$ undefined?

(A) $\dfrac{x+3}{x+1}$, 3 and -1

(B) $\dfrac{x+1}{x+3}$, -3 and 1

(C) $\dfrac{x+1}{x+3}$, 3 and -1

(D) $\dfrac{x+1}{x+3}$, -1

Solution: Answer: (B)

(1)
$$\frac{(x-1)(x+1)}{(x-1)(x+3)}$$

⇓

$$\frac{x+1}{x+3}$$

(2) The defined or undefined values of x come from the fraction before simplifying, not the fraction after simplifying.

$$x^2 + 2x - 3 = 0$$

↓

$$(x+3)(x-1) = 0$$

⇓

$$x = \text{-3 and } x = 1$$

19. How many integers greater than or equal to 200 and less than 1,000 have exactly one digit 1 ?

(A) 162

(B) 128

(C) 144

(D) 142

Solution: Answer: (C)

{ 3 sets

↓

Use Fundamental Counting Principle.

↓

Total 10 digits: 0~9

1 set   1 set   1 set

$$\boxed{8} \cdot \boxed{1} \cdot \boxed{9} = 72$$

Hundreds place   Tens place
Except 0 and 1   Only for 1

and

$$\boxed{8} \cdot \boxed{9} \cdot \boxed{1} = 72$$

⇓

$$2 \times 72 = 144$$

20. Which of the following is a simplified form of $\dfrac{a^2 - 8a + 12}{a^2 - 36}$?

(A) $\dfrac{a-2}{a-6}$

(B) $\dfrac{a-2}{a+6}$

(C) $\dfrac{a+2}{a+6}$

(D) $\dfrac{a+2}{a-6}$

Solution: Answer: (B)

$$S = \frac{a^2 - 8a + 12}{a^2 - 6^2} = \frac{a \overset{-2}{\underset{-6}{\times}} a}{(a-6)(a+6)}$$

⇓

$$S = \frac{(a-2)\cancel{(a-6)}}{\cancel{(a-6)}(a+6)} = \frac{a-2}{a+6}$$

NEXT PAGE

21.   At Milton School, there are as many twice math club members as biology club members and three times as many biology members as chemistry members. No member can be enrolled in more than one of the three clubs. There are sixty members in the 3 clubs, how many members are in the chemistry club?

(A) 12

(B) 24

(C) 6

(D) 36

Solution: Answer: (C)

Let x = # of members in chemistry club.

$$x, \quad 3x \quad, \quad 3x \cdot 2$$

biology
club

⇓

$$x + 3x + 6x = 60, \quad x = 6$$

---

22.   Each of the following is equal to $\sqrt{x^{2008}}$ except

(A) $x\sqrt{x^{2006}}$

(B) $x^{101}\sqrt{x^{1806}}$

(C) $x^{333}\sqrt{x^{1342}}$

(D) $x^{18}\sqrt{x^{1990}}$

Solution: Answer: (D)

$$\sqrt{x^{2008}} = x^{\frac{2008}{2}}$$

Use plug-in method.

↓

(A) $x^{\frac{2}{2}} \cdot x^{\frac{2006}{2}} = x^{\frac{2008}{2}}$

(B) $x^{\frac{202}{2}} \cdot x^{\frac{1806}{2}} = x^{\frac{2008}{2}}$

(C) $x^{\frac{666}{2}} \cdot x^{\frac{1342}{2}} = x^{\frac{2008}{2}}$

(D) $x^{\frac{36}{2}} \cdot x^{\frac{1990}{2}} = x^{\frac{2026}{2}} \ne x^{\frac{2008}{2}}$

⇓

Answer is (D).

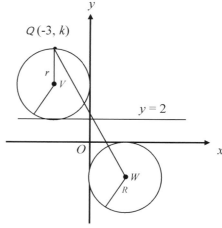

Note: Figure above not drawn to scale.

23.   In the xy-plane above, points W and V are the centers of the identical circles, which are both tangent to the y-axis, one of them tangent to x-axis, and one tangent to line $y = 2$. What is the slope of $\overline{WQ}$?

(A) $-\dfrac{11}{6}$

(B) $\dfrac{11}{6}$

(C) 3

(D) -2

Solution: Answer: (A)

Get the value of radius first.

$$x = -3$$

↓

$$r = 3$$

↓

Q (-3, 8)

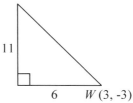

11

6   W (3, -3)

⇓

$$\text{Slope}_{\overline{WV}} = \underbrace{-}_{\substack{\text{Determined by}\\\text{the line direction}}} \frac{\text{Change of } y\text{-value}}{\text{Change of } x\text{-value}} = -\frac{11}{6}$$

NEXT PAGE

24. $f(x)$ is a linear function such that $f(6) = -7$, $f(10) = 2$, and $f(x) = 12.4$. What is the value of x ?

(A) 41.6

(B) 55.1

(C) 33.2

(D) 14.6

Solution: **Answer: (D)**

Method 1

Use the conclusion: A slope is unique for the same line.

↓

$$\frac{-7-2}{6-10} = \frac{12.4-2}{x-10}, \quad \frac{9}{4} = \frac{10.4}{x-10}$$

⇓

$$x = 10.4 \times \frac{4}{9} + 10 \approx \boxed{14.6}$$

Method 2

Use the equation of slope-intercept format.

$$y = sx + b$$

$$\begin{cases} -7 = s \cdot 6 + b \quad (1) \\ 2 = s \cdot 10 + b \quad (2) \end{cases}, \quad (2) - (1) \; 4s = 9$$

$$\boxed{s = \frac{9}{4}} \rightarrow (2), \boxed{b = -20.5}$$

⇓

$$12.4 = 2.25x - 20.5, \; x \approx \boxed{14.6}$$

Method 3

Use the equation of point-slope format.

$$y - y_o = s(x - x_o)$$

$$s = \frac{-7-2}{6-10} = \frac{9}{4}$$

$$y - 2 = \frac{9}{4}(x - 10)$$

$$12.4 - 2 = \frac{9}{4}(x - 10)$$

⇓

$$10.4 \times \frac{4}{9} = x - 10, \; x \approx 14.6$$

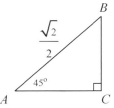

Note: Figure above not drawn to scale.

25. In the figure above, what does the perimeter equal?

(A) $1 + \dfrac{\sqrt{2}}{2}$

(B) $2 + 2\sqrt{3}$

(C) 1

(D) $4\sqrt{3}$

Solution: **Answer: (A)**

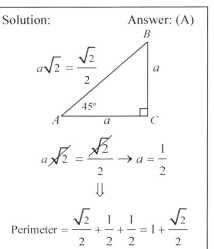

$$a\sqrt{2} = \frac{\sqrt{2}}{2} \rightarrow a = \frac{1}{2}$$

⇓

$$\text{Perimeter} = \frac{\sqrt{2}}{2} + \frac{1}{2} + \frac{1}{2} = 1 + \frac{\sqrt{2}}{2}$$

26. If the lines with the equations $y = s_1 x + 5$ and $y = s_2 x + 3$ intersect at quadrant II or III, which of the following must be the relationship between s_1 and s_2 ?

(A) $s_1 \leq s_2$

(B) $s_1 < s_2$

(C) $s_1 > s_2$

(D) $s_1 \geq s_2$

Solution: **Answer: (C)**

$$y = s_1 x + 5 \text{ and } y = s_2 x + 3$$

intersect

↓

$$s_1 x + 5 = s_2 x + 3$$

$$s_1 x - s_2 x = -2$$

$$x(s_1 - s_2) = -2, \; s_1 - s_2 = -\frac{2}{x}$$

intersection point at the left of y-axis

↓

$$x < 0$$

⇓

$$-\frac{2}{x} > 0, \; s_1 - s_2 > 0, \; \boxed{s_1 > s_2}$$

NEXT PAGE

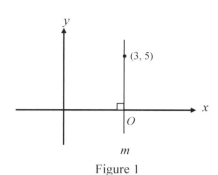

Figure 1

27. In Figure 1, the equation of line m is

(A) $y = 5$

(B) $x = 3$

(C) $y = 0$

(D) $y = 3$

Solution:	Answer: (B)

The value of x of any point on line m is equal to 3 whatever the values of y.

⇓

$x = 3$

28. $E = \sqrt[4]{\dfrac{1}{81}} = ?$

(A) $\dfrac{1}{3}$

(B) 9

(C) $\dfrac{1}{9}$

(D) 3

Solution:	Answer: (A)

$$\sqrt[4]{\frac{1}{81}} = \sqrt[4]{\frac{1}{3^4}}$$

⇓

$$E = \frac{1}{3}$$

29. If x is a prime number greater than 8 and not more than 23, then $2x + 3$ may equal any of the following except

(A) 29
(B) 25
(C) 37
(D) 24

Solution:	Answer: (D)

$$8 < x \le 23$$

↓

The prime number set $= \{11, 13, 17, 19, 23\}$

Let $x = 11, 13, 17, 19$ and 23.

↓

$2x + 3 = 25, 29, 37, 41$ and 49

⇓

$2x + 3 \ne 24$

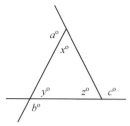

30. What is the value of $2(a + b + c)$ in the figure above?

(A) 180

(B) 360

(C) 720

(D) 380

Solution:	Answer: (C)

Method 1

$$a + x = 180, \quad b + y = 180, \quad c + z = 180$$

↓

$$a + x + b + y + c + z = 540$$

↓

$$a + b + c + \underbrace{(x + y + z)}_{180} = 540$$

↓

$$a + b + c = 360$$

⇓

$$2(a + b + c) = 720$$

Method 2

An exterior angle equals, in measure, sum of 2 non-adjacent interior angles

↓

$$a = y + z, \quad b = x + z, \quad c = x + y$$

↓

$$a + b + c = 2x + 2y + 2z$$

↓

$$2 \cdot (x + y + z) = 2 \cdot 180 = 360$$

⇓

$$2(a + b + c) = 2 \cdot 360 = 720$$

NEXT PAGE

31. A right triangle has one side of length $6\sqrt{2}$. If the lengths of the other two sides are equal, what is the area of the triangle?

Solution: Answer: 18

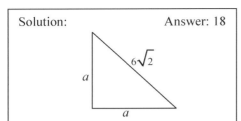

This right triangle is $45°$ right triangle.

$$\downarrow$$

$$a = 6$$

$$\Downarrow$$

$$A = \frac{a \times a}{2} = \frac{6 \times 6}{2} = 18$$

Type	Number of Bells	Rings n Times on the nth hour	Rings once on the Hour	Rings Once on the Half Hour
X	9		√	√
Y	10	√		√

32. In the table of the bell information above, what is the total number of rings of bells in the 150-minute period from $6 : 25_{pm}$ to $8 : 55_{pm}$?

Solution: Answer: 225

X: At the 7:00 and 8:00 o'clocks, one bell rings 2 times.

At the 6:30, 7:30, and 8:30, one bell rings 3 times.

Subtotal $= 9 \times (2 + 3) = 45$

Y: At the 7th and 8th hours, one bell rings $7 + 8 = 15$ times.

At the 6:30, 7:30, and 8:30, one bell rings 3 times.

Subtotal $= 10 \times (15 + 3) = 180$

$$\Downarrow$$

Total: $45 + 180 = 225$

33. A list of numbers has been arranged such that each number in the list is 16 more than the number that precedes it. If number 398 is ninth number in the list, what is the third number in the list?

Solution: Answer: 302

This is an arithmetic sequence.

$$\downarrow$$

Use the formula.

$$a_n = a_1 + (n-1)d$$

$$\downarrow$$

$$398 = a_1 + (9-1) \cdot 16$$

$$a_1 = 270$$

$$\Downarrow$$

$$a_3 = 270 + (3-1) \cdot 16 = 302$$

34. Stephanie is now five times as old as her brother Steve. After 2 years, Stephanie will be 3 times as old as Steve will be. How old was Stephanie five year ago?

Solution: Answer: 5

$$x + 2 = 3\left(\frac{1}{5}x + 2\right)$$

$$\downarrow$$

$$5x + 10 = 3(x + 10)$$

$$\downarrow$$

$$5x + 10 = 3x + 30$$

$$\Downarrow$$

$$2x = 20, \ x = 10, \ x - 5 = 5$$

NEXT PAGE

35. If the line $y = 3$ intersects the graph of the equation $y = x^2 - 3x - 25$, what is one possible x-coordinate of the intersection point of the two graphs?

Solution: Answer: 7
At an intersection point, $y = y$ and $x = x$.

$\downarrow$

$3 = x^2 - 3x - 25, \qquad x^2 - 3x - 28 = 0$

$$\begin{array}{c} x \quad\;\; 4 \\ \times \\ x \quad -7 \end{array}$$

$(x+4)(x-7) = 0$

$\Downarrow$

$x_1 = -4, \quad x_2 = \boxed{7}$

36. Eight cards in a pot are numbered 1 through 8. One card is drawn at random. The ones digit of the sum of the numbers on the remaining cards is 8. What is the number on the drawn card?

Solution: Answer: 8
Note: "through" = "from… to…".
(Including two ends)

(1). Sum $= 1 + 2 + 3 + 4 + 5 + 6 + 7 + 8 = 36$

(2). $\text{Sum}_{\text{Remaining}} = 36 - x = \begin{cases} 28 \\ 18 \\ 8 \end{cases}$

$\Downarrow$

$x = 8$

(Only 8 is one of the numbers 1 through 8.)

37. In class A, each of the 35 students contributed either a nickel or dime to the Child Foundation. If the total amount collected was \$2.05, how many students contributed a nickel?

Solution: Answer: 29
Let x = number of nickel-students;
$35 - x$ = number of dime-students.
$5x + 10(35 - x) = 205$

$\Downarrow$

$x = 29$

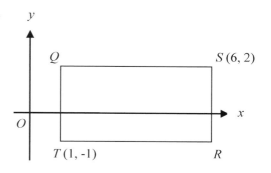

38. In the figure above, point $(a, 1)$ (not shown) is on the diagonal ST of rectangle $TQSR$. What is the value of a?

Solution: Answer: 13/3 or 4.33

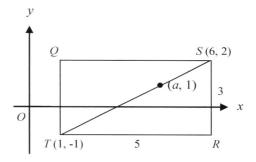

From point-intercept form and point-slope form, choose the latter form to save time for calculating the intercept.

$$y - y_o = s(x - x_o)$$

$$s = \frac{3}{5}$$

$$1 - (-1) = \frac{3}{5}(a - 1), \qquad \frac{5}{3} \cdot 2 = a - 1$$

$\Downarrow$

$$a = \frac{10}{3} + 1 = \frac{13}{3}$$

STOP

SAT Math

Practice

Test 07

Redesigned for Tests in March 2016 and Beyond

Mad Math

Math Test – No Calculator

Time: 25 Minutes
20 Questions

Notes:
- The use of a calculator is not allowed.
- All numbers used in this section are the real number.
- Figures are provided for some problems in this test. Unless otherwise indicated under the figure "Note: Figure above not drawn to scale", all figures are drawn as accurately as possible.
- All figures lie in a plane EXCEPT otherwise specified.
- Unless otherwise indicated, the domain of any function f, g or j is assumed to be the set of all real numbers x for which $f(x)$, $g(x)$, or $j(x)$ is a real number.

Reference Information

$$A = \frac{1}{2}bh$$

$$A = lw$$

$$A = \pi r^2$$

$$V = \pi r^2 h$$

$$V = lwh$$

$$c^2 = a^2 + b^2$$

$$V = \frac{1}{3}\pi r^2 h$$

$$V = \frac{4}{3}\pi r^3$$

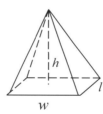

$$V = \frac{1}{3}lwh$$

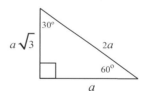

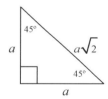

1. Which of the following is a reduced form of $\dfrac{w-2}{w^2-4}$?

(A) $\dfrac{1}{w-2}$

(B) $\dfrac{1}{w+2}$

(C) $\dfrac{w+2}{1}$

(D) $\dfrac{1}{w+1}$

3. If m is a positive integer and $4^m + 4^{m+2} = t$, what is 4^{m+1} in terms of t ?

(A) $\dfrac{17}{4t}$

(B) $4t+2$

(C) $4t-3$

(D) $\dfrac{4t}{17}$

2. The ratio of 3.5 to h is the same as the ratio of h to 4. The value of h must be

(A) ± 14

(B) -14

(C) +14

(D) $\pm\sqrt{14}$

4. If $11^m \times 11^{11} = 11^{22}$, what is the value of m ?

(A) 11

(B) 9

(C) 10

(D) 12

NEXT PAGE

Note: Figure below not drawn to scale.

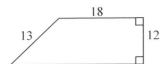

5.   What is the perimeter of the trapezoid above?

(A) 73

(B) 70

(C) 68

(D) 66

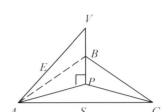

8.   In the figure above, the triangle ABC is an equilateral triangle with side S. The center of the equilateral triangle is at P. $E = S$. What is the value of the height VP in terms of S?

(A) $S\sqrt{\dfrac{11}{12}}$

(B) $\dfrac{1}{S}\sqrt{\dfrac{11}{12}}$

(C) $S\sqrt{\dfrac{2}{3}}$

(D) $S^2\sqrt{\dfrac{5}{6}}$

6.   If $b = a$, which of the following equals $bn^3 + bn^2 + b$?

(A) $a(n^3 + n^2 + 0)$

(B) $a(n^3 + n^2 + 1)$

(C) $an^3 + n^2 + 1$

(D) $an^3 + an^2 + 1$

7. $\cot x \cos x + \sin x =$

(A) $\dfrac{1}{\sin x}$

(B) $\sec x$

(C) $\tan x$

(D) $\dfrac{1}{2}\sin x$

NEXT PAGE

9. Tom's computer password consists of three 2-digit numbers. The combination is good enough for the 3 conditions below:

- One number is prime.
- One number is a multiple of 7.
- One number is day of month of Tom's father's birthday.

If every number is good enough for exact one of the conditions, what could be the combination to the password?

(A) 10-14-13
(B) 12-37-35
(C) 41-37-21
(D) 02-42-31

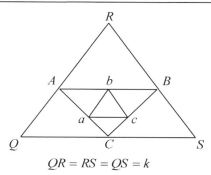

$$QR = RS = QS = k$$

Note: Figure above not drawn to scale.

11. Which of the following is the perimeter of triangle abc inside triangle QRS if A is the midpoint of $\overline{QR}$, B is the midpoint of $\overline{RS}$, and C is the midpoint of $\overline{QS}$, and if a is the midpoint of $\overline{AC}$, b is the midpoint of $\overline{AB}$, and c is the midpoint of $\overline{BC}$?

(A) $\dfrac{7k}{4}$

(B) $\dfrac{5k}{4}$

(C) $\dfrac{3k}{12}$

(D) $\dfrac{3k}{4}$

10. The quantity A is proportional to the fourth power of the quantity B, and A is 5 units if B is 3 units. What is the formula for A in terms of B?

(A) $A = \dfrac{5}{81} \sqrt[4]{B}$

(B) $A = \dfrac{81}{5} B^4$

(C) $A \geq \dfrac{5}{81} B^4$

(D) $A = \dfrac{5}{81} B^4$

NEXT PAGE

12. Which of the following is equal to 0.5 of 29 percent of 726?

(A) 29% of $\dfrac{363}{2}$

(B) 29% of 363

(C) $29\dfrac{1}{2}$% of 363

(D) $\dfrac{29}{2}$% of 363

13. If $f(x) = -(3-2x)(x+7)$, which of the following is the possible sketch for the function f ?

(A)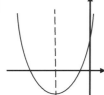

(B)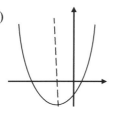

(C)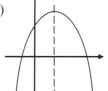

(D)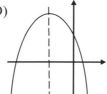

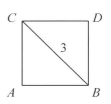

Note Figure above not drawn to scale.

14. What is the perimeter of square $ACDB$ above?

(A) $2\sqrt{2}$

(B) $6\sqrt{2}$

(C) $3\sqrt{2}$

(D) $4\sqrt{3}$

15. What are the values of x in the equation $(2x+6)^2 = 36$?

(A) $(0,-6)$

(B) $(0,5)$

(C) $(0,6)$

(D) $(0,3)$

NEXT PAGE

16. If $g(x) = \dfrac{1}{10}$ for all real numbers x, then $g\left(x - \dfrac{1}{10}\right) =$

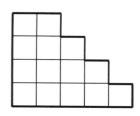

18. The figure above shows a combination of 14 squares, each with side S yards. The perimeter of the figure is P yards and the area of the figure is A square yards. If the figure area is equivalent to the figure perimeter, what is the value, in yards, of S?

$$\left(\frac{m^3}{n^2}\right)^{-2} = \left(\frac{m^3}{n^2}\right)^{-1}$$

17. If $m \neq 0$ and $n \neq 0$ in the equation above, what is the value of $n^2 - m^3$?

NEXT PAGE ⟹

$$y - 2 = 1/2(2x + 1)$$

19. What is the y-value of the y-intercept of the function above?

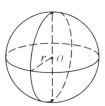

20.   What is the radius of a sphere shown above whose volume equals the volume of a right prism, which is 36π ?

STOP

No Test Contents

On This Page

Go to Next Page

Math Test – Calculator

Time: 55 Minutes
38 Questions

Notes:
- The use of a calculator is not allowed.
- All numbers used in this section are the real number.
- Figures are provided for some problems in this test. Unless otherwise indicated under the figure "Note: Figure above not drawn to scale", all figures are drawn as accurately as possible.
- All figures lie in a plane EXCEPT otherwise specified.
- Unless otherwise indicated, the domain of any function f, g or j is assumed to be the set of all real numbers x for which $f(x)$, $g(x)$, or $j(x)$ is a real number.

Reference Information

$$A = \frac{1}{2}bh$$

$$A = lw$$

$$A = \pi r^2$$

$$V = \pi r^2 h$$

$$V = lwh$$

$$c^2 = a^2 + b^2$$

$$V = \frac{1}{3}\pi r^2 h$$

$$V = \frac{4}{3}\pi r^3$$

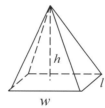

$$V = \frac{1}{3}lwh$$

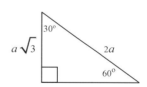

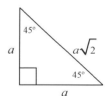

Copying or reuse of any portion of this page is illegal.

1. If the graph of the equation $y = 3x^2 - 5x + k$ is tangent to the x-axis, what is the value of k ?

(A) 12/25

(B) 25/12

(C) 10.3

(D) -25/12

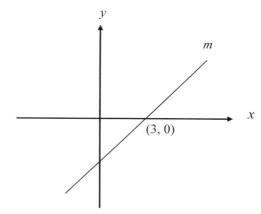

3. The figure above shows line m in the xy-plane. Line l (not shown) is obtained by horizontally translating each point on the line m 4 units to the right. If the equation of l is $y = \dfrac{4}{5}x + h$, what is the value of h?

(A) 5

(B) -6

(C) $-\dfrac{28}{5}$

(D) $-\dfrac{28}{3}$

Funds and Percent of Total Expenses Spent on 12 Projects

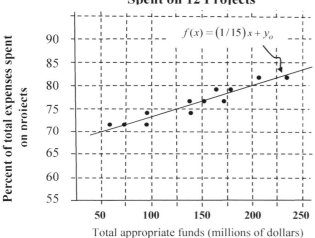

The appropriate funds are alloted to 12 research projects. The scatterplot with the line of best fit above shows data for the 12 projects.

2. What is the value of y_o of the equation of the line of best fit?

(A) $y_o = 200 / 3$

(B) $y_o = 155 / 3$

(C) $y_o = 190 / 3$

(D) $y_o = 210 / 3$

NEXT PAGE

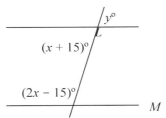

4. In the figure above, lines L and M are parallel to each other. What is the value of y?

(A) 15

(B) 75

(C) 25

(D) 30

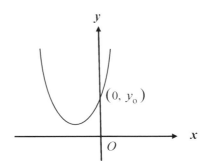

6. A parabola represented by an equation $y = ax^2 + bx + c$ is shown above. Which of the following statements must be true?

I. $b^2 - 4ac \geq 0$

II. $a < 0$

III. $b > 0$ and $c > 0$

(A) I only   (B) II only   (C) III only   (D) II and III only

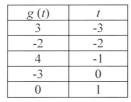

$g(t)$	t
3	-3
-2	-2
4	-1
-3	0
0	1

5. The function g is defined by the chart above. For what value of t does $t - g(t) = 0$?

(A) 2

(B) -1

(C) -2

(D) -3

NEXT PAGE

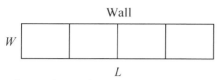

Wall

W

L

7.   In the figure above, the greatest rectangular area with dimensions W and L yards and total area 8,000 square yards is marked off on 3 sides and bounded on fourth side by a wall. In addition, the four smaller rectangles are congruent. What is the total length, in yards, of all sides except the wall side, in terms of L?

(A) $L + \dfrac{4 \times 10^4}{L}$

(B) $2L + \dfrac{4 \times 10^4}{L}$

(C) $L + \dfrac{4 \times 10^3}{2L}$

(D) $L + \dfrac{4 \times 10^4}{2L}$

8.   Which of the following does $1 \le |x + 3| \le 3$ equal?

(A) $-6 \le x \le -4$, $-2 \le x \le 0$
(B) $-6 \le x \le -4$
(C) $-2 \le x \le 0$
(D) $4 \le x \le 6$

9. $f(x)$ is a linear function such that $f(4) = -4$, $f(-3) = 5$, and $f(x) = 11.1$. What does the value of x equal?

(A) 7.78   (B) 8.77   (C) -7.74   (D) -8.77

10.   A function is defined by $f(t) = -3^t - 2$. Which of the following is the sketch of $g(t) = -f(t)$?

(A)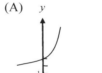

(B)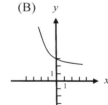

(C)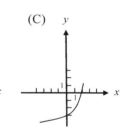

(D)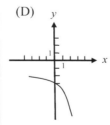

NEXT PAGE

The questions 11 and 12 refer to the information below.

Physicists' an Experiment of Ball Rolling

	Pipe 1	Pipe 2	Pipe 3
Length (miles)	87.6	70.5	88.4
Average of rolling speed (miles per hour)	35	45	40

Several physicists did an experiment. They let a special ball, which is made by mix materials, roll through three pipes, pipe 1, pipe 2, and pipe 3, which are connected by that order. Each pipe has own conditions. The records of the experiment were put into the table above.

11. The experiment started. The ball rolled directly into the pipe 1, then the pipe 2, and then the pipe 3. What is the average speed, in miles per minute, of the ball during its entire rolling process that spent five hours?

(A) 0.7

(B) 0.8

(C) 0.6

(D) 0.5

12. If the conditions of the pipe 2 are changed, the rolling time from the entrance of the pipe 2 to the exit of the pipe 2 decreases 22 percent, but the rolling times of other two pipes do not change. According to the table information, how many less minutes does the ball take to arrive at the exit of the pipe 3 than the conditions of the pipe 2 do not be changed, rounded to the nearest minute?

(A) 19

(B) 21

(C) 22

(D) 23

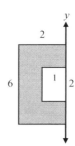

Note: Figure above not drawn to scale.

13. The two rectangles shown above are overlapped. The bigger one has dimensions 2 and 6. The smaller one has dimensions 1 and 2. If the whole figure makes one revolution on axis y, what is the volume that the shaded portion generates?

(A) 18π

(B) 20π

(C) 17π

(D) 22π

14. Which of the following value(s) must be excluded from the of $\dfrac{g(x)}{f(x)}$ if $f(x) = x^2 - 9$ and $g(x) = x - 3$?

(A) $x = -3$

(B) $x = \pm3$

(C) $x = +3$

(D) $x = 0$

NEXT PAGE

15. If $i^2 = -1$, which of the following expressions could $x^2 + 5$ equal ?

(A) $x^2 - \left(\sqrt{5}\right)^2$

(B) $x^2 + \left(\sqrt{5} \cdot i\right)^2$

(C) $\left(x - \sqrt{5} \cdot i\right)\left(x + \sqrt{5} \cdot i\right)$

(D) $\left(x - \sqrt{5} \cdot i\right)^2$

16. If $f(x) = \dfrac{1}{x}$, then $f\left(\dfrac{1}{3}\right) \cdot f\left(\dfrac{1}{x^2}\right) =$

(A) $\dfrac{1}{3x^2}$

(B) $3x^2$

(C) $\dfrac{x^2}{3}$

(D) $\dfrac{1}{x^2}$

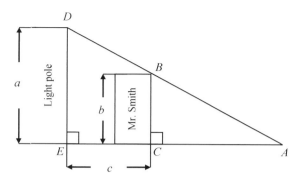

Note: Figure above not drawn to scale

17. In the figure above, Mr. Smith is $b = 7$ ft tall, the height of a light pole is $a = 14$ ft, and the distance from the base to Mr. Smith is $c = 42$ ft. If Smith's shadow is $\overline{CA}$, what is the length of $\overline{EA}$ in feet?

(A) 42

(B) 36

(C) 84

(D) 26

NEXT PAGE

18. $3\dfrac{1}{3} + 3 \cdot \dfrac{1}{3} - \dfrac{\frac{1}{3}}{\frac{1}{4}} =$

(A) $\dfrac{16}{3}$

(B) 3

(C) $\dfrac{3}{16}$

(D) $2\dfrac{1}{4}$

19. If the radius of a circle is 12 inches, what is the area of the sector whose arc length is 2π inches?

(A) 14π

(B) 12π

(C) 10π

(D) 16π

$$y/2 = 2x - 1$$

20. Change the function above to the point-slope form. What is the point?

(A) $x = 1,\ y = -2$

(B) $x = 1,\ y = 2$

(C) $x = \dfrac{1}{2},\ y = 2$

(D) $x = \dfrac{1}{2},\ y = 0$

21. What is the domain of the function f if $f(x) = \dfrac{\sqrt{x-2}}{x}$?

(A) All real integers greater than or equal to 2

(B) All real numbers except for 0

(C) All real numbers less than or equal to -2

(D) All real numbers greater than or equal to 2

NEXT PAGE

$$|z - 4| = \frac{1}{3}$$

22. What is the least value of z that satisfies the equation above?

(A) $-3\dfrac{2}{3}$

(B) $4\dfrac{1}{3}$

(C) $3\dfrac{2}{3}$

(D) $-4\dfrac{1}{3}$

24. The E-Tech Company will send a group of four people to work on a certain job. The company has 4 experienced electricians and 5 trainees. If the group consists of 2 experienced electricians and 2 trainees, how many possible distinct such groups exist?

(A) 16
(B) 30
(C) 40
(D) 60

25. Two perpendicular lines l_1 and l_2 intersect at (-4, -3). If line l_2 has a slope of $\dfrac{1}{3}$, which of the following is an equation for line l_1 ?

(A) $y = -3(x + 5)$

(B) $y = -3(x - 5)$

(C) $y = 3(x - 5)$

(D) $y = 3(x + 5)$

23. If $343^{3x} = \left(\dfrac{1}{7}\right)^{x-50}$, which of the following is the value of x ?

(A) 1

(B) 2

(C) 3

(D) 5

NEXT PAGE

26. Convert the degrees to radians or the radians to degrees for $\dfrac{\pi}{5}$ and $160°$. Which of the following a pair of results is true?

(Radians are assumed if no unit of measrement is indicated.)

(A) $36°$ and 2.79

(B) $62°$ and 4.13

(C) $20°$ and 2π

(D) $26°$ and 3.89

27. Let $f(x) = x^4 + x^3 \cdots$. If $f(4) = 0$ and $f(-3) = 0$, then $f(x)$ is divisible by

(A) $x^2 - 7x + 12$

(B) $x^2 - x + 7$

(C) $x^2 - 2x + 12$

(D) $x^2 - x - 12$

28. In the xy-plane, the graph of $-3(3x)^2 + y = b$ passes through point (1, 9). What is the value of b?

(A) -2186
(B) 18
(C) 0
(D) -18

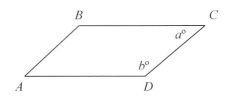

29. If $\overline{BC}$ is parallel to $\overline{AD}$ in the figure above, what is the value of $3(a + b)$?

(A) 360
(B) 450
(C) 540
(D) 600

30. In an Internet election, the voters using a certain voting program of websites cast 2.2 million votes and each vote was for either Candidate-A or Candidate-B. Candidate-A received 22,000 less votes than Candidate-B. What percent of the 2.2 million votes were cast for Candidate-B?

(A) 5.005   (B) 50.50   (C) 500.5   (D) 50.05

NEXT PAGE

$$N(t) = \frac{1}{2}t^2 - 40t + h$$

31. In the function above, $N(t)$ represents the number of certain birds on year number t for $0 < t \le 120$ and h is a constant. On what year is the number of the birds the same as it is on year number 50?

32. $\dfrac{6!}{4!} = ?$

33. Nine times a number is the same as the number added to nine. What is the number?

34. If p is the greatest prime factor of 87 and q is the least prime factor of 1,000, what is the value of $p \times q$?

35. The first term of set A is -3, and each term thereafter is 3 greater than the previous term. The Nth term of set B is given by the formula $-N + 22$. Which term of set A is the first one that value first exceeds the value of its corresponding term in set B?

36. At a high school of 679 students, each student chooses a biology course or a chemistry course or both. If 379 students of them choose biology course and 310 students of them choose chemistry course, how many students only choose chemistry course?

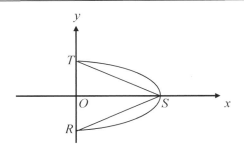

Note: Figure above not drawn to scale.

38. The figure above shows the graph of $x = g - y^2$, where g is a constant. If the area of triangle RST is 8, what is the value of g?

37. Every person of group A can insert letters in envelopes at rate of 20 per minute. Every person of group B can insert the envelopes at the rate of 32 per minute. How many people of group B are need to keep up with 16 people of group A?

STOP

Answer Key
For
SAT Math Practice Test 07

Section 3

1	B
2	D
3	D
4	A
5	D
6	B
7	A
8	C
9	B
10	D
11	D
12	B
13	B
14	B
15	A

16	1/10 or .1
17	0
18	9/7 or 1.28 or 1.29
19	2.5 or 5/2
20	3

Section 4

1	B	16	B
2	A	17	C
3	C	18	B
4	B	19	B
5	C	20	D
6	C	21	D
7	A	22	C
8	A	23	D
9	C	24	D
10	A	25	A
11	B	26	A
12	B	27	D
13	D	28	D
14	B	29	C
15	C	30	B

31	30
32	30
33	9/8
34	58
35	8
36	300
37	10
38	4

SAT Math

Practice

Test 07

Explanations

Redesigned for Tests in March 2016 and Beyond

Mad Math

Math Test – No Calculator

Time: 25 Minutes
20 Questions

Notes:
- The use of a calculator is not allowed.
- All numbers used in this section are the real number.
- Figures are provided for some problems in this test. Unless otherwise indicated under the figure "Note: Figure above not drawn to scale", all figures are drawn as accurately as possible.
- All figures lie in a plane EXCEPT otherwise specified.
- Unless otherwise indicated, the domain of any function f, g or j is assumed to be the set of all real numbers x for which $f(x)$, $g(x)$, or $j(x)$ is a real number.

Reference Information

$A = \dfrac{1}{2}bh$

$A = lw$

$A = \pi r^2$

$V = \pi r^2 h$

$V = lwh$

$c^2 = a^2 + b^2$

$V = \dfrac{1}{3}\pi r^2 h$

$V = \dfrac{4}{3}\pi r^3$

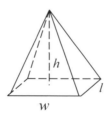

$V = \dfrac{1}{3}lwh$

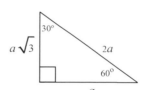

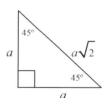

Copying or reuse of any portion of this page is illegal.

1. Which of the following is a reduced form of $\dfrac{w-2}{w^2-4}$?

(A) $\dfrac{1}{w-2}$

(B) $\dfrac{1}{w+2}$

(C) $\dfrac{w+2}{1}$

(D) $\dfrac{1}{w+1}$

Solution: Answer: (B)

$$S = \frac{w-2}{w^2-2^2} = \frac{\cancel{w-2}}{\cancel{(w-2)}(w+2)}$$

$$\Downarrow$$

$$S = \frac{1}{w+2}$$

2. The ratio of 3.5 to h is the same as the ratio of h to 4. The value of h must be

(A) ± 14

(B) -14

(C) +14

(D) $\pm\sqrt{14}$

Solution: Answer: (D)

$$\frac{3.5}{h} = \frac{h}{4}$$

$$\downarrow$$

$$h^2 = 3.5 \times 4 = 14 \Rightarrow h = \pm\sqrt{14}$$

3. If m is a positive integer and $4^m + 4^{m+2} = t$, what is 4^{m+1} in terms of t ?

(A) $\dfrac{17}{4t}$

(B) $4t+2$

(C) $4t-3$

(D) $\dfrac{4t}{17}$

Solution: Answer: (D)

$$4^m + 4^{m+2} = t \to 4^m(1+4^2) = 17\cdot 4^m$$

$$17\cdot 4^m = t,\ \ 4^m = \frac{t}{17}$$

$$4^m \cdot 4 = \frac{t}{17}\cdot 4$$

$$\Downarrow$$

$$4^{m+1} = \frac{4t}{17}$$

4. If $11^m \times 11^{11} = 11^{22}$, what is the value of m ?

(A) 11

(B) 9

(C) 10

(D) 12

Solution: Answer: (A)

$$11^m \times 11^{11} = 11^{22}$$

$$\downarrow$$

$$11^{m+11} = 11^{22}$$

$$\downarrow$$

$$m+11 = 22$$

$$\Downarrow$$

$$m = 11$$

NEXT PAGE

Note: Figure below not drawn to scale.

5. What is the perimeter of the trapezoid above?

(A) 73

(B) 70

(C) 68

(D) 66

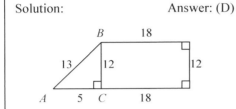

Solution: Answer: (D)

Triangle ABC is a 5-12-13 right triangle.

$$\Downarrow$$

$$p = 13 + 18 + 12 + 18 + 5 = 66$$

6. If $b = a$, which of the following equals $bn^3 + bn^2 + b$?

(A) $a(n^3 + n^2 + 0)$

(B) $a(n^3 + n^2 + 1)$

(C) $an^3 + n^2 + 1$

(D) $an^3 + an^2 + 1$

Solution: Answer: (B)

$$bn^3 + bn^2 + b = b(n^3 + n^2 + 1)$$

$$\Downarrow$$

$$a(n^3 + n^2 + 1)$$

7. $\cot x \cos x + \sin x =$

(A) $\dfrac{1}{\sin x}$

(B) $\sec x$

(C) $\tan x$

(D) $\dfrac{1}{2}\sin x$

Solution: Answer: (A)

$$\frac{\cos x}{\sin x}\cos x + \sin x$$

$$\downarrow$$

$$\frac{\cos x}{\sin x}\cos x + \sin x \frac{\sin x}{\sin x}$$

$$\Downarrow$$

$$\frac{\cos^2 x + \sin^2 x}{\sin x} = \frac{1}{\sin x}$$

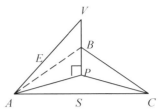

8. In the figure above, the triangle ABC is an equilateral triangle with side S. The center of the equilateral triangle is at P. $E = S$. What is the value of the height VP in terms of S?

(A) $S\sqrt{\dfrac{11}{12}}$

(B) $\dfrac{1}{S}\sqrt{\dfrac{11}{12}}$

(C) $S\sqrt{\dfrac{2}{3}}$

(D) $S^2\sqrt{\dfrac{5}{6}}$

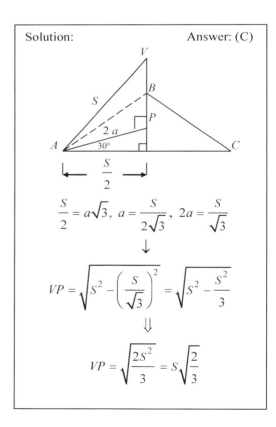

Solution: Answer: (C)

$$\frac{S}{2} = a\sqrt{3}, \; a = \frac{S}{2\sqrt{3}}, \; 2a = \frac{S}{\sqrt{3}}$$

$$\downarrow$$

$$VP = \sqrt{S^2 - \left(\frac{S}{\sqrt{3}}\right)^2} = \sqrt{S^2 - \frac{S^2}{3}}$$

$$\Downarrow$$

$$VP = \sqrt{\frac{2S^2}{3}} = S\sqrt{\frac{2}{3}}$$

NEXT PAGE

9. Tom's computer password consists of three 2-digit numbers. The combination is good enough for the 3 conditions below:

- One number is prime.
- One number is a multiple of 7.
- One number is day of month of Tom's father's birthday.

If every number is good enough for exact one of the conditions, what could be the combination to the password?

(A) 10-14-13
(B) 12-37-35
(C) 41-37-21
(D) 02-42-31

Solution: Answer: (B)

   (A) All of the three numbers can be a day of a month.

   (B) Only 12 can be a day of a month. Only number 37 is a prime number. Only 21 is a multiple of 7.

   (C) 41 and 37 both are prime.

   (D) 02 and 31 both are prime.

10. The quantity A is proportional to the fourth power of the quantity B, and A is 5 units if B is 3 units. What is the formula for A in terms of B?

(A) $A = \dfrac{5}{81}\sqrt[4]{B}$

(B) $A = \dfrac{81}{5}B^4$

(C) $A \ge \dfrac{5}{81}B^4$

(D) $A = \dfrac{5}{81}B^4$

Solution: Answer: (D)

$$A = kB^4$$
$$\downarrow$$
$$k = \frac{A}{B^4} = \frac{A}{B^4} = \frac{5}{3^4} = \frac{5}{81}$$
$$\Downarrow$$
$$A = \frac{5}{81}B^4$$

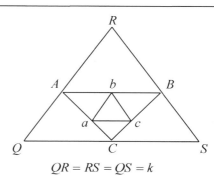

$$QR = RS = QS = k$$

Note: Figure above not drawn to scale.

11. Which of the following is the perimeter of triangle abc inside triangle QRS if A is the midpoint of $\overline{QR}$, B is the midpoint of $\overline{RS}$, and C is the midpoint of $\overline{QS}$, and if a is the midpoint of $\overline{AC}$, b is the midpoint of $\overline{AB}$, and c is the midpoint of $\overline{BC}$?

(A) $\dfrac{7k}{4}$

(B) $\dfrac{5k}{4}$

(C) $\dfrac{3k}{12}$

(D) $\dfrac{3k}{4}$

Solution: Answer: (D)

According to Triangle Midsegment Theorem, a midsegment of a triangle is parallel to a side of the triangle , and the length of the midsegment is half the length of the side.

$$QR = RS = QS = k$$
$$\downarrow$$

The triangle is a equilateral triangle.

$$\downarrow$$

$$AB = \frac{QS}{2} = \frac{k}{2}, \quad ac = \frac{AB}{2} = \frac{\frac{k}{2}}{2} = \frac{k}{4}$$
$$\Downarrow$$
$$P_{\text{Tri-}abc} = 3 \times \frac{k}{4} = \frac{3k}{4}$$

NEXT PAGE

12. Which of the following is equal to 0.5 of 29 percent of 726?

(A) 29% of $\dfrac{363}{2}$

(B) 29% of 363

(C) $29\dfrac{1}{2}$% of 363

(D) $\dfrac{29}{2}$% of 363

Solution: Answer: (B)

$$\underbrace{\dfrac{1}{2}\cdot\dfrac{29}{100}\cdot726}_{\text{Move 2}}$$

↓

$$\dfrac{29}{100}\cdot\dfrac{726}{2}$$

⇓

29% of 363

13. If $f(x) = -(3-2x)(x+7)$, which of the following is the possible sketch for the function f?

(A)
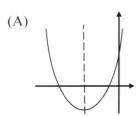

(B)
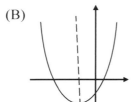

(C)
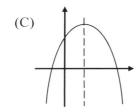

(D)
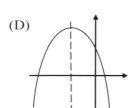

Solution: Answer: (B)

Target → factored form (intercept form),

$$f(x) = a\left(x - x_1\right)\left(x - x_2\right)$$

$$f(x) = -(-1)(2x-3)(x+7) = (2x-3)(x+7)$$

$$f(x) = 2(x-3/2)(x+7)$$

↓

$\begin{cases} a = 2 > 0 \;\to\; \text{Open-up} \\[2mm] x\text{-intercepts: } x_1 = \dfrac{3}{2} \text{ and } x_2 = -7 \end{cases}$

$$\underbrace{x = \dfrac{x_1 + x_2}{2} = \dfrac{1.5 - 7}{2} = -2.75}_{\text{equation of symmetric axis}}$$

⇓

Answer is (B).

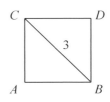

Note Figure above not drawn to scale.

14. What is the perimeter of square $ACDB$ above?

(A) $2\sqrt{2}$

(B) $6\sqrt{2}$

(C) $3\sqrt{2}$

(D) $4\sqrt{3}$

Solution: Answer: (B)

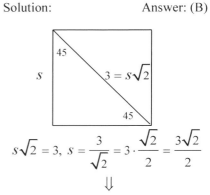

$$s\sqrt{2} = 3, \; s = \dfrac{3}{\sqrt{2}} = 3\cdot\dfrac{\sqrt{2}}{2} = \dfrac{3\sqrt{2}}{2}$$

⇓

$$P = 4s = 4\cdot\dfrac{3\sqrt{2}}{2} = 6\sqrt{2}$$

15. What are the values of x in the equation $(2x+6)^2 = 36$?

(A) $(0, -6)$

(B) $(0, 5)$

(C) $(0, 6)$

(D) $(0, 3)$

Solution: Answer: (A)

$$(2x+6)^2 - 36 = 0$$

↓

$$(2x+6)^2 - 6^2 = 0$$

↓

$$[(2x+6)-6][(2x+6)+6] = 0$$

↓

$$(2x)(2x+12) = 0$$

↓

$$2x = 0 \;\text{ or }\; 2x+12 = 0$$

⇓

$$x = 0, -6$$

NEXT PAGE

16. If $g(x) = \dfrac{1}{10}$ for all real numbers x, then $g\left(x - \dfrac{1}{10}\right) =$

Solution: Answer: 1/10 or .1

After change of value of x, the value of y corresponding with new value of x is the same value of y corresponding with old value of x.

or

$$f(x) = f(x - a)$$

$$\Downarrow$$

$$g\left(x - \dfrac{1}{10}\right) = \dfrac{1}{10}$$

$$\left(\dfrac{m^3}{n^2}\right)^{-2} = \left(\dfrac{m^3}{n^2}\right)^{-1}$$

17. If $m \neq 0$ and $n \neq 0$ in the equation above, what is the value of $n^2 - m^3$?

Solution: Answer: 0

$$\left(\dfrac{m^3}{n^2}\right)^2 = \left(\dfrac{m^3}{n^2}\right)^1$$

$$\downarrow$$

$$\dfrac{m^6}{n^4} = \dfrac{m^3}{n^2}, \quad \dfrac{m^6}{m^3} = \dfrac{n^4}{n^2}$$

$$\Downarrow$$

$$m^3 = n^2, \quad m^3 - n^2 = \boxed{0}$$

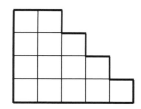

18.   The figure above shows a combination of 14 squares, each with side S yards. The perimeter of the figure is P yards and the area of the figure is A square yards. If the figure area is equivalent to the figure perimeter, what is the value, in yards, of S?

Solution: Answer: 9/7 or 1.28 or 1.29

$$\begin{cases} 14S^2 = A, \\ 18S = P, \end{cases} \text{and } P = A$$

$$\downarrow$$

$$14S^2 = 18S$$

$$\Downarrow$$

$$S = \dfrac{9}{7}$$

NEXT PAGE

$$y - 2 = 1/2\left(2x + 1\right)$$

19. What is the y-value of the y-intercept of the function above?

Solution: Answer: 2.5 or 5/2

The definition the intercept:

y-value when $x = 0$

$\downarrow$

$$y - 2 = 1/2\left(2 \times 0 + 1\right)$$

$\Downarrow$

$$y = 1/2 + 2, \quad y = 2.5$$

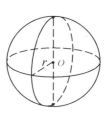

20. What is the radius of a sphere shown above whose volume equals the volume of a right prism, which is 36π ?

Solution: Answer: 3

$$V_p = 36\pi, \ V_s = \frac{4}{3}\pi r^3$$

$$V_p = V_s$$

$\downarrow$

$$36\pi = \frac{4}{3}\pi r^3$$

$$\frac{3}{4\pi} \cdot 36\pi = r^3, \ 27 = r^3$$

$\Downarrow$

$$r = \sqrt[3]{27} = \sqrt[3]{3 \cdot 3 \cdot 3} = 3$$

STOP

No Test Contents

On This Page

Go to Next Page

Math Test – Calculator

Time: 55 Minutes
38 Questions

Notes:
- The use of a calculator is not allowed.
- All numbers used in this section are the real number.
- Figures are provided for some problems in this test. Unless otherwise indicated under the figure "Note: Figure above not drawn to scale", all figures are drawn as accurately as possible.
- All figures lie in a plane EXCEPT otherwise specified.
- Unless otherwise indicated, the domain of any function f, g or j is assumed to be the set of all real numbers x for which $f(x)$, $g(x)$, or $j(x)$ is a real number.

Reference Information

$A = \dfrac{1}{2}bh$

$A = lw$

$A = \pi r^2$

$V = \pi r^2 h$

$V = lwh$

$c^2 = a^2 + b^2$

$V = \dfrac{1}{3}\pi r^2 h$

$V = \dfrac{4}{3}\pi r^3$

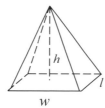

$V = \dfrac{1}{3}lwh$

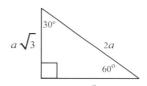

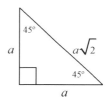

1. If the graph of the equation $y = 3x^2 - 5x + k$ is tangent to the x-axis, what is the value of k ?

(A) 12/25

(B) 25/12

(C) 10.3

(D) -25/12

> Solution: Answer: (B)
>
> "tangent to x-axis" $\rightarrow b^2 - 4ac = 0$
>
> $\Downarrow$
>
> $(-5)^2 - 4 \cdot 3 \cdot k = 0, \quad k = \dfrac{25}{12}$

Funds and Percent of Total Expenses Spent on 12 Projects

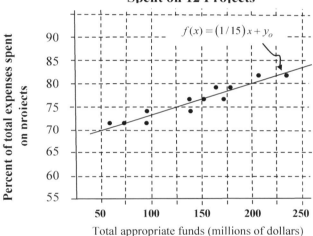

The appropriate funds are alloted to 12 research projects. The scatterplot with the line of best fit above shows data for the 12 projects.

2. What is the value of y_o of the equation of the line of best fit?

(A) $y_o = 200/3$

(B) $y_o = 155/3$

(C) $y_o = 190/3$

(D) $y_o = 210/3$

> Solution: Answer: (A)
>
> $f(x) = (1/15)x + y_o$
>
> $\downarrow$
>
> According to the line of best fit,
>
> $f(50) = 70.$
>
> $70 = \dfrac{1}{15} \cdot 50 + y_o, \quad 70 - \dfrac{10}{3} = y_o$
>
> $\Downarrow$
>
> $\dfrac{210 - 10}{3} = y_o, \quad y_o = 200/3$

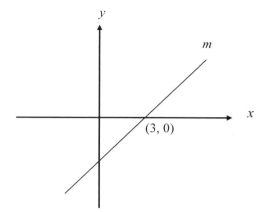

3. The figure above shows line m in the xy-plane. Line l (not shown) is obtained by horizontally translating each point on the line m 4 units to the right. If the equation of l is $y = \dfrac{4}{5}x + h$, what is the value of h?

(A) 5

(B) -6

(C) $-\dfrac{28}{5}$

(D) $-\dfrac{28}{3}$

> Solution: Answer: (C)
>
>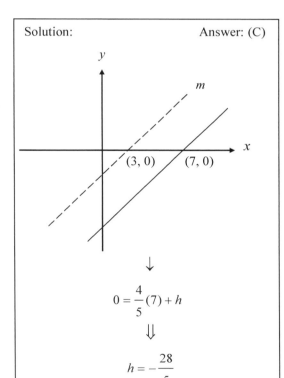
>
> $\downarrow$
>
> $0 = \dfrac{4}{5}(7) + h$
>
> $\Downarrow$
>
> $h = -\dfrac{28}{5}$

NEXT PAGE ⟩

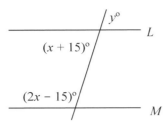

4.   In the figure above, lines L and M are parallel to each other. What is the value of y?

(A) 15

(B) 75

(C) 25

(D) 30

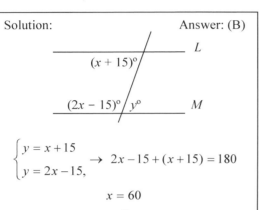

Solution: Answer: (B)

$$\begin{cases} y = x + 15 \\ y = 2x - 15, \end{cases} \rightarrow 2x - 15 + (x + 15) = 180$$

$$x = 60$$

$$\Downarrow$$

$$y = 60 + 15 = 60 + 15 = 75$$

$g(t)$	t
3	-3
-2	-2
4	-1
-3	0
0	1

5.   The function g is defined by the chart above. For what value of t does $t - g(t) = 0$?

(A) 2

(B) -1

(C) -2

(D) -3

Solution: Answer: (C)
            Refer to the table above.

$$\downarrow$$

When $t = -2$, $g(-2) = -2$.

$$\Downarrow$$

$$t - g(t) = -2 - (-2) = 0$$

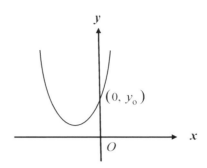

$(0, y_o)$

6.   A parabola represented by an equation $y = ax^2 + bx + c$ is shown above. Which of the following statements must be true?

I. $b^2 - 4ac \geq 0$

II. $a < 0$

III. $b > 0$ and $c > 0$

(A) I only   (B) II only   (C) III only   (D) II and III only

Solution: Answer: (C)

$$x_{1,2} = \frac{-b \pm \overset{b^2-4ac}{\sqrt{D}}}{2a} = \begin{cases} 2 \text{ real values, } D = + \\ 1 \text{ real value, } D = 0 \\ 2 \text{ non-real value, } D = - \end{cases}$$

I.   Since the curve doesn't cross the x-axis, real
     solution doesn't exist, and then $b^2 - 4ac < 0$.

$$\Downarrow$$

I is false.

II.   The curve opens up. $a > 0$.

$$\Downarrow$$

II is false.

III. (1). At a vertex, $x = -\dfrac{b}{2a}$. Because the vertex
     of the curve is in quadrant II, x-value < 0.
     And $a > 0$, then $b > 0$.

     (2). c is the y-intercept. For $y = ax^2 + bx + c$,
     when $x = 0$, $y = c$. Now c is above x-axis.
     Then $c > 0$

$$\Downarrow$$

III is true.

NEXT PAGE

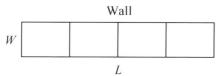

Wall

W

L

7. In the figure above, the greatest rectangular area with dimensions W and L yards and total area 8,000 square yards is marked off on 3 sides and bounded on fourth side by a wall. In addition, the four smaller rectangles are congruent. What is the total length, in yards, of all sides except the wall side, in terms of L?

(A) $L + \dfrac{4 \times 10^4}{L}$

(B) $2L + \dfrac{4 \times 10^4}{L}$

(C) $L + \dfrac{4 \times 10^3}{2L}$

(D) $L + \dfrac{4 \times 10^4}{2L}$

Solution: Answer: (A)

$$LW = 8000 \rightarrow W = \frac{8000}{L}$$

$$\text{Total} = L + 5W$$

$$\Downarrow$$

$$L + 5 \times \frac{8000}{L} = L + \frac{4 \times 10^4}{L}$$

8. Which of the following does $1 \le |x + 3| \le 3$ equal?

(A) $-6 \le x \le -4,\ -2 \le x \le 0$
(B) $-6 \le x \le -4$
(C) $-2 \le x \le 0$
(D) $4 \le x \le 6$

Solution: Answer: (A)

$$1 \le |x + 3| \le 3$$

It is equal to two inequalities.

$$\downarrow$$

(1) $1 \le +(x + 3) \le 3$
$-2 \le x \le 0$

(2) $1 \le -(x + 3) \le 3$
$-1 \ge x + 3 \ge -3$
$-3 \le x + 3 \le -1$

$$\downarrow$$

$-6 \le x \le -4$

$$\Downarrow$$

Answer is (A).

9. $f(x)$ is a linear function such that $f(4) = -4$, $f(-3) = 5$, and $f(x) = 11.1$. What does the value of x equal?

(A) 7.78   (B) 8.77   (C) -7.74   (D) -8.77

Solution: Answer: (C)

Use the conclusion: A slope is unique for the same line.

$$\downarrow$$

$$\frac{-4 - 5}{4 - (-3)} = \frac{11.1 - 5}{x - (-3)}, \quad \frac{-9}{7} = \frac{6.1}{x + 3}$$

$$\Downarrow$$

$$x = 6.1 \times \frac{7}{-9} - 3 \approx \boxed{-7.74}$$

10. A function is defined by $f(t) = -3^t - 2$. Which of the following is the sketch of $g(t) = -f(t)$?

(A) y
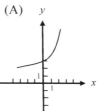
x

(B) y
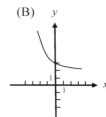
x

(C) y
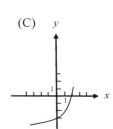
x

(D) y
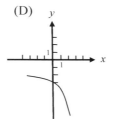
x

Solution: Answer: (A)

$$\begin{cases} f(t) = -3^t - 2 = -\left(3^t + 2\right) \\ g(t) = -f(t) = -\left(-\left(3^t + 2\right)\right) = 3^t + 2 \end{cases}$$

$$\Downarrow$$

The sketch of g is (A)

NEXT PAGE

The questions 11 and 12 refer to the information below.

Physicists' an Experiment of Ball Rolling

	Pipe 1	Pipe 2	Pipe 3
Length (miles)	87.6	70.5	88.4
Average of rolling speed (miles per hour)	35	45	40

Several physicists did an experiment. They let a special ball, which is made by mix materials, roll through three pipes, pipe 1, pipe 2, and pipe 3, which are connected by that order. Each pipe has own conditions. The records of the experiment were put into the table above.

11. The experiment started. The ball rolled directly into the pipe 1, then the pipe 2, and then the pipe 3. What is the average speed, in miles per minute, of the ball during its entire rolling process that spent five hours?

(A) 0.7
(B) 0.8
(C) 0.6
(D) 0.5

> Solution: Answer: (B)
>
> "average speed"
>
> ↓
>
> $$\text{Average speed} = \frac{\text{Total distance}}{\text{Total time}}$$
>
> $$\frac{87.6+70.5+88.4}{5} = 49.3\,(\text{mph})$$
>
> ⇓
>
> It is $\frac{49.3}{60} = 0.82$ mile per minute.

12. If the conditions of the pipe 2 are changed, the rolling time from the entrance of the pipe 2 to the exit of the pipe 2 decreases 22 percent, but the rolling times of other two pipes do not change. According to the table information, how many less minutes does the ball take to arrive at the exit of the pipe 3 than the conditions of the pipe 2 do not be changed, rounded to the nearest minute?

(A) 19
(B) 21
(C) 22
(D) 23

> Solution: Answer: (B)
>
> "times of other two pipes do not change."
>
> ↓
>
> Only need to consider the increasing part.
>
> ⇓
>
> $$t = \frac{d}{r} = \frac{70.5}{45} \times \frac{22}{100} \times 60 \approx 20.68 \approx 21 \text{ minutes}$$

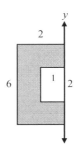

Note: Figure above not drawn to scale.

13. The two rectangles shown above are overlapped. The bigger one has dimensions 2 and 6. The smaller one has dimensions 1 and 2. If the whole figure makes one revolution on axis y, what is the volume that the shaded portion generates?

(A) 18π
(B) 20π
(C) 17π
(D) 22π

> Solution: Answer: (D)
>
> Two cylinders are formed by making on revolution. The shaded portion subtracting the smaller cylinder from the greater cylinder.
>
> $$\begin{cases} V_1 = A_1 \cdot h_1 = 2^2 \pi \cdot 6 = 24\pi \\ V_2 = A_2 \cdot h_2 = 1^2 \pi \cdot 2 = 2\pi \end{cases}$$
>
> ⇓
>
> $$V_{\text{Shaded}} = V_1 - V_2 = 24\pi - 2\pi = 22\pi$$

14. Which of the following value(s) must be excluded from the of $\frac{g(x)}{f(x)}$ if $f(x) = x^2 - 9$ and $g(x) = x - 3$?

(A) $x = -3$
(B) $x = \pm 3$
(C) $x = +3$
(D) $x = 0$

> Solution: Answer: (B)
>
> $$\frac{x-3}{x^2-9} \rightarrow x^2 - 9 = 0$$
>
> ⇓
>
> $$x = \pm\sqrt{9} = \pm 3$$

NEXT PAGE ⟩

15. If $i^2 = -1$, which of the following expressions could $x^2 + 5$ equal ?

(A) $x^2 - \left(\sqrt{5}\right)^2$

(B) $x^2 + \left(\sqrt{5} \cdot i\right)^2$

(C) $\left(x - \sqrt{5} \cdot i\right)\left(x + \sqrt{5} \cdot i\right)$

(D) $\left(x - \sqrt{5} \cdot i\right)^2$

Solution: Answer: (C)

$$x^2 + 5 = x^2 - (-5)$$
$$\downarrow$$
$$x^2 - \left(\sqrt{-5}\right)^2 = x^2 - \left(\sqrt{-1}\sqrt{5}\right)^2$$
$$\downarrow$$
$$x^2 - \left(i\sqrt{5}\right)^2$$
$$\Downarrow$$
$$(x - \sqrt{5}i)(x + \sqrt{5}i)$$

16. If $f(x) = \dfrac{1}{x}$, then $f\left(\dfrac{1}{3}\right) \cdot f\left(\dfrac{1}{x^2}\right) =$

(A) $\dfrac{1}{3x^2}$

(B) $3x^2$

(C) $\dfrac{x^2}{3}$

(D) $\dfrac{1}{x^2}$

Solution: Answer: (B)

$$f\left(\frac{1}{3}\right) = \frac{1}{\frac{1}{3}} = 3, \quad f\left(\frac{1}{x^2}\right) = \frac{1}{\frac{1}{x^2}} = x^2$$
$$\Downarrow$$
$$f\left(\frac{1}{3}\right) \cdot f\left(\frac{1}{x^2}\right) = 3 \cdot x^2$$

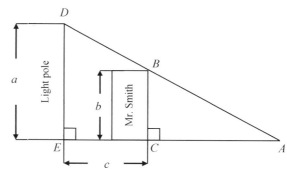

Note: Figure above not drawn to scale

17. In the figure above, Mr. Smith is $b = 7$ ft tall, the height of a light pole is $a = 14$ ft, and the distance from the base to Mr. Smith is $c = 42$ ft. If Smith's shadow is $\overline{CA}$, what is the length of $\overline{EA}$ in feet?

(A) 42

(B) 36

(C) 84

(D) 26

Solution: Answer: (C)

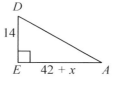

(1). $\begin{cases} \angle E = \angle C \text{ and } \angle A = \angle A \\ \text{Angle-Angle similarity} \end{cases}$

$$\downarrow$$

The 2 triangles are similar.

(2).   Similarity Ratio

$$\downarrow$$

$$\frac{x}{x + 42} = \frac{7}{14}$$

$$\downarrow$$

$$\cancel{14}^2 x = \cancel{7}\,(x + 42)$$

$$\downarrow$$

$$2x = x + 42, \quad x = 42$$

$$\Downarrow$$

$$EA = x + 42 = 42 + 42 = 84$$

NEXT PAGE

18. $3\dfrac{1}{3} + 3\cdot\dfrac{1}{3} - \dfrac{\frac{1}{3}}{\frac{1}{4}} =$

(A) $\dfrac{16}{3}$

(B) 3

(C) $\dfrac{3}{16}$

(D) $2\dfrac{1}{4}$

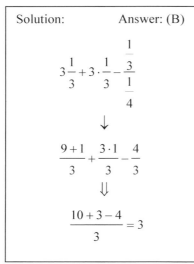

Solution: Answer: (B)

$$3\frac{1}{3} + 3\cdot\frac{1}{3} - \frac{\frac{1}{3}}{\frac{1}{4}}$$

$$\downarrow$$

$$\frac{9+1}{3} + \frac{3\cdot1}{3} - \frac{4}{3}$$

$$\Downarrow$$

$$\frac{10+3-4}{3} = 3$$

19. If the radius of a circle is 12 inches, what is the area of the sector whose arc length is 2π inches?

(A) 14π

(B) 12π

(C) 10π

(D) 16π

Solution: Answer: (B)

$$\begin{cases} s = r\theta \rightarrow 2\pi = 12\theta,\ \theta = \dfrac{\pi}{6} \\ A = \dfrac{1}{2}r^2\theta \end{cases}$$

$$\Downarrow$$

$$A = \frac{1}{2}12^2\frac{\pi}{6} = 12\pi$$

$$y/2 = 2x - 1$$

20. Change the function above to the point-slope form. What is the point?

(A) $x = 1,\ y = -2$ (B) $x = 1,\ y = 2$

(C) $x = \dfrac{1}{2},\ y = 2$ (D) $x = \dfrac{1}{2},\ y = 0$

Solution: Answer: (D)

$$\underbrace{y - y_o = s\left(x - x_o\right)}_{\text{slope-point form}}$$

$$\downarrow$$

$$y = 4x - 2,\ y = 4\left(x - 2/4\right),\ y = 4\left(x - 1/2\right)$$

$$\Downarrow$$

$$x_o = \frac{1}{2},\qquad y_o = 0$$

21. What is the domain of the function f if $f(x) = \dfrac{\sqrt{x-2}}{x}$?

(A) All real integers greater than or equal to 2

(B) All real numbers except for 0

(C) All real numbers less than or equal to -2

(D) All real numbers greater than or equal to 2

Solution: Answer: (D)

$$\begin{cases} x - 2 \ge 0 \\ x \ne 0 \end{cases} \rightarrow \begin{cases} x \ge 2 \\ x \ne 0 \end{cases}$$

The common portion of $x \ge 2$ and $x \ne 0$ is $x \ge 2$.

$$\downarrow$$

Common portion

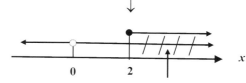

NEXT PAGE

$$|z-4|=\frac{1}{3}$$

22. What is the least value of z that satisfies the equation above?

(A) $-3\frac{2}{3}$

(B) $4\frac{1}{3}$

(C) $3\frac{2}{3}$

(D) $-4\frac{1}{3}$

Solution: Answer: (C)

$$(1)+(z-4)=\frac{1}{3},\ z=\frac{1}{3}+4=4\frac{1}{3}$$

$$(2)-(z-4)=\frac{1}{3},\ (z-4)=-\frac{1}{3},$$

$$z=4-\frac{1}{3}=3\frac{2}{3}$$

$$(3) \qquad 3\frac{2}{3}<4\frac{1}{3}$$

$$\Downarrow$$

Answer = (C)

23. If $343^{3x}=\left(\dfrac{1}{7}\right)^{x-50}$, which of the following is the value of x ?

(A) 1

(B) 2

(C) 3

(D) 5

Solution: Answer: (D)

$$\left(7^3\right)^{3x}=\left(7^{-1}\right)^{x-50}$$

$$\downarrow$$

$$7^{9x}=7^{-x+50}$$

$$\Downarrow$$

$$9x=-x+50,\quad x=5$$

24. The E-Tech Company will send a group of four people to work on a certain job. The company has 4 experienced electricians and 5 trainees. If the group consists of 2 experienced electricians and 2 trainees, how many possible distinct such groups exist?

(A) 16
(B) 30
(C) 40
(D) 60

Solution: Answer: (D)

The order doesn't matter.

(1). 2 positions and 4 elements for experienced electricians

$$m=\frac{\boxed{4}\times\boxed{3}}{2!}=6$$

(2). 2 positions and 5 elements for trainees

$$n=\frac{\boxed{5}\times\boxed{4}}{2!}=10$$

(3) 2 element sets that can be combined
→ Use Fundamental Counting Principle.

$$\Downarrow$$

$$6\times10=60$$

25. Two perpendicular lines l_1 and l_2 intersect at (-4, -3). If line l_2 has a slope of $\dfrac{1}{3}$, which of the following is an equation for line l_1 ?

(A) $y=-3(x+5)$

(B) $y=-3(x-5)$

(C) $y=3(x-5)$

(D) $y=3(x+5)$

Solution: Answer: (A)

$$s_{l_2}=\frac{1}{3}\underbrace{\longrightarrow}_{\text{Perpendicular}}s_{l_1}=-3$$

Use the point-slope form.

$$y-y_0=-3\left(x-x_0\right)$$

$$\downarrow$$

$$y-(-3)=-3\left(x-(-4)\right)$$

$$\downarrow$$

$$y+3=-3\left(x+4\right)$$

$$y=-3x-12-3$$

$$\Downarrow$$

$$y=-3x-15\ \text{ or }\ y=-3(x+5)$$

NEXT PAGE

26. Convert the degrees to radians or the radians to degrees for $\dfrac{\pi}{5}$ and $160°$. Which of the following a pair of results is true?

(Radians are assumed if no unit of measrement is indicated.)

(A) $36°$ and 2.79

(B) $62°$ and 4.13

(C) $20°$ and 2π

(D) $26°$ and 3.89

Solution: Answer: (A)

$$\frac{\pi}{5} \cdot \frac{180}{\pi} = 36°$$

and

$$160 \cdot \frac{\pi}{180} = 2.79^R$$

27. Let $f(x) = x^4 + x^3 \cdots$. If $f(4) = 0$ and $f(-3) = 0$, then $f(x)$ is divisible by

(A) $x^2 - 7x + 12$

(B) $x^2 - x + 7$

(C) $x^2 - 2x + 12$

(D) $x^2 - x - 12$

Solution   Answer: (D)

$$f(4) = 0 \text{ and } f(-3) = 0$$

↓

4 and -3 are roots of $f(x)$.

↓

$$(x - 4)(x + 3) = 0$$

↓

$f(x)$ is divisible by $(x - 4)(x + 3)$.

⇓

$$(x - 4)(x + 3) = x^2 - x - 12$$

28. In the xy-plane, the graph of $-3(3x)^2 + y = b$ passes through point $(1, 9)$. What is the value of b?

(A) -2186

(B) 18

(C) 0

(D) -18

Solution: Answer: (D)

$$-3(3^2 \cdot 1^2) + 9 = b$$

⇓

$$b = -18$$

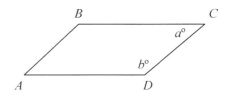

29. If $\overline{BC}$ is parallel to $\overline{AD}$ in the figure above, what is the value of $3(a + b)$?

(A) 360

(B) 450

(C) 540

(D) 600

Solution: Answer: (C)

$\overline{BC}$ is parallel to $\overline{AD}$.

↓

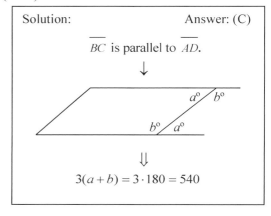

⇓

$$3(a + b) = 3 \cdot 180 = 540$$

30. In an Internet election, the voters using a certain voting program of websites cast 2.2 million votes and each vote was for either Candidate-A or Candidate-B. Candidate-A received 22,000 less votes than Candidate-B. What percent of the 2.2 million votes were cast for Candidate-B?

(A) 5.005   (B) 50.50   (C) 500.5   (D) 50.05

Solution: Answer: (B)

$$\underset{B}{x} + \underbrace{\left(x - 22 \times 10^3\right)}_{A} = 2.2 \times 10^6$$

$$2x = 22 \times 10^5 + 22 \times 10^3 = 10^3(22 \times 10^2 + 22)$$

↓

$$x = \frac{10^3(2222)}{2} = 1111 \times 10^3$$

↓

Fraction: $\dfrac{1111 \times 10^3}{2.2 \times 10^6} = \dfrac{1111 \times 10^3}{22 \times 10^2 \times 10^3} = \dfrac{1111}{2200}$

⇓

Percent: $\dfrac{1111}{2200} \times 100\% = \dfrac{1111 \times 100}{2200}\% = 50.5\%$

NEXT PAGE

$$N(t) = \frac{1}{2}t^2 - 40t + h$$

31. In the function above, $N(t)$ represents the number of certain birds on year number t for $0 < t \le 120$ and h is a constant. On what year is the number of the birds the same as it is on year number 50?

Solution: Answer: 30

$$\frac{1}{2} \cdot 50^2 - 40 \cdot 50 + \cancel{h} = \frac{1}{2}t^2 - 40t + \cancel{h}$$

$$\downarrow$$

$$1250 - 2000 = \frac{1}{2}t^2 - 40t$$

$$\downarrow$$

$$t^2 - 80t + 1500 = 0$$

$$\downarrow$$

$$(t - 30)(t - 50) = 0$$

$$\Downarrow$$

$$t = 30 \text{ or } t = 50 \text{ (given)}$$

32. $\dfrac{6!}{4!} = ?$

Solution: Answer: 30

$$\frac{6!}{4!} = \frac{6 \times 5 \times \cancel{4!}}{\cancel{4!}}$$

$$\Downarrow$$

$$6 \times 5 = 30$$

33. Nine times a number is the same as the number added to nine. What is the number?

Solution: Answer: 9/8

$$9x = x + 9$$

$$\downarrow$$

$$8x = 9$$

$$\Downarrow$$

$$x = 9/8$$

34. If p is the greatest prime factor of 87 and q is the least prime factor of 1,000, what is the value of $p \times q$?

Solution: Answer: 58

$$87 = 3 \times 29, \quad 1000 = 2 \times 500$$

$$p = 29, \ q = 2$$

$$\Downarrow$$

$$p \times q = 29 \times 2 = 58$$

35. The first term of set A is -3, and each term thereafter is 3 greater than the previous term. The Nth term of set B is given by the formula $-N + 22$. Which term of set A is the first one that value first exceeds the value of its corresponding term in set B?

Solution: Answer: 8

$$A = (\text{-3, 0, 3, 6, 9, 12, 15, 18...})$$
$$B = (-N + 22)$$
Because N represents the term number, N must represent <u>positive</u> integers.
$$N = 1, 2, 3...$$
$$B = (21, 20, 19, 18, 17, 16, 15, 14...)$$

$$8^{\text{th}} \text{ term of } A = 18$$
$$8^{\text{th}} \text{ term of } B = 14$$
$$\Downarrow$$
The <u>term</u> = 8

NEXT PAGE ⇨

36. At a high school of 679 students, each student chooses a biology course or a chemistry course or both. If 379 students of them choose biology course and 310 students of them choose chemistry course, how many students only choose chemistry course?

Solution: Answer: 300

$$T = S1 + S2 - B + N$$

T = total number of elements that overlap parts are eliminated

$S1$ and $S2$ = number of elements in sets 1 and 2

N = number of elements neither in set 1 nor set 2

B = number of elements in both sets counted twice

$\downarrow$

$$679 = 379 + 310 - B, \ B = 10$$

10 students choose chemistry and biology.

$\Downarrow$

$$\text{Students}_{\text{only choose chemistry}} = 310 - 10 = 300$$

37. Every person of group A can insert letters in envelopes at rate of 20 per minute. Every person of group B can insert the envelopes at the rate of 32 per minute. How many people of group B are need to keep up with 16 people of group A?

Solution: Answer: 10

Rate $\uparrow$, People $\downarrow$

$\downarrow$

Inverse relationship

$\downarrow$

Use $\square \cdot x = \square \cdot \square$

$\downarrow$

$$20 \cdot 16 = 32 \cdot x$$

$\Downarrow$

$$x = 10$$

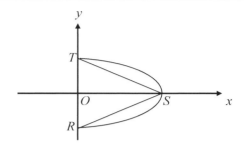

Note: Figure above not drawn to scale.

38. The figure above shows the graph of $x = g - y^2$, where g is a constant. If the area of triangle RST is 8, what is the value of g?

Solution: Answer: 4

(1) $x = 0$

$$x = -y^2 + g$$

$$0 = -y^2 + g$$

$$y^2 = g, \ y = \pm\sqrt{g}$$

$\downarrow$

$$RT = 2\sqrt{g}$$

(2) $y = 0$

$$x = -y^2 + g$$

$$x = 0 + g$$

$$x = g$$

$\downarrow$

$$OS = g$$

(3). Use the condition of area $A_{RST} = 8$.

$$A_{RST} = 8 = \frac{RT \times OS}{2} = \frac{2\sqrt{g} \times g}{2}$$

$$8 = \sqrt{g} \times g = g^{\frac{3}{2}}, \quad 8^{\frac{2}{3}} = \left(g^{\frac{3}{2}}\right)^{\frac{2}{3}}$$

$\Downarrow$

$$g = \left(\sqrt[3]{8}\right)^2 = 2^2 = 4$$

STOP

SAT Math

Practice

Test 08

Redesigned for Tests in March 2016 and Beyond

Mad Math

Math Test – No Calculator

Time: 25 Minutes
20 Questions

Notes:
- The use of a calculator is not allowed.
- All numbers used in this section are the real number.
- Figures are provided for some problems in this test. Unless otherwise indicated under the figure "Note: Figure above not drawn to scale", all figures are drawn as accurately as possible.
- All figures lie in a plane EXCEPT otherwise specified.
- Unless otherwise indicated, the domain of any function f, g or j is assumed to be the set of all real numbers x for which $f(x)$, $g(x)$, or $j(x)$ is a real number.

Reference Information

$$A = \frac{1}{2}bh$$

$$A = lw$$

$$A = \pi r^2$$

$$V = \pi r^2 h$$

$$V = lwh$$

$$c^2 = a^2 + b^2$$

$$V = \frac{1}{3}\pi r^2 h$$

$$V = \frac{4}{3}\pi r^3$$

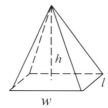

$$V = \frac{1}{3}lwh$$

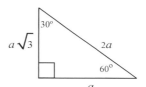

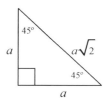

Copying or reuse of any portion of this page is illegal.

1. If $f(x) = -0.1$ for all real numbers x, what is $f(x - 0.1)$?

(A) $-\dfrac{1}{10}$

(B) -0.01

(C) $\dfrac{1}{10}$

(D) 0.05

3. What values for x would make $\dfrac{1}{\sqrt{x-1}}$ undefined ?

(A) All real numbers less than 1

(B) All real numbers greater than -1

(C) All real numbers less than -1 and equal to -1

(D) All real numbers less than 1 and equal to 1

2. Let $f(g)$ give the distance a truck can travel on g gallons The fuel economy of the truck is 16 miles per gallon, and the tank of the truck can holds a maximum of 25 gallons. What is the range of function f ?

(A) $0 < f \le 400$

(B) $0 \le f < 400$

(C) $0 < f < 400$

(D) $0 \le f \le 400$

4. What is the length of the arc intercepted by a central angle of 80° if the circle has a radius of 9 units ?

(A) $\dfrac{\pi}{4}$

(B) $\dfrac{\pi}{6}$

(C) 4π

(D) $\dfrac{2\pi}{3}$

NEXT PAGE

5. If x and y are real numbers, which of the following is the ordered pair solution for $2yi + 4i^3 = 6i^{10} + 2x$, where $i = \sqrt{-1}$?

(A) $(2, 3)$

(B) $(3, 2i)$

(C) $\left(3, \dfrac{2}{3}\right)$

(D) $(3, 2)$

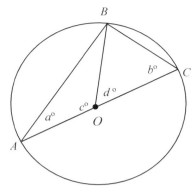

Note: Figure above not dawn to scale.

7. In the figure above, O is the center of the circle. If the ratio of c to d is $3 : 1$, what is the difference of a and b ?

(A) 30° (B) 35° (C) 40° (D) 45°

6. Which of the following is the nature of the roots of the equation $2x^2 + 2\sqrt{2}x - 1 = 0$?

(A) The equation has an imaginary root.

(B) Its roots are unequal, rational, and real numbers.

(C) Its roots are unequal, irrational, and real numbers

(D) Its roots are imaginary conjugates.

NEXT PAGE ⟹

8. If $f(x) = \sqrt[3]{-x^2 - 1}$, then which of the following is the domain of the function f ?

(A) No any solution

(B) All real numbers

(C) $-1 \le x \le 1$

(D) $x \ge 1$ or $x \le -1$

9. Convert the degrees to radians or the radians to degrees

for $\dfrac{\pi}{5}$ and 260°. Which of the following a pair of results is

true?

(Radians are assumed if no unit of measrement is indicated.)

(A) 36° and 5.45

(B) 63° and 5.45

(C) 36° and 4.54

(D) 26° and 5.34

10. $\dfrac{a^2 - b^2}{-b + a} = ?$

(A) $a + b$

(B) $a - b$

(C) $-a + b$

(D) $a^2 - b$

11. The points (3, -9), (7, 12) and (11, -5) lie on the graph of $f(x)$. If $g(x) = f(x + 2)$, which of the following points must lie on the graph of $g(x)$?

(A) (-5, -9)
(B) (1, -9)
(C) (13, -5)
(D) (9, 12)

12. Which of the following is the equivalent of the statement that three-sevenths of the square of t minus the value of r divided by the square of q equals h?

(A) $\dfrac{3t^2}{7} - \dfrac{r}{q^2} = h$

(B) $\left(\dfrac{3t}{7}\right)^2 - \left(\dfrac{r}{q}\right)^2 = h$

(C) $\dfrac{3t^2}{7} - \dfrac{r^2}{p^2} = h$

(D) $\dfrac{3}{7t^2} + \dfrac{p^2}{r} = h$

NEXT PAGE

13. If $f(x) = x^2 - 9$ and g $(x) = x + 3$, which of the following is the composition of function $(f \circ g)(x) = f(g(x))$ equal to?

(A) $(x - \sqrt{6})(x + \sqrt{6})$

(B) $(x + 6)(x - 6)$

(C) $x(x + 6)$

(D) $x^2 - 3^2$

15. What is the range of function f if $f(x) = x^2 - 10$ for $-2 \le x \le 4$?

(A) $10 \le y \le 6$

(B) $y \ge 0$

(C) $-10 \le y \le 6$

(D) $y \le 6$

14. $2\dfrac{2}{3}$ subtracted from its reciprocal is

(A) $\dfrac{55}{24}$

(B) $-\dfrac{55}{24}$

(C) $-\dfrac{73}{24}$

(D) $\dfrac{3}{8}$

NEXT PAGE

16. If p is an integer and the sum of p and next integer is larger than 11, what is the smallest possible value of p?

18. A book sells for \$66 on Internet, giving the dealer 20% profit. What was the dealer's cost?

19. The E-Tech Company will send a group of seven people to work on a certain job. The company has 4 experienced electricians and 5 trainees. If the group consists of 3 experienced electricians and 4 trainees, how many possible distinct such groups exist?

$$\begin{array}{ccc} Q & R & S \\ \bullet & \bullet & \bullet \end{array}$$

17. In the figure above, the length of $\overline{QR}$ is four more than four times the length of $\overline{RS}$, and the length of $\overline{QS}$ is 44, then what is RS ?

20. If $x^2 - 27 = 169$, then x could be equal to

STOP

Math Test – Calculator

Time: 55 Minutes
38 Questions

Notes:
- The use of a calculator is not allowed.
- All numbers used in this section are the real number.
- Figures are provided for some problems in this test. Unless otherwise indicated under the figure "Note: Figure above not drawn to scale", all figures are drawn as accurately as possible.
- All figures lie in a plane EXCEPT otherwise specified.
- Unless otherwise indicated, the domain of any function f, g or j is assumed to be the set of all real numbers x for which $f(x)$, $g(x)$, or $j(x)$ is a real number.

Reference Information

$$A = \frac{1}{2}bh$$

$$A = lw$$

$$A = \pi r^2$$

$$V = \pi r^2 h$$

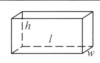

$$V = lwh$$

$$c^2 = a^2 + b^2$$

$$V = \frac{1}{3}\pi r^2 h$$

$$V = \frac{4}{3}\pi r^3$$

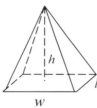

$$V = \frac{1}{3}lwh$$

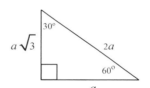

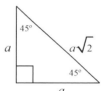

1. Several students stand in a line. Staring at one end of the line, Kevin is counted as 7th person, and starting at the other end, Kevin is counted as the 13th person. How many students are in the line?

(A) 18
(B) 21
(C) 19
(D) 20

2. $\dfrac{\dfrac{3}{\frac{1}{3}} - \dfrac{\frac{1}{3}}{3}}{} = ?$

(A) $\dfrac{82}{9}$

(B) $\dfrac{80}{9}$

(C) 7.74

(D) $\dfrac{79}{9}$

3. If $f(x) = x - 5$, $g(x) = 10x$, and $j(x) = \dfrac{x}{5}$, what does $f(j(g(5)))$ equal?

(A) 5
(B) 6
(C) 7
(D) 8

4. If $0.0029 = 0.29 \times 10^q$, what is the value of q?

(A) 3
(B) -1
(C) -2
(D) 2

NEXT PAGE

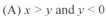
5. Line L passes through the points (0, 0) and (-6, 6). Which of the following points is located in the region between the graph of the line L and negative part of the x-axis?

(A) $x > y$ and $y < 0$
(B) $x = y$ and $y < 0$
(C) $x \geq y$ and $y < 0$
(D) $x < y$ and $y > 0$

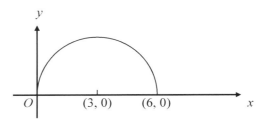

Note: Figure above not drawn to scale.

7. In the figure above, the center of the semicircle is at (3, 0). Which of the following are x-coordinates of two points on this semicircle whose y-coordinates are equal?

(A) 3 and 9
(B) 5 and 10
(C) 3 and 7
(D) 1 and 5

6. If $f(x) = (x^2 - 6x + 9)(x - 1)$, how many distinct zeros does $f(x)$ have?

(A) 1

(B) 2

(C) 3

(D) 0

8. Which of the following is $\sqrt{x^6}$ equal to

(A) x^3

(B) $\left| x^2 \right|$

(C) x^5

(D) $\left| x^3 \right|$

**RELATIONSHIP OF TEMPERATURE
AND TIME FOR MIXTURES**

Temperature T at x Second	Mixture
$T(x) = 4x - 3$	M_1
$T(x) = \dfrac{1}{4}x - 3$	M_2
$T(x) = -\dfrac{1}{4}x + 3$	M_3
$T(x) = -4x + 3$	M_4

9. The chart above shows the information of temperatures of several distinct chemical mixtures at x seconds when the mixture was formed. The temperature of which mixture goes down the greatest number of degrees during the interval from $x = 16$ to $x = 20$?

(A) M_5

(B) M_2

(C) M_3

(D) M_4

10. At a supermarket, $\dfrac{2}{7}$ of the items are discounted by 70 percent, $\dfrac{1}{7}$ of the items are discounted by 40 percent, $\dfrac{3}{14}$ of the items are discounted by 50 percent, and remaining items are not discounted. If one item is to be selected randomly, which of the following is the probability that the item is discounted by either 40 percent or 50 percent?

(A) $\dfrac{5}{14}$

(B) $\dfrac{1}{2}$

(C) $\dfrac{3}{98}$

(D) $\dfrac{3}{49}$

11. A square board is divided into m colunms of m squares each. If n of these squares lie along the boundary of the board, which of the following is a possible value of n ?

(A) 6

(B) 56

(C) 50

(D) 54

NEXT PAGE

12. What is the solution of the equation $\sqrt{x^2 - 35} = 5 - x$?

(A) no solution

(B) 5

(C) 4

(D) 7

14. If x and a are numbers such that $x < -a$ and $x > a$, which of the following must be true?

 I. $|x| < a$

 II. $|x| > a$

 III. $x > 0$

(A) I only

(B) II and III only

(C) I, II and III

(D) II only

13. If the graph of a linear function passes through the points $(p, 1)$, $(q, 5)$ and $(3, 2)$, what is the value of $3p + q$?

(A) 12
(B) 5
(C) 4
(D)-3

NEXT PAGE

15.   Which of the following could be the remainders when 3 consecutive integers are each divided by 2?

(A) 1, 2, 0
(B) 0, 1, 0
(C) 0, 2, 0
(D) 0, 1, 2

17.   In the figures above, if one of them is selected randomly, what is the probability that the number of vertices in the figure will be at least 4?

(A) 0.8

(B) $\dfrac{1}{5}$

(C) $\dfrac{2}{5}$

(D) 60%

16.   If $-1 < x < 0$, then which of the following must be true?
4.   If $-1 < x < 0$, then which of the following must be true?

(A) $\dfrac{1}{x^2} < x^5$

(B) $\dfrac{1}{x^4} < \dfrac{1}{x^3}$

(C) $x^2 < x^3$

(D) $\dfrac{1}{x^5} < \dfrac{1}{x^3}$

18.   A train travels 1,200 miles in 10 hours. Before 12:00pm the train averages 140 miles per hour. After noon the train averages 100 miles per hour. What time did the train leave?

(A) 8am
(B) 7am
(C) 9am
(D) 6am

NEXT PAGE

19. The angle formed by the hour hand and minute hand of a clock at 3:25 is

(A) 78°
(B) 67.5°
(C) 47.5°
(D) 125°

y	9	m	n
x	0	1	2

21.   The values of m and n in the chart above are related so that $(y+1)$ is directly proportional to $(x-1)$. What is the sum of m and n?

(A) 10

(B)-12

(C) 14

(D)-16

20.   Mr. Franklin chooses watermelons for his supermarket. He will choose the watermelons that weigh more than 10 pounds and less than 20 pounds. If n represents the weight of a watermelon, in pounds, he will choose, which inequalities below represents all possible values of n?

(A) $|n-15| < 10$

(B) $|n-15| > 20$

(C) $|n-15| \leq 5$

(D) $|n-15| < 5$

22.   If $f(x) = x^2 - 9$ and $g(x) = x + 3$, which of the following does the combining function $\dfrac{f}{g} = \left(\dfrac{f}{g}\right)(x) = \dfrac{f(x)}{g(x)}$ equal?

(A) $x - 3, x \neq -3$

(B) $x + 3, x \neq 3$

(C) $x + 3, x \neq -3$

(D) $x - 3$

NEXT PAGE

23.   If $16\sqrt{24} = p\sqrt{q}$, where p and q are positive integers and $p > q$, which of the following could be the value of $p - q$?

(A) $32 - \sqrt{6}$
(B) 38
(C) 46
(D) 26

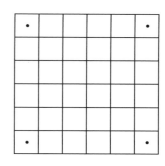

Note: Figure above not drawn to scale.

25. In the figure above, a square with side length 6 is divided into 36 squares. What is ratio of the area of the circle (not shown here) that passes through the 4 points, which are the centers of the 4 corner squares, to circumference of the circle?

(A) $\dfrac{5\sqrt{2}}{4}$

(B) $4\sqrt{2}$

(C) $5\sqrt{2}$

(D) $\dfrac{25}{\sqrt{2}}$

24.   Martin is 32 years older than his daughter May. In nine years, he will be two times as old as May will be. How old is Martin?

(A) 55

(B) 63

(C) 53

(D) 56

NEXT PAGE

26. Two sides of a triangle have lengths 6 and 19 separately. If the remaining side of the triangle has a value that is an integer, what are the largest and smallest possible perimeters of this triangle?

(A) 39 and 50
(B) 39 and 49
(C) 38 and 49
(D) 39 and 50

$$M(x) = x^2 + 3x + 6, \quad N(x) = 5x^3 + 15x^2 + 30x$$

27. If the polynomials M and N are defined above, which of the following polynomials is divisible by $5x + 5$?

(A) $f(x) = N(x) + 5M(x)$

(B) $g(x) = 5xN(x) + 5M(x)$

(C) $h(x) = 5N(x) + 5xM(x)$

(D) $j(x) = xN(x) + 5M(x)$

NEXT PAGE

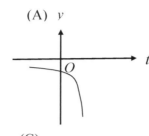

Note: Figure above not drawn to scale.

28.   In the figure above, $\overline{QS}$ and $\overline{RT}$ are perpendicular diameters of the circle. If the circle has area of 36π, which of the following is the length of $\overline{ST}$?

(A) $6\sqrt{2}$

(B) $4\sqrt{3}$

(C) $18\sqrt{2}$

(D) $8\sqrt{2}$

29. Which of the following sketches shows a relationship that is appropriately modled with the function $f(t) = ar^t$, where $a < 0$ and $r > 1$?

(A)

(B)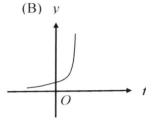

(C)

(D)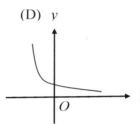

$$y + 2 = 1/2\left(2x - 1\right)$$

30.   What is the y-intercept of the function above?

(A) $\left(0, 1.5\right)$

(B) $\left(1.5,\ 0\right)$

(C) $\left(0,\ -2.5\right)$

(D) $\left(-2.5,\ 0\right)$

NEXT PAGE

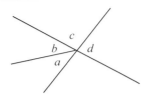

Note: Figure above not drawn to scale.

31. In the figure above, if $b = \dfrac{1}{5}a$ and $c = 4d$, what is the

value of b?

32. If $32^{2x} = \left(\dfrac{1}{2}\right)^{x-11}$, what is the value of x ?

33. The sides of a rectangular room have lengths $2s$, $3s$, and $4s$. What is the entire surface area of the room if $s = 2$?

34. Let set $S = (5, \; 10, \; 15, \; 150)$. What is the probability that the sum of any 2 numbers in S is greater than 154 ?

NEXT PAGE

Physicists' an Experiment of Ball Rolling

	Pipe 1	Pipe 2	Pipe 3
Length (meters)	200.6	200.5	108.4
Average of rolling speed (meters per minute)	35	55	40

Several physicists did an experiment. They let a special ball, which is made by mix materials, roll through three pipes, pipe 1, pipe 2, and pipe 3, which are connected by that order. Each pipe has own conditions. The records of the experiment were put into the table above.

35. The experiment started. The ball rolled directly into the pipe 1, then the pipe 2, and then the pipe 3. What is the average speed, in meters per hour, of the ball during its entire rolling process that spent ten minutes?

36. If you take 4 less than a number x and then raise this result to the 5th power, it equals 243. What is the value of x?

37. If the graph of $y = 3$ intersects the graph of $y = x^2 - 3x - 25$, what is one possible x-value of the intersection point of the graph?

38. Sarah herself can clean a room in 14 minutess, and Jay himself can clean the same room in 21 minutes. After Sarah begins the job and does $\frac{3}{7}$ of the job, Jay takes over and finishes the job. What is the entire time, in minutes, that takes Sarah and Jay to clean the room?

STOP

Answer Key
For
SAT Math Practice Test 08

Section 3

1	A
2	D
3	D
4	C
5	D
6	C
7	D
8	B
9	C
10	A
11	B
12	A
13	C
14	B
15	C

16	6
17	8
18	55
19	20
20	14

Section 4

1	C	16	D
2	B	17	A
3	A	18	B
4	C	19	C
5	D	20	D
6	B	21	B
7	D	22	A
8	D	23	D
9	D	24	A
10	A	25	A
11	B	26	B
12	A	27	A
13	A	28	A
14	D	29	A
15	B	30	C

31	6
32	1
33	208
34	1/2 or .5
35	3057
36	7
37	7
38	18

SAT Math

Practice

Test 08

Explanations

Redesigned for Tests in March 2016 and Beyond

Mad Math

Math Test – No Calculator

Time: 25 Minutes
20 Questions

Notes:
- The use of a calculator is not allowed.
- All numbers used in this section are the real number.
- Figures are provided for some problems in this test. Unless otherwise indicated under the figure "Note: Figure above not drawn to scale", all figures are drawn as accurately as possible.
- All figures lie in a plane EXCEPT otherwise specified.
- Unless otherwise indicated, the domain of any function f, g or j is assumed to be the set of all real numbers x for which $f(x)$, $g(x)$, or $j(x)$ is a real number.

Reference Information

$$A = \frac{1}{2}bh$$

$$A = lw$$

$$A = \pi r^2$$

$$V = \pi r^2 h$$

$$V = lwh$$

$$c^2 = a^2 + b^2$$

$$V = \frac{1}{3}\pi r^2 h$$

$$V = \frac{4}{3}\pi r^3$$

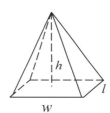
$$V = \frac{1}{3}lwh$$

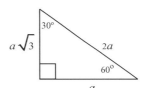

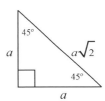

Copying or reuse of any portion of this page is illegal.

1. If $f(x) = -0.1$ for all real numbers x, what is $f(x - 0.1)$?

(A) $-\dfrac{1}{10}$

(B) -0.01

(C) $\dfrac{1}{10}$

(D) 0.05

> Solution: Answer: (A)
>
> After change of value of x, the value of y corresponding with new value of x is the same value of y corresponding with old value of x.
>
> or
>
> $$f(x) = f(x - a)$$
> $$\Downarrow$$
> $$f(x - 0.1) = -0.1 = -\frac{1}{10}$$

2. Let $f(g)$ give the distance a truck can travel on g gallons The fuel economy of the truck is 16 miles per gallon, and the tank of the truck can holds a maximum of 25 gallons. What is the range of function f ?

(A) $0 < f \le 400$

(B) $0 \le f < 400$

(C) $0 < f < 400$

(D) $0 \le f \le 400$

> Solution: Answer: (D)
>
> $$\begin{cases} \text{Input} = \text{gallons} \\ \text{Output} = \text{distance} \end{cases}$$
> $$\downarrow$$
> $$\begin{cases} \text{Domain is about gallons.} \\ \text{Range is about daitance.} \end{cases}$$
> $$\downarrow$$
> $$\begin{cases} \text{Range:} \\ \text{The least} = 0 \\ \text{The greatest} = 16 \times 25 = 400 \end{cases}$$
> $$\Downarrow$$
> $$\boxed{0 \le f \le 400}$$

3. What values for x would make $\dfrac{1}{\sqrt{x-1}}$ undefined ?

(A) All real numbers less than 1

(B) All real numbers greater than -1

(C) All real numbers less than -1 and equal to -1

(D) All real numbers less than 1 and equal to 1

> Solution: Answer: (D)
>
> $$\begin{cases} x - 1 < 0, & \rightarrow & x < 1 \\ \sqrt{x-1} = 0, & \rightarrow & x - 1 = 0^2 \end{cases}$$
> $$\Downarrow$$
> $$\begin{cases} x < 1 \\ x = 1 \end{cases}, \quad x \le 1$$

4. What is the length of the arc intercepted by a central angle of 80° if the circle has a radius of 9 units ?

(A) $\dfrac{\pi}{4}$

(B) $\dfrac{\pi}{6}$

(C) 4π

(D) $\dfrac{2\pi}{3}$

> Solution: Answer: (C)
>
> $$S = r\theta$$
> $$\Downarrow$$
> $$S = 9 \cdot 8\cancel{0} \cdot \frac{\pi}{18\cancel{0}} = 4\pi$$

NEXT PAGE

5. If x and y are real numbers, which of the following is the ordered pair solution for $2yi + 4i^3 = 6i^{10} + 2x$, where $i = \sqrt{-1}$?

(A) $(2, 3)$

(B) $(3, 2i)$

(C) $\left(3, \dfrac{2}{3}\right)$

(D) $(3, 2)$

Solution: Answer: (D)

$$\begin{cases} \underbrace{2yi + 4i^3 = 6i^{10} + 2x}_{\text{Deal with } i \text{ first.}} \\ i^3 = -i, \quad i^{10} = i^8 \cdot i^2 = -1 \end{cases}$$

$\downarrow$

$$2yi - 4i = -6 + 2x$$

$$\underbrace{0 + (2y - 4)i = -6 + 2x + 0i}_{\text{Complex number in standard form}}$$

$\Downarrow$

$$\begin{cases} 0 = -6 + 2x, \quad x = 3 \\ 2y - 4 = 0, \quad y = 2 \end{cases}$$

6. Which of the following is the nature of the roots of the equation $2x^2 + 2\sqrt{2}x - 1 = 0$?

(A) The equation has an imaginary root.

(B) Its roots are unequal, rational, and real numbers.

(C) Its roots are unequal, irrational, and real numbers

(D) Its roots are imaginary conjugates.

Solution: Answer: (C)

$$b^2 - 4ac = \left(2\sqrt{2}\right)^2 - 4 \cdot 2 \cdot \left(-1\right) = 8 + 8 = 16 > 0$$

$$x_{1 \text{ and } 2} = \frac{-2\sqrt{2} \pm 4}{2 \cdot 2}$$

$\Downarrow$

Its roots $x_{1 \text{ and } 2}$ are unequal, irrational, and real.

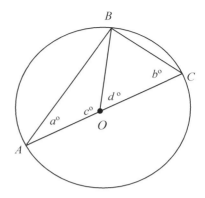

Note: Figure above not dawn to scale.

7. In the figure above, O is the center of the circle. If the ratio of c to d is $3 : 1$, what is the difference of a and b ?

(A) 30° (B) 35° (C) 40° (D) 45°

Solution: Answer: (D)

$$\begin{cases} c + d = 180 \\ c : d = 3k : k \end{cases} \rightarrow 3k + k = 180$$

$\downarrow$

$$4k = 180 \rightarrow k = 45 \rightarrow \begin{cases} c = 3k = 135 \\ d = k = 45 \end{cases}$$

$\downarrow$

In triangle OCB, $OB = OC =$ radius and $b = m\angle C$.

$\downarrow$

$$b = \frac{180 - d}{2} = \frac{180 - 45}{2} = 67.5$$

and

In triangle OAB, $OA = OB =$ radius and $a = m\angle A$.

$\downarrow$

$$a = \frac{180 - c}{2} = \frac{180 - 135}{2} = 22.5$$

$\Downarrow$

$$a - b = 67.5 - 22.5 = 45$$

NEXT PAGE ⇨

8. If $f(x) = \sqrt[3]{-x^2 - 1}$, then which of the following is the domain of the function f ?

(A) No any solution

(B) All real numbers

(C) $-1 \le x \le 1$

(D) $x \ge 1$ or $x \le -1$

> Solution: Answer: (B)
>
> $(-x^2 - 1)$ is not under even-root
>
> such as $\sqrt[2]{}$ or $\sqrt[4]{}$.
>
> $\Downarrow$
>
> x can be any real number.

9. Convert the degrees to radians or the radians to degrees for $\dfrac{\pi}{5}$ and $260°$. Which of the following a pair of results is true?

(Radians are assumed if no unit of measrement is indicated.)

(A) $36°$ and 5.45

(B) $63°$ and 5.45

(C) $36°$ and 4.54

(D) $26°$ and 5.34

> Solution: Answer: (C)
>
> $\dfrac{\pi}{5} \cdot \dfrac{180}{\pi} = 36°$
>
> and
>
> $260 \cdot \dfrac{\pi}{180} \approx 4.54^R$

10. $\dfrac{a^2 - b^2}{-b + a} = ?$

(A) $a + b$

(B) $a - b$

(C) $-a + b$

(D) $a^2 - b$

> Solution: Answer: (A)
>
> $\dfrac{a^2 - b^2}{a - b}$
>
> $\downarrow$
>
> $\dfrac{(a - b)(a + b)}{a - b}$
>
> $\Downarrow$
>
> $a + b$

11. The points (3, -9), (7, 12) and (11, -5) lie on the graph of $f(x)$. If $g(x) = f(x + 2)$, which of the following points must lie on the graph of $g(x)$?

(A) (-5, -9)
(B) (1, -9)
(C) (13, -5)
(D) (9, 12)

> Solution: Answer: (B)
>
> By $f(x + 2) \rightarrow$ all values of x of the points of the function graph are shifted 2 units left, but all values of y before and after its corresponding x is shifted, should have no change.
>
> The y value of y in choice (B) has no change when x value is shifted 2 units left from $x = 3$ to $x = 1$.
>
> $\Downarrow$
>
> Answer is (B).

12. Which of the following is the equivalent of the statement that three-sevenths of the square of t minus the value of r divided by the square of q equals h?

(A) $\dfrac{3t^2}{7} - \dfrac{r}{q^2} = h$

(B) $\left(\dfrac{3t}{7}\right)^2 - \left(\dfrac{r}{q}\right)^2 = h$

(C) $\dfrac{3t^2}{7} - \dfrac{r^2}{p^2} = h$

(D) $\dfrac{3}{7t^2} + \dfrac{p^2}{r} = h$

> Solution: Answer: (A)
>
> $\dfrac{3}{7} \times t^2 - \dfrac{r}{q^2} = h$
>
> $\Downarrow$
>
> $\dfrac{3t^2}{7} - \dfrac{r}{q^2} = h$

NEXT PAGE ⇨

13. If $f(x) = x^2 - 9$ and $g(x) = x + 3$, which of the following is the composition of function $(f \circ g)(x) = f(g(x))$ equal to?

(A) $(x - \sqrt{6})(x + \sqrt{6})$

(B) $(x + 6)(x - 6)$

(C) $x(x + 6)$

(D) $x^2 - 3^2$

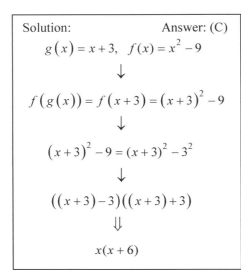

Solution: Answer: (C)

$$g(x) = x + 3, \quad f(x) = x^2 - 9$$
$$\downarrow$$
$$f(g(x)) = f(x+3) = (x+3)^2 - 9$$
$$\downarrow$$
$$(x+3)^2 - 9 = (x+3)^2 - 3^2$$
$$\downarrow$$
$$((x+3)-3)((x+3)+3)$$
$$\Downarrow$$
$$x(x+6)$$

14. $2\dfrac{2}{3}$ subtracted from its reciprocal is

(A) $\dfrac{55}{24}$

(B) $-\dfrac{55}{24}$

(C) $-\dfrac{73}{24}$

(D) $\dfrac{3}{8}$

Solution: Answer: (B)

(1). $2\dfrac{2}{3} = \dfrac{8}{3}$

Its reciprocal $= \dfrac{3}{8}$

(2).

"subtracted from its reciprocal"
$$\Downarrow$$
$$\dfrac{3}{8} - \dfrac{8}{3} = \dfrac{9-64}{24} = -\dfrac{55}{24}$$

15. What is the range of function f if $f(x) = x^2 - 10$ for $-2 \le x \le 4$?

(A) $10 \le y \le 6$

(B) $y \ge 0$

(C) $-10 \le y \le 6$

(D) $y \le 6$

Solution: Answer: (C)

Method 1

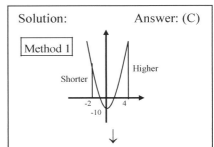

$$\downarrow$$

Choose $x = 4$.
$$\begin{cases} f(4) = 4^2 - 10 = 6 \\ \text{Figure 6} \end{cases}$$
$$\Downarrow$$
Answer is (C).

Method 2

$$f(x) = x^2 - 10 \text{ for } -2 \le x \le 4$$
$$\downarrow$$
The smallest one:
$$f(0) = 0^2 - 10 = -10$$
The greatest one:
$$f(4) = 4^2 - 10 = 6$$
$$\Downarrow$$
$$-10 \le y \le 6$$

NEXT PAGE

16. If p is an integer and the sum of p and next integer is larger than 11, what is the smallest possible value of p?

> Solution: Answer: 6
>
> Let n = next integer.
>
> (1) If $p = 5$, then $n = 6$.
>
> $p + n = 5 + 6 = 11, \text{not} > 11.$
>
> (2) If $p = 6$, then $n = 7$
>
> $p + n = 6 + 7 = 13 > 11$
>
> $\Downarrow$
>
> $p = 6$

17. In the figure above, the length of $\overline{QR}$ is four more than four times the length of $\overline{RS}$, and the length of $\overline{QS}$ is 44, then what is RS?

> Solution: Answer: 8
>
>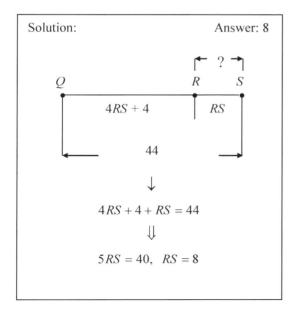
>
> $4RS + 4 + RS = 44$
>
> $\Downarrow$
>
> $5RS = 40, \quad RS = 8$

18. A book sells for \$66 on Internet, giving the dealer 20% profit. What was the dealer's cost?

> Solution: Answer: 55
>
> $66 = 1.2x \qquad x = 55$

19. The E-Tech Company will send a group of seven people to work on a certain job. The company has 4 experienced electricians and 5 trainees. If the group consists of 3 experienced electricians and 4 trainees, how many possible distinct such groups exist?

> Solution: Answer: 20
>
> $\begin{cases} \text{1 element set} \\ \qquad \downarrow \\ \text{Use the counting method of} \\ \text{permutations or combinations.} \end{cases}$
>
> Order doesn't matter.
>
> $\downarrow$
>
> Use the counting method of combinations
>
> $\downarrow$
>
> (1) 3 positions and 4 elements for experienced pilots
>
> $m = \dfrac{\boxed{4} \times \boxed{3} \times \boxed{2}}{3!} = 4$
>
> (2) 4 positions and 5 elements for trainees
>
> $n = \dfrac{\boxed{5} \times \boxed{4} \times \boxed{3} \times \boxed{2}}{4!} = 5$
>
> (3) 2 element sets and they can be combined in practice.
>
> $\downarrow$
>
> Use Fundamental Counting Principle.
>
> $\Downarrow$
>
> $m \times n = 4 \times 5 = 20$

20. If $x^2 - 27 = 169$, then x could be equal to

> Solution: Answer: 14
>
> $x^2 - 27 = 169$
>
> $\downarrow$
>
> $x^2 = 196$
>
> $\Downarrow$
>
> $x = \pm\sqrt{196} = \pm 14 \Rightarrow 14$

STOP

Math Test – Calculator

Time: 55 Minutes
38 Questions

Notes:
- The use of a calculator is not allowed.
- All numbers used in this section are the real number.
- Figures are provided for some problems in this test. Unless otherwise indicated under the figure "Note: Figure above not drawn to scale", all figures are drawn as accurately as possible.
- All figures lie in a plane EXCEPT otherwise specified.
- Unless otherwise indicated, the domain of any function f, g or j is assumed to be the set of all real numbers x for which $f(x)$, $g(x)$, or $j(x)$ is a real number.

Reference Information

$$A = \frac{1}{2}bh$$

$$A = lw$$

$$A = \pi r^2$$

$$V = \pi r^2 h$$

$$V = lwh$$

$$c^2 = a^2 + b^2$$

$$V = \frac{1}{3}\pi r^2 h$$

$$V = \frac{4}{3}\pi r^3$$

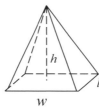

$$V = \frac{1}{3}lwh$$

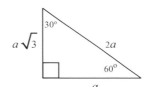

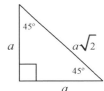

Copying or reuse of any portion of this page is illegal.

1. Several students stand in a line. Staring at one end of the line, Kevin is counted as 7th person, and starting at the other end, Kevin is counted as the 13th person. How many students are in the line?

(A) 18
(B) 21
(C) 19
(D) 20

Solution: **Answer: (C)**

7th

13th

$13 + 7 = 20$
But Kevin's position is repeatedly counted.
⇓
$20 - 1 = 19$

---

2. $\dfrac{\frac{3}{\frac{1}{3}} - \frac{\frac{1}{3}}{3}} = ?$

(A) $\dfrac{82}{9}$

(B) $\dfrac{80}{9}$

(C) 7.74

(D) $\dfrac{79}{9}$

Solution: **Answer: (B)**

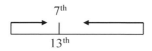

↓

$3 \times 3 - \dfrac{1}{3 \times 3}$

⇓

$9 - \dfrac{1}{9} = \dfrac{80}{9}$

---

3. If $f(x) = x - 5$, $g(x) = 10x$, and $j(x) = \dfrac{x}{5}$, what does $f(j(g(5)))$ equal?

(A) 5
(B) 6
(C) 7
(D) 8

Solution: **Answer: (A)**

$g(5) = 10 \cdot 5 = 50$

↓

$j(50) = \dfrac{50}{5} = 10$

⇓

$f(10) = 10 - 5 = 5$

---

4. If $0.0029 = 0.29 \times 10^q$, what is the value of q?

(A) 3
(B) -1
(C) -2
(D) 2

Solution: **Answer: (C)**

$\dfrac{\cancel{29}}{100\,\cancel{00}} = \dfrac{\cancel{29}}{1\,\cancel{00}} \times 10^q$

↓

$\dfrac{1}{100} = 10^q, \quad 10^{-2} = 10^q$

⇓

$q = -2$

NEXT PAGE

5. Line L passes through the points $(0, 0)$ and $(-6, 6)$. Which of the following points is located in the region between the graph of the line L and negative part of the x-axis?

(A) $x > y$ and $y < 0$
(B) $x = y$ and $y < 0$
(C) $x \geq y$ and $y < 0$
(D) $x < y$ and $y > 0$

Solution: Answer: (D)

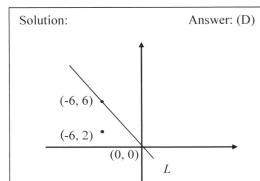

Choose one point with the x-coordinate -6 between the graph of the line L and negative part of the x-axis.

$$x = -6, \ y = 2$$
$$\Downarrow$$
$$x < y \text{ and } y > 0$$

6. If $f(x) = (x^2 - 6x + 9)(x - 1)$, how many distinct zeros does $f(x)$ have?

(A) 1

(B) 2

(C) 3

(D) 0

Solution: Answer: (B)

$$(x^2 - 6x + 9)(x - 1) = 0$$
$$(x - 3)^2 (x - 1) = 0$$
$$\downarrow$$
$$(x - 3)^2 = 0 \text{ or } (x - 1) = 0$$
$$x = 3, \ 3, \ x = 1$$
$$\Downarrow$$
$$f(x) \text{ has 2 different zeros.}$$

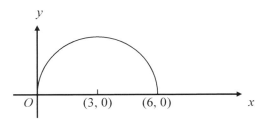

Note: Figure above not drawn to scale.

7. In the figure above, the center of the semicircle is at $(3, 0)$. Which of the following are x-coordinates of two points on this semicircle whose y-coordinates are equal?

(A) 3 and 9
(B) 5 and 10
(C) 3 and 7
(D) 1 and 5

Solution: Solution: (D)

The semicircle is a symmetric graph.

From $x = 3$ to $x = 1$, the distance = 2.
From $x = 3$ to $x = 5$, the distance = 2.

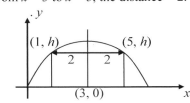

Only $x = 1$ and $x = 5$ can make the same distance from $x = 3$. So only values of y corresponding the values of $x = 1$ and $x = 5$ are equal.

8. Which of the following is $\sqrt{x^6}$ equal to

(A) x^3

(B) $|x^2|$

(C) x^5

(D) $|x^3|$

Solution: Answer: (D)

$$\sqrt{x^6} = \sqrt{\left(x^3\right)^2}$$

x can be negative, 0, or positive.

$$\Downarrow$$
$$|x^3|$$

NEXT PAGE

RELATIONSHIP OF TEMPERATURE AND TIME FOR MIXTURES

Temperature T at x Second	Mixture
$T(x) = 4x - 3$	M_1
$T(x) = \dfrac{1}{4}x - 3$	M_2
$T(x) = -\dfrac{1}{4}x + 3$	M_3
$T(x) = -4x + 3$	M_4

9.   The chart above shows the information of temperatures of several distinct chemical mixtures at x seconds when the mixture was formed. The temperature of which mixture goes down the greatest number of degrees during the interval from $x = 16$ to $x = 20$?

(A) M_5

(B) M_2

(C) M_3

(D) M_4

Solution: Answer: (D)

If the slopes are greater than 0, the temperatures

   go up. So choices (A) and (B) are canceled.

The slope of (C) is $-\dfrac{1}{4}$ and slope of (D) is -4.

For each second,

   one temperature goes down 4 units and

another temperature goes down $\dfrac{1}{4}$ units.

$\Downarrow$

The temperature of (D) goes down faster.

---

10.   At a supermarket, $\dfrac{2}{7}$ of the items are discounted by 70 percent, $\dfrac{1}{7}$ of the items are discounted by 40 percent, $\dfrac{3}{14}$ of the items are discounted by 50 percent, and remaining items are not discounted. If one item is to be selected randomly, which of the following is the probability that the item is discounted by either 40 percent or 50 percent?

(A) $\dfrac{5}{14}$

(B) $\dfrac{1}{2}$

(C) $\dfrac{3}{98}$

(D) $\dfrac{3}{49}$

Solution: Answer: (A)

For a probability question, "or" = "+".

$\Downarrow$

$$\dfrac{1}{7} + \dfrac{3}{14} = \dfrac{2}{14} + \dfrac{3}{14} = \dfrac{5}{14}$$

11. A square board is divided into m colunms of m squares each. If n of these squares lie along the boundary of the board, which of the following is a possible value of n ?

(A) 6

(B) 56

(C) 50

(D) 54

Solution: Answer: (B)

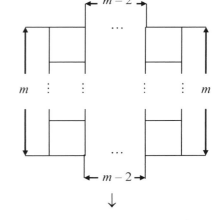

$$n = 2(m-2) + 2m = 4m - 4$$

When $m = 15$, $n = 60 - 4 = \boxed{56}$

$\Downarrow$

Answer is (B).

NEXT PAGE

12. What is the solution of the equation $\sqrt{x^2 - 35} = 5 - x$?

(A) no solution

(B) 5

(C) 4

(D) 7

Solution: Answer: (A)

$$\left(\sqrt{x^2 - 35}\right)^2 = \left(5 - x\right)^2$$

$$x^2 - 35 = 25 - 10x + x^2$$

$$x = 6$$

Because of squaring action, check $x = 6$.

$$\text{Left side} = \sqrt{6^2 - 35} = 1$$

$$\text{Right side} = 5 - 6 = -1$$

$$\text{Left side} \neq \text{Right side}$$

⇓

$\left(\sqrt{x^2 - 35}\right)^2 = \left(5 - x\right)^2$ has on solution.

13. If the graph of a linear function passes through the points $(p, 1)$, $(q, 5)$ and $(3, 2)$, what is the value of $3p + q$?

(A) 12
(B) 5
(C) 4
(D) -3

Solution: Answer: (A)

$$\frac{1-5}{p-q} = \frac{5-2}{q-3}, \quad \frac{p-q}{-4} = \frac{q-3}{3}$$

↓

$$3(p - q) = -4(q - 2)$$

↓

$$3p - 3q = -4(q - 3) = -4q + 12$$

⇓

$$3p + q = 12$$

14. If x and a are numbers such that $x < -a$ and $x > a$, which of the following must be true?

   I. $|x| < a$

   II. $|x| > a$

   III. $x > 0$

(A) I only

(B) II and III only

(C) I, II and III

(D) II only

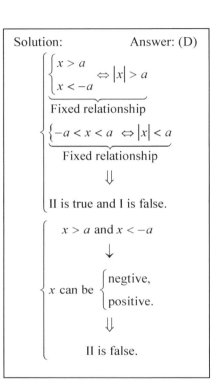

Solution: Answer: (D)

$$\underbrace{\begin{cases} x > a \\ x < -a \end{cases} \Leftrightarrow |x| > a}_{\text{Fixed relationship}}$$

$$\underbrace{\left\{ -a < x < a \; \Leftrightarrow \; |x| < a \right.}_{\text{Fixed relationship}}$$

⇓

II is true and I is false.

$$\begin{cases} x > a \text{ and } x < -a \\ \qquad\qquad \downarrow \\ x \text{ can be } \begin{cases} \text{negtive,} \\ \text{positive.} \end{cases} \end{cases}$$

⇓

II is false.

NEXT PAGE ⟹

15. Which of the following could be the remainders when 3 consecutive integers are each divided by 2?

(A) 1, 2, 0
(B) 0, 1, 0
(C) 0, 2, 0
(D) 0, 1, 2

Solution: Answer: (B)

$$\frac{x}{2}, \frac{x+1}{2}, \frac{x+2}{2}$$

↓

Use plug-in method.

↓

When $x = 2$, remainders $= 0, 1, 0$

⇓

Answer is (B).

16. If $-1 < x < 0$, then which of the following must be true?

(A) $\frac{1}{x^2} < x^5$

(B) $\frac{1}{x^4} < \frac{1}{x^3}$

(C) $x^2 < x^3$

(D) $\frac{1}{x^5} < \frac{1}{x^3}$

Solution: Answer: (D)

$\begin{cases} \dfrac{1}{x^2}, \ \dfrac{1}{x^4}, \text{ and } x^2 \text{ are positive or 0.} \\ \qquad \downarrow \\ \text{(A), (B), (C), and (E) are eliminated.} \end{cases}$

Let $x = -\dfrac{1}{2}$ to test.

$$\frac{1}{\left(-\frac{1}{2}\right)^3} = \frac{1}{\frac{1}{-8}} = -8, \quad \frac{1}{\left(-\frac{1}{2}\right)^5} = -32$$

↓

$-32 < -8$

⇓

Answer is (D)

17. In the figures above, if one of them is selected randomly, what is the probability that the number of vertices in the figure will be at least 4?

(A) 0.8

(B) $\dfrac{1}{5}$

(C) $\dfrac{2}{5}$

(D) 60%

Solution: Answer: (A)

"at least 4" = 4, 5 and 6
4 figures have vertices equal or more than 4.

⇓

$$P = \frac{4}{5} = \frac{8}{10} = 0.8$$

18. A train travels 1,200 miles in 10 hours. Before 12:00pm the train averages 140 miles per hour. After noon the train averages 100 miles per hour. What time did the train leave?

(A) 8am
(B) 7am
(C) 9am
(D) 6am

Solution: Answer: (B)

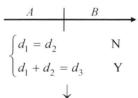

$\begin{cases} d_1 = d_2 & \text{N} \\ d_1 + d_2 = d_3 & \text{Y} \end{cases}$

↓

$140x + 100(10 - x) = 1200$
$140x + 1000 - 100x = 1200$
$40x = 200$

↓

$x = 5$

⇓

$12:00\text{pm} - 5 = 7\text{am}$

NEXT PAGE

19. The angle formed by the hour hand and minute hand of a clock at 3:25 is

(A) 78°
(B) 67.5°
(C) 47.5°
(D) 125°

Solution: Answer: (C)

Hour hand:

It has reactions for both hours and minutes.
3 hours: $3 \cdot 30° = 90°$
25 minutes: $25 \cdot 0.5° = 12.5°$
$90 + 12.5 = 102.5°$

Minute hand:

It only has the reaction for minutes.

25 minutes: $25 \cdot 6° = 150°$

The angle degrees between 2 hands:
⇓
$150° - 102.5° = 47.5°$

20. Mr. Franklin chooses watermelons for his supermarket. He will choose the watermelons that weigh more than 10 pounds and less than 20 pounds. If n represents the weight of a watermelon, in pounds, he will choose, which inequalities below represents all possible values of n?

(A) $|n - 15| < 10$
(B) $|n - 15| > 20$
(C) $|n - 15| \leq 5$
(D) $|n - 15| < 5$

Solution: Answer: (D)
Interpret English to math first.
$$10 < n < 20$$
$$\boxed{-b < x + a < b}$$
One row
⇕
$$|x + a| < b$$

Use plug-in method.
↓
(D): $|n - 15| < 5$
$$-5 < n - 15 < 5$$
$$10 < n < 20$$
⇓
Answer is (D).

y	9	m	n
x	0	1	2

21. The values of m and n in the chart above are related so that $(y + 1)$ is directly proportional to $(x - 1)$. What is the sum of m and n?

(A) 10
(B) -12
(C) 14
(D) -16

Solution: Answer: (B)

(1) Get the constant k first.
$$9 + 1 = k(0 - 1), \quad k = -10$$
↓

(2) Get m and n, respectively.
Proportion given: $y + 1 = k(x - 1)$
$$m + 1 = (-10)(1 - 1), \quad m = -1$$
$$n + 1 = (-10)(2 - 1), \quad n = -11$$
(1) and (2)
↓

(3) Get the sum.
⇓
$$m + n = -1 + (-11) = -12$$

22. If $f(x) = x^2 - 9$ and g $(x) = x + 3$, which of the following does the combining function $\dfrac{f}{g} = \left(\dfrac{f}{g}\right)(x) = \dfrac{f(x)}{g(x)}$ equal?

(A) $x - 3, x \neq -3$
(B) $x + 3, x \neq 3$
(C) $x + 3, x \neq -3$
(D) $x - 3$

Solution: Answer: (A)

(1) $\dfrac{x^2 - 9}{x + 3}$
⇓
$x + 3 \neq 0, \; x \neq \boxed{-3}$

(2) $\dfrac{x^2 - 9}{x + 3}$
$\dfrac{\cancel{(x + 3)}(x - 3)}{\cancel{x + 3}}$
⇓
$\boxed{x - 3}$

NEXT PAGE ⟩

23.   If $16\sqrt{24} = p\sqrt{q}$, where p and q are positive integers and $p > q$, which of the following could be the value of $p - q$?

(A) $32 - \sqrt{6}$
(B) 38
(C) 46
(D) 26

Solution: Answer: (D)

$$16\sqrt{24} = 16\sqrt{4 \cdot 6} = 16 \cdot 2\sqrt{6} = 32\sqrt{6}$$

$$32 > 6, \ p > q$$

$$\Downarrow$$

$$p - q = 32 - 6 = 26$$

24.   Martin is 32 years older than his daughter May. In nine years, he will be two times as old as May will be. How old is Martin?

(A) 55

(B) 63

(C) 53

(D) 56

Solution: Answer: (A)

$$\begin{cases} \text{Let } x = \text{Martin's current age.} \\ \quad\quad\downarrow \\ x - 32 = \text{May's current age.} \end{cases}$$

$$\downarrow$$

$$\underbrace{x + 9}_{\text{Martin's age}} = 2\underbrace{\left(x - 32 + 9\right)}_{\text{May's age}}$$

$$\Downarrow$$

$$x = 55$$

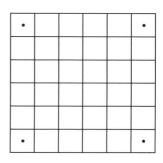

Note: Figure above not drawn to scale.

25. In the figure above, a square with side length 6 is divided into 36 squares. What is ratio of the area of the circle (not shown here) that passes through the 4 points, which are the centers of the 4 corner squares, to circumference of the circle?

(A) $\dfrac{5\sqrt{2}}{4}$

(B) $4\sqrt{2}$

(C) $5\sqrt{2}$

(D) $\dfrac{25}{\sqrt{2}}$

Solution: Answer: (A)

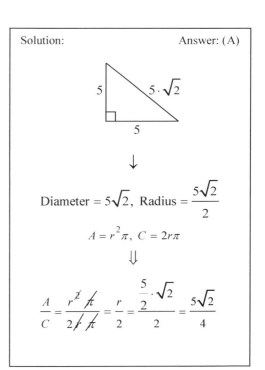

$$\text{Diameter} = 5\sqrt{2}, \ \text{Radius} = \frac{5\sqrt{2}}{2}$$

$$A = r^2\pi, \ C = 2r\pi$$

$$\Downarrow$$

$$\frac{A}{C} = \frac{r^{\cancel{2}}\cancel{\pi}}{2\cancel{r}\cancel{\pi}} = \frac{r}{2} = \frac{\frac{5}{2} \cdot \sqrt{2}}{2} = \frac{5\sqrt{2}}{4}$$

NEXT PAGE

26. Two sides of a triangle have lengths 6 and 19 separately. If the remaining side of the triangle has a value that is an integer, what are the largest and smallest possible perimeters of this triangle?

(A) 39 and 50
(B) 39 and 49
(C) 38 and 49
(D) 39 and 50

$$M(x) = x^2 + 3x + 6, \quad N(x) = 5x^3 + 15x^2 + 30x$$

27. If the polynomials M and N are defined above, which of the following polynomials is divisible by $5x + 5$?

(A) $f(x) = N(x) + 5M(x)$

(B) $g(x) = 5xN(x) + 5M(x)$

(C) $h(x) = 5N(x) + 5xM(x)$

(D) $j(x) = xN(x) + 5M(x)$

Solution: Answer: (B)

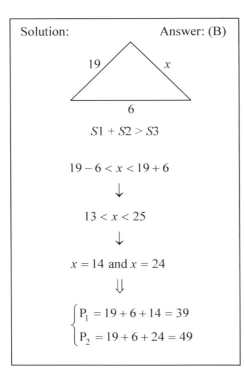

$$S1 + S2 > S3$$

$$19 - 6 < x < 19 + 6$$

$$\downarrow$$

$$13 < x < 25$$

$$\downarrow$$

$$x = 14 \text{ and } x = 24$$

$$\Downarrow$$

$$\begin{cases} P_1 = 19 + 6 + 14 = 39 \\ P_2 = 19 + 6 + 24 = 49 \end{cases}$$

Solution: Answer: (A)

N and M have the relationship:

$$N(x) = 5x\left(x^2 + 3x + 6\right) = 5x \cdot M(x)$$

When $P(x)$ is divided by $5x + 5$, it can be written as

$$\frac{P(x)}{5x + 5} = M(x) + \frac{r}{5x + 5}.$$

If remaunder $r = 0$, $P(x)$ is called "P is divisible by $5x + 5$."

It is $\underbrace{P(x) = M(x)\left(5x + 5\right)}$.

Use this conclusion.

Plug-in

$$P(x) = N(x) + 5M(x) = 5xM(x) + 5M(x) = M(x)\left(5x + 5\right)$$

$$f(x) = P(x)$$

$$\Downarrow$$

Answer is (A).

NEXT PAGE

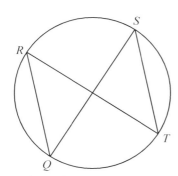

Note: Figure above not drawn to scale.

28.   In the figure above, $\overline{QS}$ and $\overline{RT}$ are perpendicular diameters of the circle. If the circle has area of 36π, which of the following is the length of $\overline{ST}$?

(A) $6\sqrt{2}$

(B) $4\sqrt{3}$

(C) $18\sqrt{2}$

(D) $8\sqrt{2}$

Solution: Answer: (A)

$$A = r^2\pi \;\rightarrow\; 36\cancel{\pi} = r^2\cancel{\pi}$$

$$\downarrow$$

$$r = 6$$

$$\frac{\overline{QS}}{2} = \frac{\overline{RT}}{2} = r$$

$$\Downarrow$$

$$ST = \sqrt{r^2 + r^2} = \sqrt{2\cdot 36} = 6\sqrt{2}$$

29.   Which of the following sketches shows a relationship that is appropriately modled with the function $f(t) = ar^t$, where $a < 0$ and $r > 1$?

(A) y 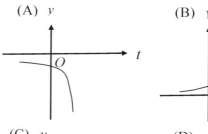   (B) y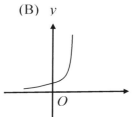

(C) y 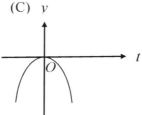   (D) y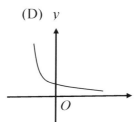

Solution: Answer: (A)

It is an exponential functions $f(t). = ar^t$.

$$r > 1 \text{ and } a > 0 \;\rightarrow\; (B)$$

But $r > 1$ and $a < 0$

$$\Downarrow$$

The sketch will be similar to (A).

$$y + 2 = 1/2\,(2x - 1)$$

30.   What is the y-intercept of the function above?

(A) $(0, 1.5)$

(B) $(1.5,\ 0)$

(C) $(0,\ -2.5)$

(D) $(-2.5,\ 0)$

Solution: Answer: (C)

The definition the intercept:

y-value when $x = 0$

$$\downarrow$$

$$y + 2 = 1/2\,(2\times 0 - 1)$$

$$\Downarrow$$

$$y = -1/2 - 2, \quad y = -2.5$$

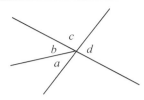

Note: Figure above not drawn to scale.

31. In the figure above, if $b = \frac{1}{5}a$ and $c = 4d$, what is the value of b?

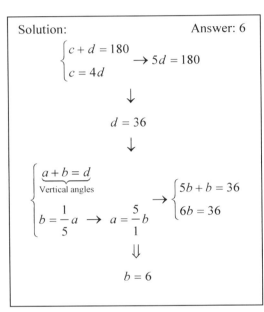

Solution: Answer: 6

$$\begin{cases} c + d = 180 \\ c = 4d \end{cases} \rightarrow 5d = 180$$

$$\downarrow$$

$$d = 36$$

$$\downarrow$$

$$\underbrace{\begin{cases} a + b = d \\ \text{Vertical angles} \\ b = \frac{1}{5}a \rightarrow a = \frac{5}{1}b \end{cases}} \rightarrow \begin{cases} 5b + b = 36 \\ 6b = 36 \end{cases}$$

$$\Downarrow$$

$$b = 6$$

32. If $32^{2x} = \left(\frac{1}{2}\right)^{x-11}$, what is the value of x ?

Solution: Answer: 1

$$\left(2^5\right)^{2x} = \left(2^{-1}\right)^{x-11}, \qquad 2^{10x} = 2^{-x+11}$$

$$\Downarrow$$

$$10x = -x + 11, \qquad x = \boxed{1}$$

33. The sides of a rectangular room have lengths $2s$, $3s$, and $4s$. What is the entire surface area of the room if $s = 2$?

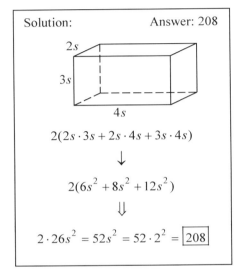

Solution: Answer: 208

$$2(2s \cdot 3s + 2s \cdot 4s + 3s \cdot 4s)$$

$$\downarrow$$

$$2(6s^2 + 8s^2 + 12s^2)$$

$$\Downarrow$$

$$2 \cdot 26s^2 = 52s^2 = 52 \cdot 2^2 = \boxed{208}$$

34. Let set $S = (5, 10, 15, 150)$. What is the probability that the sum of any 2 numbers in S is greater than 154 ?

Solution: Answer: 1/2 or .5

$$\underbrace{5 + 150, \ 10 + 150, \text{ and } 15 + 150}_{\text{3 possibilies}} > 154$$

$$\Downarrow$$

$$P = \frac{3}{\begin{array}{c}\text{Total} \\ \text{possibilities}\end{array} \begin{cases} \boxed{4}\boxed{3} \\ 2! \end{cases}} = \frac{1}{2}$$

NEXT PAGE ⟩

Physicists' an Experiment of Ball Rolling

	Pipe 1	Pipe 2	Pipe 3
Length (meters)	200.6	200.5	108.4
Average of rolling speed (meters per minute)	35	55	40

Several physicists did an experiment. They let a special ball, which is made by mix materials, roll through three pipes, pipe 1, pipe 2, and pipe 3, which are connected by that order. Each pipe has own conditions. The records of the experiment were put into the table above.

35. The experiment started. The ball rolled directly into the pipe 1, then the pipe 2, and then the pipe 3. What is the average speed, in meters per hour, of the ball during its entire rolling process that spent ten minutes?

Solution: Answer: 3057

$$\text{Average speed} \neq \frac{\text{Speed 1} + \text{Speed 2} + \text{Speed 3}}{3}$$

"average speed"

$$\downarrow$$

$$\text{Average speed} = \frac{\text{Total distance}}{\text{Total time}}$$

$$\Downarrow$$

$$\frac{200.6 + 200.5 + 108.4}{\frac{1\!\!\!/0}{6\!\!\!/0}} = 509.5 \times 6 = 3057 \,(\text{meters per hour})$$

36.   If you take 4 less than a number x and then raise this result to the 5th power, it equals 243. What is the value of x?

Solution: Answer: 7

$$x - 4, \qquad (x-4)^5 = 243$$

$$\downarrow$$

$$\left((x-4)^5\right)^{\frac{1}{5}} = \sqrt[5]{243}$$

$$\Downarrow$$

$$x - 4 = \sqrt[5]{3 \cdot 3 \cdot 3 \cdot 3 \cdot 3} = 3, \quad x = \boxed{7}$$

37.   If the graph of $y = 3$ intersects the graph of $y = x^2 - 3x - 25$, what is one possible x-value of the intersection point of the graph?

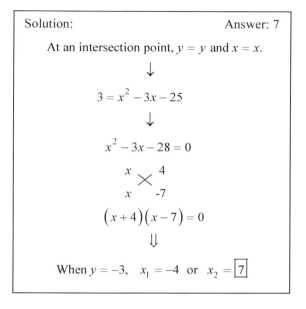

Solution: Answer: 7

At an intersection point, $y = y$ and $x = x$.

$$\downarrow$$

$$3 = x^2 - 3x - 25$$

$$\downarrow$$

$$x^2 - 3x - 28 = 0$$

$$\begin{matrix} x & 4 \\ x & -7 \end{matrix}$$

$$(x+4)(x-7) = 0$$

$$\Downarrow$$

When $y = -3$, $x_1 = -4$ or $x_2 = \boxed{7}$

38.   Sarah herself can clean a room in 14 minutess, and Jay himself can clean the same room in 21 minutes. After Sarah begins the job and does $\frac{3}{7}$ of the job, Jay takes over and finishes the job. What is the entire time, in minutes, that takes Sarah and Jay to clean the room?

Solution: Answer: 18

$$"\frac{3}{7} \text{ of the job"}$$

$$\downarrow$$

1 is the entire job as fraction.

$$\downarrow$$

$$\begin{cases} T_{\text{Sarah}} = 14 \cdot \dfrac{3}{7} = 6 \\ T_{\text{Jay}} = 21 \cdot \dfrac{4}{7} = 12 \end{cases}$$

$$\Downarrow$$

$$T_{\text{Entire}} = 6 + 12 = 18$$

STOP

SAT Math

Practice

Test 09

Redesigned for Tests in March 2016 and Beyond

Mad Math

Math Test – No Calculator

Time: 25 Minutes
20 Questions

Notes:
- The use of a calculator is not allowed.
- All numbers used in this section are the real number.
- Figures are provided for some problems in this test. Unless otherwise indicated under the figure "Note: Figure above not drawn to scale", all figures are drawn as accurately as possible.
- All figures lie in a plane EXCEPT otherwise specified.
- Unless otherwise indicated, the domain of any function f, g or j is assumed to be the set of all real numbers x for which $f(x)$, $g(x)$, or $j(x)$ is a real number.

Reference Information

$$A = \frac{1}{2}bh$$

$$A = lw$$

$$A = \pi r^2$$

$$V = \pi r^2 h$$

$$V = lwh$$

$$c^2 = a^2 + b^2$$

$$V = \frac{1}{3}\pi r^2 h$$

$$V = \frac{4}{3}\pi r^3$$

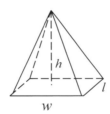

$$V = \frac{1}{3}lwh$$

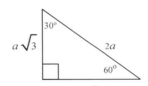

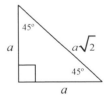

1. The domain of function $f(x) = \dfrac{x^2 - 4}{x^2 + 2x}$ is

(A) all real numbers except –2.
(B) all real numbers except 0.
(C) all real numbers.
(D) all real numbers except -2 and 0.

2. What is the length of the arc intercepted by a central angle of 150° if the circle has a radius of 10 units ?

(A) $\dfrac{50\pi}{3}$

(B) $\dfrac{25\pi}{3}$

(C) $\dfrac{5\pi}{6}$

(D) $\dfrac{2\pi}{3}$

3. If $f(x) = \dfrac{f(x+1)}{2}$ and $f(3) = 6$, then $f(2) + f(3) =$

(A) 8

(B) 9

(C) 10

(D) 11

4. The angle formed by the hour hand and minute hand of a clock at 7:24 is

(A) 78°
(B) 67.5°
(C) 72.5°
(D) 125°

NEXT PAGE

5. $\tan\dfrac{\pi}{2} = ?$

(A) $\sin 0$

(B) $\sin\dfrac{\pi}{2}$

(C) $\cot 0$

(D) $\cos\dfrac{3\pi}{2}$

7. Which of the following has the same solution(s) as $|x-4| = 3$?

(A) $x^2 + 8x - 7$

(B) $x^2 + 8x + 7$

(C) $x^2 - 8x + 7$

(D) $x^2 - 8x - 7$

6. In the xy-plane, what is the x-intercept of a line that has a slope of $\dfrac{1}{3}$ and passes through the point (-3, 3) ?

(A) (0, -12)

(B) (12, 0)

(C) (-12, 0)

(D) (4, 0)

8. Which of the following is the nature of the roots of the equation $2x^2 + 2\sqrt{2}x + 1 = 0$?

(A) The equation has an imaginary root.

(B) Its roots are unequal, rational, and real numbers.

(C) Its roots are unequal, irrational, and real numbers

(D) Its roots are equal, irrational, and real.

NEXT PAGE ⟫

9. $\left(10^{10}\right)^{10} =$

(A) $10 \cdot 10 \cdot 10$

(B) $10^{10^{10}}$

(C) 10^{100}

(D) 10^{20}

Note that figure not drawn to scale.

11.   Point O is the center of the circle above. What fraction of the area of the the circle is the area of the shaded portion?

(A) $\dfrac{8}{5}$

(B) $\dfrac{5}{8}$

(C) $\dfrac{3}{8}$

(D) $\dfrac{7}{18}$

10.   If $m^2 + mn + n^2 = 7$ and $mn = 6$, what is the value of $(m-n)^2$?

(A) -11

(B) 12

(C) 1

(D) 2

12. For all real number x, $g(3x) = 3x^2 + x - 3$. What is an expression for $g(x)$ in terms of x ?

(A) $x^2 + \dfrac{x}{3} - 3$

(B) $\dfrac{x^2}{3} + \dfrac{x}{2} - 3$

(C) $\dfrac{x^2}{3} + \dfrac{x}{3} - 3$

(D) $\dfrac{x^2}{3} + x - 3$

NEXT PAGE

13. Which of the following expression is a simplified form of

$$\frac{-2y^2 + y + 1}{2y^2 - 4y + 2}?$$

(A) $\dfrac{2y-1}{2(y+1)}$

(B) $\dfrac{2(y+1)}{2y-1}$)

(C) $\dfrac{y+1}{2(y-1)}$

(D) $\dfrac{2y+1}{2(1-y)}$

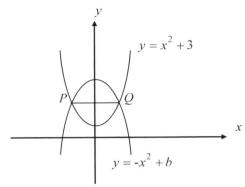

15.   The figure above shows the graphs of $y = x^2 + 3$ and $y = -x^2 + b$ for some constant b. If $PQ = 6$, what is the value of b?

(A) 10
(B) 13
(C) 21
(D) 20

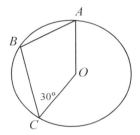

Note: Figure above not drawn to scale.

14.   In the figure above, points A, B, and C lie on the circumference of the circle centered at O. If $m\angle OAB = 20°$, then $m\angle AOC = ?$

(A) 150°
(B) 20°
(C) 280°
(D) 260°

NEXT PAGE

16.   80 students try out for a school volleyball team. Of these, 32 can play the infield, 38 can play the outfield, and 16 can play both the infield and outfield. How many of the eighty students can play neither the infield nor the outfield?

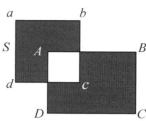

Note: Figure above not drawn to scale.

19. In the figure above, the bigger square *abcd* and rectangle *ABCD* are overlapped each other. The point *A* is located at the center of the bigger square. If the area of the bigger square is 16, what is the area of the white region?

17. James, the owner of a bike store, sells a bike $120 that makes 20% profit. During an on sale period, the profit is cut to 8%. What is the final price of the bike?

18.   When $x = 7$, $(x-1)(x-k) > 0$ and when $x = 6$, $(x-1)(x-k) < 0$. What is one possible value for k ?

20.   The least integer and greatest integer of a set of consecutive odd integers are –21 and 27. What is the sum of the all integers in the set?

STOP

Math Test – Calculator

Time: 55 Minutes
38 Questions

Notes:
- The use of a calculator is not allowed.
- All numbers used in this section are the real number.
- Figures are provided for some problems in this test. Unless otherwise indicated under the figure "Note: Figure above not drawn to scale", all figures are drawn as accurately as possible.
- All figures lie in a plane EXCEPT otherwise specified.
- Unless otherwise indicated, the domain of any function f, g or j is assumed to be the set of all real numbers x for which $f(x)$, $g(x)$, or $j(x)$ is a real number.

Reference Information

$$A = \frac{1}{2}bh$$

$$A = lw$$

$$A = \pi r^2$$

$$V = \pi r^2 h$$

$$V = lwh$$

$$c^2 = a^2 + b^2$$

$$V = \frac{1}{3}\pi r^2 h$$

$$V = \frac{4}{3}\pi r^3$$

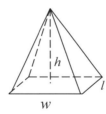

$$V = \frac{1}{3}lwh$$

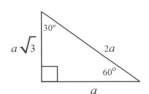

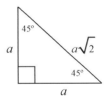

1. If $0 < x < 1$ and $0 < y < 1$, which of the following must be true?

(A) $\dfrac{x^3}{y^2} > 0$

(B) $\dfrac{1}{x} \cdot y = 1$

(C) $y - x > 0$

(D) $x - y > 0$

3. If perimeter of a rectangle is 60 feet, the greatest area of the rectangle must be

(A) 200 ft^2

(B) 400 ft^2

(C) 300 ft^2

(D) 225 ft^2

2. Both $x = -4$ and $x = 5$ are solutions for which of the following equations?

  I. $(x - 4)(x + 5) = 0$

  II. $3x = -15$

  III. $(x + 4)(x - 5) = 0$

(A) I only

(B) II only

(C) III only

(D) I and II only

4. $a \neq 0,\ b \neq 0,\ \dfrac{b}{100} \div \dfrac{a}{1000} =$

(A) $\dfrac{10a}{b}$

(B) $\dfrac{ab}{10^5}$

(C) $b10^3 a10^2$

(D) $\dfrac{10b}{a}$

NEXT PAGE

5. If $f(x) = x + 2$, $g(x) = 4x$, and $j(x) = \dfrac{2}{x}$, what does

$g(f(j(4)))$ equal?

(A) 6

(B) 9

(C) 10

(D) 12

6. Eric left his home at 8:00am, traveling along Route 1 at 50 miles per hour. At 11:00am, Victor left home and started after him on the same road at 80 miles per hour. At what time did Victor catch up to Eric?

(A) 2:00pm
(B) 4:00pm
(C) 3:00pm
(D) 1:00pm

7. Which of the following sketches shows a relationship that is appropriately modled with the function $f(x) = ax^b + c$, where $f(x) = 0$, $a < 0$, $b = 1$, and $c < 0$?

(A)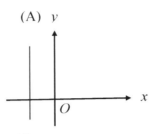

(B)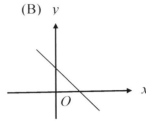

(C)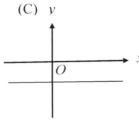

(D)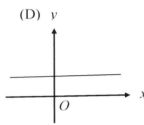

NEXT PAGE

8. If the radius of a circle is 6 feet, what is the area of the sector whose arc length is 6π feet?

(A) 12.5π

(B) 25π

(C) 24π

(D) 18π

9. Monica is 6 years younger than her sister Michelle. In eight years, Monica's age will be $\dfrac{5}{8}$ of Michelle's age. How old is Michelle now?

(A) 6

(B) 14

(C) 8

(D) 13

10. If $-1 < x < 0$, then which of the following must be true?

I. $x^2 > x^3$

II. $x^3 > x^5$

III. $x^2 > x^4$

(A) I only

(B) II only

(C) I and III only

(D) II and III only

NEXT PAGE

Questions 11 and 12 refer to the information below.

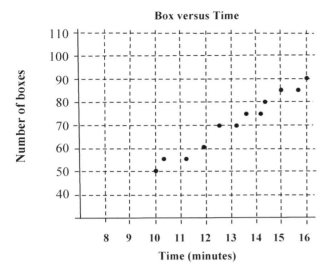

Box versus Time

Group	Rate of Packing (boxes per minute)
group 1	7/2
group 2	5/2
group 3	17/4
group 4	5
group 5	20/3
group 6	7
group 7	4

Calculating the approximate number, N, of the boxes packed by people is easy: N = Time × Rate of packing. The scatterlpot and table above provide the relationship of time and box, and the names of seven packing groups and their rates of packing.

11. According to the information of the scatterplot and table, if group 4 and group 7 both each now have twenty boxes to pack, which of the following will be closest to the absolute difference, in minutes, of their time?

(A) 1.5   (B) 2.0   (C) 1   (D) 2.5

12. By the scatterplot providing the time ploted against box for 12 people of a single group, the packing rate is closest to that of which the following groups?

(A) group 2
(B) group 5
(C) group 4
(D) group 3

13. If Maria wants to get a solution that is 6% salt from 510 quarts of solution that is 5% salt, how much water, in quarts, must be evaporated?

(A) 85
(B) 60
(C) 65
(D) 70

NEXT PAGE

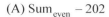

14. The sum of all even integrs from 0 to 204 is Sum_{even}.

What is the sum of all even integers from 4 to 202?

(A) $\text{Sum}_{\text{even}} - 202$

(B) $\text{Sum}_{\text{even}} - 200$

(C) $\text{Sum}_{\text{even}} - 206$

(D) $\text{Sum}_{\text{even}} - 208$

15. If n is an integer greater than zero, let ◼ n ◼ be defined as the set of all multiples of n. All of the numbers in which of the following sets are also in all three of the sets ◼ 2 ◼, ◼ 4 ◼ , and ◼ 5 ◼?

(A) ◼ 10 ◼

(B) ◼ 30 ◼

(C) ◼ 40 ◼

(D) ◼ 50 ◼

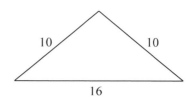

Note: Figure above not drawn to scale.

16. In the figure above, what is the area of a triangle whose sides are 10, 10, and 16?

(A) 48

(B) 24

(C) 12

(D) 60

17. A and B both are constant and $4x^2 + Ax - 6$ is equivalent to $(x-2)(4x+B)$. What is the value of A?

(A) -11

(B) 5

(C) 11

(D) -5

NEXT PAGE

18. What is the domain of $f(x) = \dfrac{a}{|x| - x}$ is, where $a > 0$?

(A) $x > 0$

(B) $x > a$

(C) $x < 0$

(D) $x = a$

19. The price of a CD player was reduced from $180 to $120. What was the percent of decrease in the price of the unit?

(A) 33%

(B) $\left(66 + \dfrac{2}{3}\right)\%$

(C) 66%

(D) $\left(33 + \dfrac{1}{3}\right)\%$

20. If $s = 5q$, $q = 4r$, $3r = p$, and $p \neq 0$, then $s/p =$

(A) 4

(B) $\dfrac{20}{3}$

(C) 10

(D) -4

NEXT PAGE

21. If the fraction $\dfrac{1}{26}$ is equivalent to the repeating decimal 0.3846153846153…, what is the 68th digit after the decimal point of the repeating decimal?

(A) 4
(B) 7
(C) 9
(D) 8

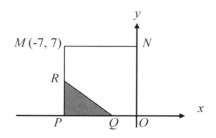

Note: Figure above not drawn to scale.

23. In the figure above, the coordinates of R are $(-7, k)$ and the coordinates of Q are $(-1, 0)$. One point in square $MNOP$ is to be chosen randomly. If the probability that the point will be in the shaded triangle is 10%, what is the value of k ?

(A) $\dfrac{49}{30}$

(B) 3/2

(C) 2.5

(D) 5.2

22. The first term of set A is -2, and each term thereafter is 2 greater than the previous term. The Nth term of set B is given by the formula $-N + 12$. What is the value of the term of set A that first exceeds the value of its corresponding term in set B?

(A) 6
(B) 8
(C) 7
(D) 5

NEXT PAGE

24. If $f(x) = \sqrt{-x^2 + 1}$, then which of the following is the domain of the function f ?

(A) $x \le -1$ or $x \ge 1$

(B) $x \le -1$

(C) $-1 \le x \le 1$

(D) All real numbers

25. $(a + b - 3)(a + b + 3) = ?$

(A) $(a + b)^2 - 9$

(B) $(a - b)^2 - 9$

(C) $(a + b)^2 + 9$

(D) $a^2 - 2ab + b^2 + 3$

26. At JFK Academy, the ratio of girls to boys is 2 to 3. If three-fifths of the boys are on a team and the remaining 30 boys are not, how many girls are in this school?

(A) 90
(B) 50
(C) 80
(D) 300

NEXT PAGE

27. Which of the following is the zeros, vertex, domain, and range of function $f(x) = \dfrac{1}{4}(2x-1)(2x-11)$?

(A) Zeros $= (5.5,\ 1/2\ )$, $\begin{pmatrix} \text{Vertex} = (3,\ -25/4) \\ \text{Domain} = \text{All real numbers} \\ \text{Open up, Range} \geq -25/4 \end{pmatrix}$

(B) Zeros $= (5.5,\ 1/2\ )$, $\begin{pmatrix} \text{Vertex} = (-25/4,\ 3,) \\ \text{Domain} = \text{All real numbers} \\ \text{Open up, Range} \geq -25/4 \end{pmatrix}$

(C) Zeros $= (1/2,\ 5.5)$, $\begin{pmatrix} \text{Vertex} = (-25/4,\ 3) \\ \text{Domain} = \text{All real numbers} \\ \text{Open up, Range} \geq 3 \end{pmatrix}$

(D) Zeros $= (1/2,\ 5.5)$, $\begin{pmatrix} \text{Vertex} = (3,\ -25/4) \\ \text{Domain} = \text{All real numbers} \\ \text{Open up, Range} \geq -25/4 \end{pmatrix}$

Questions 28 and 29 refer to the following figure:

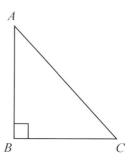

28. What is $\tan A$?

(A) $\dfrac{AB}{BC}$ (B) $\dfrac{BC}{AB}$ (C) $\dfrac{AC}{BC}$ (D) $\dfrac{BC}{AC}$

29. If $AC = \sqrt{2}$, what is the area of the triangle?

(A) $\sin C \cos C$ (B) $\dfrac{\sin C \cos C}{2}$

(C) $\sin A \cos A$ (D) $\dfrac{\sin A \cos A}{2}$

NEXT PAGE

30. Which scatterplot below shows a relationship that is approximately modeled with the equation $f(x) = ax^k$, where a is positive and k is a positive non-integer?

(A)

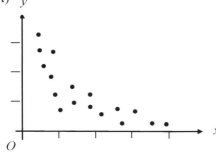

(B)

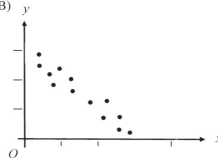

(C)

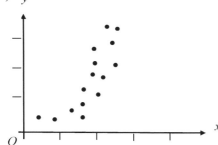

(D)

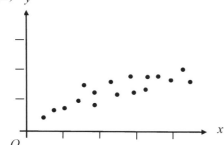

NEXT PAGE

31. Robot-1 and Robot-2 stand shoulder-to-shoulder on one line. Then each of them takes 16 steps in opposite direction away and stops. And then Robot-1 goes back, walks toward Robot-2 and reaches Robot-2 in 22 steps. The size of one of Robot-1's steps is how many times the size of one of Robot-2's steps?

Note: All of Robot-1's steps designed are the same size and all of Robot-2's steps designed are the same size also.

32. For how many integers m is $(3m+1)(4m-17)$ a negative number?

33. If a 3-digit number is selected randomly, what is the probability that all 3 digits are even numbers?

34. Jennifer filled 5/7 of John's swimming pool with 2800 cube feet. What is the total capacity of John's swimming pool?

NEXT PAGE

Note: Figure below not drawn to scale.

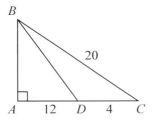

35. In the figure above, what is the the area of triangle ABD?

36. What does $|x - 7| < 2$ equal?

37. In the figure above, if the length of OO' of the regular hexagon with a center O is $3\sqrt{3}$, what is the perimeter of the hexagon?

38. Let @ be defined by $m @ w = m^w$. If $A = 2 @ a$, $B = 2 @ b$, and $a - b = 4$, what is the value of $\dfrac{A}{B}$?

STOP

Answer Key
For
SAT Math Practice Test 09

Section 3

1	D
2	B
3	B
4	A
5	C
6	C
7	C
8	D
9	C
10	A
11	B
12	C
13	D
14	D
15	C

16	26
17	108
18	$6 < x < 7$
19	4
20	75

Section 4

1	A	16	A
2	C	17	D
3	D	18	C
4	D	19	D
5	C	20	B
6	B	21	D
7	A	22	B
8	D	23	A
9	C	24	C
10	C	25	A
11	C	26	B
12	B	27	D
13	A	28	B
14	C	29	A
15	C	30	D

31	8/3 or 2.66 or 2.67
32	5
33	1/9 or .111
34	3920
35	72
36	$5 < x < 9$
37	36
38	16 or 16/1

SAT Math

Practice

Test 09

Explanations

Redesigned for Tests in March 2016 and Beyond

Mad Math

Math Test – No Calculator

Time: 25 Minutes
20 Questions

Notes:
- The use of a calculator is not allowed.
- All numbers used in this section are the real number.
- Figures are provided for some problems in this test. Unless otherwise indicated under the figure "Note: Figure above not drawn to scale", all figures are drawn as accurately as possible.
- All figures lie in a plane EXCEPT otherwise specified.
- Unless otherwise indicated, the domain of any function f, g or j is assumed to be the set of all real numbers x for which $f(x)$, $g(x)$, or $j(x)$ is a real number.

Reference Information

$A = \dfrac{1}{2}bh$

$A = lw$

$A = \pi r^2$

$V = \pi r^2 h$

$V = lwh$

$c^2 = a^2 + b^2$

$V = \dfrac{1}{3}\pi r^2 h$

$V = \dfrac{4}{3}\pi r^3$

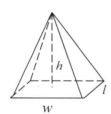
$V = \dfrac{1}{3}lwh$

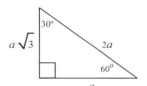

1. The domain of function $f(x) = \dfrac{x^2 - 4}{x^2 + 2x}$ is

(A) all real numbers except –2.
(B) all real numbers except 0.
(C) all real numbers.
(D) all real numbers except -2 and 0.

Solution: Answer: (D)

$$x^2 + 2x \neq 0, \rightarrow x(x+2) \neq 0$$

$$\Downarrow$$

$$\begin{cases} x \neq 0 \\ (x+2) \neq 0 \end{cases} \rightarrow \boxed{x \neq 0,\ x \neq -2}$$

2. What is the length of the arc intercepted by a central angle of $150°$ if the circle has a radius of 10 units ?

(A) $\dfrac{50\pi}{3}$

(B) $\dfrac{25\pi}{3}$

(C) $\dfrac{5\pi}{6}$

(D) $\dfrac{2\pi}{3}$

Solution: Answer: (B)

$$S = r\theta = \cancel{10} \cdot 150 \cdot \frac{\pi}{\cancel{180}}$$

$$\Downarrow$$

$$\frac{50\pi}{6} = \frac{25\pi}{3}$$

3. If $f(x) = \dfrac{f(x+1)}{2}$ and $f(3) = 6$, then $f(2) + f(3) =$

(A) 8
(B) 9
(C) 10
(D) 11

Solution: Answer: (B)

$$f(x) = \frac{f(x+1)}{2} \text{ and } f(3) = 6$$

$$\downarrow$$

$$f(2) = \frac{f(2+1)}{2} = \frac{f(3)}{2} = \frac{6}{2} = 3$$

$$\Downarrow$$

$$f(2) + f(3) = 3 + 6 = 9$$

4. The angle formed by the hour hand and minute hand of a clock at 7:24 is

(A) 78°
(B) 67.5°
(C) 72.5°
(D) 125°

Solution: Answer: (A)

Hour hand:
     7 hours: 7 · 30° = 210°
     24 minutes: 24 · 0.5° = 12°
         210 + 12 = 222°
Minute hand:
     24 minutes: 24 · 6° = 144°

$$\Downarrow$$

The angles between 2 hands:
     222° – 144° = 78°

NEXT PAGE

5. $\tan \dfrac{\pi}{2} = ?$

(A) $\sin 0$

(B) $\sin \dfrac{\pi}{2}$

(C) $\cot 0$

(D) $\cos \dfrac{3\pi}{2}$

Solution: Answer: (C)

$$\tan \dfrac{\pi}{2} = \text{undefined}$$

$$\cot 0 = \text{undefined}$$

$$\Downarrow$$

$$\tan \dfrac{\pi}{2} = \cot 0$$

---

6. In the xy-plane, what is the x-intercept of a line that has a slope of $\dfrac{1}{3}$ and passes through the point (-3, 3) ?

(A) (0, -12)

(B) (12, 0)

(C) (-12, 0)

(D) (4, 0)

Solution: Answer: (C)

$$x\text{-intercept} \rightarrow (x,\ 0)$$

$$\dfrac{0-3}{x-(-3)} = \dfrac{1}{3}, \qquad \dfrac{x+3}{3} = 3$$

$$\Downarrow$$

$$x = \boxed{-12}$$

---

7. Which of the following has the same solution(s) as $|x-4| = 3$?

(A) $x^2 + 8x - 7$

(B) $x^2 + 8x + 7$

(C) $x^2 - 8x + 7$

(D) $x^2 - 8x - 7$

Solution: Answer: (C)

$$\begin{cases} +(x-4) = 3 \\ \quad x_1 = 7 \\ -(x-4) = 3 \\ \quad x - 4 = -3 \\ \quad x_2 = 1 \end{cases}$$

$$\downarrow$$

$$\text{Factors} = (x-7) \text{ and } (x-1)$$

$$\downarrow$$

$$(x-7)\cdot(x-1) = x^2 - 7x - x + 7$$

$$\Downarrow$$

$$x^2 - 8x + 7$$

---

8. Which of the following is the nature of the roots of the equation $2x^2 + 2\sqrt{2}x + 1 = 0$?

(A) The equation has an imaginary root.

(B) Its roots are unequal, rational, and real numbers.

(C) Its roots are unequal, irrational, and real numbers

(D) Its roots are equal, irrational, and real.

Solution: Answer: (D)

$$b^2 - 4ac = \left(2\sqrt{2}\right)^2 - 4\cdot 2\cdot 1 = 8 - 8 = 0$$

$$x_{1 \text{ and } 2} = \dfrac{-2\sqrt{2} \pm 0}{2\cdot 2} = \dfrac{-2\sqrt{2}}{2\cdot 2}$$

$$\Downarrow$$

$$x_{1 \text{ and } 2} \text{ are equal, irrational, and real.}$$

NEXT PAGE ⟹

9. $\left(10^{10}\right)^{10} =$

(A) $10 \cdot 10 \cdot 10$

(B) $10^{10^{10}}$

(C) 10^{100}

(D) 10^{20}

Solution: Answer: (C)

$$\left(a^m\right)^n = a^{mn}$$

$\downarrow$

$$\left(10^{10}\right)^{10} = 10^{10 \cdot 10}$$

$\Downarrow$

$$10^{100}$$

---

10. If $m^2 + mn + n^2 = 7$ and $mn = 6$, what is the value of $(m-n)^2$?

(A) -11

(B) 12

(C) 1

(D) 2

Solution: Answer: (A)

$$m^2 + mn - 3mn + n^2 = 7 - 3mn$$

$\downarrow$

$$m^2 - 2mn + n^2 = 7 - 3 \times 6$$

$\Downarrow$

$$(m-n)^2 = -11$$

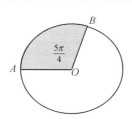

Note that figure not drawn to scale.

11. Point O is the center of the circle above. What fraction of the area of the the circle is the area of the shaded portion?

(A) $\dfrac{8}{5}$

(B) $\dfrac{5}{8}$

(C) $\dfrac{3}{8}$

(D) $\dfrac{7}{18}$

Solution: Answer: (B)

In the same circle, arc, area, and measure of angle have the same ratio.

$\begin{cases} \text{if getting ratio from area, you can use} \\ \text{it to obtain arc or angle measure.} \end{cases}$

$\begin{cases} \text{if getting ratio from arc, you can use} \\ \text{it to obtain area or angle measure.} \end{cases}$

$\begin{cases} \text{if getting ratio from angle measure,} \\ \text{you can use it to obtain area or arc.} \end{cases}$

$\Downarrow$

$$\frac{\frac{5\pi}{4}}{2\pi} = \frac{5\pi}{8\pi} = \frac{5}{8}$$

---

12. For all real number x, $g(3x) = 3x^2 + x - 3$. What is an expression for $g(x)$ in terms of x ?

(A) $x^2 + \dfrac{x}{3} - 3$

(B) $\dfrac{x^2}{3} + \dfrac{x}{2} - 3$

(C) $\dfrac{x^2}{3} + \dfrac{x}{3} - 3$

(D) $\dfrac{x^2}{3} + x - 3$

Solution: Answer: (C)

Use plug-in method.

(C) $g(x) = \dfrac{x^2}{3} + \dfrac{x}{3} - 3$

$\downarrow$

$$g(3x) = \frac{(3x)^2}{3} + \frac{3x}{3} - 3$$

$\Downarrow$

$$3x^2 + x - 3$$

NEXT PAGE ⟶

13. Which of the following expression is a simplified form of

$$\frac{-2y^2 + y + 1}{2y^2 - 4y + 2}?$$

(A) $\dfrac{2y-1}{2(y+1)}$

(B) $\dfrac{2(y+1)}{2y-1}$)

(C) $\dfrac{y+1}{2(y-1)}$

(D) $\dfrac{2y+1}{2(1-y)}$

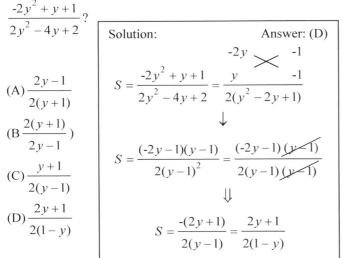

Solution: Answer: (D)

$$S = \frac{-2y^2 + y + 1}{2y^2 - 4y + 2} = \frac{y \quad -1}{2(y^2 - 2y + 1)}$$

$$-2y \times -1$$

$$S = \frac{(-2y-1)(y-1)}{2(y-1)^2} = \frac{(-2y-1)\,(y-1)}{2(y-1)\,(y-1)}$$

$$S = \frac{-(2y+1)}{2(y-1)} = \frac{2y+1}{2(1-y)}$$

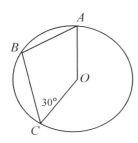

Note: Figure above not drawn to scale.

14.   In the figure above, points A, B, and C lie on the circumference of the circle centered at O. If $m\angle OAB = 20°$, then $m\angle AOC = ?$

(A) 150°
(B) 20°
(C) 280°
(D) 260°

Solution: Answer: (D)

Draw a segment $\overline{OB}$ in the figure below.

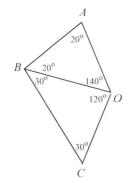

$OA = OC = OB = $ Radius

$\Downarrow$

$m\angle AOC = 140 + 120 = 260$

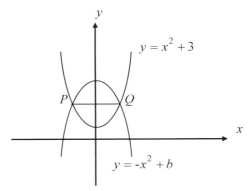

15.   The figure above shows the graphs of $y = x^2 + 3$ and $y = -x^2 + b$ for some constant b. If $PQ = 6$, what is the value of b?

(A) 10
(B) 13
(C) 21
(D) 20

Solution: Answer: (C)

(1) At the intersection points

$$y = y$$

$\downarrow$

$$x^2 + 3 = -x^2 + b$$

(2) $PQ = 6 \rightarrow x = \pm 3$

$\downarrow$

$$(\pm 3)^2 + 3 = -(\pm 3)^2 + b$$

$\downarrow$

$$12 = -9 + b$$

$\Downarrow$

$$b = 21$$

NEXT PAGE

16. 80 students try out for a school volleyball team. Of these, 32 can play the infield, 38 can play the outfield, and 16 can play both the infield and outfield. How many of the eighty students can play neither the infield nor the outfield?

Solution: Answer: 26

$$T = S1 + S2 - B + N$$

T = total number of elements that overlap parts are eliminated

$S1$ and $S2$ = number of elements in sets 1 and 2

N = number of elements neither in set 1 nor set 2

B = number of elements in both sets counted twice

↓

$$80 = 32 + 38 - 16 + N$$

⇓

$$N = 26$$

17. James, the owner of a bike store, sells a bike $120 that makes 20% profit. During an on sale period, the profit is cut to 8%. What is the final price of the bike?

Solution: Answer: 108

$$120 = 1.2c, \quad c = 100$$

⇓

$$x = 100 \times 1.08 = 108$$

18. When $x = 7$, $(x-1)(x-k) > 0$ and when $x = 6$, $(x-1)(x-k) < 0$. What is one possible value for k?

Solution: Answer: $6 < k < 7$

$(1).\ (7-1)(7-k) > 0$

↓

$7 - k > 0,\ k < 7$

$(2).\ (6-1)(6-k) < 0$

↓

$6 - k > 0,\ k > 6$

$(1) + (2)$

⇓

$(3).\quad 6 < k < 7$

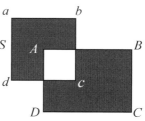

Note: Figure above not drawn to scale.

19. In the figure above, the bigger square *abcd* and rectangle *ABCD* are overlapped each other. The point A is located at the center of the bigger square. If the area of the bigger square is 16, what is the area of the white region?

Solution: Answer: 4

Point A is at the center of the bigger square.

↓

the white region is a square.

↓

The length of side of white square is $\sqrt{16} \div 2 = 2$.

⇓

$$A_{\text{white}} = 2 \times 2 = 4$$

20. The least integer and greatest integer of a set of consecutive odd integers are –21 and 27. What is the sum of the all integers in the set?

Solution: Answer: 75

$$\underbrace{-21, \ldots -1, 1, \ldots 21}_{\text{subsum}=0}, 23, 25, 27$$

⇓

$$\text{Sum} = 0 + 23 + 25 + 27 = 75$$

STOP

Math Test – Calculator

Time: 55 Minutes
38 Questions

Notes:
- The use of a calculator is not allowed.
- All numbers used in this section are the real number.
- Figures are provided for some problems in this test. Unless otherwise indicated under the figure "Note: Figure above not drawn to scale", all figures are drawn as accurately as possible.
- All figures lie in a plane EXCEPT otherwise specified.
- Unless otherwise indicated, the domain of any function f, g or j is assumed to be the set of all real numbers x for which $f(x)$, $g(x)$, or $j(x)$ is a real number.

Reference Information

$$A = \frac{1}{2}bh$$

$$A = lw$$

$$A = \pi r^2$$

$$V = \pi r^2 h$$

$$V = lwh$$

$$c^2 = a^2 + b^2$$

$$V = \frac{1}{3}\pi r^2 h$$

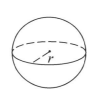

$$V = \frac{4}{3}\pi r^3$$

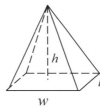

$$V = \frac{1}{3}lwh$$

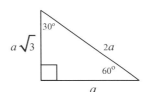

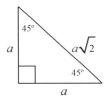

1. If $0 < x < 1$ and $0 < y < 1$, which of the following must be true?

(A) $\dfrac{x^3}{y^2} > 0$

(B) $\dfrac{1}{x} \cdot y = 1$

(C) $y - x > 0$

(D) $x - y > 0$

Solution: Answer: (A)

Not enough information except (A)

$$x > 0,\ y > 0$$
$$\downarrow$$
$$x^3 > 0 \text{ and } y^2 > 0$$
$$\Downarrow$$
$$\dfrac{x^3}{y^2} > 0$$

2. Both $x = -4$ and $x = 5$ are solutions for which of the following equations?

   I. $(x - 4)(x + 5) = 0$

   II. $3x = -15$

   III. $(x + 4)(x - 5) = 0$

(A) I only

(B) II only

(C) III only

(D) I and II only

Solution: Answer: (C)

   I. $(x - 4)(x + 5) = 0$

   $(x - 4) = 0,\ x = \boxed{+4}$

   $(x + 5) = 0,\ x = \boxed{-5}$

   II. $3x = -15,\ x = \boxed{-5}$

   III. $(x + 4)(x - 5) = 0$

   $(x + 4) = 0,\ x = \boxed{-4}$

   $(x - 5) = 0,\ x = \boxed{+5}$

   $\Downarrow$

   Only III is true.

3. If perimeter of a rectangle is 60 feet, the greatest area of the rectangle must be

(A) 200 ft^2

(B) 400 ft^2

(C) 300 ft^2

(D) 225 ft^2

Solution: Answer: (D)

A square is a special rectangle.

When a rectangle is a square with the same perimeter of a rectangle that is not a square, the square has the greater area than the rectangle.

$$\downarrow$$
$$\dfrac{60}{4} = 15$$

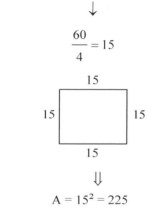

$$\Downarrow$$
$$A = 15^2 = 225$$

4. $a \neq 0,\ b \neq 0,\ \dfrac{b}{100} \div \dfrac{a}{1000} =$

(A) $\dfrac{10a}{b}$

(B) $\dfrac{ab}{10^5}$

(C) $b10^3 a10^2$

(D) $\dfrac{10b}{a}$

Solution: Answer: (D)

$$\dfrac{b}{100} \times \dfrac{10\,00}{a}$$
$$\Downarrow$$
$$\dfrac{10b}{a}$$

NEXT PAGE

5. If $f(x) = x + 2$, $g(x) = 4x$, and $j(x) = \dfrac{2}{x}$, what does

$g(f(j(4)))$ equal?

(A) 6

(B) 9

(C) 10

(D) 12

Solution: Answer: (C)

$$j(4) = \frac{2}{4} = \frac{1}{2}$$

$$f\left(\frac{1}{2}\right) = \frac{1}{2} + 2 = 2.5$$

$$\Downarrow$$

$$g(2.5) = 4 \times 2.5 = 10$$

---

6. Eric left his home at 8:00am, traveling along Route 1 at 50 miles per hour. At 11:00am, Victor left home and started after him on the same road at 80 miles per hour. At what time did Victor catch up to Eric?

(A) 2:00pm
(B) 4:00pm
(C) 3:00pm
(D) 1:00pm

Solution: Answer: (B)

$\dfrac{A \text{ Earlier}}{B \text{ Later}}$ ⟶

$$\begin{cases} d_1 = d_2 & Y \\ d_1 + d_2 = d_3 & N \end{cases}$$

$$\downarrow$$

$$50y = 80(y - 3)$$

$$y = 8$$

$$\Downarrow$$

$$x = 8:00\text{am} + 8 = 4:00\text{pm}$$

---

7. Which of the following sketches shows a relationship that is appropriately modled with the function $f(x) = ax^b + c$, where $f(x) = 0$, $a < 0$, $b = 1$, and $c < 0$?

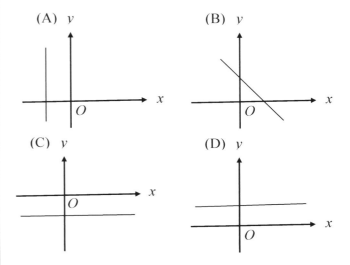

(A) y

(B) y

(C) y

(D) y

Solution: Answer: (A)

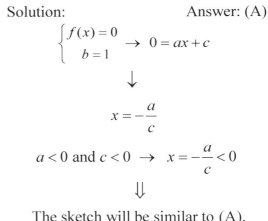

$$\begin{cases} f(x) = 0 \\ b = 1 \end{cases} \rightarrow 0 = ax + c$$

$$\downarrow$$

$$x = -\frac{a}{c}$$

$$a < 0 \text{ and } c < 0 \rightarrow x = -\frac{a}{c} < 0$$

$$\Downarrow$$

The sketch will be similar to (A).

NEXT PAGE ⟹

8. If the radius of a circle is 6 feet, what is the area of the sector whose arc length is 6π feet?

(A) 12.5π

(B) 25π

(C) 24π

(D) 18π

Solution:　　　　　　　Answer: (D)

Use the formulas:

$$\begin{cases} s = r\theta \rightarrow 6\pi = 6\theta, \ \theta = \pi \\ A = \dfrac{1}{2}r^2\theta \end{cases}$$

$$\Downarrow$$

$$A = \dfrac{1}{2} \cdot 6^2 \cdot \pi = 18\pi$$

9. Monica is 6 years younger than her sister Michelle. In eight years, Monica's age will be $\dfrac{5}{8}$ of Michelle's age. How old is Michelle now?

(A) 6

(B) 14

(C) 8

(D) 13

Solution:　　　　　　Answer: (C)

$$x - 6 + 8 = \dfrac{5}{8}(x + 8)$$

$$\Downarrow$$

$$x = 8$$

10. If $-1 < x < 0$, then which of the following must be true?

I. $x^2 > x^3$

II. $x^3 > x^5$

III. $x^2 > x^4$

(A) I only

(B) II only

(C) I and III only

(D) II and III only

Solution:　　　　　　　Answer: (C)

$$\begin{cases} \text{I. } x^2 > x^3 \\ x^2 > 0, \ x < 0 \\ \Downarrow \\ \text{I is true.} \end{cases}$$

Use $x = -\dfrac{1}{2}$ to test.

II. $x^3 > x^5$

$$\left(-\dfrac{1}{2}\right)^3 = -\dfrac{1}{8}, \ \left(-\dfrac{1}{2}\right)^5 = -\dfrac{1}{32}$$

$$-\dfrac{1}{32} > -\dfrac{1}{8} \rightarrow x^3 < x^5$$

$$\Downarrow$$

II is false.

III. $x^2 > x^4$

$$\left(-\dfrac{1}{2}\right)^2 = \dfrac{1}{4}, \ \left(-\dfrac{1}{2}\right)^4 = \dfrac{1}{16}$$

$$\dfrac{1}{4} > \dfrac{1}{16} \rightarrow x^2 > x^4$$

$$\Downarrow$$

III is true.

NEXT PAGE

Questions 11 and 12 refer to the information below.

Box versus Time

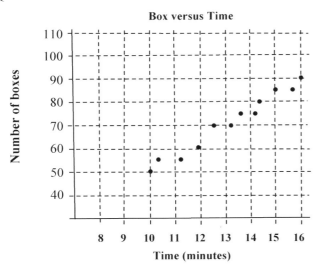

Group	Rate of Packing (boxes per minute)
group 1	7/2
group 2	5/2
group 3	17/4
group 4	5
group 5	20/3
group 6	7
group 7	4

Calculating the approximate number, N, of the boxes packed by people is easy: N = Time × Rate of packing. The scatterlpot and table above provide the relationship of time and box, and the names of seven packing groups and their rates of packing.

11. According to the information of the scatterplot and table, if group 4 and group 7 both each now have twenty boxes to pack, which of the following will be closest to the absolute difference, in minutes, of their time?

   (A) 1.5   (B) 2.0   (C) 1   (D) 2.5

Solution: Answer: (C)

$\begin{cases} \text{The rate of group 4 is 5. That means } \dfrac{1}{5} \text{ minute per box.} \\ \text{The rate of group 7 is 4. That means } \dfrac{1}{4} \text{ minute per box.} \end{cases}$

$$\Downarrow$$

$$\left(\frac{1}{4}\times 20\right)-\left(\frac{1}{5}\times 20\right)=5-4=1$$

12. By the scatterplot providing the time ploted against box for 12 people of a single group, the packing rate is closest to that of which the following groups?

(A) group 2

(B) group 5

(C) group 4

(D) group 3

Solution: Answer: (B)

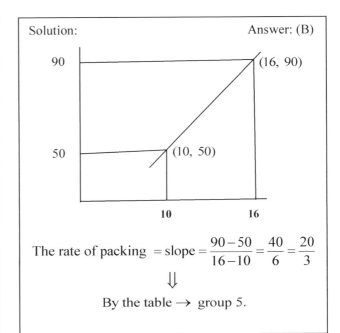

$$\text{The rate of packing } = \text{slope} = \frac{90-50}{16-10}=\frac{40}{6}=\frac{20}{3}$$

$$\Downarrow$$

By the table → group 5.

13. If Maria wants to get a solution that is 6% salt from 510 quarts of solution that is 5% salt, how much water, in quarts, must be evaporated?

(A) 85
(B) 60
(C) 65
(D) 70

Solution: Answer: (A)

$$A + B = M$$

$$510\times 5 - 0x = 6\times(510-x)$$

or

$$510\times\frac{5}{100}-\frac{0}{100}x=\frac{6}{100}\times(510-x)$$

$$\Downarrow$$

$$x = \boxed{85}$$

NEXT PAGE ⇨

14. The sum of all even integrs from 0 to 204 is Sum_{even}.

What is the sum of all even integers from 4 to 202?

(A) $\text{Sum}_{even} - 202$

(B) $\text{Sum}_{even} - 200$

(C) $\text{Sum}_{even} - 206$

(D) $\text{Sum}_{even} - 208$

Solution: Answer: (C)

$$\text{Sum}_{even} - (2 + 204) = \text{Sum}_{even} - 206$$

---

15. If n is an integer greater than zero, let ◼ n ◼ be defined as the set of all multiples of n. All of the numbers in which of the following sets are also in all three of the sets ◼ 2 ◼, ◼ 4 ◼ , and ◼ 5 ◼?

(A) ◼ 10 ◼

(B) ◼ 30 ◼

(C) ◼ 40 ◼

(D) ◼ 50 ◼

Solution: Answer: (C)

Set ◼ 2 ◼ = (2, 4, 6, …40…80…).
Set ◼ 4 ◼ = (4, 8, 12, …40…80…).
Set ◼ 5 ◼ = (5, 10, 15, …40…80…).

Number 10 in (A), number 30 in (B), number in (C), and number 70 in (E) are not in set ◼ 4 ◼.

◼ 40 ◼ = (40, 80…)

⇓

All of the numbers in (C) are in the 3 sets.

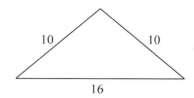

Note: Figure above not drawn to scale.

16. In the figure above, what is the area of a triangle whose sides are 10, 10, and 16?

(A) 48

(B) 24

(C) 12

(D) 60

Solution: Answer: (A)

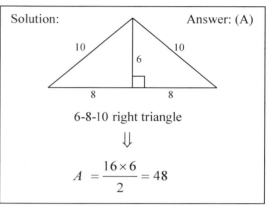

6-8-10 right triangle

⇓

$$A = \frac{16 \times 6}{2} = 48$$

17. A and B both are constant and $4x^2 + Ax - 6$ is equivalent to $(x - 2)(4x + B)$. What is the value of A?

(A) -11

(B) 5

(C) 11

(D) -5

Solution: Answer: (D)

(1).

$$(x - 2)(4x + B)$$

↓

$$4x^2 - 2 \cdot 4x + Bx - 2B$$

↓

$$4x^2 + (B - 8)x - 2B$$

(2).

Compare the coefficients.

↓

$$\begin{cases} -2B = -6 \\ B - 8 = A \end{cases}$$

⇓

$$B = 3 \text{ and } A = \boxed{-5}$$

NEXT PAGE

18. What is the domain of $f(x) = \dfrac{a}{|x| - x}$ is, where $a > 0$?

(A) $x > 0$

(B) $x > a$

(C) $x < 0$

(D) $x = a$

Solution: Answer: (C)

Use a TI graph calculator.

The main steps:

$\boxed{Y =}$, at sign $\backslash Y_1 =$, type

$10/(|x| - x) \rightarrow \boxed{GRAPH}$.

↑

$\begin{cases} \text{The steps for getting } |x|: \\ \boxed{MATH} \rightarrow NUM \rightarrow 1: abs(\end{cases}$

The graph should be like the

sketch below.

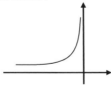

From the sketch above, the conclution

should be that the doamin is all $x < 0$.

19. The price of a CD player was reduced from \$180 to \$120. What was the percent of decrease in the price of the unit?

(A) 33%

(B) $\left(66 + \dfrac{2}{3}\right)\%$

(C) 66%

(D) $\left(33 + \dfrac{1}{3}\right)\%$

Solution: Answer: (D)

$\dfrac{(180 - 120)}{180} = \dfrac{1}{3}$

↓

$\dfrac{1}{3} = \dfrac{1}{3} \times 1 = \dfrac{1}{3} \times 100\%$

↓

$\dfrac{100}{3}\%$

⇓

$33\dfrac{1}{3}\% = (33 + \dfrac{1}{3})\%$

20. If $s = 5q$, $q = 4r$, $3r = p$, and $p \neq 0$, then $s / p =$

(A) 4

(B) $\dfrac{20}{3}$

(C) 10

(D) -4

Solution: Answer: (B)

The question asks value of s / p.

↓

q and r should be canceled.

Let $q = 1$.

↓

$\begin{cases} s = 5 \cdot 1 = \boxed{5} \\ 1 = 4r, \; r = \boxed{\dfrac{1}{4}} \end{cases} \rightarrow p = 3 \cdot \dfrac{1}{4} = \dfrac{3}{4}$

⇓

$\dfrac{s}{p} = \dfrac{5}{\frac{3}{4}} = \dfrac{20}{3}$

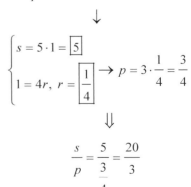

NEXT PAGE

21. If the fraction $\dfrac{1}{26}$ is equivalent to the repeating decimal 0.3846153846153…, what is the 68th digit after the decimal point of the repeating decimal?

(A) 4
(B) 7
(C) 9
(D) 8

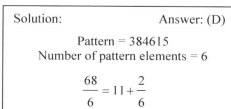

Solution: Answer: (D)

Pattern = 384615
Number of pattern elements = 6

$$\frac{68}{6} = 11 + \frac{2}{6}$$

remainder = 2

↓

68th digit is at the 2nd pattern position

⇓

68th digit = 8

22. The first term of set A is -2, and each term thereafter is 2 greater than the previous term. The Nth term of set B is given by the formula $-N + 12$. What is the value of the term of set A that first exceeds the value of its corresponding term in set B?

(A) 6
(B) 8
(C) 7
(D) 5

Solution: Answer: (B)

$A = (-2, 0, 2, 4, 6, 8…)$
$B = (-N + 12)$
Because N represents the term number,
N must represent positive integers.
$N = 1, 2, 3…$
$B = (11, 10, 9, 8, 7, 6…)$

6th term of $A = 8$
6th term of $B = 6$
⇓
The underlined value is 8

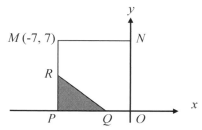

Note: Figure above not drawn to scale.

23. In the figure above, the coordinates of R are $(-7, k)$ and the coordinates of Q are $(-1, 0)$. One point in square $MNOP$ is to be chosen randomly. If the probability that the point will be in the shaded triangle is 10%, what is the value of k ?

(A) $\dfrac{49}{30}$

(B) 3/2

(C) 2.5

(D) 5.2

Solution: Answer: (A)

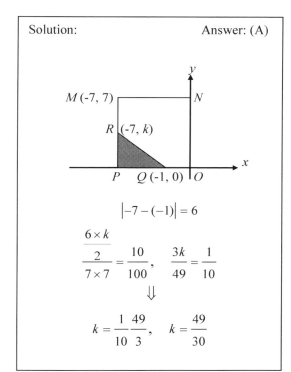

$$|-7 - (-1)| = 6$$

$$\frac{\frac{6 \times k}{2}}{7 \times 7} = \frac{10}{100}, \quad \frac{3k}{49} = \frac{1}{10}$$

⇓

$$k = \frac{1}{10} \cdot \frac{49}{3}, \quad k = \frac{49}{30}$$

NEXT PAGE ⟩

24. If $f(x) = \sqrt{-x^2 + 1}$, then which of the following is the domain of the function f ?

(A) $x \leq -1$ or $x \geq 1$

(B) $x \leq -1$

(C) $-1 \leq x \leq 1$

(D) All real numbers

Solution: Answer: (C)

$$-x^2 + 1 \geq 0$$

Use a TI graphing calculator.

Press $\boxed{Y=}$. Enter $-x^2 + 1$.

Press $\boxed{GRAPH}$. You will see the graph roughly like the sketch below:

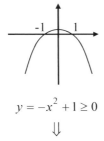

$$y = -x^2 + 1 \geq 0$$
$$\Downarrow$$
$$-1 \leq x \leq 1$$

---

25. $(a + b - 3)(a + b + 3) = ?$

(A) $(a + b)^2 - 9$

(B) $(a - b)^2 - 9$

(C) $(a + b)^2 + 9$

(D) $a^2 - 2ab + b^2 + 3$

Solution: Answer: (A)

Use the formula:
$$x^2 - y^2 = (x - y)(x + y).$$
$$\downarrow$$
$$(a + b)^2 - 3^2$$
$$\Downarrow$$
$$(a + b)^2 - 9$$

---

26.   At JFK Academy, the ratio of girls to boys is 2 to 3. If three-fifths of the boys are on a team and the remaining 30 boys are not, how many girls are in this school?

(A) 90
(B) 50
(C) 80
(D) 300

Solution: Answer: (B)

$$\frac{2}{5}b = 30, \ b = \frac{30 \times 5}{2} = 75$$
$$\Downarrow$$
$$\frac{g}{b} = \frac{2}{3}, g = \frac{2}{3}b = \frac{2}{3} \times 75 = 50$$

---

27. Which of the following is the zeros, vertex, domain, and range of function $f(x) = \dfrac{1}{4}(2x-1)(2x-11)$?

(A) Zeros $= (5.5,\ 1/2\ )$, $\begin{pmatrix} \text{Vertex} = (3,\ -25/4) \\ \text{Domain = All real numbers} \\ \text{Open up, Range} \geq -25/4 \end{pmatrix}$

(B) Zeros $= (5.5,\ 1/2\ )$, $\begin{pmatrix} \text{Vertex} = (-25/4,\ 3,) \\ \text{Domain = All real numbers} \\ \text{Open up, Range} \geq -25/4 \end{pmatrix}$

(C) Zeros $= (1/2,\ 5.5)$, $\begin{pmatrix} \text{Vertex} = (-25/4,\ 3) \\ \text{Domain = All real numbers} \\ \text{Open up, Range} \geq 3 \end{pmatrix}$

(D) Zeros $= (1/2,\ 5.5)$, $\begin{pmatrix} \text{Vertex} = (3,\ -25/4) \\ \text{Domain = All real numbers} \\ \text{Open up, Range} \geq -25/4 \end{pmatrix}$

Solution: Answer: (D)

Use the factor form.

$$f(x) = k(x-r_1)(x-r_2)$$

$$\downarrow$$

$$\frac{1}{4}\left(2\left(x-\frac{1}{2}\right)\cdot 2\left(x-\frac{11}{2}\right)\right) = \left(x-\frac{1}{2}\right)\cdot(x-5.5)$$

$$\Downarrow$$

$$\boxed{\text{Zeros} = \frac{1}{2} \text{ and } 5.5}$$

Use the vertex form.

$$f(x) = k(x-x_m)^2 + y_m$$

$$\frac{1}{4}\left(4x^2 - 2x - 22x + 11\right)$$

$$x^2 - 6x + 3^2 - 3^2 + \frac{11}{4} = (x-3)^2 - \frac{25}{4}$$

$$\Downarrow$$

$$\boxed{\begin{array}{c} \text{Vertex} = \left(3,\ -\dfrac{25}{4}\right) \\ \text{Domain = All real numbers} \\ \dfrac{1}{4} > 0 \rightarrow \text{Open up, Range} \geq -\dfrac{25}{4} \end{array}}$$

Questions 28 and 29 refer to the following figure:

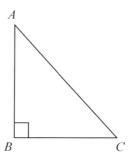

28. What is $\tan A$?

(A) $\dfrac{AB}{BC}$ (B) $\dfrac{BC}{AB}$ (C) $\dfrac{AC}{BC}$ (D) $\dfrac{BC}{AC}$

Solution   Answer: (B)

The definition of tangent

$$\Downarrow$$

$$\tan A = \frac{BC}{AB} \text{ (for } A \text{, not for } C)$$

29. If $AC = \sqrt{2}$, what is the area of the triangle?

(A) $\sin C \cos C$ (B) $\dfrac{\sin C \cos C}{2}$

(C) $\sin A \cos A$ (D) $\dfrac{\sin A \cos A}{2}$

Solution: Answer: (A)

$$\sin C = \frac{AB}{AC}, \quad AB = AC\sin C$$

$$\cos C = \frac{BC}{AC}, \quad BC = AC\cos C$$

$$\downarrow$$

$$\begin{cases} A = \dfrac{AB \cdot BC}{2} = \dfrac{AC\sin C \cdot AC\cos C}{2} \\ AC = \sqrt{2} \end{cases}$$

$$\Downarrow$$

$$A = \frac{\left(\sqrt{2}\right)^2 \sin C \cdot \cos C}{2}$$

NEXT PAGE ⇨

30. Which scatterplot below shows a relationship that is approximately modeled with the equation $f(x) = ax^k$, where a is positive and k is a positive non-integer?

(A)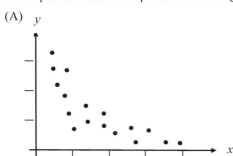

(B)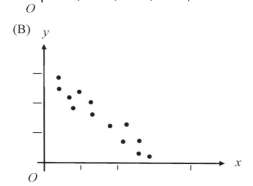

(C)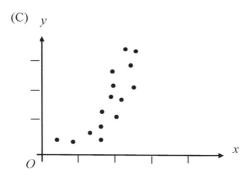

(D)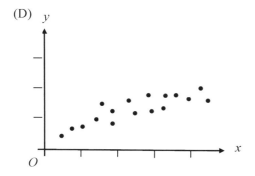

Solution: Answer: (D)

$f(x) = ax^k$ is a power function.

It can be $y = x^{1/2} = \sqrt{x}$.

$\Downarrow$

Answer is (D).

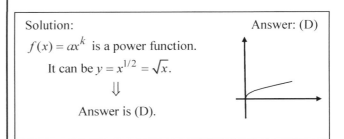

NEXT PAGE

31. Robot-1 and Robot-2 stand shoulder-to-shoulder on one line. Then each of them takes 16 steps in opposite direction away and stops. And then Robot-1 goes back, walks toward Robot-2 and reaches Robot-2 in 22 steps. The size of one of Robot-1's steps is how many times the size of one of Robot-2's steps?
Note: All of Robot-1's steps designed are the same size and all of Robot-2's steps designed are the same size also.

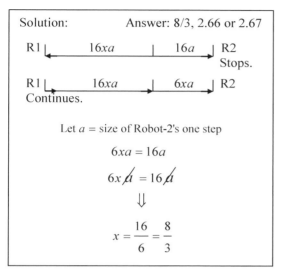

Solution: Answer: 8/3, 2.66 or 2.67

R1 |⟵ 16xa | 16a ⟶| R2
                             Stops.

R1 |⟶ 16xa | 6xa ⟶| R2
Continues.

Let a = size of Robot-2's one step

$$6xa = 16a$$

$$6x\cancel{a} = 16\cancel{a}$$

⇓

$$x = \frac{16}{6} = \frac{8}{3}$$

32. For how many integers m is $(3m+1)(4m-17)$ a negative number?

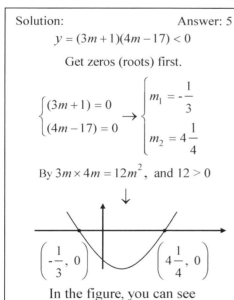

Solution: Answer: 5

$$y = (3m+1)(4m-17) < 0$$

Get zeros (roots) first.

$$\begin{cases} (3m+1) = 0 \\ (4m-17) = 0 \end{cases} \rightarrow \begin{cases} m_1 = -\frac{1}{3} \\ m_2 = 4\frac{1}{4} \end{cases}$$

By $3m \times 4m = 12m^2$, and $12 > 0$

↓

$\left(-\frac{1}{3}, 0\right)$ $\left(4\frac{1}{4}, 0\right)$

In the figure, you can see when each value of $y < 0$,

$$\underbrace{-\frac{1}{3} < m < 4\frac{1}{4}}_{m=0,\ 1,\ 2,\ 3,\ 4}$$

⇓

5 integers

33. If a 3-digit number is selected randomly, what is the probability that all 3 digits are even numbers?

Solution: Answer: 1/9 or .111

$$\boxed{9} \cdot \boxed{10} \cdot \boxed{10} = 900$$

Five even digits: 0, 2, 4, 6, 8

If the first digit is 0, it becomes a 2-digit number. The first digit cannot be 0.

The question does not indicate that the 3 digits are different. So the 3-digit number can have the same digits.

3 element sets

↓

$$\boxed{4} \cdot \boxed{5} \cdot \boxed{5} = 100$$

↑   ↖↗

| 2, 4, 6, 8 | | 0, 2, 4, 6, 8 |

⇓

$$P = \frac{100}{900} = \frac{1}{9} = .111$$

34. Jennifer filled 5/7 of John's swimming pool with 2800 cube feet. What is the total capacity of John's swimming pool?

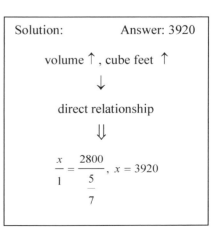

Solution: Answer: 3920

volume ↑, cube feet ↑

↓

direct relationship

⇓

$$\frac{x}{1} = \frac{2800}{\frac{5}{7}}, \quad x = 3920$$

NEXT PAGE ⟹

Note: Figure below not drawn to scale.

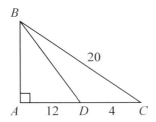

35. In the figure above, what is the the area of triangle ABD?

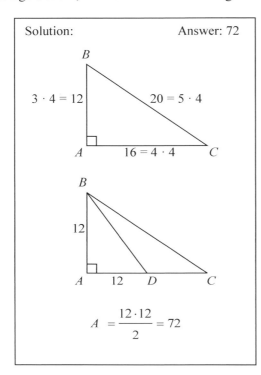

Solution: Answer: 72

$3 \cdot 4 = 12$ $20 = 5 \cdot 4$

$16 = 4 \cdot 4$

$A = \dfrac{12 \cdot 12}{2} = 72$

36. What does $|x - 7| < 2$ equal?

Solution: Answer: $5 < x < 9$

$$|x - 7| < 2$$
$$\downarrow$$
$$-2 < x - 7 < 2$$
$$\Downarrow$$
$$5 < x < 9$$

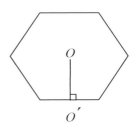

37. In the figure above, if the length of OO' of the regular hexagon with a center O is $3\sqrt{3}$, what is the perimeter of the hexagon?

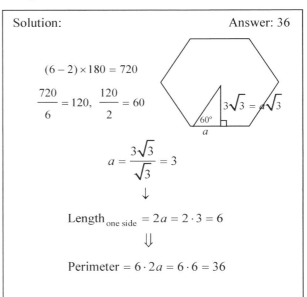

Solution: Answer: 36

$(6 - 2) \times 180 = 720$

$\dfrac{720}{6} = 120, \quad \dfrac{120}{2} = 60$

$3\sqrt{3} = a\sqrt{3}$

$a = \dfrac{3\sqrt{3}}{\sqrt{3}} = 3$

$\downarrow$

$\text{Length}_{\text{one side}} = 2a = 2 \cdot 3 = 6$

$\Downarrow$

$\text{Perimeter} = 6 \cdot 2a = 6 \cdot 6 = 36$

38. Let @ be defined by $m @ w = m^{w}$. If $A = 2 @ a$, $B = 2 @ b$, and $a - b = 4$, what is the value of $\dfrac{A}{B}$?

Solution: Answer: 16 or 16/1

$$A = 2 @ a = 2^{a}, \quad B = 2 @ b = 2^{b}$$
$$\downarrow$$
$$\frac{A}{B} = \frac{2^{a}}{2^{b}} = 2^{a} \cdot 2^{-b} = 2^{a-b}$$
$$a - b = 4$$
$$\Downarrow$$
$$\frac{A}{B} = 2^{4} = 16$$

STOP

SAT Math

Practice

Test 10

Redesigned for Tests in March 2016 and Beyond

Mad Math

Math Test – No Calculator

Time: 25 Minutes
20 Questions

Notes:

- The use of a calculator is not allowed.
- All numbers used in this section are the real number.
- Figures are provided for some problems in this test. Unless otherwise indicated under the figure "Note: Figure above not drawn to scale", all figures are drawn as accurately as possible.
- All figures lie in a plane EXCEPT otherwise specified.
- Unless otherwise indicated, the domain of any function f, g or j is assumed to be the set of all real numbers x for which $f(x)$, $g(x)$, or $j(x)$ is a real number.

Reference Information

$$A = \frac{1}{2}bh$$

$$A = lw$$

$$A = \pi r^2$$

$$V = \pi r^2 h$$

$$V = lwh$$

$$c^2 = a^2 + b^2$$

$$V = \frac{1}{3}\pi r^2 h$$

$$V = \frac{4}{3}\pi r^3$$

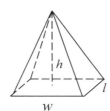

$$V = \frac{1}{3}lwh$$

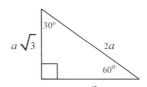

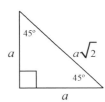

Copying or reuse of any portion of this page is illegal.

1. If $\sqrt{q^2} = q$, which of the following is the set of all real numbers q ?

(A) nonnegative real integers only

(B) positive real numbers only

(C) nonnegative real numbers only

(D) nonpositive real numbers only

3. If $i = \sqrt{-1}$, then $|-6 + 3i| =$

(A) $\sqrt{95}$

(B) 35

(C) $3\sqrt{5}$

(D) 19

2. What is the product of the zeros of $f(x) = 22^{11}x^2 + 22^{11}$?

(A) 22

(B) 2

(C) 0

(D) 1

4. For all real number x, $g(2x) = 2x^2 + x - 1$. What is an expression for $g(x)$ in terms of x ?

(A) $g(x) = x^2 + \dfrac{x}{2} - 1$ (B) $g(x) = \dfrac{x^2}{4} + \dfrac{x}{2} - 1$

(C) $g(x) = \dfrac{x^2}{2} + x - 1$ (D) $g(x) = \dfrac{x^2}{2} + \dfrac{x}{2} - 1$

NEXT PAGE

5. If $x^2(2s-1) + 3x - 2 = 0$ has no real solutions, what is the greatest integer value of s ?

(A) 1

(B) 0

(C) 2

(D) -1

6. Let $f(t)$ give the entire amount earned, in dollars, in a week by James as a function of the number of hours worked. James earns $10.5 per hour and must work 3 to 5 days each week from 6 to 8 hours each day. What is the domain of function f ?

(A) $18 \leq t \leq 40$

(B) $18 < t \leq 40$

(C) $18 \leq t, t \geq 40$

(D) $18 \leq t < 40$

7. Where defined, $\dfrac{\sin x - \cos x}{1 - \tan x}$ is equal to

(A) $\cos x$

(B) $\tan x$

(C) $-\csc x$

(D) $-\cos x$

NEXT PAGE

8. What is the domain of function $f(x) = \dfrac{100}{x^2 + 0.0001}$?

(A) All real numbers including -0.01

(B) $x \neq -\dfrac{1}{10000}$

(C) $-0.001 \leq x \leq 0.001$

(D) $-\sqrt{0.001} \leq x \leq \sqrt{0.001}$

9. The median of a list of 139 consecutive integers is 73. What is the greatest integer in the list?

(A) 142

(B) 143

(C) 144

(D) 145

10. Four years from now, Kevin's age will be $4x + 2$. Which of the following represents his age four years ago?

(A) $4x - 2$

(B) $4x - 3$

(C) $4x - 5$

(D) $4x - 6$

11. Which of the following is the zeros, vertex, domain, and range of function $f(x) = \dfrac{1}{4}(2x - 1)(2x - 4)$?

(A) Zeros $= (1/2, 2)$, $\begin{pmatrix} \text{Vertex} = (5/4, \text{-}9/16) \\ \text{Domain} = \text{All real numbers} \\ \text{Range} \geq \text{-}9/16 \end{pmatrix}$

(B) Zeros $= (2, 1/2)$, $\begin{pmatrix} \text{Vertex} = (\text{-}9/16, 5/4) \\ \text{Domain} = \text{All real numbers} \\ \text{Range} \geq 5/4 \end{pmatrix}$

(C) Zeros $= (1/2, 2)$, $\begin{pmatrix} \text{Vertex} = (\text{-}9/16, 5/4) \\ \text{Domain} = \text{All real numbers} \\ \text{Range} \leq \text{-}9/16 \end{pmatrix}$

(D) Zeros $= (2, 1/2)$, $\begin{pmatrix} \text{Vertex} = (\text{-}9/16, 5/4) \\ \text{Domain} = \text{All real numbers} \\ \text{Range} \leq 5/4 \end{pmatrix}$

NEXT PAGE ⇨

12. Which domain of the following functions does not include 10 ?

(A) $y = \dfrac{x}{x^2 - 10x}$

(B) $y = \dfrac{x^2}{x^3 + 10x}$

(C) $y = \dfrac{x^2 - 1}{x^5 + 10x}$

(D) $y = \dfrac{x}{x^7 + 10x}$

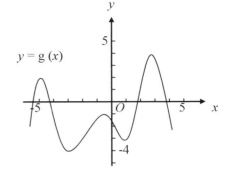

14. The figure above shows the graph of $y = g(x)$, where $-5 \le x \le 5$. For what value of x does the function g obtain its least value?

(A) -4
(B) -3
(C) 3
(D) -1

13. If Kathie completely travels a circular path in 30 minutes, how many degrees does she travel by 0.5 minute?

(A) 3

(B) 4

(C) 6

(D) 5

15. If an isosceles right triangle whose legs are 3 is rotated about its one leg to produce a right circular cone, what is the volume of the cone?

(A) 18π

(B) 10π

(C) 6π

(D) 9π

NEXT PAGE

16.   If $0.047 = 4.7 \times 10^{p}$, what is the value of $(-p)$?

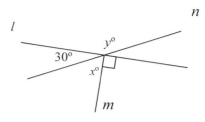

Note: Figure above not drawn to scale.

19.   In the figure above, lines l, m, and n meet at a point and line l is perpendicular to m. What is the value of $y - x$?

17.   If $b + \dfrac{1}{b} = 6$, then $b^{2} + \dfrac{1}{b^{2}} =$

20.   If John, Jack, and James can clean a building in 6 hours, and John and Jack working together can do it in 9 hours, how long will it take James alone to clean the building?

18.   Michael can travel from Bedminster to New York City by his own car or taxi. He can then travel to Boston by plane, train, ship, or bus. From Boston, he can travel to Jackson Academy by bus, or taxi. In how many different ways can Michael travel from Bedminster to New York City to Boston and then to Jackson Academy?

STOP

Math Test – Calculator

Time: 55 Minutes
38 Questions

Notes:
- The use of a calculator is not allowed.
- All numbers used in this section are the real number.
- Figures are provided for some problems in this test. Unless otherwise indicated under the figure "Note: Figure above not drawn to scale", all figures are drawn as accurately as possible.
- All figures lie in a plane EXCEPT otherwise specified.
- Unless otherwise indicated, the domain of any function f, g or j is assumed to be the set of all real numbers x for which $f(x)$, $g(x)$, or $j(x)$ is a real number.

Reference Information

$$A = \frac{1}{2}bh$$

$$A = lw$$

$$A = \pi r^2$$

$$V = \pi r^2 h$$

$$V = lwh$$

$$c^2 = a^2 + b^2$$

$$V = \frac{1}{3}\pi r^2 h$$

$$V = \frac{4}{3}\pi r^3$$

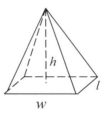
$$V = \frac{1}{3}lwh$$

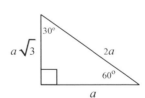

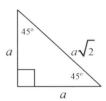

1. If a function defined by $g(x) = \sqrt[3]{7x^2 - 3}$, what is the domain of the function?

(A) The set of all real integers

(B) $x \geq 1$

(C) $x > 1$

(D) The set of all real numbers

2. If the radius of a circle is 5 feet, what is the area of the sector whose arc length is 5π feet?

(A) 12.5π

(B) 25π

(C) 24π

(D) 18π

3. The price of a CD player was increased from $120 to $200. What was the percentage of increase in the price of the unit?

(A) 33%

(B) $66\dfrac{2}{3}\%$

(C) 66%

(D) $33\dfrac{1}{3}\%$

4. The vertices of a triangle are (-2, 6), (-2, 1), and (2, 1). The area of the triangle is

(A) 14

(B) 54

(C) 10

(D) 12

NEXT PAGE

5. Which of the following is $\sqrt[4]{d^{12}}$ equal to

(A) $-d^3$

(B) $\left|d^3\right|$

(C) d^6

(D) $\left|d^2\right|$

6. If for all real numbers x, a function f is defined by

$$f(x) = \begin{cases} 5, & x = 11 \\ 6, & x \neq 11 \end{cases}, \text{ then } f(6) - f(5) =$$

(A) 3

(B) 0

(C) 1

(D) 2

7. If $\dfrac{1}{3}$ of a cup apple juice is filled up to 2-cup mark of a measuring container with a mixture containing equal amounts of apple and pineapple juices, what is the ratio of apple juice to final mixture?

(A) $\dfrac{5}{12}$

(B) $\dfrac{7}{12}$

(C) $\dfrac{6}{11}$

(D) $\dfrac{2}{3}$

8. If $\sqrt{q^2} = -q$, which of the following is the set of all real numbers q?

(A) all negative integers and zero only

(B) all positive real numbers only

(C) all nonzero real numbers only

(D) all negative real numbers and zero only

NEXT PAGE

9. Jack is a car salesperson. He sells two kinds of cars. For one of them, the selling price is $32,000, and for another one, the selling price is $48,000. Last week, Jack's goal was to sell at least 10 cars. He met his goal. The total value of the cars he sold was no more than $360,000. Let x be the number of $32,000 cars, and y be the number of $48,000 cars, that Jack sold last week. Which system of inequalities below represents the conditions described?

(A) $x + y \geq 10$, $32,000x + 48,000y < 360,000$

(B) $x + y \geq 10$, $32,000x + 48,000y \geq 360,000$

(C) $x + y \geq 10$, $32,000x + 48,000y \leq 360,000$

(D) $x + y > 10$, $32,000x + 48,000y \leq 360,000$

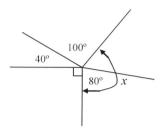

11.   In the figure above, what is the value of x?

(A) 80

(B) 130

(C) 100

(D) 70

\

10.   If the surface area of a sphere is 144π, what is the volume of the sphere?

(A) 36π

(B) 25π

(C) 256π

(D) 288π

12.   Let M1 be the median and M2 be the mode of the following set of numbers, 3, 5, 3, 4, 1, 2, 3, 6, 7, 8, and 2. What is the average (arithmetic mean) of M1 and M2?

(A) 3
(B) 4
(C) 5
(D) 6

NEXT PAGE

13.   If $f(x) = x^2 - 3x + 4$, $\dfrac{f(x-k)-f(x)}{k}$ is equal to

(A) $k + 2x - 3$

(B) $k + 2x + 3$

(C) $k - 2x + 3$

(D) $k^2 - 2x + 3$

15.   A 25-gallon mixture of ammonia and water contains 5 gallons of ammonia. If 5 more gallons of ammonia are added, what percent of the new mixture is water?

(A) 33

(B) 66

(C) $33\dfrac{1}{3}$

(D) $66\dfrac{2}{3}$

14.   Five points, A, B, C, D, and E, lie on a line, not necessarily in that order. The length of $\overline{AB}$ is 36. Point C is midpoint of $\overline{AB}$, and point D is the midpoint of $\overline{AC}$. If the distance between D and E is 7, what are all possible distances between A and E?

   (A) 2 and 16   (B) 16   (C) 8   (D) 2

NEXT PAGE

16. Erica takes 10 seconds to run a distance of 150 feet. What is the runner's speed in yards per hour?

(A) 18,000
(B) 16,000
(C) 15,000
(D) 17,000

17. What is $\dfrac{1}{3}$ percent of 3 percent ?

(A) $\dfrac{1}{3 \times 10^4}$

(B) $\dfrac{1}{10^4}$

(C) $\dfrac{3}{10^4}$

(D) $\dfrac{1}{10 \times 3^4}$

18. Which of the following is the graph of all values of x for $9 \le x^2 \le 25$?

(A)

(B)

(C)

(D)

NEXT PAGE

CAROLINE'S TOUR EXPENSES

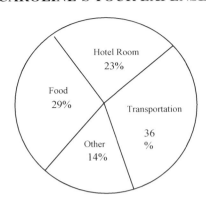

19.   In the circle graph above, it shows the distribution of Caroline's $1,050 tour expenses. The amount Caroline paid for the transportation was only portion of the total cost of transportation. She shared the cost of transportation with five other girls equally. What was the total cost of the transportation?

(A) 1,839
(B) 2,019
(C) 2,268
(D) 2,228

20.   Toni is 29 years old and her sister, Jody, is 17. How many years ago was Toni's age two times as old as Jody's?

(A) 6
(B) 5
(C) 4
(D) 7

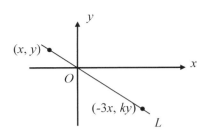

Note: Figure above not drawn to scale.

21.   In the figure above, the straight line L passes through origin point $(0, 0)$. What is the value of k?

(A) 3
(B) 1/3
(C) 1
(D) -3

22. $(k^2 - 1)(k^2 - 3) =$

(A) $(k^2 + 2k - 1)(k^2 - 3)$

(B) $(k - 1)(k - 1)(k - \sqrt{3})(k - \sqrt{3})$

(C) $(k^2 - 2k + 1)(k^2 - 3)$

(D) $(k - 1)(k + 1)(k - \sqrt{3})(k + \sqrt{3})$

NEXT PAGE

23. A green box contains 6 items, of which four are good and the rest are defective, and a yellow box contains 5 items, of which three are good and the rest are defective. An item is drawn randomly from each box. What is the probability that one item is good and one is defective?

(A) $\dfrac{2}{225}$

(B) $\dfrac{7}{15}$

(C) 0.65

(D) 0.30

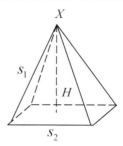

Note: Figure above not drawn to scale.

25.   The pyramid shown above has height H and a square base of side s_2. The 4 edges each have length s_1 and meet at X. X is the vertex of the pyramid. $s_1 = s_2$. What is the value of height H in terms of s_1?

(A) $s_1\sqrt{3}$

(B) $\dfrac{s_1\sqrt{2}}{3}$

(C) $\dfrac{s_1\sqrt{3}}{3}$

(D) $\dfrac{s_1\sqrt{2}}{2}$

24.   The least integer and greatest integer of a set of consecutive even integers are -20 and 26. What is the sum of all integers in the set?

(A) 46
(B) 50
(C) 26
(D) 72

NEXT PAGE

26. Jack and Tony left their respective schools at the same time for a run to a library. Jack ran at an average rate of 6 miles per hour. Tony ran at an average rate of 7 miles per hour. They arrived at the library at the same time. If Tony ran 0.5 mile farther than Jack, what is the distance, in miles, did Tony run?

(A) 4.0

(B) 3.5

(C) 5.5

(D) 2.5

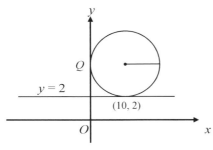

27. In the xy-plane above, the circle is tangent to the line $y = 2$ and y-axis. What are the coordinates (x, y) of point Q?

(A) (0, 10)
(B) (10, 0)
(C) (0, 2)
(D) (0, 12)

28. Let $f(t)$ give the entire amount earned, in dollars, in a week by James as a function of the number of hours worked. James earns \$10.5 per hour and must work 3 to 5 days each week from 6 to 8 hours each day. What is the domain and range of function f ?

(A) $18 < t < 40$
    $189 < f < 420$

(B) $18 < t \leq 40$
    $189 \leq f < 420$

(C) $18 \leq t \leq 40$
    $189 \leq f \leq 420$

(D) $18 \leq t < 40$
    $189 \leq f < 420$

NEXT PAGE

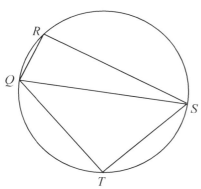

Note: Figure above not drawn to scale.

29.   In the figure above, if $QR = 5, QS = 13,$ $ST = 12,$ and $\overline{QS}$ is a diameter of the circle, which of the following is the area of triangle QST ?

(A) 78

(B) 65

(C) 30

(D) 32.5

30.   If $x^2 + 8x - 9 \le 0$ and $f(x) = x^2 + 6x + 8,$ what is the range of $f(x)$?

(A) $-1 \le f(x) \le 35$

(B) $15 < f(x) \le 35$

(C) $-1 < f(x) \le 35$

(D) $0 \le f(x) \le 35$

NEXT PAGE

31. James places a 13-foot ladder against a vertical wall of a building. The bottom of the ladder stands on concrete 5 feet from the base of the building. If the top of the ladder slips down 7 feet, how many feet the bottom of the ladder will slide out

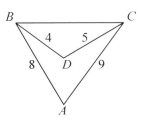

33.   In the figure above, how much smaller is the perimeter of triangle *BDC* than the perimeter of triangle *ABC* ?

34. The Tech Service that is a company of technical services will send a group of 6 people to work on a certain job. The company has six experienced electricians and five trainees. If the group consists of three experienced electricians and 3 trainees, how many possible distinct such groups exist?

32. Company *A* is owned by four men and one woman, each of them has equal shares. If one of the men sells one-third of his shares to the woman, and another of men keeps one-third of his shares and sells the rest to the woman, what fraction of the company will the woman own?

NEXT PAGE ⟩

35. Several students stand in a line. Staring at one end of the line, Kevin is counted as 8th person, and starting at the other end, Kevin is counted as the 12th person. How many students are in the line?

36. James has six blank cards. Each card is written with one of the following letters: *A, B, C, D, E* or *F*. Each of six cards does not have the same letter. If *E* and *F* are always the center letters in the arrangements, how many possible distinct six-letter arrangements can James create?

37. Cynthia cuts a cube object with volume 1cubic inches in half in all 3 directions, what is the total surface area of the separated smaller cubes, in square inches?

38. If Maria wants to get a solution that is 6% alcohol from 510 quarts of solution that is 5% alcohol, how much water, in quarts, must be evaporated?

STOP

Answer Key
For
SAT Math Practice Test 10

Section 3

1	C
2	D
3	C
4	D
5	D
6	A
7	D
8	A
9	A
10	D
11	A
12	A
13	C
14	B
15	D

16	2
17	34
18	16
19	90
20	18

Section 4

1	D	16	A
2	A	17	B
3	B	18	C
4	C	19	C
5	B	20	B
6	B	21	D
7	B	22	D
8	D	23	B
9	C	24	D
10	D	25	D
11	B	26	B
12	A	27	D
13	C	28	C
14	A	29	C
15	D	30	A

31	7
32	2/5 or .4
33	8
34	200
35	19
36	48
37	12
38	85

SAT Math

Practice

Test 10

Explanations

Redesigned for Tests in March 2016 and Beyond

Mad Math

Math Test – No Calculator

Time: 25 Minutes
20 Questions

Notes:

- The use of a calculator is not allowed.
- All numbers used in this section are the real number.
- Figures are provided for some problems in this test. Unless otherwise indicated under the figure "Note: Figure above not drawn to scale", all figures are drawn as accurately as possible.
- All figures lie in a plane EXCEPT otherwise specified.
- Unless otherwise indicated, the domain of any function f, g or j is assumed to be the set of all real numbers x for which $f(x)$, $g(x)$, or $j(x)$ is a real number.

Reference Information

$A = \dfrac{1}{2}bh$

$A = lw$

$A = \pi r^2$

$V = \pi r^2 h$

$V = lwh$

$c^2 = a^2 + b^2$

$V = \dfrac{1}{3}\pi r^2 h$

$V = \dfrac{4}{3}\pi r^3$

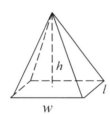

$V = \dfrac{1}{3}lwh$

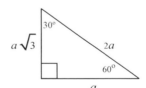

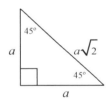

1. If $\sqrt{q^2} = q$, which of the following is the set of all real numbers q?

(A) nonnegative real integers only

(B) positive real numbers only

(C) nonnegative real numbers only

(D) nonpositive real numbers only

Solution: Answer: (C)

If ☐ is inside $\sqrt{}$,

☐ ≥ 0 and $\sqrt{☐} \geq 0$.

⇓

$\sqrt{q^2} = q, \qquad q \geq 0$

2. What is the product of the zeros of $f(x) = 22^{11}x^2 + 22^{11}$?

(A) 22

(B) 2

(C) 0

(D) 1

Solution: Answer: (D)

Use the formula of product of the zeros of the quadratic function.

⇓

$\text{Product}_{zeros} = \dfrac{c}{a} = \dfrac{22^{11}}{22^{11}} = 1$

3. If $i = \sqrt{-1}$, then $|-6 + 3i| =$

(A) $\sqrt{95}$

(B) 35

(C) $3\sqrt{5}$

(D) 19

Solution: Answer: (C)

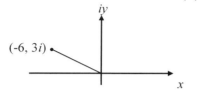

The absolute value $|a + bi|$ of a complex number $a + bi$ is the distance between origin $(0, 0)$ and point $(a, \; bi)$.

↓

$|a + bi| = \sqrt{(a-0)^2 + (b-0)^2} = \sqrt{a^2 + b^2}$

⇓

$|6 + 3i| = \sqrt{(-6)^2 + 3^2} = \sqrt{45} = 3\sqrt{5}$

4. For all real number x, $g(2x) = 2x^2 + x - 1$. What is an expression for $g(x)$ in terms of x?

(A) $g(x) = x^2 + \dfrac{x}{2} - 1$ (B) $g(x) = \dfrac{x^2}{4} + \dfrac{x}{2} - 1$

(C) $g(x) = \dfrac{x^2}{2} + x - 1$ (D) $g(x) = \dfrac{x^2}{2} + \dfrac{x}{2} - 1$

Solution: Answer: (D)

Use plug-in method.

↓

(C) $g(x) = \dfrac{x^2}{2} + \dfrac{x}{2} - 1$

↓

$g(2x) = \dfrac{(2x)^2}{2} + \dfrac{2x}{2} - 1$

⇓

$2x^2 + x - 1$

NEXT PAGE ⟩

5. If $x^2(2s-1)+3x-2=0$ has no real solutions, what is the greatest integer value of s ?

(A) 1

(B) 0

(C) 2

(D) -1

Solution: Answer: (D)

$$3^2 - 4(2s-1)(-2) < 0$$

$$\Downarrow$$

$$16s < -1, \quad s < -\frac{1}{16}, \quad s = -1$$

6. Let $f(t)$ give the entire amount earned, in dollars, in a week by James as a function of the number of hours worked. James earns \$10.5 per hour and must work 3 to 5 days each week from 6 to 8 hours each day. What is the domain of function f ?

(A) $18 \le t \le 40$

(B) $18 < t \le 40$

(C) $18 \le t, t \ge 40$

(D) $18 \le t < 40$

Solution: Answer: (A)

$\begin{cases} \text{Input} = \text{hours} \\ \text{Output} = \text{total dollars} \end{cases}$

$\begin{cases} \text{Domain is about hours.} \\ \text{Range is about total dollars.} \end{cases}$

$\begin{cases} \text{Domain:} \\ \text{The least} = 3 \times 6 = 18 \\ \text{The greatest} = 5 \times 8 = 40 \end{cases}$

$$\Downarrow$$

$$\boxed{18 \le t \le 40}$$

7. Where defined, $\dfrac{\sin x - \cos x}{1 - \tan x}$ is equal to

(A) $\cos x$

(B) $\tan x$

(C) $- \csc x$

(D) $- \cos x$

Solution: Answer: (D)

Method 1

$$\frac{\sin x - \cos x}{1 - \tan x} = \frac{\sin x - \cos x}{1 - \dfrac{\sin x}{\cos x}} \cdot \frac{\cos x}{\cos x}$$

$$\downarrow$$

$$\frac{(\sin x - \cos x)\cos x}{\cos x - \sin x} = \frac{-(\cos x - \sin x)\cos x}{\cos x - \sin x}$$

$$\Downarrow$$

$$\boxed{-\cos x}$$

Method 2

$$\frac{\sin x - \cos x}{1 - \tan x} = \frac{\sin x - \cos x}{1 - \dfrac{\sin x}{\cos x}}$$

$$\downarrow$$

$$\frac{\sin x - \cos x}{\dfrac{\cos x - \sin x}{\cos x}} = \frac{-(\cos x - \sin x)}{\dfrac{\cos x - \sin x}{\cos x}}$$

$$\downarrow$$

$$\frac{-(\cos x - \sin x)\cos x}{\cos x - \sin x}$$

$$\Downarrow$$

$$\boxed{-\cos x}$$

NEXT PAGE

8. What is the domain of function $f(x) = \dfrac{100}{x^2 + 0.0001}$?

(A) All real numbers including -0.01

(B) $x \neq -\dfrac{1}{10000}$

(C) $-0.001 \leq x \leq 0.001$

(D) $-\sqrt{0.001} \leq x \leq \sqrt{0.001}$

Solution: Answer: (A)

The denominator has no any chance to be 0.

⇓

All real numbers

9. The median of a list of 139 consecutive integers is 73. What is the greatest integer in the list?

(A) 142

(B) 143

(C) 144

(D) 145

Solution: Answer: (A)

$139 - 1 = 138$

(1 number position for 73)

$138 \div 2 = 69$

•••, 73, •••

↑   ↑

69   69

numbers   numbers

$73 + 69 = 142$

10. Four years from now, Kevin's age will be $4x + 2$. Which of the following represents his age four years ago?

(A) $4x - 2$

(B) $4x - 3$

(C) $4x - 5$

(D) $4x - 6$

Solution: Answer: (D)

Current age $= 4x + 2 - 4 = 4x - 2$

⇓

4 years ago $= 4x - 2 - 4 = 4x - 6$

11. Which of the following is the zeros, vertex, domain, and range of function $f(x) = \dfrac{1}{4}(2x - 1)(2x - 4)$?

(A) Zeros $= (1/2, 2)$, $\begin{pmatrix} \text{Vertex} = (5/4,\ \text{-9/16}) \\ \text{Domain} = \text{All real numbers} \\ \text{Range} \geq \text{-9/16} \end{pmatrix}$

(B) Zeros $= (2, 1/2)$, $\begin{pmatrix} \text{Vertex} = (\text{-9/16},\ 5/4) \\ \text{Domain} = \text{All real numbers} \\ \text{Range} \geq 5/4 \end{pmatrix}$

(C) Zeros $= (1/2, 2)$, $\begin{pmatrix} \text{Vertex} = (\text{-9/16},\ 5/4) \\ \text{Domain} = \text{All real numbers} \\ \text{Range} \leq \text{-9/16} \end{pmatrix}$

(D) Zeros $= (2, 1/2)$, $\begin{pmatrix} \text{Vertex} = (\text{-9/16},\ 5/4) \\ \text{Domain} = \text{All real numbers} \\ \text{Range} \leq 5/4 \end{pmatrix}$

Solution: Answer: (A)

Use the factor form: $f(x) = k(x - r_1)(x - r_2)$

$$\dfrac{1}{4}\left(2\left(x - \dfrac{1}{2}\right) \cdot 2\left(x - \dfrac{4}{2}\right)\right) = \left(x - \dfrac{1}{2}\right) \cdot (x - 2)$$

⇓

$\text{Zeros} = \dfrac{1}{2}$ and 2

Use the vertex form: $f(x) = k(x - x_m)^2 + y_m$

$$\dfrac{1}{4}\left(4x^2 - 10x + 4\right) = x^2 - \left(\dfrac{5}{2}\right)x + 1$$

$$x^2 - \left(\dfrac{5}{2}\right)x + \left(\dfrac{\frac{5}{2}}{2}\right)^2 - \left(\dfrac{\frac{5}{2}}{2}\right)^2 + 1$$

$$(x - 5/4)^2 - 25/16 + 1 = (x - 5/4)^2 - 9/16$$

⇓

$\text{Vertex} = (5/4,\ -9/16)$

$\text{Domain} = \text{All real numbers}$

$\text{Range} \geq -9/16$

12. Which domain of the following functions does not include 10 ?

(A) $y = \dfrac{x}{x^2 - 10x}$

(B) $y = \dfrac{x^2}{x^3 + 10x}$

(C) $y = \dfrac{x^2 - 1}{x^5 + 10x}$

(D) $y = \dfrac{x}{x^7 + 10x}$

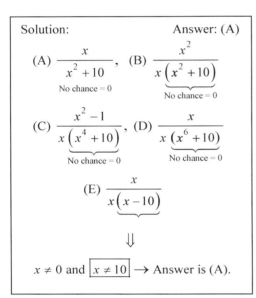

Solution: Answer: (A)

(A) $\dfrac{x}{x^2 + 10}$, (B) $\dfrac{x^2}{x(x^2 + 10)}$

No chance = 0   No chance = 0

(C) $\dfrac{x^2 - 1}{x(x^4 + 10)}$, (D) $\dfrac{x}{x(x^6 + 10)}$

No chance = 0   No chance = 0

(E) $\dfrac{x}{x(x - 10)}$

No chance = 0

⇓

$x \neq 0$ and $\boxed{x \neq 10}$ → Answer is (A).

13. If Kathie completely travels a circular path in 30 minutes, how many degrees does she travel by 0.5 minute?

(A) 3

(B) 4

(C) 6

(D) 5

Solution: Answer: (C)

minutes ↑, degrees ↑

↓

direct relationship

⇓

$\dfrac{x}{\tfrac{1}{2}} = \dfrac{360}{30}$, $x = \dfrac{360 \times \tfrac{1}{2}}{30} = 6$

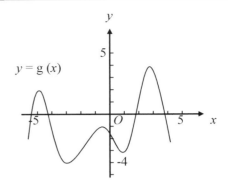

$y = g(x)$

14. The figure above shows the graph of $y = g(x)$, where $-5 \le x \le 5$. For what value of x does the function g obtain its least value?

(A) -4

(B) -3

(C) 3

(D) -1

Solution: Answer: (B)

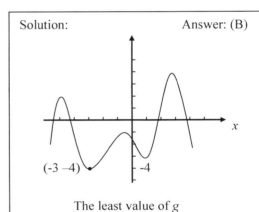

(-3 –4)   -4

The least value of g

15. If an isosceles right triangle whose legs are 3 is rotated about its one leg to produce a right circular cone, what is the volume of the cone?

(A) 18π

(B) 10π

(C) 6π

(D) 9π

(E) 12π

Solution: Answer: (D)

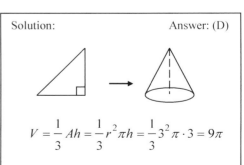

$V = \dfrac{1}{3} Ah = \dfrac{1}{3} r^2 \pi h = \dfrac{1}{3} 3^2 \pi \cdot 3 = 9\pi$

NEXT PAGE

16. If $0.047 = 4.7 \times 10^p$, what is the value of $(-p)$?

Solution: Answer: 2

$$\frac{47}{1000} = \frac{47}{10} \times \frac{1}{100} = 4.7 \times 10^{-2}$$

$$\downarrow$$

$$10^{-2} = 10^p$$

$$\Downarrow$$

$$p = -2, \quad -p = 2$$

17. If $b + \dfrac{1}{b} = 6,$ then $b^2 + \dfrac{1}{b^2} =$

Solution: Answer: 34

$$\left(b + \frac{1}{b}\right)^2 = b^2 + 2b \cdot \frac{1}{b} + \left(\frac{1}{b}\right)^2 = 6^2$$

$$\downarrow$$

$$b^2 + 2b \cdot \frac{1}{b} + \left(\frac{1}{b}\right)^2 = b^2 + 2 + \frac{1}{b^2} = 36$$

$$\Downarrow$$

$$b^2 + \frac{1}{b^2} = 36 - 2 = 34$$

18. Michael can travel from Bedminster to New York City by his own car or taxi. He can then travel to Boston by plane, train, ship, or bus. From Boston, he can travel to Jackson Academy by bus, or taxi. In how many different ways can Michael travel from Bedminster to New York City to Boston and then to Jackson Academy?

Solution: Answer: 16

(car, taxi), (plane, train, ship, bus), (bus, taxi)

$$\downarrow$$

3 element sets

$$\downarrow$$

Use the counting method of
Fundamental Counting Principle.

$$\Downarrow$$

$$m \times n \times p = 2 \times 4 \times 2 = 16$$

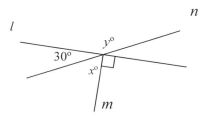

Note: Figure above not drawn to scale.

19. In the figure above, lines l, m, and n meet at a point and line l is perpendicular to m. What is the value of $y - x$?

Solution: Answer: 90

$$y = 180 - 30 = 150$$

$$\downarrow$$

$$x = 90 - 30 = 60$$

$$\Downarrow$$

$$y - x = 150 - 60 = 90$$

20. If John, Jack, and James can clean a building in 6 hours, and John and Jack working together can do it in 9 hours, how long will it take James alone to clean the building?

Solution: Answer: 18

$$\text{Type: } \frac{T}{t_{a1}} + \frac{T}{t_{a2}} = 1$$

T = time of working together

t_{a1} = time of working alone

t_{a2} = time of working alone

$$\downarrow$$

$$\frac{6}{9} + \frac{6}{\text{James}} = 1, \quad \frac{2}{3} + \frac{6}{\text{James}} = 1$$

$$\downarrow$$

$$\frac{2 \cdot \text{James} + 3 \times 6}{3 \cdot \text{James}} = 1$$

$$2 \cdot \text{James} + 18 = 3 \cdot \text{James}$$

$$\Downarrow$$

$$\text{James} = 18$$

STOP

Math Test – Calculator

Time: 55 Minutes
38 Questions

Notes:
- The use of a calculator is not allowed.
- All numbers used in this section are the real number.
- Figures are provided for some problems in this test. Unless otherwise indicated under the figure "Note: Figure above not drawn to scale", all figures are drawn as accurately as possible.
- All figures lie in a plane EXCEPT otherwise specified.
- Unless otherwise indicated, the domain of any function f, g or j is assumed to be the set of all real numbers x for which $f(x)$, $g(x)$, or $j(x)$ is a real number.

Reference Information

$$A = \frac{1}{2}bh$$

$$A = lw$$

$$A = \pi r^2$$

$$V = \pi r^2 h$$

$$V = lwh$$

$$c^2 = a^2 + b^2$$

$$V = \frac{1}{3}\pi r^2 h$$

$$V = \frac{4}{3}\pi r^3$$

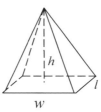

$$V = \frac{1}{3}lwh$$

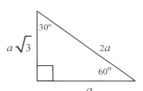

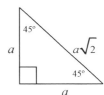

1. If a function defined by $g(x) = \sqrt[3]{7x^2 - 3}$, what is the domain of the function?

(A) The set of all real integers

(B) $x \geq 1$

(C) $x > 1$

(D) The set of all real numbers

Solution:	Answer: (D)

The radicand in a cube root = negative, 0 or positive.

$\Downarrow$

The domain can be all real numbers.

2. If the radius of a circle is 5 feet, what is the area of the sector whose arc length is 5π feet?

(A) 12.5π

(B) 25π

(C) 24π

(D) 18π

Solution:	Answer: (A)

Use the formulas:

$$\begin{cases} s = r\theta \rightarrow 5\pi = 5\theta, \ \theta = \pi \\ A = \dfrac{1}{2}r^2\theta \end{cases}$$

$\Downarrow$

$$A = \frac{1}{2} \cdot 5^2 \cdot \pi = 12.5\pi$$

3. The price of a CD player was increased from \$120 to \$200. What was the percentage of increase in the price of the unit?

(A) 33%

(B) $66\dfrac{2}{3}\%$

(C) 66%

(D) $33\dfrac{1}{3}\%$

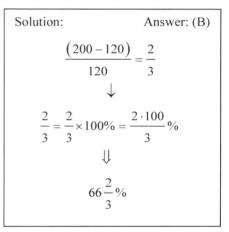

Solution:	Answer: (B)

$$\frac{(200 - 120)}{120} = \frac{2}{3}$$

$\downarrow$

$$\frac{2}{3} = \frac{2}{3} \times 100\% = \frac{2 \cdot 100}{3}\%$$

$\Downarrow$

$$66\frac{2}{3}\%$$

4. The vertices of a triangle are (-2, 6), (-2, 1), and (2, 1). The area of the triangle is

(A) 14
(B) 54
(C) 10
(D) 12

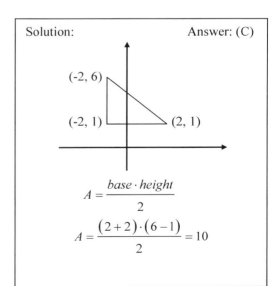

Solution:	Answer: (C)

$$A = \frac{base \cdot height}{2}$$

$$A = \frac{(2 + 2) \cdot (6 - 1)}{2} = 10$$

NEXT PAGE

5. Which of the following is $\sqrt[4]{d^{12}}$ equal to

(A) $-d^3$

(B) $\left|d^3\right|$

(C) d^6

(D) $\left|d^2\right|$

Solution: Answer: (B)

$$\sqrt[4]{d^{12}} = \sqrt[4]{\left(d^3\right)^4}$$

d can be negative, 0, or positive.

$\Downarrow$

$$\left|d^3\right|$$

---

6. If for all real numbers x, a function f is defined by

$$f(x) = \begin{cases} 5, & x = 11 \\ 6, & x \neq 11 \end{cases}, \text{ then } f(6) - f(5) =$$

(A) 3

(B) 0

(C) 1

(D) 2

Solution: Answer: (B)

$$f(x) = 6 \text{ except } x = 11.$$

$\Downarrow$

$$f(6) - f(5) = 6 - 6 = 0$$

---

7. If $\dfrac{1}{3}$ of a cup apple juice is filled up to 2-cup mark of a measuring container with a mixture containing equal amounts of apple and pineapple juices, what is the ratio of apple juice to final mixture?

(A) $\dfrac{5}{12}$

(B) $\dfrac{7}{12}$

(C) $\dfrac{6}{11}$

(D) $\dfrac{2}{3}$

Solution: Answer: (B)

$\begin{cases} \text{Before } \dfrac{1}{3} \text{ of a cup apple juice was filled up to} \\ \text{2-cup mark of the container, the container had} \\ \text{contained } 2 - \dfrac{1}{3} = \dfrac{6-1}{3} = \dfrac{5}{3} \text{ cup mixed juice.} \end{cases}$

$\downarrow$

$$\text{Ratio} = \dfrac{\dfrac{1}{3} + \dfrac{\frac{5}{3}}{2}}{2}$$

$\downarrow$

$$\dfrac{\dfrac{1}{3} + \dfrac{5}{6}}{2} = \dfrac{\dfrac{1}{3} + \dfrac{5}{6}}{2} \cdot \dfrac{6}{6}$$

$\Downarrow$

$$\dfrac{2+5}{12} = \dfrac{7}{12}$$

---

8. If $\sqrt{q^2} = -q$, which of the following is the set of all real numbers q?

(A) all negative integers and zero only

(B) all positive real numbers only

(C) all nonzero real numbers only

(D) all negative real numbers and zero only

Solution: Answer: (D)

$$\sqrt{q^2} = -q \;\rightarrow\; -q \geq 0 \;\Rightarrow\; \boxed{q \leq 0}$$

NEXT PAGE

9. Jack is a car salesperson. He sells two kinds of cars. For one of them, the selling price is $32,000, and for another one, the selling price is $48,000. Last week, Jack's goal was to sell at least 10 cars. He met his goal. The total value of the cars he sold was no more than $360,000. Let x be the number of $32,000 cars, and y be the number of $48,000 cars, that Jack sold last week. Which system of inequalities below represents the conditions described?

(A) $x+y \geq 10, \quad 32,000x + 48,000y < 360,000$

(B) $x+y \geq 10, \quad 32,000x + 48,000y \geq 360,000$

(C) $x+y \geq 10, \quad 32,000x + 48,000y \leq 360,000$

(D) $x+y > 10, \quad 32,000x + 48,000y \leq 360,000$

Solution: Answer: (C)

$$\begin{cases} \text{"at least"} \to \text{ Use sign } \geq, \\ \quad \text{and "met his goal"} \\ \qquad \downarrow \\ \quad \text{Use sign } \geq. \end{cases}$$

"no more than" $\to$ Use sign $\leq$.

$$\Downarrow$$

$$x + y \geq 10$$

$$32,000x + 48,000y \leq 360,000$$

10. If the surface area of a sphere is 144π, what is the volume of the sphere?

(A) 36π

(B) 25π

(C) 256π

(D) 288π

Solution: Answer: (D)

$$4r^2 \cancel{\pi} = 144\cancel{\pi}, \; r^2 = 36, \; r = 6$$

$$\Downarrow$$

$$V = \frac{4}{3}r^3\pi = \frac{4}{3} \cdot 6^3 \pi = \frac{4 \cdot 6 \cdot 6^2}{3}\pi = 288\pi$$

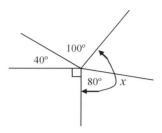

11.   In the figure above, what is the value of x?

(A) 80

(B) 130

(C) 100

(D) 70

\

Solution: Answer: (B)

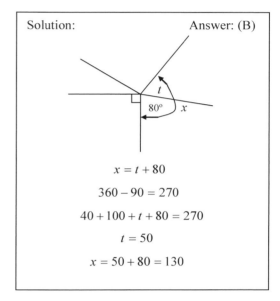

$$x = t + 80$$

$$360 - 90 = 270$$

$$40 + 100 + t + 80 = 270$$

$$t = 50$$

$$x = 50 + 80 = 130$$

12.   Let M1 be the median and M2 be the mode of the following set of numbers, 3, 5, 3, 4, 1, 2, 3, 6, 7, 8, and 2. What is the average (arithmetic mean) of M1 and M2?

(A) 3
(B) 4
(C) 5
(D) 6

Solution: Answer: (A)

Increasing order : $1, 2, 2, 3, 3, 3, 4, 5, 6, 7, 8$

Median $= 3$

Mode $= 3$

Average $= \dfrac{\text{Median+Mode}}{2} = \dfrac{3+3}{2} = 3$

NEXT PAGE ⟶

13.   If $f(x) = x^2 - 3x + 4$, $\dfrac{f(x-k) - f(x)}{k}$ is equal to

(A) $k + 2x - 3$

(B) $k + 2x + 3$

(C) $k - 2x + 3$

(D) $k^2 - 2x + 3$

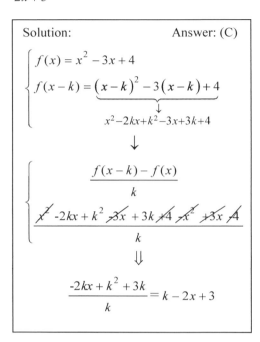

Solution: Answer: (C)

$$\begin{cases} f(x) = x^2 - 3x + 4 \\ f(x-k) = \underbrace{(x-k)^2 - 3(x-k) + 4} \\ \qquad\quad x^2 - 2kx + k^2 - 3x + 3k + 4 \end{cases}$$

↓

$$\begin{cases} \dfrac{f(x-k) - f(x)}{k} \\[2mm] \dfrac{\cancel{x^2} - 2kx + k^2 \cancel{-3x} + 3k \cancel{+4}\ \cancel{-x^2}\ \cancel{+3x}\ \cancel{-4}}{k} \end{cases}$$

⇓

$$\dfrac{-2kx + k^2 + 3k}{k} = k - 2x + 3$$

14.   Five points, A, B, C, D, and E, lie on a line, not necessarily in that order. The length of $\overline{AB}$ is 36. Point C is midpoint of $\overline{AB}$, and point D is the midpoint of $\overline{AC}$. If the distance between D and E is 7, what are all possible distances between A and E?

(A) 2 and 16   (B) 16   (C) 8   (D) 2

Solution: Answer: (A)

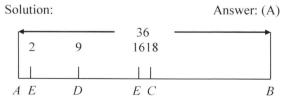

By the information, the order of A, B, C, and D are fixed, but E is not. E can be located at two distinct positions as shown above.

⇓

$AE = 2$ or 16

15.   A 25-gallon mixture of ammonia and water contains 5 gallons of ammonia. If 5 more gallons of ammonia are added, what percent of the new mixture is water?

(A) 33

(B) 66

(C) $33\dfrac{1}{3}$

(D) $66\dfrac{2}{3}$

Solution: Answer: (D)

$$\dfrac{P}{100} = \dfrac{5}{25}, \quad P = 20$$

$$\begin{cases} P = 20 \\ A + B = M \end{cases}$$

↓

$$25 \times 20 + 5 \times 100 = (25 + 5)y$$

$$1000 = 30y$$

$$y = \dfrac{100}{3} = 33\dfrac{1}{3}$$

⇓

$$x = \boxed{66\dfrac{2}{3}}$$

NEXT PAGE

16. Erica takes 10 seconds to run a distance of 150 feet. What is the runner's speed in yards per hour?

(A) 18,000
(B) 16,000
(C) 15,000
(D) 17,000

Solution: Answer: (A)

Change unit first.

$$\frac{10}{60} = \frac{1}{6}\text{ minutes}, \quad \frac{150}{3} = 50\text{ yards}$$

minutes ↑ , yards ↑

↓

direct proportion

↓

Use the proportion equation.

$$\frac{x}{\Box} = \frac{\Box_x}{\Box}$$

↓

$$\frac{x}{60} = \frac{50}{\frac{1}{6}}$$

⇓

$$x = 18000$$

17. What is $\frac{1}{3}$ percent of 3 percent ?

(A) $\dfrac{1}{3 \times 10^4}$

(B) $\dfrac{1}{10^4}$

(C) $\dfrac{3}{10^4}$

(D) $\dfrac{1}{10 \times 3^4}$

Solution: Answer: (B)

$$\frac{\frac{1}{3}}{100} \times \frac{3}{100}$$

↓

$$\frac{1}{\cancel{3} \times 100} \times \frac{\cancel{3}}{100}$$

⇓

$$\frac{1}{10^4}$$

18. Which of the following is the graph of all values of x for $9 \le x^2 \le 25$?

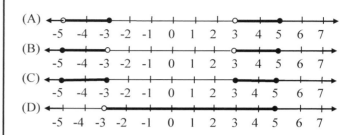

Solution: Answer: (C)

Method 1 Use the input and output concepts.

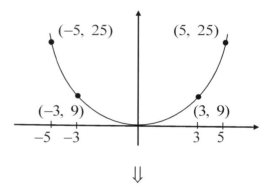

⇓

Answer is (C).

Method 2

If $b > 0$, now 9 and 25 > 0,

(1). $x^2 \le b \to \underbrace{-\sqrt{b} \le x \le \sqrt{b}}_{\text{One row}}$, $\quad x^2 \le 25 \to \underbrace{-5 \le x \le 5}_{\text{One row}}$

(2). $x^2 \ge b \to \underbrace{\begin{cases} x \ge \sqrt{b} \\ x \le -\sqrt{b} \end{cases}}_{\text{Two rows}}$, $\quad x^2 \ge 9 \to \underbrace{\begin{cases} x \ge 3 \\ x \le -3 \end{cases}}_{\text{Two rows}}$

Combine the results of (1) and (2).

⇓

$$-5 \le x \le -3, \quad 3 \le x \le 5$$

NEXT PAGE

CAROLINE'S TOUR EXPENSES

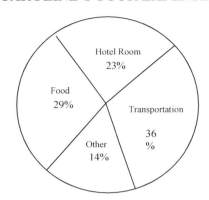

19. In the circle graph above, it shows the distribution of Caroline's $1,050 tour expenses. The amount Caroline paid for the transportation was only portion of the total cost of transportation. She shared the cost of transportation with five other girls equally. What was the total cost of the transportation?

(A) 1,839
(B) 2,019
(C) 2,268
(D) 2,228

Solution: Answer: (C)

$$105\cancel{0} \times \frac{36}{10\cancel{0}} = 378$$

$$\frac{378}{x} = \frac{1}{6}$$

⇓

$$x = 6 \times 378 = 2268$$

20. Toni is 29 years old and her sister, Jody, is 17. How many years ago was Toni's age two times as old as Jody's?

(A) 6
(B) 5
(C) 4
(D) 7

Solution: Answer: (B)

$$29 - x = 2(17 - x)$$

⇓

$$x = 5$$

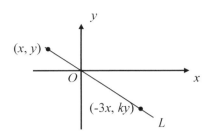

Note: Figure above not drawn to scale.

21. In the figure above, the straight line L passes through origin point (0, 0). What is the value of k?

(A) 3
(B) 1/3
(C) 1
(D) -3

Solution: Answer: (D)

$$\begin{cases} \text{One line has a unique slope.} \\ \text{Slope} = \frac{y_1 - y_2}{x_1 - x_2} \end{cases}$$

All points on the same line

↓

$$\text{slope}_1 = \text{slope}_2$$

The line passes through origin.

↓

$$\frac{\cancel{y}}{\cancel{x}} = \frac{k\cancel{y}}{-3\cancel{x}}$$

⇓

$$k = -3$$

22. $(k^2 - 1)(k^2 - 3) =$

(A) $(k^2 + 2k - 1)(k^2 - 3)$

(B) $(k - 1)(k - 1)(k - \sqrt{3})(k - \sqrt{3})$

(C) $(k^2 - 2k + 1)(k^2 - 3)$

(D) $(k - 1)(k + 1)(k - \sqrt{3})(k + \sqrt{3})$

Solution: Answer: (D)

$$(k^2 - 1)(k^2 - 3)$$

⇓

$$(k - 1)(k + 1)(k - \sqrt{3})(k + \sqrt{3})$$

NEXT PAGE

23. A green box contains 6 items, of which four are good and the rest are defective, and a yellow box contains 5 items, of which three are good and the rest are defective. An item is drawn randomly from each box. What is the probability that one item is good and one is defective?

(A) $\dfrac{2}{225}$

(B) $\dfrac{7}{15}$

(C) 0.65

(D) 0.30

Solution: Answer: (B)

$$\left\{ \begin{array}{l} P_{1 \text{ green good and 1 yellow defective}} = \dfrac{4}{6} \times \dfrac{2}{5} = \dfrac{4}{15} \\[2mm] P_{1 \text{ yellow good and 1 green defective}} = \dfrac{3}{5} \times \dfrac{2}{6} = \dfrac{3}{15} \end{array} \right.$$

Either event

"1 green good and 1 yellow defective"

or

"1 yellow good and 1 green defective" accur.

↓

$P_{1 \text{ green good and 1 yellow defective}} + P_{1 \text{ yellow good and 1 green defective}}$

⇓

$$\dfrac{4}{15} + \dfrac{3}{15} = \dfrac{7}{15}$$

24. The least integer and greatest integer of a set of consecutive even integers are -20 and 26. What is the sum of all integers in the set?

(A) 46
(B) 50
(C) 26
(D) 72

Solution: Answer: (D)

$$\underbrace{-20,\ldots-12,-10,\ldots-2}_{0},\mathbf{0},\underbrace{2,\ldots10,12,\ldots20}_{0},\underbrace{22,24,26}_{22+24+26=\,72}$$

⇓

$$\text{Sum} = 22 + 24 + 26 = 72$$

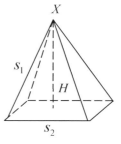

Note: Figure above not drawn to scale.

25. The pyramid shown above has height H and a square base of side s_2. The 4 edges each have length s_1 and meet at X. X is the vertex of the pyramid. $s_1 = s_2$. What is the value of height H in terms of s_1?

(A) $s_1\sqrt{3}$

(B) $\dfrac{s_1\sqrt{2}}{3}$

(C) $\dfrac{s_1\sqrt{3}}{3}$

(D) $\dfrac{s_1\sqrt{2}}{2}$

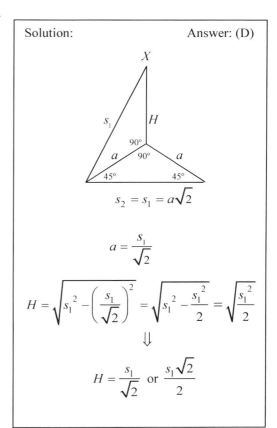

Solution: Answer: (D)

$$s_2 = s_1 = a\sqrt{2}$$

$$a = \dfrac{s_1}{\sqrt{2}}$$

$$H = \sqrt{s_1^{\,2} - \left(\dfrac{s_1}{\sqrt{2}}\right)^2} = \sqrt{s_1^{\,2} - \dfrac{s_1^{\,2}}{2}} = \sqrt{\dfrac{s_1^{\,2}}{2}}$$

⇓

$$H = \dfrac{s_1}{\sqrt{2}} \text{ or } \dfrac{s_1\sqrt{2}}{2}$$

NEXT PAGE

26. Jack and Tony left their respective schools at the same time for a run to a library. Jack ran at an average rate of 6 miles per hour. Tony ran at an average rate of 7 miles per hour. They arrived at the library at the same time. If Tony ran 0.5 mile farther than Jack, what is the distance, in miles, did Tony run?

(A) 4.0

(B) 3.5

(C) 5.5

(D) 2.5

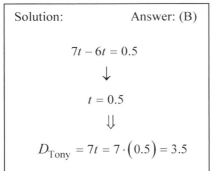

Solution: Answer: (B)

$$7t - 6t = 0.5$$
$$\downarrow$$
$$t = 0.5$$
$$\Downarrow$$
$$D_{\text{Tony}} = 7t = 7 \cdot (0.5) = 3.5$$

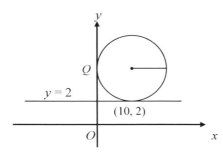

27. In the xy-plane above, the circle is tangent to the line $y = 2$ and y-axis. What are the coordinates (x, y) of point Q?

(A) (0, 10)
(B) (10, 0)
(C) (0, 2)
(D) (0, 12)

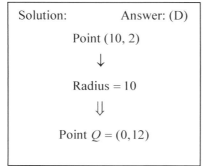

Solution: Answer: (D)

Point (10, 2)
$$\downarrow$$
Radius = 10
$$\Downarrow$$
Point $Q = (0, 12)$

28. Let $f(t)$ give the entire amount earned, in dollars, in a week by James as a function of the number of hours worked. James earns \$10.5 per hour and must work 3 to 5 days each week from 6 to 8 hours each day. What is the domain and range of function f ?

(A) $18 < t < 40$
$189 < f < 420$

(B) $18 < t \le 40$
$189 \le f < 420$

(C) $18 \le t \le 40$
$189 \le f \le 420$

(D) $18 \le t < 40$
$189 \le f < 420$

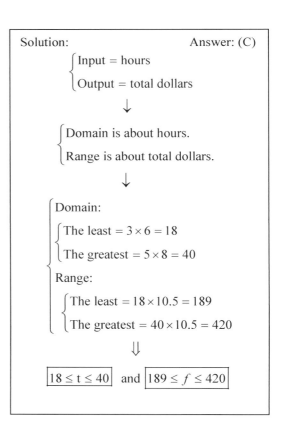

Solution: Answer: (C)

$$\begin{cases} \text{Input} = \text{hours} \\ \text{Output} = \text{total dollars} \end{cases}$$
$$\downarrow$$
$$\begin{cases} \text{Domain is about hours.} \\ \text{Range is about total dollars.} \end{cases}$$
$$\downarrow$$

Domain:
$$\begin{cases} \text{The least} = 3 \times 6 = 18 \\ \text{The greatest} = 5 \times 8 = 40 \end{cases}$$
Range:
$$\begin{cases} \text{The least} = 18 \times 10.5 = 189 \\ \text{The greatest} = 40 \times 10.5 = 420 \end{cases}$$
$$\Downarrow$$
$\boxed{18 \le t \le 40}$ and $\boxed{189 \le f \le 420}$

NEXT PAGE

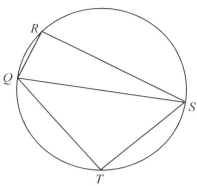

Note: Figure above not drawn to scale.

29.   In the figure above, if $QR = 5, QS = 13$, $ST = 12$, and $\overline{QS}$ is a diameter of the circle, which of the following is the area of triangle QST ?

(A) 78

(B) 65

(C) 30

(D) 32.5

Solution: **Answer: (C)**

$\underbrace{\angle R = \angle T}_{\text{They faces half circle, respectively.}} = 90°$

$\dfrac{QS}{2} = \dfrac{180}{2} = 90$

$QR = 5, QS = 13,\ ST = 12$

↓

$QST = QSR$ both are a 5-12-13 right triangle.

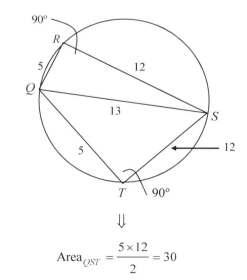

⇓

$\text{Area}_{QST} = \dfrac{5 \times 12}{2} = 30$

---

30.   If $x^2 + 8x - 9 \le 0$ and $f(x) = x^2 + 6x + 8$, what is the range of $f(x)$?

(A) $-1 \le f(x) \le 35$

(B) $15 < f(x) \le 35$

(C) $-1 < f(x) \le 35$

(D) $0 \le f(x) \le 35$

Solution: **Answer: (A)**

Get the domain first.

$\begin{cases} \underset{\text{value of } y}{x^2 + 8x - 9} \le 0 \\ \text{The leading coefficient} > 0. \\ \underset{\text{value of } y}{(x-1)(x+9)} \le 0 \end{cases}$

↓

$\underbrace{-9 \le x \le 1}_{\substack{\text{This domian makes} \\ \text{all values of } y \le 0.}}$

Use a graphing calculator to see if the lowest point is between $x = -9$ and $x = 1$.

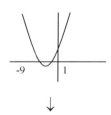

The lowest point is between

$x = -9$ and $x = 1$.

↓

$x = \dfrac{-b}{2a} = \dfrac{-6}{2} = -3$

$f(-3) = \left(-3\right)^2 + 6\left(-3\right) + 8 = -1$

$f(-9) = (-9)^2 + 6(-9) + 8 = 35$

↓

$-1 \le f(x) \le 35$

⇓

Answer is (A).

NEXT PAGE

31. James places a 13-foot ladder against a vertical wall of a building. The bottom of the ladder stands on concrete 5 feet from the base of the building. If the top of the ladder slips down 7 feet, how many feet the bottom of the ladder will slide out

Solution: Answer: 7

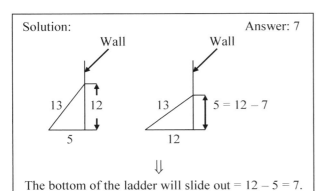

The bottom of the ladder will slide out $= 12 - 5 = 7$.

32. Company A is owned by four men and one woman, each of them has equal shares. If one of the men sells one-third of his shares to the woman, and another of men keeps one-third of his shares and sells the rest to the woman, what fraction of the company will the woman own?

Solution: Answer: 2/5 or .4

Let total shares be 1.

↓

Each person had $\dfrac{1}{5}$ of the total shares.

⇓

$$\frac{1}{5} + \frac{1}{5} \times \frac{1}{3} + \frac{1}{5} \times \left(1 - \frac{1}{3}\right) = \frac{2}{5}$$

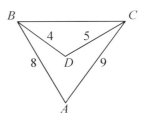

33.   In the figure above, how much smaller is the perimeter of triangle BDC than the perimeter of triangle ABC?

Solution: Answer: 8

$$P_{ABC} - P_{BDC}$$

↓

$$(8 + 9 + BC) - (4 + 5 + BC)$$

⇓

$$17 + \cancel{BC} - 9 - \cancel{BC} = 8$$

34. The Tech Service that is a company of technical services will send a group of 6 people to work on a certain job. The company has six experienced electricians and five trainees. If the group consists of three experienced electricians and 3 trainees, how many possible distinct such groups exist?

Solution: Answer: 200

The order doesn't matter.

(1) 3 positions and 6 elements for experienced tutors

$$m = \frac{\boxed{6} \times \boxed{5} \times \boxed{4}}{3!} = 20$$

(2). 3 positions and 5 elements for trainees

$$n = \frac{\boxed{5} \times \boxed{4} \times \boxed{3}}{3!} = 10$$

(3)   2 element sets

They can be combined in this case.

↓

Fundamental Counting Principle

⇓

$$m \times n = 20 \times 10 = 200$$

NEXT PAGE ⇨

35. Several students stand in a line. Staring at one end of the line, Kevin is counted as 8th person, and starting at the other end, Kevin is counted as the 12th person. How many students are in the line?

Solution: Answer: 19

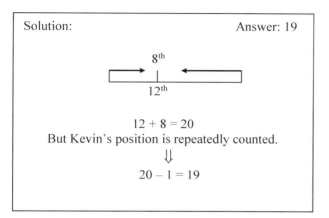

$12 + 8 = 20$
But Kevin's position is repeatedly counted.
$\Downarrow$
$20 - 1 = 19$

36. James has six blank cards. Each card is written with one of the following letters: *A, B, C, D, E* or *F*. Each of six cards does not have the same letter. If *E* and *F* are always the center letters in the arrangements, how many possible distinct six-letter arrangements can James create?

Solution: Answer: 48

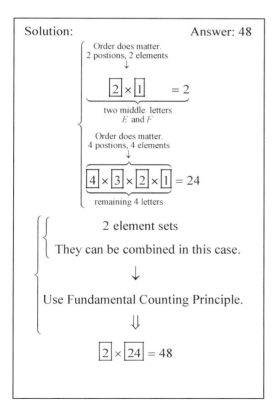

Order does matter.
2 postions, 2 elements
$\downarrow$
$\boxed{2} \times \boxed{1} = 2$
two middle letters
E and *F*

Order does matter.
4 postions, 4 elements
$\downarrow$
$\boxed{4} \times \boxed{3} \times \boxed{2} \times \boxed{1} = 24$
remaining 4 letters

2 element sets
They can be combined in this case.
$\downarrow$
Use Fundamental Counting Principle.
$\Downarrow$
$\boxed{2} \times \boxed{24} = 48$

37. Cynthia cuts a cube object with volume 1 cubic inches in half in all 3 directions, what is the total surface area of the separated smaller cubes, in square inches?

Solution: Answer: 12

(1) $1 = s^3,\ s = 1,\ A_1 = s^2 = 1^2 = 1$
$\downarrow$
$A_{\text{original}} = 6 \times 1 = 6$

Each of 3 cutting creates 2 more surfaces with area 1.

Three cuttings create 6 more surfaces with area 1.

$A_{\text{extra-6}} = 6 \times 1 = 6$
$\Downarrow$

(2) $A_{\text{total}} = A_{\text{extra-6}} + A_{\text{original}}$
$A_{\text{total}} = 6 + 6 = 12$

38. If Maria wants to get a solution that is 6% alcohol from 510 quarts of solution that is 5% alcohol, how much water, in quarts, must be evaporated?

Solution: Answer: 85

$A - B = M$
$\downarrow$
$\underbrace{\frac{5}{100} \cdot 510}_{\text{Pure alcohol}} - \frac{0}{100} \cdot x = \underbrace{\frac{6}{100} \times (510 - x)}_{\text{Pure alcohol}}$
$\downarrow$
$2550 = 3060 - 6x,\ 6x = 510$
$\Downarrow$
$x = 85$

STOP

SAT Math

Practice

Test 11

Redesigned for Tests in March 2016 and Beyond

Mad Math

Math Test – No Calculator

Time: 25 Minutes
20 Questions

Notes:

- The use of a calculator is not allowed.
- All numbers used in this section are the real number.
- Figures are provided for some problems in this test. Unless otherwise indicated under the figure "Note: Figure above not drawn to scale", all figures are drawn as accurately as possible.
- All figures lie in a plane EXCEPT otherwise specified.
- Unless otherwise indicated, the domain of any function f, g or j is assumed to be the set of all real numbers x for which $f(x)$, $g(x)$, or $j(x)$ is a real number.

Reference Information

$$A = \frac{1}{2}bh$$

$$A = lw$$

$$A = \pi r^2$$

$$V = \pi r^2 h$$

$$V = lwh$$

$$c^2 = a^2 + b^2$$

$$V = \frac{1}{3}\pi r^2 h$$

$$V = \frac{4}{3}\pi r^3$$

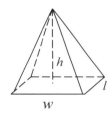

$$V = \frac{1}{3}lwh$$

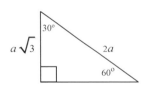

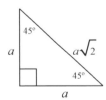

1. If $f(x) = -x^3 - 1$, what does $f(4x)$ equal?

(A) $-4x^4 - 1$

(B) $-64x - 1$

(C) $-4x^4 - 4x$

(D) None above

2. What percent of 72 is 24 ?

(A) $\dfrac{1}{3}$

(B) 33

(C) $33\dfrac{1}{3}$

(D) 0.34

3. Which of the following expressions is equal to 0 for the values of x?

(A) $|x - 2| + 4$

(B) $|x - 3| + 2$

(C) $|x - 2| + 3$

(D) $|1 - x| - 5$

4. The ordered pairs $(3x + 1,\ 4)$ and $\left(x - 5,\ 1 + \dfrac{y}{2} \right)$ are equal, Which of the following does (x, y) equal?

(A) $(-3, 6)$

(B) $(-6, 3)$

(C) $(3, -6)$

(D) $(-2, 5)$

5. Johnson made a training plan for swimming, in which the distance of his swimming each day increased by a constant amount. If Johnson's training plan requires that his swimming in day 7 is a distance of 200 meters and in day 13 is a distance of 380 meters, which of the following best describes how the distance changes between day 7 and day13 of Johnson's training plan?

(A) Johnson increases the distance by 30% per day.

(B) Johnson increases the distance by 1.5 times per day.

(C) Johnson increases the distance by 20 meters per day.

(D) Johnson increases the distance by 30 meters per day.

NEXT PAGE

6. Which of the following must be true about a polynomial $P(x)$ if the value of $P(-5) = -7$?

(A) $x - 5$ is a factor of $P(x)$.

(B) $x + 5$ is a factor of $P(x)$.

(C) The remainder is -7 if $P(x)$ is divided by $x - 5$.

(D) The remainder is -7 if $P(x)$ is divided by $x + 5$.

$$f(x) = \frac{5}{7}x - b$$

7. In the function above, b is a constant. When $f(-7) = 7$, what is the value of $f(7)$?

(A) 19

(B) -5

(C) 17

(D) 7

8. If $f(x) = -x^2 - x$, what is $f(-19x)$ equivalent to?

(A) $19x^2 + 19x$

(B) $-19x^2 + 19x$

(C) $-361x^2 + 19x$

(D) $19x^3 + 19x^2$

9. James made a training plan for run, in which the distance of his run each day increased by some rate. If James's training plan requires that his run in day 8 is a distance of 10 miles and in day 11 is a distance of 12.5 miles, which of the following best describes how the distance changes between day 8 and day 11 of James's training plan?

(A) James increases the distance by 22% per day.

(B) James increases the distance by 1.020 times per day.

(C) James increases the distance by 0.833 miles per day.

(D) James increases the distance by 1.077 times per day.

10. If $a \neq 0, b \neq 0, \dfrac{b}{100} \div \dfrac{a}{1000} =$

(A) $\dfrac{10a}{b}$ (B) $\dfrac{ab}{10^5}$ (C) $b10^3 a10^2$ (D) $\dfrac{10b}{a}$

NEXT PAGE

$$\begin{cases} h(x) = x^2 + 5x + 4 \\ j(x) = 3x^4 + 15x^3 + 12x^2 \end{cases}$$

11. If the polynomials h and j are defined above, which of the following polynomials is divisible by $3x^2 + 5$?

(A) $N(x) = 3x^2 j(x) + 5h(x)$ (B) $M(x) = j(x) + 5h(x)$

(C) $A(x) = 2 j(x) + 5h(x)$ (D) $B(x) = 3x^2 j(x) + (1/5) h(x)$

12. A rectangle was changed by decreasing its length by 20% and increasing its width by 10%. If these changes decreased the area of the rectangle by $X\%$, what is the value of X?

(A) 20

(B) 10

(C) 30

(D) 12

13. The registrar's office of Milton Academy receives the exam scores of AP Calculus AB from 1 to 5. If the office received the score in the first 8 scores was 4.5 that was the average (arithmetic mean), what is the least value the office can receive for the 12th score and still be able to have an average of at least 4.6 for the first 15 scores?

(A) 5

(B) 4

(C) 2

(D) 3

NEXT PAGE

Questions 14 and 15 refer to the information below.

After registered a construction company in a month, Michael obtained a project. For this project because his investment was limited, he could not buy every thing. For some tools, he needed to rent them. The following table shows the costs of the materials and weekly rental for distinct companies X, Y and Z.

Company	X	Y	Z
Materials Cost M	$2,400	$1,800	$1,900
Rental of Tool-1 Cost T1	$150	$200	$250
Rental of Tool-2 Cost T2	$400	$600	$500
Rental of Tool-3 Cost T3	$300	$350	$350

The toal cost, $C(w)$, for buying and renting in terms of the number of weeks, w, is given by

$$C(w) = (T1 + T2 + T3)w + M.$$

14.   For what number of weeks will the total cost from Company X be greater than or equal to the total cost from Company Z?

(A) $w \geq 2$
(B) $w \leq 2$
(C) $w \geq 3$
(D) $w \leq 3$

15.   If the relationship of the total cost, $C(w)$, and weeks, w, is graphed in the xy-plane, what does the initial value of the curve represent?

(A) w
(B) M
(C) $C(w)$
(D) $T1 + T2 + T3$

16. From January 1, 2016 to December 31, 2016, the price of a certain stock increased by 215 percent, and from January 1, 2017 to December 31, 2017, the price of the stock increased by 60 percent. Over the period of the two years, by what percentage did the stock rise?

17. If 3 feet lengthen each side of a square, the area is increased by 21 square yards. What is the length, in yards, of a side of the original square?

18. If $m^2 + mn + n^2 = 7$ and $mn = 6$, what is the value of $(m+n)^2$?

19. 65% of 98 is the same as 49% of what number?

$$\begin{cases} f(x) \le -8x + 240 \\ \quad f(x) \le 2x \end{cases}$$

20. In the xy-plan, if a point (x_1, y_1) lies in the solution set of the system of inequalities above, what is the maximum possible value of y_1 ?

STOP

Math Test – Calculator

Time: 55 Minutes
38 Questions

Notes:
- The use of a calculator is not allowed.
- All numbers used in this section are the real number.
- Figures are provided for some problems in this test. Unless otherwise indicated under the figure "Note: Figure above not drawn to scale", all figures are drawn as accurately as possible.
- All figures lie in a plane EXCEPT otherwise specified.
- Unless otherwise indicated, the domain of any function f, g or j is assumed to be the set of all real numbers x for which $f(x)$, $g(x)$, or $j(x)$ is a real number.

Reference Information

$$A = \frac{1}{2}bh$$

$$A = lw$$

$$A = \pi r^2$$

$$V = \pi r^2 h$$

$$V = lwh$$

$$c^2 = a^2 + b^2$$

$$V = \frac{1}{3}\pi r^2 h$$

$$V = \frac{4}{3}\pi r^3$$

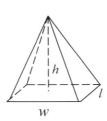

$$V = \frac{1}{3}lwh$$

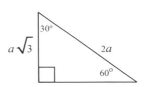

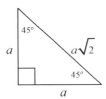

Copying or reuse of any portion of this page is illegal.

1. What are all values of x for which $|x - 2| - 2 < 0$?

(A) $x < 0, \ x > 4$

(B) $x < -4, \ x > 4$

(C) $x < -2, \ x > 2$

(D) $0 < x < 4$

2. If $\dfrac{y}{x} = \dfrac{5}{8}$, what is the value of $\dfrac{8x}{5y}$?

(A) 1

(B) $\left(\dfrac{8}{5}\right)^2$

(C) $\dfrac{16}{10}$

(D) $\dfrac{25}{64}$

3. Which of the following is a reduced form of $\dfrac{a^2 - 8a + 12}{a^2 - 36}$?

(A) $\dfrac{a-2}{a-6}$

(B) $\dfrac{a-2}{a+6}$

(C) $\dfrac{a+2}{a+6}$

(D) $\dfrac{a+2}{a-6}$

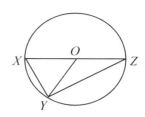

Note: Figure above not drawn to scale

4. In the figure above, triangle XYZ is inscribed in the circle that has center O. If $XY = OX$, which of the following is the measure, in degree, of angle OYZ?

(A) 60

(B) 45

(C) 70

(D) 30

5. $\left(k^2 - 1\right)\left(k^2 - 2\right) =$

(A) $(k^2 + 2k - 1)(k^2 - 2)$ (B) $(k^2 + 2k + 1)(k^2 - 2)$

(C) $(k^2 - 2k + 1)(k^2 - 2)$ (D) $(k - 1)(k + 1)(k - \sqrt{2})(k + \sqrt{2})$

6. Four years from now, Kevin's age will be $4x + 2$. Which of the following represents his age four years ago?

(A) $4x - 2$

(B) $4x - 3$

(C) $4x - 5$

(D) $4x - 6$

NEXT PAGE

7. If x and y are numbers such that $-y < x < y$, which of the following must be true?

    I. $|x| > y$

    II. $|x| < y$

    III. $y < 0$

(A) I only

(B) II only

(C) I and III only

(D) I, II and III

8. If $f(x) = -(x-9)^2 - 7$, what are the equation of its symmetric axis and vertex coordinates?

(A) $\begin{cases} \text{Vertex: } (-9, 7) \\ \text{Equation: } x = -9 \end{cases}$ (B) $\begin{cases} \text{Vertex: } (9, 7) \\ \text{Equation: } x = 9 \end{cases}$

(C) $\begin{cases} \text{Vertex: } (-9, 7) \\ \text{Equation: } x = 7 \end{cases}$ (D) $\begin{cases} \text{Vertex: } (9, -7) \\ \text{Equation: } x = 9 \end{cases}$

$$\begin{cases} y = (x+3)(x-3) \\ x^2 - 9 = y \end{cases}$$

9. How many ordered pairs (x, y) satisfy the system of equations shown above?

(A) one

(B) two

(C) zero

(D) infinity

10. If $f(x) = (2x+1)(x+7)$, what is the equation of its symmetric axis?

(A) 3.75

(B) 4

(C) –4

(D) –3.75

11. If the first two terms of a sequence are 14 and 23 and each subsequence is the sum of the two preceding terms, how many of the first 1000 terms are even and how many of the first 1000 terms are odd?

(A) 334 and 666

(B) 333 and 667

(C) 334 and 667

(D) 332 and 665

12. If $f(x) = (x-3)(x+7)$, which of the following is equivalent to the function f ?

(A) $(x-2)^2 - 21$

(B) $(x-2)^2 - 25$

(C) $(x+2)^2 - 25$

(D) $(x+2)^2 + 25$

13. What are the factored form of $f(x) = 2x^2 - 7x + 5$ and its roots ?

(A) $\begin{cases} (2x-5)(x-1) \\ x = 5 \text{ and } x = 1 \end{cases}$

(B) $\begin{cases} (2x-5)(x-1) \\ x = -5 \text{ and } x = -1 \end{cases}$

(C) $\begin{cases} 2\left(x-\dfrac{5}{2}\right)(x-1) \\ x = \dfrac{5}{2} \text{ and } x = 1 \end{cases}$

(D) $\begin{cases} 2\left(x-\dfrac{5}{2}\right)(x-1) \\ x = -\dfrac{5}{2} \text{ and } x = -1 \end{cases}$

14. If $f(x) = (1-4x)^2 - 36$, which of the following is equivalent to the function f ?

(A) $4(x+5/4)(x-7/4)$

(B) $4(x-5/4)(x+7/4)$

(C) $16(x-5/4)(x+7/4)$

(D) $16(x-7/4)(x+5/4)$

NEXT PAGE

15. In the universe, the mesosphere is the layer of a planet's atmosphere. The mesosphere of some planet is between 40,000 m and 56,000 m above the planet's surface. At the distance of 40,000 m, the temperature in the mesosphere is $-10°$F, and at the distance of 56,000 m, the temperature in the mesosphere is $-70°$F. For each additional 4,000 m from the planet's surface, the temperature in the layer decreases by $a°$F, where a is a constant. Which of the following is the value of a?

(A) 3   (B) 12   (C) 15   (D) 10

16. Johnson made a training plan for his swimming. Johnson himself modeled the training plan by the equation $D = \dfrac{t + 120}{3}$, where D is distance in meters and t is time in days. Accordiing to the model, by how many meters will the distance increase per day?

(A) $0.\overline{3}$

(B) 120

(C) 40

(D) 3

$$\begin{cases} 3(x+2) = y \\ \dfrac{y}{x} = 7 \end{cases}$$

17. If (x, y) is the solution to the system of equations above, what is the y-value?

(A) 6.5

(B) 8.4

(C) 10.5

(D) 10.4

18. If b is less than a and $b > 0$, which of the following is the least value?

(A) $\dfrac{a}{a - b}$

(B) $\dfrac{1}{b - a}$

(C) $\dfrac{1}{a + b}$

(D) $\dfrac{1}{a - b}$

NEXT PAGE

$$x^2 - (m/4)x = -2k$$

19. In the quadratic function above, m and k are constants. Which of the following is the solutions for x?

(A) $x = \dfrac{m \pm \sqrt{m^2 - 128k}}{8}$

(B) $x = \dfrac{m}{8} \pm \dfrac{\sqrt{m^2 + 128k}}{8}$

(C) $x = \dfrac{m \pm \sqrt{m^2 - 8k}}{8}$

(D) $x = \dfrac{-m \pm \sqrt{m^2 - 128k}}{8}$

$$y - 2 = 3/2(2x + 1)$$

20. What is the y-intercept of the function above?

(A) $(0, -0.5)$

(B) $(-0.5, 0)$

(C) $(0, 3.5)$

(D) $(-3.5, 0)$

21. Michael Johnson, a town council, did a survey to determine whether the residents in a large town prefer building a new park. The council asked 125 shoppers who visited a local mall on a Sunday, and 5 of those refused respond. Which of the following makes it less likely that a reliable conclusion can be drawn about the park-building preference of all residents in this town?

(A) The population size

(B) The place the survey was given

(C) The amount of people who refused to respond

(D) None above

Questions 22 and 23 refer to the information below.

The stock price of a certain share is worth \$356 today. After conducting, May concludes that the stock will decrease \$12 of its value per years for the next seven years. May uses the linear function $v(t) = st + b$ to model the value, $v(t)$, of the stock in t years.

22   What correct value should May use for s ?

(A) 356

(B) -12

(C)   84

(D) 272

23. What will the value, in dollars, of the stock will be at the end of seven years?

(A) 272

(B) 440

(C) -440

(D) -272

24.   Which of the following sketches shows a relationship that is appropriately modled with the function $f(t) = ar^t$, where $a \geq 1$ and $0 < r < 1$?

(A) v

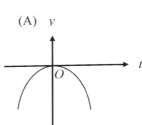

(B) v

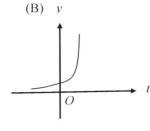

(C) v

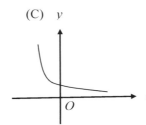

(D) v

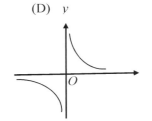

NEXT PAGE

25. Which of the following sketches shows a relationship that is appropriately modled with the function $y = ax^b + c,$ where $a = 0$ and $c < 0$?

(A) y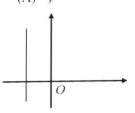

(B) y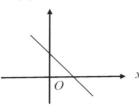

(C) y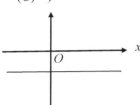

(D) y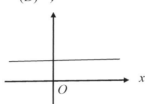

26. If $|Q - h| - 2 < 0,$ Q and h both are integers, and $2006 < Q < 2014,$ what are all possible values of h?

(A) 2010 and 2011

(B) 2008 and 2012

(C) From 2009 to 2011

(D) 2011 and 2012

27. If a cube is inscribed in a sphere of radius 10, which of the following is the volume of the cube, to the nearest tenth?

(A) 1.0   (B) 3519.6   (C) 1539.6   (D) 6583.1

NEXT PAGE

$$g(x) = |2x - 13|$$

28. For the equation above, what is one possible value of b for which $g(b) < b$?

(A) 13

(B) 14

(C) 12

(D) $4\dfrac{1}{3}$

Questions 29 and 30 refer to the information below.

An animal scientist uses a formula as a tool for his research about the population of rabbits. The population of the rabbits that this scientist expects to grow next month N_N can be calculated from the population current month N_C by the following formula.

$$N_N = N_C - 0.3 N_C \left(\frac{N_C}{C} - 1 \right)$$

The C in the formula is an envirobmental constant. Its value is determined by envirobmental conditions.

29. If the population of the rabbits current month N_C is 200 and C is 300, what will be the population of rabbits two months from current month? (Round your answer to a whole number.)

(A) 235

(B) 238

(C) 233

(D) 232

30. If the animal scientist wants to increase the population of rabbits, he needs to improve the environmenal conditions. If the animal scientist's target is that the population of rabbits will increase from 200 this month to 230 next month, after improving the environmental conditions, what should the value of C be equal to?

(A) 415

(B) 410

(C) 380

(D) 400

NEXT PAGE

31. In triangle ABC, $m\angle C$ is $90°$. What is $\cos(90° - B)$ equal to if $\sin B = 0.3$ and B is an acute angle in degree measure?

32. A river boat paddled at 10 miles per hour, stopped and rested for 2.5 hours, then paddled back at 15 miles per hour. How far downstream did the boat travel if the entire time for the trip, including the rest, was 8.5 hours?

33. What is the absolute value of the difference between the lengths of the two legs of a right triangle if the length of one of the legs is 4 meters shorter than the other, and the area of the triangle is 70 square meters?

34. Each of 4 boys played a computer game with each of 5 girls, and then each girl played a computer game with each of the other girls. How many computer games were played?

NEXT PAGE

35. What is the probability of getting exactly two tails when flipping three coins?

36. Since beginning of this quarter, Mary has taken 6 history exams. If she earns a 75 on the next exam, her exam average (arithmetic mean) will be decreased by three points. what is her current exam average?

Questions 37 and 38 refer to the information below.

In a certain county, there are two toll stations A and B of high ways. If cars, during business hours, enter any one of the two toll stations at an average rate of s cars per minute and each car stays at the station for an average time t minutes, the average number of cars at the station, n, during business hours at any time is given by the formula

$$n(t) = st.$$

37. The manager of the toll station A determines that cars, during business hours, enter the station at an average rate of 30 cars per minute and all of them each stay an average of 1.4 minutes. About what average number of cars should at the toll station A at any time during business hours?

38. The manager of the toll station B determines that cars, during business hours, enter the station at an average rate of 2,400 cars per hour and all of them each stay an average of 1.2 minutes. The average number of cars at the station B at any time during business hours is what percent more than the average number of cars at the station A at any time during business hours? (Note: Ignore the percent symbol when you entering your answer.)

STOP

Answer Key
For
SAT Math Practice Test 11

Section 3

1	B
2	C
3	D
4	A
5	D
6	D
7	C
8	D
9	D
10	D
11	B
12	D
13	D
14	B
15	B

16	274
17	10
18	13
19	130
20	48

Section 4

1	D	16	A
2	B	17	C
3	B	18	B
4	D	19	A
5	D	20	C
6	D	21	B
7	B	22	B
8	D	23	A
9	D	24	C
10	D	25	C
11	A	26	B
12	C	27	C
13	C	28	C
14	D	29	B
15	C	30	D

31	.3
32	36
33	4
34	30
35	3/8 or .375
36	96
37	42
38	14.2 or 14.3

SAT Math

Practice

Test 11

Explanations

Redesigned for Tests in March 2016 and Beyond

Mad Math

Math Test – No Calculator

Time: 25 Minutes
20 Questions

Notes:

- The use of a calculator is not allowed.
- All numbers used in this section are the real number.
- Figures are provided for some problems in this test. Unless otherwise indicated under the figure "Note: Figure above not drawn to scale", all figures are drawn as accurately as possible.
- All figures lie in a plane EXCEPT otherwise specified.
- Unless otherwise indicated, the domain of any function f, g or j is assumed to be the set of all real numbers x for which $f(x)$, $g(x)$, or $j(x)$ is a real number.

Reference Information

$A = \dfrac{1}{2}bh$

$A = lw$

$A = \pi r^2$

$V = \pi r^2 h$

$V = lwh$

$c^2 = a^2 + b^2$

$V = \dfrac{1}{3}\pi r^2 h$

$V = \dfrac{4}{3}\pi r^3$

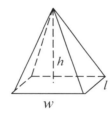

$V = \dfrac{1}{3}lwh$

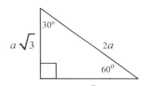

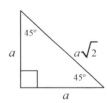

1. If $f(x) = -x^3 - 1$, what does $f(4x)$ equal?

(A) $-4x^4 - 1$

(B) $-64x - 1$

(C) $-4x^4 - 4x$

(D) None above

Solution: Answer: (B)

$$f(4x) = -(4x)^3 - 1$$

$$\Downarrow$$

$$-64x^3 - 1$$

2. What percent of 72 is 24 ?

(A) $\dfrac{1}{3}$

(B) 33

(C) $33\dfrac{1}{3}$

(D) 0.34

Solution: Answer: (C)

$$\frac{x}{100} \cdot 72 = 24$$

$$\downarrow$$

$$x = 24 \cdot \frac{100}{72}$$

$$\Downarrow$$

$$x = \frac{100}{3} = 33\frac{1}{3}$$

3. Which of the following expressions is equal to 0 for the values of x?

(A) $|x - 2| + 4$

(B) $|x - 3| + 2$

(C) $|x - 2| + 3$

(D) $|1 - x| - 5$

Solution: Answer: (D)

$\begin{cases} \text{(A)} \ |x - 2| = -4 \\ \text{(B)} \ |x - 3| = -2 \\ \text{(C)} \ |x - 2| = \text{-}3 \\ \text{(D)} \ |1 - x| = 5 \end{cases}$

An absolute value can not be negative.

$$\downarrow$$

(A), (B), and (C) are canceled.

$$\Downarrow$$

Answer is (D).

4. The ordered pairs $(3x + 1, \ 4)$ and $\left(x - 5, \ 1 + \dfrac{y}{2}\right)$ are equal, Which of the following does (x, y) equal?

(A) $(-3, 6)$

(B) $(-6, 3)$

(C) $(3, -6)$

(D) $(-2, 5)$

Solution: Answer: (A)

$$3x + 1 = x - 5, \ 2x = -6, \ \boxed{x = -3}$$

$$4 = 1 + \frac{y}{2}, \quad 3 = \frac{y}{2}, \qquad \boxed{y = 6}$$

$$\Downarrow$$

$$(-3, 6)$$

5. Johnson made a training plan for swimming, in which the distance of his swimming each day increased by a constant amount. If Johnson's training plan requires that his swimming in day 7 is a distance of 200 meters and in day 13 is a distance of 380 meters, which of the following best describes how the distance changes between day 7 and day 13 of Johnson's training plan?

(A) Johnson increases the distance by 30% per day.

(B) Johnson increases the distance by 1.5 times per day.

(C) Johnson increases the distance by 20 meters per day.

(D) Johnson increases the distance by 30 meters per day.

Solution: Answer: (D)

"increased by a constant amount."

$$\downarrow$$

The relationship between input days and output distances can be represented by a linear function, and the constant amount is the slope s in $f(t) = st + b$.

$$\Downarrow$$

$$s = \frac{380 - 200}{13 - 7} = 30$$

NEXT PAGE ⟹

6. Which of the following must be true about a polynomial $P(x)$ if the value of $P(-5) = -7$?

(A) $x - 5$ is a factor of $P(x)$.

(B) $x + 5$ is a factor of $P(x)$.

(C) The remainder is -7 if $P(x)$ is divided by $x - 5$.

(D) The remainder is -7 if $P(x)$ is divided by $x + 5$.

Solution: Answer: (D)

When $P(x)$ is divided by $x + 5$, it can be written as

$$\frac{P(x)}{x+5} = Q(x) + \frac{-7}{x+5}.$$

$\downarrow$

$$P(x) = (x+5)Q(x) + \cancel{(x+5)}\frac{-7}{\cancel{(x+5)}}$$

$$P(x) = (x+5)Q(x) - 7, \quad P(-5) = 0 - 7 = -7$$

$\Downarrow$

Answer is (D).

$$f(x) = \frac{5}{7}x - b$$

7. In the function above, b is a constant. When $f(-7) = 7$, what is the value of $f(7)$?

(A) 19

(B) -5

(C) 17

(D) 7

Solution: Answer: (C)

$$7 = \frac{5}{7} \cdot (-7) - b, \quad b = -5 - 7 = -12$$

$\downarrow$

$$f(x) = \frac{5}{7}x + 12$$

$\Downarrow$

$$f(7) = \frac{5}{7} \cdot 7 + 12 = 17$$

---

8. If $f(x) = -x^2 - x$, what is $f(-19x)$ equivalent to?

(A) $19x^2 + 19x$

(B) $-19x^2 + 19x$

(C) $-361x^2 + 19x$

(D) $19x^3 + 19x^2$

Solution: Answer: (C)

$$f(-19x) = -(-19x)^2 - (-19x)$$

$\Downarrow$

$$-361x^2 + 19x$$

---

9. James made a training plan for run, in which the distance of his run each day increased by some rate. If James's training plan requires that his run in day 8 is a distance of 10 miles and in day 11 is a distance of 12.5 miles, which of the following best describes how the distance changes between day 8 and day 11 of James's training plan?

(A) James increases the distance by 22% per day.

(B) James increases the distance by 1.020 times per day.

(C) James increases the distance by 0.833 miles per day.

(D) James increases the distance by 1.077 times per day.

Solution: Answer: (D)

"increased by some rate."

$\downarrow$

The relationship between input days and output distances can be represented by an exponential function, and the rate is the growth factor r in the function $f(t) = a_o r^t$.

$\Downarrow$

$$\frac{12.5}{10} = \frac{a_o r^{11}}{a_o r^8}, \quad 1.25 = r^3, \quad \boxed{r = 1.077}$$

---

10. If $a \neq 0$, $b \neq 0$, $\dfrac{b}{100} \div \dfrac{a}{1000} =$

(A) $\dfrac{10a}{b}$ (B) $\dfrac{ab}{10^5}$ (C) $b10^3 a 10^2$ (D) $\dfrac{10b}{a}$

Solution: Answer: (D)

$$\frac{b}{100} \times \frac{1000}{a} = \frac{10b}{a}$$

$$\begin{cases} h(x) = x^2 + 5x + 4 \\ j(x) = 3x^4 + 15x^3 + 12x^2 \end{cases}$$

11. If the polynomials h and j are defined above, which of the following polynomials is divisible by $3x^2 + 5$?

(A) $N(x) = 3x^2 j(x) + 5h(x)$ (B) $M(x) = j(x) + 5h(x)$

(C) $A(x) = 2j(x) + 5h(x)$ (D) $B(x) = 3x^2 j(x) + (1/5) h(x)$

Solution: Answer: (B)

j and h have the relationship:

$$j(x) = 3x^2 \left(x^2 + 5x + 4 \right) = 3x^2 h(x)$$

When $M(x)$ is divided by $3x^2 + 5$, it can be written as

$$\frac{M(x)}{3x^2 + 5} = h(x) + \frac{r}{3x^2 + 5}.$$

If remaunder $r = 0$, $P(x)$ is called "P is divisible by $3x^2 + 5$."

It is $\underbrace{M(x) = h(x)\left(3x^2 + 5 \right)}_{\text{Use this conclusion.}}$

Plug-in

$$M(x) = j(x) + 5h(x) = 3x^2 h(x) + 5h(x) = h(x)\left(3x^2 + 5 \right)$$

$$\left(\text{It is } \frac{M(x)}{3x^2 + 5} = h(x) + \frac{0}{3x^2 + 5}. \right)$$

$$\Downarrow$$

Answer is (B).

12. A rectangle was changed by decreasing its length by 20% and increasing its width by 10%. If these changes decreased the area of the rectangle by $X\%$, what is the value of X?

(A) 20

(B) 10

(C) 30

(D) 12

Solution: Answer: (D)

$$\frac{\frac{80}{100}\cancel{x} \cdot \frac{110}{100}\cancel{y}}{\cancel{xy}} = 1 - \frac{X}{100}$$

$$\downarrow$$

$$\frac{8\cancel{0}}{\cancel{100}} \cdot \frac{11\cancel{0}}{\cancel{100}} = \frac{100 - X}{\cancel{100}}$$

$$\Downarrow$$

$$88 = 100 - X, \quad X = 12$$

13. The registrar's office of Milton Academy receives the exam scores of AP Calculus AB from 1 to 5. If the office received the score in the first 8 scores was 4.5 that was the average (arithmetic mean), what is the least value the office can receive for the 12th score and still be able to have an average of at least 4.6 for the first 15 scores?

(A) 5

(B) 4

(C) 2

(D) 3

Solution: Answer: (D)

Total of the first 8 scores

$$8 \times 4.5 = 36$$

If $\underbrace{\text{from 9th to 15th except 12th}}_{15 - 9 = 6 \text{ scores}}$ each

score is 5, $6 \times 5 = 30$.

$$\frac{36 + 30 + x}{15} = 4.6, \quad 66 + x = 69$$

If you use an average greater than 4.6, the x-value will not be the least one.

$$\Downarrow$$

$$x = 3$$

NEXT PAGE

Questions 14 and 15 refer to the information below.

After registered a construction company in a month, Michael obtained a project. For this project because his investment was limited, he could not buy every thing. For some tools, he needed to rent them. The following table shows the costs of the materials and weekly rental for distinct companies X, Y and Z.

Company	X	Y	Z
Materials Cost M	$2,400	$1,800	$1,900
Rental of Tool-1 Cost T1	$150	$200	$250
Rental of Tool-2 Cost T2	$400	$600	$500
Rental of Tool-3 Cost T3	$300	$350	$350

The toal cost, $C(w)$, for buying and renting in terms of the number of weeks, w, is given by
$$C(w) = (T1 + T2 + T3)w + M.$$

14. For what number of weeks will the total cost from Company X be greater than or equal to the total cost from Company Z?

(A) $w \geq 2$
(B) $w \leq 2$
(C) $w \geq 3$
(D) $w \leq 3$

Solution: Answer: (B)

$$C(w)_X = (150 + 400 + 300)w + 2400$$
$$C(w)_Z = (250 + 500 + 350)w + 1900$$
$$C(w)_X \geq C(w)_Z$$
$$850w + 2400 \geq 1100w + 1900$$
$$\Downarrow$$
$$500 \geq 250w, \quad w \leq 2$$

15. If the relationship of the total cost, $C(w)$, and weeks, w, is graphed in the xy-plane, what does the initial value of the curve represent?

(A) w
(B) M
(C) $C(w)$
(D) $T1 + T2 + T3$

Solution: Answer: (B)

$$C(w) = (T1 + T2 + T3)w + M$$
$$\downarrow$$
It is the slope-intercept form of linear function
$$f(x) = sx + b.$$
When the input $x = 0$. $f(0) = b$.
$$\begin{cases} b \text{ is the intercept.} \\ b \text{ is the initial value also.} \end{cases}$$
M is at the position of b.
$$\Downarrow$$
M is the initial value.

NEXT PAGE

16. From January 1, 2016 to December 31, 2016, the price of a certain stock increased by 215 percent, and from January 1, 2017 to December 31, 2017, the price of the stock increased by 60 percent. Over the period of the two years, by what percentage did the stock rise?

Solution: Answer: 404

$(1 + 2.15) = 3.15$ (on December 31, 2016)

$3.15 \times 1.6 = 5.04$ (on December 31, 2017)
⇓
$504\% - 100\% = 404\%$

17. If 3 feet lengthen each side of a square, the area is increased by 21 square yards. What is the length, in yards, of a side of the original square?

Solution: Answer: 10

$(x+1)^2 - (x)^2 = 21, \quad x^2 + 2x + 1 - x^2 = 21$
⇓
$2x + 1 = 21, \qquad x = 10$

18. If $m^2 + mn + n^2 = 7$ and $mn = 6$, what is the value of $(m+n)^2$?

Solution: Answer: 13

$m^2 + mn + mn + n^2 = 7 + mn, \quad m^2 + 2mn + n^2 = 7 + 6$
⇓
$(m+n)^2 = 13$

19. 65% of 98 is the same as 49% of what number?

Solution: Answer: 130

$\dfrac{65}{100} \times 98 = \dfrac{49}{100} x, \quad 65 \times 98^2 = 49 x$
⇓
$x = 130$

$$\begin{cases} f(x) \le -8x + 240 \\ f(x) \le 2x \end{cases}$$

20. In the xy-plan, if a point (x_1, y_1) lies in the solution set of the system of inequalities above, what is the maximum possible value of y_1 ?

Solution: Answer: 48

$y = -8x + 240$

$\begin{cases} x = 0 \\ y = 240 \end{cases}$ and $\begin{cases} y = 0 \\ x = 30 \end{cases}$ $y = 2x$
↓   ↓

$\begin{cases} y \le -8x + 240 \\ y \le 2x \end{cases}$ →

Intersection point

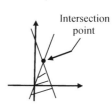

Solve for the value of y.

$\begin{cases} \dfrac{y - 240}{-8} = x \\ \dfrac{y}{2} = x \end{cases}$, $x = x$ → $\dfrac{y}{2} = \dfrac{y - 240}{-8}$

To cancel x

$-4y = y - 240, \quad 5y = 240, \quad y = 48$
⇓

It is the maximum y_1 from the bottom graph.

STOP

Math Test – Calculator

Time: 55 Minutes
38 Questions

Notes:
- The use of a calculator is not allowed.
- All numbers used in this section are the real number.
- Figures are provided for some problems in this test. Unless otherwise indicated under the figure "Note: Figure above not drawn to scale", all figures are drawn as accurately as possible.
- All figures lie in a plane EXCEPT otherwise specified.
- Unless otherwise indicated, the domain of any function f, g or j is assumed to be the set of all real numbers x for which $f(x)$, $g(x)$, or $j(x)$ is a real number.

Reference Information

$$A = \frac{1}{2}bh$$

$$A = lw$$

$$A = \pi r^2$$

$$V = \pi r^2 h$$

$$V = lwh$$

$$c^2 = a^2 + b^2$$

$$V = \frac{1}{3}\pi r^2 h$$

$$V = \frac{4}{3}\pi r^3$$

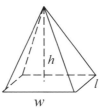

$$V = \frac{1}{3}lwh$$

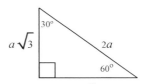

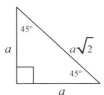

Copying or reuse of any portion of this page is illegal.

1. What are all values of x for which $|x - 2| - 2 < 0$?

(A) $x < 0, \ x > 4$

(B) $x < -4, \ x > 4$

(C) $x < -2, \ x > 2$

(D) $0 < x < 4$

Solution: Answer: (D)

$$|x - 2| < 2$$

$$\downarrow$$

$$-2 < x - 2 < 2$$

$$\downarrow$$

$$+2 - 2 < x < 2 + 2$$

$$\Downarrow$$

$$0 < x < 4$$

2. If $\dfrac{y}{x} = \dfrac{5}{8}$, what is the value of $\dfrac{8x}{5y}$?

(A) 1

(B) $\left(\dfrac{8}{5}\right)^2$

(C) $\dfrac{16}{10}$

(D) $\dfrac{25}{64}$

Solution: Answer: (B)

$$\frac{y}{x} = \frac{5}{8}, \quad \frac{x}{y} = \frac{8}{5}$$

$$\downarrow$$

$$\left(\frac{8}{5}\right) \times \frac{x}{y} = \frac{8}{5} \times \left(\frac{8}{5}\right)$$

$$\Downarrow$$

$$\frac{8x}{5y} = \frac{64}{25} = \frac{8^2}{5^2} = \left(\frac{8}{5}\right)^2$$

3. Which of the following is a reduced form of $\dfrac{a^2 - 8a + 12}{a^2 - 36}$?

(A) $\dfrac{a - 2}{a - 6}$

(B) $\dfrac{a - 2}{a + 6}$

(C) $\dfrac{a + 2}{a + 6}$

(D) $\dfrac{a + 2}{a - 6}$

Solution: Answer: (B)

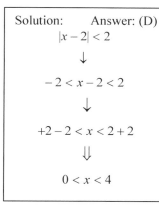

$$\frac{(a - 2)(a - 6)}{(a - 6)(a + 6)}$$

$$\Downarrow$$

$$\frac{(a - 2)\,(a - 6)}{(a - 6)(a + 6)} = \frac{a - 2}{a + 6}$$

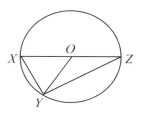

Note: Figure above not drawn to scale

4. In the figure above, triangle XYZ is inscribed in the circle that has center O. If $XY = OX$, which of the following is the measure, in degree, of angle OYZ?

(A) 60

(B) 45

(C) 70

(D) 30

Solution: Answer: (D)

The radii form an equilateral triangle OYX and an isosceles triangle YOZ.

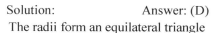
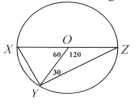

5. $\left(k^2 - 1\right)\left(k^2 - 2\right) =$

(A) $(k^2 + 2k - 1)(k^2 - 2)$

(B) $(k^2 + 2k + 1)(k^2 - 2)$

(C) $(k^2 - 2k + 1)(k^2 - 2)$

(D) $(k - 1)(k + 1)(k - \sqrt{2})(k + \sqrt{2})$

Solution: Answer: (D)

$$\left(k^2 - 1^2\right)\left(k^2 - \left(\sqrt{2}\right)^2\right)$$

$$\Downarrow$$

$$(k - 1)(k + 1)\left(k - \sqrt{2}\right)\left(k + \sqrt{2}\right)$$

6. Four years from now, Kevin's age will be $4x + 2$. Which of the following represents his age four years ago?

(A) $4x - 2$

(B) $4x - 3$

(C) $4x - 5$

(D) $4x - 6$

Solution: Answer: (D)

Current age $= 4x + 2 - 4 = 4x - 2$

$$\Downarrow$$

4 years ago $= 4x - 2 - 4 = 4x - 6$

NEXT PAGE

7. If x and y are numbers such that $-y < x < y$, which of the following must be true?

    I. $|x| > y$

    II. $|x| < y$

    III. $y < 0$

(A) I only

(B) II only

(C) I and III only

(D) I, II and III

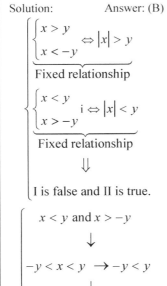

Solution: Answer: (B)

$\begin{cases} x > y \\ x < -y \end{cases} \Leftrightarrow |x| > y$

$\underbrace{\qquad\qquad}_{\text{Fixed relationship}}$

$\begin{cases} x < y \\ x > -y \end{cases} \text{i} \Leftrightarrow |x| < y$

$\underbrace{\qquad\qquad}_{\text{Fixed relationship}}$

$\Downarrow$

I is false and II is true.

$x < y \text{ and } x > -y$

$\downarrow$

$-y < x < y \rightarrow -y < y$

$\downarrow$

y must be greater than 0.

$\Downarrow$

III is false.

8. If $f(x) = -(x-9)^2 - 7$, what are the equation of its symmetric axis and vertex coordinates?

(A) $\begin{cases} \text{Vertex: } (-9, 7) \\ \text{Equation: } x = -9 \end{cases}$
  (B) $\begin{cases} \text{Vertex: } (9, 7) \\ \text{Equation: } x = 9 \end{cases}$

(C) $\begin{cases} \text{Vertex: } (-9, 7) \\ \text{Equation: } x = 7 \end{cases}$
  (D) $\begin{cases} \text{Vertex: } (9, -7) \\ \text{Equation: } x = 9 \end{cases}$

Solution: Answer: (D)

Change the equation to the vertex form.

$$f(x) = a\left(x - x_m\right)^2 + y_m$$

$$f(x) = -(x-9)^2 + \left(-7\right)$$

$\Downarrow$

$\begin{cases} \text{Vertex: } (9, -7) \\ \text{The equation: } x = 9 \end{cases}$

$\begin{cases} y = (x+3)(x-3) \\ x^2 - 9 = y \end{cases}$

9. How many ordered pairs (x, y) satisfy the system of equations shown above?

(A) one

(B) two

(C) zero

(D) infinity

Solution: Answer: (D)

$$x^2 - 9 = y \quad \rightarrow \quad y = (x+3)(x-3)$$

$\downarrow$

The two equations are the same one.

$\downarrow$

They have exactly the same curve.

$\Downarrow$

∞ ordered pairs

10. If $f(x) = (2x+1)(x+7)$, what is the equation of its symmetric axis?

(A) 3.75

(B) 4

(C) -4

(D) -3.75

Solution: Answer: (D)

Change the equation to the factored form (intercept form),

$$f(x) = a\left(x - x_1\right)\left(x - x_2\right)$$

$$f(x) = 2\left(x + \frac{1}{2}\right)\left(x + 7\right)$$

$\Downarrow$

$$x = \frac{x_1 + x_2}{2} = \frac{\left(-1/2\right) - 7}{2} = -3.75$$

NEXT PAGE ⟩

11. If the first two terms of a sequence are 14 and 23 and each subsequence is the sum of the two preceding terms, how many of the first 1000 terms are even and how many of the first 1000 terms are odd?

(A) 334 and 666

(B) 333 and 667

(C) 334 and 667

(D) 332 and 665

Solution: Answer: (A)

The first term is 14. It is not 0.

$$\underbrace{14,\ 23,\ 37}_{\text{1 even number}},\ \underbrace{60,\ 97,\ 157}_{\text{1 even number}},\ \cdots$$

↓

Each 3 terms include an even number.

Each 3 terms include 2 odd numbers.

⇓

$$\frac{999}{3}+1=334,\qquad \frac{999}{3}\times 2=666$$

↑

Value of 1000th term is even.

12. If $f(x)=(x-3)(x+7)$, which of the following is equivalent to the function f?

(A) $(x-2)^2-21$

(B) $(x-2)^2-25$

(C) $(x+2)^2-25$

(D) $(x+2)^2+25$

Solution: Answer: (C)

$$\begin{cases}\text{Factored form} \to \text{Vertex form}\\ f(x)=a\left(x-x_{\text{m}}\right)^2+y_{\text{m}}\end{cases}$$

$$x^2-3x+7x-21$$

↓

$$x^2+4x+2^2-2^2-21$$

⇓

$$(x+2)^2-25$$

13. What are the factored form of $f(x)=2x^2-7x+5$ and its roots?

(A) $\begin{cases}(2x-5)(x-1)\\ x=5 \text{ and } x=1\end{cases}$

(B) $\begin{cases}(2x-5)(x-1)\\ x=-5 \text{ and } x=-1\end{cases}$

(C) $\begin{cases}2\left(x-\dfrac{5}{2}\right)(x-1)\\ x=\dfrac{5}{2} \text{ and } x=1\end{cases}$

(D) $\begin{cases}2\left(x-\dfrac{5}{2}\right)(x-1)\\ x=-\dfrac{5}{2} \text{ and } x=-1\end{cases}$

Solution: Answer: (C)

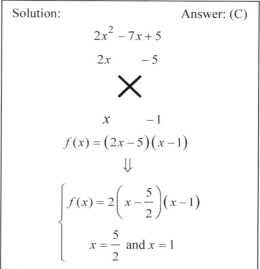

$$2x^2-7x+5$$

$2x \qquad -5$

$x \qquad -1$

$$f(x)=(2x-5)(x-1)$$

⇓

$$\begin{cases}f(x)=2\left(x-\dfrac{5}{2}\right)(x-1)\\ x=\dfrac{5}{2} \text{ and } x=1\end{cases}$$

14. If $f(x)=(1-4x)^2-36$, which of the following is equivalent to the function f?

(A) $4(x+5/4)(x-7/4)$

(B) $4(x-5/4)(x+7/4)$

(C) $16(x-5/4)(x+7/4)$

(D) $16(x-7/4)(x+5/4)$

Solution: Answer: (D)

$$\begin{cases}\text{Target} \to \underbrace{\text{Factored form}}_{\text{Intercept form}}\\ f(x)=a\left(x-x_1\right)\left(x-x_2\right)\end{cases}$$

$$f(x)=\left((-1)(4x-1)\right)^2-36$$

$$f(x)=\left(4(x-1/4)\right)^2-36 \to a=4^2=16$$

$$0=(1-4x)^2-36,\quad 36=(1-4x)^2$$

$$\begin{cases}-6=1-4x\\ +6=1-4x\end{cases} \to \begin{cases}x_1=7/4\\ x_2=-5/4\end{cases}$$

⇓

$$f(x)=16(x-7/4)(x+5/4)$$

NEXT PAGE ⟹

15. In the universe, the mesosphere is the layer of a planet's atmosphere. The mesosphere of some planet is between 40,000 m and 56,000 m above the planet's surface. At the distance of 40,000 m, the temperature in the mesosphere is -10°F, and at the distance of 56,000 m, the temperature in the mesosphere is -70°F. For each additional 4,000 m from the planet's surface, the temperature in the layer decreases by a°F, where a is a constant. Which of the following is the value of a?

(A) 3   (B) 12   (C) 15   (D) 10

> Solution: Answer: (C)
>
> "decreases by a°F, where a is a constant"
>
> means
>
> "decreased by a constant amount."
>
> The relationship between input distances and output temperature can be represented by a linear function, and the constant amount is the slope s in $y = sx + b$.
>
> $\Downarrow$
>
> $s = \dfrac{y_2 - y_1}{x_2 - x_1} = \dfrac{-70 - (-10)}{\dfrac{56000 - 40000}{4000}} = -15, \quad a = 15$

16. Johnson made a training plan for his swimming. Johnson himself modeled the training plan by the equation $D = \dfrac{t + 120}{3}$, where D is distance in meters and t is time in days. Accordiing to the model, by how many meters will the distance increase per day?

(A) $0.\overline{3}$

(B) 120

(C) 40

(D) 3

> Solution: Answer: (A)
>
> The model is a linear function $y = sx + b$.
>
> $D = \dfrac{t + 120}{3} = \dfrac{t}{3} + \dfrac{120}{3} = \dfrac{1}{3}t + 40$
>
> "distance increase per day" = slope s.
>
> $\Downarrow$
>
> $s = \dfrac{1}{3} = 0.\overline{3}$

$$\begin{cases} 3(x+2) = y \\ \dfrac{y}{x} = 7 \end{cases}$$

17. If (x, y) is the solution to the system of equations above, what is the y-value?

(A) 6.5

(B) 8.4

(C) 10.5

(D) 10.4

> Solution: Answer: (C)
>
> $\begin{cases} \\ \\ \\ \end{cases}$ The target is y.
>
> $\downarrow$
>
> Use $x = x$ to let x be eleminated.
>
> $3(x+2) = y, \quad x = \dfrac{y}{3} - 2$
>
> $\dfrac{y}{x} = 7, \quad x = \dfrac{y}{7}$
>
> $x = x$
>
> $21 \cdot \dfrac{y}{7} = \left(\dfrac{y}{3} - 2 \right) 21, \quad 3y = 7y - 42$
>
> $\Downarrow$
>
> $4y = 42, \quad y = 10.5$

18. If b is less than a and $b > 0$, which of the following is the least value?

(A) $\dfrac{a}{a - b}$

(B) $\dfrac{1}{b - a}$

(C) $\dfrac{1}{a + b}$

(D) $\dfrac{1}{a - b}$

> Solution: Answer: (B)
>
> $a > b$ and $b > 0$
>
> $\downarrow$
>
> $b - a < 0$
>
> $\downarrow$
>
> Only $\dfrac{1}{b - a} < 0$
>
> $\Downarrow$
>
> Answer is (B).

NEXT PAGE

$$x^2 - (m/4)x = -2k$$

19. In the quadratic function above, m and k are constants. Which of the following is the solutions for x?

(A) $x = \dfrac{m \pm \sqrt{m^2 - 128k}}{8}$

(B) $x = \dfrac{m}{8} \pm \dfrac{\sqrt{m^2 + 128k}}{8}$

(C) $x = \dfrac{m \pm \sqrt{m^2 - 8k}}{8}$

(D) $x = \dfrac{-m \pm \sqrt{m^2 - 128k}}{8}$

Solution: Answer: (A)

$$x^2 - \frac{m}{4}x + 2k = 0$$

$$x = \frac{\dfrac{m}{4} \pm \sqrt{\left(-\dfrac{m}{4}\right)^2 - 4 \cdot 1 \cdot (2k)}}{2 \cdot 1} = \frac{\dfrac{m}{4} \pm \sqrt{\dfrac{m^2}{16} - 8k}}{2}$$

$$\frac{\dfrac{m}{4} \pm \sqrt{\dfrac{m^2 - 128k}{16}}}{2} = \frac{\dfrac{m}{4} \pm \dfrac{1}{4}\sqrt{m^2 - 128k}}{2} \cdot \frac{4}{4}$$

$$\Downarrow$$

$$x = \frac{m \pm \sqrt{m^2 - 128k}}{8}$$

$$y - 2 = 3/2(2x+1)$$

20. What is the y-intercept of the function above?

(A) $(0, -0.5)$

(B) $(-0.5, 0)$

(C) $(0, 3.5)$

(D) $(-3.5, 0)$

Solution: Answer: (C)

The definition the intercept:

y-value when $x = 0$

$\downarrow$

$y - 2 = 3/2(2 \times 0 + 1)$

$\Downarrow$

$y = 3/2 + 2, \quad y = 3.5$

21. Michael Johnson, a town council, did a survey to determine whether the residents in a large town prefer building a new park. The council asked 125 shoppers who visited a local mall on a Sunday, and 5 of those refused respond. Which of the following makes it less likely that a reliable conclusion can be drawn about the park-building preference of all residents in this town?

(A) The population size

(B) The place the survey was given

(C) The amount of people who refused to respond

(D) None above

Solution: Answer: (B)

If a large enough sample is chosen randomly from a population, whether the population size is small or large, a reliable conclusion can be drawn.

$\Downarrow$

(A) is incorrect.

If the participants have been chosen randomly, as a survey, even though fewer participants refuse to respond, a reliable conclusion can still be drawn about the population.

$\Downarrow$

(C) is incorrect.

The participants should be at random chosen from entire population. This survey conducted was not at random chosen because the residents who were not at the mall had no chance of being chosen. So this method is less likely to result in a biased sample because a wide range of residents will be surveyed.

$\Downarrow$

(B) is correct.

NEXT PAGE

Questions 22 and 23 refer to the information below.

The stock price of a certain share is worth $356 today. After conducting, May concludes that the stock will decrease $12 of its value per years for the next seven years. May uses the linear function $v(t) = st + b$ to model the value, $v(t)$, of the stock in t years.

22   What correct value should May use for s ?

(A) 356

(B) -12

(C)   84

(D) 272

Solution: Answer: (B)

"decrease $12"

↓

The slope of a linear function

⇓

$s = -12$

23. What will the value, in dollars, of the stock will be at the end of seven years ?

(A) 272

(B) 440

(C) -440

(D) -272

Solution: Answer: (A)

$$f(7) = -12 \times 7 + 356$$

⇓

$$f(7) = 272$$

24.   Which of the following sketches shows a relationship that is appropriately modled with the function $f(t) = ar^t$, where $a \geq 1$ and $0 < r < 1$?

(A) v

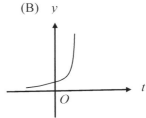

(B) v

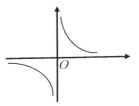

(C) v

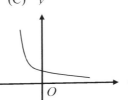

(D) v

Solution: Answer: (C)

It is an exponential functions $f(t). = ar^t$.

$$0 < r < 1$$

⇓

The sketch will be similar to (C).

NEXT PAGE

25. Which of the following sketches shows a relationship that is appropriately modled with the function $y = ax^b + c$, where $a = 0$ and $c < 0$?

(A) y

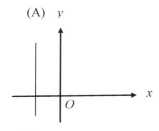

(B) y

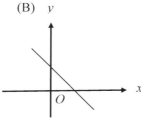

(C) y

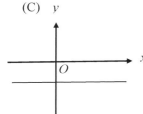

(D) y

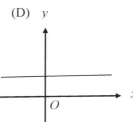

Solution: Answer: (C)
$$a = 0 \rightarrow y = c$$
$$c < 0$$
$$\Downarrow$$
The sketch will be similar to (C).

Note that (A) is for $x = c$.

26. If $|Q - h| - 2 < 0$, Q and h both are integers, and $2006 < Q < 2014$, what are all possible values of h?

(A) 2010 and 2011

(B) 2008 and 2012

(C) From 2009 to 2011

(D) 2011 and 2012

Solution: Answer: (B)
$$\begin{cases} |Q - h| < 2 \\ \downarrow \\ -2 < Q - h < 2 \\ \downarrow \\ h - 2 < Q < 2 + h \end{cases}$$
$$2006 < Q < 2014$$
$$\downarrow$$
$$\begin{cases} 2 + h = 2014 \\ h - 2 = 2006 \end{cases}$$
$$\Downarrow$$
$$\begin{cases} h = 2012 \\ h = 2008 \end{cases}$$

27. If a cube is inscribed in a sphere of radius 10, which of the following is the volume of the cube, to the nearest tenth?

(A) 1.0   (B) 3519.6   (C) 1539.6   (D) 6583.1

Solution: Answer: (C)

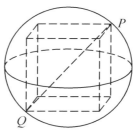

Volue $V = s^3 \rightarrow$ Target: s

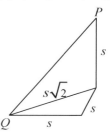

Method 1

$$PQ = \sqrt{s^2 + \left(s\sqrt{2}\right)^2}$$
$$\sqrt{s^2 + 2s^2} = \sqrt{3s^2}$$
$$PQ = s\sqrt{3}, \quad PQ = 2 \cdot 10 = 20$$
$$\downarrow$$
$$s\sqrt{3} = 20, \quad s = \frac{20}{\sqrt{3}}$$
$$\Downarrow$$
$$V = s^3 = \left(\frac{20}{\sqrt{3}}\right)^3 = 1539.6$$

Method 2

Directly use the conclusion
for any cube: $\underline{PQ = s\sqrt{3}}$.
$$\downarrow$$
$$20 = s\sqrt{3}, \quad s = \frac{20}{\sqrt{3}}$$
$$\Downarrow$$
$$V = s^3 = \left[\frac{20}{\sqrt{3}}\right]^3 = 1539.5$$

NEXT PAGE

$$g(x) = |2x - 13|$$

28. For the equation above, what is one possible value of b for which $g(b) < b$?

(A) 13

(B) 14

(C) 12

(D) $4\dfrac{1}{3}$

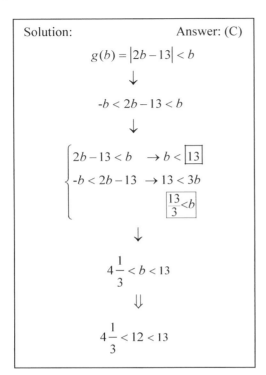

Solution: Answer: (C)

$$g(b) = |2b - 13| < b$$

$$\downarrow$$

$$-b < 2b - 13 < b$$

$$\downarrow$$

$$\begin{cases} 2b - 13 < b \rightarrow b < \boxed{13} \\ -b < 2b - 13 \rightarrow 13 < 3b \\ \phantom{-b < 2b - 13 \rightarrow} \boxed{\dfrac{13}{3} < b} \end{cases}$$

$$\downarrow$$

$$4\dfrac{1}{3} < b < 13$$

$$\Downarrow$$

$$4\dfrac{1}{3} < 12 < 13$$

Questions 29 and 30 refer to the information below.

An animal scientist uses a formula as a tool for his research about the population of rabbits. The population of the rabbits that this scientist expects to grow next month N_N can be calculated from the population current month N_C by the following formula.

$$N_N = N_C - 0.3 N_C \left(\dfrac{N_C}{C} - 1 \right)$$

The C in the formula is an envirobmental constant. Its value is determined by envirobmental conditions.

29. If the population of the rabbits current month N_C is 200 and C is 300, what will be the population of rabbits two months from current month? (Round your answer to a whole number.)

(A) 235 (B) 238 (C) 233 (D) 232

Solution: Answer: (B)

(1). $N_{N-1} = 200 - 0.3 \cdot 200 \left(\dfrac{200}{300} - 1 \right)$

$N_{N-1} = 200 - 60 \left(-\dfrac{1}{3} \right) = 220$

(2). $N_{N-2} = 220 - 0.3 \cdot 220 \left(\dfrac{220}{300} - 1 \right)$

$N_{N-2} = 220 - 66 \left(-\dfrac{8}{30} \right)$

$N_{N-2} = 220 + 17.6 \approx 237.6 \approx \boxed{238}$

30. If the animal scientist wants to increase the population of rabbits, he needs to improve the environmenal conditions. If the animal scientist's target is that the population of rabbits will increase from 200 this month to 230 next month, after improving the environmental conditions, what should the value of C be equal to?

(A) 415

(B) 410

(C) 380

(D) 400

Solution: Answer: (D)

$$230 = 200 - 0.3 \cdot 200 \left(\dfrac{200}{C} - 1 \right), \quad 30 = -60 \left(\dfrac{200}{C} - 1 \right)$$

$$\Downarrow$$

$$3 = -\dfrac{1200}{C} + 6, \quad \dfrac{1200}{C} = 3, \quad C = 400$$

NEXT PAGE ⟩

31. In triangle ABC, $m\angle C$ is $90°$. What is $\cos(90° - B)$ equal to if $\sin B = 0.3$ and B is an acute angle in degree measure?

Solution: Answer: 0.3

$(90° - B)$ and B are complementary.

$$\sin(90° - B) = \cos B$$
$$\Downarrow$$
$$\sin(90° - B) = 0.3$$

32. A river boat paddled at 10 miles per hour, stopped and rested for 2.5 hours, then paddled back at 15 miles per hour. How far downstream did the boat travel if the entire time for the trip, including the rest, was 8.5 hours?

Solution: Answer: 36

$$\frac{d}{r} = t, \quad t_1 + t_2 = t_3, \qquad \frac{d}{10} + \frac{d}{15} = 8.5 - 2.5$$
$$\Downarrow$$
$$30 \cdot \left(\frac{d}{10} + \frac{d}{15}\right) = 6 \cdot 30, \quad 3d + 2d = 180, \quad d = 36$$

33. What is the absolute value of the difference between the lengths of the two legs of a right triangle if the length of one of the legs is 4 meters shorter than the other, and the area of the triangle is 70 square meters?

Solution: Answer: 4

$$A_{\text{Tri}} = \frac{b \cdot h}{2}, \qquad 70 = \frac{x \cdot (x - 4)}{2}$$
$$140 = x^2 - 4x, \quad x^2 - 4x - 140 = 0$$
$$(x - 14)(x + 10) = 0$$
$$\underbrace{x = -10}_{\substack{\text{Cannot be negative} \\ \text{for sides of a triangle.}}}, \quad x = 14$$
$$\Downarrow$$
$$x - (x - 4) = 14 - (14 - 4) = 4$$

34. Each of 4 boys played a computer game with each of 5 girls, and then each girl played a computer game with each of the other girls. How many computer games were played?

Solution: Answer: 30

(1) Boys playing with girls

2 element sets
(Boy set and girl set)
$$\downarrow$$
Use Fundamental Counting Principle.

1 boy set   1 girl set
$$\boxed{4} \times \boxed{5} = 20$$

(2) Girls playing with girls

$\Big\{$ 1 element set
$$\downarrow$$
Use Permutations or Combinations.

$\Big\{$ Order doesn't matter.
$$\downarrow$$
Use Combinations.

$$\downarrow$$

2 positions, 5 elements
$$\frac{\boxed{5} \times \boxed{4}}{2!} = 10$$

(3) Two sets cannot be combined in this case.
$$\downarrow$$
Use addition.
$$\Downarrow$$
$$20 + 10 = 30$$

NEXT PAGE

35. What is the probability of getting exactly two tails when flipping three coins?

Solution: Answer: 3/8 or .375

Only two states: tails and heads.
Use $T = 2^n$ to get the total possibilities, where n is the number of coins.

$$T = 2^3 = 8$$

Order doesn't matter. There are 3 elements. For "exact two tails": 2 positions for 2 tails

Possibilities of "exact two tails": $\dfrac{3 \times 2}{2!} = 3$

$$\Downarrow$$

$$P_{\text{Exact 2 tails}} = \frac{3}{8}$$

36. Since beginning of this quarter, Mary has taken 6 history exams. If she earns a 75 on the next exam, her exam average (arithmetic mean) will be decreased by three points. what is her current exam average?

Solution: Answer: 96

$$\frac{6x + 75}{6 + 1} = x - 3$$

$$\downarrow$$

$$6x + 75 = 7x - 21$$

$$\downarrow$$

$$21 + 75 = 7x - 6x$$

$$\Downarrow$$

$$x = 96$$

Questions 37 and 38 refer to the information below.

In a certain county, there are two toll stations A and B of high ways. If cars, during business hours, enter any one of the two toll stations at an average rate of s cars per minute and each car stays at the station for an average time t minutes, the average number of cars at the station, n, during business hours at any time is given by the formula

$$n(t) = st.$$

37. The manager of the toll station A determines that cars, during business hours, enter the station at an average rate of 30 cars per minute and all of them each stay an average of 1.4 minutes. About what average number of cars should at the toll station A at any time during business hours?

Solution: Answer: 42

$$n(t) = st$$

$$\Downarrow$$

$$n(1.4) = 30 \times 1.4 = 42$$

38. The manager of the toll station B determines that cars, during business hours, enter the station at an average rate of 2,400 cars per hour and all of them each stay an average of 1.2 minutes. The average number of cars at the station B at any time during business hours is what percent more than the average number of cars at the station A at any time during business hours? (Note: Ignore the percent symbol when you entering your answer.)

Solution: Answer: 14.3 or 14.2

$$n(1.2) = \frac{2400}{60} \times 1.2 = 48$$

$$\Downarrow$$

$$\frac{48 - 42}{42} \times 100\% = \frac{600}{42}\% \approx 14.3\% \text{ or } 14.2\%$$

STOP

SAT Math

Practice

Test 12

Redesigned for Tests in March 2016 and Beyond

Mad Math

Math Test – No Calculator

Time: 25 Minutes
20 Questions

Notes:

- The use of a calculator is not allowed.
- All numbers used in this section are the real number.
- Figures are provided for some problems in this test. Unless otherwise indicated under the figure "Note: Figure above not drawn to scale", all figures are drawn as accurately as possible.
- All figures lie in a plane EXCEPT otherwise specified.
- Unless otherwise indicated, the domain of any function f, g or j is assumed to be the set of all real numbers x for which $f(x)$, $g(x)$, or $j(x)$ is a real number.

Reference Information

$$A = \frac{1}{2}bh$$

$$A = lw$$

$$A = \pi r^2$$

$$V = \pi r^2 h$$

$$V = lwh$$

$$c^2 = a^2 + b^2$$

$$V = \frac{1}{3}\pi r^2 h$$

$$V = \frac{4}{3}\pi r^3$$

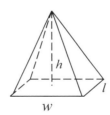

$$V = \frac{1}{3}lwh$$

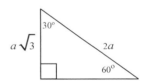

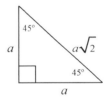

1. If $f(x) = x - \sqrt{x-1}$, at which of the following values of x is $f(x)$ undefined?

(A) 0

(B) 3

(C) 2

(D) 1

2. If $x^2 = 8$, what is the value of $(x-1)(x+1)$?

(A) 0
(B) 9
(C) 7
(D) 5

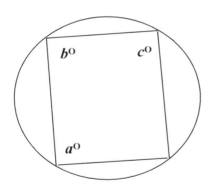

Note: Figure above is not drawn to scale.

3. In the figure above, a circle comscribes a quadrilateral. Which of the following must be true?

(A) $a° + c° = 180°$
(B) $b° + c° = 180°$
(C) $b° + a° = 180°$
(D) $b° + c° + a° = 270°$

4. $\cot 0 = ?$

(A) $\sin 0$

(B) $\sin \dfrac{\pi}{2}$

(C) $\tan \dfrac{\pi}{2}$

(D) $\cos \dfrac{3\pi}{2}$

5. If $g(x) = 3x - 2$ and $g(x-1) - g(x) = 5x$, then $x =$

(A) $\dfrac{5}{3}$

(B) $-\dfrac{5}{3}$

(C) $\dfrac{3}{5}$

(D) $-\dfrac{3}{5}$

6. Which of the following expression is not equal to $\dfrac{2}{3}$?

(A) $\dfrac{\frac{5}{6} - \frac{1}{6}}{4}$

(B) $\dfrac{\frac{3}{4}}{\frac{1}{2}}$

(C) $\dfrac{\frac{3}{4}}{\frac{2}{}}$

(D) $\sqrt{\dfrac{16}{36}}$

NEXT PAGE

7. $\dfrac{\sqrt{3}-1}{1-\sqrt{5}} =$

(A) $\dfrac{\left(\sqrt{3}-1\right)\left(1+\sqrt{5}\right)}{6}$

(B) $\dfrac{\left(\sqrt{3}-1\right)\left(1-\sqrt{5}\right)}{4}$

(C) $-\dfrac{\left(\sqrt{3}-1\right)\left(1+\sqrt{5}\right)}{4}$

(D) $\dfrac{\left(\sqrt{3}-1\right)\left(1\pm\sqrt{5}\right)}{4}$

8. Tom, an owner of a computer retail store, sells a computer of $780. It makes a 30% profit. During an on sale period, the profit is cut to 16%. What is the final price of the computer?

(A) 616
(B) 612
(C) 722
(D) 696

9. Tim is a car salesperson. He sells two kinds of cars. For one of them, the selling price is $32,000, and for another one, the selling price is $48,000. Last week, Tim's goal was to sell 10 cars. He did not meet his goal. The total value of the cars he sold was at least $360,000. Let x be the number of $32,000 cars, and y be the number of $48,000 cars, that Tim sold last week. Which system of inequalities below represents the conditions described?

(A) $x+y \geq 10,\quad 32,000x+48,000y < 360,000$
(B) $x+y < 10,\quad 32,000x+48,000y \geq 360,000$
(C) $x+y > 10,\quad 32,000x+48,000y \leq 360,000$
(D) $x+y \geq 10,\quad 32,000x+48,000y \geq 360,000$

10. If r men can paint a house in t days, how long will it take s men to do the same job?

(A) $\dfrac{rs}{t}$

(B) rst

(C) $\dfrac{rt}{s}$

(D) $\dfrac{st}{r}$

NEXT PAGE

Price per Pound of Materials

Materials	USDs ($)	EUROs (€)
A	3	2.49
B	9	7.48
C	15	12.46
D	9	7.48

The chart above gives the prices of four different materials expressed in both USDs and EUROs. Let u be USDs and e be EUROs.

11. If the $ 24,000 in a shipment come entirely from a pounds of material A, b pounds of material B, and d pounds of material D, which of the following represents a in terms of b and d ?

(A) $a = 8000 + 3(b+d)$

(B) $a = 8000 - 9(b+d)$

(C) $a = 8000 - 9(b-d)$

(D) $a = 8000 - 3(b+d)$

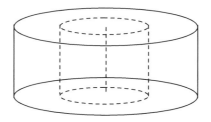

12. In the figure above, the right circular cylinder has a radius of 2 units and a height of 3 units. A cylindrical hole is made through the center as shown, with a diameter of 2 units. What is the area of the total surfaces of the solid?

(A) 32π

(B) 16π

(C) 24π

(D) 12π

13. Which of the following shifts of the graph of $y = x^2$ can result in the graph of $y = x^2 - 12x + h$, where h is a constant less than 36 ?

(A) Right 6 units and down $(h - 36)$

(B) Right 6 units and down $|h - 36|$

(C) Left 6 units and down $(h - 6)$

(D) Right 6 units and up $|h - 36|$

14. A circle is circumscribed about a given square and another circle is inscribed in the same square. What is the ratio of the radius of the inscribed circle to the radius of the circumscribed circle?

(A) $\sqrt{2} : 1$

(B) $\sqrt{2} : 2$

(C) $1 : 2$

(D) $2 : \sqrt{2}$

15 If $2p + 2(r + 2) = q$, what is $r - 2$ in terms of p and q ?

(A) $\dfrac{q}{2} - 2p$

(B) $\dfrac{q}{2} - p - 4$

(C) $\dfrac{2p - q}{2}$

(D) $\dfrac{q}{2} - p + 4$

NEXT PAGE

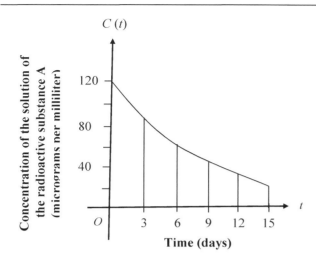

In the graph and chart above show the information about the concentration of the solution of the radioactive substance A and the corresponding time.

16. By the chart, how many more micrograms of the substance are present in 6 milliliters 6 days after the time beginning than are present in 8 milliliters 12 days after the time beginning?

Time (days)	Concentration of the solution of the radioactive substance A (micrograms per milliliter)
0	120
3	85
6	61
9	43
12	31
15	21

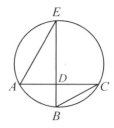

Note: Figure above not drawn to scale.

17. If $\overline{BE}$ is perpendicular to $\overline{AC}$, $DE = 8$, $BD = 3$, and $DC = 4$, what is AE?

NEXT PAGE

Questions 18 and 19 are followed the information below:

The acceleration of a motorcycle is a function involving time elapsed. *T* represents the time, in seconds, lapsed and

$$A\ (T) = 15T^2 + 120T + 86$$

represents the acceleration of the motorcycle.

18. What is the time when the acceleration is 386?

19. What is the acceleration when the time is 5 seconds?

20.   If a company charge *d* dollars for their product, where $0 \le d \le 100$, the income from the product will be $I(d) = 1000d - 10d^2$ dollars per day. By this model, for what values of *d* would the company's daily income for the product be the maximum?

STOP

No Test Contents

On This Page

Go to Next Page

Math Test – Calculator

Time: 55 Minutes
38 Questions

Notes:
- The use of a calculator is not allowed.
- All numbers used in this section are the real number.
- Figures are provided for some problems in this test. Unless otherwise indicated under the figure "Note: Figure above not drawn to scale", all figures are drawn as accurately as possible.
- All figures lie in a plane EXCEPT otherwise specified.
- Unless otherwise indicated, the domain of any function f, g or j is assumed to be the set of all real numbers x for which $f(x)$, $g(x)$, or $j(x)$ is a real number.

Reference Information

$$A = \frac{1}{2}bh$$

$$A = lw$$

$$A = \pi r^2$$

$$V = \pi r^2 h$$

$$V = lwh$$

$$c^2 = a^2 + b^2$$

$$V = \frac{1}{3}\pi r^2 h$$

$$V = \frac{4}{3}\pi r^3$$

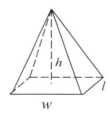

$$V = \frac{1}{3}lwh$$

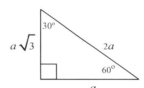

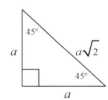

1. For all positive t, function f is defined by $f(t) = \left(\dfrac{1}{x}\right)^t$, where x is a non-zero constant. Which of the following is equal to $f(3t)$?

(A) $3f(t)$

(B) $6f(t)$

(C) $\left(f(t)\right)^3$

(D) $9f(t)$

2 If m is 25% of q and p is 35% of q, what is $x = p - m$, in terms of q?

(A) $10\%q$

(B) $20\%q$

(C) $30\%q$

(D) $40\%q$

3. If $125^{\frac{4}{x}} = 25$, then x is equal to

(A) 4

(B) 3

(C) 6

(D) 5

4. In right triangle ABC, if the hypotenuse $AB = 15$, $BC = 12$, and $AC = 9$, then the cosine of $\angle B$ is

(A) $\dfrac{1}{5}$

(B) $\dfrac{4}{5}$

(C) $\dfrac{3}{5}$

(D) $\dfrac{5}{3}$

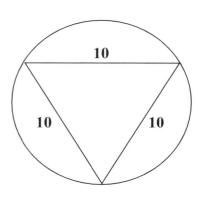

5. In the figure above, the triangle is an equilateral one. It is inscribed in the circle. What is the area A of the non-triangle inside the circle?

(A) $\dfrac{100}{3}\pi - 25\sqrt{2}$ (B) $\dfrac{100}{3}\pi - 25\sqrt{3}$ (C) $\dfrac{104}{3}\pi - 25\sqrt{3}$

(D) $\dfrac{100}{3}\pi - 24\sqrt{3}$

NEXT PAGE

Median	82
Mean	77
Standard Deviation	8
Lower quartile	75
Upper quartile	90

6.   The statistical information above provides a summary

of math scores of 200 students at West Water High School.

Approximate 100 of the students in the statistical information

have math scores

(A) from 70 to 89.

(B) less than 77.

(C) from 75 to 90.

(D) less than 90.

7.   If $\dfrac{\pi}{2} < x_1 < \pi$ and $\pi < x_2 < \dfrac{3\pi}{2}$, which of the

following equations must be false?

(A) $\cos x_1 = \cos x_2$

(B) $\tan x_1 = \sin x_2$

(C) $\tan x_1 = \cos x_2$

(D) $\sin x_1 = \cos x_2$

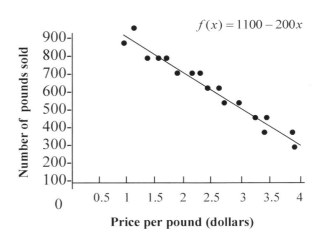

A supermarket sells pounds of peanutbutters and decides the

price per pound every month. The scatterplot above shows

the price and the number of pounds of peanutbutters sold for

17 months with the line of best fit and the equation for the line.

8.   What is the best explanation of the meaning of the

y-intercept of the line of best fit?

(A)   The y-intercept is -200. This means that for every dollar,

the supermarket expects to sell 200 fewer pounds of peanutbutters,

but the price of a pound of peanutbutters increases.

(B) The y-intercept is 1,100. We should only trust the prediction of

sales for the prices between $1 and $4.

(C) The y-intercept is 1,100. We should only trust the prediction of

sales for the prices between $0 and $4.

(D) The y-intercept is 5.5. We should only trust the prediction of

sales for the prices between $1 and $4.

NEXT PAGE

9. If $x > 0$, $y > 0$, and y is directly proportional to square root of x, which of the following is inversely proportional to $\sqrt{y}$?

(A) $y^{\frac{1}{4}}$

(B) $x^{\frac{1}{4}}$

(C) $y^{-\frac{1}{4}}$

(D) $x^{-\frac{1}{4}}$

10. If $k = 7^b$, then $7^{3b-3} =$

(A) $\dfrac{k^3}{343}$

(B) k^{3+7^3}

(C) 7^{3+k^3}

(D) $343k^3$

11. If $i = \sqrt{-1}$, what are the real numbers?

I. $i^{25} - i^{26}$

II. i^{25}

III. $i^{25} + i^{26} + i^{27}$

(A) I only

(B) II only

(C) III only

(D) I and II only

NEXT PAGE

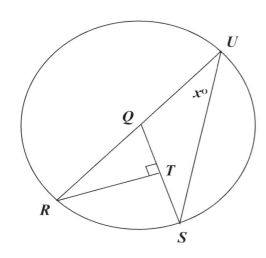

12. In the figure above, $\overline{RU}$ is a diameter and $\overline{RT}$ bisects radius QS, which of the following is the value of $2x$?

(A) 30   (B) 15   (C) 45   (D) 60

13. A box is shifting along the line $y = -0.5x + 3$ at a speed of 3 yards per minute. How many minutes will it take for the box to touch the y-axis if the box starts at x-intercept and shifts to the left along the line?

(A) 6.71

(B) 2.24

(C) 4.42

(D) 1.67

NEXT PAGE

14 If $\dfrac{y}{x} = \dfrac{6}{7}$, what is the value of $\dfrac{7y}{6x}$?

(A) 1

(B) $\left(\dfrac{7}{6}\right)^2$

(C) $\dfrac{14}{12}$

(D) $\dfrac{36}{49}$

p	q
1	1
2	4
3	9

16. Several values for the variables p and q are shown in the chart above. Which of the following could be inversely proportional to p ?

(A) q^2

(B) $\sqrt{q}$

(C) $\left(\sqrt{q}\right)^{-1}$

(D) $\dfrac{q}{2}$

$$\dfrac{x}{24} = \dfrac{6}{x}$$

15. What is one possible value of x that could be the solution of the equation above?

(A) -12

(B) $\dfrac{1}{4}$

(C) 144

(D) 10

NEXT PAGE

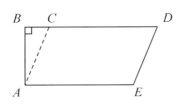

Note: Figure above not drawn to scale.

17. In the figure above, the length of segment $\overline{AB}$ is 8, and the length of each side of quadrilareral $ACDE$ is 10. What is the area of quadrilareral $ABDE$?

(A) 128

(B) 104

(C) 108

(D) 106

18.   If k kilometers are equal to m miles, how many kilometers are equal to M miles?

(A) km

(B) kmM

(C) $\dfrac{kM}{m}$

(D) kM

19. If a and b are integers such that $a^2 = 64$ and $3b^3 = 81$, which of the following could be true ?

  I. $a = 8$
  II. $b = -3$
  III. $a + b = -5$

(A) I only

(B) I and III

(C) II and III

(D) II only

NEXT PAGE

20. The expression $\dfrac{2x-1}{3}+\dfrac{x+5}{3}$ is how much more than

$x-1$?

(A) 7/3

(B) 3/7

(C) 7/4

(D) 4/7

y	9	m	n
x	0	1	2

22. The values of m and n in the chart above are related so that $(y+1)$ is directly proportional to $(x-1)$. What is the sum of m and n?

(A) 10

(B)-12

(C) 14

(D)-16

21. If the equations of 2 lines are $y = 4x + 3$ and $y = 3x + 4$, respectively, and the two lines intersect, what is the absolute value of the difference of the x-coordinate and y-coordinate?

(A) 5

(B) 6

(C) 4

(D) 3

NEXT PAGE

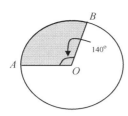

Note that figure not drawn to scale.

23.   Point O is the center of the circle above. What fraction of the area of the the circle is the area of the shaded portion?

(A) $\dfrac{18}{7}$

(B) $\dfrac{7}{16}$

(C) $\dfrac{11}{18}$

(D) $\dfrac{7}{18}$

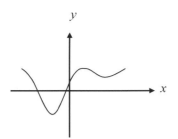

24.   The graph of a function $f(x)$ is shown above. Which of the following could be the graph of $\left| f(x) \right|$?

(A)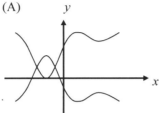

(B)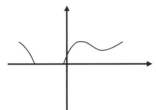

(C)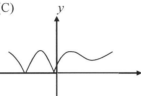

(D)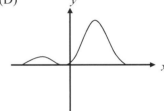

NEXT PAGE

25. What are the values of x in the equation $(2x + 4)^2 = 16$?

(A) $(0, 4)$

(B) $(4, 0)$

(C) $(-4, 0)$

(D) $(0, -4)$

27. At East River School, the volleyball club has 12 members and the basketball club has 16 members. If a total of 20 students belong to only either volleyball club or basketball club, how many students belong to both clubs?

(A) 8
(B) 4
(C) 9
(D) 7

28. A 16-liter solution of acid and water is 25% acid. How many liters of acid must be added to increase the concentration of acid in the solution to 50%?

(A) 8
(B) 4
(C) 5
(D) 6

26. What is the solution to the equation $\sqrt{x - 2} = -4$?

(A) no solution

(B) 18

(C) 16

(D) 12

NEXT PAGE

29. If $\sin x = -u$, $u > 0$, in $\dfrac{\pi}{2} < x < \dfrac{3}{2}\pi$, which of the

following must be true for $\tan x$?

(A) $\dfrac{u}{\sqrt{1^2 - u^2}}$

(B) $\dfrac{\sqrt{1^2 - u^2}}{u}$

(C) $\sqrt{1^2 - u^2}$

(D) $\pm \dfrac{u}{\sqrt{1^2 - u^2}}$

30. An insect population is growing in such a way: number in each generation is approximately 2 times of the previous generation. If there are 1,000 insects in the first generation, approximately how many insects will there be in the fifth generation?

(A) 32,000
(B) 10,000
(C) 8,000
(D) 16,000

NEXT PAGE

31. If $x - 2$ is 1 less than $y + 5$, then $x + 3$ exceeds y by what amount?

32. At a snack bar, Frank bought 5 hamburgers and 3 bottled waters for a total of $16. Henry paid the same prices for the hamburger and bottled water. Henry bought 4 hamburgers and 2 bottled waters for a total of $12. What is the the total cost of one hamburger and one bottled water? (Disregard the sign $ when gridding)

33. If Harry takes 3 minutes to travel from place P to place Q at a constant speed of 30 miles per one-half of hour, how many minutes does he take to travel the same route from place Q to place P at a constant speed of 40 miles per hour?

34. Martin is 32 years older than his daughter May. In nine years, he will be two times as old as May will be. How old is Martin?

NEXT PAGE

35. Jennifer, a salesperson of a computer wholesale company, sells a computer of $840. It makes a 20% profit. During an on sale period, the profit is cut to 6%. What is the final price of the computer? (Disregard the sign $ when gridding.)

x	$g(x)$	$f(x)$
2	-1	2
1	0	-1
0	1	-2
-1	2	3
-2	3	4

37 According to chart above, what is the value of $g(-2) - f(1)$?

38. The area of a garden enclosed is a rectangle. The three sides of the rectangle are enclosed by 80 feet of fence and another side is bounded by the wall of a building. What is the value of the width if the garden reaches its maximum area?

36. At Whitewater High School, a history class has 25 students in it. Of those students, 12 are enrolled in biology and 14 are enrolled in chemistry. What is the minimum percent of the students in the history class who are also enrolled in biology and chemistry? (Disregard the sign % when gridding.)

STOP

Answer Key
For
SAT Math Practice Test 12

Section 3

1	A
2	C
3	A
4	C
5	D
6	B
7	C
8	D
9	B
10	C
11	D
12	C
13	B
14	B
15	B

16	118
17	10
18	2
19	1061
20	50

Section 4

1	C	16	C
2	A	17	B
3	C	18	C
4	B	19	B
5	B	20	A
6	C	21	B
7	D	22	B
8	B	23	D
9	D	24	C
10	A	25	D
11	C	26	A
12	D	27	B
13	B	28	A
14	A	29	A
15	A	30	D

31	9
32	4
33	9/2 or 4.5
34	55
35	742
36	4
37	4
38	20

SAT Math

Practice

Test 12

Explanations

Redesigned for Tests in March 2016 and Beyond

Mad Math

Math Test – No Calculator

Time: 25 Minutes
20 Questions

Notes:
- The use of a calculator is not allowed.
- All numbers used in this section are the real number.
- Figures are provided for some problems in this test. Unless otherwise indicated under the figure "Note: Figure above not drawn to scale", all figures are drawn as accurately as possible.
- All figures lie in a plane EXCEPT otherwise specified.
- Unless otherwise indicated, the domain of any function f, g or j is assumed to be the set of all real numbers x for which $f(x)$, $g(x)$, or $j(x)$ is a real number.

Reference Information

$A = \dfrac{1}{2}bh$

$A = lw$

$A = \pi r^2$

$V = \pi r^2 h$

$V = lwh$

$c^2 = a^2 + b^2$

$V = \dfrac{1}{3}\pi r^2 h$

$V = \dfrac{4}{3}\pi r^3$

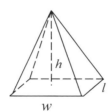

$V = \dfrac{1}{3}lwh$

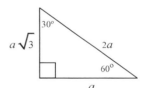

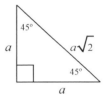

1. If $f(x) = x - \sqrt{x-1}$, at which of the following values of x is $f(x)$ undefined?

(A) 0

(B) 3

(C) 2

(D) 1

> Solution: Answer: (A)
> $$x - 1 < 0, \quad x < 1$$
> $$\Downarrow$$
> Only $x = 0$ is less than
> 1 among the 4 choices.

2. If $x^2 = 8$, what is the value of $(x-1)(x+1)$?

(A) 0
(B) 9
(C) 7
(D) 5

> Solution: Answer: (C)
> $$(x-1)(x+1) = x^2 - 1$$
> $$\Downarrow$$
> $$8 - 1 = 7$$

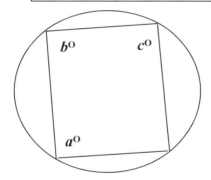

Note: Figure above is not drawn to scale.

3. In the figure above, a circle comscribes a quadrilateral. Which of the following must be true?

(A) $a° + c° = 180°$

(B) $b° + c° = 180°$

(C) $b° + a° = 180°$

(D) $b° + c° + a° = 270°$

> Solution: Answer: (A)
> A quadrilateral may not a parallerogram.
> Use the conclusion: If a quadrilateral is inscribed
> in a circle, the sum of the opposite angles are $180°$.

4. $\cot 0 = ?$

(A) $\sin 0$

(B) $\sin \dfrac{\pi}{2}$

(C) $\tan \dfrac{\pi}{2}$

(D) $\cos \dfrac{3\pi}{2}$

> Solution: Answer: (C)
> $$\tan \frac{\pi}{2} = \text{undefined}$$
> $$\cot 0 = \text{undefined}$$
> $$\Downarrow$$
> $$\tan \frac{\pi}{2} = \cot 0$$

5. If $g(x) = 3x - 2$ and $g(x-1) - g(x) = 5x$, then $x =$

(A) $\dfrac{5}{3}$

(B) $-\dfrac{5}{3}$

(C) $\dfrac{3}{5}$

(D) $-\dfrac{3}{5}$

> Solution: Answer: (D)
> $$g(x-1) = 3(x-1) - 2$$
> $$\downarrow$$
> $$3x - 3 - 2 = 3x - 5$$
> $$\downarrow$$
> $$g(x-1) - g(x)$$
> $$\downarrow$$
> $$(3x - 5) - (3x - 2) = -3$$
> By the condition of this question,
> $$g(x-1) - g(x) = 5x$$
> $$\Downarrow$$
> $$-3 = 5x, \quad x = -\frac{3}{5}$$

6. Which of the following expression is not equal to $\dfrac{2}{3}$?

(A) $\dfrac{5}{6} - \dfrac{1}{6}$

(B) $\dfrac{\frac{4}{3}}{\frac{1}{2}}$

(C) $\dfrac{\frac{4}{3}}{2}$

(D) $\sqrt{\dfrac{16}{36}}$

> Solution: Answer: (B)
> Use plug-in method.
> $$\Downarrow$$
> $$(B) = \frac{\frac{4}{3}}{\frac{1}{2}} = \frac{\frac{4}{3} \times 6}{\frac{1}{2} \times 6} = \frac{8}{3} \neq \frac{2}{3}$$

NEXT PAGE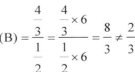

7. $\dfrac{\sqrt{3}-1}{1-\sqrt{5}} =$

(A) $\dfrac{\left(\sqrt{3}-1\right)\left(1+\sqrt{5}\right)}{6}$

(B) $\dfrac{\left(\sqrt{3}-1\right)\left(1-\sqrt{5}\right)}{4}$

(C) $-\dfrac{\left(\sqrt{3}-1\right)\left(1+\sqrt{5}\right)}{4}$

(D) $\dfrac{\left(\sqrt{3}-1\right)\left(1\pm\sqrt{5}\right)}{4}$

Solution: Answer: (C)

$$\dfrac{\sqrt{3}-1}{1-\sqrt{5}} = \dfrac{\sqrt{3}-1}{1-\sqrt{5}} \cdot \dfrac{1+\sqrt{5}}{1+\sqrt{5}}$$

$$\downarrow$$

$$\dfrac{\left(\sqrt{3}-1\right)\left(1+\sqrt{5}\right)}{1^2 - \left(\sqrt{5}\right)^2}$$

$$\Downarrow$$

$$-\dfrac{\left(\sqrt{3}-1\right)\left(1+\sqrt{5}\right)}{4}$$

8. Tom, an owner of a computer retail store, sells a computer of $780. It makes a 30% profit. During an on sale period, the profit is cut to 16%. What is the final price of the computer?

(A) 616
(B) 612
(C) 722
(D) 696

Solution: Answer: (D)

$$780 = 1.3y$$

$$\downarrow$$

$$78\overset{6}{\cancel{0}}00 = \cancel{13}\,y$$

$$y = 600$$

$$\downarrow$$

$$600 \times 1.16 = 696$$

$$\Downarrow$$

$$x = 6 \times 116 = 696$$

9. Tim is a car salesperson. He sells two kinds of cars. For one of them, the selling price is $32,000, and for another one, the selling price is $48,000. Last week, Tim's goal was to sell 10 cars. He did not meet his goal. The total value of the cars he sold was at least $360,000. Let x be the number of $32,000 cars, and y be the number of $48,000 cars, that Tim sold last week. Which system of inequalities below represents the conditions described?

(A) $x+y \geq 10$, $32,000x + 48,000y < 360,000$

(B) $x+y < 10$, $32,000x + 48,000y \geq 360,000$

(C) $x+y > 10$, $32,000x + 48,000y \leq 360,000$

(D) $x+y \geq 10$, $32,000x + 48,000y \geq 360,000$

Solution: Answer: (B)

$\begin{cases} \text{"goal was to sell 10 cars"} \rightarrow \text{Use sign =,} \\ \qquad \text{but "did not meet his goal"} \end{cases}$

$$\downarrow$$

Use sign $<$.

"at least" $\rightarrow$ Use sign $\geq$.

$$\Downarrow$$

$$x + y < 10$$
$$32,000x + 48,000y \geq 360,000$$

10. If r men can paint a house in t days, how long will it take s men to do the same job?

(A) $\dfrac{rs}{t}$

(B) rst

(C) $\dfrac{rt}{s}$

(D) $\dfrac{st}{r}$

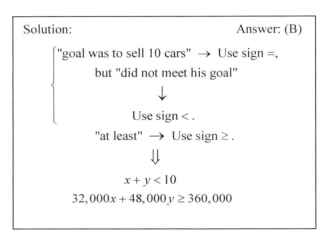

Solution: Answer: (C)

men $\uparrow$, days $\downarrow$

$$\downarrow$$

inverse proportionrelationship

Use the equation below.

$$\square_3 \cdot x = \square_1 \cdot \square_2$$

$$\Downarrow$$

$$x \cdot s = r \cdot t, \quad x = \boxed{\dfrac{rt}{s}}$$

NEXT PAGE ⟩

Price per Pound of Materials

Materials	USDs ($)	EUROs (€)
A	3	2.49
B	9	7.48
C	15	12.46
D	9	7.48

The chart above gives the prices of four different materials expressed in both USDs and EUROs. Let u be USDs and e be EUROs.

11. If the $ 24,000 in a shipment come entirely from a pounds of material A, b pounds of material B, and d pounds of material D, which of the following represents a in terms of b and d ?

(A) $a = 8000 + 3(b+d)$

(B) $a = 8000 - 9(b+d)$

(C) $a = 8000 - 9(b-d)$

(D) $a = 8000 - 3(b+d)$

Solution: Answer: (D)
$$24000 = 3a + 9b + 9d$$
$$\downarrow$$
$$24000 = 3a + 9(b+d), \quad 24000 - 9(b+d) = 3a$$
$$\Downarrow$$
$$a = 8000 - 3(b+d)$$

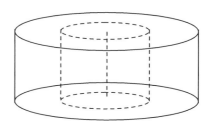

12. In the figure above, the right circular cylinder has a radius of 2 units and a height of 3 units. A cylindrical hole is made through the center as shown, with a diameter of 2 units. What is the area of the total surfaces of the solid?

(A) 32π

(B) 16π

(C) 24π

(D) 12π

Solution: Answer: (C)

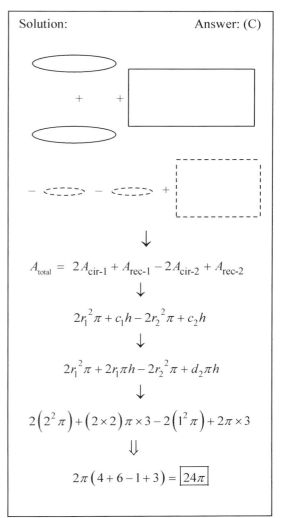

$$A_{\text{total}} = 2A_{\text{cir-1}} + A_{\text{rec-1}} - 2A_{\text{cir-2}} + A_{\text{rec-2}}$$
$$\downarrow$$
$$2r_1^2\pi + c_1h - 2r_2^2\pi + c_2h$$
$$\downarrow$$
$$2r_1^2\pi + 2r_1\pi h - 2r_2^2\pi + d_2\pi h$$
$$\downarrow$$
$$2(2^2\pi) + (2 \times 2)\pi \times 3 - 2(1^2\pi) + 2\pi \times 3$$
$$\Downarrow$$
$$2\pi(4 + 6 - 1 + 3) = \boxed{24\pi}$$

NEXT PAGE ⟶

13. Which of the following shifts of the graph of $y = x^2$ can result in the graph of $y = x^2 - 12x + h$, where h is a constant less than 36 ?

(A) Right 6 units and down $(h - 36)$

(B) Right 6 units and down $|h - 36|$

(C) Left 6 units and down $(h - 6)$

(D) Right 6 units and up $|h - 36|$

Solution: Answer: (B)

$$y = x^2 - 12x + h$$

$$\downarrow$$

$$y = x^2 - 12x + 6^2 + h - 6^2$$

$$\downarrow$$

$$y = (x - 6)^2 + \left(h - 36\right)$$

$$(x - 6)^2 \text{ and } h < 36$$

$$\Downarrow$$

Right 6 units and down $|h - 36|$ units

14. A circle is circumscribed about a given square and another circle is inscribed in the same square. What is the ratio of the radius of the inscribed circle to the radius of the circumscribed circle?

(A) $\sqrt{2} : 1$

(B) $\sqrt{2} : 2$

(C) $1 : 2$

(D) $2 : \sqrt{2}$

Solution: Answer: (B)

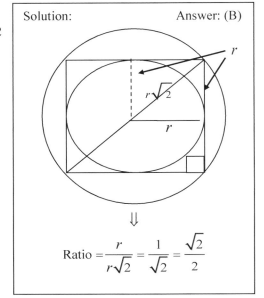

$$\Downarrow$$

$$\text{Ratio} = \frac{r}{r\sqrt{2}} = \frac{1}{\sqrt{2}} = \frac{\sqrt{2}}{2}$$

15 If $2p + 2(r + 2) = q$, what is $r - 2$ in terms of p and q ?

(A) $\dfrac{q}{2} - 2p$

(B) $\dfrac{q}{2} - p - 4$

(C) $\dfrac{2p - q}{2}$

(D) $\dfrac{q}{2} - p + 4$

Solution: Answer: (B)

$$2(r + 2) = q - 2p$$

$$\downarrow$$

$$r + 2 = \frac{q - 2p}{2}$$

$$\downarrow$$

$$r + 2 - \left(4\right) = \frac{q - 2p}{2} - \left(4\right)$$

$$\downarrow$$

$$\frac{q}{2} - \frac{2p}{2} - \left(4\right)$$

$$\Downarrow$$

$$\frac{q}{2} - p - 4$$

NEXT PAGE

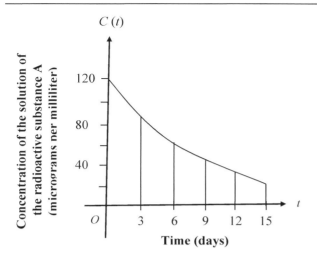

Time (days)	Concentration of the solution of the radioactive substance A (micrograms per milliliter)
0	120
3	85
6	61
9	43
12	31
15	21

In the graph and chart above show the information about the concentration of the solution of the radioactive substance A and the corresponding time.

16. By the chart, how many more micrograms of the substance are present in 6 milliliters 6 days after the time beginning than are present in 8 milliliters 12 days after the time beginning?

Solution: Answer: 118
$$(6 \times 61) - (8 \times 31)$$
$$\Downarrow$$
$$366 - 248 = 118$$

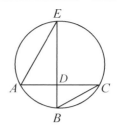

Note: Figure above not drawn to scale.

17. If $\overline{BE}$ is perpendicular to $\overline{AC}$, $DE = 8$, $BD = 3$, and $DC = 4$, what is AE?

Solution: Answer: 10

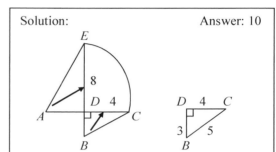

$\angle AEB$ and $\angle ACB$ face the same arc AB.

$\downarrow$

They have the same angle measure.

The 2 triangles have the same 3 pairs of angles.
                                    interior

$\downarrow$

They are similar triangles.

$\downarrow$

The ratios of the corresponding sides are equal.

$\downarrow$

$$\frac{AE}{BC} = \frac{8}{4}$$

$\Downarrow$

$$\frac{AE}{5} = \frac{8}{4}, \quad AE = \boxed{10}$$

NEXT PAGE

Questions 18 and 19 are followed the information below:

The acceleration of a motorcycle is a function involving time elapsed. T represents the time, in seconds, lapsed and
$$A(T) = 15T^2 + 120T + 86$$
represents the acceleration of the motorcycle.

18. What is the time when the acceleration is 386?

> Solution: Answer: 2
>
> $$386 = 15T^2 + 120T + 86$$
> $\downarrow$
> $$T^2 + 8T - 20 = 0,\ (T + 10)(T-2) = 0$$
> $\Downarrow$
> $$T = 2, -10$$

19. What is the acceleration when the time is 5 seconds?

> Solution: Answer: 1061
>
> $$A(5) = 15 \cdot 5^2 + 120 \cdot 5 + 86 = 1061$$

20. If a company charge d dollars for their product, where $0 \le d \le 100$, the income from the product will be $I(d) = 1000d - 10d^2$ dollars per day. By this model, for what values of d would the company's daily income for the product be the maximum?

> Solution: Answer: 50
>
> $\begin{cases} \text{This function is a quadratic function.} \\ \qquad\qquad \downarrow \\ \text{Its graph is a parabola.} \end{cases}$
>
> The graph opens down because $a = -10 < 0$.
>
> When $d = -\dfrac{b}{2a}$, $I(d) =$ maximum value.
>
> $$b = 1000,\ a = -10$$
> $\Downarrow$
> $$d = -\frac{1000}{2 \cdot (-10)} = 50$$

STOP

No Test Contents

On This Page

Go to Next Page

Math Test – Calculator

Time: 55 Minutes
38 Questions

Notes:
- The use of a calculator is not allowed.
- All numbers used in this section are the real number.
- Figures are provided for some problems in this test. Unless otherwise indicated under the figure "Note: Figure above not drawn to scale", all figures are drawn as accurately as possible.
- All figures lie in a plane EXCEPT otherwise specified.
- Unless otherwise indicated, the domain of any function f, g or j is assumed to be the set of all real numbers x for which $f(x)$, $g(x)$, or $j(x)$ is a real number.

Reference Information

$$A = \frac{1}{2}bh$$

$$A = lw$$

$$A = \pi r^2$$

$$V = \pi r^2 h$$

$$V = lwh$$

$$c^2 = a^2 + b^2$$

$$V = \frac{1}{3}\pi r^2 h$$

$$V = \frac{4}{3}\pi r^3$$

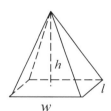

$$V = \frac{1}{3}lwh$$

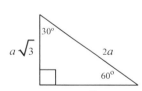

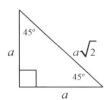

Copying or reuse of any portion of this page is illegal.

1. For all positive t, function f is defined by $f(t) = \left(\dfrac{1}{x}\right)^t$, where x is a non-zero constant. Which of the following is equal to $f(3t)$?

(A) $3f(t)$

(B) $6f(t)$

(C) $\left(f(t)\right)^3$

(D) $9f(t)$

Solution: Answer: (C)

x is a letter. Now it is not an input.

$$f(3t) = \left(\frac{1}{x}\right)^{3t} = \left(\left(\frac{1}{x}\right)^t\right)^3$$

$\Downarrow$

$$f(3t) = \left(f(t)\right)^3$$

2. If m is 25% of q and p is 35% of q, what is $x = p - m$, in terms of q?

(A) $10\%q$

(B) $20\%q$

(C) $30\%q$

(D) $40\%q$

Solution: Answer: (A)

$$p - m = \frac{35}{100}q - \frac{25}{100}q$$

$\Downarrow$

$$\frac{10}{100}q$$

3. If $125^{\frac{4}{x}} = 25$, then x is equal to

(A) 4

(B) 3

(C) 6

(D) 5

Solution: Answer: (C)

$$\left(5^3\right)^{\frac{4}{x}} = 5^2 \rightarrow 5^{\frac{12}{x}} = 5^2$$

$\Downarrow$

$$\frac{12}{x} = 2, \quad x = 6$$

4. In right triangle ABC, if the hypotenuse $AB = 15$, $BC = 12$, and $AC = 9$, then the cosine of $\angle B$ is

(A) $\dfrac{1}{5}$

(B) $\dfrac{4}{5}$

(C) $\dfrac{3}{5}$

(D) $\dfrac{5}{3}$

Solution: Answer: (B)

$\Downarrow$

$$\cos B = \frac{12}{15} = \frac{4}{5}$$

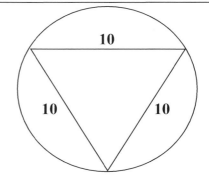

5. In the figure above, the triangle is an equilateral one. It is inscribed in the circle. What is the area A of the non-triangle inside the circle?

(A) $\dfrac{100}{3}\pi - 25\sqrt{2}$

(B) $\dfrac{100}{3}\pi - 25\sqrt{3}$

(C) $\dfrac{104}{3}\pi - 25\sqrt{3}$

(D) $\dfrac{100}{3}\pi - 24\sqrt{3}$

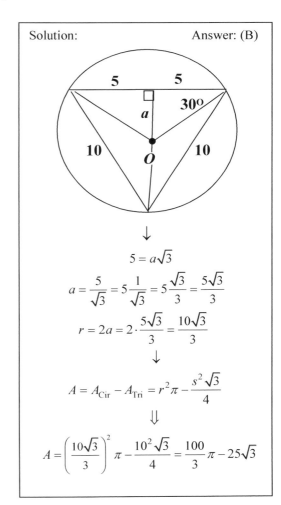

Solution: Answer: (B)

$\downarrow$

$$5 = a\sqrt{3}$$

$$a = \frac{5}{\sqrt{3}} = 5\frac{1}{\sqrt{3}} = 5\frac{\sqrt{3}}{3} = \frac{5\sqrt{3}}{3}$$

$$r = 2a = 2 \cdot \frac{5\sqrt{3}}{3} = \frac{10\sqrt{3}}{3}$$

$\downarrow$

$$A = A_{\text{Cir}} - A_{\text{Tri}} = r^2\pi - \frac{s^2\sqrt{3}}{4}$$

$\Downarrow$

$$A = \left(\frac{10\sqrt{3}}{3}\right)^2 \pi - \frac{10^2\sqrt{3}}{4} = \frac{100}{3}\pi - 25\sqrt{3}$$

NEXT PAGE

Median	82
Mean	77
Standard Deviation	8
Lower quartile	75
Upper quartile	90

6.   The statistical information above provides a summary of math scores of 200 students at West Water High School. Approximate 100 of the students in the statistical information have math scores

(A) from 70 to 89.

(B) less than 77.

(C) from 75 to 90.

(D) less than 90.

Solution: Answer: (C)

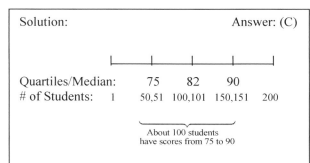

Quartiles/Median: 75   82   90
# of Students: 1   50,51   100,101   150,151   200

About 100 students
have scores from 75 to 90

Note: Number 75 represents the lower quartile;
       Number 90 represents the upper quartile.

7.   If $\dfrac{\pi}{2} < x_1 < \pi$ and $\pi < x_2 < \dfrac{3\pi}{2}$, which of the following equations must be false?

(A) $\cos x_1 = \cos x_2$

(B) $\tan x_1 = \sin x_2$

(C) $\tan x_1 = \cos x_2$

(D) $\sin x_1 = \cos x_2$

Solution: Answer: (D)

The value of $\sin x_1 > 0$

The value of $\cos x_2 < 0$

$\Downarrow$

$\sin x_1 \neq \cos x_2$

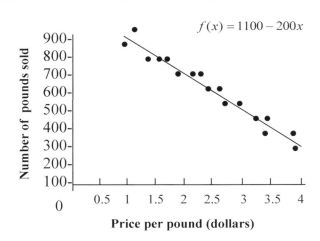

$f(x) = 1100 - 200x$

A supermarket sells pounds of peanutbutters and decides the price per pound every month. The scatterplot above shows the price and the number of pounds of peanutbutters sold for 17 months with the line of best fit and the equation for the line.

8.   What is the best explanation of the meaning of the y-intercept of the line of best fit?

(A) The y-intercept is -200. This means that for every dollar, the supermarket expects to sell 200 fewer pounds of peanutbutters, but the price of a pound of peanutbutters increases.

(B) The y-intercept is $1,100$. We should only trust the prediction of sales for the prices between $1 and $4.

(C) The y-intercept is $1,100$. We should only trust the prediction of sales for the prices between $0 and $4.

(D) The y-intercept is 5.5. We should only trust the prediction of sales for the prices between $1 and $4.

Solution: Answer: (B)

   The y-intercept is $1,100$. We should only trust the prediction of sales for the prices between $1 and $4. When $x = \$0$, y-intercept $= 1,100$. That means 1.100 pounds of peanutbutters are free. In general, it is not realistic.

NEXT PAGE ⟩

9. If $x > 0$, $y > 0$, and y is directly proportional to square root of x, which of the following is inversely proportional to $\sqrt{y}$?

(A) $y^{\frac{1}{4}}$

(B) $x^{\frac{1}{4}}$

(C) $y^{-\frac{1}{4}}$

(D) $x^{-\frac{1}{4}}$

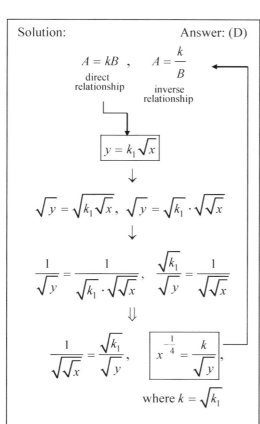

Solution:　　　　　　　　Answer: (D)

$A = kB$,　　$A = \dfrac{k}{B}$

direct relationship　　inverse relationship

$y = k_1 \sqrt{x}$

$\sqrt{y} = \sqrt{k_1 \sqrt{x}}, \quad \sqrt{y} = \sqrt{k_1} \cdot \sqrt{\sqrt{x}}$

$\dfrac{1}{\sqrt{y}} = \dfrac{1}{\sqrt{k_1} \cdot \sqrt{\sqrt{x}}}, \quad \dfrac{\sqrt{k_1}}{\sqrt{y}} = \dfrac{1}{\sqrt{\sqrt{x}}}$

$\Downarrow$

$\dfrac{1}{\sqrt{\sqrt{x}}} = \dfrac{\sqrt{k_1}}{\sqrt{y}}, \quad \boxed{x^{-\frac{1}{4}} = \dfrac{k}{\sqrt{y}}},$

where $k = \sqrt{k_1}$

10. If $k = 7^b$, then $7^{3b-3} =$

(A) $\dfrac{k^3}{343}$

(B) k^{3+7^3}

(C) 7^{3+k^3}

(D) $343k^3$

Solution:　　　　　Answer: (A)

$7^{3b-3} = 7^{3b} \cdot 7^{-3} = \left(7^b\right)^3 \cdot 7^{-3}$

$k = 7^b$

$\Downarrow$

$\left(k\right)^3 \cdot 7^{-3} = \dfrac{k^3}{7^3} = \dfrac{k^3}{343}$

11. If $i = \sqrt{-1}$, what are the real numbers?

I.　$i^{25} - i^{26}$

II.　i^{25}

III.　$i^{25} + i^{26} + i^{27}$

(A) I only

(B) II only

(C) III only

(D) I and II only

Solution:　　　　　　　　Answer: (C)

$\begin{cases} i^4 = 1 \\ i^{25} = i^{24} + i^1 = i \end{cases}$

I.　$i^{25} - i^{26} = i^{25}(1 - i)$

$\downarrow$

$i(1 - i) = i - i^2 = 1 + i$

(not real number)

II.　　　　$i^{25} = i$

(not real number)

III. $i^{25} + i^{26} + i^{27} = i^{25}(1 + i + i^2)$

$\downarrow$

$i(1 + i - 1) = i^2 = -1$

(real number)

$\Downarrow$

Answer is (C).

NEXT PAGE ⇨

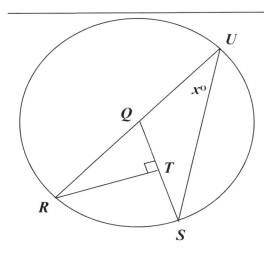

12. In the figure above, $\overline{RU}$ is a diameter and $\overline{RT}$ bisects radius QS, which of the following is the value of $2x$?

(A) 30   (B) 15   (C) 45   (D) 60

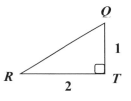

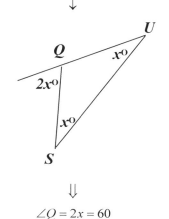

Solution: Answer: (D)

$$QS = QR$$

$$QT = \frac{1}{2}QS = \frac{1}{2}QR, \quad \frac{QR}{QT} = \frac{2}{1}$$

$\angle R = 30°, \quad \angle Q = 60°$

1 extrerio angle = sum of 2 non-adjacent angles

$\Downarrow$

$\angle Q = 2x = 60$

13. A box is shifting along the line $y = -0.5x + 3$ at a speed of 3 yards per minute. How many minutes will it take for the box to touch the y-axis if the box starts at x-intercept and shifts to the left along the line?

(A) 6.71
(B) 2.24
(C) 4.42
(D) 1.67

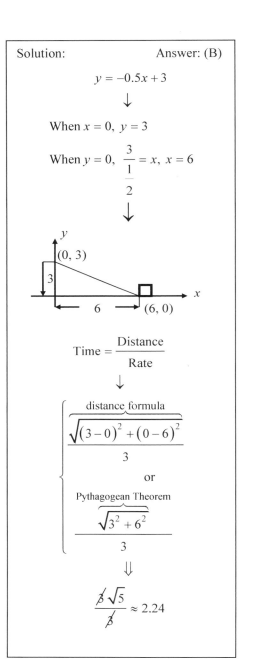

Solution: Answer: (B)

$$y = -0.5x + 3$$

$\downarrow$

When $x = 0$, $y = 3$

When $y = 0$, $\dfrac{3}{\frac{1}{2}} = x$, $x = 6$

$\downarrow$

$$\text{Time} = \frac{\text{Distance}}{\text{Rate}}$$

$\downarrow$

distance formula
$$\frac{\sqrt{(3-0)^2 + (0-6)^2}}{3}$$

or

Pythagogean Theorem
$$\frac{\sqrt{3^2 + 6^2}}{3}$$

$\Downarrow$

$$\frac{\cancel{3}\sqrt{5}}{\cancel{3}} \approx 2.24$$

NEXT PAGE

14 If $\dfrac{y}{x} = \dfrac{6}{7}$, what is the value of $\dfrac{7y}{6x}$?

(A) 1

(B) $\left(\dfrac{7}{6}\right)^2$

(C) $\dfrac{14}{12}$

(D) $\dfrac{36}{49}$

Solution: Answer: (A)

$$\dfrac{y}{x} = \dfrac{6}{7}$$

↓

$$\left(\dfrac{7}{6}\right) \times \dfrac{x}{y} = \dfrac{6}{7} \times \left(\dfrac{7}{6}\right)$$

⇓

$$\dfrac{7y}{6x} = 1$$

$$\dfrac{x}{24} = \dfrac{6}{x}$$

15. What is one possible value of x that could be the solution of the equation above?

(A) -12

(B) $\dfrac{1}{4}$

(C) 144

(D) 10

Solution: Answer: (A)

$$\dfrac{x}{24} = \dfrac{6}{x}$$

↓

$$x^2 = 24 \times 6 = 144$$

⇓

$$x = \pm\sqrt{144} = \pm 12$$

p	q
1	1
2	4
3	9

16.   Several values for the variables p and q are shown in the chart above. Which of the following could be inversely proportional to p ?

(A) q^2

(B) $\sqrt{q}$

(C) $\left(\sqrt{q}\right)^{-1}$

(D) $\dfrac{q}{2}$

Solution: Answer: (C)

$$A = \dfrac{k}{B}$$

↓

Change positions of p and q

"could be" → Let $k = 1$.

$$q = \dfrac{1}{p} \qquad\qquad q = \dfrac{1}{p}$$

1	1	$\left(\sqrt{1}\right)^{-1} = 1$
4	$\dfrac{1}{2}$	$\left(\sqrt{4}\right)^{-1} = \dfrac{1}{2}$
9	$\dfrac{1}{3}$	$\left(\sqrt{9}\right)^{-1} = \dfrac{1}{3}$

⇓

$$\left(\sqrt{q}\right)^{-1} = \dfrac{1}{p}$$

NEXT PAGE

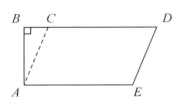

Note: Figure above not drawn to scale.

17. In the figure above, the length of segment $\overline{AB}$ is 8, and the length of each side of quadrilareral $ACDE$ is 10. What is the area of quadrilareral $ABDE$?

(A) 128

(B) 104

(C) 108

(D) 106

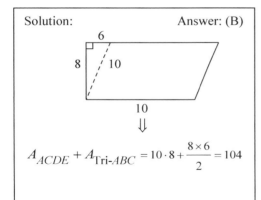

Solution: Answer: (B)

$$A_{ACDE} + A_{\text{Tri-}ABC} = 10 \cdot 8 + \frac{8 \times 6}{2} = 104$$

18. If k kilometers are equal to m miles, how many kilometers are equal to M miles?

(A) km

(B) kmM

(C) $\dfrac{kM}{m}$

(D) kM

Solution: Answer: (C)

kilometers ↑ , miles ↑

↓

direct relationship

↓

Use the equation.

$$\frac{x}{\Box_3} = \frac{\Box_{1x}}{\Box_2}$$

↓

$$\frac{x}{M} = \frac{k}{m}$$

⇓

$$x = \frac{kM}{m}$$

19. If a and b are integers such that $a^2 = 64$ and $3b^3 = 81$, which of the following could be true?

     I. $a = 8$

     II. $b = -3$

     III. $a + b = -5$

(A) I only

(B) I and III

(C) II and III

(D) II only

Solution: Answer: (B)

"Could be"

$$a^2 = 64, \ \left(\pm 8 \right)^2 = 64, \ a = \pm 8$$

$$3b^3 = 81, \ b^3 = 27, \ b = +3$$

↓

     I. $a = 8$ (could be)

     II. $b \neq -3$ (never)

     III. $a + b = -8 + 3 = -5$ (could be)

⇓

I and III

NEXT PAGE

20. The expression $\dfrac{2x-1}{3} + \dfrac{x+5}{3}$ is how much more than $x - 1$?

(A) 7/3

(B) 3/7

(C) 7/4

(D) 4/7

Solution: Answer: (A)

Use one denominator.

$\downarrow$

$$\dfrac{2x-1+x+5-3(x-1)}{3}$$

$\Downarrow$

$$\dfrac{\cancel{3}x + 4 \,\cancel{-3x} + 3}{3} = \dfrac{7}{3}$$

21. If the equations of 2 lines are $y = 4x + 3$ and $y = 3x + 4$, respectively, and the two lines intersect, what is the absolute value of the difference of the x-coordinate and y-coordinate?

(A) 5

(B) 6

(C) 4

(D) 3

Solution: Answer: (B)

At the intersection point, $y = y$.

$\downarrow$

$$4x + 3 = 3x + 4$$

$$x = 1$$

By $y = 4x + 3$, $y = 7$

$\Downarrow$

$$|x - y| = |1 - 7| = 6$$

y	9	m	n
x	0	1	2

22. The values of m and n in the chart above are related so that $(y + 1)$ is directly proportional to $(x - 1)$. What is the sum of m and n?

(A) 10

(B)-12

(C) 14

(D)-16

Solution: Answer: (B)

Proportion: $y + 1 = k(x - 1)$

(1) Get the constant k first.

$$9 + 1 = k(0 - 1), \quad k = -10$$

$\downarrow$

(2) Get m and n, respectively.

$$m + 1 = (-10)(1 - 1), \quad m = -1$$

$$n + 1 = (-10)(2 - 1), \quad n = -11$$

(1) and (2)

(3) Get the sum.

$\Downarrow$

$$m + n = -1 + (-11) = -12$$

NEXT PAGE

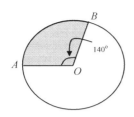

Note that figure not drawn to scale.

23.   Point O is the center of the circle above. What fraction of the area of the the the circle is the area of the shaded portion?

(A) $\dfrac{18}{7}$

(B) $\dfrac{7}{16}$

(C) $\dfrac{11}{18}$

(D) $\dfrac{7}{18}$

Solution: Answer: (D)

In the same circle, arc, area, and measure of angle have the same ratio.

$\begin{cases} \text{if getting ratio from area, you can use} \\ \text{it to obtain arc or angle measure.} \end{cases}$

$\begin{cases} \text{if getting ratio from arc, you can use} \\ \text{it to obtain area or angle measure.} \end{cases}$

$\begin{cases} \text{if getting ratio from angle measure,} \\ \text{you can use it to obtain area or arc.} \end{cases}$

$\Downarrow$

$$\dfrac{140}{360} = \dfrac{7}{18}$$

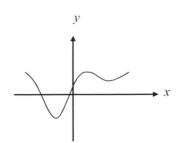

24.   The graph of a function $f(x)$ is shown above. Which of the following could be the graph of $\left| f(x) \right|$?

(A) y 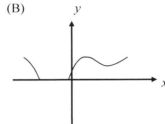 (B) y

(C) y 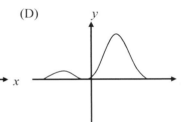 (D) y

Solution: Answer: (C)

Note: (1) $f(x)$ happens first, then $\left| f(x) \right|$ happens.

(2) Absolute sign only affects values of y, not x.

NEXT PAGE

25. What are the values of x in the equation $(2x+4)^2 = 16$?

(A) (0, 4)

(B) (4, 0)

(C) (-4, 0)

(D) (0, -4)

> Solution: Answer: (D)
>
> **Method 1**
>
> $$2x + 4 = \pm 4$$
>
> ↓
>
> $$\begin{cases} 2x = 4 - 4 \\ 2x = -4 - 4 \end{cases}$$
>
> ⇓
>
> $$x = 0, \ -4$$
>
> **Method 2**
>
> $$(2x+4)^2 - 4^2 = 0$$
>
> $$[(2x+4)-4][(2x+4)+4] = 0$$
>
> ↓
>
> $$(2x)(2x+8) = 0$$
>
> ⇓
>
> $$x = 0, -4$$

26. What is the solution to the equation $\sqrt{x-2} = -4$?

(A) no solution

(B) 18

(C) 16

(D) 12

> Solution: Answer: (A)
>
> The SAT-I convention,
>
> ↓
>
> $$\sqrt{x-2} \neq -4$$
>
> ⇓
>
> $\sqrt{x-2} = -4$ has no solution.

27. At East River School, the volleyball club has 12 members and the basketball club has 16 members. If a total of 20 students belong to only either volleyball club or basketball club, how many students belong to both clubs?

(A) 8

(B) 4

(C) 9

(D) 7

> Solution: Answer: (B)
>
> Note: Two layers
>
> $$(12+16) - 20 = 8$$
>
> Half of 8 is counted twice.
>
> ↓
>
> $$\frac{8}{2} = 4$$
>
> ⇓
>
> 4 the members belong to both clubs.

28. A 16-liter solution of acid and water is 25% acid. How many liters of acid must be added to increase the concentration of acid in the solution to 50%?

(A) 8

(B) 4

(C) 5

(D) 6

> Solution: Answer: (A)
>
> $$A + B = M$$
>
> $$\underbrace{16 \times 25 + 100x = 50 \cdot (16 + x)}$$
>
> ↑
>
> $$\begin{cases} 16 \times \frac{25}{100} + \frac{100}{100}x = \frac{50}{100} \cdot (16+x) \\ \\ \text{Do not need write down the 100s.} \end{cases}$$
>
> $$400 + 100x = 50 \cdot (16 + x)$$
>
> ↓
>
> $$\overset{2}{\cancel{100}} (4 + x) = \cancel{50} \cdot (16 + x)$$
>
> ↓
>
> $$8 + 2x = 16 + x$$
>
> ⇓
>
> $$x = \boxed{8}$$

NEXT PAGE

29. If $\sin x = -u$, $u > 0$, in $\dfrac{\pi}{2} < x < \dfrac{3}{2}\pi$, which of the following must be true for $\tan x$?

(A) $\dfrac{u}{\sqrt{1^2 - u^2}}$

(B) $\dfrac{\sqrt{1^2 - u^2}}{u}$

(C) $\sqrt{1^2 - u^2}$

(D) $\pm\dfrac{u}{\sqrt{1^2 - u^2}}$

Solution: Answer: (A)

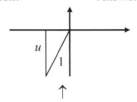

$\sin x = -u = -\dfrac{u}{1}$

↓

$\sin x$ occurs in quadrant III.

↓

$\cos x = -\dfrac{\sqrt{1^2 - u^2}}{1} = -\sqrt{1^2 - u^2}$

$\tan x = \dfrac{\sin x}{\cos x}$

⇓

$\tan x = \dfrac{-u}{-\sqrt{1^2 - u^2}} = +\dfrac{u}{\sqrt{1^2 - u^2}}$

30. An insect population is growing in such a way: number in each generation is approximately 2 times of the previous generation. If there are 1,000 insects in the first generation, approximately how many insects will there be in the fifth generation?

(A) 32,000
(B) 10,000
(C) 8,000
(D) 16,000

Solution   Answer: (D)

$\begin{cases} \text{Exponential function } f(n) = a_0 r^n, \\ \text{where } n \text{ is an integer} \geq 0. \end{cases}$

$\begin{cases} \text{Geometric sequence } a_n = a_1 r^{n-1}, \\ \text{where } n \text{ is an integer} \geq 1 \text{ because } 0 \\ \text{term should not exist.} \end{cases}$

Which formula above should we choose? Generally speaking, use the formula of exponential function for some problems involving population and investment; use the geometric sequence if a question includes the word "geometric sequence".

↓

Use formula $f(n) = a_0 r^n$.
$n = 5 - 1 = 4$

⇓

$f(4) = 1000(2)^4 = 16000$

NEXT PAGE

31. If $x - 2$ is 1 less than $y + 5$, then $x + 3$ exceeds y by what amount?

Solution: Answer: 9

$$x - 2 = y + 5 - 1$$
$$\downarrow$$
$$x - 2 = y + 4$$
$$\downarrow$$
$$x - 2 + 5 = y + 4 + 5$$
$$\Downarrow$$
$$x + 3 - y = 9$$

32. At a snack bar, Frank bought 5 hamburgers and 3 bottled waters for a total of $16. Henry paid the same prices for the hamburger and bottled water. Henry bought 4 hamburgers and 2 bottled waters for a total of $12. What is the the total cost of one hamburger and one bottled water? (Disregard the sign $ when gridding)

Solution: Answer: 4

$$5x + 3y = 16 \quad (1)$$
$$4x + 2y = 12 \quad (2)$$
$$(1) - (2)$$
$$\Downarrow$$
$$x + y = 4$$

33. If Harry takes 3 minutes to travel from place P to place Q at a constant speed of 30 miles per one-half of hour, how many minutes does he take to travel the same route from place Q to place P at a constant speed of 40 miles per hour?

Solution: Answer: 9/2 or 4.5

$$s_1 = 60, \quad t_1 = 3$$
$$s_2 = 40, \quad x = t_2$$
$$\text{speed} \uparrow, \quad \text{time} \downarrow$$
$$\downarrow$$

Use inverse proportion.

$$x \cdot \square_3 = \square_1 \cdot \square_2$$
$$4\cancel{0} \cdot t_2 = 6\cancel{0} \cdot 3$$
$$\Downarrow$$
$$t_2 = \frac{18}{4} = \frac{9}{2} = 4.5$$

34. Martin is 32 years older than his daughter May. In nine years, he will be two times as old as May will be. How old is Martin?

Solution: Answer: 55

Let x = Martin's current age.
$$\downarrow$$
$x - 32$ = May's current age.
$$\downarrow$$
$$\underset{\text{Martin' age}}{x + 9} = 2\underset{\text{Martin' age}}{\underbrace{(x - 32 + 9)}}$$
$$\Downarrow$$
$$x = 55$$

NEXT PAGE

35.   Jennifer, a salesperson of a computer wholesale company, sells a computer of $840. It makes a 20% profit. During an on sale period, the profit is cut to 6%. What is the final price of the computer? (Disregard the sign $ when gridding.)

Solution: Answer: 742

$$840 = 1.2y, \quad 84\,\overset{7}{\cancel{0}}0 = \cancel{12}y$$

$$\downarrow$$

$$y = 700$$

$$\Downarrow$$

$$x = 700 \times 1.06 = 742$$

36.   At Whitewater High School, a history class has 25 students in it. Of those students, 12 are enrolled in biology and 14 are enrolled in chemistry. What is the minimum percent of the students in the history class who are also enrolled in biology and chemistry? (Disregard the sign % when gridding.)

Solution: Answer: 4

$$25 = 12 + 14 - B + N$$

$$B = 1 + N, \text{ when } N = 0, B = 1$$

$$\Downarrow$$

$$\frac{1}{25} \times 100\% = 4\%$$

x	$g(x)$	$f(x)$
2	-1	2
1	0	-1
0	1	-2
-1	2	3
-2	3	4

37   According to chart above, what is the value of $g(-2) - f(1)$?

Solution: Answer: 4

$$\begin{cases} g(-2) = 3 \\ f(1) = -1 \end{cases}$$

$$\Downarrow$$

$$g(-2) - f(1) = 3 - (-1) = 4$$

38.   The area of a garden enclosed is a rectangle. The three sides of the rectangle are enclosed by 80 feet of fence and another side is bounded by the wall of a building. What is the value of the width if the garden reaches its maximum area?

Solution: Answer: 20

$$A(W) = L \cdot W = (80 - 2W)W = -2W^2 + 80W$$

If $f(x) = ax + bx + c$ has its maximum value, $x = \dfrac{-b}{2a}$.

$$\Downarrow$$

$$W = \frac{-80}{2(-2)} = 20$$

STOP

SAT Math

Practice

Test 13

Redesigned for Tests in March 2016 and Beyond

Mad Math

Math Test – No Calculator

Time: 25 Minutes
20 Questions

Notes:
- The use of a calculator is not allowed.
- All numbers used in this section are the real number.
- Figures are provided for some problems in this test. Unless otherwise indicated under the figure "Note: Figure above not drawn to scale", all figures are drawn as accurately as possible.
- All figures lie in a plane EXCEPT otherwise specified.
- Unless otherwise indicated, the domain of any function f, g or j is assumed to be the set of all real numbers x for which $f(x)$, $g(x)$, or $j(x)$ is a real number.

Reference Information

$A = \dfrac{1}{2}bh$

$A = lw$

$A = \pi r^2$

$V = \pi r^2 h$

$V = lwh$

$c^2 = a^2 + b^2$

$V = \dfrac{1}{3}\pi r^2 h$

$V = \dfrac{4}{3}\pi r^3$

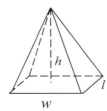

$V = \dfrac{1}{3}lwh$

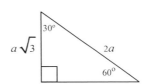

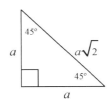

1. Which of the following expressions with positive exponents only is equal to $\dfrac{m^{-1}n}{n^{-1}-m^{-1}}$?

(A) $m(m-n)$

(B) $n(m-n)$

(C) $\dfrac{n^2}{(m-n)}$

(D) $m(n-m)$

2. Ryan buys two pencils and a pen for \$2.15. If a pencil costs \$0.35 less than a pen, how much does the pen cost?

(A) \$0.95
(B) \$0.85
(C) \$0.75
(D) \$0.65

3. If p_1 represents the greatest prime number less than 96 and p_2 represents the least prime number greater than 8, which of the following is the value of $p_1 - p_2$?

(A) 81

(B) 80

(C) 82

(D) 78

4. $\dfrac{m^2-m-6}{m+2}= ?$

(A) $m+3$

(B) $m+2$

(C) $m-2$

(D) $m-3$

5. If x is a positive integer and $\dfrac{1}{7}<\dfrac{4}{x}<\dfrac{1}{5}$, what is the number of all possible values of x?

(A) 21
(B) 9
(C) 22
(D) 7

NEXT PAGE

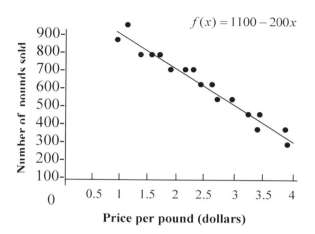

$f(x) = 1100 - 200x$

Price per pound (dollars)

A supermarket sells pounds of peanutbutters and decides the price per pound every month. The scatterplot above shows the price and the number of pounds of peanutbutters sold for 17 months with the line of best fit and the equation for the line.

6. By the line of best fit above, how many pounds of peanut-butters should the supermarket expect to sell in a month when the price of peanutbutter is $4.00 each pound?

(A) 700

(B) 800

(C) 300

(D) 500

7. By the line of best fit on the left, what is the price of peanutbutters the supermarket expects to sell in a month when the peanutbutters are 600 pounds?

(A) $3.00

(B) $2.50

(C) $3.70

(D) $2.10

$$\begin{cases} 3x - 1 > 5 \\ y > 3x + 1 \end{cases}$$

8. Which of the following consists of the y-coordinates of all the points that satisfy the system of inequalities above?

(A) $y > 6$

(B) $y > 5$

(C) $y > 7$

(D) $y > -7$

NEXT PAGE

$$g(x) = |2x - 13|$$

9. For the equation above, what is one possible value of b for which $g(b) < b$?

(A) 13

(B) 14

(C) 12

(D) $4\frac{1}{3}$

$$y - 2 = 3/2(2x + 1)$$

10. What is the slope of the function above?

(A) 3/2

(B) 2

(C) −1.5

(D) 3

11. A list of numbers has been arranged such that each number in the list is 16 more than the number that precedes it. If number 298 is the tenth number in the list, what is the third number in the list?

(A) 410

(B) 280

(C) 168

(D) 186

NEXT PAGE

12. If m is $\dfrac{3}{2}$ of n and n is $\dfrac{5}{3}$ of r, what is the value of $\dfrac{m}{r}$?

(A) $\dfrac{5}{2}$

(B) $\dfrac{10}{3}$

(C) $\dfrac{2}{5}$

(D) $\dfrac{10}{6}$

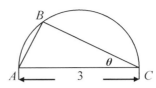

15. In figure above, a triangle is inscribed in a semicircle with diameter 3. What is the perimeter of the triangle in terms of θ?

(A) $\dfrac{9\sin\theta \cdot \cos\theta}{2}$ 　　　　 (B) $\dfrac{6\sin\theta \cdot \cos\theta}{2}$

(C) $3\sin\theta + \cos\theta + 3$ 　　 (D) $3(\sin\theta + \cos\theta + 1)$

13. If x is a real number such that $(x+1)^2 < 4$, which of the following must be true?

(A) $x \le 1$ 　　(B) $x < -3$ 　　(C) $-3 < x < 1$ 　　(D) $-1 < x, \ x > 1$

14. On the first day of a sale, customers numbered 119 through 201 were waited on. How many customers were waited on the first day?

(A) 82
(B) 83
(C) 81
(D) 152

NEXT PAGE ⟩

16. Six cards in a pot are numbered 1 through 6. One card is drawn at random. The ones digit of the sum of the numbers on the remaining cards is 0. What is the number on the drawn card?

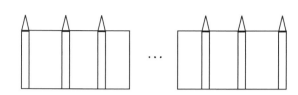

19. The figure above represents a stretch of wall, which is 1,120 yards long. The wall posts are placed at two ends and also placed every 5.6 yards along the wall. How many the posts totally are there in the wall stretch?

17. Four times the first of three consecutive even integers is 4 more than twice the third. What is the third integer?

20. The number of birds on each of swamplands S_1 and S_2 keeps constant from year to year, however the birds migrate between the two swamplands S_1 and S_2 . In one year, 30% of the birds on swampland S_1 have migrated to swampland S_2 , 20% of the birds on swampland S_2 have migrated to swampland S_1 . If the entire number of birds is 20,000, how many birds are on swampland S_1 ?

18. The median of seven consecutive integers is 38. What is the greatest one of these seven integers?

STOP

Math Test – Calculator

Time: 55 Minutes
38 Questions

Notes:
- The use of a calculator is not allowed.
- All numbers used in this section are the real number.
- Figures are provided for some problems in this test. Unless otherwise indicated under the figure "Note: Figure above not drawn to scale", all figures are drawn as accurately as possible.
- All figures lie in a plane EXCEPT otherwise specified.
- Unless otherwise indicated, the domain of any function f, g or j is assumed to be the set of all real numbers x for which $f(x)$, $g(x)$, or $j(x)$ is a real number.

Reference Information

$A = \dfrac{1}{2}bh$

$A = lw$

$A = \pi r^2$

$V = \pi r^2 h$

$V = lwh$

$c^2 = a^2 + b^2$

$V = \dfrac{1}{3}\pi r^2 h$

$V = \dfrac{4}{3}\pi r^3$

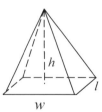

$V = \dfrac{1}{3}lwh$

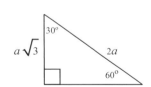

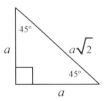

1. If $6p = 5q = 2m = 5n$, then $\dfrac{mn}{pq} =$

(A) 5

(B) 4

(C) 3

(D) 2

$$x^2 - 6x + 9 \leq 0$$

3. The solution set of the inequality above consists of all real numbers is

(A) $x \geq 3$

(B) $x \leq 3$

(C) $x = 3$

(D) $-\infty < x < \infty$

$\overset{\longleftarrow\ \ 2x+3\ \ \longrightarrow}{P \qquad\qquad Q}\quad\overset{\longleftarrow\ \ 2x-1\ \ \longrightarrow}{S \qquad\qquad R}$

2. In the figure above, if the length of segment PR is $4x + 3$, what is the length of segment QS?

(A) $4x + 1$
(B) $x + 3$
(C) $6x - 5$
(D) 1

4. If n is $\dfrac{2}{3}$ of s and p is $\dfrac{4}{5}$ of s, what is the value of $\dfrac{n}{p}$?

$(A)\dfrac{5}{2}$

$(B)\dfrac{10}{3}$

$(C)\dfrac{5}{6}$

$(D)\dfrac{15}{8}$

NEXT PAGE ⟩

Price per Pound of Materials

Materials	EUROs (€)	USDs ($)
A	3	3.64
B	5	6.06
C	200	243
D	3	3.64

The chart above gives the prices of four different materials expressed in both USDs and EUROs. Let u be USDs and e be EUROs.

5.   Which of the following equations best represents the relationship between u and e?

(A) $e = 1.21u$

(B) $u = 2.12e$

(C) $u = 1.21e$

(D) $u = \dfrac{e}{1.21}$

6.   The sum of the digits of a three-digit number is 10. If the hundreds place is 2 times the tens place and the units place is $\dfrac{1}{3}$ of the tens place, what is the hundreds place of the number?

(A) 6
(B) 4
(C) 3
(D) 2

7.   If Jonathon plans to obtain a solution that is 50% alcohol from 20 pounds of a solution that is 35% alcohol, how many pounds of pure alcohol must be added?

(A) 2
(B) 4
(C) 5
(D) 6

8. The sum of the digits of a three-digit number is 10. If the hundreds place is 2 times the tens place and the units place is $\dfrac{1}{3}$ of the tens place, what is the units place of the number?

(A) 6
(B) 4
(C) 1
(D) 2

NEXT PAGE

g(x)	x
0	−1
1	0
0	3

9. Three of whose values are shown in the chart above. If g is a polynomial of degree 3, what could $g(x)$ be equal to?

(A) $(x-3)\left(x-\dfrac{3}{2}\right)(x+3)$

(B) $(x+1)(x-3)(x+3)$

(C) $(x-1)\left(x-\dfrac{3}{2}\right)(x+3)$

(D) $(x+1)(x-3)\left(x-\dfrac{1}{3}\right)$

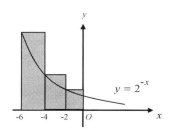

10. In the figure above, the curve is a portion of the graph of $y = 2^{-x}$. What is the sum of the areas of the three shaded rectangles?

(A) 84

(B) 48

(C) 168

(D) 186

NEXT PAGE

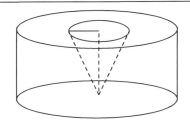

11. In the figure above, the right circular cylinder has a radius of 2 units and a height of 3 units. The hole of a right cone is made by a special machine through the center as shown, with a diameter of 2 units. About what is the area of the total surfaces of the solid (Lateral area of a right circular cone is $A = \frac{1}{2}cl$, where c is circumference and l is slant height)?

(A) 69.62

(B) 107π

(C) 82.36

(D) 26.58

12. In the xy-plane, points (2, 1) and (4, 3) define a line, and points (-2, -3) and (-4, -2) define another line. At which of the following (x, y) points do the two lines intersect?

(A) (2, 3)

(B) $(-\frac{4}{3}, -\frac{5}{3})$

(C) (-2, -3)

(D) (3, 2)

NEXT PAGE

13. 5 points, *A, B, C, D*, and *E*, lie on a line, not necessarily in that order. $\overline{AB}$ has a length of 36. Point *C* is the midpoint of $\overline{AB}$, and point *D* is the midpoint of $\overline{AC}$. If the distance between *D* and *E* is 7, what are all possible distances between *A* and *E*?

(A) 2
(B) 16
(C) 8
(D) 2 and 16

14. Monica can travel from Bedminster to New York City by her own car or taxi. She can then travel to Boston by plane, train, ship, or bus. From Boston, she can travel to MTY Academy by bus, or taxi. In how many different ways can Monica travel from Bedminster to New York City to Boston and then to MTY Academy?

(A) 8
(B) 10
(C) 24
(D) 16

15. On a number line, if point *A* has coordinate –4 and point *B* has coordinate 14, what is the coordinate of the point that is located $\dfrac{2}{3}$ of the way from *A* to *B*?

(A) 8
(B) 4
(C) -6
(D) 2

NEXT PAGE

16. For how many integers m is $(3m+1)(4m-17)$ a negative number?

(A) 4

(B) 6

(C) 2

(D) 5

17. On the number line above, if the tick marks are equally spaced, the expression of b in terms of a must be

(A) $a+3$ (B) $4a-1$ (C) $4a-3$ (D) $2a-1$

18. A certain integer greater than 1 has only three positive integer factors: 1, itself, and its square root. And one of the factors is a prime number. Which of the following is the certain number?

(A) 25
(B) 16
(C) 81
(D) 256

NEXT PAGE

19. If five more than m is a negative number and if 7 more than m is a positive number, which of the following could be the value of m?

(A) -4
(B) -7
(C) -5
(D) -6

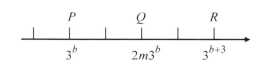

21. On the number line above, point Q is the midpoint of $\overline{PR}$. If the tick marks are equally spaced, and b is greater than zero, what is the value of m?

(A) $\dfrac{10}{4}$

(B) $\dfrac{26}{4}$

(C) 8

(D) 7

20. If a $3,000 deposit earns 6% simple annual interest, which of the following is the interest earned in 6 years?

(A) 108

(B) 416

(C) 1,080

(D) 800

22. The daily cost of running a certain heater is p cents per hour for the first r hours, and q cents per hour for each additional hour over r hours. Which of the following expressions represents the cost, in dollars, of running this heater for h hours each day, for d days, if $r < h < 24$?

(A) $\dfrac{pr + q(h - r)}{100d}$

(B) $\dfrac{d\left[pr + dq(h - r)\right]}{100}$

(C) $\dfrac{dpr + q(h - r)}{100}$

(D) $\dfrac{d\left[pr + q(h - r)\right]}{100}$

NEXT PAGE

23. Michael is a car salesperson. He sells two kinds of cars. For one of them, the selling price is $32,000, and for another one, the selling price is $48,000. Last week, Michael's goal was to sell at least 10 cars. He did not meet his goal. The total value of the cars he sold was over $360,000. Let x be the number of $32,000 cars, and y be the number of $48,000 cars, that Michael sold last week. Which system of inequalities below represents the conditions described?

(A) $x + y > 10$
$\quad 32,000x + 48,000y < 360,000$

(B) $x + y > 10$
$\quad 32,000x + 48,000y > 360,000$

(C) $x + y < 10$
$\quad 32,000x + 48,000y > 360,000$

(D) $x + y < 10$
$\quad 32,000x + 48,000y < 360,000$

24. The sum of six distinct integers is zero. What is the least number of these integers that must be positive?

(A) 8

(B) 6

(C) 1

(D) 3

$$A \quad B \quad C \quad D \quad E \quad F \quad G \quad H \quad I$$

25.   In the figure above, the letters represent consecutive integers on a number line. If $3C + G = 24$, what is the value of D?

(A) 8
(B) 6
(C) 5
(D) 12

26. Points A and B are the endpoints of a line segment, and the length of the segment is at most 28. There are four other points on the segment, $P, Q, R,$ and S, which are located at distances of 5, 7, 14, and 15, respectively, from point A. which of the points could be the midpoint of AB?

(A) P
(B) Q
(C) R
(D) S

NEXT PAGE

123456…484950…899100

27. The integer above is formed by writing the integers from 1 to 100, in order, next to each other. If the integer is read from left to right, what is 170th digit from the left?

(A) 5
(B) 1
(C) 2
(D) 9

28 The sum of all even integers from 2 to 206 is 10,712.

What is the sum of all even integers from 4 to 204 ?

(A) 10916

(B) 10504

(C) 10918

(D) 10819

29. What are the solutions to $6x^2 + 24x - 12 = 0$?

(A) $-2 \pm \sqrt{6}$

(B) $\pm 2 - \sqrt{6}$

(C) $\pm 2 + \sqrt{6}$

(D) $+2 \pm \sqrt{6}$

30. If $\cos x = \dfrac{\sqrt{2}}{\sqrt{5}}$, where $\dfrac{3\pi}{2} < x < 2\pi$, what is $\tan x$?

(A) $-\dfrac{\sqrt{6}}{2}$

(B) -1.11

(C) -3.42

(D) 2.28

NEXT PAGE

Questions 31 and 32 refer to the information

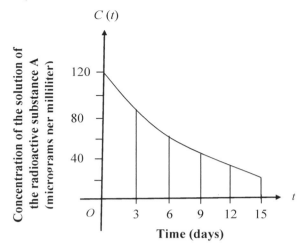

$C(t)$

Time (days)

Time (days)	Concentration of the solution of the radioactive substance A (micrograms per milliliter)
0	120
3	85
6	61
9	43
12	31
15	21

In the graph and chart above show the information about the concentration of the solution of the radioactive substance A and the corresponding time.

31.   If the concentration of the solution of the radioactive substance is 120 micrograms per milliliter, it is modeled by the function C defined by $C(t) = 120r^{(t/3)}$, where C is the concentration of the solution, in micrograms, and t is the time, in days. If C approximates the values in the chart, what is the value of r, rounded to the nearest hundredth?

32. By the chart, how many less micrograms of the substance are present in 8 milliliters 12 days after the time beginning than are present in 9 milliliters 15 days after the time beginning?

33. How many of the first 200 positive integers are multiples of either 6 or 15?

34. If a rectangular solid has length 10 centimeters, width 2 centimeters, and height 50 centimeters, then how many of the rectangular solids have a volume of five cubic meters when they are combined?

NEXT PAGE

Note: Figure below not drawn to scale.

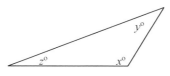

35 If in the figure above, $x > 90$, $z = y - 1$, and y is an integer, what is the greatest possible value of z ?

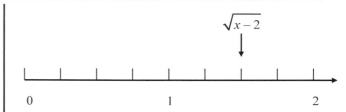

37. In the figure above, there are eight equal intervals between 0 and 2 on the number line. What is the value of x?

36. Judy is 28 years old and her sister, Jody, is 17. How many years ago was Judy' age two times as old as Jody's?

38. At a store, two sevenths of the items are discounted by 70 percent, one seventh of the items are discounted by 40 percent, three fourteenths of the items are discounted by 50 percent, and rest items are not discounted. If one item is to be selected randomly, what is the probability that the item is discounted by 40 percent, 50 percent or 70 percent?

STOP

Answer Key
For
SAT Math Practice Test 13

Section 3

1	C
2	A
3	D
4	D
5	D
6	C
7	B
8	C
9	C
10	D
11	D
12	A
13	C
14	B
15	D

16	1
17	10
18	41
19	201
20	8000

Section 4

1	C	16	D
2	D	17	C
3	C	18	A
4	C	19	D
5	C	20	C
6	A	21	D
7	D	22	D
8	C	23	C
9	D	24	C
10	C	25	B
11	A	26	C
12	C	27	D
13	D	28	B
14	D	29	A
15	A	30	A

31	0.71
32	59
33	40
34	5000
35	44
36	6
37	17/4 or 4.25
38	9/14 or .642 or .643

SAT Math

Practice

Test 13

Explanations

Redesigned for Tests in March 2016 and Beyond

Mad Math

Math Test – No Calculator

Time: 25 Minutes
20 Questions

Notes:
- The use of a calculator is not allowed.
- All numbers used in this section are the real number.
- Figures are provided for some problems in this test. Unless otherwise indicated under the figure "Note: Figure above not drawn to scale", all figures are drawn as accurately as possible.
- All figures lie in a plane EXCEPT otherwise specified.
- Unless otherwise indicated, the domain of any function f, g or j is assumed to be the set of all real numbers x for which $f(x)$, $g(x)$, or $j(x)$ is a real number.

Reference Information

$$A = \frac{1}{2}bh$$

$$A = lw$$

$$A = \pi r^2$$

$$V = \pi r^2 h$$

$$V = lwh$$

$$c^2 = a^2 + b^2$$

$$V = \frac{1}{3}\pi r^2 h$$

$$V = \frac{4}{3}\pi r^3$$

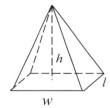

$$V = \frac{1}{3}lwh$$

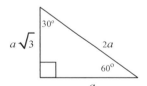

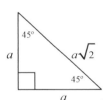

1. Which of the following expressions with positive exponents only is equal to $\dfrac{m^{-1}n}{n^{-1}-m^{-1}}$?

(A) $m(m-n)$

(B) $n(m-n)$

(C) $\dfrac{n^2}{(m-n)}$

(D) $m(n-m)$

Solution: Answer: (C)

$$\dfrac{m^{-1}n}{n^{-1}-m^{-1}}=\dfrac{\dfrac{1}{m}n}{\dfrac{1}{n}-\dfrac{1}{m}}$$

$$\dfrac{n}{m}\cdot\dfrac{1}{\dfrac{m-n}{mn}}=\dfrac{n^2}{(m-n)}$$

2. Ryan buys two pencils and a pen for \$2.15. If a pencil costs \$0.35 less than a pen, how much does the pen cost?

(A) \$0.95
(B) \$0.85
(C) \$0.75
(D) \$0.65

Solution: Answer: (A)

$$x+2(x-35)=215$$
$$\downarrow$$
$$x+2x-70=215$$
$$\Downarrow$$
$$3x=285,\ x=95$$

3. If p_1 represents the greatest prime number less than 96 and p_2 represents the least prime number greater than 8, which of the following is the value of p_1-p_2 ?

(A) 81

(B) 80

(C) 82

(D) 78

Solution: Answer: (D)

$$p_1=89,\quad p_2=11$$
$$\Downarrow$$
$$p_1-p_2=89-11=78$$

4. $\dfrac{m^2-m-6}{m+2}=?$

(A) $m+3$

(B) $m+2$

(C) $m-2$

(D) $m-3$

Solution: Answer: (D)

$$m^2-m-6$$
$$\downarrow$$
$$(m-3)(m+2)$$
$$\downarrow$$
$$\dfrac{m^2-m-6}{m+2}$$
$$\downarrow$$
$$\dfrac{(m-3)\ \cancel{(m+2)}}{\cancel{m+2}}$$
$$\Downarrow$$
$$m-3$$

5. If x is a positive integer and $\dfrac{1}{7}<\dfrac{4}{x}<\dfrac{1}{5}$, what is the number of all possible values of x?

(A) 21
(B) 9
(C) 22
(D) 7

Solution: Answer: (D)

$$\dfrac{1}{7}<\dfrac{4}{x}<\dfrac{1}{5}$$

$$\boxed{\dfrac{1}{5}}\quad \dfrac{4}{x}\quad \boxed{\dfrac{1}{7}}$$
$$\downarrow$$
$$\dfrac{5}{1}<\dfrac{x}{4}<\dfrac{7}{1}$$
$$\downarrow$$
$$20<x<28$$
$$\downarrow$$
$$x=21,22,23,24,25,26,27$$
$$\Downarrow$$
$$N=7$$

NEXT PAGE

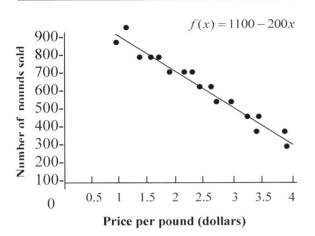

$$f(x) = 1100 - 200x$$

A supermarket sells pounds of peanutbutters and decides the price per pound every month. The scatterplot above shows the price and the number of pounds of peanutbutters sold for 17 months with the line of best fit and the equation for the line.

6.   By the line of best fit above, how many pounds of peanut-butters should the supermarket expect to sell in a month when the price of peanutbutter is $4.00 each pound?

(A) 700

(B) 800

(C) 300

(D) 500

Solution: Answer: (C)

"expect to sell"

↓

values of the line, not values of the points.

↓

$$f(4) = 1100 - 200 \cdot 4$$

⇓

$$f(4) = 300$$

---

7. By the line of best fit on the left, what is the price of peanutbutters the supermarket expects to sell in a month when the peanutbutters are 600 pounds?

(A) $3.00

(B) $2.50

(C) $3.70

(D) $2.10

Solution: Answer: (B)

"expect to sell"

↓

values of the line, not values of the points.

↓

$$600 = 1100 - 200x, \quad 2x = 5$$

⇓

$$x = 2.5$$

$$\begin{cases} 3x - 1 > 5 \\ y > 3x + 1 \end{cases}$$

8. Which of the following consists of the y-coordinates of all the points that satisfy the system of inequalities above?

(A) $y > 6$

(B) $y > 5$

(C) $y > 7$

(D) $y > -7$

Solution: Answer: (C)

$a > b$ and $b > c$ → $a > c$

$$\begin{cases} 3x - 1 > 5 \\ \qquad\downarrow \qquad \rightarrow 3x + 1 > 7 \\ 3x - 1 + 2 > 5 + 2 \end{cases}$$

⇓

$$y > 3x + 1 > 7, \quad y > 7$$

NEXT PAGE

$$g(x) = |2x - 13|$$

9. For the equation above, what is one possible value of b for which $g(b) < b$?

(A) 13

(B) 14

(C) 12

(D) $4\dfrac{1}{3}$

> Solution: Answer: (C)
>
> $$g(b) = |2b - 13| < b$$
>
> $$\downarrow$$
>
> $$-b < 2b - 13 < b$$
>
> $$\downarrow$$
>
> $$\begin{cases} 2b - 13 < b \quad \rightarrow b < \boxed{13} \\ -b < 2b - 13 \quad \rightarrow 13 < 3b \\ \qquad\qquad\qquad \boxed{\dfrac{13}{3} < b} \end{cases}$$
>
> $$\downarrow$$
>
> $$4\dfrac{1}{3} < b < 13$$
>
> $$\Downarrow$$
>
> $$4\dfrac{1}{3} < 12 < 13$$

$$y - 2 = 3/2 \left(2x + 1\right)$$

10. What is the slope of the function above?

(A) 3/2

(B) 2

(C) −1.5

(D) 3

> Solution: Answer: (D)
>
> $$\underbrace{y - y_o = s(x - x_o)}_{\text{slope-point form}}$$
>
> $$\downarrow$$
>
> $$y - 2 = \frac{3}{2} \cdot 2\left(x + \frac{1}{2}\right)$$
>
> $$\Downarrow$$
>
> $$s = 3$$

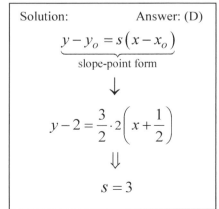

11. A list of numbers has been arranged such that each number in the list is 16 more than the number that precedes it. If number 298 is the tenth number in the list, what is the third number in the list?

(A) 410

(B) 280

(C) 168

(D) 186

> Solution: Answer: (D)
>
> Use the formula of arithmetic sequences.
>
> $$a_n = a_1 + (n-1)d$$
>
> $$\downarrow$$
>
> $$298 = a_1 + 9 \cdot 16, \quad 298 - 144 = a_1$$
>
> $$\downarrow$$
>
> $$a_1 = 154$$
>
> $$\Downarrow$$
>
> $$a_3 = 154 + 2 \cdot 16 = 186$$

NEXT PAGE

12. If m is $\dfrac{3}{2}$ of n and n is $\dfrac{5}{3}$ of r, what is the value of $\dfrac{m}{r}$?

(A) $\dfrac{5}{2}$

(B) $\dfrac{10}{3}$

(C) $\dfrac{2}{5}$

(D) $\dfrac{10}{6}$

> Solution: Answer: (A)
>
> $$m = \frac{3}{2}n, \quad n = \frac{5}{3}r$$
>
> The question asks $\dfrac{m}{r}$ that has no n.
>
> Let $n = 2$.
>
> $$m = 3 \text{ and } r = \frac{6}{5}$$
>
> $\Downarrow$
>
> $$\frac{m}{r} = \frac{3}{\frac{6}{5}} = \frac{3 \times 5}{6} = \boxed{\frac{5}{2}}$$

13. If x is a real number such that $(x+1)^2 < 4$, which of the following must be true?

(A) $x \le 1$ (B) $x < -3$ (C) $-3 < x < 1$ (D) $-1 < x, \; x > 1$

> Solution: Answer: (C)
>
> Use the conclusions $\sqrt{x^2} = |x|$ and
>
> $$|x+a| < b \;\to\; -b < x+a < b.$$
>
> $\downarrow$
>
> $$\sqrt{(x+1)^2} < \sqrt{4}, \quad |x+1| < 2$$
>
> $\downarrow$
>
> $$-2 < x+1 < 2$$
>
> $\Downarrow$
>
> $$-3 < x < 1$$

14. On the first day of a sale, customers numbered 119 through 201 were waited on. How many customers were waited on the first day?

(A) 82
(B) 83
(C) 81
(D) 152

> Solution: Answer: (B)
>
> $$N_{\text{last}} - N_{\text{first}} + 1$$
>
> $\Downarrow$
>
> $$201 - 119 + 1 = 83$$

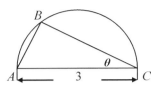

15. In figure above, a triangle is inscribed in a semicircle with diameter 3. What is the perimeter of the triangle in terms of θ?

(A) $\dfrac{9\sin\theta \cdot \cos\theta}{2}$ (B) $\dfrac{6\sin\theta \cdot \cos\theta}{2}$

(C) $3\sin\theta + \cos\theta + 3$ (D) $3(\sin\theta + \cos\theta + 1)$

> Solution: Answer: (D)
>
> semicircle
>
> $\downarrow$
>
> $\overline{AC} = $ diameter
>
>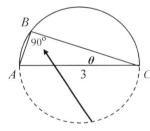
>
> Value of $AC = 180°$
>
> $\downarrow$
>
> $$\angle ABC = \underbrace{\frac{\text{Value of } AC}{2}}_{\text{A rule}} = \frac{180°}{2} = 90°$$
>
> $\downarrow$
>
> $$\sin\theta = \frac{AB}{3}, \quad AB = 3\sin\theta$$
>
> $$\cos\theta = \frac{BC}{3}, \quad BC = 3\cos\theta$$
>
> $\downarrow$
>
> $$\text{Perimeter} = AB + BC + AC$$
>
> $\downarrow$
>
> $$3\sin\theta + 3\cos\theta + 3$$
>
> $\Downarrow$
>
> $$3(\sin\theta + \cos\theta + 1)$$

NEXT PAGE

16. Six cards in a pot are numbered 1 through 6. One card is drawn at random. The ones digit of the sum of the numbers on the remaining cards is 0. What is the number on the drawn card?

Solution: Answer: 1

$$\begin{cases} \text{Sum} = 1+2+3+4+5+6 = 21 \\ \text{Sum}_{\text{Remaining}} = 21 - x = \begin{cases} 0 \\ 10 \\ 20 \end{cases} \\ x \leq 6 \end{cases}$$

$$\Downarrow$$

$$x = 1$$

17. Four times the first of three consecutive even integers is 4 more than twice the third. What is the third integer?

Solution: Answer: 10

Let $(x-4)$, $(x-2)$, and x be the

3 consecutive even integers.

$$\downarrow$$

$$4(x-4) = 2x+4$$

$$\downarrow$$

$$4x-16 = 2x+4$$

$$\Downarrow$$

$$x = 10$$

18. The median of seven consecutive integers is 38. What is the greatest one of these seven integers?

Solution: Answer: 41

The median 38 uses 1 position.

Either side of the median uses

$$\frac{7-1}{2} = 3 \text{ positions.}$$

$$\downarrow$$

$$\underbrace{38,}_{3} \; \underbrace{39, 40, 41}_{3}$$

$$\Downarrow$$

$$38 + 3 = 41$$

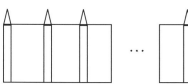 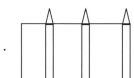

19. The figure above represents a stretch of wall, which is 1,120 yards long. The wall posts are placed at two ends and also placed every 5.6 yards along the wall. How many the posts totally are there in the wall stretch?

Solution: Answer: 201

$$\frac{1120}{5.6}+1 \quad \rightarrow \quad \frac{11200}{56}+1$$

$$\Downarrow$$

$$200 + 1 = 201$$

20. The number of birds on each of swamplands S_1 and S_2 keeps constant from year to year, however the birds migrate between the two swamplands S_1 and S_2. In one year, 30% of the birds on swampland S_1 have migrated to swampland S_2, 20% of the birds on swampland S_2 have migrated to swampland S_1. If the entire number of birds is 20,000, how many birds are on swampland S_1?

Solution: Answer: 8000

$$\begin{cases} S_1 + S_2 = 20000 \\ \dfrac{70}{100}S_1 + \dfrac{20}{100}S_2 = S_1 \end{cases}$$

$$\downarrow$$

$$\frac{70}{100}S_1 + \frac{20}{100}(20000 - S_1) = S_1$$

$$\downarrow$$

$$7\cancel{0}S_1 + 2\cancel{0}(20000 - S_1) = 10\cancel{0}S_1$$

$$7S_1 + 40000 - 2S_1 = 10S_1$$

$$40000 = 5S_1$$

$$\Downarrow$$

$$S_1 = 8000$$

STOP

Math Test – Calculator

Time: 55 Minutes
38 Questions

Notes:

- The use of a calculator is not allowed.
- All numbers used in this section are the real number.
- Figures are provided for some problems in this test. Unless otherwise indicated under the figure "Note: Figure above not drawn to scale", all figures are drawn as accurately as possible.
- All figures lie in a plane EXCEPT otherwise specified.
- Unless otherwise indicated, the domain of any function f, g or j is assumed to be the set of all real numbers x for which $f(x)$, $g(x)$, or $j(x)$ is a real number.

Reference Information

$$A = \frac{1}{2}bh$$

$$A = lw$$

$$A = \pi r^2$$

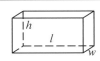

$$V = \pi r^2 h$$

$$V = lwh$$

$$c^2 = a^2 + b^2$$

$$V = \frac{1}{3}\pi r^2 h$$

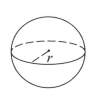

$$V = \frac{4}{3}\pi r^3$$

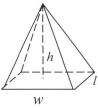

$$V = \frac{1}{3}lwh$$

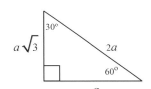

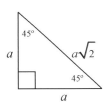

1. If $6p = 5q = 2m = 5n$, then $\dfrac{mn}{pq} =$

(A) 5

(B) 4

(C) 3

(D) 2

Solution: Answer: (C)

$$\frac{mn}{pq} = \frac{m}{p} \times \frac{n}{q}$$

$$\downarrow$$

(1). $6p = 2m$, $\boxed{\dfrac{m}{p} = 3}$

(2). $5q = 5n$, $\boxed{\dfrac{n}{q} = 1}$

$$\Downarrow$$

$$\frac{mn}{pq} = 3 \times 1 = \boxed{3}$$

$$\overset{2x + 3}{\longleftrightarrow} \qquad \overset{2x - 1}{\longleftrightarrow}$$

$P \qquad\qquad Q \qquad S \qquad\qquad R$

2. In the figure above, if the length of segment PR is $4x + 3$, what is the length of segment QS?

(A) $4x + 1$

(B) $x + 3$

(C) $6x - 5$

(D) 1

Solution: Answer: (D)

$$QS = 4x + 3 - [(2x + 3) + (2x - 1)]$$

$$\Downarrow$$

$$QS = 4x + 3 - 4x - 2 = 1$$

$$x^2 - 6x + 9 \le 0$$

3. The solution set of the inequality above consists of all real numbers is

(A) $x \ge 3$

(B) $x \le 3$

(C) $x = 3$

(D) $-\infty < x < \infty$

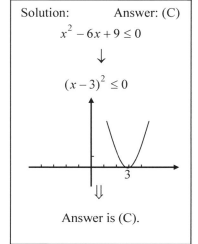

Solution: Answer: (C)

$$x^2 - 6x + 9 \le 0$$

$$\downarrow$$

$$(x - 3)^2 \le 0$$

Answer is (C).

4. If n is $\dfrac{2}{3}$ of s and p is $\dfrac{4}{5}$ of s, what is the value of $\dfrac{n}{p}$?

(A) $\dfrac{5}{2}$

(B) $\dfrac{10}{3}$

(C) $\dfrac{5}{6}$

(D) $\dfrac{15}{8}$

Solution: Answer: (C)

$$n = \frac{2}{3}s, \quad p = \frac{4}{5}s$$

The question asks $\dfrac{n}{p}$ that has no s.

Let $s = 3$.

$$\downarrow$$

$$n = 2 \text{ and } p = \frac{12}{5}$$

$$\Downarrow$$

$$\frac{n}{p} = \frac{2}{\dfrac{12}{5}} = \frac{2 \times 5}{12} = \boxed{\dfrac{5}{6}}$$

NEXT PAGE

Price per Pound of Materials

Materials	EUROs (€)	USDs ($)
A	3	3.64
B	5	6.06
C	200	243
D	3	3.64

The chart above gives the prices of four different materials expressed in both USDs and EUROs. Let u be USDs and e be EUROs.

5. Which of the following equations best represents the relationship between u and e?

(A) $e = 1.21u$

(B) $u = 2.12e$

(C) $u = 1.21e$

(D) $u = \dfrac{e}{1.21}$

Solution: Answer: (C)

$$\frac{3.64}{3} \approx 1.21, \quad \frac{6.06}{5} \approx 1.21, \quad \frac{243}{200} \approx 1.21$$

$$\downarrow$$

$$\frac{u}{e} = 1.21$$

$$\Downarrow$$

$$u = 1.21e \quad \text{or} \quad e = \frac{u}{1.21}$$

6. The sum of the digits of a three-digit number is 10. If the hundreds place is 2 times the tens place and the units place is $\dfrac{1}{3}$ of the tens place, what is the hundreds place of the number?

(A) 6
(B) 4
(C) 3
(D) 2

Solution: Answer: (A)

The question asks the value of hundreds place.
Let x = value of hundreds place.

$$x + \frac{1}{2}x + \frac{1}{3}\left(\frac{1}{2}x\right) = 10$$

$$\frac{6x + 3x + x}{6} = 10$$

$$\Downarrow$$

$$x = 6$$

7. If Jonathon plans to obtain a solution that is 50% alcohol from 20 pounds of a solution that is 35% alcohol, how many pounds of pure alcohol must be added?

(A) 2
(B) 4
(C) 5
(D) 6

Solution: Answer: (D)

$$A + B = M$$

$$20 \times 35 + 100x = 50 \cdot (20 + x)$$

$$\downarrow$$

$$700 + 100x = 50 \cdot (20 + x)$$

$$\downarrow$$

$$\cancel{100}^{2} \cdot (7 + x) = \cancel{50} \cdot (20 + x)$$

$$\Downarrow$$

$$x = \boxed{6}$$

8. The sum of the digits of a three-digit number is 10. If the hundreds place is 2 times the tens place and the units place is $\dfrac{1}{3}$ of the tens place, what is the units place of the number?

(A) 6
(B) 4
(C) 1
(D) 2

Solution: Answer: (C)

The question asks the value of units place.
Let x = value of units place.

$$\downarrow$$

$$2 \cdot (3x) + 3x + x = 10$$

$$\Downarrow$$

$$x = 1$$

NEXT PAGE

$g(x)$	x
0	-1
1	0
0	3

9. Three of whose values are shown in the chart above. If g is a polynomial of degree 3, what could $g(x)$ be equal to?

(A) $(x-3)\left(x-\dfrac{3}{2}\right)(x+3)$

(B) $(x+1)(x-3)(x+3)$

(C) $(x-1)\left(x-\dfrac{3}{2}\right)(x+3)$

(D) $(x+1)(x-3)\left(x-\dfrac{1}{3}\right)$

Solution: Answer: (D)

$$g(-1) = 0 \text{ and } g(3) = 0$$

$(x+1)$ and $(x-3)$ are factors of $g(x)$.

This means that $g(x)$ can be written as $g(x) = (x+1)(x-3)(x-k)$ for a certain real number k.

(A) and (C) are cancelled.

When $x = 0$, $g(0) = 1$.

↓

$$(0+1)(0-3)(0-k) = 1, \rightarrow k = \dfrac{1}{3}$$

⇓

$$(x+1)(x-3)(x-\dfrac{1}{3})$$

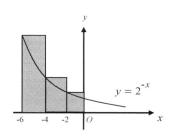

$y = 2^{-x}$

10. In the figure above, the curve is a portion of the graph of $y = 2^{-x}$. What is the sum of the areas of the three shaded rectangles?

(A) 84

(B) 48

(C) 168

(D) 186

Solution: Answer: (C)

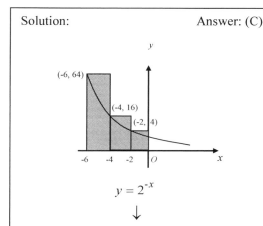

$y = 2^{-x}$

↓

$\begin{cases} \text{Heights of rectangles} \\ f(-2) = 2^2 = 4 \\ f(-4) = 2^4 = 16 \\ f(-6) = 2^6 = 64 \end{cases}$

each base of each rectangle $= 1$

⇓

$$\text{Sum} = 4 \cdot 2 + 16 \cdot 2 + 64 \cdot 2 = 168$$

NEXT PAGE

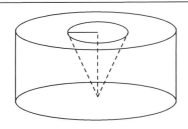

11. In the figure above, the right circular cylinder has a radius of 2 units and a height of 3 units. The hole of a right cone is made by a special machine through the center as shown, with a diameter of 2 units. About what is the area of the total surfaces of the solid (Lateral area of a right circular cone is $A = \frac{1}{2}cl$, where c is circumference and l is slant height)?

(A) 69.62

(B) 107π

(C) 82.36

(D) 26.58

Solution: Answer: (A)

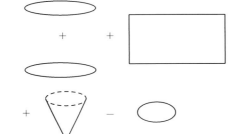

$$A_{total} = 2A_{circ} + A_{rect} + A_{late} - A_{cone\text{-}base}$$

$$\downarrow$$

$$2r_1^2\pi + c_1h + \frac{1}{2}c_2l - r_2^2\pi$$

$$l = \sqrt{1^2 + 3^2} = \sqrt{10}$$

$$\downarrow$$

$$2r_1^2\pi + 2r_1\pi h + \frac{1}{2}\cdot 2r_2\pi\sqrt{10} - r_2^2\pi$$

$$\downarrow$$

$$2\left(2^2\pi\right) + 2\cdot 2\pi\cdot 3 + 1\cdot\pi\sqrt{10} - \left(1^2\pi\right)$$

$$8\pi + 12\pi + \pi\sqrt{10} - \pi = \pi(19 + \sqrt{10})$$

$$\Downarrow$$

$$A_{total} = 69.62$$

12. In the xy-plane, points (2, 1) and (4, 3) define a line, and points (-2, -3) and (-4, -2) define another line. At which of the following (x, y) points do the two lines intersect?

(A) (2, 3)

(B) $(-\frac{4}{3}, -\frac{5}{3})$

(C) (-2, -3)

(D) (3, 2)

Solution: Answer: (C)

$$y - y_0 = s(x - x_0)$$

where $s = $ slope $= \dfrac{y_2 - y_1}{x_2 - x_1}$.

$$(1) \quad y - 1 = \frac{3-1}{4-2}(x-2)$$

$$y = x - 1$$

$$(2) \quad y + 3 = \frac{-3+2}{-2+4}(x+2)$$

$$y = -\frac{1}{2}x - 4$$

At an intersection point,

$$y = y$$

$$x - 1 = -\frac{1}{2}x - 4, \; x = -2$$

Only (C) has $x = -2$.

$$\Downarrow$$

Answer is (C).

NEXT PAGE

13. 5 points, *A, B, C, D*, and *E*, lie on a line, not necessarily in that order. $\overline{AB}$ has a length of 36. Point *C* is the midpoint of $\overline{AB}$, and point *D* is the midpoint of $\overline{AC}$. If the distance between *D* and *E* is 7, what are all possible distances between *A* and *E*?

(A) 2
(B) 16
(C) 8
(D) 2 and 16

Solution: Answer: (D)

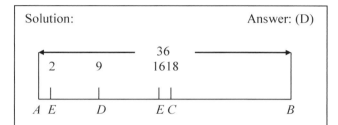

By the information, *A, B, C*, and *D* are fixed. But *E* is not fixed. It can be located at two distinct positions.

14.   Monica can travel from Bedminster to New York City by her own car or taxi. She can then travel to Boston by plane, train, ship, or bus. From Boston, she can travel to MTY Academy by bus, or taxi. In how many different ways can Monica travel from Bedminster to New York City to Boston and then to MTY Academy?

(A) 8
(B) 10
(C) 24
(D) 16

Solution: Answer: (D)

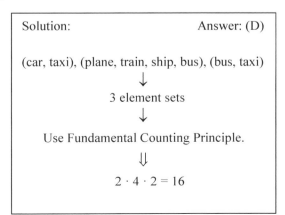

(car, taxi), (plane, train, ship, bus), (bus, taxi)
↓
3 element sets
↓
Use Fundamental Counting Principle.
⇓
$2 \cdot 4 \cdot 2 = 16$

15. On a number line, if point *A* has coordinate –4 and point *B* has coordinate 14, what is the coordinate of the point that is located $\dfrac{2}{3}$ of the way from *A* to *B*?

(A) 8
(B) 4
(C) -6
(D) 2

Solution: Answer: (A)

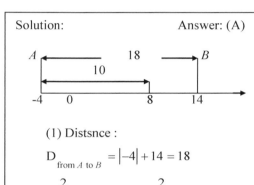

(1) Distsnce :

$$D_{\text{from } A \text{ to } B} = |-4| + 14 = 18$$

$$\frac{2}{3} \text{Way}_{\text{from } A \text{ to } B} = \frac{2}{3} \times 18 = 12$$

⇓

(2) Coordinate:

$$\frac{2}{3} C_{\text{from } A \text{ to } B} = 8$$

NEXT PAGE

16. For how many integers m is $(3m+1)(4m-17)$ a negative number?

(A) 4

(B) 6

(C) 2

(D) 5

Solution: Answer: (D)

$$y = (3m+1)(4m-17) < 0$$

$$\begin{cases} y = (3m+1)(4m-17) = 0 \\ \text{Get zeros (roots) first.} \end{cases}$$

$$\begin{cases} (3m+1) = 0 \\ (4m-17) = 0 \end{cases} \rightarrow \begin{cases} m_1 = -\dfrac{1}{3} \\ m_2 = 4\dfrac{1}{4} \end{cases}$$

By $3m \times 4m = 12m^2$, and $12 > 0$

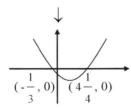

$$\left(-\dfrac{1}{3}, 0\right) \quad \left(4\dfrac{1}{4}, 0\right)$$

In the figure, you can see when each value of $y < 0$,

$$\underbrace{-\dfrac{1}{3} < m < 4\dfrac{1}{4}}_{m = 0, 1, 2, 3, 4}$$

$$\Downarrow$$

5 integers

1   a b

17. On the number line above, if the tick marks are equally spaced, the expression of b in terms of a must be

(A) $a+3$ (B) $4a-1$ (C) $4a-3$ (D) $2a-1$

Solution: Answer: (C)

1   a b

"equally spaced"

$$\downarrow$$

$$b - a = 3(a-1)$$

$$\Downarrow$$

$$b - a = 3a - 3, \quad b = 4a - 3$$

18. A certain integer greater than 1 has only three positive integer factors: 1, itself, and its square root. And one of the factors is a prime number. Which of the following is the certain number?

(A) 25

(B) 16

(C) 81

(D) 256

Solution: Answer: (A)

1 is not a prime number.

Use plug-in method.

$$\downarrow$$

$$\begin{cases} \text{25 has only 3 positive integer factors:} \\ 1, 25, \text{ and } \sqrt{25} = 5. \\ \text{5 is a prime number.} \\ \qquad 1, N, \sqrt{N} \end{cases}$$

$$\Downarrow$$

Answer is (A).

NEXT PAGE

19. If five more than m is a negative number and if 7 more than m is a positive number, which of the following could be the value of m?

(A) -4
(B) -7
(C) -5
(D) -6

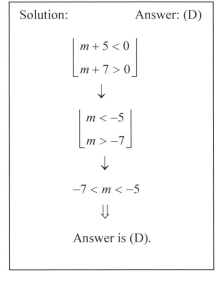

Solution: Answer: (D)

$$\begin{bmatrix} m+5 < 0 \\ m+7 > 0 \end{bmatrix}$$

$\downarrow$

$$\begin{bmatrix} m < -5 \\ m > -7 \end{bmatrix}$$

$\downarrow$

$$-7 < m < -5$$

$\Downarrow$

Answer is (D).

20. If a \$3,000 deposit earns 6% simple annual interest, which of the following is the interest earned in 6 years?

(A) 108

(B) 416

(C) 1,080

(D) 800

Solution: Answer: (C)

Formula for simple interest:
$$i = art$$
Formula for simple interest:
$$b = a(1 + rt)$$
Formula for compound interest:
$$b = a(1 + r)^t$$

where
i is year interest,
b is the balance,
a is starting value,
r is the annual interest rate,
t is the time in years.

$$i = art = 30\,00 \times \frac{6}{1\,00} \times 6$$

$\Downarrow$

$$i = 1,080$$

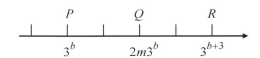

$$P \qquad Q \qquad R$$
$$3^b \qquad 2m3^b \qquad 3^{b+3}$$

21. On the number line above, point Q is the midpoint of $\overline{PR}$. If the tick marks are equally spaced, and b is greater than zero, what is the value of m?

(A) $\dfrac{10}{4}$

(B) $\dfrac{26}{4}$

(C) 8

(D) 7

Solution: Answer: (D)

$$2m3^b - 3^b = 3^{b+3} - 2m3^b$$

$$2m3^b - 3^b = 3^b \cdot 3^3 - 2m3^b$$

$\downarrow$ factoring

$$3^b(2m-1) = 3^b(3^3 - 2m)$$

$$\cancel{3^b}(2m-1) = \cancel{3^b}(3^3 - 2m)$$

$\downarrow$

$$2m - 1 = 27 - 2m$$

$\Downarrow$

$$4m = 28, \quad m = 7$$

22. The daily cost of running a certain heater is p cents per hour for the first r hours, and q cents per hour for each additional hour over r hours. Which of the following expressions represents the cost, in dollars, of running this heater for h hours each day, for d days, if $r < h < 24$?

(A) $\dfrac{pr + q(h-r)}{100d}$

(B) $\dfrac{d[pr + dq(h-r)]}{100}$

(C) $\dfrac{dpr + q(h-r)}{100}$

(D) $\dfrac{d[pr + q(h-r)]}{100}$

Solution: Answer: (D)

Basic portion + Additional portion

days

$\downarrow$

$$d[pr + q(h-r)] \text{ (cents)}$$

$\Downarrow$

$$d\left[\frac{pr + q(h-r)}{100}\right] \text{ (dollars)}$$

NEXT PAGE ⟩

23. Michael is a car salesperson. He sells two kinds of cars. For one of them, the selling price is $32,000, and for another one, the selling price is $48,000. Last week, Michael's goal was to sell at least 10 cars. He did not meet his goal. The total value of the cars he sold was over $360,000. Let x be the number of $32,000 cars, and y be the number of $48,000 cars, that Michael sold last week. Which system of inequalities below represents the conditions described?

(A) $x + y > 10$
$32,000x + 48,000y < 360,000$

(B) $x + y > 10$
$32,000x + 48,000y > 360,000$

(C) $x + y < 10$
$32,000x + 48,000y > 360,000$

(D) $x + y < 10$
$32,000x + 48,000y < 360,000$

Solution: Answer: (C)

$\begin{cases} \text{"at least"} \to \text{Use sign } \geq, \\ \text{but "did not meet his goal"} \end{cases}$

$\downarrow$

Use sign $<$.

"over" $\to$ Use sign $>$.

$\Downarrow$

$x + y < 10$
$32,000x + 48,000y > 360,000$

24. The sum of six distinct integers is zero. What is the least number of these integers that must be positive?

(A) 8

(B) 6

(C) 1

(D) 3

Solution: Answer: (C)

Let $N_n < 0, M > 0,$

and

$N_1 + N_2 +,\dots + N_5 = -M.$

$\downarrow$

$N_1 + N_2 +,\dots + N_5 + M = 0$

$\Downarrow$

The least number of the integers is 1.

$A \quad B \quad C \quad D \quad E \quad F \quad G \quad H \quad I$

25. In the figure above, the letters represent consecutive integers on a number line. If $3C + G = 24$, what is the value of D?

(A) 8
(B) 6
(C) 5
(D) 12

Solution: Answer: (B)

$3C + G = 24$

$\downarrow$

$3C + G = 3(A + 2) + (A + 6)$

$\downarrow$

$3(A + 2) + (A + 6) = 24$

$\downarrow$

$A = 3$

"consecutive"

$\Downarrow$

$D = A + 1 + 1 + 1 = 3 + 3 = 6$

26. Points A and B are the endpoints of a line segment, and the length of the segment is at most 28. There are four other points on the segment, P, Q, R, and S, which are located at distances of 5, 7, 14, and 15, respectively, from point A. which of the points could be the midpoint of AB?

(A) P
(B) Q
(C) R
(D) S

Solution: Answer: (C)

Mid

5	10	→ 14, 15 outside	Wrong
7	14	→ 15 outside	Wrong
14	28	→ every point inside	Correct
15	30	→ over 28	Wrong

$\Downarrow$

Answer is (C).

NEXT PAGE

123456…484950…899100

27. The integer above is formed by writing the integers from 1 to 100, in order, next to each other. If the integer is read from left to right, what is 170th digit from the left?

(A) 5
(B) 1
(C) 2
(D) 9

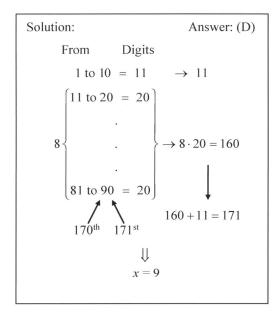

Solution: Answer: (D)

From		Digits
1 to 10	=	11 → 11
11 to 20	=	20
.		
8 { .		} → 8·20 = 160
.		
81 to 90	=	20

160 + 11 = 171

170th 171st

$x = 9$

28. The sum of all even integers from 2 to 206 is 10,712.

What is the sum of all even integers from 4 to 204?

(A) 10916

(B) 10504

(C) 10918

(D) 10819

(E) 10405

Solution: Answer: (B)

$$10712 - (2 + 206)$$
$$\Downarrow$$
$$10712 - 208 = 10504$$

29. What are the solutions to $6x^2 + 24x - 12 = 0$?

(A) $-2 \pm \sqrt{6}$

(B) $\pm 2 - \sqrt{6}$

(C) $\pm 2 + \sqrt{6}$

(D) $+2 \pm \sqrt{6}$

Solution: Answer: (A)

$$6\left(x^2 + 4x - 2\right) = 0$$
$$\downarrow$$

Use $x_{1,2} = \dfrac{-b \pm \sqrt{b^2 - 4ac}}{2a}$

$$\downarrow$$

$$x_{1,2} = \frac{-4 \pm \sqrt{16 + 8}}{2} = \frac{-4 \pm \sqrt{4 \cdot 6}}{2}$$
$$\Downarrow$$
$$\frac{-4 \pm 2\sqrt{6}}{2} = -2 \pm \sqrt{6}$$

30. If $\cos x = \dfrac{\sqrt{2}}{\sqrt{5}}$, where $\dfrac{3\pi}{2} < x < 2\pi$, what is $\tan x$?

(A) $-\dfrac{\sqrt{6}}{2}$

(B) -1.11

(C) -3.42

(D) 2.28

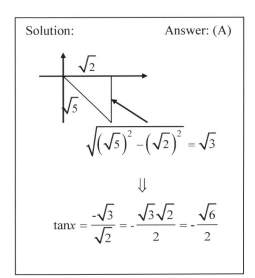

Solution: Answer: (A)

$$\sqrt{\left(\sqrt{5}\right)^2 - \left(\sqrt{2}\right)^2} = \sqrt{3}$$
$$\Downarrow$$
$$\tan x = \frac{-\sqrt{3}}{\sqrt{2}} = -\frac{\sqrt{3}\sqrt{2}}{2} = -\frac{\sqrt{6}}{2}$$

NEXT PAGE

Questions 31 and 32 refer to the information

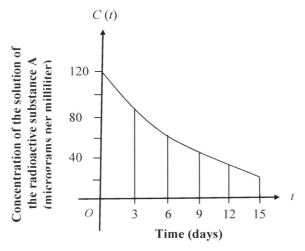

Time (days)	Concentration of the solution of the radioactive substance A (micrograms per milliliter)
0	120
3	85
6	61
9	43
12	31
15	21

In the graph and chart above show the information about the concentration of the solution of the radioactive substance A and the corresponding time.

31.   If the concentration of the solution of the radioactive substance is 120 micrograms per milliliter, it is modeled by the function C defined by $C(t) = 120r^{(t/3)}$, where C is the concentration of the solution, in micrograms, and t is the time, in days. If C approximates the values in the chart, what is the value of r, rounded to the nearest hundredth?

Solution: Answer: .71
You may use the 2 values of any row
in the chart except the first row.

$$\begin{cases} C(3) = 85 = 120r^{(3/3)} \\ 85/120 = r \\ \Downarrow \\ r \approx 0.71 \end{cases} \text{ or } \begin{cases} C(6) = 61 = 120r^{(6/3)} \\ 61/120 = r^2 \\ \Downarrow \\ r = \sqrt{61/120} \approx 0.71 \end{cases}$$

32. By the chart, how many less micrograms of the substance are present in 8 milliliters 12 days after the time beginning than are present in 9 milliliters 15 days after the time beginning?

Solution: Answer: 59
$$(8 \times 31) - (9 \times 21)$$
$$\Downarrow$$
$$248 - 189 = 59$$

33.   How many of the first 200 positive integers are multiples of either 6 or 15?

Solution: Answer: 40

$$\begin{pmatrix} 1 \times 6 \\ 2 \times 6 \\ \vdots \\ 5 \times 6 \\ \vdots \\ \underbrace{33 \times 6 = 198}_{\text{Most close to 200}} \end{pmatrix}, \begin{pmatrix} 1 \times 15 \\ 2 \times 15 \\ \vdots \\ \underbrace{13 \times 15 = 195}_{\text{Most close to 200}} \end{pmatrix}, \begin{pmatrix} 1 \times 30 \\ 2 \times 30 \\ \vdots \\ \underbrace{6 \times 30 = 180}_{\text{Most close to 200}} \end{pmatrix}$$

$$\Downarrow$$

$$33 + 13 - \underbrace{6}_{\substack{\text{Amount} \\ \text{counted} \\ \text{twice}}} = \boxed{40}$$

34. If a rectangular solid has length 10 centimeters, width 2 centimeters, and height 50 centimeters, then how many of the rectangular solids have a volume of five cubic meters when they are combined?

Solution: Answer: 5000

$$\begin{cases} V = S_1 \cdot S_2 \cdot S_3 \\ 1 \text{ meter} = 100 \text{ centimeters} \end{cases}$$

$$V = \frac{1\!\!\!/0}{1\!\!\!/00} \cdot \frac{2}{100} \cdot \frac{5\!\!\!/0}{100} = \frac{1}{1000}$$

$$\Downarrow$$

$$x = \frac{5}{\dfrac{1}{1000}} = 5000$$

NEXT PAGE

Note: Figure below not drawn to scale.

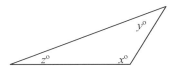

35 If in the figure above, $x > 90$, $z = y - 1$, and y is an integer, what is the greatest possible value of z ?

Solution: Answer: 44

$y°$ is an integer. $\to x°$ and $z°$ are integers.

$$y = z + 1$$
$$x + (z + 1) + z = 180$$
$$z = \frac{179 - x}{2}$$

According to the equation above, when x has the least value, z has the greatest value.

$$\Downarrow$$

$$z = \frac{179 - 91}{2} = 44$$

---

36. Judy is 28 years old and her sister, Jody, is 17. How many years ago was Judy' age two times as old as Jody's?

Solution: Answer: 6

Let x = number of years ago.

$$28 - x = \underbrace{2(17 - x)}_{\text{Judy's age}}$$
$$\underset{\text{Judy's age}}{}$$

$$\Downarrow$$

$$x = 6$$

$$\sqrt{x - 2}$$
$$\downarrow$$

```
|___|___|___|___|___|___|___|___|___>
0           1               2
```

37. In the figure above, there are eight equal intervals between 0 and 2 on the number line. What is the value of x?

Solution: Answer: 17/4 or 4.25

$$\frac{6}{4} = \frac{3}{2} = \sqrt{x - 2} \to \left(\frac{3}{2}\right)^2 = x - 2$$

$$\Downarrow$$

$$2 + \frac{9}{4} = x, \quad \frac{8 + 9}{4} = x, \quad x = \frac{17}{4} \text{ or } 4.25$$

---

38. At a store, two sevenths of the items are discounted by 70 percent, one seventh of the items are discounted by 40 percent, three fourteenths of the items are discounted by 50 percent, and rest items are not discounted. If one item is to be selected randomly, what is the probability that the item is discounted by 40 percent, 50 percent or 70 percent?

Solution: Answer: 9/14 or .642 or .643

$$"\text{or}" = "+"$$

$$\Downarrow$$

$$\frac{2}{7} + \frac{1}{7} + \frac{3}{14} = \frac{9}{14}$$

STOP

SAT Math

Practice

Test 14

Redesigned for Tests in March 2016 and Beyond

Mad Math

Math Test – No Calculator

Time: 25 Minutes
20 Questions

Notes:
- The use of a calculator is not allowed.
- All numbers used in this section are the real number.
- Figures are provided for some problems in this test. Unless otherwise indicated under the figure "Note: Figure above not drawn to scale", all figures are drawn as accurately as possible.
- All figures lie in a plane EXCEPT otherwise specified.
- Unless otherwise indicated, the domain of any function f, g or j is assumed to be the set of all real numbers x for which $f(x)$, $g(x)$, or $j(x)$ is a real number.

Reference Information

$$A = \frac{1}{2}bh$$

$$A = lw$$

$$A = \pi r^2$$

$$V = \pi r^2 h$$

$$V = lwh$$

$$c^2 = a^2 + b^2$$

$$V = \frac{1}{3}\pi r^2 h$$

$$V = \frac{4}{3}\pi r^3$$

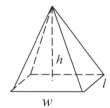

$$V = \frac{1}{3}lwh$$

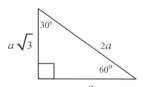

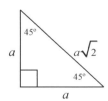

1. Five cards in a pot are numbered 1 through 5. One card is drawn at random. The ones digit of the sum of the numbers on the remaining cards is 1. What is the number on the drawn card?

(A) 4
(B) 2
(C) 1
(D) 3

2. If p_1 represents the greatest prime number less than 101

and p_2 represents the least prime number greater than 47,

which of the following is the value of $p_1 + p_2$?

(A) 152

(B) 150

(C) 154

(D) 156

3. Two times the first of three consecutive even integers is 20 less than four times the third. What is the second integer?

(A) 7
(B) 6
(C) 5
(D) 4

4. Which of the following does $\sqrt{x^2}$ equal?

(A) $-x$

(B) $\sqrt{x}$

(C) x

(D) $|x|$

5. If $y_m = 1 + (-1)^m$, where $m = 1, 2, 3, 4, ...$, which of the following statements is true?

(A) For all m, $y_m = 2$ or $y_m = 1$.

(B) For all m, $y_m = 0$ only.

(C) For all m, $y_m = 0$ or $y_m = 2$.

(D) For all m, $y_m = 1$ or $y_m = 2$.

NEXT PAGE

Price per Pound of Materials

Materials	EUROs (€)	USDs ($)
A	3	3.64
B	5	6.06
C	200	243
D	3	3.64

The chart above gives the prices of four different materials expressed in both USDs and EUROs. Let u be USDs and e be EUROs.

6. If the € 36,000 in a shipment come entirely from a pounds of material A, b pounds of material B, and d pounds of material D, which of the following represents b in terms of a and d?

(A) $b = 7200 - \dfrac{5}{3}(a + d)$

(B) $b = 7200 - \dfrac{3}{5}(a + d)$

(C) $b = 7200 + \dfrac{3}{5}(a + d)$

(D) $b = 7200 + \dfrac{5}{3}(a + d)$

7. A sprinkler is set to spray water over a distance of 1 yard and rotates through an angle of 330°. What is the area, in square yards, watered by the sprinkler?

(A) $\dfrac{11\pi}{5}$

(B) 330

(C) $\dfrac{11\pi}{12}$

(D) $\dfrac{11\pi}{3}$

NEXT PAGE

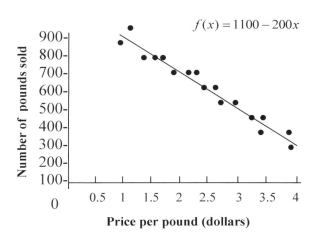

$f(x) = 1100 - 200x$

Price per pound (dollars)

A supermarket sells pounds of peanutbutters and decides the price per pound every month. The scatterplot above shows the price and the number of pounds of peanutbutters sold for 17 months with the line of best fit and the equation for the line.

8.   By the line of best fit above, how many pounds of peanutbutters should the supermarket expect to sell in a month when the price of peanutbutter is $2.00 each pound?

(A) 700

(B) 800

(C) 300

(D) 500

9. By the line of best fit on the left, what is the price of peanutbutters the supermarket expects to sell in a month when the peanutbutters are 680 pounds?

(A) $3.00

(B) $2.50

(C) $3.70

(D) $2.10

10.   If $216^{\frac{5}{x}} = 36$, then x is equal to

(A) 19

(B) 21

(C) 15

(D) 7.5

NEXT PAGE

Questions 11 and 12 refer to the information below.

Box versus Time

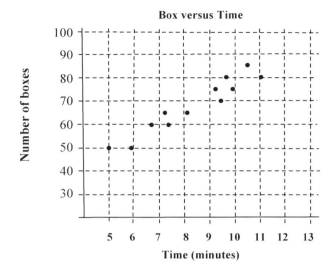

Team	Rate of Packing (boxes per minute)
team 1	6.00
team 2	2.50
team 3	4.25
team 4	6.25
team 5	5.00
team 6	7.00
team 7	4.00

Calculating the approximate number, N, of the boxes packed by people is easy: N = Time × Rate of packing. The scatterlpot and table above provide the relationship of time and box, and the names of seven packing teams and their rate of packing.

11. According to the information of the scatterplot and table, if team 3 and team 7 both have finished 1/10 hour for packing boxes, then each of them now have 15 boxes to pack, which of the following will be closest to the sum, in minutes, of their time?

(A) 18   (B) 20   (C) 32   (D) 16

12. By the scatterplot providing the time ploted against box for 12 people of a single team, the rate of packing is closest to that of which the following teams?

(A) team 2

(B) team 5

(C) team 1

(D) team 3

NEXT PAGE

r	q
0	200
1	400
2	600
3	800

13. The table above shows data of a function. What could be the graph of the function?

(A) a graph of an exponential function

(B) a circle

(C) a hyperbola

(D) a straight line

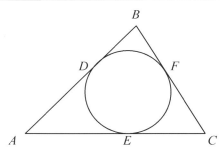

Note: Figure above not drawn to scale.

15. In the figure above, if circle is inscribed in triangle ABC, $AD = 8$ and $CF = 2$ what is the length of the side AC?

(A) 16
(B) 12
(C) 14
(D) 10

14. Which of the following could be the remainders when 3 consecutive integers are each divided by 2?

(A) 1, 2, 0
(B) 0, 1, 0
(C) 0, 2, 0
(D) 0, 1, 2

16. Several students stand in a line. Starting at one end of the line, Maria is counted as 8th person, and starting at the other end, Maria is counted as the 13th person. How many students are in the line?

17. What is the number that satisfies the following three conditions?

4. It is an integer greater than 2000 and less than 3,200.
5. The sum of its digits is 29.
6. It tens and units digits are the same.

18. On a restaurant menu, there are four desserts, four appetizers and six main courses. How many different dinners can be ordered if each dinner consists of one dessert, one appetizer and one course?

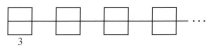

Note: Figure above not drawn to scale.

19. The figure above shows some squares, each side measuring 3 units, placed at one end of a 104-unit straight-line segment. If there are 2-unit spaces between consecutive squares and the center of each square is on the segment, what is the maximum number of such squares that could be placed on the 104-unit segment?

20. In how many distinct ways can four people arrange themselves in the four person seats of a car if only two of the people can drive the car?

STOP

Copying or reuse of any portion of this page is illegal.

No Test Contents

On This Page

Go to Next Page

Math Test – Calculator

Time: 55 Minutes
38 Questions

Notes:
- The use of a calculator is not allowed.
- All numbers used in this section are the real number.
- Figures are provided for some problems in this test. Unless otherwise indicated under the figure "Note: Figure above not drawn to scale", all figures are drawn as accurately as possible.
- All figures lie in a plane EXCEPT otherwise specified.
- Unless otherwise indicated, the domain of any function f, g or j is assumed to be the set of all real numbers x for which $f(x)$, $g(x)$, or $j(x)$ is a real number.

Reference Information

$$A = \frac{1}{2}bh$$

$$A = lw$$

$$A = \pi r^2$$

$$V = \pi r^2 h$$

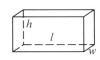

$$V = lwh$$

$$c^2 = a^2 + b^2$$

$$V = \frac{1}{3}\pi r^2 h$$

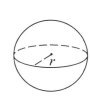

$$V = \frac{4}{3}\pi r^3$$

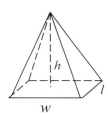

$$V = \frac{1}{3}lwh$$

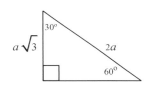

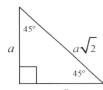

Copying or reuse of any portion of this page is illegal.

$$\begin{cases} 3x > 5 \\ y > 3x + 1 \end{cases}$$

1. Which of the following consists of the y-coordinates of all the points that satisfy the system of inequalities above?

(A) $y > 4$

(B) $y > 5$

(C) $y > 6$

(D) $y > \dfrac{5}{3}$

2. If $\dfrac{p}{r} = \dfrac{4}{7}$ and $\dfrac{r}{q} = \dfrac{2}{5}$, then $\dfrac{q}{p} =$

(A) $\dfrac{43}{20}$

(B) $\dfrac{35}{8}$

(C) $\dfrac{14}{20}$

(D) $\dfrac{12}{7}$

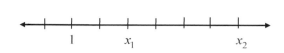

3. On the number line above, if the tick marks are equally spaced, the expression of x_2 in terms of x_1 must be

(A) $3x_1 - 2$ (B) $3x_1 + 2$ (C) $x_1 - 2$ (D) $3x_1 - 1$

4. If $9x - 27 = 36$, then the value of $(x + 3)$ is

(A) 4

(B) 6

(C) 5

(D) 10

NEXT PAGE

5. If $t_1 = \dfrac{W}{R_1}$ and $t_2 = \dfrac{W}{R_2}$, then $T = \dfrac{W}{R_1 + R_2}$ is equal to

(A) $\dfrac{t_2}{T} + \dfrac{T}{t_1} = 1$

(B) $\dfrac{T}{t_1} + \dfrac{T}{t_2} = 1$

(C) $\dfrac{t_1}{T} + \dfrac{t_2}{T} = 1$

(D) $\dfrac{t_1}{T} + \dfrac{t_2}{T} + 1 = 0$

$$-\dfrac{y}{2} - 1 = 2x + 1$$

7. What is the slope of the function above?

(A) 1

(B) -2

(C) -4

(D) 4

8. If four more than m is a negative number and if six more than m is a positive number, which of the following could be the value of m?

(A) -4
(B) 3
(C) -5
(D) -6

6. Five points, A, B, C, D, and E, lie on a line, not necessarily in that order. $\overline{AB}$ has a length of 36. Point C is the midpoint of $\overline{AB}$, and point D is the midpoint of $\overline{AC}$. If the distance between D and E is 7, what is one possible distance between B and E?

(A) 16 or 14
(B) 6
(C) 20 or 34
(D) 26

NEXT PAGE

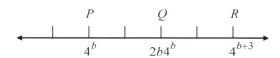

9. On the number line above, point Q is the midpoint of $\overline{PR}$. If b is greater than zero, and the tick marks are equally spaced, what is the value of b?

(A) $\dfrac{63}{4}$

(B) 5

(C) 3

(D) $\dfrac{65}{4}$

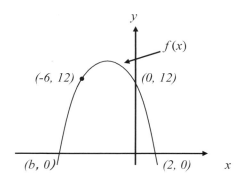

10. The diagram above shows the graph of a quadratic function f. What is the value of b?

(A) -8

(B) -5

(C) -7

(D) -9

NEXT PAGE

11. Points A and B are the endpoints of a line segment, and the length of the segment is less than 28. There are four other points on the segment, P, Q, R, and S, which are located at distances of 7, 11, 14, and 15, respectively, from point A. which of the points could be the midpoint of AB?

(A) P
(B) Q
(C) R
(D) S

13. A 16-liter solution of acid and water is 25% acid. How many liters of water must be added to reduce the concentration of acid in the solution to 10%?

(A) 26
(B) 22
(C) 24
(D) 20

12. To celebrate Anthony's birthday, his n friends agree to share equally to a dinner that costs a total of x dollars. If q of the friends can't share the cost, which of the following represents the additional amount, in dollars, that each of the remaining friends must share to pay for the dinner?

(A) $\dfrac{-qx}{n(n-q)}$

(B) $-\dfrac{n(n-q)}{qx}$

(C) $\dfrac{-n(n+q)}{qx}$

(D) $\dfrac{qx}{n(n-q)}$

NEXT PAGE

14   Let the function g be defined by $g(x) = k(x-a)^2$, where k is a negtive constant and a is a positive constant. For what value of x will the function g have its maximum value?

(A) k

(B) $-k$

(C) $-a$

(D) a

15.   The sides of a rectangular solid have lengths $4s$, $5s$, and $7s$. Which of the following is the entire surface area of the rectangular solid, in terms of s ?

(A) $83s^2$

(B) $166s^2$

(C) $176s^2$

(D) $186s^2$

$$A \quad B \quad C \quad D \quad E \quad F \quad G \quad H \quad I$$

16.   In the figure above, the letters represent consecutive integers on a number line. If $2C + E = 23$, what is the value of F?

(A) 10

(B) 6

(C) 5

(D) 12

123456…484950…899100

17.   The integer above is formed by writing the integers from 1 to 100, in order, next to each other. If the integer is read from left to right, what is 90th digit from the left?

(A) 5

(B) 1

(C) 2

(D) 9

NEXT PAGE

18. If the perimeter of a regular polygon is 18, which of the following could be the length of one side of the polygon?

(A) 18
(B) 3
(C) 5
(D) 7

19. If the first two terms of a sequence are 14 and 23 and each subsequence is the sum of the two preceding terms, how many of the first 1000 terms are even and how many of the first 1000 terms are odd?

(A) 334 and 666

(B) 333 and 667

(C) 334 and 667

(D) 332 and 665

20. A function is defined by $f(t) = -(1/2)^t + 4$. Which of the following is the sketch of $f(t)$?

(A)

(B)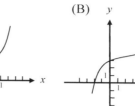

(C)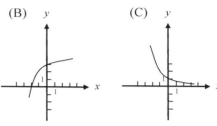

(D)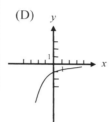

NEXT PAGE

21. In the sequence k_1, k_2, k_3, $k_4, \ldots$, where k_1 is the first term, k_m is equal to $6m + 1$. If S_m represents the sum of the first m terms, which of th following is the value of S_{61} ?

(A) 11,407

(B) 2,275

(C) 11,704

(D) 2,257

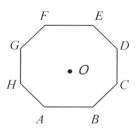

Note: Figure above not drawn to scale.

22. In the regular octagon $ABCDEFGH$ above, if O is the center of the octagon, what is the degree measure of $\dfrac{\angle B}{2}$?

(A) $135°$

(B) $67.5°$

(C) $45°$

(D) $90°$

23. If $3x^2 + 7x + K$ is divided by $x + 2$, then remainder is 1. Which of the following is the value of K ?

(A) 1

(B) 2

(C) 3

(D) 4

NEXT PAGE

24. On a number line, if point B has coordinate -4 and point A has coordinate -10, what is the coordinate of the point that is located $\dfrac{1}{3}$ of the way from B to A?

(A) 6
(B) 4
(C) -6
(D) 2

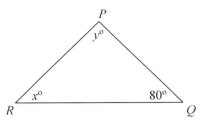

Note: Figure above not drawn to scale.

26. In the figure above, $PR < PQ$. Which of the following must be true?

(A) $x^\circ > 81^\circ$
(B) $x^\circ = y^\circ$
(C) $y^\circ < 20^\circ$
(D) $x^\circ < y^\circ$

25. The function g is defined by $g(x) = (x+2)(x-5)$. The graph of g in the xy-plane is a parabola. Which interval below contains the x-coordinate of the vertex of the graph of g ?

(A) $-5 < x \le 1$
(B) $-3 < x \le 0$
(C) $-2 \le x < 1.5$
(D) $-3 < x \le 1.5$

27. In the sequence 9, 15, 33, 87... where 9 is the first term, which of the following could denote the nth term?

(A) n^9

(B) $9 \times n$

(C) 9^n

(D) $3^n + 6$

NEXT PAGE

28. If the sequence $p - 2$, $p + 2$, and $2p - 3$ form an arithmetic sequence, what is the value of p?

(A) 9
(B) -3
(C) 8
(D) 6

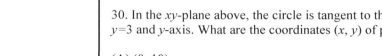

30. In the xy-plane above, the circle is tangent to the line $y = 3$ and y-axis. What are the coordinates (x, y) of point Q?

(A) $(0, 10)$
(B) $(10, 0)$
(C) $(0, 3)$
(D) $(0, 13)$

29. If $\dfrac{1}{2}$ of a cup pineapple juice is filled to a $1\dfrac{1}{2}$-cup mark of a measuring container with a mixture containing equal amounts of apple and pineapple juices, what is the ratio of the apple juice to the final mixture?

(A) $\dfrac{5}{12}$

(B) $\dfrac{7}{12}$

(C) $\dfrac{1}{3}$

(D) $\dfrac{2}{3}$

NEXT PAGE

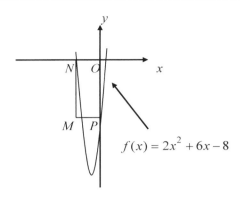

$$f(x) = 2x^2 + 6x - 8$$

31. In the figure above, the graph of $f(x)$ intersects the y-axis at point P and the x-axis at point N. What is the area of rectangle $MNOP$?

32. How many three-digit numbers have the hundreds digit equal to 2 and the units digit equal to 3?

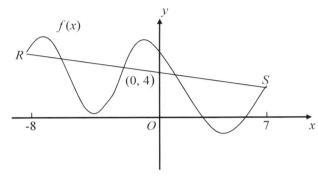

33. The figure above shows the graph of the function g and segment $\overline{RS}$ that has a y-intercept of 4. For how many values of x between -8 and 7 does $f(x) = 4$?

34. The vertices of a triangle are $(3, 1)$, $(3, 5)$, and $(6, 1)$. The area of the triangle is

NEXT PAGE

35. What is 33.5 percent of 60 ?

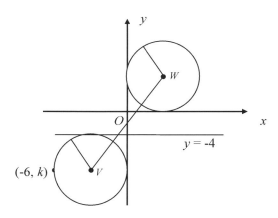

Note: Figure above not drawn to scale.

36. The old equipment of Dr. Bush's office is broken. To fix it will cost $280. New energy-efficient equipment costing $580 will save Dr. Bush's $20 on his monthly bill. If buying the new equipment, Dr. Bush, after *m* months, will save an amount equal to the difference between the cost of the new equipment and the cost of fixing the old one. What is the value of *m?*

38. In the *xy*-plane above, points *W* and *V* are the centers of the identical circles, which are both tangent to the *y*-axis, one of them tangent to *x*-axis, and one tangent to line *y* = -4. What is the slope of $\overline{WV}$?

37. If one of distinct seven books, book *M*, has to be placed in the middle on a bookshelf, how many distinct ways can the seven books be arranged on the bookshelf?

STOP

Answer Key
For
SAT Math Practice Test 14

Section 3

1	A
2	B
3	D
4	D
5	C
6	B
7	C
8	A
9	D
10	D
11	A
12	C
13	D
14	B
15	D

16	20
17	2999
18	96
19	21
20	12

Section 4

1	C	16	A
2	B	17	A
3	A	18	B
4	D	19	A
5	B	20	B
6	C	21	A
7	C	22	B
8	C	23	C
9	D	24	C
10	A	25	D
11	B	26	C
12	D	27	D
13	C	28	A
14	D	29	C
15	B	30	D

31	32
32	10
33	3
34	6
35	20.1
36	15
37	720
38	5/3 or 1.66 or 1,67

SAT Math

Practice

Test 14

Explanations

Redesigned for Tests in March 2016 and Beyond

Mad Math

Math Test – No Calculator

Time: 25 Minutes
20 Questions

Notes:
- The use of a calculator is not allowed.
- All numbers used in this section are the real number.
- Figures are provided for some problems in this test. Unless otherwise indicated under the figure "Note: Figure above not drawn to scale", all figures are drawn as accurately as possible.
- All figures lie in a plane EXCEPT otherwise specified.
- Unless otherwise indicated, the domain of any function f, g or j is assumed to be the set of all real numbers x for which $f(x)$, $g(x)$, or $j(x)$ is a real number.

Reference Information

$$A = \frac{1}{2}bh$$

$$A = lw$$

$$A = \pi r^2$$

$$V = \pi r^2 h$$

$$V = lwh$$

$$c^2 = a^2 + b^2$$

$$V = \frac{1}{3}\pi r^2 h$$

$$V = \frac{4}{3}\pi r^3$$

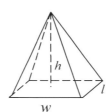

$$V = \frac{1}{3}lwh$$

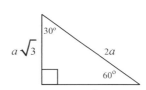

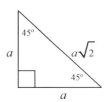

1. Five cards in a pot are numbered 1 through 5. One card is drawn at random. The ones digit of the sum of the numbers on the remaining cards is 1. What is the number on the drawn card?

(A) 4
(B) 2
(C) 1
(D) 3

Solution: Answer: (A)

$$\begin{cases} \text{Sum} = 1+2+3+4+5 = 15 \\ \text{Sum}_{\text{Remaining}} = 15 - x = \begin{cases} 1 \\ 11 \end{cases} \\ x \le 5 \end{cases}$$

$$\Downarrow$$

$$x = 4$$

2. If p_1 represents the greatest prime number less than 101 and p_2 represents the least prime number greater than 47, which of the following is the value of $p_1 + p_2$?

(A) 152
(B) 150
(C) 154
(D) 156

Solution: Answer: (B)

$$p_1 = 97, \quad p_2 = 53$$

$$\Downarrow$$

$$p_1 + p_2 = 97 + 53 = 150$$

3. Two times the first of three consecutive even integers is 20 less than four times the third. What is the second integer?

(A) 7
(B) 6
(C) 5
(D) 4

Solution: Answer: (D)

Let $(x-2)$, x, and $(x+2)$ be the 3 consecutive even integers.

$$\downarrow$$

$$2(x-2) = 4(x+2) - 20$$

$$\downarrow$$

$$2x - 4 = 4x + 8 - 20$$

$$\Downarrow$$

$$x = 4$$

4. Which of the following does $\sqrt{x^2}$ equal?

(A) $-x$

(B) $\sqrt{x}$

(C) x

(D) $|x|$

Solution: Answer: (D)

$$\begin{cases} x^2 \ge 0, \ \left(x^2\right)^{\frac{1}{2}} \ge (0)^{\frac{1}{2}} \\ \downarrow \\ \sqrt{x^2} \ge 0 \quad \text{and} \\ \underbrace{\text{The question condition } x < 0 \text{ or } x \ge 0} \end{cases}$$

This question does indicate the the domain of $\sqrt{x^2}$.
The values of x could be in the interval above.

$$\Downarrow$$

$$\sqrt{x^2} = |x|$$

5. If $y_m = 1 + (-1)^m$, where $m = 1, 2, 3, 4, ...$, which of the following statements is true?

(A) For all m, $y_m = 2$ or $y_m = 1$.
(B) For all m, $y_m = 0$ only.
(C) For all m, $y_m = 0$ or $y_m = 2$.
(D) For all m, $y_m = 1$ or $y_m = 2$.

Solution: Answer: (C)

$$y_1 = 1 + (-1)^1 = 0, \ y_2 = 1 + (-1)^2 = 2$$
$$y_3 = 1 + (-1)^3 = 0, \ y_4 = 1 + (-1)^4 = 2$$

$$\Downarrow$$

$$0, 2, 0, 2, ...$$

NEXT PAGE

Price per Pound of Materials

Materials	EUROs (€)	USDs ($)
A	3	3.64
B	5	6.06
C	200	243
D	3	3.64

The chart above gives the prices of four different materials expressed in both USDs and EUROs. Let u be USDs and e be EUROs.

6.   If the € 36,000 in a shipment come entirely from a pounds of material A, b pounds of material B, and d pounds of material D, which of the following represents b in terms of a and d?

(A) $b = 7200 - \dfrac{5}{3}(a+d)$

(B) $b = 7200 - \dfrac{3}{5}(a+d)$

(C) $b = 7200 + \dfrac{3}{5}(a+d)$

(D) $b = 7200 + \dfrac{5}{3}(a+d)$

Solution: Answer: (B)
$$36000 = 3a + 5b + 3d$$
$$\Downarrow$$
$$36000 = 5b + 3(a+d), \quad 36000 - 3(a+d) = 5b$$
$$\Downarrow$$
$$b = 7200 - \frac{3}{5}(a+d)$$

7.   A sprinkler is set to spray water over a distance of 1 yard and rotates through an angle of $330°$. What is the area, in square yards, watered by the sprinkler?

(A) $\dfrac{11\pi}{5}$

(B) 330

(C) $\dfrac{11\pi}{12}$

(D) $\dfrac{11\pi}{3}$

Solution: Answer: (C)
$$A = \frac{1}{2}R^2\theta^r = \frac{1}{2}\cdot 1^2 \cdot 330 \cdot \frac{\pi}{180} = 11 \cdot \frac{\pi}{12}$$
or
$$A = \frac{1}{2}R^2\theta^r = \frac{1}{2}\cdot 1^2 \cdot \frac{11\pi}{6}$$
$$\Downarrow$$
$$A = \frac{11\pi}{12}$$

NEXT PAGE ⟹

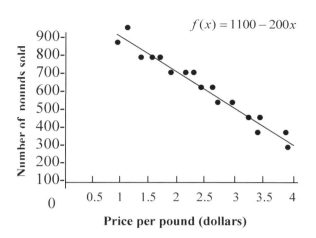

$f(x) = 1100 - 200x$

Price per pound (dollars)

A supermarket sells pounds of peanutbutters and decides the price per pound every month. The scatterplot above shows the price and the number of pounds of peanutbutters sold for 17 months with the line of best fit and the equation for the line.

8.   By the line of best fit above, how many pounds of peanutbutters should the supermarket expect to sell in a month when the price of peanutbutter is $2.00 each pound?

(A) 700

(B) 800

(C) 300

(D) 500

Solution: Answer: (A)

"expect to sell"

↓

values of the line, not values of the points.

↓

$f(2) = 1100 - 200 \cdot 2$

⇓

$f(2) = 700$

9.   By the line of best fit on the left, what is the price of peanutbutters the supermarket expects to sell in a month when the peanutbutters are 680 pounds?

(A) $3.00

(B) $2.50

(C) $3.70

(D) $2.10

Solution: Answer: (D)

"expect to sell"

↓

values of the line, not values of the points.

↓

$680 = 1100 - 200x, \quad 200x = 420$

⇓

$x = \dfrac{42}{20} = \dfrac{21}{10} = 2.1$

10.   If $216^{\frac{5}{x}} = 36$, then x is equal to

(A) 19

(B) 21

(C) 15

(D) 7.5

Solution: Answer: (D)

$\left(6^3\right)^{\frac{5}{x}} = 6^2 \rightarrow 6^{\frac{15}{x}} = 6^2$

⇓

$\dfrac{15}{x} = 2, \quad x = 7.5$

NEXT PAGE ⇨

Questions 11 and 12 refer to the information below.

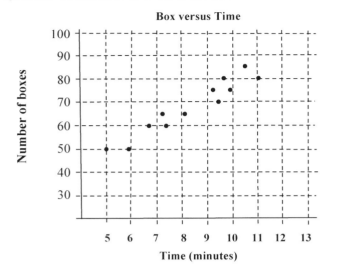

Box versus Time

Team	Rate of Packing (boxes per minute)
team 1	6.00
team 2	2.50
team 3	4.25
team 4	6.25
team 5	5.00
team 6	7.00
team 7	4.00

Calculating the approximate number, N, of the boxes packed by people is easy: N = Time × Rate of packing. The scatterlpot and table above provide the relationship of time and box, and the names of seven packing teams and their rate of packing.

11. According to the information of the scatterplot and table, if team 3 and team 7 both have finished 1/10 hour for packing boxes, then each of them now have 15 boxes to pack, which of the following will be closest to the sum, in minutes, of their time?

(A) 18   (B) 20   (C) 32   (D) 16

Solution: Answer: (A)

$$(1/10) \text{ hour} = 6 \text{ minutes}$$

$$\begin{cases} \text{Rate of group 3 is } \dfrac{17}{4}. \text{ That means } \dfrac{4}{17} \text{ minute per box.} \\ \\ \text{Rate of group 7 is 4. That means } \dfrac{1}{4} \text{ minute per box.} \end{cases}$$

$$\downarrow$$

$$\left(6 + \frac{4}{17} \times 15\right) + \left(6 + \frac{1}{4} \times 15\right) \approx 9.53 + 9.75$$

A box cannot be 0.53 or 0.75 one.

$$\Downarrow$$

$$S = 9 + 9 = 18$$

12. By the scatterplot providing the time ploted against box for 12 people of a single team, the rate of packing is closest to that of which the following teams?

(A) team 2

(B) team 5

(C) team 1

(D) team 3

Solution: Answer: (C)

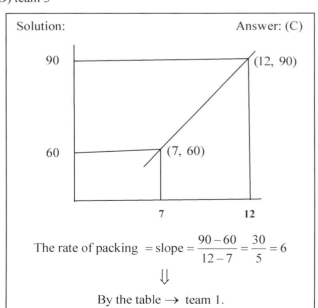

The rate of packing $= \text{slope} = \dfrac{90 - 60}{12 - 7} = \dfrac{30}{5} = 6$

$$\Downarrow$$

By the table → team 1.

NEXT PAGE

r	q
0	200
1	400
2	600
3	800

13. The table above shows data of a function. What could be the graph of the function?

(A) a graph of an exponential function

(B) a circle

(C) a hyperbola

(D) a straight line

Solution: Answer: (D)

q and r should be output and input, respectively.

The values of function q increase by 200 as r increases by 1, so this is a linear function with slope $s = 200$. Because $g(0) = 200$, the vertical intercept is 200.

$$g(r) = 200 + 200r$$
$$\Downarrow$$

Its graph is a straight line.

14. Which of the following could be the remainders when 3 consecutive integers are each divided by 2?

(A) 1, 2, 0
(B) 0, 1, 0
(C) 0, 2, 0
(D) 0, 1, 2

Solution: Answer: (B)

$$\frac{x}{2}, \quad \frac{x+1}{2}, \quad \frac{x+2}{2}$$

Use plug-in method.
$$\downarrow$$

When $x = 2$,

remainders = 0, 1, 0.
$$\Downarrow$$

Answer is (B).

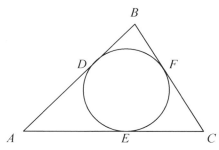

Note: Figure above not drawn to scale.

15. In the figure above, if circle is inscribed in triangle ABC, $AD = 8$ and $CF = 2$ what is the length of the side AC?

(A) 16
(B) 12
(C) 14
(D) 10

Solution: Answer: (D)

Type: A circle is tangent by segments.

The circle is tangent by the segments PQ and PS.
$$\downarrow$$
$$PQ = PS.$$
$$AE = AD = 8 \text{ and } EC = CF = 2$$
$$\Downarrow$$
$$AC = AE + EC = 8 + 2 = 10$$

16. Several students stand in a line. Starting at one end of the line, Maria is counted as 8th person, and starting at the other end, Maria is counted as the 13th person. How many students are in the line?

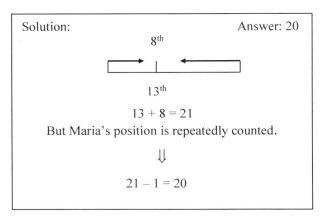

Solution: Answer: 20

$$13 + 8 = 21$$

But Maria's position is repeatedly counted.

⇓

$$21 - 1 = 20$$

17. What is the number that satisfies the following three conditions?

1. It is an integer greater than 2000 and less than 3,200.
2. The sum of its digits is 29.
3. It tens and units digits are the same.

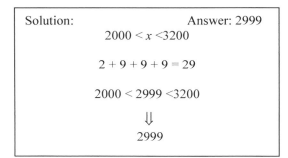

Solution: Answer: 2999

$$2000 < x < 3200$$

$$2 + 9 + 9 + 9 = 29$$

$$2000 < 2999 < 3200$$

⇓

2999

18. On a restaurant menu, there are four desserts, four appetizers and six main courses. How many different dinners can be ordered if each dinner consists of one dessert, one appetizer and one course?

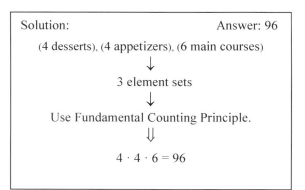

Solution: Answer: 96

(4 desserts), (4 appetizers), (6 main courses)

↓

3 element sets

↓

Use Fundamental Counting Principle.

⇓

$$4 \cdot 4 \cdot 6 = 96$$

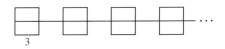

Note: Figure above not drawn to scale.

19. The figure above shows some squares, each side measuring 3 units, placed at one end of a 104-unit straight-line segment. If there are 2-unit spaces between consecutive squares and the center of each square is on the segment, what is the maximum number of such squares that could be placed on the 104-unit segment?

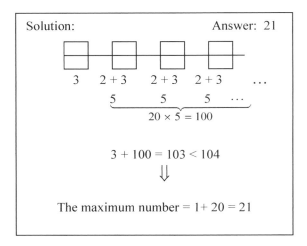

Solution: Answer: 21

3   2 + 3   2 + 3   2 + 3   ...
       5   5   5   ...
$$20 \times 5 = 100$$

$$3 + 100 = 103 < 104$$

⇓

The maximum number $= 1 + 20 = 21$

20. In how many distinct ways can four people arrange themselves in the four person seats of a car if only two of the people can drive the car?

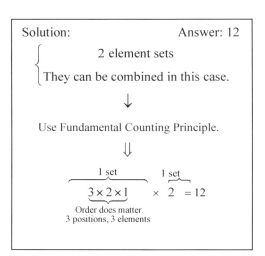

Solution: Answer: 12

{ 2 element sets
  They can be combined in this case.

↓

Use Fundamental Counting Principle.

⇓

1 set   1 set
$$3 \times 2 \times 1 \times 2 = 12$$
Order does matter.
3 positions, 3 elements

STOP

No Test Contents

On This Page

Go to Next Page

Math Test – Calculator

Time: 55 Minutes
38 Questions

Notes:
- The use of a calculator is not allowed.
- All numbers used in this section are the real number.
- Figures are provided for some problems in this test. Unless otherwise indicated under the figure "Note: Figure above not drawn to scale", all figures are drawn as accurately as possible.
- All figures lie in a plane EXCEPT otherwise specified.
- Unless otherwise indicated, the domain of any function f, g or j is assumed to be the set of all real numbers x for which $f(x)$, $g(x)$, or $j(x)$ is a real number.

Reference Information

$A = \dfrac{1}{2}bh$

$A = lw$

$A = \pi r^2$

$V = \pi r^2 h$

$V = lwh$

$c^2 = a^2 + b^2$

$V = \dfrac{1}{3}\pi r^2 h$

$V = \dfrac{4}{3}\pi r^3$

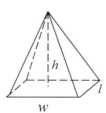

$V = \dfrac{1}{3}lwh$

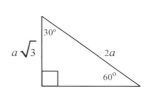

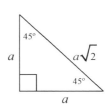

$$\begin{cases} 3x > 5 \\ y > 3x + 1 \end{cases}$$

1. Which of the following consists of the y-coordinates of all the points that satisfy the system of inequalities above?

(A) $y > 4$

(B) $y > 5$

(C) $y > 6$

(D) $y > \dfrac{5}{3}$

Solution: Answer: (C)

$a > b$ and $b > c \rightarrow a > c$

$$\begin{cases} 3x > 5 \\ \quad\downarrow \\ 3x + 1 > 5 + 1 \end{cases} \rightarrow 3x + 1 > 6$$

$\Downarrow$

$y > 3x + 1 > 6, \ y > 6$

2. If $\dfrac{p}{r} = \dfrac{4}{7}$ and $\dfrac{r}{q} = \dfrac{2}{5}$, then $\dfrac{q}{p} =$

(A) $\dfrac{43}{20}$

(B) $\dfrac{35}{8}$

(C) $\dfrac{14}{20}$

(D) $\dfrac{12}{7}$

Solution: Answer: (B)

The question asks $\dfrac{q}{p}$ that has no r.

Let $r = 1$.

$\downarrow$

$$\begin{cases} p = \dfrac{4}{7} \\ \dfrac{1}{q} = \dfrac{2}{5} \rightarrow q = \dfrac{5}{2} \end{cases}$$

$\Downarrow$

$\dfrac{q}{p} = \dfrac{\frac{5}{2}}{\frac{4}{7}} = \dfrac{5 \times 7}{2 \times 4} = \boxed{\dfrac{35}{8}}$

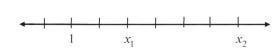

3. On the number line above, if the tick marks are equally spaced, the expression of x_2 in terms of x_1 must be

(A) $3x_1 - 2$ (B) $3x_1 + 2$ (C) $x_1 - 2$ (D) $3x_1 - 1$

Solution: Answer: (A)

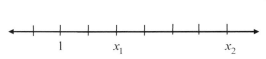

"equally spaced"

$\downarrow$

$x_2 - x_1 = 2(x_1 - 1)$

$\Downarrow$

$x_2 - x_1 = 2x_1 - 2, \ x_2 = 3x_1 - 2$

4.   If $9x - 27 = 36$, then the value of $(x + 3)$ is

(A) 4
(B) 6
(C) 5
(D) 10

Solution: Answer: (D)

$9(x - 3) = 36^{\,4}$

$\downarrow$

$x - 3 = 4$

$\downarrow$

$x - 3 + (6) = 4 + (6)$

$\Downarrow$

$x + 3 = 10$

NEXT PAGE

5. If $t_1 = \dfrac{W}{R_1}$ and $t_2 = \dfrac{W}{R_2}$, then $T = \dfrac{W}{R_1 + R_2}$ is equal to

(A) $\dfrac{t_2}{T} + \dfrac{T}{t_1} = 1$

(B) $\dfrac{T}{t_1} + \dfrac{T}{t_2} = 1$

(C) $\dfrac{t_1}{T} + \dfrac{t_2}{T} = 1$

(D) $\dfrac{t_1}{T} + \dfrac{t_2}{T} + 1 = 0$

Solution:　　　　Answer: (B)

$$\begin{cases} t_1 = \dfrac{W}{R_1} \rightarrow R_1 = \dfrac{W}{t_1} \\[2mm] t_2 = \dfrac{W}{R_2} \rightarrow R_2 = \dfrac{W}{t_2} \end{cases}$$

↓

$$\begin{cases} T = \dfrac{W}{R_1 + R_2} \\[4mm] T = \dfrac{W}{\dfrac{W}{t_1} + \dfrac{W}{t_2}} = \dfrac{\cancel{W}}{\cancel{W}\left(\dfrac{1}{t_1} + \dfrac{1}{t_2}\right)} \end{cases}$$

↓

$$\left(\dfrac{1}{t_1} + \dfrac{1}{t_2}\right) T = 1$$

⇓

$$\dfrac{T}{t_1} + \dfrac{T}{t_2} = 1$$

6. Five points, $A,\ B,\ C,\ D,$ and E, lie on a line, not necessarily in that order. $\overline{AB}$ has a length of 36. Point C is the midpoint of $\overline{AB}$, and point D is the midpoint of $\overline{AC}$. If the distance between D and E is 7, what is one possible distance between B and E?

(A) 16 or 14
(B) 6
(C) 20 or 34
(D) 26

Solution:　　　　　　　　　　Answer: (C)

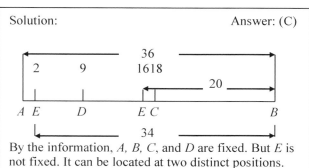

By the information, A, B, C, and D are fixed. But E is not fixed. It can be located at two distinct positions.

$$-\dfrac{y}{2} - 1 = 2x + 1$$

7. What is the slope of the function above?

(A) 1

(B) -2

(C) -4

(D) 4

Solution:　　　　　　Answer: (C)

$$-\dfrac{y}{2} = 2x + 2, \quad y = -4x - 4$$

$$\underbrace{y = sx + b}_{\text{slope-intercept form}}$$

⇓

$$s = -4$$

8. If four more than m is a negative number and if six more than m is a positive number, which of the following could be the value of m?

(A) -4
(B) 3
(C) -5
(D) -6

Solution:　　　Answer: (C)

$$\begin{bmatrix} m + 4 < 0 \\ m + 6 > 0 \end{bmatrix}$$

↓

$$\begin{bmatrix} m < -4 \\ m > -6 \end{bmatrix}$$

↓

$$-6 < m < -4$$

⇓

Answer is (C).

NEXT PAGE

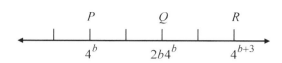

9. On the number line above, point Q is the midpoint of $\overline{PR}$. If b is greater than zero, and the tick marks are equally spaced, what is the value of b?

(A) $\dfrac{63}{4}$

(B) 5

(C) 3

(D) $\dfrac{65}{4}$

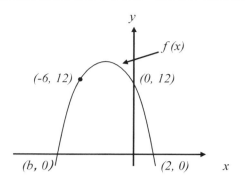

10. The diagram above shows the graph of a quadratic function f. What is the value of b?

(A) -8

(B) -5

(C) -7

(D) -9

Solution: Answer: (D)

$$2b4^b - 4^b = 4^{b+3} - 2b4^b$$

$$2b4^b - 4^b = 4^b \cdot 4^3 - 2b4^b$$

$$\downarrow \text{ factoring}$$

$$4^b(2b-1) = 4^b(4^3 - 2b)$$

$$\cancel{4^b}(2b-1) = \cancel{4^b}(4^3 - 2b)$$

$$2b - 1 = 64 - 2b$$

$$\Downarrow$$

$$4b = 65, \quad b = \frac{65}{4}$$

Solution: Answer: (A)

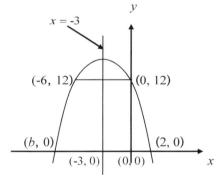

Obtain the symmetrical line first.

symmetrical line $x = \dfrac{-6+0}{2} = -3$

distance between points (-3, 0) and (2, 0) = 5

A parabola is a symmetric graph.

$$\downarrow$$

distance between points (-3, 0) and (b, 0) = 5

$$\Downarrow$$

$$b = -8$$

NEXT PAGE

11. Points A and B are the endpoints of a line segment, and the length of the segment is less than 28. There are four other points on the segment, P, Q, R, and S, which are located at distances of 7, 11, 14, and 15, respectively, from point A. which of the points could be the midpoint of AB?

(A) P
(B) Q
(C) R
(D) S

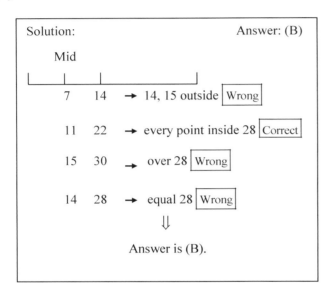

Solution: Answer: (B)

Mid

| 7 | 14 | → 14, 15 outside | Wrong |

| 11 | 22 | → every point inside 28 | Correct |

| 15 | 30 | → over 28 | Wrong |

| 14 | 28 | → equal 28 | Wrong |

⇓

Answer is (B).

12. To celebrate Anthony's birthday, his n friends agree to share equally to a dinner that costs a total of x dollars. If q of the friends can't share the cost, which of the following represents the additional amount, in dollars, that each of the remaining friends must share to pay for the dinner?

(A) $\dfrac{-qx}{n(n-q)}$

(B) $-\dfrac{n(n-q)}{qx}$

(C) $\dfrac{-n(n+q)}{qx}$

(D) $\dfrac{qx}{n(n-q)}$

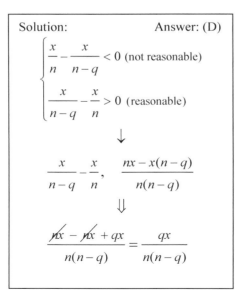

Solution: Answer: (D)

$$\begin{cases} \dfrac{x}{n} - \dfrac{x}{n-q} < 0 \ \text{(not reasonable)} \\[2mm] \dfrac{x}{n-q} - \dfrac{x}{n} > 0 \ \text{(reasonable)} \end{cases}$$

↓

$$\dfrac{x}{n-q} - \dfrac{x}{n}, \quad \dfrac{nx - x(n-q)}{n(n-q)}$$

⇓

$$\dfrac{\cancel{nx} - \cancel{nx} + qx}{n(n-q)} = \dfrac{qx}{n(n-q)}$$

13. A 16-liter solution of acid and water is 25% acid. How many liters of water must be added to reduce the concentration of acid in the solution to 10%?

(A) 26
(B) 22
(C) 24
(D) 20

Solution: Answer: (C)

$$A + B = M$$

$$16 \times 25 + 0 \cdot x = 10 \cdot (16 + x)$$

$$\begin{cases} 16 \times \dfrac{25}{100} + \dfrac{0}{100} \cdot x = \dfrac{10}{100} \cdot (16+x) \\[2mm] \downarrow \\ \text{Do not need write down the 100s.} \end{cases}$$

↓

$$40\cancel{0} = \cancel{10} \cdot (16 + x)$$

⇓

$$x = \boxed{24}$$

NEXT PAGE ⟩

14 Let the function g be defined by $g(x) = k(x-a)^2$, where k is a negtive constant and a is a positive constant. For what value of x will the function g have its maximum value?

(A) k

(B) $-k$

(C) $-a$

(D) a

Solution: Answer: (D)

Method 1

$$g(x) = k(x-a)^2 = k\left(x^2 - 2ax + a^2\right)$$

↓

$$g(x) = kx^2 - 2akx + ka^2$$

$$g(x) = Ax^2 + Bx + C$$

$A < 0$, when $x = \dfrac{-B}{2A}$, function

g has its maximum value.

⇓

$$x = \frac{-(-2ak)}{2k} = a$$

Method 2

Vertex form of quadratic function:

$$f(x) = k\left(x - x_m\right) + y_m$$

⇓

$$x_m = a$$

15. The sides of a rectangular solid have lengths $4s$, $5s$, and $7s$. Which of the following is the entire surface area of the rectangular solid, in terms of s ?

(A) $83s^2$

(B) $166s^2$

(C) $176s^2$

(D) $186s^2$

Solution: Answer: (B)

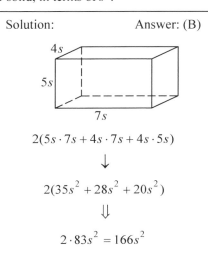

$$2(5s \cdot 7s + 4s \cdot 7s + 4s \cdot 5s)$$

↓

$$2(35s^2 + 28s^2 + 20s^2)$$

⇓

$$2 \cdot 83s^2 = 166s^2$$

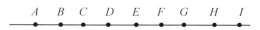

16. In the figure above, the letters represent consecutive integers on a number line. If $2C + E = 23$, what is the value of F?

(A) 10

(B) 6

(C) 5

(D) 12

Solution: Answer: (A)

$$2(A+2) + (A+4) = 23$$

↓

$$A = 5$$

"consecutive"

⇓

$$F = A + 1 + 1 + 1 + 1 + 1 = 5 + 5 = 10$$

123456…484950…899100

17. The integer above is formed by writing the integers from 1 to 100, in order, next to each other. If the integer is read from left to right, what is 90th digit from the left?

(A) 5

(B) 1

(C) 2

(D) 9

Solution: Answer: (A)

From   Digits

1 to 10 = 11   → 11

$4\begin{cases} 11 \text{ to } 20 = 20 \\ \quad . \\ \quad . \\ \quad . \\ 41 \text{ to } 50 = 20 \end{cases}$ → $4 \cdot 20 = 80$

↓

$$80 + 11 = 91$$

90th

⇓

$$x = 5$$

NEXT PAGE

18. If the perimeter of a regular polygon is 18, which of the following could be the length of one side of the polygon?

(A) 18
(B) 3
(C) 5
(D) 7

Solution: Answer: (B)

(1) Any regular polygon has at least 3 sides.

↓

Choices (A) and (E) are eliminated.

(2) $S_{\text{side length}} = \dfrac{\text{Perimeter}}{\text{\# of sides}} \rightarrow \dfrac{\text{Perimeter}}{\text{Integer}}$

$\dfrac{18}{\text{Integer}} \neq 5 \text{ or } 7$ $\dfrac{18}{\text{Integer}} = \dfrac{18}{6} = 3$

↓   ⇓

(C) and (D) are liminated.   Answer is (B).

19. If the first two terms of a sequence are 14 and 23 and each subsequence is the sum of the two preceding terms, how many of the first 1000 terms are even and how many of the first 1000 terms are odd?

(A) 334 and 666

(B) 333 and 667

(C) 334 and 667

(D) 332 and 665

Solution: Answer: (A)

The first term is 14. It is not 0.

$\underbrace{14,\ 23,\ 37}_{\text{1 even number}},\ \underbrace{60,\ 97,\ 157}_{\text{1 even number}},\ \cdots$

↓

Each 3 terms include an even number.

Each 3 terms include 2 odd numbers.

⇓

$\dfrac{999}{3} + 1 = 334,$ $\dfrac{999}{3} \times 2 = 666$

↑

Value of 1000th

term is even.

20. A function is defined by $f(t) = -(1/2)^{t} + 4$. Which of the following is the sketch of $f(t)$?

(A)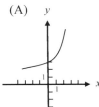

(B)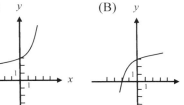

(C)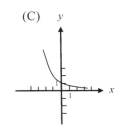

(D)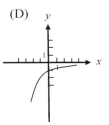

Solution: Answer: (B)

$\begin{cases} h(t) = (1/2)^{t} \text{ and } 0 < 1/2 < 1 \\ \text{Its sketch is (C).} \end{cases}$

$\begin{cases} j(x) = -h(x) \\ \text{The graph of } h \text{ flips about } x\text{-axis.} \end{cases}$

The sketch of $j(t) = -(1/2)^{t}$ is (D).

⇓

The sketch of $f(t) = -(1/2)^{t} + 4$ is (B).

21. In the sequence k_1, k_2, k_3, k_4,..., where k_1 is the first term, k_m is equal to $6m+1$. If S_m represents the sum of the first m terms, which of th following is the value of S_{61} ?

(A) 11, 407

(B) 2, 275

(C) 11, 704

(D) 2, 257

Solution: Answer: (A)

$$k_m = 6m + 1$$

When $m = 1, 2, 3, 4,...,$

$$k_1 = 6 \cdot 1 + 1 = 7$$
$$k_2 = 6 \cdot 2 + 1 = 13$$
$$k_3 = 6 \cdot 3 + 1 = 19$$
$$k_4 = 6 \cdot 4 + 1 = 25$$

$\downarrow$

It is an arithmetic sequence.

The difference is equal to 6.

Use formulas of arithmetic sequence.

$$\begin{cases} a_n = a_1 + (n-1)d \\ S_n = \dfrac{a_1 + a_n}{2} \cdot n \end{cases}$$

or

$$S_n = \frac{2a_1 + (n-1)d}{2} \cdot n$$

$\downarrow$

$$S_{61} = \frac{2 \cdot 7 + 60 \cdot 6}{2} \cdot 61$$

$\Downarrow$

$$\boxed{11407}$$

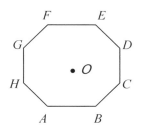

Note: Figure above not drawn to scale.

22. In the regular octagon $ABCDEFGH$ above, if O is the center of the octagon, what is the degree measure of $\dfrac{\angle B}{2}$?

(A) $135°$

(B) $67.5°$

(C) $45°$

(D) $90°$

Solution: Answer: (B)

$$(n-2) \times 180$$

$\downarrow$

$$(8-2) \times 180 = 1080$$

$\Downarrow$

$$\frac{m\angle B}{2} = \frac{\dfrac{1}{8} \cdot 1040}{2} = \frac{1080}{8 \cdot 2} = 67.5$$

---

23. If $3x^2 + 7x + K$ is divided by $x + 2$, then remainder is 1. Which of the following is the value of K ?

(A) 1

(B) 2

(C) 3

(D) 4

Solution: Answer: (C)

The remainder theorem:

If $\dfrac{P(x)}{x-c}$, the remainder $= P(c)$.

$\downarrow$

$$3 \cdot (-2)^2 + 7(-2) + K = 1$$
$$12 - 14 + K = 1$$

$\Downarrow$

$$K = 3$$

NEXT PAGE

24. On a number line, if point B has coordinate -4 and point A has coordinate -10, what is the coordinate of the point that is located $\dfrac{1}{3}$ of the way from B to A?

(A) 6
(B) 4
(C) -6
(D) 2

Solution: Answer: (C)

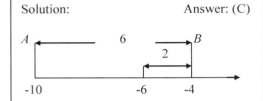

(1) Distsnce:

$$D_{\text{from } B \text{ to } A} = \left|-10\right| - \left|-4\right| = 6$$

$$\frac{1}{3}\text{Way}_{\text{from } B \text{ to } A} = \frac{1}{3} \times 6 = 2$$

⇓

(2) Coordinate:

$$\frac{1}{3}C_{\text{from } B \text{ to } A} = -6$$

25. The function g is defined by $g(x) = (x+2)(x-5)$. The graph of g in the xy-plane is a parabola. Which interval below contains the x-coordinate of the vertex of the graph of g?

(A) $-5 < x \le 1$
(B) $-3 < x \le 0$
(C) $-2 \le x < 1.5$
(D) $-3 < x \le 1.5$

Solution: Answer: (D)

$$0 = (x+2)(x-5)$$

↓

Roots or zeros: $x = -2$ and $x = 5$

⇓

The vertex x-coordinate $= \dfrac{x_1 + x_2}{2} = \dfrac{-2+5}{2} = 1.5$

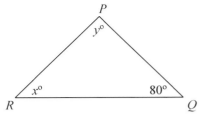

Note: Figure above not drawn to scale.

26. In the figure above, $PR < PQ$. Which of the following must be true?

(A) $x° > 81°$
(B) $x° = y°$
(C) $y° < 20°$
(D) $x° < y°$

Solution: Answer: (C)

In any triangle, the greater side subtends the greater angle, and vice versa.

↓

$$PR < PQ$$
$$x > 80°$$

↓

$$(80° + x°) > 160°$$

⇓

The degrees of the third angle $y° < 20°$

27. In the sequence 9, 15, 33, 87... where 9 is the first term, which of the following could denote the nth term?

(A) n^9
(B) $9 \times n$
(C) 9^n
(D) $3^n + 6$

Solution: Answer: (D)

$$n = 1, 2, 3, 4...$$

(Note: Because there is no zero term, $n \ne 0$)

Use plug-in method.

↓

(D) $3^n + 6$

$$3^1 + 6 = 9$$
$$3^2 + 6 = 15$$
$$3^3 + 6 = 33$$
$$3^4 + 6 = 87$$

⋮

⇓

Answer is (D).

NEXT PAGE

28. If the sequence $p - 2$, $p + 2$, and $2p - 3$ form an arithmetic sequence, what is the value of p?

(A) 9
(B) -3
(C) 8
(D) 6

> **Solution:**   **Answer: (A)**
>
> For any arithmetic sequence a, b, c,
>
> $$b - a = c - b$$
>
> $\downarrow$
>
> $$(p+2) - (p-2) = (2p-3) - (p+2)$$
>
> $\Downarrow$
>
> $$4 = p - 5, \quad p = \boxed{9}$$

29. If $\frac{1}{2}$ of a cup pineapple juice is filled to a $1\frac{1}{2}$-cup mark of a measuring container with a mixture containing equal amounts of apple and pineapple juices, what is the ratio of the apple juice to the final mixture?

(A) $\dfrac{5}{12}$

(B) $\dfrac{7}{12}$

(C) $\dfrac{1}{3}$

(D) $\dfrac{2}{3}$

> **Solution:**   **Answer: (C)**
>
> Before $\dfrac{1}{2}$ of a cup apple juice was filled
>
> to a $1\dfrac{1}{2}$-cup container, the container had
>
> contained $\left(\dfrac{3}{2} - \dfrac{1}{2} \right)$ cup mixed juice.
>
> $\Downarrow$
>
> $$\text{Ratio} = \dfrac{\dfrac{3}{2} - \dfrac{1}{2}}{\dfrac{3}{2}} = \dfrac{\dfrac{1}{2}}{\dfrac{3}{2}} = \dfrac{1}{3}$$

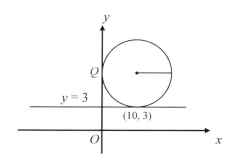

30. In the xy-plane above, the circle is tangent to the line $y=3$ and y-axis. What are the coordinates (x, y) of point Q?

(A) $(0, 10)$
(B) $(10, 0)$
(C) $(0, 3)$
(D) $(0, 13)$

> **Solution:**   **Answer: (D)**
>
> point $(10, 3)$
>
> $\downarrow$
>
> radius $= 10$
>
> $\Downarrow$
>
> Point $Q = (0, 13)$

NEXT PAGE

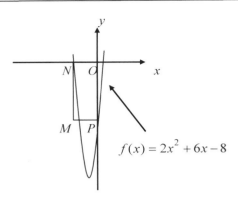

$$f(x) = 2x^2 + 6x - 8$$

31. In the figure above, the graph of $f(x)$ intersects the y-axis at point P and the x-axis at point N. What is the area of rectangle $MNOP$?

Solution: Answer: 32

$$f(x) = y = 2x^2 + 6x - 8$$

(1) $\underbrace{\text{When } x = 0, \ y = -8}_{\text{for point } P}$.

(2) $\underbrace{\text{When } y = 0, \ 0 = 2x^2 + 6x - 8.}_{\text{for point } N}$

$$x^2 + 3x - 4 = 0$$

$$(x + 4)(x - 1) = 0$$

$$x = 1, \qquad x = -4$$

It is not on the rectangle.

(3) $A_{MNOP} = |-8| \cdot |-4| = 32$

32. How many three-digit numbers have the hundreds digit equal to 2 and the units digit equal to 3?

Solution: Answer: 10

$$203, 213, 223 \ldots 283, 293$$

⇓

$$x = 10$$

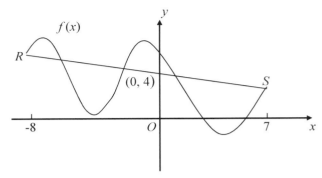

33. The figure above shows the graph of the function g and segment $\overline{RS}$ that has a y-intercept of 4. For how many values of x between -8 and 7 does $f(x) = 4$?

Solution: Answer: 3

Draw a horizontal line, which passes through the point $(0, 4)$. The function of the line is $y = 4$. The line intersects the graph of f at 3 points between -8 and 7.

⇓

Answer = 3

34. The vertices of a triangle are $(3, 1)$, $(3, 5)$, and $(6, 1)$. The area of the triangle is

Solution: Answer: 6

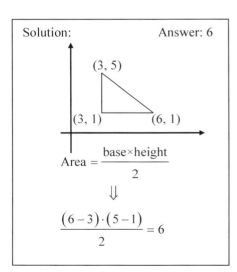

$$\text{Area} = \frac{\text{base} \times \text{height}}{2}$$

⇓

$$\frac{(6 - 3) \cdot (5 - 1)}{2} = 6$$

NEXT PAGE

35.   What is 33.5 percent of 60 ?

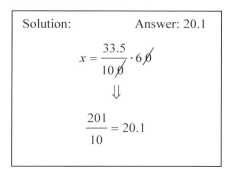

Solution: Answer: 20.1

$$x = \frac{33.5}{10\cancel{0}} \cdot 6\cancel{0}$$

$$\Downarrow$$

$$\frac{201}{10} = 20.1$$

36. The old equipment of Dr. Bush's office is broken. To fix it will cost $280. New energy-efficient equipment costing $580 will save Dr. Bush's $20 on his monthly bill. If buying the new equipment, Dr. Bush, after *m* months, will save an amount equal to the difference between the cost of the new equipment and the cost of fixing the old one. What is the value of *m?*

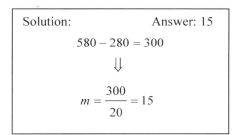

Solution: Answer: 15

$$580 - 280 = 300$$

$$\Downarrow$$

$$m = \frac{300}{20} = 15$$

37.   If one of distinct seven books, book *M*, has to be placed in the middle on a bookshelf, how many distinct ways can the seven books be arranged on the bookshelf?

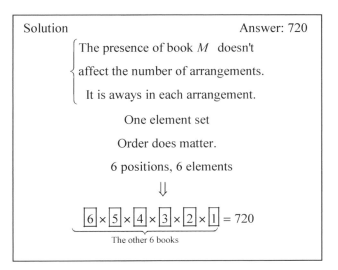

Solution   Answer: 720

⎧ The presence of book *M* doesn't
⎨ affect the number of arrangements.
⎩ It is aways in each arrangement.

One element set

Order does matter.

6 positions, 6 elements

$$\Downarrow$$

$$\boxed{6} \times \boxed{5} \times \boxed{4} \times \boxed{3} \times \boxed{2} \times \boxed{1} = 720$$

The other 6 books

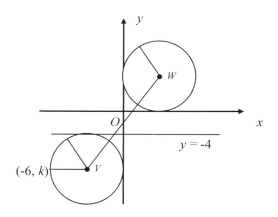

Note: Figure above not drawn to scale.

38.   In the *xy*-plane above, points *W* and *V* are the centers of the identical circles, which are both tangent to the *y*-axis, one of them tangent to *x*-axis, and one tangent to line *y* = -4. What is the slope of $\overline{WV}$?

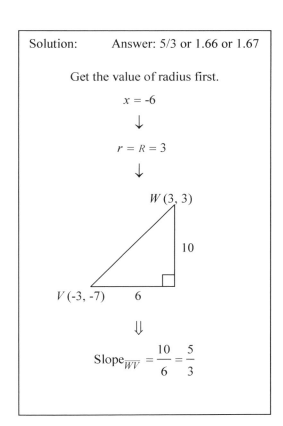

Solution: Answer: 5/3 or 1.66 or 1.67

Get the value of radius first.

$$x = -6$$

$$\downarrow$$

$$r = R = 3$$

$$\downarrow$$

$$\text{Slope}_{\overline{WV}} = \frac{10}{6} = \frac{5}{3}$$

STOP

SAT Math

Practice

Test 15

Redesigned for Tests in March 2016 and Beyond

Mad Math

Math Test – No Calculator

Time: 25 Minutes
20 Questions

Notes:
- The use of a calculator is not allowed.
- All numbers used in this section are the real number.
- Figures are provided for some problems in this test. Unless otherwise indicated under the figure "Note: Figure above not drawn to scale", all figures are drawn as accurately as possible.
- All figures lie in a plane EXCEPT otherwise specified.
- Unless otherwise indicated, the domain of any function f, g or j is assumed to be the set of all real numbers x for which $f(x)$, $g(x)$, or $j(x)$ is a real number.

Reference Information

$$A = \frac{1}{2}bh$$

$$A = lw$$

$$A = \pi r^2$$

$$V = \pi r^2 h$$

$$V = lwh$$

$$c^2 = a^2 + b^2$$

$$V = \frac{1}{3}\pi r^2 h$$

$$V = \frac{4}{3}\pi r^3$$

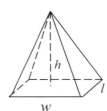

$$V = \frac{1}{3}lwh$$

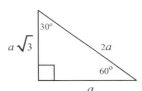

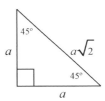

1. On the last day of a sale, customers numbered integer n through integer m, $m > n > 0$, were waited on. How many customers were waited on this day?

(A) $m - n$
(B) $n - m$
(C) $n - m + 1$
(D) $m - n + 1$

2. That $x - 2$ is subtracted from $x - 3$ equals

(A) 1

(B) -1

(C) -2

(D) 2

3. If $p = \dfrac{1}{a}$ and $q = \dfrac{1}{b}$ and $a = 3$, $b = 2$, what is the value

of $\dfrac{1}{p} - \dfrac{1}{q}$?

(A) 1
(B) 2
(C) 3
(D) 4

4. If p_1 represents the greatest prime number less than 83 and p_2 represents the least prime number greater than 59, which of the following is the value of $p_1 - p_2$?

(A) 20

(B) 18

(C) 22

(D) 21

5. If $x - 5$ is 2 more than $y + 4$, then $x + 1$ exceeds y by what amount?

(A) 4
(B) 6
(C) 10
(D 12

6. If $x^2 + y^2 = 256$ and $xy = 25$, what is the value of $(x - y)^2$?

(A) 306
(B) 206
(C) 302
(D) 216

NEXT PAGE

x	f(x)
0	200
1	400
2	800
3	1600

7. The table above shows data of a function. What could be the graph of the function?

(A) a graph of an exponential function

(B) a hyperbola

(C) a parabola

(D) a line

8. Which scatterplot below shows a relationship that is approximately modeled with the equation $f(x) = ar^x$, where $a > 0$ and $r > 1$?

(A)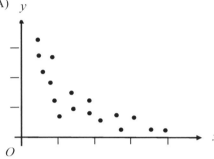

(B)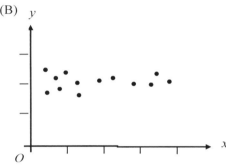

(C)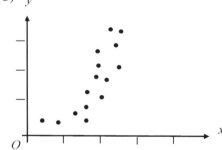

(D)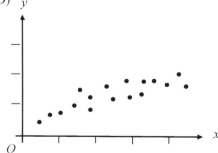

NEXT PAGE

9. What is the least possible value of y if $0 < x \leq y$ and $(x + y)^2 - (x - y)^2 \geq 81$?

(A) 1.5

(B) 2.5

(C) 3.5

(D) 4.5

10. Five points, $A, B, C, D,$ and E, lie on a line, not necessarily in that order. $\overline{AB}$ has a length of 40. Point C is the midpoint of $\overline{AB}$, and point D is the midpoint of $\overline{AC}$. If the distance between D and E is 7, what are all possible distances between B and E?

(A) 23
(B) 37
(C) 17 and 3
(D) 37 and 23

11. John wants to buy a mixture of red tea and green tea. Its price is $20/lb. He has 3 pounds of red tea at $18 per pound. How many pounds of green tea at $26 each pound does John have to purchase?

(A) 3
(B) 1
(C) 5
(D) 2

12. The sum of the digits of a three-digit number is 10. If the hundreds place is 2 times the tens place and the units place is $\frac{1}{3}$ of the tens place, what is the tens place of the number?

(A) 6
(B) 4
(C) 3
(D) 2

NEXT PAGE

13. If a $2,000 bond earns 7% simple annual interest, which of the following is the interest earned in 5 years?

(A) 70

(B) 700

(C) 35

(D) 140

14. In the number line above, the tick marks are equally spaced on the line. How many the tick marks would there be on the number line between the tick marks at 9 and 12?

(A) 13
(B) 11
(C) 9
(D) 8

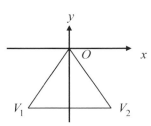

15. In the xy-coordinate plane above, points V_1, O, and V_2 are the 3 vertices of a certain triangle. The coordinates of V_1 are (-2, b) and the coordinates of V_2 are (2, b). Which of the following is one possible value of b if the area of triangle V_1OV_2 is less than 7 and greater than 6 ?

(A) $-\dfrac{15}{4}$

(B) $-\dfrac{13}{4}$

(C) $-\dfrac{11}{4}$

(D) $-\dfrac{7}{2}$

NEXT PAGE

16. The median of eleven consecutive integers is 41. What is the least one of these eleven integers?

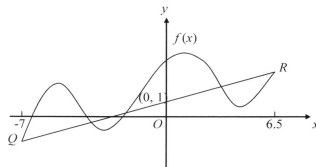

19. The figure above shows the graph of the function f and segment $\overline{QR}$ that has a y-intercept of 1. For how many values of x between -7 and 6.5 does $f(x) = 1$?

17. Maria is both the 11th shortest and 11th tallest student in her math class. If the height of each student in her class is different, how many students are in the class?

20. Shirley can select one or more following four toppings for her pizza: Meatballs, Sausage, Green Peppers, and Mushrooms. If she selects one or more, how many different combinations of the pizza toppings are possible?

18. A certain town has 1800 telephones. Three-fourths of the phones have dials. If push-button phones replace one-third of the dial phones, how many dial phones remain?

STOP

Math Test – Calculator

Time: 55 Minutes
38 Questions

Notes:
- The use of a calculator is not allowed.
- All numbers used in this section are the real number.
- Figures are provided for some problems in this test. Unless otherwise indicated under the figure "Note: Figure above not drawn to scale", all figures are drawn as accurately as possible.
- All figures lie in a plane EXCEPT otherwise specified.
- Unless otherwise indicated, the domain of any function f, g or j is assumed to be the set of all real numbers x for which $f(x)$, $g(x)$, or $j(x)$ is a real number.

Reference Information

$A = \dfrac{1}{2}bh$

$A = lw$

$A = \pi r^2$

$V = \pi r^2 h$

$V = lwh$

$c^2 = a^2 + b^2$

$V = \dfrac{1}{3}\pi r^2 h$

$V = \dfrac{4}{3}\pi r^3$

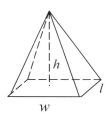

$V = \dfrac{1}{3}lwh$

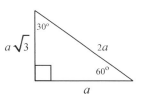

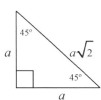

1. In some election, several people collected signatures to place a candidate on the ballot. Of these signatures, 35 percent were thrown out as invalid. Then a further 20 percent of those remaining signatures were eliminated. What percent of the original number of signatures were left?

(A) 52%

(B) 46%

(C) 55%

(D) 70%

2. Jeff was 20 years old x years ago. Which of the following represents his age in y years from now?

(A) $20 + x - y$

(B) $20 - x - y$

(C) $20 + x + y$

(D) $20 + y - x$

3. How many even 2-digit integers less than 90 are there?

(A) 32

(B) 40

(C) 36

(D) 30

4. If the fraction 1/26 is equal to the repeating decimal 0.3846153846153…, what is the 68th digit after the decimal point of the repeating decimal?

(A) 4
(B) 7
(C) 9
(D) 8

5. A list of numbers has been arranged such that each number in the list is 6 less than the number that precedes it. If 98 is the sixth number in the list, what is the second number in the list?

(A) 74
(B) 80
(C) 68
(D) 122

NEXT PAGE

```
3 | 5  6
4 | 1  3
5 | 8  9
6 | 2  4  6  7
7 | 0  7  8
```

3 | 6 represents 36.

6. The stem-and-leaf plot above shows the statistic data. What is the median value of the statistic data?

(A) 59

(B) 64

(C) 62

(D) 58

7. In the xy-plane, the center of a circle has coordinates (3, 11), and the circle touches the x-axis at one point. What is the radius of the circle?

(A) 3

(B) 11

(C) 8

(D) 14

8. The shortest distance from the center of a circle to a chord AB is 8. If the diameter of the center is 20, what is the length of the chord?

(A) 10
(B) 12
(C) 6
(D) 13

9. Which of the following shifts of the graph of $y = x^2$ can result in the graph of $y = x^2 + 14x + h$, where h is a constant less than 49 ?

(A) 7 units right and $(h - 49)$ up

(B) 7 units right and $(h - 49)$ down

(C) 7 units left and $|h - 49|$ up

(D) 7 units left and $|h - 49|$ down

NEXT PAGE

10. In an office supply store, Doris bought 6 items from aisles 2 through 5 and 8 items from aisles 3 through 10. Which of the following could be the total number of items that Doris bought?

(A) 6
(B) 7
(C) 15
(D) 13

11. How many distinct positive four-digit integers can be formed if the first digit must be 3, the last cannot be 3, and digits can be used more than one time?

(A) 900

(B) 1,000

(C) 8,000

(D) 7,200

12. A function is defined by $f(t) = -3^t + 2$. Which of the following is the sketch of $g(t) = f(-t)$?

(A)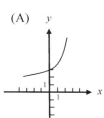

(B)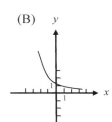

(C)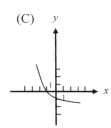

(D)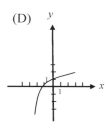

NEXT PAGE

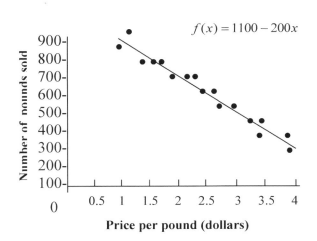

$f(x) = 1100 - 200x$

A supermarket sells pounds of peanutbutters and decides the price per pound every month. The scatterplot above shows the price and the number of pounds of peanutbutters sold for 17 months with the line of best fit and the equation for the line.

13. By the line of best fit above, how many pounds of peanutbutters should the supermarket expect to sell in a month when the price of peanutbutter is $1.50 each pound?

(A) 700

(B) 800

(C) 300

(D) 500

14. By the line of best fit on the left, what is the price of peanutbutters the supermarket expect to sell in a month when the peanutbutters are 360 pounds?

(A) $3.00

(B) $2.50

(C) $3.70

(D) $2.10

15. If the resulting graph represents the graph of $g(x)$ from the graph of $f(x) = 4x^2$ translated 4 units right and 4 units up, what is the value of $g(4.4)$?

(A) 6.34

(B) 3.72

(C) 5.31

(D) 4.64

NEXT PAGE

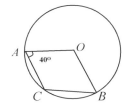

Note: Figure above not drawn to scale.

16. In the figure above, points A, B, and C lie on the circumference of the circle centered at O. If $m\angle OBC = 60^\circ$, $m\angle AOB = ?$

(A) 110
(B) 120
(C) 160
(D) 140

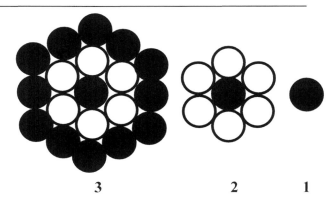

3   2   1

17. The figure sequence above starts with one circle. If each coming figure is structured by adding a ring of the identical circles around the immediately preceding figure, which of the following is the total number of circles in the sixth figure of the sequence?

(A) 71

(B) 81

(C) 64

(D) 91

NEXT PAGE

18. In the xy-plane, A and B are distinct points, which have the same y-coordinate and lie on the parabola whose equation is $y = -x^2 + 5x + 30$. Which of the following is the x-coordinate of the midpoint of $\overline{AB}$?

(A) $\dfrac{5}{2}$

(B) $-\dfrac{2}{5}$

(C) $\dfrac{2}{5}$

(D) $-\dfrac{5}{3}$

19. If a company charge d dollars for their product, where $0 \le d \le 100$, the income from the product will be $I(d) = 1000d - 10d^2$ dollars per day. By this model, for which of the following values of d would the company's daily income for the product be the maximum?

(A) -50
(B) 30
(C) 50
(D) -30

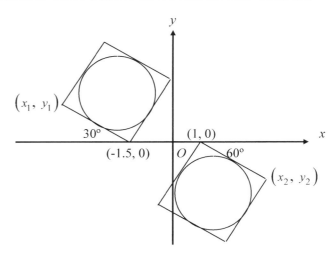

20. In the figure above, 2 identical circles with radius 3 are inscribed in 2 squares, respectively. Which of the following are the values of x_2 and y_1 ?

(A) $x_2 = 4$, $y_1 = -3$
(B) $x_2 = -4$, $y_1 = 3$
(C) $x_2 = 4\sqrt{3}$, $y_1 = 3$
(D) $x_2 = 4$, $y_1 = 3$

NEXT PAGE ⇨

$$\begin{cases} x = z^2 \\ x = \sqrt{y} \\ y = 9z \end{cases}$$

21. In the system of equations above, if $x > 0$, what is the value of x ?

(A) $3\sqrt[3]{3}$

(B) $3\sqrt{3}$

(C) 3

(D) 4

Note: Figure above not drawn to scale.

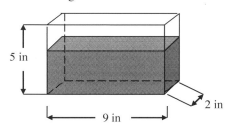

22. The figure above shows the dimensions of a rectangular container sealed up. There is 20 cubic inches of sand in the container. The container will be repositioned on level ground so that the container places on one, which has the least area, of the six surfaces. If it has been repositioned, which of the following will be ratio of the height of the non-sand to the height of the sand?

(A) $\dfrac{2}{7}$

(B) $\dfrac{5}{2}$

(C) $\dfrac{3}{7}$

(D) $\dfrac{7}{2}$

NEXT PAGE ⟶

$$\begin{cases} 3y+1 > 5 \\ x > 3y-2 \end{cases}$$

23. Which of the following consists of the *x*-coordinates of all the points that satisfy the system of inequalities above?

(A) $x < 2$

(B) $x > -2$

(C) $x > 2$

(D) $x > 1$

The fish and beef weighed 5 pounds.
The fish and chicken weighed 6 pounds.
The beef and chicken weighed 7 pounds.

24. By the information above, what is the weight of the chicken?

(A) 4 Pounds
(B) 7 Pounds
(C) 9 Pounds
(D) $\dfrac{5}{2}$ Pounds

25. About what is the ratio of the volume of the cylinder to volume of the sphere if a cylinder whose base radius is 4 is inscribed in a sphere of radius 5 ?

(A) 2.46

(B) 0.44

(C) 4.00

(D) 0.58

26. Michelle, a college graduate, goes to work for D dollars per month. In several months the company she works for gives all employees a 20% pay cut. A few months later, the company gives all employees a 20% raise. What is Michelle's new salary?

(A) D

(B) $0.96D$

(C) $1.2D$

(D) $0.8D$

NEXT PAGE

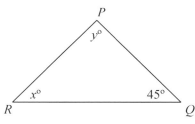

Note: Figure above not drawn to scale.

27. In the figure above, $PR > PQ$. Which of the following must be true?

(A) $x° > 45°$
(B) $x° = y°$
(C) $x° > y°$
(D) $x° < 45°$

28. One ball is dropped from a height of 256 inches and begins bouncing on a floor. If the height of each bounce is three-fourths the height of the previous bounce, what is the height , in inches, between the floor and highest point that the balls can reach after the ball fourth time hits the floor?

(A) 343

(B) 245

(C) 243

(D) 241

29. If $3x^2 + 7x + W$ is divided by $x + 3$, then remainder is 3. Which of the following is the value of W ?

(A) -2

(B) 2

(C) -3

(D) 4

30. Machine A itself can finish a job in a hours, and Machine B itself can finish a job in b hours, where $a > 0$ and $b > 0$. After Machine A begins the job and does $3/4$ of the job, Machine B takes over and finishes the remaining job. Which of the following is the entire time, in hours, that takes Machine A and Machine B to finish the job?

(A) $\dfrac{3a + 2b}{4}$

(B) $\dfrac{2a - b}{4}$

(C) $\dfrac{2a - 3b}{2}$

(D) $\dfrac{3a + b}{4}$

NEXT PAGE

The questions 31 and 32 refer to the information below.

Number of Competitors by Score and Morning

	Score 10 / 10	Score 9 / 10	Score 8 / 10	Score ≤ 7 / 10	Total
Morning 1	3	3	4	8	18
Morning 2	2	4	3	9	18
Morning 3	4	3	6	5	18
Morning 4	3	4	4	7	18
Total	12	14	17	29	72

The number of competitors obtaining a given score in each of four mornings is shown in the chart above. In order to win some certain awards, the same eighteen competitors, in each of four mornings, solved ten math problems. Each competitor obtained one point for each correct solution.

31. What is the average score of the competitors who obtained at least score 8 points in Morning 3, rounded to the nearest hundredth?

32. If a competitor is chosen randomly, and no competitor obtained the same score in two distinct mornings, what is the probability that the chosen competitor obtained a score 9 points in Mornings 3 and 4, given that the competitor obtained a score of 9 points in one of the four mornings?

33. If the equations of 2 lines are $y = 4x + 3$ and $y = 3x + 4$, respectively, and the two lines intersect, what is the absolute value of the difference of the x-coordinate and y-coordinate?

NEXT PAGE

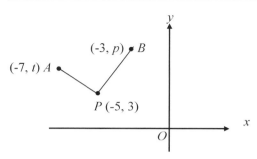

Note: Figure above not drawn to scale.

34. In the figure above, $\overline{AP}$ is perpendicular to $\overline{BP}$, $p = 7$, what is the value of t?

35. James has six blank cards. Each card is written with one of the following letters: *A, B, C, D, E* or *F*. Each of six cards does not have the same letter. If *E* and *F* are always the center letters in each arrangement, how many possible distinct six-letter arrangements can James create?

NEXT PAGE

36   At a college, in a class of 90 juniors, there are 4 girls for every 6 boys. In a senior class, there are 5 girls for every 2 boys. If the two classes are combined, and in the combined class, the number of girls is twice the number of boys, how many boys are in the senior class?

37.   A certain number is any integer greater than 1 that has only three positive integer factors: 1, itself, and its square root. And, one of the factors is a prime number. What is the certain number?

38. The three angles of a triangle have measures of $3m$, m, and $2n$, where $m > 9°$. If m and n are integers, what is the greatest possible value of n?

STOP

Answer Key
For
SAT Math Practice Test 15

Section 3

1	D
2	B
3	A
4	B
5	D
6	B
7	A
8	C
9	D
10	D
11	B
12	C
13	B
14	B
15	B

16	36
17	21
18	900
19	5
20	15

Section 4

1	A	16	C
2	C	17	D
3	B	18	A
4	D	19	C
5	D	20	D
6	C	21	A
7	B	22	D
8	B	23	C
9	D	24	A
10	D	25	D
11	A	26	B
12	D	27	D
13	B	28	C
14	C	29	C
15	D	30	D

31	8.85
32	3/49 Or .061
33	6
34	4
35	48
36	144
37	49
38	70

SAT Math

Practice

Test 15

Explanations

Redesigned for Tests in March 2016 and Beyond

Mad Math

Math Test – No Calculator

Time: 25 Minutes
20 Questions

Notes:
- The use of a calculator is not allowed.
- All numbers used in this section are the real number.
- Figures are provided for some problems in this test. Unless otherwise indicated under the figure "Note: Figure above not drawn to scale", all figures are drawn as accurately as possible.
- All figures lie in a plane EXCEPT otherwise specified.
- Unless otherwise indicated, the domain of any function f, g or j is assumed to be the set of all real numbers x for which $f(x)$, $g(x)$, or $j(x)$ is a real number.

<u>**Reference Information**</u>

$$A = \frac{1}{2}bh$$

$$A = lw$$

$$A = \pi r^2$$

$$V = \pi r^2 h$$

$$V = lwh$$

$$c^2 = a^2 + b^2$$

$$V = \frac{1}{3}\pi r^2 h$$

$$V = \frac{4}{3}\pi r^3$$

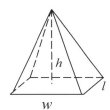

$$V = \frac{1}{3}lwh$$

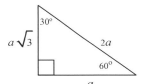

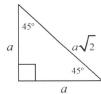

1. On the last day of a sale, customers numbered integer n through integer m, $m > n > 0$, were waited on. How many customers were waited on this day?

(A) $m - n$
(B) $n - m$
(C) $n - m + 1$
(D) $m - n + 1$

Solution: Answer: (D)

$$N_{last} - N_{first} + 1$$
$$\Downarrow$$
$$m - n + 1$$

2. That $x - 2$ is subtracted from $x - 3$ equals

(A) 1

(B) -1

(C) -2

(D) 2

Solution: Answer: (B)

$$x - 3 - (x - 2)$$
$$\Downarrow$$
$$x - 3 - x + 2 = -1$$

3. If $p = \dfrac{1}{a}$ and $q = \dfrac{1}{b}$ and $a = 3$, $b = 2$, what is the value of $\dfrac{1}{p} - \dfrac{1}{q}$?

(A) 1
(B) 2
(C) 3
(D) 4

Solution: Answer: (A)

$$a = \frac{1}{p} = 3, \quad b = \frac{1}{q} = 2$$
$$\Downarrow$$
$$\frac{1}{p} - \frac{1}{q} = 3 - 2 = 1$$

4. If p_1 represents the greatest prime number less than 83 and p_2 represents the least prime number greater than 59, which of the following is the value of $p_1 - p_2$?

(A) 20

(B) 18

(C) 22

(D) 21

Solution: Answer: (B)

$$p_1 = 79, \quad p_2 = 61$$
$$\Downarrow$$
$$p_1 - p_2 = 79 - 61 = 18$$

5. If $x - 5$ is 2 more than $y + 4$, then $x + 1$ exceeds y by what amount?

(A) 4
(B) 6
(C) 10
(D 12

Solution: Answer: (D)

$$x - 5 = y + 4 + 2 = y + 6$$
$$\downarrow$$
$$x - 5 + \left(6\right) = y + 6 + \left(6\right)$$
$$\Downarrow$$
$$\left(x + 1\right) - y = 12$$

6. If $x^2 + y^2 = 256$ and $xy = 25$, what is the value of $(x - y)^2$?

(A) 306
(B) 206
(C) 302
(D) 216

Solution: Answer: (B)

$$x^2 - 2xy + y^2 = 256 - 2xy$$
$$\Downarrow$$
$$(x - y)^2 = 256 - 2 \times 25 = 206$$

NEXT PAGE

x	f(x)
0	200
1	400
2	800
3	1600

7. The table above shows data of a function. What could be the graph of the function?

(A) a graph of an exponential function

(B) a hyperbola

(C) a parabola

(D) a line

Solution:　　　　　　　　Answer: (A)

The function $f(x)$ increase by distinct values as r increases by 1, so this is not a linear function. To determine if f may be an exponential function, check ratios of consecutive values:

$$\frac{400}{200} = \frac{800}{400} = \frac{1600}{800} = 2$$

↓

The value of $f(x)$ increases by a factor of 2 when each time x increases by 1. Because $f(0) = 200$, y-intercept = 200.

⇓

$$f(r) = 200(2)^x$$

8. Which scatterplot below shows a relationship that is approximately modeled with the equation $f(x) = ar^x$, where $a > 0$ and $r > 1$?

(A)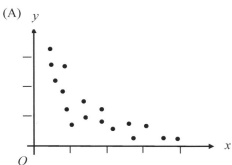

(B)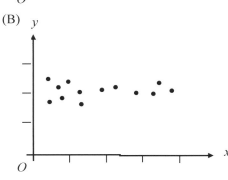

(C)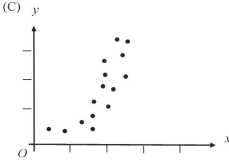

(D)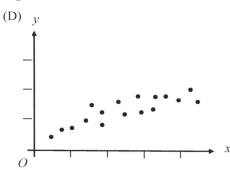

Solution:　　　　　　　　Answer: (C)

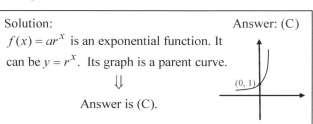

$f(x) = ar^x$ is an exponential function. It can be $y = r^x$. Its graph is a parent curve.

⇓

Answer is (C).

NEXT PAGE

9. What is the least possible value of y if $0 < x \leq y$ and $(x+y)^2 - (x-y)^2 \geq 81$?

(A)1.5

(B) 2.5

(C) 3.5

(D) 4.5

> Solution: Answer: (D)
>
> (1). $x^2 + 2xy + y^2 - (x^2 - 2xy + y^2) \geq 81$
>
> $\cancel{x^2} + 2xy + \cancel{y^2} \cancel{-x^2} + 2xy \cancel{-y^2} \geq 81$
>
> $4xy \geq 81, \quad xy \geq \dfrac{81}{4}, \quad y \geq \dfrac{81}{4x}$
>
> (2). $0 < x \leq y$
>
>   ↓
>
> When $x = y$, y has the least value.
>
> $y \geq \dfrac{81}{4y}, \quad yy = y^2 \geq \dfrac{81}{4}$
>
> $\begin{cases} y > 0 \\ \\ y \geq +\sqrt{\dfrac{81}{4}} = \dfrac{9}{2} \end{cases}$
>
>   ⇓
>
> $y_{\text{least one}} = \dfrac{9}{2} = 4.5$

10. Five points, A, B, C, D, and E, lie on a line, not necessarily in that order. $\overline{AB}$ has a length of 40. Point C is the midpoint of $\overline{AB}$, and point D is the midpoint of $\overline{AC}$. If the distance between D and E is 7, what are all possible distances between B and E?

(A) 23

(B) 37

(C) 17 and 3

(D) 37 and 23

> Solution: Answer: (D)
>
>   40
>
> 3   10   1720
>
> A E   D   E C   B
>
> By the information, A, B, C, and D are fixed. But E is not fixed. It can be located at two distinct positions. So, there are two distances.
>
>   ⇓
>
> $40 - 17 = 23$ or $40 - 3 = 37$.

11. John wants to buy a mixture of red tea and green tea. Its price is \$20/lb. He has 3 pounds of red tea at \$18 per pound. How many pounds of green tea at \$26 each pound does John have to purchase?

(A) 3

(B) 1

(C) 5

(D) 2

> Solution: Answer: (B)
> $A + B = M$
>
> $3 \times 18 + 26x = 20(3 + x)$
>
>   ⇓
>
> $x = \boxed{1}$

12. The sum of the digits of a three-digit number is 10. If the hundreds place is 2 times the tens place and the units place is $\dfrac{1}{3}$ of the tens place, what is the tens place of the number?

(A) 6

(B) 4

(C) 3

(D) 2

> Solution: Answer: (C)
>
> The question asks the value of tens place.
> Let x = value of tens place.
>
>   ↓
>
> $2x + x + \dfrac{1}{3}x = 10$
>
>   ↓
>
> $\dfrac{6x + 3x + x}{3} = 10$
>
>   ⇓
>
> $x = 3$

NEXT PAGE ⟩

13. If a $2,000 bond earns 7% simple annual interest, which of the following is the interest earned in 5 years?

(A) 70

(B) 700

(C) 35

(D) 140

14. In the number line above, the tick marks are equally spaced on the line. How many the tick marks would there be on the number line between the tick marks at 9 and 12?

(A) 13
(B) 11
(C) 9
(D) 8

Solution: Answer: (B)

$$x = 3 + 5 + 3 = 11$$

<u>Note</u>: "between…and…" = "excluding two ends"

Solution: Answer: (B)

$$
\begin{cases}
\text{Formula for simple interest:} & \text{where} \\
\quad i = art & i \text{ is year interest,} \\
\text{Formula for simple interest:} & b \text{ is the balance,} \\
\quad b = a(1+rt) & a \text{ is starting value,} \\
\text{Formula for compound interest:} & r \text{ is the annual interest rate,} \\
\quad b = a(1+r)^t & t \text{ is the time in years.}
\end{cases}
$$

$$\downarrow$$

$$i = art = 20\,\cancel{00} \times \frac{7}{1\cancel{00}} \times 5$$

$$\Downarrow$$

$$i = 700$$

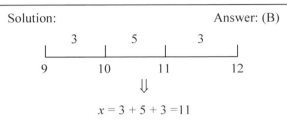

15. In the xy-coordinate plane above, points V_1, O, and V_2 are the 3 vertices of a certain triangle. The coordinates of V_1 are $(-2, b)$ and the coordinates of V_2 are $(2, b)$. Which of the following is one possible value of b if the area of triangle V_1OV_2 is less than 7 and greater than 6 ?

(A) $-\dfrac{15}{4}$

(B) $-\dfrac{13}{4}$

(C) $-\dfrac{11}{4}$

(D) $-\dfrac{7}{2}$

Solution: Answer: (B)

Base $2 + 2 = 4$ and height $|b|$

$$A = \frac{\text{Base} \times \text{height}}{2}, \quad 6 < \frac{\cancel{4}^{2} \cdot |b|}{\cancel{2}} < 7$$

$$b < 0 \;\rightarrow\; \frac{6}{2} < -b < \frac{7}{2}$$

$$\Downarrow$$

$$-\frac{7}{2} < b < -\frac{6}{2}, \quad -\frac{14}{4} < b < -\frac{12}{4}$$

NEXT PAGE

16. The median of eleven consecutive integers is 41. What is the least one of these eleven integers?

Solution: Answer: 36

The median 41 uses 1 position.

Either side of the median uses

$$\frac{11-1}{2} = 5 \text{ positions.}$$

↓

$$\underbrace{36,37,38,39,40,}_{5} 41, \underbrace{\qquad}_{5}$$

⇓

$$41 - 5 = 36$$

17. Maria is both the 11th shortest and 11th tallest student in her math class. If the height of each student in her class is different, how many students are in the class?

Solution: Answer: 21

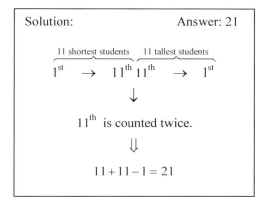

11th is counted twice.

⇓

$$11 + 11 - 1 = 21$$

18. A certain town has 1800 telephones. Three-fourths of the phones have dials. If push-button phones replace one-third of the dial phones, how many dial phones remain?

Solution: Answer: 900

$$1800 \cdot \frac{\cancel{3}}{4} \cdot \frac{2}{\cancel{3}}$$

⇓

900

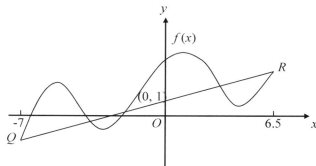

19. The figure above shows the graph of the function f and segment $\overline{QR}$ that has a y-intercept of 1. For how many values of x between -7 and 6.5 does $f(x) = 1$?

Solution: Answer: 5

Draw a horizontal line, which passes through the point $(0, 1)$. The function of the line is $y = 1$. The line intersects the graph of f at 5 points between -7 and 6.5.

⇓

Answer = 5

20. Shirley can select one or more following four toppings for her pizza: Meatballs, Sausage, Green Peppers, and Mushrooms. If she selects one or more, how many different combinations of the pizza toppings are possible?

Solution: Answer: 15

The order of toppings does not matter.

(1) One topping: 4 Combinations
(2) Two toppings:
    2 positions, 4 elements

$$\frac{\boxed{4} \times \boxed{3}}{2!} = 6 \quad \text{Combinations}$$

(3) Three toppings:
    3 positions, 4 elements

$$\frac{\boxed{4} \times \boxed{3} \times \boxed{2}}{3!} = 4 \quad \text{Combinations}$$

(4) Four toppings: 1 Combination
    The sets above cannot be combined.

↓

Use addition.

⇓

(5) Total combinations = 4 + 6 + 4 + 1 = 15

STOP

Math Test – Calculator

Time: 55 Minutes
38 Questions

Notes:

- The use of a calculator is not allowed.
- All numbers used in this section are the real number.
- Figures are provided for some problems in this test. Unless otherwise indicated under the figure "Note: Figure above not drawn to scale", all figures are drawn as accurately as possible.
- All figures lie in a plane EXCEPT otherwise specified.
- Unless otherwise indicated, the domain of any function f, g or j is assumed to be the set of all real numbers x for which $f(x)$, $g(x)$, or $j(x)$ is a real number.

Reference Information

$$A = \frac{1}{2}bh$$

$$A = lw$$

$$A = \pi r^2$$

$$V = \pi r^2 h$$

$$V = lwh$$

$$c^2 = a^2 + b^2$$

$$V = \frac{1}{3}\pi r^2 h$$

$$V = \frac{4}{3}\pi r^3$$

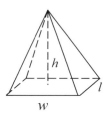

$$V = \frac{1}{3}lwh$$

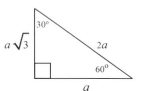

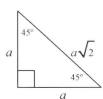

Copying or reuse of any portion of this page is illegal.

1. In some election, several people collected signatures to place a candidate on the ballot. Of these signatures, 35 percent were thrown out as invalid. Then a further 20 percent of those remaining signatures were eliminated. What percent of the original number of signatures were left?

(A) 52%

(B) 46%

(C) 55%

(D) 70%

> Solution: Answer: (A)
> "Remaining" of "remaining"
> $\Downarrow$
> $0.65 \cdot 0.8 = 0.52 = 52\%$

2. Jeff was 20 years old x years ago. Which of the following represents his age in y years from now?

(A) $20 + x - y$

(B) $20 - x - y$

(C) $20 + x + y$

(D) $20 + y - x$

> Solution: Answer: (C)
> Current age $= 20 + x$
> $\Downarrow$
> y years from now $= 20 + x + y$

3. How many even 2-digit integers less than 90 are there?

(A) 32

(B) 40

(C) 36

(D) 30

> Solution: Answer: (B)
> 0 cannot be at tens's place.
> Otherwise, it becomes 1 digit number.
> $\Downarrow$
> $\boxed{8} \cdot \boxed{5} = 40$
> 1,2,···,8   0,2,4,6,8

4. If the fraction 1/26 is equal to the repeating decimal 0.3846153846153..., what is the 68th digit after the decimal point of the repeating decimal?

(A) 4

(B) 7

(C) 9

(D) 8

> Solution: Answer: (D)
> Pattern $= 384615$
> $\downarrow$
> Number of pattern elements $= 6$
> $$\frac{68}{6} = 11 + \frac{2}{6}$$
> $\downarrow$
> remainder $= 2$
> $\downarrow$
> 4th digit is at the second pattern position.
> $\Downarrow$
> 68th digit $= 8$

5. A list of numbers has been arranged such that each number in the list is 6 less than the number that precedes it. If 98 is the sixth number in the list, what is the second number in the list?

(A) 74

(B) 80

(C) 68

(D) 122

> Solution: Answer: (D)
> Use the formula of arithmetic sequences.
> $$a_n = a_1 + (n-1)d$$
> $\downarrow$
> $98 = a_1 + (6-1)(-6)$
> $\downarrow$
> $a_1 = 128$
> $\Downarrow$
> $a_2 = 128 + (2-1)(-6) = 122$

3	5 6
4	1 3
5	8 9
6	2 4 6 7
7	0 7 8

3 | 6 represents 36.

6. The stem-and-leaf plot above shows the statistic data. What is the median value of the statistic data?

(A) 59

(B) 64

(C) 62

(D) 58

Solution: Answer: (C)

13 (odd) numbers
↓
The 7th number is middle one.
⇓
The median number is 62.

7. In the xy-plane, the center of a circle has coordinates $(3, 11)$, and the circle touches the x-axis at one point. What is the radius of the circle?

(A) 3

(B) 11

(C) 8

(D) 14

Solution   Answer: (B)

Method: Draw a sketch.

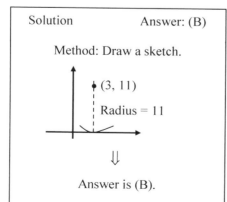

Radius = 11

⇓

Answer is (B).

8. The shortest distance from the center of a circle to a chord AB is 8. If the diameter of the center is 20, what is the length of the chord?

(A) 10

(B) 12

(C) 6

(D) 13

Solution: Answer: (B)

6- 8-10 right triangle

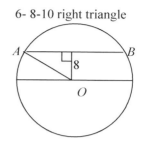

$$\text{Radius} = \frac{\text{Diameter}}{2} = \frac{20}{2} = 10$$
↓
$$OA = 10 = \text{radius}$$
⇓
$$\frac{AB}{2} = 6, \; AB = 12$$

9. Which of the following shifts of the graph of $y = x^2$ can result in the graph of $y = x^2 + 14x + h$, where h is a constant less than 49 ?

(A) 7 units right and $(h - 49)$ up

(B) 7 units right and $(h - 49)$ down

(C) 7 units left and $|h - 49|$ up

(D) 7 units left and $|h - 49|$ down

Solution: Answer: (D)

$$y = x^2 + 14x + h$$
↓
$$y = x^2 + 14x + 7^2 + h - 7^2$$
↓
$$y = (x + 7)^2 + h - 49$$
$$h < 49$$
⇓
The graph is translated
7 units left and $|h - 49|$ down

NEXT PAGE

10. In an office supply store, Doris bought 6 items from aisles 2 through 5 and 8 items from aisles 3 through 10. Which of the following could be the total number of items that Doris bought?

(A) 6
(B) 7
(C) 15
(D) 13

Solution: Answer: (D)

Repeated aisles

| 0 item | 6 items | 2 items |

Repeated aisles

| 6 items | 0 item | 8 items |

Consider 2 situations (1) and (2) below.
(1). The 6 items of 8 items came from repeated aisles.
↓
The least number of items = 8
(2). All the 8 items from aisles 3 through 10 were bought from not repeated aisles.
↓
The greatest number of items = 6 + 8 = 14.
↓
$8 \le x \le 14$
⇓
Answer is (D).

11. How many distinct positive four-digit integers can be formed if the first digit must be 3, the last cannot be 3, and digits can be used more than one time?

(A) 900

(B) 1,000

(C) 8,000

(D) 7,200

Solution: Answer: (A)
4-digit integer
↓
4 element sets
↓
Use Fundamental Counting Principle.
⇓

| 1 set | 1 set | 1 set | 1 set |

$\boxed{1} \cdot \boxed{10} \cdot \boxed{10} \cdot \boxed{9} = 900$

3   0–9   0–9   0–9
                    except 3

12. A function is defined by $f(t) = -3^t + 2$. Which of the following is the sketch of $g(t) = f(-t)$?

(A)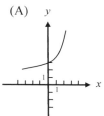

(B)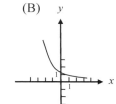

(C)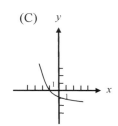

(D)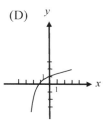

Solution: Answer: (D)

$$\begin{cases} f(t) = -3^t + 2 = -\left(3^t - 2\right) \\ g(t) = f(-t) = -\left(3^{-t} - 2\right) = -\left(\left(\frac{1}{3}\right)^t - 2\right) \end{cases}$$

$h(t) = \left(\frac{1}{3}\right)^t$ → The sketch of h is (B).

$j(t) = \left(\frac{1}{3}\right)^t - 2$ → The sketch of j is (C).

$g(t) = f(-t) = -j(t)$
↓
The sketch of j flips about x-axis.
⇓
The sketch of g is (D).

NEXT PAGE

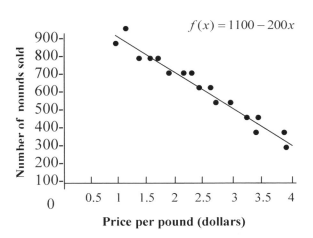

$f(x) = 1100 - 200x$

Price per pound (dollars)

A supermarket sells pounds of peanutbutters and decides the price per pound every month. The scatterplot above shows the price and the number of pounds of peanutbutters sold for 17 months with the line of best fit and the equation for the line.

13.   By the line of best fit above, how many pounds of peanutbutters should the supermarket expect to sell in a month when the price of peanutbutter is \$1.50 each pound?

(A) 700

(B) 800

(C) 300

(D) 500

Solution: Answer: (B)

"expect to sell"

↓

values of the line, not values of the points.

↓

$f(3/2) = 1100 - 200 \cdot (3/2)$

⇓

$f(3/2) = 800$

14.   By the line of best fit on the left, what is the price of peanutbutters the supermarket expect to sell in a month when the peanutbutters are 360 pounds?

(A) \$3.00

(B) \$2.50

(C) \$3.70

(D) \$2.10

Solution: Answer: (C)

"expect to sell"

↓

values of the line, not values of the points.

↓

$360 = 1100 - 200x, \quad 200x = 740$

⇓

$x = \dfrac{74}{20} = \dfrac{37}{10} = 3.7$

15. If the resulting graph represents the graph of $g(x)$ from the graph of $f(x) = 4x^2$ translated 4 units right and 4 units up, what is the value of $g(4.4)$?

(A) 6.34

(B) 3.72

(C) 5.31

(D) 4.64

Solution: Answer: (D)

$g(x) = 4(x-4)^2 + 4$

↓

$g(4.4) = 4(4.4 - 4)^2 + 4$

⇓

$4(0.4)^2 + 4 = 0.64 + 4 = 4.64$

NEXT PAGE

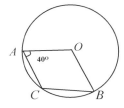

Note: Figure above not drawn to scale.

16.   In the figure above, points A, B, and C lie on the circumference of the circle centered at O. If $m\angle OBC = 60^\circ$, $m\angle AOB = ?$

(A) 110
(B) 120
(C) 160
(D) 140

Solution: Answer: (C)

Draw a segment $\overline{OC}$ in the figure below.

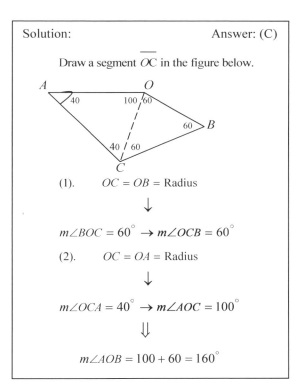

(1). $OC = OB = $ Radius

↓

$m\angle BOC = 60^\circ \rightarrow m\angle OCB = 60^\circ$

(2). $OC = OA = $ Radius

↓

$m\angle OCA = 40^\circ \rightarrow m\angle AOC = 100^\circ$

⇓

$m\angle AOB = 100 + 60 = 160^\circ$

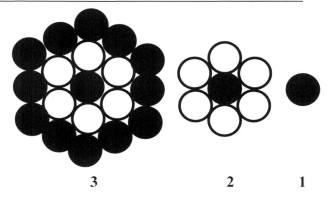

|3|2|1|

17.   The figure sequence above starts with one circle. If each coming figure is structured by adding a ring of the identical circles around the immediately preceding figure, which of the following is the total number of circles in the sixth figure of the sequence?

(A) 71

(B) 81

(C) 64

(D) 91

Solution: Answer: (D)

Try to figure a law out.

↓

The law is that the number of the circles of each ring is a multiple of 6

$1 + 1\times 6 + 2\times 6 + 3\times 6 + 4\times 6 + 5\times 6$

⇓

$1 + 6\left(1 + 2 + 3 + 4 + 5\right) = 1 + 15\times 6 = \boxed{91}$

NEXT PAGE

18. In the xy-plane, A and B are distinct points, which have the same y-coordinate and lie on the parabola whose equation is $y = -x^2 + 5x + 30$. Which of the following is the x-coordinate of the midpoint of $\overline{AB}$?

(A) $\dfrac{5}{2}$

(B) $-\dfrac{2}{5}$

(C) $\dfrac{2}{5}$

(D) $-\dfrac{5}{3}$

> Solution: Answer: (A)
>
> $$y = -x^2 + 5x + 30$$
>
> $$\Downarrow$$
>
> $$x = -\frac{b}{2a} = -\frac{5}{-2 \cdot 1} = \frac{5}{2}$$

19. If a company charge d dollars for their product, where $0 \le d \le 100$, the income from the product will be $I(d) = 1000d - 10d^2$ dollars per day. By this model, for which of the following values of d would the company's daily income for the product be the maximum?

(A) -50
(B) 30
(C) 50
(D) -30

> Solution: Answer: (C)
>
> $\begin{cases} \text{This function is a quadratic function.} \\ \quad\quad\quad\downarrow \\ \text{Its graph is a parabola.} \end{cases}$
>
> The graph opens down because $a = -10 < 0$.
>
> When $d = -\dfrac{b}{2a}$, $I(d) = $ maximum value.
>
> $b = 1000, \ a = -10$
>
> $$\Downarrow$$
>
> $$d = -\frac{1000}{2 \cdot (-10)} = 50$$

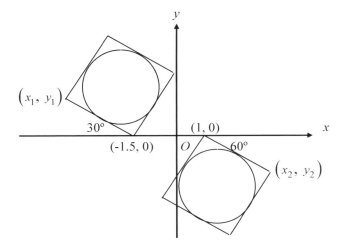

20. In the figure above, 2 identical circles with radius 3 are inscribed in 2 squares, respectively. Which of the following are the values of x_2 and y_1 ?

(A) $x_2 = 4, \ y_1 = -3$

(B) $x_2 = -4, \ y_1 = 3$

(C) $x_2 = 4\sqrt{3}, \ y_1 = 3$

(D) $x_2 = 4, \ y_1 = 3$

> Solution: Answer: (D)
>
> Use the conclusion:
>
> $\begin{cases} \text{If a circle is inscribed in a square,} \\ \text{diameter of circle} = \text{side of square} \end{cases}$
>
> $$r = 3, \ d = 6$$
>
>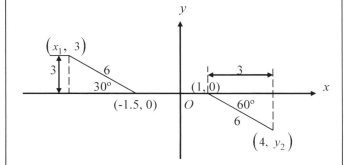
>
> $$\Downarrow$$
>
> $$x_2 = 1 + 3 = 4, \quad y_1 = 3$$
>
>

$$\begin{cases} x = z^2 \\ x = \sqrt{y} \\ y = 9z \end{cases}$$

21. In the system of equations above, if $x > 0$, what is the value of x ?

(A) $3\sqrt[3]{3}$

(B) $3\sqrt{3}$

(C) 3

(D) 4

Note: Figure above not drawn to scale.

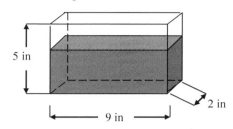

22. The figure above shows the dimensions of a rectangular container sealed up. There is 20 cubic inches of sand in the container. The container will be repositioned on level ground so that the container places on one, which has the least area, of the six surfaces. If it has been repositioned, which of the following will be ratio of the height of the non-sand to the height of the sand?

(A) $\dfrac{2}{7}$

(B) $\dfrac{5}{2}$

(C) $\dfrac{3}{7}$

(D) $\dfrac{7}{2}$

Solution: Answer: (A)

The question asks x-value.

↓

Cancel y and z.

Cannot find easier way to do elimination.

↓

Use the common substitution method.

$$\begin{cases} x = z^2 \\ x = \sqrt{y} \\ y = 9z \quad (1) \end{cases} \rightarrow \begin{cases} \pm\sqrt{x} = z \quad (2) \\ x^2 = y \quad (3) \end{cases}$$

↓

$(2), (3) \rightarrow (1)$

↓

$x^2 = 9(\pm\sqrt{x})$

↓

$\left(x^2\right)^2 = \left(9(\pm\sqrt{x})\right)^2$

↓

$x^4 = 81x$

$x > 0$

↓

$x^3 = 81, \quad x = \sqrt[3]{81} = \sqrt[3]{3 \times 3 \times 3 \times 3}$

⇓

$\sqrt[3]{3 \times 3 \times 3} \cdot \sqrt[3]{3} = 3\sqrt[3]{3}$

Solution: Answer: (D)

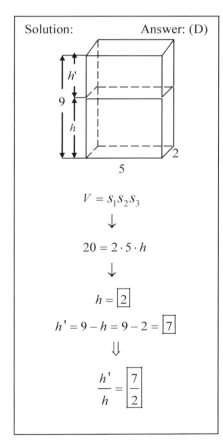

$V = s_1 s_2 s_3$

↓

$20 = 2 \cdot 5 \cdot h$

↓

$h = \boxed{2}$

$h' = 9 - h = 9 - 2 = \boxed{7}$

⇓

$\dfrac{h'}{h} = \boxed{\dfrac{7}{2}}$

NEXT PAGE ⟩

$$\begin{cases} 3y+1>5 \\ x>3y-2 \end{cases}$$

23. Which of the following consists of the x-coordinates of all the points that satisfy the system of inequalities above?

(A) $x<2$

(B) $x>-2$

(C) $x>2$

(D) $x>1$

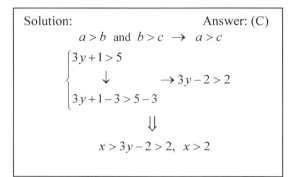

Solution: Answer: (C)

$$a>b \text{ and } b>c \rightarrow a>c$$

$$\begin{cases} 3y+1>5 \\ \quad\downarrow \qquad\qquad \rightarrow 3y-2>2 \\ 3y+1-3>5-3 \end{cases}$$

$$\Downarrow$$

$$x>3y-2>2, \; x>2$$

The fish and beef weighed 5 pounds.
The fish and chicken weighed 6 pounds.
The beef and chicken weighed 7 pounds.

24. By the information above, what is the weight of the chicken?

(A) 4 Pounds

(B) 7 Pounds

(C) 9 Pounds

(D) $\dfrac{5}{2}$ Pounds

Solution: Answer: (A)

$$\begin{cases} f+b=5 \; (1) \\ f+c=6 \; (2) \\ b+c=7 \; (3) \end{cases}$$

The question asks c.

$$\downarrow$$

$$\begin{cases} \text{The target is } c. \\ \text{Cancel } b \text{ and } f. \end{cases}$$

$$(2)-(1)$$

$$-b+c=1 \; (4)$$

$$(4)+(3)$$

$$\Downarrow$$

$$2c=8, \boxed{c=4}$$

25. About what is the ratio of the volume of the cylinder to volume of the sphere if a cylinder whose base radius is 4 is inscribed in a sphere of radius 5 ?

(A) 2.46

(B) 0.44

(C) 4.00

(D) 0.58

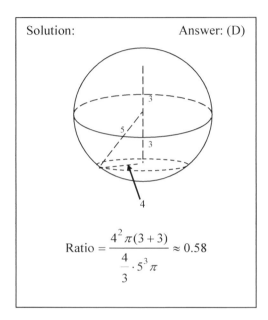

Solution: Answer: (D)

$$\text{Ratio} = \frac{4^2\pi(3+3)}{\dfrac{4}{3}\cdot 5^3\pi} \approx 0.58$$

26. Michelle, a college graduate, goes to work for D dollars per month. In several months the company she works for gives all employees a 20% pay cut. A few months later, the company gives all employees a 20% raise. What is Michelle's new salary?

(A) D

(B) $0.96D$

(C) $1.2D$

(D) $0.8D$

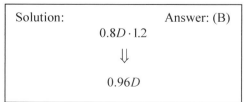

Solution: Answer: (B)

$$0.8D \cdot 1.2$$

$$\Downarrow$$

$$0.96D$$

NEXT PAGE ⇨

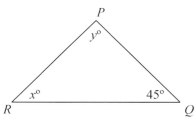

Note: Figure above not drawn to scale.

27. In the figure above, $PR > PQ$. Which of the following must be true?

(A) $x° > 45°$
(B) $x° = y°$
(C) $x° > y°$
(D) $x° < 45°$

> **Solution:**   **Answer: (D)**
>
> In any triangle, the greater side subtends the greater angle, and vice versa.
>
> $\downarrow$
>
> $PR > PQ$
>
> Angle of $45°$ is opposite PR.
> $x°$ is opposite PQ.
>
> $\Downarrow$
>
> $x° < 45°$

28. One ball is dropped from a height of 256 inches and begins bouncing on a floor. If the height of each bounce is three-fourths the height of the previous bounce, what is the height , in inches, between the floor and highest point that the balls can reach after the ball fourth time hits the floor?

(A) 343

(B) 245

(C) 243

(D) 241

> **Solution:**   **Answer: (C)**
>
>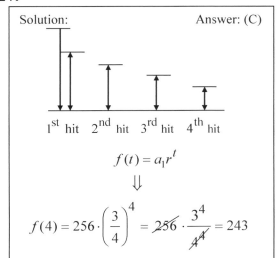
>
> 1st hit 2nd hit 3rd hit 4th hit
>
> $f(t) = a_1 r^t$
>
> $\Downarrow$
>
> $f(4) = 256 \cdot \left(\dfrac{3}{4}\right)^4 = \cancel{256} \cdot \dfrac{3^4}{\cancel{4^4}} = 243$

29. If $3x^2 + 7x + W$ is divided by $x + 3$, then remainder is 3. Which of the following is the value of W ?

(A) -2

(B) 2

(C) -3

(D) 4

> **Solution:**   **Answer: (C)**
>
> The remainder theorem:
>
> If $\dfrac{P(x)}{x - c}$, the remainder $= P(c)$.
>
> $\downarrow$
>
> $3 \cdot (-3)^2 + 7(-3) + W = 3$
>
> $\downarrow$
>
> $27 - 21 + W = 3$
>
> $\Downarrow$
>
> $W = -3$

30. Machine A itself can finish a job in a hours, and Machine B itself can finish a job in b hours, where $a > 0$ and $b > 0$. After Machine A begins the job and does $3/4$ of the job, Machine B takes over and finishes the remaining job. Which of the following is the entire time, in hours, that takes Machine A and Machine B to finish the job?

(A) $\dfrac{3a + 2b}{4}$

(B) $\dfrac{2a - b}{4}$

(C) $\dfrac{2a - 3b}{2}$

(D) $\dfrac{3a + b}{4}$

> **Solution:**   **Answer: (D)**
>
> $3/4$ of job $= 3/4$ of time
> $1/4$ of job $= 1/4$ of time
>
> $\downarrow$
>
> $\begin{cases} T_A = \dfrac{3}{4}a \\ T_B = \dfrac{1}{4}b \end{cases}$
>
> $\Downarrow$
>
> $T = T_A + T_B = \dfrac{3a}{4} + \dfrac{b}{4} = \dfrac{3a + b}{4}$

NEXT PAGE

The questions 31 and 32 refer to the information below.

Number of Competitors by Score and Morning

	Score 10 / 10	Score 9 / 10	Score 8 / 10	Score ≤ 7 / 10	Total
Morning 1	3	3	4	8	18
Morning 2	2	4	3	9	18
Morning 3	4	3	6	5	18
Morning 4	3	4	4	7	18
Total	12	14	17	29	72

The number of competitors obtaining a given score in each of four mornings is shown in the chart above. In order to win some certain awards, the same eighteen competitors, in each of four mornings, solved ten math problems. Each competitor obtained one point for each correct solution.

31. What is the average score of the competitors who obtained at least score 8 points in Morning 3, rounded to the nearest hundredth?

Solution: Answer: 8.85

$$\text{Average} = \frac{\text{Total values}}{\text{Total frequencies}}$$

$$\Downarrow$$

$$\frac{4 \times 10 + 3 \times 9 + 6 \times 8}{4 + 3 + 6} = \frac{40 + 27 + 54}{13} \approx 8.85$$

32. If a competitor is chosen randomly, and no competitor obtained the same score in two distinct mornings, what is the probability that the chosen competitor obtained a score 9 points in Mornings 3 and 4, given that the competitor obtained a score of 9 points in one of the four mornings?

Solution: Answer: 3/49 or .061

$$P_{M-3} = \frac{3}{14}, \quad P_{M-4} = \frac{4}{14} = \frac{2}{7}$$

$$\text{"and"}$$

$$\Downarrow$$

$$P_{M-3} \times P_{M-4} = \frac{3}{\cancel{14}^{7}} \times \frac{\cancel{2}}{7} = \frac{3}{49}$$

33. If the equations of 2 lines are $y = 4x + 3$ and $y = 3x + 4$, respectively, and the two lines intersect, what is the absolute value of the difference of the x-coordinate and y-coordinate?

Solution: Answer: 6

At the intersection point, $y = y$.

$$\downarrow$$

$$4x + 3 = 3x + 4$$

$$x = 1$$

By $y = 4x + 3$, $y = 7$

$$\Downarrow$$

$$|x - y| = |1 - 7| = 6$$

NEXT PAGE

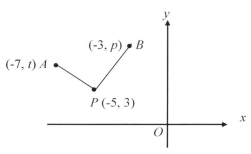

Note: Figure above not drawn to scale.

34. In the figure above, $\overline{AP}$ is perpendicular to $\overline{BP}$, $p = 7$, what is the value of t?

Solution: Answer: 4

The two segments are perpendicular.

↓

$$s_2 \cdot s_1 = -1$$

↓

$$\frac{t-3}{-7-(-5)} \cdot \frac{7-3}{-3-(-5)} = -1$$

↓

$$\frac{t-3}{-2} \cdot \frac{4}{2} = -1$$

⇓

$$t = 4$$

35. James has six blank cards. Each card is written with one of the following letters: A, B, C, D, E or F. Each of six cards does not have the same letter. If E and F are always the center letters in each arrangement, how many possible distinct six-letter arrangements can James create?

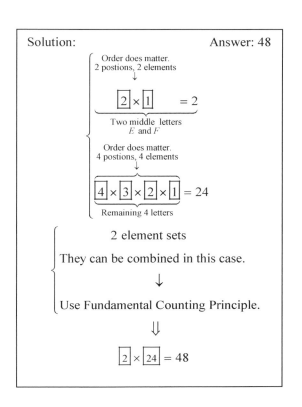

NEXT PAGE

36 At a college, in a class of 90 juniors, there are 4 girls for every 6 boys. In a senior class, there are 5 girls for every 2 boys. If the two classes are combined, and in the combined class, the number of girls is twice the number of boys, how many boys are in the senior class?

Solution: Answer: 144

$$\begin{cases} \text{4 girls for every 6 boys} \\ \text{Number of } A \text{ for every number of } B \end{cases}$$

↓

This is the question involving the ratio.

↓

(1) $\dfrac{4}{1\cancel{0}} \cdot 9\cancel{0} = 36$, $\dfrac{6}{1\cancel{0}} \cdot 9\cancel{0} = 54$

(2). Girls are twice boys.

↓

$$36 + 5k = 2(54 + 2k)$$
$$36 + 5k = 108 + 4k$$
$$k = 72$$

⇓

$$2k = 2 \cdot 72 = 144$$

37. A certain number is any integer greater than 1 that has only three positive integer factors: 1, itself, and its square root. And, one of the factors is a prime number. What is the certain number?

Solution: Answer: 49

1 is not a prime number.

Use plug-in method.

↓

$$\begin{cases} \text{49 has only 3 positive integer factors:} \\ \text{1, 49, and } \sqrt{49} = 7. \\ \text{7 is a prime number.} \\ 1, N, \sqrt{N} \end{cases}$$

⇓

$$N = 49$$

38. The three angles of a triangle have measures of $3m$, m, and $2n$, where $m > 9°$. If m and n are integers, what is the greatest possible value of n?

Solution: Answer: 70

$$3m + m + 2n = 180$$

↓

$$4m + 2n = 180, \ 2n = 180 - 4m$$

↓

$$n = \frac{180 - 4m}{2} = 90 - 2m$$

⇓

$$n = 90 - 2 \times 10 = 70$$

STOP

Made in the USA
Middletown, DE
15 May 2019